BRITAIN AN̲ ̲ ̲ ̲ ̲ ̲T̲ ̲ ̲ ̲ ̲ ̲ ̲ ̲PY

Britain and the World in the Twentieth Century
Ever-decreasing Circles

Michael J. Turner

continuum

Continuum UK, The Tower Building, 11 York Road, London SE1 7NX
Continuum US, 80 Maiden Lane, Suite 704, New York, NY 10038

www.continuumbooks.com

First published 2010

British Library Cataloguing-in-Publication Data
A catalogue record for this book is available from the British Library.

ISBN 978 1 44118 983 7 [hardcover]
ISBN 978 1 44111 157 9 [paperback]

Typeset by Pindar NZ, Auckland, New Zealand
Printed and bound by MPG Books Ltd, Cornwall, Great Britain

Contents

Introduction

'As I look out upon the future of our country in the changing scene of human destiny, I feel the existence of three great circles among the free nations and democracies ...' This is how Winston Churchill prefaced the statements he repeatedly made about the international situation after the Second World War. Addressing the Conservative Party's annual conference, on 9 October 1948, he went on to describe the 'three circles' of world power and to suggest that Britain would continue to play a leading role in international affairs. The first 'circle' was the empire-Commonwealth. The second was the 'English-speaking world', in which co-operation between Britain and the United States of America had become so important. The third was 'United Europe'.

> These three majestic circles are co-existent and if they are linked together there is no force or combination which could overthrow them or ever challenge them. Now, if you think of the three interlinked circles you will see that we are the only country which has a great part in every one of them. We stand, in fact, at the very point of junction, and ... we have the opportunity of joining them all together.[1]

Churchill was not alone in thinking that this unique position, as a participant in each of the 'three circles' and as the only means of connecting them, would guarantee Britain's survival as a great power. Many people at home and abroad expected Britain to maintain its role and influence after 1945, just as it had done in previous times. It proved to be more difficult to do this than anyone could have predicted, and the twentieth century is generally seen as a century of relative decline for Britain.

One of the core premises of this book is that if we want to understand British foreign policy, we need to consider the multiple pressures and possibilities facing those who made the key decisions. It is easy to assume that Britain's great power status was lost because the resources were not available for extended commitments in each of the 'three circles', and that British leaders would have done better to concentrate on only one of the 'circles' (probably, in view of the way things turned out, Europe); but *all* of the 'circles' were problematic in their own way, and long-term trends in policy were not necessarily based on the wrong choices.

This book balances those accounts that exaggerate or otherwise misrepresent the nature of Britain's decline as a world power. What might be called the 'literature of decline' has emerged as an important part of the historiography of modern Britain. Much of this work has been extremely influential, and rightly so, but there has been a tendency to go too far, with analyses that are unwarrantably negative and condemnatory. It has become almost axiomatic that 'a hard-headed calculation of national interest . . . was neglected in favour of unrealistic ambitions and ideals'.[2] The suggestion is that Britain's main problem was a failure of leadership; that British policy making was fundamentally flawed; and that Britain lost influence and status in the world because of decisions made by blinkered and foolish individuals. These interpretations must be challenged. British leaders were not uninformed, or unreflective, or unsuccessful in managing decline and sustaining Britain's influence. By examining the circumstances in which they were placed, the options that were available to them, the goals they had in view and the international environment that conditioned all, this book demonstrates that British leaders did a much better job than many historians have recognized.

Diplomacy has been compared to a game of cards: the point is to play one's hand to best effect. In analysing Britain's foreign policy in the twentieth century, this book explains how and why the cards were played as they were, and casts light on the alternative courses that might have been available at critical moments.

The book is presented as a contribution to ongoing debates about British decline. It is concerned with Britain's changing position in the world. It places British policy making in the appropriate domestic and international contexts; stresses the interconnectedness of events; explores the various determinants of political, military, economic, strategic, diplomatic and other decisions; and makes use of primary sources while also synthesizing the work of other historians in order to provide a fair and detailed account of Britain's involvement in the 'three circles'. These were decreasing circles in that the scope for British activity in each of them gradually narrowed. Nevertheless, what is most noteworthy is not Britain's relative decline, but Britain's ability to manage and minimize decline.

Acknowledgements

I would like to thank everyone connected with the commissioning, production and publication of this book, especially Tony Morris, Michael Greenwood, Alice Eddowes and Kim Pillay. I would also like to thank those students who have taken my courses in international history over the years. For good or ill, my decision to write about British foreign policy was a direct response to their comments and questions in class.

I am very grateful to colleagues and friends at Appalachian State University. They have provided a wonderfully supportive environment in which I was able finally to complete the manuscript. Most of all I want to thank Catherine, Grace, Jill and Ethan, and the rest of the family across Britain and America. Nobody could wish for better allies!

Any errors or shortcomings in this book are entirely my own responsibility.

MJT
Boone, North Carolina
June 2009

The Era of the Two World Wars

At the end of the nineteenth century, Britain was one of the leading world powers with a large empire and strong navy, a tradition of political stability and diplomatic influence, and the ability to defend its interests in all the strategically important parts of the globe. The ascendancy of the mid-Victorian period had given way, however, to more challenging circumstances.[1] The rise of Germany reduced Britain's involvement in European affairs, and Britain's economic strength relative to that of its main competitors – the United States, Germany and France – was not what it had been.[2] Tensions were building up, notably in central Europe and the Balkans, where longstanding rivalries were exacerbated by sovereignty disputes and the pursuit of colonies. Instability was spreading in those parts of Africa, the Middle East and Asia where the European powers had been constructing territorial and trading empires.[3] British leaders had for years presented Britain's 'isolation' from European quarrels as a virtue, but there had to be a reassessment at the beginning of the twentieth century, in part because of the Boer War of 1899–1902.[4]

This war was fought by Britain to maintain its authority in southern Africa.[5] It showed up some weaknesses, especially in military organization, and led to much talk of the dangers of 'isolation' in a world that was changing. Lord Salisbury, who served as Conservative prime minister between 1895 and 1902, once remarked that 'isolation' rarely entailed serious practical inconvenience, but he added that British governments had never denied the need for co-operation with other powers in certain circumstances. In the early 1900s, in many parts of the world, new ways had to be found to shore up Britain's position. It would be an exaggeration to suggest that there was a dramatic change in policy, however, for Britain was still reluctant to enter into formal alliances and take on extra military responsibilities.[6] Britain did not suddenly become vulnerable, but remained a world power and was in many regions pre-eminent.[7] Though there was some ambivalence about Europe, this was less a sign of weakness than a continuation of traditional routines. The key was to keep options open for as long as possible.[8]

The Far East was identified by Salisbury as an area of special concern. An understanding here with the United States[9] or with Germany[10] might have been preferable, but with neither of them disposed to be helpful, London had to look elsewhere – to Japan, an increasingly assertive regional power. Japan posed a potential threat to Britain's interests, but by far the biggest threat in the region was posed by Russia, and Japan shared Britain's suspicions about Russian expansionism. In 1901 the Japanese proposed a formal alliance. Britain agreed and the alliance was concluded in 1902. This was the first modern pact between a European power and an Asian power. Britain and Japan agreed to co-operate in China and the Yellow Sea and to respect the independence of China and Korea, though Japan's special interest in the latter was recognized. If Britain or Japan went to war, the uninvolved ally was to remain neutral, but if another power joined in against Britain or Japan, the uninvolved ally would be obliged to fight. The alliance gave Japan a free hand in Korea, Britain did not have to spend so much defending its Asian possessions, and Russia's advance was countered. The alliance was renewed in 1905 and 1911.[11]

In Europe, meanwhile, London's main concern was the rapid growth in Germany's military capability, combined as it was with Berlin's confrontational tone. Particularly alarming was the expansion of the German navy. Admiral Alfred von Tirpitz, secretary of state for the imperial navy from 1897 to 1916, wanted to use the navy to intimidate the British and push them into an accommodation.[12]

Though British governments wished to trim the defence budget and were reluctant to engage in an arms race, they could not allow their freedom of action to be limited. Edward Grey, who was foreign secretary in the Liberal governments of 1905–15, saw a strong fleet as an essential for Britain, with its overseas empire and dependence on maritime trade, whereas Germany was really a continental power, needing a strong army but not the navy that was being built. Winston Churchill, who had defected from the Conservatives to the Liberals in 1904 and was appointed as first lord of the admiralty in 1911, agreed with Grey. More money was provided for the Royal Navy and the idea spread that it might become necessary to resolve disagreements with Germany's enemies France and Russia.[13]

France and Russia had concluded an alliance in 1894. French leaders were suspicious of Germany and the memory of defeat in the Franco-Prussian War of 1870–71 continued to affect French policy in the early twentieth century. The alliance with Russia was essential to French strategy and for Germany it raised the possibility of having to fight a war on two fronts. Alliance with France suited the Russians, all the more so after they were embarrassed by defeat in the Russo-Japanese War of 1904–5. According to Russia's foreign minister (1906–10) Alexander Isvolsky, the way to restore prestige was through gains in the Balkans. The alliance with France, it was hoped, would prevent Germany from interfering when Russia made its move, for the Russians were bound to clash with Austria-Hungary, Germany's ally since 1879.[14]

In the late nineteenth century Britain came close to war with both France and Russia because of imperial struggles.[15] Seeking to improve relations with France, in view of the danger posed by Germany and the need to stabilize spheres of influence outside Europe, British foreign secretary (1900–5) Lord Lansdowne negotiated the entente of April 1904. This agreement was not the same as the Anglo-Japanese alliance, for it involved no military commitments, and there was still some reserve in London's dealings with Paris. French foreign minister (1898–1905) Theophile Delcasse wanted a change, however, believing that France could not stand up to Germany in Europe and Britain in Africa at the same time. The entente recognized Britain's interests in Egypt and French interests in Morocco, and arrangements were settled with respect to frontiers in West Africa, fishing rights off Newfoundland, and involvement in South East Asia, Madagascar and the New Hebrides. From the outset the French attached more importance to the entente than did the British.[16]

When Grey became foreign secretary in December 1905, he inherited improving Anglo-French relations. Co-operation was soon reinforced by the Algeciras Conference of January to April 1906. Germany had been complaining about French involvement in Morocco, but when representatives of the great powers met at Algeciras in Spain to discuss the situation, only Austria-Hungary backed Germany. London and Paris had already agreed to work together on Morocco, and although the Russians were angry because France had not assisted them during the Russo-Japanese War, there was no chance that Russia would act against the French. The Moroccan crisis made Britain and France psychologically closer, and they became closer still as Germany tried to separate them. The Liberal government in Britain – led by Henry Campbell-Bannerman until April 1908 and thereafter by H.H. Asquith – valued the entente, and under its prime minister (1906–9) Georges Clemenceau, the French government avoided colonial friction with Britain and directed nationalist sentiment against Germany. There was still no formal, binding commitment to France, but Grey sanctioned Anglo-French military conversations. He did not inform his cabinet colleagues.[17] At the same time a process of reform began, to improve Britain's fighting capacity, initiated by the secretary of state for war (1905–12) Richard Haldane.[18]

Though contacts with Germany continued, German unfriendliness led the British to pay more attention to the causes of Anglo-Russian antagonism. An entente with Russia was concluded in August 1907. The Russians were wary of ongoing British resistance in frontier regions, feared the long-term implications of the Anglo-Japanese alliance, and hoped to prevent a pact between London and Berlin to extinguish Russian influence in the Middle East. By the entente Persia was partitioned into spheres of influence and the neutrality of Afghanistan was recognized, as were Britain's special interests in the Persian Gulf. Tibet was to be a buffer zone. Britain and Russia agreed to respect the integrity of the Ottoman

Empire, and there was a vague statement about access for Russian vessels from the Black Sea into the Mediterranean.[19] Consultation with the French became an established feature of British foreign policy, whereas contact with Russia was less frequent and less useful. Despite its limitations, however, the Anglo-Russian entente angered German leaders.[20]

Alleviating some of the tension in Anglo-Russian relations was a reasonable goal for the British government with regard to the balance of power in Europe, yet imperial considerations were probably paramount and it is also possible that Lansdowne had favoured an entente with France not because he feared Germany but because he wanted to secure the empire and, in particular, defend India from Russia. London may have decided that the Anglo-Japanese alliance did not represent a sufficient deterrent, and it was likely that Indian nationalists would try even harder to throw off British authority if they saw that it rested, even in part, on Japanese assistance.[21]

The ententes assumed greater importance to Britain because of Germany's policy. Grey was not prepared to sacrifice good relations with France or Russia, especially the former, and could make no bargain with Berlin that cut across these relations. He was increasingly concerned about Europe, but he thought that the main effect of the ententes was to enable Britain to retain its naval superiority and its empire. These advantages might be lost if Britain sided with Germany. Early in 1907 the senior clerk in the western department of the foreign office, Eyre Crowe, remarked that German policy could be interpreted either as a calculated bid for hegemony or as a confused set of measures, drifting along by its own momentum. Either way, the result would be war. Grey was of a similar opinion. He believed that the isolation of Germany would lead to war, and that German domination of Europe would also mean war. There was a wide area of possibility between these two scenarios, and Grey wanted to keep great power relations within this space. As time passed, he thought that the Germans were preventing him from doing so.[22]

To his detractors Crowe was unduly pessimistic and his warnings made war more likely, but Crowe was only one of many experts who had a role in the shaping of British policy, and policy was not made exclusively in the foreign office but owed something to a variety of political, economic, military and strategic imperatives.[23] Crowe's wish for a harder line was satisfied in some respects, for this was a period in which more ruthlessness crept into Britain's approach to international issues.[24]

Fear and tension increased. Austria-Hungary's annexation of Bosnia-Herzegovina in 1908, with German approval, caused further instability in the Balkans. Bosnia-Herzegovina had been administered by the Austrians since 1878, though it was nominally part of the Ottoman Empire. Russian foreign minister Isvolsky had been working on a deal whereby Russia would accept formal annexation in return for Vienna's support for the opening of the Bosporus and Dardanelle Straits to Russian ships, but Vienna announced the annexation while he was still preparing the ground. The result was more ill feeling between Russia and Austria-Hungary. The strongest Balkan state, Serbia, condemned Austria-Hungary's action and appealed to Russia, but the latter had to limit its response because Britain and France refused to intervene.[25]

Willing to see Russia challenged in the Balkans, the Germans also continued their coercive tactics with respect to the French in Morocco. The arrival of a German gunboat at Agadir in June 1911 alarmed the British, who feared the establishment of a German naval base on the Atlantic coast of North Africa. What Germany really wanted was compensation for accepting French control of Morocco, and soon Berlin was offered territory in central Africa, but before the crisis passed Britain issued a clear warning. Chancellor of the exchequer David Lloyd George declared that although Britain wanted to remain at peace, if pushed too far Britain would fight. The Agadir crisis augmented Anglo-French co-operation and Grey told the cabinet of the military conversations that had been going on since 1906. Some of his colleagues were uneasy, especially Asquith, but Grey stood firm. If an expectation arose in Paris that Britain would assist France in war, he argued, this could not be helped, and it would not be to Britain's benefit to abandon the military conversations.[26]

The possibility of war was accepted in sections of the British government. An awareness of danger was also spreading among the public. Some newspapers, notably the *Daily Mail*, recommended that Britain had to strengthen itself in order to prevent war. Prominent intellectuals mused over changing times, among them the writer H.G. Wells, who in 1909 used the first aeroplane flight across the English Channel (by French aviator Louis Blériot) to make the point that Britain was being drawn towards the continent. There was a schism among British socialists. Some opposed war while others actively contributed to anti-German sentiment. Public opinion was also affected by the way the media depicted war. There was a tendency to gloss over the negative aspects.[27]

That suspicion of Germany continued to grow was due primarily to the arms race. This was the age of the 'Dreadnoughts', which were more powerful than all previous battleships. In 1909 there were claims that Germany had secretly accelerated its construction programme and that the development of new vessels made Britain's superiority in pre-'Dreadnought' battleships irrelevant. The government decided to build four new 'Dreadnoughts'. Naval chiefs wanted six, the popular cry was for eight, but the government was reluctant to spend so heavily. Diplomatic initiatives came to nothing. Britain promised to offer no opposition to Germany's colonial expansion and to join no aggressive combination against the Germans if they slowed down their naval building. Berlin insisted that the arms race could only be suspended if Britain undertook to remain neutral in the event of a European war. This meant that Britain would have to desert France in return for German friendship. Grey ruled this out.[28]

The situation was not helped by rising Anglophobia in Germany.[29] In contrast, anti-German opinion in Britain was not so much a cause of the First World War as the result of it, and it was widely thought that Britain and Germany drifted apart from the 1890s not because they were inevitable enemies but because their interests diverged: Germany could not help Britain to preserve its empire, and Britain could not protect or threaten Germany's position in Europe. Though questions relating to trade and colonies might have been settled by negotiation, the snag was Germany's determination to increase its influence, which involved ending British naval supremacy.[30]

In the aftermath of the Agadir affair, Italy took advantage of instability in the Ottoman Empire to seize Tripolitania, Cyrenaica and the Dodecanese Islands. Italy's success intensified nationalist fervour in the Balkans. Serbia was intent on freeing the area from the control of both Istanbul and Vienna, which for generations had stood at the head of two great multi-national empires. Serbia made gains in the Balkan Wars of 1912–13 and the country's prime minister, Nikola Pašić, satisfied that the Turks had effectively been dealt with, planned next to break Austria-Hungary's influence in the region. The Balkan Wars surprised the great powers, forced Turkey to cede almost all of its territory in Europe, and greatly inconvenienced Grey, who was hard pressed to localize the conflict and arrange for mediation.[31]

National self-determination was one of the popular causes of the period, and as Turkish rule in south-eastern Europe ended, it seemed likely that Austria-Hungary would have to make a similar adjustment. Vienna tried to resist. In February 1913 the chief of the German general staff, Helmuth von Moltke, suggested to his Austrian counterpart that the next war would pitch German against Slav. Moltke looked forward to this, though he stressed that public opinion in Germany, Austria-Hungary and elsewhere would be more easily managed if Russia could be presented as the aggressor.[32]

To Austrian emperor Franz Joseph and his advisers, a satisfactory settlement in the Balkans could only be achieved by a general war. On 28 June 1914, Franz Joseph's nephew and heir Franz Ferdinand was murdered in the Bosnian capital Sarajevo. Since the assassins had links with a secret society in Belgrade, the Austrians blamed Serbia. Here was an opportunity to exterminate the Serbian challenge and deal also with the nationalities issue within the empire, and in this determination Vienna was backed by Kaiser Wilhelm II and the government of Germany.[33]

Grey called upon France, Italy and Germany to join Britain in an effort to broker an agreement, but the Austrians declared war on Serbia, and Belgrade was bombarded on 28 July 1914. The Russians mobilized when Serbia appealed for help and Germany declared war on Russia on 1 August. Berlin offered France the opportunity to remain neutral, provided the military bases at Toulon and Verdun were handed over to Germany. The French response was to mobilize, and Germany declared war on France on 3 August.[34]

The great powers had lost control over events. From the late nineteenth century the pattern of alliances changed, states feared war less than they feared standing alone when war broke out, and a formerly stable international states system crumbled.[35] A confused mixture of ambiguity and rigidity made it impossible to solve the final crisis. The Germans believed that their security was at stake. The Russians believed that Austrian intervention in the Balkans would undermine Russia's security. All the interested powers thought that delay would rob them of the initiative. Mobilization plans were inflexible and alliances largely unconditional and offensive. Britain and France could not demand that the Russians limit themselves to defensive actions only, and needed to preserve their relationship with Russia for their own protection. French security depended on the maintenance of Russian power. Britain did not realize that German mobilization would mean war and that, in order to prevent this, Britain would need to stop Russia from mobilizing first. Perhaps British policy was not sufficiently firm, and this misled the Germans, yet British leaders were unsure about the German policy to which they were reacting and the Germans had necessarily to keep their plans secret, particularly the intention to attack France through Belgium.[36]

Britain refused a German proposal at the beginning of August 1914 because it would have entailed abandoning France and bargaining away the longstanding British interest in the integrity of Belgium, which in turn affected the approaches to the North Sea and English Channel, vital to British security. Grey persuaded the cabinet to authorize the Royal Navy to defend French coasts and shipping from the Germans. Then Belgium appealed for British protection. Britain was a signatory to the international convention of 1839 that guaranteed Belgium, and had reasserted its commitment to Belgium in 1870 during the Franco-Prussian War. Now German forces invaded Belgium in order to facilitate their offensive against France. In Britain, popular sympathy for Belgium and outrage at German aggression created a wave of support for war. The invasion of Belgium also united the Asquith government, some members of which had insisted that Britain should not join in the European conflict. The government sent an ultimatum to the Germans, requesting their withdrawal from Belgian territory. Germany did not comply and the ultimatum expired at midnight on 4 August.[37]

Grey had tried to prolong the peace while preserving for Britain the freedom to make decisions up to the last minute should war break out. He had also ensured that if the British had to fight they would not lack friends. Though the ententes were not alliances, Anglo-French co-operation in particular had developed in such a way as to make it unlikely that Britain would stay out of a war in which

France and Germany faced each other. The German invasion of Belgium had a bearing on cabinet deliberations, but by itself it did not bring Britain into the war. The cabinet decided on 29 July that the commitment to Belgium fell collectively, not individually, upon the five signatories to the 1839 agreement (Britain, France, Russia, Austria and Prussia). Asquith informed King George V that if Britain went to war, it would be a matter of policy rather than obligation. In London, during the weekend of 1 to 3 August, there were mass demonstrations in favour of war, and by 3 August the cabinet had agreed that Britain would fight. The main reasons for this were the sense of duty to France, anxiety about control of the English Channel, and the idea that if Britain stayed out of the war, and Germany won, sooner or later Britain would have to confront a greatly strengthened adversary.[38]

This decision was not easily reached, though, and there was much confusion in late July and early August 1914, in Berlin as well as in London. The German government had for some time been listening to advisers who doubted Britain's will to fight, while nobody in Britain except Grey knew how far Britain was committed to France.[39] Uncertainty went hand in hand with error. On the British side, wider strategic questions were not properly addressed in the months before August 1914. For the Liberal party leadership the primary task was to avoid a government split.[40]

Grey had no doubt that Britain was bound to fight alongside the French, but he could never be sure how far cabinet, parliament and public opinion would be willing to go. In his speech in the House of Commons on 3 August 1914, he admitted that Britain had made no binding promises to France. There was friendship, however, and this had evolved so far that Grey considered it to equate to a commitment, one that accorded rather than clashed with British objectives. Indeed, self-interest coincided with moral duty. To stand aside, Grey declared, would be to forfeit Britain's good name and to jeopardize the nation's essential interests.[41]

After the war, a defeated Germany took responsibility for causing it. The 'war guilt clause' was included in the Treaty of Versailles of 1919 and was controversial at the time and afterwards.[42] While it is clear that Germany acted in a way that made war more likely, it is also the case that war was greeted enthusiastically at élite and popular levels in all the belligerent nations, which indicates that they all believed they had a reason to fight. Some historians have suggested that the war began because governments wished to turn attention away from domestic problems by means of an adventurous foreign policy.[43]

It is true that Asquith's government faced difficulties at home (social welfare, Ireland, votes for women, the prerogatives of the House of Lords, the economy, industrial relations). But if the government really wanted to divert attention with a war, the prime minister would hardly have objected as he did to Anglo-French military conversations; Grey would not have tried so hard to prevent escalation in the Balkans, and the cabinet would not have been divided on the question of going to war until the last moment in the summer of 1914.[44] There were problems in the empire,[45] and the war was partly fought for imperial reasons, but this is not the same as fighting a war to take attention away from domestic issues.

Still, one might ask why the statesmen of the day were so sensitive about war guilt. This was a constant theme in both wartime propaganda and post-war claims. For Britain and its allies, freedom from blame was needed in order to justify the peace terms. For the Germans it was important to deny responsibility for the war in order to bolster allegations about unfair treatment by the victorious powers. It is probable that Germany had not wanted a major war of the kind that broke out in 1914.[46]

The idea that Britain should have stayed out of the war runs counter to the view taken at the time and afterwards that Germany had to be prevented from dominating Europe.[47] Questions might still be asked, however, about the choices made by Grey. Under Salisbury and Lansdowne, British policy was flexible, and by the time the Liberals took office in 1905, Britain's diplomatic position was stronger than it had been for some time. These facts were not sufficiently appreciated by Grey, according to modern critics who think that he was wrong to see Germany as a threat and wrong to attach such importance to co-operation with France and Russia.[48]

One problem here is that British policy was directly influenced by German policy. Grey did not simply act on his own whims. He had to take account of what was happening in Europe and beyond. Berlin might genuinely have wanted an agreement with Britain, but the German government made a mistake in thinking that the way to get this was to expose British weaknesses. Since London was convinced by 1914 that the Germans would not rest until they were ascendant in Europe, it made sense to help France and fight against Germany when war broke out. The Germans had added naval strength to their existing military power on the continent and seemed to believe that war was necessary if their nation was to fulfil its destiny.[49]

Germany's determination to challenge Britain cannot be discounted, and in 1914 the German government did not opt for war only because of British policy. Remaining neutral was not a viable prospect for Britain, meanwhile, and Grey had grounds to regard Germany as dangerous. He was not alone: members of the Conservative opposition in parliament were even more suspicious of Germany. Moreover, to exaggerate the difference between pre- and post-1905 British policy and to accuse Grey of a rigid, proactive approach that contravened the non-committal methods perfected by Salisbury, without taking proper account of changes in the international environment, is to do a serious disservice to Grey.

It must also be remembered that Britain fought in 1914 for imperial reasons, alongside the concern about the future of Europe. The British had to safeguard their far-flung territories, not just the home islands, and believed that victory for Germany and its allies would endanger the whole empire. The government called on the colonies and dominions to help, and help they did, with troops and resources.[50]

To suggest that there was a fundamental shift in British policy in the early twentieth century – the relinquishing of 'isolation'[51] – is to overstate what happened, and it is no less misleading to exaggerate the change than it is to argue that everything stayed the same. As international circumstances made it more difficult for Britain to sustain its global position, no government and no foreign secretary could afford to ignore the needs and opportunities of the day.

The title of a book published by H.G. Wells in 1914 set the tone for post-war attitudes in Britain: *The War That Will End War*. The political failures, social hardship, moral disorder and terrible carnage associated with the 'Great War' made people think that it could never be allowed to happen again, which helped to create the appeasement mood of the 1920s and 1930s. Appeasement has come to have negative connotations, yet appeasement was meant to keep the peace, an aspiration of which few did not approve. It was not an admission of weakness. In fact, its supporters saw it as a policy of strength and honour. It was meant to pacify and satisfy other states. The context in which British governments tried to do this changed enormously as the relatively calm 1920s became the hazardous 1930s.[52]

Many historians have disparaged appeasement. To Correlli Barnett, for example, appeasement is best defined as a preference for so-called 'morality' over power, and a readiness to yield to pressure.[53] Measures of appeasement seemed appropriate to contemporaries, however, and with respect to Germany were widely accepted as necessary. The main impulse in the 1920s stemmed from the shocking impact of the First World War and the feeling that the war had been futile, disastrous and wrong.[54]

In the 1920s there was real faith in international harmony and stability. In January 1919 the peace conference in Paris approved a proposal for the formation of the League of Nations. This body was dedicated to disarmament, arbitration and collective security. Its influence proved in the long run to be limited, for it lacked an army and depended on the great powers to implement its resolutions, and it suffered considerably from the stance of the Americans, who did not join the League and minimized their involvement in European affairs in the interwar period. Still, in the mid- to late 1920s there was the 'Locarno spirit', a reference to the Locarno conference of October 1925, which demonstrated that the victorious powers of 1918 were committed to a normalization of their relations with the new democratic republic of Germany, ruled from Weimar. Locarno was taken as proof that disputes could be resolved amicably. Britain was an active participant, and international co-operation was a principal goal of successive governments, irrespective of their party complexion. The Conservatives were in office under Andrew Bonar Law in 1922–23 and under Stanley Baldwin in 1923–24 and 1924–29. Labour was in office from January to November 1924 under James Ramsay MacDonald, and again under MacDonald in 1929–31. Conservative-dominated national coalition governments were in office under MacDonald in 1931–35 and Baldwin in 1935–37.[55]

In this era of peace and promise it seemed appropriate for the British to scale down their armaments. Ironically, in view of his later reputation as an anti-appeaser, the retrenchment drive was presided over by Winston Churchill, who served as chancellor of the exchequer, 1924–29, after rejoining the Conservatives. At the time the reductions had much support, but they put Britain at a disad-vantage when it came to efforts to influence others in the 1930s. The First World War had transformed international affairs and problems of adjustment were particularly acute in the foreign office. Whatever the difficulties facing policy makers, though, public opinion was for peace and this was clearly reflected in sections of the British press.[56]

British power after the First World War was still considerable. Some historians argue that economic, political and military circumstances prompted compro-mises, with the result that Britain's influence and independence were eroded.[57] In fact, the 1920s saw no headlong retreat on Britain's part. In terms of prestige, geopolitical position and the skill of its statesmen, Britain continued to do well. Economic problems were increasing, but influence rested on more than the performance of the economy.[58]

German foreign policy in the time of the Weimar Republic was designed above all to amend the Treaty of Versailles, which, it was felt, had been unduly harsh on Germany. The Versailles terms were evaded in various ways, sometimes prompting Britain and especially France into retaliation, but with the rise of the 'Locarno spirit' there was more willingness in London and Paris to negotiate, and this was exploited by the leading figure in German politics between 1923 and 1929, Gustav Stresemann.[59] Germany joined the League of Nations in 1926. In 1927 Britain and France agreed that the occupying force in the Rhineland should be reduced in size and declared that the rights of German minorities outside Germany must be respected. In 1928 Germany was one of sixty-five states to sign the Kellogg Briand Pact, which rejected war as an instrument of national policy (Frank Kellogg was US secretary of state and Aristide Briand French foreign minister). The vexed question of war reparations was settled in 1929. These were useful developments, but the economic and political chaos engendered by global depression, at its worst between 1929 and 1932, had a dramatic impact in Germany, where Adolf Hitler and the Nazis were able to overturn the Weimar Republic in 1933. Hitler left the League of Nations and massively increased Germany's military spending.[60]

This exacerbated the difficulties British leaders had been experiencing when trying to decide on the best course to take in Europe and beyond. Some thought of withdrawing from Europe after the First World War and focusing on the empire; others insisted that Britain must play a leading role in Europe, but could not agree on whether to pursue stability through the League of Nations or to arrange for smaller bargains to improve relations between France and Germany. Although a detailed scheme of disarmament did not arise in the 1920s, in part because Germany resented the limits placed on its military capacity,[61] British leaders wanted Germany to be admitted to the League and there was less talk of war guilt and more talk of the need to rehabilitate Germany.[62] Co-operation between Germany and the Soviet Union brought complications. These two outcast states had concluded the Treaty of Rapallo in April 1922. They established diplomatic and economic links and renounced financial claims arising from the First World War, and secretly agreed to assist each other with military training and weapons testing. British concerns about the impact of this relationship increased the eagerness to act as mediator between France and Germany, so as to stabilize Western Europe and turn Germany away from the Soviets. The Locarno conference was important to Britain for these reasons,[63] but it left many matters unresolved and there were quarrels between Britain and France before and after the conference, indicating a fundamental disagreement about how to handle European problems.[64]

The main terms of the Treaty of Versailles and the British view that Germany had a right to complain about them have prompted much debate.[65] International relations in the 1920s and 1930s were materially shaped by differing opinions about revisions to Versailles, and these in turn were related to the ongoing problem of disarmament. After the lack of progress in the 1920s, a new effort was made at the Geneva disarmament conference of 1932–34. The British were reluctant to press for a substantial treaty, however, because after downsizing their own military establishment they required other governments to follow Britain's example. They were not prepared to make further reductions themselves.[66]

As Hitler established himself in power in Germany, the British grew concerned about his intentions, but they were much more worried about Japanese expansion in Asia and about the schemes of Josef Stalin, dictator of the Soviet Union. Japan had fought in the First World War against Germany and its allies, and subsequently in the Russian civil war against the Bolsheviks. Political, economic and cultural influences combined to increase Japan's wish for territory and influence, while Britain, France and the United States pressed Japan to abide by collective agreements and, in particular, to keep out of China. The Anglo-Japanese alliance was allowed to lapse. By treaties signed in Washington DC in 1921–22, a ratio of 5:5:3 for naval strength was agreed for America, Britain and Japan; these three powers plus France guaranteed one another's possessions in the Pacific; and China's independence was recognized. The idea spread among Japanese leaders, and especially its army chiefs, that friendship with the Western powers was incompatible with Japan's needs and ambitions, and this notion was reinforced as economic depression hit the West in 1929–32 and appeared to weaken its ability to withstand Japanese designs in Asia. A puppet state was set up in Manchuria in 1932 and in 1933 Japan left the League of Nations.[67]

British suspicion of Russia, which had been so strong in the nineteenth century and was not entirely allayed in the years before the First World War, quickly revived as a result of the Bolshevik coup of 1917 and the establishment of the Union of Soviet Socialist Republics in 1922. Stalin became leader of the USSR in 1924. In his statements on foreign policy he stressed his desire for peace and trade while warning other powers not to interfere in Soviet affairs. After 1933 he treated Nazi Germany as the main threat. In this he was correct, but otherwise Stalin's decisions owed a lot to his own paranoia. Determined to prevent the army from becoming a rival power base within the Soviet Union, he removed more than half his generals during the purges of the mid-1930s. He was also convinced that Britain and France were willing for Germany to grow strong because they hoped in due course to turn Germany against the Soviet Union.[68]

Worried about Germany and Japan, suspicious of the Soviet Union, conscious of US isolationism and unsure about the reliability of France, Britain became more apprehensive. In the 1920s, circumstances had been different and measures of appeasement – constructive efforts to promote agreement, solve problems and reduce tension – had been successful. In Europe, the primary task was to control Germany's post-war revival and gradually to bring Germany back into the comity of nations. Britain was ready to reduce the reparations bill and grant Germany equal rights. After 1933 reparations had been stopped and Hitler had left the League on the grounds that Germany was being denied equal rights, so these bargaining tools were gone. The need now was to find out what Hitler wanted. There were hopes that in making agreements with Germany, a concession on one side would be met with a concession on the other. Under the Anglo-German Naval Agreement of June 1935, Germany promised not to build more than 35 per cent of the Royal Navy's strength in all classes of vessel, and Britain agreed that submarines would not be subject to this ceiling. While London viewed this bargain as a measure of arms limitation that would help in restraining Germany, Berlin, on the other hand, saw it as a means of pressurizing France and the Soviet Union. It was controversial because it contradicted the disarmament clauses in the Treaty of Versailles, and the French and Italian governments complained about Britain's failure to consult them.[69]

If the appeasement policy was to remain robust, it was important to bargain from a position of strength and to obtain something back for everything offered. As circumstances changed, the policy fell apart. So anxious were they to keep the peace that the chief appeasers were prepared to make unilateral concessions. The motives remained correct, it might be argued, but the methods were flawed. It is not easy to see how matters could have been better managed: the Germans pretended to be appeaseable.

The task of reaching an understanding with the Nazi regime was hindered by internal problems. Negotiations often involved economic incentives, for instance, and the foreign office wanted to be more proactive in this. In the treasury and the Bank of England there was resistance. Although economic aid offered a possible antidote to German extremism, there was no agreement about the way it should be used.[70] International economic relations formed the essential backdrop and it is possible that assessments of the general situation were unduly pessimistic.[71] If this is true, Britain's diplomacy in the 1930s must have been affected more by political errors than by economic failures, a supposition that reinforces the claims of those historians who wish to attach blame to particular individuals or government bodies.

The treasury was the most influential department because it controlled the public purse. Alfred Duff Cooper, secretary of state for war 1935–36 and first lord of the admiralty 1936–38, considered the treasury's influence excessive. More recently it has been argued that the treasury determined defence priorities, and that senior Conservative ministers attached more importance to financial stability than to national security. Some historians have defended the treasury, pointing out that careful supervision was needed to ensure that resources were not wasted. By setting limits the treasury made sure that all available funds had not already been spent when war came in 1939. The treasury's main concern in the 1930s was to maintain Britain's economic competitiveness and future earning capacity.[72]

In addition to fear of distorting the economy and losing exports, there was concern about the shortage of skilled labour in Britain and a determination to avoid a cycle of boom and bust. The depression of 1929–32 was like a spectre that haunted legislators and there was no wish to jeopardize recovery through incautious measures of intervention. This was the position of Neville Chamberlain, who was chancellor of the exchequer from November 1931 and succeeded Baldwin as prime minister in May 1937. Only after the 'Anschluss' of March 1938, the union of Germany and Austria, forbidden at Versailles, was Chamberlain willing to abandon the principle that rearmament should not encroach on Britain's foreign trade. The treasury's assumptions were really those of the established order in politics and society. One had only to look abroad to see that extremists thrived in times of economic distress. An ambitious rearmament programme would cost too much, and if money had to be printed to pay for it, inflation would set in and business confidence would plummet. Conservative ministers, MPs and supporters in the country did not want to endanger the social and economic structures from which they benefited.[73]

Nevertheless, the situation in Europe required a more energetic response on Britain's part. When he was in office, many observers thought Baldwin inattentive when it came to international affairs. Meanwhile the Germans continued to be inconsistent and awkward. Hopes were raised towards the end of 1934 and it seemed that negotiations might be leading somewhere. Permanent under-secretary at the foreign office (1930–38) Robert Vansittart thought so, but then the Nazi leadership became more truculent.[74] Britain's dealings with Germany were also affected by the attitude of the French, who became nervous and demanding. After the First World War they had expected to make Germany harmless, and this had not happened. France might have been more confident had the old alliance with Russia remained intact, but the establishment of the Bolshevik regime in Russia meant that some other way had to be found to create the prospect of war on two fronts for Germany if it resorted to aggression. Links were established in the 1920s with Poland and with the 'Little Entente' of Czechoslovakia, Yugoslavia and Rumania, but these were no substitute for Tsarist Russia when it came to deterring Germany. In 1934 the Polish government agreed a non-aggression pact with Germany. As for the 'Little Entente', it was never a robust alliance and from 1935 Yugoslavia pursued a pro-German policy.[75]

Anglo-French relations were hampered by errors on both sides. On naval construction, disarmament, intelligence, economic links, co-operation in and outside Europe, and on what to do about Germany and Italy, London and Paris had common interests and yet worked together intermittently. Partly this was due to British insularity and the traditional notion that Britain should rise above the European powers and arbitrate between them.[76]

Without a strong eastern ally the French became more dependent on Britain. Since Eastern Europe was not strategically important to Britain, and since it had been tensions there that had triggered off the First World War, the British were unwilling to get involved in the region or to make any commitments concerning it, and they warned the French not to provoke Berlin. The French put together a security plan that they thought would ensure peace in Europe. British leaders initially went along with it, hoping to promote what they really wanted: Anglo-French-Italian co-operation against Germany. The French envisaged a system of pacts covering Eastern Europe; an air pact; Germany's return to the League of Nations, and a relaxation of the limits on German rearmament. Much to their disappointment, nobody else approved of this package in its entirety. The British ambassador in Berlin (1933–37) Eric Phipps commented that the real need was for a bargain that would have enough 'teeth' to satisfy the French, while being sufficiently 'toothless' to satisfy the Germans. Phipps did think that an understanding with Hitler was possible; his main proviso related to territorial concessions, which he did not consider appropriate. In the mid-1930s, evidently, the right mix of teeth and toothlessness was not within reach. It is also clear that the Nazis did not have to contend with a united opposition as they pursued their schemes for German revival. Washington DC distanced itself from European problems. London and Paris did not see eye to eye, and neither trusted Stalin, though France signed a treaty with the Soviet Union in May 1935 that provided for mutual aid in case of unprovoked aggression. The British hoped to preserve a common front with France and Italy, but Italian leader Benito Mussolini decided that he could get more out of friendship with Hitler.[77]

The French could obtain no guarantees from Britain while the Germans stepped up their propaganda relating to frontier disputes and the presence of German minorities in Eastern Europe. Fortunately for Hitler, Britain, Poland and the Soviet Union did not combine together. They each thought that security would come not through multilateral co-operation but through better relations with Germany, and they did not explore the interdependency of their policies and the potential for collective restraints on Germany.[78]

As for Mussolini, one of his aims was the extension of Italy's possessions in Africa. Tension on the border between independent Ethiopia and neighbouring Italian areas led to an incident in December 1934. The matter was referred to the League of Nations, but the League procrastinated because Britain and France wished to avoid alienating Italy. Mussolini's forces invaded Ethiopia in October 1935. The League condemned Italy and imposed sanctions, but these inconvenienced the Italians hardly at all. Hitler took advantage of the controversy to send German troops into the Rhineland, which Versailles had demilitarized. The British were annoyed; they had planned to bring up the Rhineland in new talks with Germany. Foreign secretary (1935–38) Anthony Eden remarked that once again, by taking something that was about to be offered, the Germans had robbed Britain of the initiative.[79]

Attempts to accommodate Hitler were complicated by the machinations of Mussolini, who thought that victory in Ethiopia could be used to challenge the British in North Africa and the Mediterranean. Mussolini grew bolder because of the prospect of an alliance with Hitler. He expected to clash with Britain and France and knew that Italy, too weak to win alone, needed German support.[80]

Officials in London reasoned that Hitler wanted territory. Versailles had stripped Germany of its empire and some former German colonies were being administered as League of Nations mandates. Perhaps they could be returned to Germany. Perhaps the French would agree to hand over some of their possessions. Perhaps there could be a repartitioning of Africa. These ideas developed in the mid-1930s and demonstrate how serious the British were about pacifying a resurgent Germany. The belief was that peace could be maintained, but that this would require territorial adjustments. In February 1936 Vansittart wrote that a settlement with Germany could not be made unless it provided for German expansion, and, since an offer could not be made at the expense of others in Europe, it would have to be at Britain's own expense in Africa. Vansittart insisted that this transaction would have to be conditional on concessions from Germany. In return for territory, he thought, the Germans should agree to limit their armaments, abandon territorial claims in Europe and return to the League. Eden went further and argued that the colonial question was one for Germany, not Britain, to raise.[81]

Military planning was central to the policy of appeasement. With faith in collective security relatively strong in the 1920s, British defence spending fell both in absolute terms and as a share of national wealth. The largest share of the available money went to the Royal Navy, essential for the protection of trade and empire, although aircraft carriers were neglected. The Royal Air Force was developed primarily as long-range artillery for the destruction of enemy cities. This focus on bombers, however, meant that air defence was largely overlooked. As for the army, its main function was to provide for the internal security of British possessions. Little was spent on mechanization and new weapons and equipment. In the 1930s there was a change. Concerns about Japanese policy in Asia and German policy in Europe prompted the service chiefs to demand more money. Chamberlain's budget of 1937 was the first to make serious provision for rearmament.[82]

Still, there was inertia and delay, and for too long conciliation, not deterrence, was the goal. In some quarters there was a wish for closer co-operation with France. In others this was opposed, in case it encouraged the French to make demands of Germany. There were disagreements about the bomber force, seen as necessary by some but as a hindrance to diplomacy by others. The bombers gave Britain the ability to damage Germany, yet this could not prevent Germany from launching a first strike and made an arms race inevitable. Appeasement, if it could deliver a reduction in armaments, seemed preferable.[83]

British planning rested on a global system. The entire empire had to be defended and the principal threat to the empire was posed by Japan. After consolidating their position in Manchuria in 1931–32, the Japanese coveted the whole of northern China and the colonies of the European powers in South East Asia and the Pacific, especially those that had oil, iron ore, tin and rubber. For the British, Japanese expansionism endangered Australia and New Zealand, Malaya, Burma, India, and potentially also the Persian Gulf and British East Africa. In this context, one advantage of the Anglo-German Naval Agreement of 1935 was that it freed the Royal Navy to meet commitments in the Far East. Navy chiefs did not want to take on extra responsibilities in European waters. Army chiefs also prioritized the empire: this was an actual commitment, whereas Europe was a hypothetical commitment. These opinions were strengthened when Germany and Japan signed the Anti-Comintern Pact in November 1936. The pact provided for joint action against international communism (Comintern had been set up by the Bolsheviks in 1919 to guide revolutionary movements abroad). Italy signed in

November 1937. Even as the situation in Europe became more ominous, global concerns were still taking precedence. The actions of Japan in Asia and those of Italy in Africa put at risk Britain's imperial possessions and communications. So did instability in the Middle East. From 1936 there was serious disorder in Palestine, which Britain administered as a League mandate.[84] Japan's conduct in the Far East worried the Americans as well as the British, and there was some co-operation there, but it was mostly limited and informal, and it did not make up for China's inability to resist Japan.[85]

If limited resources, the needs of imperial defence and events in the Far East appeared to make appeasement appropriate in Europe, so did Britain's vulnerability to attack from the air. Until 1937 it was assumed that no effective air defence was possible. The bomber deterrent represented the military side of appeasement. The plan was to use it alongside diplomatic efforts to bring the Germans to the negotiating table, and the favoured concept between 1934 and 1937 was parity deterrence: numerical equality with the Germans to show them that they would never be allowed air superiority.[86]

Britain lacked the means greatly to increase its responsibilities in Europe and in the wider world. The cardinal necessity, as the defence requirements sub-committee made clear in a report of 1935, was to avoid simultaneous hostilities on three fronts: with Germany in Europe, Japan in Asia and Italy in Africa. The minister for the co-ordination of defence (1936–39), Thomas Inskip, declared in February 1938 that it was beyond Britain's capacity to provide for the defence of Britain and the empire against three powers in three different theatres.[87]

The defence requirements sub-committee had been appointed by the cabinet in October 1933 to investigate deficiencies in Britain's global system. Its reports indicated that navy, army and air force all had to be improved, but initially it focused on the Far East as the area that was most in need of attention. A quarrel developed as a result of the German threat closer to home. For the treasury, naval spending could be minimized by means of a thaw in relations with Japan. The foreign office disliked this idea, not least because it would offend the United States, but chancellor of the exchequer Neville Chamberlain was less concerned about offending the Americans than he was about the strength of the German air force. He advocated a rapprochement with Japan, which never materialized, and such influences on rearmament policy had consequences later on as Britain was reduced to a weaker bargaining position.[88]

British policy was directly shaped by intelligence. During the 1930s the British government had little accurate information about the strength of potential aggressors. There were breaches of security, and assessments about the course of events in Europe, the Far East and elsewhere varied wildly. The regimes that the British were trying to keep tabs on – in Berlin, Tokyo, Moscow and Rome – were unpredictable and deceitful. Neglect did not help, for the intelligence service was

not properly funded and the machinery for collecting and evaluating information was inadequate. This encouraged misconceptions: an underestimation of
German air power, for instance, and the belief that the German navy would operate primarily in the Baltic. Britain's navy chiefs lacked details about the capability
of German vessels and put their faith in the Anglo-German Naval Agreement,
which Berlin eventually repudiated in April 1939.[89] Better information would
probably have altered British policy in the 1930s.

Intelligence failings with regard to Japan matched those concerning Germany.
Racial prejudice played a part in British underestimation of Japan's military
strength, for assumptions about British superiority merged with an old impression that Japan was essentially cautious. In addition, the system for gathering
information in Asia was not only under-resourced but was directed against Soviet
influence in Asia and especially against anti-British activity in India, not just the
activities of Japan.[90]

If appeasement rested on poor intelligence, another influence was the mindset
of Britain's political and social élites. Within the governing class there was an
abhorrence of communism and the idea of co-operation with the Soviet Union
had little backing. The French were not liked or trusted, and there was in some
quarters an affinity with Germany, a sense of Anglo-Saxon kinship that had
cultural and historical supports. The change of regime in Germany in 1933 was
seen by many as akin to a normal change of government in Britain. Hitler was
an elected national leader. If encouraged, it was thought, he would be reasonable,
and the case for revision of the Treaty of Versailles was incontestable. When
Hitler remilitarized the Rhineland in 1936, Lord Lothian suggested that the
Germans were merely walking into their own back garden. Lothian, who had
been a member of the British delegation at the Paris peace conference and served
briefly in government in 1931–32, considered appeasement a decent, pragmatic
and helpful policy in the mid-1930s, and many people agreed with him.[91] Lord
Londonderry, who had been secretary of state for air (1931–35), thought that
the Germans had right on their side when they marched into the Rhineland.
Londonderry later declared the 'Anschluss' to be justifiable, since Austrians were
Germanic and wanted to be part of Germany (in fact, some estimates indicate
that fewer than half of the Austrian people favoured union with Germany).
Londonderry believed in appeasement and was sure that it would work.[92]

Appeasement had a reasonable and constructive side to it, especially before
Chamberlain became prime minister in 1937. Among foreign policy profession-
als it seemed proper for Britain to admit that Versailles was flawed. Vansittart
approved of the 'war guilt clause' while also, in 1931, suggesting that the military
clauses in the treaty could be dispensed with so as to allow Germany to introduce
conscription and to build up to French naval strength. In November 1935, a joint
memorandum by Orme Sargent and Ralph Wigram, the heads of the central

department in the foreign office 1928–33 and 1933–36 respectively, described parts of the Treaty of Versailles as untenable and indefensible. Such remarks show that the need for a settlement was recognized and that Versailles was seen as the logical place to start.[93]

These ideas and admissions do not mean that Britain was weak, and it is not the case that Germany was uninfluenced by British policy. Britain in the 1930s was certainly a great power, with its empire and global reach; its role in the League of Nations; its active foreign policy; its determination to maintain stability in important parts of the world and to co-operate with other powers when necessary to do this; its large navy and network of bases, and its economic and financial strength, which was still considerable despite the First World War and Great Depression. Senior Nazis thought of Britain as the main obstacle to their designs, though British leaders were conscious that their influence over Germany would be limited until rearmament was well under way.[94]

Appeasement was shaped at crucial times by the personnel involved, among them Nevile Henderson, the ambassador in Berlin from the spring of 1937. Henderson believed that Hitler was amenable, and when the crisis over Czechoslovakia developed in 1938 and it was clear that the Nazis would be satisfied with nothing less than annexation of the German-speaking areas of that country, Henderson insisted that this was not worth fighting over. He thought that if Britain was going to rearm, it should do so secretly rather than publicly in order to avoid any suggestion that Britain was prepared to go to war with Germany.[95]

On the Czech issue Henderson argued that Hitler wished to avoid war and that German claims were morally justified. For Henderson, and for others who thought as he did, there was a danger that Britain might be used as a pawn by France. Henderson thought that there need be no direct clash between Britain, dominant on the oceans, and Germany, which wanted to dominate Europe, and he made this point more than once to foreign secretary (1938–40) Lord Halifax. Even after the outbreak of the Second World War there were some who wanted to come to terms with Hitler. This was partly because of British suspicion of the Soviet Union.[96]

Britain's failure to conclude an agreement with the Soviets in this period has been called one of the greatest mistakes in the history of British diplomacy.[97] There was no enthusiasm for an agreement in London, however, while in Moscow there was anger at the tendency of British policy in the 1930s and particularly the failure to restrain Germany. From 1935 the British knew that their relations with the Soviets would be ruined if Britain tried unilaterally to negotiate with Hitler using territory in Eastern Europe. This, in effect, is what happened over Czechoslovakia in 1938. By the Munich Agreement of September 1938, Britain and France accepted Germany's annexation of the Sudetenland, the

German-speaking parts of Czechoslovakia. Chamberlain thought that he had ensured peace and that Hitler had given up any designs on the rest of Czechoslovakia, but Germany invaded in March 1939. In April Chamberlain offered to guarantee Poland, thought to be Hitler's next target. This guarantee could not possibly be effective without Soviet assistance, and Chamberlain lost leverage in that the agreement with Poland was simultaneously a guarantee for the Soviets, since the Germans could only attack the USSR through Poland. During April and May Britain also made agreements with Greece, Rumania and Turkey, but nothing was agreed with the Soviet Union. Chamberlain did not consider the Soviets to be militarily strong, and to his mind they needed Britain more than Britain needed them. Stalin hoped to postpone war between Germany and the Soviet Union, which coincided with the German desire to avoid a war on two fronts. Hitler did not want to fight the Soviets until he was ready. Therefore, in August 1939 Germany and the Soviet Union, to general surprise, concluded a non-aggression pact.[98]

Chamberlain was accused of a serious blunder. By the spring of 1939, for instance, Winston Churchill was urging the government to make friendly over-tures to Moscow. Yet Stalin would probably not have chosen Britain and France over Germany. He doubted that the British and French were strong enough to deter the Germans.[99]

Until the summer of 1939, most people in Britain opposed involvement in another European war. Efforts to keep the peace were widely supported. Signs of the public mood during the 1930s include the East Fulham by-election of October 1933, which resulted in what was hailed as a 'victory for pacifism' (the Labour candidate won the seat, overturning a large Conservative majority). During the early 1930s the League of Nations Union, which had been formed in 1918, organized a 'peace ballot' based on house-to-house canvassing. More than eleven million people participated, and when the results were published in 1935 they revealed overwhelming support for peace and disarmament. A Peace Pledge Union was established in 1936. At a debate in the Oxford Union in February 1933, the majority voted against fighting 'for king and country', which attracted enormous attention at home and abroad. The *Daily Express* considered it 'contemptible and indecent', while the *Manchester Guardian* argued that Oxford students were right to wonder why Britain had fought wars in the past and to consider the basis upon which they might be justified in the future. Public opinion polls, though they must be treated cautiously, indicate that British people did not want war and, when war came, had mistaken notions about what it would entail. Chamberlain and his colleagues believed that they were faith-fully reflecting the nation's preferences in their measures of appeasement. After Munich Chamberlain was a national hero, although the joke went round that he had turned all four cheeks to Hitler.[100] One of the leading peace campaigners in

Britain, Lord Cecil, a strong supporter of the League of Nations who had been in government during and after the First World War, later wrote of the peace ballot as a highly significant endeavour that had some influence on British policy, though not as much as he had hoped.[101]

For the chiefs of staff the most important consideration was that Britain could not fight a war on three fronts. Appeasement was therefore in the nation's best interests. The chiefs wanted as little to do with European problems as possible. They stressed that Britain did not have a continental-sized army. Disheartened by financial constraints, they considered Britain unprepared for war and in their annual reports of 1932 and 1937 stressed the under-spending since the First World War and the military strength of potential enemies.[102]

When serious problems arose, the government and chiefs of staff tried to find a way out, one that would restore calm and keep up appearances so that domestic and foreign observers would continue to believe in negotiation. The Czech crisis brought this endeavour to the point of collapse. London realized that the 'Anschluss' of March 1938 made more likely a German effort to dismember Czechoslovakia, especially as demonstrations broke out in the Sudetenland and Berlin accused the Czech authorities of mistreating German people there. Chamberlain asked the chiefs of staff to consider the military implications. The resulting assessment utilized outdated information and made Czechoslovakia seem more vulnerable than it really was. In August 1938 Chamberlain sent Walter Runciman, who had previously served in Liberal and national coalition governments, on a mission to the Sudetenland, ostensibly to listen to both sides but in fact to put pressure on the Czech government. Runciman agreed with Chamberlain on the need to avoid war: Britain was not ready to fight and war would ruin Britain's world position. The Runciman report was worded so as to justify the meeting at Munich. German interests apparently mattered more than the survival of Czechoslovakia, and what London really wanted was to remove impediments to peace and trade with Germany. But Munich had unfortunate consequences. It marked the abandonment of a democratic country and a well-defended frontier; it meant that France could no longer count on the Germans being distracted in Eastern Europe; and the loss of Czechoslovakia was the loss of a small but strong army, a thriving armaments industry, and a considerable amount of modern equipment and military stocks.[103]

When the Czech crisis demanded a solution, Chamberlain honestly believed that he was the man to take charge. He had been a successful mayor of Birmingham and entered parliament relatively late in life, but he had a sense of what mattered most to prosperous middle-class Conservatives and he rose quickly, serving as minister of health during the 1920s and then as chancellor of the exchequer, a post in which he won renown for paring down the defence estimates. Chamberlain was a strong debater and highly confident in his own judgement, but as prime minister this made him stubborn. Trusting in the ability of intelligent men to reason together, he thought of diplomacy as a series of businesslike dealings, for this was his experience in English provincial politics. His attitude, and his meddling in foreign policy, prompted the resignation of foreign secretary Anthony Eden in February 1938. Chamberlain was insisting on the need to keep Germany and Italy apart, which for him necessitated negotiations with Mussolini. Eden did not trust the Italian dictator, pointed to Italy's invasion of Ethiopia and intervention in the Spanish civil war, which had broken out in 1936, and argued that Chamberlain was wrong not to seek the help of US president Franklin D. Roosevelt and wrong to turn his back on the League of Nations and on the possibility of co-operation with the Soviet Union.[104]

To Chamberlain, the League was not fit for purpose. He did not respect the foreign office much, either, and this led to a break from the past in diplomatic concepts and methods.[105] The prime minister had some fixed ideas about the international order. He believed that his predecessor Baldwin had neglected European affairs and that this had damaged Britain's standing. He was convinced that Britain had no reliable allies and that the collective security sponsored by the League was obsolete. He had little confidence in the French or the Americans and did not trust the Soviets. Stalin's purges made him think that the Soviet Union was weaker than it appeared, and he thought that the price of Soviet help would be the spread of communism in Eastern Europe. In addition, the government was aware that opinion in the empire was very much against war. Indeed, it was not clear that the dominions would help if Britain fought in Europe for European reasons. In view of all this, Chamberlain thought that peace had to be preserved through personal diplomacy.[106]

Chamberlain treated the dispute between Berlin and Czechoslovakia as an obstacle to appeasement. In November 1937, British and French representatives met to discuss German policy and it was agreed that if Hitler proceeded with the 'Anschluss' no action would be taken, but French foreign minister (1936–38) Yvon Delbos pointed out that France and Czechoslovakia were allies. If the Czechs were attacked, France would have to fight. British leaders saw that, rather than risk another German conquest of France, which would lead to even greater difficulties in the future, Britain would also have to fight. The only way to avoid this was to put together a bargain that was acceptable to both the Czechs and the Germans. As the weaker party, it was Czechoslovakia that had to be pushed into making concessions. With the Munich Agreement Chamberlain assumed that the crisis had passed, that his approach had worked, and that Hitler's signature on an Anglo-German declaration of friendship reflected the German leader's prudence and good faith.[107]

The Labour MP Jack Lawson, who accepted the post of deputy commissioner for civil defence in the northern counties of England in April 1939, later recalled the sense at that time that war was coming and could not be averted. Labourites opposed Chamberlain's appeasement, but Lawson reckoned that a different policy would not have worked because Hitler could not be swayed by 'any combination of wisdom or power on this earth'. Lawson did not allow his opposition to Chamberlain to prevent him from serving his community: 'What I thought of Mr Chamberlain was one thing: the need for preparing shelters and succour for the people among whom my life had been spent, was another thing.'[108]

The Munich Agreement did allow Britain more time to prepare. Between September 1938 and September 1939, the country became more united; the Labour Party accepted rearmament; appeasement was discredited; the dominions became more likely to assist Britain, and defences were strengthened. Fighter aircraft and radar stations, in particular, helped to preserve Britain from invasion in the early part of the war. On the other hand, in the same twelve months the German army doubled in size, Czechoslovakia was lost, all chance of Soviet assistance was forfeited, French morale was undermined, and the reputations of Britain and France suffered all over the world.[109]

Britain and France lacked the will to fight Germany in 1938. By September 1939 the French were stronger militarily, but there were political divisions and economic problems.[110] It is not easy to see any great improvement in Britain's military position relative to Germany's in 1938–39, a year during which Germany spent five times more than Britain did on defence. Even radar was not effective until after the war started. Indeed, Britain was stronger militarily in 1940 than in 1939. It is true that the British were unprepared for war in 1938, but it does not follow that they were at a bigger disadvantage then than they were in 1939, when Germany was also better armed and no longer had to worry about an attack from the east.[111] The idea that September 1938 was a lost opportunity is not very sound. Perhaps March 1936, when Hitler remilitarized the Rhineland, better fits the bill. Germany was certainly more beatable in 1936 than in 1938 or 1939. Again, though, the probable outcome of war in 1936 is open to debate, as is the outcome of war in 1938.[112]

The pros and cons of Munich, and of Chamberlain's policy as a whole, will continue to be contested. In the 1940s Chamberlain was strongly condemned, but he was also defended, and in the 1960s there were both negative and sympathetic treatments.[113] Attempts were made thereafter to validate what Chamberlain did. The idea that he was weak and naïve was rejected; appeasement was presented as the best available policy and one that was realistic and had popular support. The prime minister, it was argued, knew that Britain needed time to rearm. Britain's strategic situation was worse than it had been in 1914, and, according to this interpretation, Chamberlain should not be reproached for trying to prevent war and then to postpone it when it became more likely.[114] As chancellor of the exchequer he had realized that Britain's resources had to be husbanded carefully, and he was also aware of the impact of the First World War and Great Depression and of the British public's aversion to high taxes and rearmament. The longer war was delayed, the better chance Britain had of surviving it.[115] Recent biographers of Chamberlain admit to his arrogance and impatience, but a plea is also made that it would have been beyond *anyone* (not only Chamberlain) to advance Britain more quickly towards war readiness.[116]

The revised, kinder assessment of Chamberlain's appeasement does not enjoy universal approval. In negative accounts, much is made of the pitfalls of personal diplomacy and of Chamberlain's inability to avoid them. He was too quick to rule out other options, it is thought, and erroneously presumed that he alone could remedy international problems.[117] Despite a growing appreciation of the political, economic and imperial problems and the cultural influences that shaped the thinking of Chamberlain and his colleagues, it is suggested that personality and individual choice cannot be discounted and that blame should not be removed from Chamberlain and placed elsewhere. Another claim is that Chamberlain engaged in misrepresentation and manipulation, controlling the public relations side of foreign policy and making it seem that government and nation were more solidly behind appeasement than they really were.[118]

Before he became prime minister, appeasement was on firmer ground and had more support. Its priority was to keep the peace by addressing genuine German grievances. Under Chamberlain, however, appeasement became more of a personal crusade, and he persisted with it after many in government, parliament and the nation had turned against it. He believed it was working. Though not weak or foolish, he deceived himself. The desire for stability was not in itself discreditable, but the premise here is that it would have been possible to stop Hitler had British policy been different.[119]

Since it is difficult to tell whether alternative options were viable, we cannot be certain that they would have worked, which also means that we cannot be certain that Chamberlain's policy, in the circumstances of the time, was incorrect. Any British prime minister would have faced the same problem that Chamberlain did: how to preserve Britain's global interests at a time when resources were already overstretched.[120] It is important also to remember that responsibility for what happened in 1938–39 was not Chamberlain's alone. In government and society it was a fundamental precept that war must be avoided, for war would mean economic ruin and the break-up of the empire. It was difficult to think differently.[121]

Appeasement failed because Nazi foreign policy was assertive and destabilizing, but this failure does not automatically mean that appeasement was unrealistic. It only became so later on, in 1938–39, when the Hitler regime proved itself to be bent on aggrandizement through military aggression. No settlement with the Nazis was possible. In the course of international relations, though, it has to be admitted that this was an unusual situation. The normal assumption was that agreements *were* possible. While this assumption remained intact, appeasement had necessity, morality and expediency to recommend it. Once it became obvious that appeasement would not work, thoughts turned to its abandonment, but it was not unreasonable to try to salvage something first.[122]

After the outbreak of war there were calls for Britain to make an early peace with Germany. Churchill became prime minister in May 1940. Some historians have emphasized his failure to ensure Britain's survival as an independent world power. They think he could have negotiated an end to the fighting, or fought a limited war so as to avoid the exhaustion of Britain's resources. As it turned out, declaring for total victory committed the nation to a conflict that cost more than Britain could afford to pay. Victory may have had noble connotations, but with it came the end of Britain's role and status in the world.[123]

Privately, Churchill did consider a negotiated peace with Germany. In public, however, he appeared resilient, which was essential if he was to bolster the national spirit. Unconditional surrender did not become a war aim until 1943, when the Americans and Soviets as well as the British were fighting against Germany. In 1940 it would have been impossible for Britain alone to win total victory.[124] Negative assessments of Churchill's war leadership are outnumbered by more favourable accounts, although these often allow Churchill's own version of events to determine the interpretative agenda.[125]

The ramifications of a long and exhausting war in terms of Britain's control over its empire are also important here, for an early peace with Germany might have allowed Britain to defend key possessions in Asia, which fell to the Japanese.[126] Military defeat at the hands of Japan weakened Britain's authority when the colonies were regained after the war. On the other hand, it is not clear that British reinforcements could have been transferred from Europe to Asia in sufficient numbers, and post-war independence movements in the empire had wider foundations than simply the previous territorial expansion of Japan. Britain's future international role would also be significantly affected by the massive expansion of American and Soviet power in the 1940s.[127]

During and after the Second World War there was a shift in focus, for the main threat to the security of Britain and the empire was seen to be the Soviet Union rather than Germany, and debates in London about deterrence, Europe and future strategy were increasingly shaped by assumptions about Stalin's designs. In some ways this marked a reversion to tradition. Before the 1910s Russia had been regarded as Britain's most dangerous geopolitical rival.[128]

As the world's leading power at the end of the nineteenth century, Britain wanted stability. Major change in international relations and the reorientation of political and economic networks across the globe were bound to inconvenience Britain: as top nation, the only way was down. To maintain the established order was to ensure continued primacy, but wars tend to be motors of change, and this is certainly true of the conflicts of 1914–18 and 1939–45. Though Britain did not lose these wars, it did lose its ascendancy. The governments of the late nineteenth century knew that wars could happen. Much thought was given to such questions as how to win wars when they could not be avoided, and how to make sure that the changes wrought by war did not damage Britain's economic and military strength in the long term. By 1945 Britain's future as a world power was at stake, but Churchill appeared confident – and not without reason. Each of the 'three circles' offered Britain the scope and opportunity to exercise influence, maintain status and so shape power relationships as to demonstrate continued independence, initiative and importance. As a contingent and relative quality, however, there could be no guarantee that Britain's power would not decrease. Indeed, it was clear by 1945 that in some parts of the world, Britain would need the help of allies, especially the United States. Uneven patterns of economic progress and the reconfiguration of international politics between the late nineteenth century and the mid-twentieth century, accelerated and accentuated by wars, greatly affected the economic basis of British power and relationships within the empire. Yet recovery was expected, and substantially achieved within five years of the end of the Second World War. Then events intruded and challenges arose to cast doubt on the long-term viability of the global role.

2

Post-war Adjustments

On 19 February 1947, British foreign secretary Ernest Bevin instructed Lord Inverchapel, Britain's ambassador in Washington DC, to inform the US state department that, owing to financial constraints, Britain could no longer support Greece and Turkey against communist insurgency and external pressure. The Americans would have to step in and take over. This was a turning point in post-war history. Bevin's success in persuading the United States to commit itself to security arrangements in Europe was regarded at the time and afterwards as a notable accomplishment, but was it a sign of British influence and ingenuity, or of failure and weakness? The desire to obtain American support did not mean that Britain was no longer a great power. London was able to provide for the security of Britain, the empire and a range of global interests, and to promote a European settlement after the Second World War, pursuing these ends both independently and in league with others. In Europe and beyond Britain played a leading role in post-war international relations, but economic problems imposed limitations, as did the need to work with allies. The British had to reassess aims and methods because they could not afford not to, but in the circumstances they did well. Prestige and influence were sustained.

This was a period in which the international order was rapidly changing. The disruption wrought by the Second World War necessitated adjustments on the part of all the great powers. The desire for peace and co-operation had led to the establishment of the United Nations on 24 October 1945, but the existence of the UN did not mean that the post-war years were free of tension.

In the historiography of the Cold War, most attention is paid to the United States and the USSR, though the focus is often on Europe, where the distinction between rival political and economic systems became most pronounced. Europe was the front line.[1] Some historians are of the opinion that Britain shares responsibility for the beginning of the Cold War, and this concentration on the actions of Britain (and other states) has drawn attention away from the USA and USSR and given rise to a more 'de-polarized' framework.[2] British leaders regarded the USSR as dangerous before the Americans did, and although the Cold War developed into a mainly US–Soviet contest, Britain influenced its course. Sometimes the British even prompted actions in the West before the purposes of the Soviet Union had been properly assessed. Anti-Soviet attitudes in the foreign office and the continuation of imperial concerns meant that the Cold War carried forward an already established enmity.[3]

Britain's imperial agenda was one of the causes of the Cold War. By 1945 the need to protect the empire had fostered the belief that Britain must have a say in what happened across Europe as well as in Asia, Africa and the Middle East. Britain had also to take into account American hostility towards British imperialism, as well as US opposition to Soviet aggrandizement. There could be no bargain with Stalin, even if he insisted that he would be satisfied with a security buffer in Eastern Europe and would not meddle in Britain's spheres of influence. Although the British had less influence than the United States and the USSR in the post-war world, they still had the potential to exercise power, especially through the empire, a global system upon which Britain could base its effort to regain equal status with the Americans and Soviets.[4]

The two superpowers could not ignore Britain. It is true that the Second World War had stretched Britain to the limit and that the military and economic resources needed to compete with the USA and USSR were not available, but past successes, trade, empire and high levels of defence spending gave the British a prominence in the world, and a sense of autonomy, that their real strength probably did not merit.[5]

In Britain, before and after the Second World War, the USSR was thought to represent an ideological, military, imperial and power-political threat.[6] During the war Churchill, who held the premiership until July 1945, knew that the Soviets' co-operation was necessary, but he hoped to prevent the formation of a closed Soviet bloc after the war. On this point he tried hard to win over the US president, Roosevelt, whose attitude was more equivocal.[7] Mistrust of Britain increased during 1944–45 in the US Congress and press, where it was claimed that the British would not repay their war debts and that their goal was to trick the United States into sustaining Britain's international position.[8]

At the Yalta conference early in 1945, Roosevelt sought to reassure the Soviets that the United States and Britain were not acting together against them. In return for the promise that American troops would leave Europe within two years, Stalin agreed that Poland and other parts of occupied Eastern Europe could choose their own forms of government.[9] It soon emerged that Stalin would not stick to this. Soviet foreign minister Vyacheslav Molotov admitted as much in March 1945. Roosevelt died in April. Instead of waiting until American troops had left Europe, and allowing British and American suspicions to decrease, the Soviets began to tighten their grip in Eastern Europe.[10]

Roosevelt's successor as president was Harry Truman, who declared that Stalin must abide by the Yalta agreements. Even so, the new president did not wish to annoy the Soviets, believing that their military help was still needed in Europe and against Japan. Truman later admitted that he had been too hasty in rejecting

Churchill's advice, and Churchill regretted that he had not gone to America to meet Truman immediately after Roosevelt's death.[11]

Germany surrendered in May 1945, and in July a Labour government took office in Britain. If there were great expectations at home for reform and improvement, the Cold War meant that changes in policy would not be so dramatic abroad. The new prime minister, Clement Attlee, and the foreign secretary, Bevin, shared Churchill's concern about the Soviets.

As one of the victorious allies, Britain shared in the occupation of Germany, and, despite emerging weakened from the war, Britain was incontestably the strongest regional state, spending more on defence in 1948 than all the other European countries combined. Political leaders, whether Conservative or Labour, saw Britain as a global power. Europe was important, but British interests were not confined to Europe.[12] Since the Soviets appeared to be intent on undermining not only European security but also the British empire, there was no option but for British forces to remain stationed all over the world, whatever the drain on resources. In December 1947 Bevin suggested to the US secretary of state (1947–49) George Marshall that there should be an English-speaking alliance to counter the Soviets *everywhere*, and Bevin began negotiating along these lines with Australia, New Zealand and Canada.

Stalin did not see Britain and America as inevitable partners. The Truman administration's abrupt ending of lend-lease, by which the Americans had provided aid to their wartime allies, was taken by the Soviets as a sign of American ruthlessness and was certainly a serious blow to Britain.[13] Ill feeling between Britain and the United States increased in 1945 and 1946.

Britain sought enhanced security for the empire and for Europe, and US help in achieving this. Attlee wished to balance continental commitments with the preservation of the empire. This meant refusing to commit substantial forces to Europe unless the obligation was shared by the United States. Bevin agreed. He wanted to show that Britain could be a reliable ally to America and to use this position to influence US policy. He was a tough negotiator. 'He talks a bit, rather rambling and portentous', noted the under-secretary of state for foreign affairs, Christopher Mayhew; 'I don't think he's got at all a disciplined mind. It's all shrewdness, experience and personality.' The anti-communist Bevin disliked the Soviet regime and decided that British interests would not be served if he tried to hold a balance between the two superpowers, or play them off against each other. He saw stability in Europe as the basis for lasting peace throughout the world. Therefore it was vital to persuade the Americans not to withdraw from European affairs.[14]

The Truman administration and US armed service chiefs were initially reluctant to commit. It looked as if there would be no special favours for Britain. Not only had lend-lease been ended as soon as Japan surrendered in August 1945, but the McMahon Act of 1946 ended atomic co-operation with Britain. Although British forces had helped to defeat Japan, moreover, the Americans directed occupation policy and the restoration of the Japanese economy had implications for Britain's own economic prospects.[15] Meanwhile the Soviets continued to interfere in Poland, the Balkans and central Asia, and to make demands about the future of Germany and Europe. Stalin had already made gains, particularly on occupation zones in Germany, at the 'Big Three' conferences in Teheran (November 1943), Yalta (February 1945) and Potsdam (July 1945), and these offered a foundation on which to build.[16] British disappointment about American policy deepened. Instead of demonizing British imperialism, it was thought, America should be doing something about Soviet expansionism. There was consternation at the rapid demobilization of US forces.[17]

Before his death, Roosevelt had decided to join with Britain in confronting Stalin. Truman and his advisers reversed this plan, preferring a more independent line. Until 1947 the US government chose not to challenge Stalin directly on such matters as democratic elections across Eastern Europe. This frustrated Bevin, who wanted Anglo-American co-operation against the Soviet Union. Bevin was also hindered by Britain's need for financial aid. Washington DC was ready to provide funds, but not to the extent that Britain desired, and American leaders saw an opportunity to weaken Britain's empire and British trade. Some accused the British of exaggerating their problems and insisted that Britain with its colonies must not be allowed to rise and challenge the United States economically. A loan of $3.75 billion was agreed in December 1945, but the Americans charged commercial rates (2 per cent interest over fifty years). They also argued that Britain should abandon imperial preference, yet retained their own high tariffs to protect US industries.[18]

Anglo-American relations further deteriorated as Britain was excluded from the USA's treaty with Nationalist China in November 1946, as the Americans exploited Britain's withdrawal from India in 1947 with a massive expansion in US exports to the former British possession, and as Britain tried in vain to gain US assistance in the eastern Mediterranean and Palestine. A civil war was raging in Greece, with British forces assisting the Greek government against communist rebels, while in Palestine, which Britain held as a UN mandate after 1945, there was violent conflict between Jews and Arabs. Britain decided to give up this mandate in 1947, and partition was agreed for 1948. London's pleas for US help were rebuffed. Bevin favoured the establishment of a single, bi-national Palestinian state. When circumstances ruled this out, his main concern was that the British should not lose Arab friendship. He also feared an increase in Soviet influence in the Middle East. But the Palestinian crisis was costing Britain £40 million a year by 1947 and was tying down 10 per cent of Britain's armed forces. Withdrawal was unavoidable.[19]

Christopher Mayhew thought that the British were undone by the actions of others, so that it became impossible to keep order in Palestine while trying to fulfil the pledges made in the Balfour Declaration of 1917: that is, promoting the establishment of a Jewish state while safeguarding the interests of the indigenous population. The Americans and Soviets both supported partition at the UN, probably because each hoped to replace Britain as the leading power in the Middle East.[20]

Britain still had worldwide commitments, and the strain of these prompted Attlee's government to look for ways to save money. The prime minister, treasury and board of trade recommended a rapid scaling down of overseas activity, but Bevin and the foreign office, and the chiefs of staff, warned that the Soviets would move into areas evacuated by Britain. Keeping imperial communications open, protecting investments and Britain's oil supply, defending free peoples against communism and Soviet aggrandizement, upholding British prestige and influence in the world: these and other needs had to be weighed carefully in order to make best use of the money and manpower available. The withdrawal from Palestine was difficult to accept. Might Britain not be pushed out of the Middle East altogether, and the empire cut in half? The chiefs of staff laid particular stress on air bases in the Middle East, which were within striking distance of Soviet oil fields and industrial centres.[21]

Unfortunately for Britain, extreme nationalism was developing in the Middle East and its leaders and beneficiaries were not in the mood for negotiation. Bevin's plans for regional economic development had little impact: Britain lacked the funds to make them work and most Arab leaders were so annoyed by what was happening in Palestine that they rejected proposals for a new Anglo-Arab understanding. Nationalism placed the ruling élites under pressure, as did religious militancy and fears about the spread of communism. For domestic reasons, some Arab rulers had to turn against Britain.[22]

In London, considerations of world status possibly mattered more than the perceived need to protect the Middle East or remain within striking distance of the USSR, although it is true that Egypt assumed a new strategic importance to Britain in the early Cold War. Britain was determined to maintain air bases in Egypt, and the Americans approved, despite their suspicions of British imperialism.[23] Then again, was the intention really to deter the USSR? Perhaps policy was only presented this way in order to build consensus at home and win US support for Britain's imperial objectives. The government did not wish to abandon too many commitments too quickly. There was an enduring belief in Britain's great-power status: hence the successful resistance to Attlee's notion of abandoning the Middle East and holding instead to a defensive line across Africa from Nigeria to Kenya.[24] There was still a determination to remain strong in the Middle East and to exclude others, the Americans as well as the Soviets.

While Attlee hoped that the Soviet Union would negotiate, and Bevin and the chiefs of staff opposed radical retrenchments in the belief that these would erode influence, nobody could deny that Britain's global position was weaker than before. Concern about the Middle East was matched by concern about Asia. Japanese victories in the war had a huge impact on Asians, for the European colonial powers lost their image of superiority. India gained its independence in 1947. Though it joined the Commonwealth, the loss of the Indian army depleted the manpower Britain required to defend the empire. Other former colonies did not join the Commonwealth, notably Burma.[25]

The link between metropolis and colonies was changing, but decolonization was not the straightforward result of any one factor. Britain's effort to remain a global power ruled out a hasty retreat from empire. Rather, there was a careful reordering of relationships, and in many places this went according to plan.[26] The dilemmas of empire were not unique to Britain, but they brought into sharper relief the need to reassess military and financial capabilities and manage commitments accordingly.

In Europe there were ongoing anxieties. Cold War mentality developed quickly before, during and after the Potsdam conference. The Soviets had refused to give way on many issues, and the British and Americans hoped that agreements on these could be worked out later as part of a full peace settlement. At this stage they still wanted to preserve 'Big Three' co-operation. During 1945 the Soviets were willing to talk. They wanted security guarantees and US economic assistance, but by February 1946 Stalin was suggesting that nothing much could be gained by compromising with the capitalist West.[27]

European recovery was retarded and tension increased. Stalin's demand for an enlarged Poland had implications for Germany. Although London and Washington DC decided that hindering Germany's economic recovery would be disastrous for the rest of Europe, there was also a desire to avoid a final breach with Stalin, and some policy makers in Britain and the United States were more worried about German revival than about Soviet expansion. There was much discussion about how to penalize Germany. Occupation zones had been agreed at Yalta but disputes arose with the Soviets on reparations and the most suitable system of government for post-war Germany.[28]

Moscow wanted maximum reparations from Germany and wished to prevent the incorporation of Germany into a military-economic bloc led by America.[29] The reparations issue was never settled. US secretary of state (1945–47) James Byrnes suggested that a deal could be postponed. In the meantime, the occupying powers would use resources from their own zones and the western zones would send industrial material into the Soviet zone in return for food. Despite discussions over following years, no progress was made.[30]

Alec Cairncross, head of the Economics Advisory Council in Berlin in 1945 and subsequently an adviser to the British government, later argued that the occupying powers ought to have made separate arrangements because the attempt to find common ground merely increased rancour. London and Washington DC were moved by German protests. The British and Americans wanted, in time, to make Germany self-supporting and this was not compatible with heavy reparations demands. The French made difficulties. They wanted to strengthen themselves and weaken Germany. The Soviets preferred centralization and a command economy, with an opportunity for German communists led by Walter Ulbricht to dominate, while the United States and Britain wanted a federal system and free enterprise. In the summer of 1946 the British, Americans and French stopped sending reparations to the Soviets and arranged for the economic union of their three zones. In September Truman announced that US forces would remain in Germany until stability was assured.[31]

European co-operation was widely regarded as the most promising basis for a new post-war order. American leaders were in favour of this because they wanted Europeans to be self-reliant, so that US involvement could be reduced. In contemplating European unity, the British wanted limited collective agreements with no loss of independent action. To Bevin, and to the senior Conservatives Churchill and Eden, Britain was still a world power. Co-operation with the Europeans was appropriate, but it was not the priority. Bevin's main goal remained unchanged: binding the Americans to Europe.[32]

As Bevin told the House of Commons in February 1947, Anglo-American friendship was an end in itself, but it was also part of the bigger picture. Without it, what hope could there be of restoring economies and establishing peace and security in Europe? A reinvigorated West would discourage the Soviets from taking risks, Bevin thought; but if the West appeared weak and divided, the Soviets would seek to control all of Europe.[33]

The fact that Washington DC was exhibiting greater unease about Stalin's plans led Bevin to contemplate a firmer Anglo-American alliance, based on history, ideals and strategy. The American attitude was more pragmatic: the key was to decide how *useful* Britain could be. Soviet leaders, though they knew that the Americans were more powerful than the British, regarded Britain as the more astute and so the more implacable enemy.[34]

For a time Bevin's policy was not overtly or automatically anti-Soviet. There were serious disagreements between London and Washington DC and it still seemed possible to create an independent British-led 'third force' in world affairs that would be the equal of the United States and USSR. As events unfolded, however, Bevin abandoned all hope of a deal with Stalin, and in the foreign office it became axiomatic that the Soviet Union was intent on ascendancy.[35]

Churchill's 'iron curtain' speech, delivered in Fulton, Missouri, on 5 March 1946, reinforced opinions that were already taking shape. Seeking to alarm the

Americans and threaten Moscow, Churchill reiterated earlier points about the Soviet menace and spoke of a divided Europe, whereupon Bevin stepped up his efforts to make the Americans realize that they had to be more proactive if they wanted security for themselves and their friends. Coincidentally, some of Truman's advisers had been recommending a more assertive attitude, notably George Kennan, head of the policy planning staff at the US state department. This set the scene for the exchanges of February 1947, when the British informed Washington DC that they could no longer combat communist pressure in Greece and Turkey.[36]

Within the British government there had been arguments about defence expenditure. Chancellor of the exchequer Hugh Dalton led the demand for cuts, and although Attlee decided not to go as far as Dalton wanted, some activities had to be dropped in order for others to continue. Withdrawal from Greece did not mean that the British presence in the eastern Mediterranean and Middle East would cease. Moreover, the decisions of early 1947 about Greece and Turkey, and about Palestine and India, were taken before ministers knew the full extent of Britain's financial problems, which suggests that imperial strategy – and not just retrenchment – affected their thinking.[37]

Attlee still envisaged a settlement with Stalin after Bevin had decided it was impossible. This added to the pressure on Bevin, who was already worried about Palestine and India. He complained that the prime minister and others in the government and Labour Party did not appreciate what was at stake in Greece and Turkey. A communist Greece would transform the regional situation, and British withdrawal might damage Anglo-American relations.[38] Bevin and the chiefs of staff objected to the ending of aid to Greece and Turkey, but with Dalton warning about the costs, and Attlee unconvinced that vital British interests were at stake, Bevin accepted that economic assistance should cease. He expected British support for the Greek army to continue in some form. The Americans were surprised by the British message of February 1947, but the state department decided to use it to rally Congress and the American people behind a more active policy. Truman now favoured such a course, as did the heads of key government departments, the joint chiefs of staff, and US ambassadors in Athens, Moscow and elsewhere.[39]

Willingness to act, however, did not mean that the Truman administration was pleased about Britain's message. Some US officials objected that the problem had been dumped on them. Some took the British intention to withdraw from Greece and Turkey as proof of the impending disintegration of Britain's empire. British leaders did not see it this way. Specifically, there was no question of leaving the Middle East, or of inviting America in. Far from being on the point of collapse, it was thought, the empire would be strengthened by a reallocation of resources. In later years, as expected, the Americans found that sustaining British power in specific regions was an expedient way of waging the Cold War.[40]

This lay in the future. In the early weeks of 1947 the main concern of the British government was to manage a limited disengagement in a way that would save money and satisfy the Labour Party, parliament and public opinion. At the same time, it had to be accomplished in a manner that did not lead other governments to think of Britain as a spent force. Clearly, disengagement would be much easier with American help. As *The Times* noted: 'The old complaint that British chestnuts are being pulled out of the fire will be heard again, to which the response that they are as much American as British in the world of today may lack effectiveness.' In the event, Britain could rely on the growing American realization that Soviet expansion had to be checked and that Britain was an indispensable ally in this endeavour.[41]

In an address to Congress on 12 March 1947, Truman announced that the United States would assist free peoples to resist armed minorities and outside pressure. This was the basis of the Truman Doctrine. It involved a guarantee of military and diplomatic support for America's friends and a clear warning to America's foes. The situation in Europe was its essential context, for purges and trials across Eastern Europe indicated that the Soviets were taking firmer control.[42]

Whether it was the product of genuine fear or of political and territorial ambition, Soviet intransigence had pushed the United States and Britain closer together.[43] American resolve was further demonstrated by the 1947 Defence Act, which created a combined department of defence to co-ordinate military organization, and the establishment of the National Security Council and Central Intelligence Agency.[44] The US commitment to Europe was formalized by collective security arrangements of 1947 to 1949. The Truman Doctrine was just the beginning. American personnel and $400 million in aid were made available for Greece and Turkey. This period saw the end of US isolation and the adoption (at least in official circles) of containment and the 'domino theory': the idea that if one state fell to communism, others in the vicinity would follow.[45]

It was not inevitable that Truman's speech of 12 March 1947 would give life to a global anti-communist effort.[46] Yet the controversy surrounding it in the United States indicates that many people thought he had gone too far. Truman's critics claimed that he was commencing an ideological crusade and destroying all hope of agreement with the Soviets. Perhaps he was: the American response to the British note of February 1947 owed a lot to deliberations that had already taken place.[47]

In parliament, meanwhile, the Attlee government was pressed to explain its position. On 5 March 1947 Christopher Mayhew confirmed that Anglo-American discussions were taking place. On 13 March there were calls for a full debate on Truman's address to Congress, and on 17 March MPs demanded information about the talks with the Americans. Hector McNeil, minister of state at the foreign office, admitted that the British government had not been informed beforehand about Truman's address. Related issues would continue to be pursued through the usual diplomatic channels, however, and McNeil said that, as far as he knew, the Americans would provide aid with no strings attached. Some MPs suggested that the Americans should be urged to reconsider, because US involvement in Greece and Turkey would be 'inflammatory', but McNeil did not accept this.[48]

Bevin was relieved that the Americans were responding to his appeal and that Greece would be protected, but it would be wrong to assume that the Truman administration had been tricked into taking a course it would not otherwise have taken. For Britain, the pleasing outcome came as much by luck as by design. British machinations should not be underestimated, though, for Bevin, Attlee and their colleagues knew what they were doing, and they knew what they wanted to happen. *The Times* saw far-reaching principles behind Truman's offer of aid to Greece and Turkey, argued that British exertions in Greece were now being rewarded, and commended those American commentators who had decided that American and British interests in the region were identical. The *Manchester Guardian* hailed a 'revolutionary change in US policy'.[49]

The gap between British and American thinking had closed as US-Soviet relations worsened during 1946. Truman shared Britain's desire to prevent a communist triumph in Greece, though he had to be wary, if only for domestic political reasons.[50] The Truman Doctrine was partly but not solely a response to Britain's conduct. It was also a response to the actions of the USSR. Soviet policy opened the way for closer collaboration between the United States and Britain. Perhaps the Truman Doctrine gave the British more than they really desired. The ideological aspects and worldwide implications of what Truman said were unsettling because Britain's interests were bound to be affected by an expansive US foreign policy.

That 1947 marks a turning point is underlined by the events that followed Truman's speech. In May 1947 Dean Acheson, the US under-secretary of state, spoke of long-term help for any people seeking to preserve its independence, and on 5 June 1947 secretary of state George Marshall promised economic aid to European governments if they made proposals for reconstruction. The Marshall Plan was based on the premise that there could be no security without prosperity. A related concern was that if recovery was delayed, communist parties would attract support in Europe and Soviet influence would spread.[51]

The main point of Acheson's speech of May 1947 was that American economic muscle should be used abroad for political purposes. As for Marshall, a difficult foreign ministers' meeting in Moscow in April 1947 had convinced him that America should take the initiative in Europe. There was a slight hitch when Christopher Mayhew responded to Soviet claims about British economic weakness by declaring that all was well, but the resulting controversy abated once American legislators accepted that Soviet provocation had led Mayhew to exaggerate.[52]

Marshall soon confirmed that the USSR was included in the offer of economic aid. The US government wanted to present the plan as a collective effort, realizing that it would be useful to emphasize concert and goodwill. As expected, the Soviets refused to join in. Stalin had no wish for co-operation along the lines Marshall had indicated, and would have preferred to keep Western Europe weak and divided. Moscow condemned Marshall Aid and ordered satellite regimes in Eastern Europe to stay out of the plan. Despite the USSR's need for assistance, Stalin decided that to join the Marshall Plan would be to fall into a trap. Participation would reveal the true condition of the Soviet economy and make the USSR dependent on the United States.[53]

The Marshall Plan encouraged the Soviets to strengthen their position in Eastern Europe. They suspected that the United States, Britain and Germany would form a revived capitalist system, and that Germany's restored military-industrial strength would be directed against the USSR. Poland and Czechoslovakia were less hostile to the Marshall Plan and wanted to accept American help, but Stalin could not allow their economies to be integrated with those of Western Europe. There had to be a closed buffer zone between Germany and the USSR. The solution was to impose more restrictions. Communists in Eastern Europe who protested were removed from office; some were imprisoned. Cominform, the Communist Information Bureau, was established in September 1947. It was designed to bind the satellites together and also included the French and Italian communist parties as members. Soviet thinking came to rest on the 'two camp' doctrine. The world was now divided into the imperialists led by America and the anti-imperialists led by the USSR.[54]

The Marshall Plan convinced Moscow that the two camps were irreconcilable. Stalin had tried to gain as much as he could within the wartime framework of co-operation with Britain and the United States. This framework had disintegrated, mainly because of the deadlock over Germany, and the Marshall Plan led Stalin to think that his security agenda was in jeopardy. The consolidation of the eastern bloc proceeded apace with mutual assistance treaties and then the establishment of Comecon, the Council for Mutual Economic Assistance, in 1949. There was some resistance to Soviet control, though, especially from the Yugoslavian leader Josip Broz Tito.[55]

Integration in the eastern bloc was organized around the needs of the USSR, and Moscow was quick to use repression when necessary. This was repeatedly emphasized in the West, where there was considerable alarm after the Czech coup of 1948, when communists seized power in a state with an established democratic tradition, and when Cominform organized strikes in France and Italy to dissuade their governments from accepting Marshall Aid and US leadership.[56]

Throughout the West it had been agreed that European recovery would be impossible without German recovery, and as Germany became the front line in the Cold War, it moved rapidly towards political division. In the summer of 1946 the American and British zones were combined as 'Bizonia'. This, and the fact that the two leading German politicians, Kurt Schumacher of the Social Democrats and Konrad Adenauer of the Christian Democrats, were both anti-communist, further encouraged the Soviets to tighten their grip in the eastern zone.[57]

The economic reconstruction of Germany became an urgent necessity for the Western allies, especially Britain, because of occupation expenses. The goal was to develop German industry as quickly as possible, despite Soviet protests that a revived Germany would be aggressive. Germany became the biggest drain on Britain's resources. With no peace settlement, the occupation had to continue, and Germany's economic collapse meant that the basic needs in each zone had to be supplied by the occupying power. The British zone was in north-west Germany. In 1946 British taxpayers paid for about 70 per cent of its food supply. Hugh Dalton complained that Britain was paying reparations to Germany rather than the other way around. He predicted occupation costs of £80 million for 1946. The actual expenditure was £120 million. The government had to ration bread in Britain, a measure avoided during the Second World War, in order to maintain the supply of American wheat to feed Germans. The wheat was paid for out of the US loan to Britain, and the loan itself was controversial. The government was accused of mortgaging the empire and surrendering to American pressure.[58]

Germany's future had to be settled, and French security interests had somehow to be balanced against the consideration that to hamper German recovery would be economically to disadvantage Western Europe. The West was also concerned about the influence of communism in unstable parts of Europe, and wished to keep Germany and the Soviet Union apart.[59]

The British seem quickly to have accepted that Germany and Europe would be divided. The Truman Doctrine and Marshall Aid were exactly what Bevin had been hoping for, and he made sure that Britain and the Europeans organized themselves to apply for US help. In July 1947 he and the French foreign minister, Georges Bidault, put together a committee and presented the United States with a plan to boost production and exports, promote financial stability and foster economic co-operation among participating nations. In April 1948, in Paris, a permanent body was established to administer Marshall Aid. This was the Organization for European Economic Co-operation (OEEC), of which sixteen governments were members.[60]

Although contemporaries praised the Marshall Plan for promoting recovery, historians have disagreed about its impact. Economic growth began before the plan was implemented, and the idea that the plan saved Western Europe for democracy has been questioned.[61] Some commentators have argued that the importance of the Marshall Plan was political rather than economic and financial. What is clear is that conditions varied: if Germany, Austria and Italy were in crisis, other parts of Europe were not. Certainly the Marshall Plan contributed greatly to the economic reconstruction and political rehabilitation of West Germany, which facilitated wider economic co-operation and encouraged the growth of institutions that met the security concerns of Germany's neighbours.[62]

In practice, the Marshall Plan was not an exclusively American project. The leaders of Britain and Western Europe influenced what happened in their own countries.[63] At the same time, if they did their best to determine the type of assistance they received from the Americans, there was always the worry that it might be reduced if they made too many stipulations. Britain sometimes suffered by giving way to US pressure. One of the conditions attached to the US loan concerned the convertibility of sterling. In July 1947 the British government did as it had promised and sterling was made convertible, but the rapid shrinkage of Britain's gold and dollar reserves forced an immediate volte-face. The situation improved once Marshall Aid began to flow, though the British remained cautious thereafter about adopting measures to reform trade and stabilize currencies before they were ready for them.[64] British politicians and civil servants treated the difficulties of 1947 as the result of excessive expenditure overseas and the premature switch to convertibility.

Those who believed that the Marshall Plan would prevent economic collapse jolted the sceptics into accepting it. In London, the debate turned largely on a treasury report of June 1948, which suggested that non-involvement with the Marshall Plan would reduce the supply of food, oil and raw materials. Unemployment would rise, food rationing would go on, and consumption would fall. Perhaps this forecast was unduly alarmist,[65] but even without the treasury recommendations it would have been difficult for Attlee's government not to join in the Marshall Plan.

The Marshall Plan can also be viewed in a global perspective. American policy was shaped by suspicion of Soviet intentions and had ramifications beyond Europe, touching the civil war in China as well as the insurrection in Greece; the economic disruption in Japan as well as that in Germany; the rise of national-ism in Indochina, Indonesia, Egypt and India as well as the financial chaos in Western Europe, and the popularity of the communist parties in France and Italy. Washington DC thought that the worldwide situation, already bad, was getting worse.[66]

Bevin, though not directly responsible for the Marshall Plan, did much to fashion it. Marshall's comments of June 1947 were vague and Bevin took an imaginative leap to ensure that substantial aid would materialize. According to

Denis Healey, then secretary of the Labour Party's International Department, Bevin decided to act 'the moment he heard a report of the speech on his bedside radio'. When it was suggested that the British ambassador in Washington DC should seek a meeting with Marshall, to find out what he really meant, Bevin vetoed the idea. What Marshall had already said would suit Britain's purposes well enough.[67]

The escalation of the Cold War was promoted not only by the Truman Doctrine and the Marshall Plan, but also by propaganda and ideological warfare. Britain played an active part in this. At the end of 1947 the Information Research Department (IRD) was set up in the foreign office. Christopher Mayhew had recommended this move because the Soviets were using the UN 'without inhibition' as a propaganda platform. Western delegates chose not to respond, preferring to set an example of respect for the UN, but Mayhew considered this inadequate. Bevin took up Mayhew's plan for ideological warfare, and, with Attlee's help, gained cabinet approval for the establishment of the IRD, which was soon supplying material for broadcasts and speeches. By the autumn of 1948 a great deal of information had been gathered about the USSR. The IRD expanded quickly and fed material to contacts abroad, mainly through Britain's embassies and high commissions, and to newspapers, publishers, trade union officials, MPs and others at home.[68]

This was also a time when integrationist tendencies increased in Western Europe. Bevin had persuaded European leaders to work together so that the Marshall Plan would benefit all concerned, and this brought forth further suggestions for collective action, on military as well as economic matters. The Americans welcomed joint European ventures and decided that Washington DC's links with London would be more helpful if the British became closely involved in Europe, but British political leaders, whether Labour or Conservative, remained hesitant. Though they agreed that European co-operation was necessary, their aversion to supra-nationalism was solid. They favoured bargains between sovereign states and disliked bodies that could act independently of the governments that set them up. There was also an idea that Britain did not need Europe, because of the 'special relationship' with America and global interests in the empire and Commonwealth.[69] As the Americans urged Britain to discard its anti-integrationist preferences, Bevin resisted. In October 1949 he made it plain to the US ambassador in London that Britain was a world power and would not risk its own strength and independence by associating too closely with Western Europe.[70]

What Bevin really wanted was a European security system to which the Americans would adhere. He knew he was more likely to draw America in if he worked with the Europeans. In March 1947 Britain and France concluded a fifty-year defensive alliance, the Treaty of Dunkirk. Next came the formation of the Western Union under the Treaty of Brussels of May 1948, a mutual defence agreement involving Britain, France, Belgium, Luxembourg and the Netherlands.[71]

The French government attached great importance to the Treaty of Dunkirk. British leaders did not. Indeed, they initially had no wish to extend the treaty and rebuffed French requests for closer military relations. Still, the usefulness of broader arrangements could not be gainsaid, and Bevin was a leading mover behind the formation of the Western Union. The development of this security system was encouraged by the USSR's condemnation of it, and the Brussels Pact received a favourable reception in the British press, particularly in *The Times*, which argued that its members were wholly right to pursue 'that unity which alone can produce the maximum strength from their separate resources'.[72]

Although Bevin's plan for the Western Union included co-operation over a range of activities, not only defence, his commitment was conditional. In his speeches on the matter in the early part of 1948, he probably went further than he had intended. Britain's embassies abroad were inundated with requests for more information, and some European leaders even assumed that Bevin had turned integrationist. They would soon be brought back to reality.[73]

Commending the Brussels Pact to the Commons on 4 May 1948, Bevin repeated previous comments about the need for a coalition of the free nations of Western Europe, including Britain. Although he envisaged a larger Western Union, however, Bevin stressed that there could be no 'pooling of sovereignty' and no 'European federated state'. One had to be practical, he explained, and the whole point of the Western Union was, gradually and methodically, to unite only those interests that *could* be united. None of this was meant to be confrontational: 'we are concocting nothing aggressive against anyone'.[74] Despite this assurance, the Soviets reacted to the formation of Western Union by deepening the crisis over the future of Germany. The blockade of Berlin, from June 1948 to May 1949, brought a dangerous increase in East-West tension.

The West saw Germany as a barrier against Soviet aggression and believed that the Soviets would not relinquish their occupation zone in eastern Germany. This explains the determination to make sure that the western part of Germany would have parliamentary democracy and economic liberalism and be tied into the West's defence system. Despite continuing talks, the Soviets seemed unwilling to finalize a deal, and Britain and the United States decided that the western zones should unite. A new currency, the Deutschmark, was introduced, and preparations were made for the possibility of a separate German state and a military alliance involving the United States, Canada, Britain and Western Europe.[75]

Claiming that the Brussels Pact was directed against them, the Soviets restricted access to Berlin, a divided city since the end of the war and over a hundred miles inside the Soviet zone. They withdrew from the joint administration in Berlin.

They introduced a currency reform in East Berlin, to increase their control, but this prompted the Western powers to extend their new currency to West Berlin. In June 1948 the Soviets tried to cut off West Berlin completely, closing all access by land from the western zones, but supplies were brought in by air. The Soviets resorted to a blockade in order to force the Western powers to negotiate for a united, neutral, demilitarized Germany. The blockade demonstrated the extent of Soviet fear at the prospect of a strong Germany allied to the West. It was ended in return for the promise of new talks, but a subsequent conference of foreign ministers in Paris settled nothing.[76]

The British government's position was clear throughout the crisis. Bevin set the tone in its early stages, most notably in a speech of 30 June 1948 in which he maintained that although the Soviets said they wanted reunification, their policies made the division of Germany more likely. Europe's economic recovery was being held back, Bevin declared, and the Western powers wanted to support German reconstruction by granting responsible government. The Soviets had to accept, moreover, that the Western powers were not in Berlin on sufferance: they had obligations there. Despite some misgivings, Attlee accepted Bevin's view that Britain had to stand with the Americans and break the blockade. In the British press there was also strong support for a robust policy, and when the blockade was lifted *The Times* commented that the whole experience had made the West stronger. The *Observer* suggested that Stalin's blockade was doomed from the start, owing to the USSR's relative economic weakness: the Soviets lacked the means to 'nourish all of East Europe'.[77]

Some commentators thought that Bevin and Attlee had been too cautious during the crisis and that the Labour Party's internal divisions were having an undue influence on policy. Complaints were also made about the fruitless talks in Paris. Bevin hit back. Though there had been no settlement of outstanding issues, he said in July 1949, Britain and its allies would continue to strive for a breakthrough and could feel proud that they had 'put up a good fight' in Berlin.[78]

The Berlin crisis fostered greater military co-operation between the British and Americans. On Bevin's suggestion, US bombers were stationed in Britain. In time the presence of US bases became highly contentious, and once the USSR developed its atomic bomb the bases were a stark reminder that Britain was a Soviet target. Nevertheless, by the end of the Berlin crisis a basic strategy had been adopted. In the absence of massive ground forces the Soviets were to be deterred by the threat of atomic assault. In 1948–49 this threat had effect. Rejecting other options, including UN mediation, the Americans relied on their atomic monopoly.[79]

No less important was the decision to create a separate republic in Germany. German representatives negotiated together, and with the British, Americans and French, a constitution was drawn up, and after elections in August 1949

Konrad Adenauer became chancellor of the new Federal Republic of Germany (FRG).[80] The Soviets had not originally planned to establish a separate German state in their zone, but after the establishment of the FRG they set up the German Democratic Republic (GDR) in October 1949. A divided Germany suited both superpowers. They accommodated themselves to the fact that the German question could not be solved, and in the long run division meant that a resurgent Germany could not by itself cause another war. Yet this also suggested that there could be no end to the Cold War, for the division of Germany created a lasting atmosphere of danger.[81]

More than one scholar has claimed that Stalin never wanted a separate communist East German state, that it was really the German communist leader, Ulbricht, who prevented a four-power agreement on Germany, and that, had it not been for Ulbricht, Stalin would have tolerated a unified non-communist Germany.[82] American policy has also been scrutinized. Although the US government had not intended to divide Germany, there is evidence to suggest that American leaders decided at an early stage that partition accorded with their long-range plans for the type of relationship they wanted with Europe.[83] Or was it the British who took the lead in the division of Germany and creation of a western bloc? Reflecting on the lessons of the interwar years, ignoring signs that Moscow wanted to continue the 'Big Three' co-operation of wartime, and anxious to draw America further into post-war European affairs as a prop for Britain's great-power status, the British chose to treat the USSR as untrustworthy and adopted containment long before the doctrine was formally elaborated. By February 1947 Bevin was arguing for the division of Germany, to be accomplished in such a way that the blame could be placed on Moscow.[84]

Whether they desired it from the outset, for their own reasons, or came to see it as a regrettable necessity, or only accepted it at the last moment in response to Soviet conduct, American and British leaders, and the leaders of Western Europe, decided that the division of Germany would benefit their countries and West Germany, if they built up the necessary economic and security arrangements. The FRG enjoyed political rehabilitation thanks to the exigencies of the Cold War, and economic prosperity thanks to the Marshall Plan and the 'managed capitalism' or 'social market economy' favoured by the government in Bonn. Adenauer condemned the division of Germany, though he was in no hurry about reunification and committed the FRG to collective security and economic co-operation.[85]

The most significant development of these post-war years in terms of mutual defence was the foundation of NATO, the North Atlantic Treaty Organization, in April 1949. With the Berlin crisis following the Czech coup in quick succession, it was thought to be incumbent upon the West to respond. This was the view of Truman and his advisers, and Bevin also saw the need for firm action, as did most of his counterparts in Western Europe.[86]

On 11 June 1948, the US Senate passed a resolution in favour of treaties for international aid and security.[87] The Truman administration had already approved talks with Canada and the Western Union, and by January 1949 Truman was speaking confidently about the expected alliance. In April the North Atlantic Treaty was signed by the United States, Canada, the original Western Union powers, Denmark, Norway, Portugal, Italy and Iceland. These participants were later joined by Greece and Turkey. The coverage was therefore much wider than the 'North Atlantic' and the treaty marked a considerable enlargement of the Western Union concept, much to Bevin's satisfaction.[88]

Bevin had realized that continued pressure from the Soviets was creating more eagerness in the West for thorough precautionary measures. He wanted Britain and Western Europe to come together and maintained that no security system could work without the Americans. In helping to convince them to make the necessary commitment, Bevin's contribution was decisive. When the Brussels Pact had been signed, there was opposition in Washington DC to stronger US ties to Western Europe, but the pact showed conclusively that Britain and the Europeans were organizing for self-defence even before they had any guarantee of US assistance. Bevin knew how important this was to the Americans.[89]

That NATO was not an inevitable outcome of Cold War developments, however, is indicated by the arguments it caused in the United States. It was not easy for the Truman administration to build support for the treaty and some US strategists did not welcome the shift from an economic focus, seen in the Marshall Plan, towards a military focus (soon to be strengthened by the Korean War). George Kennan, for instance, never thought of containment as primarily military in nature.[90] On the other hand, the Marshall Plan did have a military dimension. The goal of economic recovery was not separated from the need for security, and some recipients of Marshall Aid used it for military strengthening. The shift from an economic to a military focus, however, is easier to discern in Washington DC than in the capitals of Western Europe, where the preferred method of resisting communism was through economic and social reconstruction, not military spending. The Americans paid more of the costs for collective security than did their allies, who were unwilling massively to increase defence budgets. Of all the allies, Britain did most to pay its way. Britain's military expenditure remained unusually high by West European standards.

There was a change in British attitudes, with military considerations gradually taking precedence over economic concerns. One of Britain's priorities after the war had been to obtain American aid. This had been a difficult undertaking, during which quarrels arose on account of Washington DC's wish for Britain to move closer to Europe (a course that Attlee's government decided would not be in keeping with Britain's great-power status) and because of American pressure for free trade and freely convertible currencies (which threatened Britain's interests with respect to the Commonwealth, the sterling area and domestic policies designed to restore full employment). The Marshall Plan was strategically as well as economically important. It increased American involvement in Europe and encouraged Bevin to believe that a security system could be established to accompany economic recovery. During 1948–49 the British were reluctant to increase their defence spending unless the United States promised to help. The formation of NATO indicated that this matter was being resolved, and the military side of containment gained the ascendancy thereafter because of the ways in which American and British leaders thought they should respond to Soviet actions.[91]

The Times stated, correctly, that the North Atlantic Treaty was based on 'a common principle rather than a geographical area'. NATO gave hope and confidence to the West, proved that America would not turn away from European problems, and represented a warning to Moscow.[92]

The establishment of NATO was another departure in international affairs. America openly took up a leadership role and supported the West's security arrangements. Bevin considered this his greatest achievement. He was helped by the Berlin blockade and by the Brussels Pact. He had demonstrated Britain's readiness to share security burdens. The primary importance of the Brussels Pact to the British may well have been that it gave them leverage: they were far more interested in gaining American assistance than in combining with Europeans.[93] At the same time, Bevin had hoped that the Brussels treaty would open the door for broader co-operation between Britain and Western Europe on economic, cultural and other matters. Links with the continent were important to Britain, Bevin thought, because they would limit dependence upon the United States, and the Brussels Pact was more than just a ploy to obtain a definite US commitment to European security. Unfortunately for Bevin, he could not control the process of European co-operation. He began scheming against integrationists as they advanced their own agenda.[94]

The British were irritated by pressure from Washington DC with regard to European integration, for they were still prioritizing a global strategy. While Britain was prepared to consider economic, political and military agreements with Western Europe on an inter-governmental basis, the Americans decided that much closer bonds were advisable.[95] There was another complication, in that some British leaders continued to think that US isolationism might resurface. They were pleased, though, that NATO created a different prospect to that of 1944–45 when the Americans had seen Britain, not the Soviets, as the main obstacle to peace in the post-war world. Stalin had miscalculated again: the Berlin crisis had had results he did not want, just as his opposition to the Marshall Plan had done previously.

Nevertheless, the North Atlantic Treaty was so worded that the use of armed force was an option, not a pledge. Washington DC could decide whether or not to resort to arms in a crisis. This must have added to the lingering fear in London about US isolationism. While he actively pushed for NATO, Bevin was keen that the Americans should appear to be taking the lead. The alliance would perish, he was sure, if it came to be regarded in America as a British project. He adjusted his position according to what he thought the US Senate was willing to ratify, and in February 1949 he wrote that a limited treaty would be better than no treaty at all. The terminology was relatively unimportant. Bevin was confident that if a war did break out, 'the United States would not be able to avoid being involved'.[96]

Through the North Atlantic Treaty, Britain obtained the best guarantee of Western Europe's security that was available at the time. A price had to be paid, however, and certain goals abandoned, especially the search for an independent role for Britain. Bevin continued to be assailed by critics, particularly on the left of the Labour Party. They considered him too fond of the Americans, needlessly hostile towards the USSR, and deluded about Britain's position in the world. They said he was tied to the past, yet NATO was a break with British tradition in that it evolved into a firm and lasting commitment of a kind that had been eschewed in previous decades. Moreover, Bevin *was* ready to argue with the Americans. The problem was that nobody but the Americans could provide the economic aid needed by post-war Britain.[97]

Lord Ismay, who after a distinguished military and diplomatic career became the first secretary-general of NATO (1952–57), remarked that NATO's original purpose was to keep the Americans in, the Soviets out, and the Germans down.[98] The FRG would not be down for long: by the mid-1950s the West's security arrangements had to include the FRG as a full partner. But as for binding the Americans to Europe and deterring Soviet aggression, NATO served Britain's interests very well.[99]

In August 1949 the Soviets tested an atomic bomb. Officially announced in March 1950, this event caused a panic in the United States and Britain because it had not been expected so soon. Britain was in range of the USSR's weapons, and its leaders knew that, ultimately, the United States would not make sacrifices to save Britain. The British needed their own atomic bomb. This would enable them to deter the Soviets and remain a great power.[100]

During the Second World War, awareness of German efforts to develop an atomic weapon had prompted the British to commence their own programme, which was overtaken in 1942 by the much larger American operation. Churchill and Roosevelt concluded the Quebec Agreement of 1943 and Hyde Park Agreement of 1944 on atomic co-operation, but in 1946 the US Congress brought this to an end.[101] Britain's post-war decision to develop the atomic bomb was tinged with not a little resentment, and although the Attlee government argued for international arms control through the United Nations Atomic Energy

Commission, there was no question of abandoning Britain's own programme.[102] On more than one occasion the Americans indicated that talks could recommence, but when the British requested specific technological information this was refused. Though broad international co-operation on atomic matters had appeal, Britain could not give up its hard-won advantages in the field and it was also important not to let the atomic quarrel with America jeopardize the 'special relationship' as a whole.[103]

There were detailed discussions in Britain about atomic weapons. In October 1946 Bevin insisted that Britain must have the bomb, and he overcame objections from colleagues that the country could not afford it. One of the key points Bevin used to back up his case was the attitude of the Americans: they would be more likely to take British interests into account, he thought, if Britain was an atomic power. This was also Attlee's view. Without the atomic bomb, the prime minister argued, Britain would be reliant on the Americans with no guarantee of their help. The decision to develop the bomb was made in January 1947.[104]

Bevin and Attlee were not acting from a sense of irreversible decline. They and the chiefs of staff were determined not to accept a US monopoly of atomic weapons, and believed that the West would be safer once Britain had an atomic capability, since potential enemies would be easier to deter if they knew that atomic weapons were being manufactured in Britain as well as in America. The weapons programme did create difficulties, however, because of the cost and because the programme added to rivalries between the armed services as they competed for resources and influence.[105]

The possibility of war with the USSR, not the resurgence of Germany, was now the primary concern. Military strategists, who were ahead of the foreign office in proposing containment of the Soviets, had been arguing since 1945 that Europe could not be defended against a Soviet land attack, and this led them into an early advocacy of German rearmament. They wanted more American support and a British withdrawal from the continent in the event of Soviet aggression. The atomic bomb was vital for deterrence and for manipulating Soviet perceptions.[106]

The determination to develop atomic weapons accorded with Britain's ambition in international affairs and with the contemporary understanding, abroad as well as at home, of Britain's place and influence in the world. The British were ready to contribute to collective security and played a leading role in the UN and NATO and in the construction of Western Europe's defence system. The British had a say in the organization of post-war affairs in the Middle East and Far East as well as in Europe. With limited means, Britain maintained its global reach. A delicate balancing act was necessary, though, as some responsibilities were given up in order for others to be confirmed and new ones added in line with Britain's long-range interests.

3

Asia, the Middle East, Europe: No Respite (I)

At the beginning of the 1950s the British were looking for answers to the central question they faced: how could they shape the new international order so that it suited Britain? They expected to be involved in the Pacific and the Indian Ocean, in Asia, the Middle East and Europe, but they were unsure about how best to accomplish their goals in these different regions, and about how and where to co-operate with the Americans. They knew, also, that Britain's economic strength and military capacity would need to be enhanced if the global reach was to remain intact. Attlee's government hoped for quieter times, in order to preserve British influence and prestige in a cost-effective way. Instead, the government had to respond to mounting pressure.

In June 1950 the Korean War broke out after forces from the communist north invaded the south (Korea had been partitioned after the Second World War into Soviet and US spheres of influence). The United Nations condemned this aggression, with Truman taking advantage of the temporary absence of Soviet representatives. The Korean War proved to be the making of NATO as a working military alliance. The North Atlantic Treaty contained an element of discretion regarding the use of military force, but Truman decided that Stalin must have approved the North Korean invasion, which had ramifications for Europe. London and Washington DC agreed that NATO had to be strong enough to deter. Britain also backed the UN position on Korea.[1]

Bevin's health gave way and his successor as foreign secretary was Herbert Morrison, who held the post from March to October 1951. Morrison lacked Bevin's vision and experience. He was also unlucky. Korea was not the only worry. In 1951 a spy scandal brought forth accusations of laxity at the foreign office and undermined the credibility of British intelligence. Then Australia and New Zealand concluded a security agreement with the United States in which Britain was not included. Though the British presence in the Far East did not become unimportant overnight, exclusion from the ANZUS Pact was seen in London as a sign that the Americans were out to increase their own role in the region to the detriment of British interests there. There was also a danger that Australia and New Zealand would focus on the Pacific and offer no help to Britain in the Middle East. The chiefs of staff decided that this was a price worth paying for an American guarantee of their security and that there was no need for Britain to join the pact unless it was opened to others. Attlee agreed.[2]

Despite an effort to minimize the significance of the ANZUS Pact, it troubled British leaders. Even more alarming was the deterioration of Britain's position in the Middle East. Iran took control of the Anglo-Iranian Oil Company in May 1951 and in Egypt there were demands that British troops should be removed from the large base at Suez.

The cabinet's view was that Iran's decision could not be reversed. Attlee decided against the use of force. The Americans would not help, and Britain was unable to take quick action on the scale needed. Therefore British personnel were withdrawn from Iran and Attlee referred the matter to the UN. Concern increased about the impact of this on the British economy and on public opinion, about the possibility of Soviet intervention, and about the effect on Britain's international standing. The Korean War and Britain's rearmament programme entailed a massive increase in spending, and the nationalization of the Anglo-Iranian Oil Company meant that Britain had to buy American oil. All this put pressure on sterling and reduced Britain's dollar reserves. Dean Acheson, the US secretary of state (1949–53), praised the British for seeking an accommodation with Iran, but his comment did not comfort ministers who were agitated by allegations at home that they were squandering Britain's reputation.[3]

Though the government had to appear reasonable, in order not to alienate Washington DC or important Arab states, there was a determination to gain either a new oil concession or compensation for loss of revenue. Thoughts turned to the possibility of bringing down the Iranian regime, and the British secret service engaged in discussions with the CIA. An effort was made to deprive Iran of income by hindering its production and exportation of oil. Churchill initially wanted military action, but by the time he returned as prime minister in October 1951 he had reconsidered.[4]

Damaged in Iran, British interests were also at stake in Egypt. The Egyptian government had been pressing for a revision of previous agreements with Britain. Anglo-American military conversations in October 1950 confirmed that the Middle East would continue to be a British and Commonwealth responsibility. Suez was regarded as an essential headquarters, both for reasons of regional security and because of the West's need for oil. Britain's military chiefs had envisaged a security pact with Egypt as a willing partner, but Egypt confirmed in the autumn of 1951 that it would not participate in any defence plan that included Britain. Though Bevin had tried to conclude an agreement on the Suez base, his overtures were in vain. There was little he could do, for he was convinced that Britain should not get involved in Egypt's internal affairs. Morrison and Attlee were of the same opinion.[5]

Some of Britain's problems in the Middle East had less to do with Arab nationalism than with Britain's economic weaknesses. Egypt was probably an exception, because nationalism became virulent there, but otherwise Britain could not do more in the region because it lacked the wherewithal to do so. The situation was not helped by instability in the Middle East. There was no unity among the Arab states and they never had an agreed method of dealing with one another or with Britain, yet Britain could not expect to maintain its position simply by manipulating inter-Arab rivalries. Other methods had to be tried. Attempts to widen the basis of co-operation with Arab states had mostly collapsed by the early 1950s. Britain could not fund extensive social and economic reforms and Arab nationalism was largely anti-British in character.[6]

The Attlee government regarded the Middle East as a pillar of British global strategy, and hoped to preserve Britain's primacy there and exclude the Americans. During Churchill's premiership of 1951–55, however, circumstances changed. In part because nuclear weapons made the presence of British forces there less needful, and in part because Britain's economic problems prompted a ceaseless reassessment of commitments, Churchill pushed for greater US involvement in the Middle East.

Arab nationalism, the establishment of Israel, the Soviet threat and Britain's limited resources led London to devise plans for a regional defence organization that would be British-led, but in which others would share the burden. The Americans refused to participate, as did key Arab states. London was frequently confused by US policy because, while seeking more influence for themselves in the region, the Americans were still encouraging Britain to take the lead there and recognized the special importance of the Middle East in British strategy. Washington DC was never enthusiastic about British proposals for the region, however, and preferred to explore alternatives such as an increased US presence in the Mediterranean, or the promotion of a 'northern tier' as the front line against the Soviets.[7]

Army officers seized power in Egypt in 1952 and King Farouk, Britain's ally, was overthrown. Egypt became a republic in 1953. The garrison in the Suez Canal zone swelled to over 80,000 strong, which represented the largest concentration of British forces anywhere in the world. The Egyptian demand for British withdrawal grew louder and in London it was decided that the financial and political costs of remaining were too high. Withdrawal had to be carefully managed, however, so that it did not look like surrender or encourage the Soviets to intervene. The foreign office and chiefs of staff eventually agreed that since Suez would have to be relinquished, the main defensive effort would focus on the northern approaches to the Middle East. Really, Britain was making a virtue out of necessity. The new plan would require a smaller number of troops and would therefore be cheaper. Britain would maintain a reduced garrison in the Middle East, with a strategic reserve that could be sent into the region at short notice.[8]

The chiefs of staff stressed the continuing importance of the Middle East in a report of July 1952. Anthony Eden, who had taken over as foreign secretary in October 1951, told cabinet colleagues and Commonwealth leaders at the end of 1952 that more advantage should be taken of Turkey's membership of NATO and that it would be safe to retreat from Suez if agreements could be made for the stationing of British forces elsewhere in the vicinity. Nor did Eden rule out a defence agreement with the new Egyptian regime.[9]

In Europe, meanwhile, Germany's future was still in dispute and it was feared that Moscow's support for North Korea increased the risk of Soviet aggression against Western Europe as the United States was distracted in Asia. There was some talk of a European army, but opinion differed as to whether it should include troops from the FRG. The Truman administration endorsed the idea of incorporating German forces, but Britain objected to the integrationist aspects of European army proposals and there was general unease about a militarily strong Germany. A conference in September 1950 in New York resulted in a compromise. Western Europe would be defended by a NATO army under an American supreme commander, Dwight Eisenhower, formerly the allied commander in Europe during the Second World War, and the United States would deploy further troops in Europe. The deal was another success for Bevin before he had to leave the foreign office. He had not embraced the idea of a European army and the New York agreement meant that there would be more US involvement in Europe and, for the time being, no German rearmament and no concessions to the integrationists, although the latter soon pushed forward their plans for economic co-operation, resulting in the formation of the European Coal and Steel Community (ECSC) in April 1951. By this time German rearmament was a major issue in international relations. At war in Korea, the Americans wanted German rearmament so that Europe would not be vulnerable.[10]

Bevin had persuaded the British cabinet, and Acheson, that the best course would be to strengthen Western Europe's defences first, by reorganizing NATO, and only then to consider the FRG's role. He was ready to accept German rearmament in return for a more extensive US commitment to Europe. He grew annoyed by French objections and hoped that a solution could be found using the machinery provided by the Brussels Pact and the North Atlantic Treaty. He expected the French to relax as the US military presence in Europe increased.[11]

Bevin and Attlee appreciated the need to make commitments to allies in Europe, as a means to other ends, but remained unenthusiastic. Churchill also saw Britain as a special case. If Britain was to encourage integration, Churchill thought, it should do so from the outside. To Churchill, European peace depended on friendship between the French and Germans. He was happy to facilitate this but did not see why Britain had to get involved in European structures. Churchill was thinking in terms of Britain's traditional role of creating a balance of power on the continent, while the Cold War made him anxious to deny the Soviets any advantage that might accrue from division in the West.[12]

French misgivings were partly allayed by schemes of integration that offered the means to control German rearmament. The establishment of the ECSC affected industrial-military potential, and, by joining France and the FRG together, made war between them almost impossible; but there was still a long way to go before anything like a consensus would emerge as to the best way to organize Western Europe's defences.[13]

Though the British remained concerned about the possible consequences of West Germany's rearmament and economic development, fear of Germans had by now been superseded by fear of the Soviets. The Korean War also helped to convince London that the FRG should be brought into the West's defence and economic systems. This had to happen in a way that did not harm Britain, however, and anxiety increased in the spring of 1952 when the foreign office warned that the FRG might soon be in a dominant position in Western markets.[14]

At the same time, the consolidation of NATO was more than welcome. From the American perspective it was important to reassure allies and make NATO strong, but there was also a reluctance to commit resources unless there was a coherent package of measures to which Western Europe made a significant contribution. Complete unity of purpose was not guaranteed because individual members of the alliance had their own interests to pursue.[15] Some of NATO's advocates saw it as more than a military body. Indeed, they probably had wider goals in mind from the beginning, for they wanted peace, stability, economic progress and a new pattern for security and diplomacy in the West. In America there may even have been an expectation that NATO, by encouraging greater European self-sufficiency, would eventually allow US withdrawal.[16] This prospect did not go down well in London or in Western Europe.

One of the most disturbing developments in this period was the 'fall of China'. The Chinese civil war ended in victory for Mao Tse-tung and the communists and in 1950 the USSR signed a treaty with the new People's Republic of China.[17] Britain was prepared to recognize Mao's republic, but American leaders still regarded the nationalist Chiang Kai-shek as the true leader of China, even though his forces had been pushed off the mainland to the island of Taiwan. Britain decided to recognize both the new Chinese government *and* the nationalist regime on Taiwan, and controversy continued because the latter retained China's seat on the UN security council under US patronage. Bevin's view was that recognition of Mao's regime would be useful: if China had good relations with the West, he reasoned, the Soviets would be easier to contain. The British also had business interests in China and concerns about the safety of Hong Kong. Britain recognized communist China in January 1950.[18]

In June 1950, when the minister of state at the foreign office, Kenneth Younger, confirmed that there had been contact with Peking and that Chinese representation at the UN was under discussion, he added that 'there is no question of a deal or appeasement in this matter'. *The Times* declared that although it might not change Peking's policies or improve Britain's trade with China, recognition was a sensible move. Instead of trying to reverse what had happened in China, the point now was to prevent the same thing from happening elsewhere in Asia.[19]

For the foreign office and chiefs of staff, the main goal was stability. This was seen to require the co-operation of all the major powers involved in the region. Continued unrest would be damaging to Britain, necessitating a greater commitment of resources to police the sea-lanes and defend British interests, and American suspicion of British colonialism and the fact that Chiang Kai-shek resented Britain's possession of Hong Kong meant that London had to tread carefully.[20] British leaders had other regional concerns in mind, including their wish for cordial relations with India and the need to sustain Britain's position in Singapore and Malaya. A clash with Mao's China was avoidable, London believed, and China could be prevented from committing itself irreversibly to the USSR. In this connection Bevin complained that American leaders were overly influenced by domestic political considerations; they seemed unable to treat the China question in a pragmatic as opposed to an ideological manner.[21]

By the summer of 1950 Bevin was disappointed that recognition of the People's Republic of China had not brought the expected benefits. British firms were not making more money in China, and Soviet advisers and technicians were well established there. Bevin thought that US aid to Taiwan was leading Mao to rely more on the Soviets. He hoped that the Americans would cut this aid and negotiate on the matter of China's seat at the UN.[22]

Attlee told the Americans towards the end of 1950 (with the Korean War in its sixth month) that rather than confront China, the West should attempt to divide China from the Soviet Union. Acheson pointed out that while the USA was resisting communism in Europe, it would be inconsistent to accept the spread of communism in Asia. He also stressed that if Taiwan fell to communism, Japan and the Philippines might follow, and that Chiang Kai-shek had sympathizers in the US Congress. Attlee was concerned about the cohesion of the UN and argued that the West must respect opinion in Asia, in order not to lose support there, but Acheson repeated that the United States would not bargain with China. The British view was that Taiwan and South Korea could both be protected through diplomacy. Attlee wanted a regional settlement and reasoned that China's admission to the UN would facilitate this. When China rejected proposals for a ceasefire in Korea, Washington DC became even more impatient with the British, though the tension eased when Britain backed a motion condemning Chinese aggression in Korea, passed at the UN on 1 February 1951.[23]

Having committed troops to Korea in the hope of influencing US policy, the

Labour government was alarmed whenever Truman threatened to use atomic weapons, and there was controversy about whether or not the Americans had to have British consent before adopting certain measures in Korea. Bevin's successor Morrison gave mixed signals, urging that the Korean War should not spread while agreeing that British forces might be used beyond Korea under the doctrine of containment. To Attlee's frustration, the US government seemed not to notice that Britain was already making sacrifices for the common cause. In Malaya British forces fought Chinese-backed guerrillas from 1948, a commitment that eventually required 100,000 troops and cost £50 million per year.[24]

America had discontinued the exchange of atomic information and technology in 1946. The British pressed ahead to develop their own atomic bomb, which was tested in October 1952. Britain could now claim to be on an equal footing with the USA and USSR, atomic powers since 1945 and 1949 respectively. Perhaps Washington DC would take Britain more seriously in future. This had been one of the main motives behind the British weapons programme. In the absence of an international agreement to stop the production of atomic weapons, moreover, other governments sought to develop them, which made it even more important for Britain to do so. France had the atomic bomb by 1960 and China by 1962. Another motive for Britain was a wish to look into the use of atomic energy for economic purposes.[25]

British defence planners knew it was vital to have the ability to respond in case of Soviet attack, and related to this was the pursuit of defensive arrangements involving the United States. Britain's success in building an atomic bomb was important in both respects, and also helped to deal with another problem, the political trouble involved in retaining bases outside Britain. New weaponry meant that fewer bases were needed. The financial aspects of defence were less easily addressed. It was expensive to maintain adequate nuclear and conventional forces.[26]

American leaders did not doubt that British friendship was worth having. A united front against the Soviets was essential, as was the presence of US bases, weapons and personnel on British soil. The US government seemed to accept Britain's claim still to be a *world* power and not just a European one, supporting sterling during its devaluation in September 1949 and looking upon France as the more likely leader of European integration. The Americans were pleased when Britain's armed forces were expanded: national service began in 1949. A report by US strategists in August 1951 concluded that Britain alone among America's allies had the resources of an independent military power. Therefore the United States could not treat the British just like any other nation.[27]

Preserving Britain's military strength through national service was important, both in itself and because the Americans approved, but it was not uncontroversial. Serious misgivings were voiced in parliament regarding expense and efficiency. Among British newspapers *The Times* was generally complimentary about Labour's defence policy, while the *Manchester Guardian* emphasized Attlee's confession that there would have to be 'sacrifices' and 'some reduction in the standard of living'. Churchill insisted that with proper reorganization Britain and the Commonwealth could have security at a lower cost.[28]

In January 1950 Truman authorized the development of a hydrogen bomb (the American bomb was ready in 1952, the Soviet one in 1953). Increasingly, the Americans opted for a policy of coercion based on superior military strength, which entailed massive spending in response to the Soviet threat in Europe and Asia,[29] and the Cold War was truly militarized.[30] Whatever the merits and demerits of America's confrontational stance, one thing is clear. In view of growing concerns about the global balance of power, the Americans – and some of their allies – felt themselves bound to fight in Korea.

In November 1943 Roosevelt, Churchill and Chiang Kai-shek had agreed on a multi-power trusteeship for Korea after the Second World War. Stalin accepted this arrangement, and when Soviet forces moved into northern Korea in 1945 the Americans proposed that there should be two occupation zones, divided at the thirty-eighth parallel. The beginning of the Cold War meant that neither side wanted to be the first to withdraw.[31]

Negotiations made little progress, while in Korea there was political polarization. Truman referred the problem to the UN. Occupying forces withdrew and the UN agreed to sponsor elections. Stalin decided not to allow elections in the northern part of Korea, which became the communist Democratic People's Republic of Korea under Kim Il Sung. Syngman Rhee became leader of the new Republic of Korea in the south. Both Kim and Rhee wanted to unify the country on their own terms, and civil war started before the international war did.[32] Nevertheless, the specifically Korean causes of the Korean War do not tell the whole story, for Kim's forces invaded the south with the permission of both Stalin and Mao, who had their own ends in view and would increasingly find themselves competing for influence in Asia.[33]

Stalin had been trying to cultivate China's friendship because he did not want Mao to become another Tito. The breach between the USSR and Yugoslavia seemed to Washington DC to be worth exploiting. The Churchill government agreed, and Eden visited Belgrade in September 1952. Stalin treated Mao cautiously in order to avoid the same kind of trouble. Rather than issuing threats or offering economic co-operation, he sought to bring China into the Soviet sphere by raising Mao's security concerns. The plan worked in that the Korean War postponed the Sino-Soviet split for almost a decade. In other respects, however, the situation was mishandled. Stalin wrongly assumed that the United States would keep out, and his preference was for the North Koreans to take only limited action and for the crisis to pass quickly. Instead, the whole North Korean army was mobilized.[34]

The war was initiated, therefore, by North Korea. Moscow and Peking had some involvement, but they did not order the invasion. The Americans, meanwhile, appear not to have taken seriously enough the prospect of an impending military clash. More could have been done, perhaps, to restrain both North and South Korea, and the war broke out partly because of the ideological and political division in Korea that had been encouraged by outsiders, including the Americans.[35]

Before June 1950 American policy in Asia focused on Taiwan. The Korean War made the US government even more determined to resist Mao's China and protect Taiwan. American involvement in Indochina was also stepped up, as was aid to the Philippines, and progress quickened towards a peace treaty and an economic and security relationship with Japan. US commitments to South Korea obviously increased as well. Truman decided that Stalin was out to test American resolve in Korea and that communist aggression could not go unanswered. He also wished to demonstrate American willingness to uphold international law through the UN.[36]

The Americans proposed the 'Uniting for Peace' procedure, which was adopted so that the United Nations general assembly could assume functions of the security council when action by the latter was prevented by a veto. In addition, the Korean War prompted the UN to identify 'enemy states', China and North Korea. The naming of aggressors was made possible by the absence of the Soviets, who were boycotting the UN in protest at the refusal to grant China's seat to the People's Republic of China rather than Taiwan.[37]

North Korea launched its attack across the thirty-eighth parallel on 24 June 1950. The next day the security council condemned the invasion and instructed the North Koreans to withdraw. On 27 June Truman confirmed that the United States would help South Korea to repel the invasion and the security council called for assistance. Twelve UN members agreed to provide troops and equipment.[38]

The North Koreans were soon repulsed but China's intervention in November 1950 changed everything. America had to respond with a much greater effort than the Truman administration had envisaged. Stalin was also disappointed, realizing that Mao would be a rival, not a client. Mao sent a large army into Korea after an ill-advised push north by the headstrong American general Douglas MacArthur, who had been appointed to command UN forces (and was also in charge of the occupation of Japan). MacArthur advanced to the Chinese frontier. Already alarmed by US naval activity in the Taiwan Straits, Mao feared an American attack on China and decided to strike first, even though Stalin refused to help. China used the crisis to annex Tibet and forced MacArthur into a rapid retreat at the end of 1950. Truman eventually sacked MacArthur in April 1951 because he refused to follow orders. The Soviets sent fighter aircraft into Korea, but no bombers, and the Americans threatened to employ atomic weapons. Attlee and Bevin objected strongly to all such talk.[39]

Truman's concerns about the way things were going in Korea were deepened by political problems at home. His remark to the press late in November 1950, that the use of atomic weapons was under consideration, reflected his frustration. That London made so much of the matter shows the extent of the fear in Britain and Western Europe that there would be war between America and China and that, by prioritizing Asia, US leaders were neglecting North Atlantic security.

Truman and Acheson thought that they could fight a limited war in Asia *and* strengthen NATO. While seeking to reassure America's allies, for domestic reasons they continued to talk tough on Korea. In response to Attlee's insistence that China was independent of Moscow, Truman declared that China was acting like a Soviet satellite and that although he did not want war with China, there could be no question of abandoning South Korea. As for the atomic bomb, Truman said that he had not authorized its use and that he would not do so without consulting the British, but he refused to put this in writing when pressed by Attlee.[40]

On the question of atomic weapons, British and American leaders arrived at different understandings of what was agreed by Attlee and Truman when they met in Washington DC in December 1950. Truman spoke of consultation, while Attlee told colleagues back in London that he had obtained a firm commitment from Truman and that, in effect, the atomic bomb was a joint possession. Clearly the British prime minister had to present the talks as a success, but atomic weapons were not discussed at length and the talks focused more on European defence, the shortage of raw materials, which was affecting British rearmament, and co-operation in the Far East. American and British leaders were not paying enough attention to the domestic political circumstances that shaped each other's statements and conduct on international affairs, and Attlee's visit to Washington DC did not resolve this problem.[41]

Attlee and his colleagues had hoped for a period of calm after the crises of the immediate post-war years, and they were not enthusiastic about sending British troops to Korea. They did so in order to be a moderating influence upon the Americans. Yet they had to give way to US pressure on many points, and some in the government advocated a firmer line and argued that Britain should not be identified so closely with American policy. The decision to fight in Korea went hand in hand with the desire for more American help in Europe.[42]

Korea was of marginal importance to Britain. Even so, Bevin, Attlee and their advisers held the Soviets responsible for North Korea's invasion and thought that Britain should support Truman's call for intervention. With US forces close by in Japan and the Soviets absent from the UN, circumstances were favourable, and it was expected that military action would have salutary effects with regard to British Malaya and French Indochina. Bevin argued that Korea could not be viewed in isolation, but some of his colleagues opined that it would be disastrous if the Americans associated Korea too closely with other issues, particularly Taiwan. Bevin accepted that any action taken by the UN should be confined to Korea, and the cabinet agreed to back the United States on this basis.[43]

Though it was committed to containment in Asia, the government feared that Western Europe was becoming more vulnerable to Soviet pressure. Britain lacked the means to act alone as Western Europe's protector, and as for the new and sudden obligation to fight in Korea, the chiefs of staff opposed a substantial diversion of manpower and resources from other tasks.[44]

Attlee informed parliament on 26 June 1950 that the UN security council had condemned North Korea and on 27 June Attlee stated that Britain would support the American proposal that members of the UN should assist South Korea. In a subsequent broadcast to the nation, the prime minister recalled the 1930s and the failure then to deal firmly with aggressors.[45]

Bevin was ill in this period, but he did try to persuade Washington DC of the need for a quick settlement in Korea. The Soviets should be invited to negotiate, he thought, and, since China's UN seat and the status of Taiwan were bound to crop up, it would be better if American leaders did not make categorical statements about these matters in public. Acheson was quick to defend US policy. Matters became more complicated as India called for a ceasefire in Korea, an ending of the Soviet boycott of UN meetings, and the transfer of China's seat on the security council. Though the British had no wish to annoy India and other Asian members of the Commonwealth, they assured Truman and Acheson of their determination to see aggressors confronted, and asked only that the Americans should not allow Moscow to use the Taiwan issue to turn Asian countries against the West. India's mediation plan collapsed primarily because of US opposition. A British approach to Moscow achieved nothing. Still, Attlee repeatedly reminded the Americans of the international demand for a settlement in Korea.[46]

The swift response to aggression, declared the *Economist*, had 'stiffened the political stamina of the free world', and *The Times* suggested that the communist nations, having expected an easy victory in Korea, were shocked by the determination and unity evinced at the UN. Military action was necessary and in keeping with UN rules, argued *The Times*, but there should be no talk of conquering the whole of Korea: intervention should be aimed only at driving the aggressors back to the frontier they had crossed.[47]

Despite ongoing suspicion of American designs, the foreign office approved the inclusion of British troops, ships and aircraft in the UN operation. The chiefs of staff protested that Britain's forces were already overstretched, but the foreign office view prevailed: there could be no hope of persuading the Truman administration to take more notice of London's opinion if Britain refused to fight. At the same time, Western Europe and the Middle East mattered much more to Britain, and it was thought that if the Korean War were not brought to a rapid conclusion, the Americans would grow impatient and take actions that would bring China and the Soviets into a larger conflagration.[48]

The Attlee government's difficulties were compounded by circumstances at home. The general election of February 1950 had left Labour in office, but with a reduced majority. The Conservatives sought to take advantage and the international situation was a favourite topic for them. Churchill impugned every move that jeopardized the Anglo-American 'special relationship'. This set a limit to what the government tried to do in Washington DC, but any hint of deference immediately raised objections on the Labour left, which also opposed increases in defence expenditure. In the foreign office there were still hopes that Korea would be unified under UN supervision. Though it was realized that Moscow would probably not agree, the British lobbied for elections for the whole of Korea. Much more urgent, though, was the need to stem the increase of tension between America and China.[49]

The British government and chiefs of staff were alarmed by MacArthur's rapid advance to the Chinese border. They recommended a halt further south. Had their wishes prevailed, it is possible that China would not have unleashed its huge 'volunteer' force in November 1950, for China had indicated a readiness to compromise on the basis of a rump communist state as a barrier between itself and the rest of Korea.[50] The British had been optimistic, for it seemed that the fighting could be ended quickly, to be followed by elections sooner rather than later. The Americans, and Syngman Rhee, were not about to rush into elections that the communists might win, however, and then China's intervention made it clear that the UN operation in Korea would have to be extended. Britain called for a ceasefire and the establishment of a buffer zone, to separate UN and Chinese forces. It was too late.[51]

These developments suggested that Britain would not be able to restrain the Americans. Attlee's government, and subsequently the Churchill government that replaced it, were in an awkward position. They advised caution because they wanted to avoid a bigger war in Asia and keep the United States interested in Europe, but they also wished to demonstrate that Britain was a useful ally to the Americans. In public Bevin stressed Anglo-American friendship. In private he condemned US policies, as did other British leaders. Criticism was openly expressed by many MPs, as in a foreign affairs debate of 29 November 1950, and there were stark differences of opinion with respect to the role of the Americans in Korea.[52]

London had not taken kindly to US pressure on matters such as economic integration in Europe and British rearmament. When the British complained about US policy, the Americans responded in kind. They wondered how reliable Britain really was, and angrily rebuffed attempts by Britain to lecture the United States about the best way forward in world affairs.[53]

The foreign office remained sceptical about US policy, which seemed likely to extend the war beyond Korea. This would mean either a breach between Britain and America, or British involvement in an Asian war that would divide the Commonwealth, waste resources and weaken Britain's defences. In the early part of 1951 MacArthur pressed for an escalation in order to avoid being forced to leave Korea altogether.[54] Acheson wanted Britain to support resolutions against China at the UN. Britain continued to seek a ceasefire. In the foreign office there was disappointment that no common Anglo-American policy had emerged, amazement at Washington DC's lack of concern about how its actions looked to the rest of the world, and much annoyance when Acheson warned that any further British criticisms would revive isolationist sentiment in the United States. More welcome was the dismissal of MacArthur.[55]

Washington DC and Peking took up irreconcilable positions. The Americans were ready to talk about a ceasefire but the Chinese argued that this could not be arranged unless it was part of a full settlement. Eventually the British decided to back a resolution at the UN that condemned China while mentioning the possibility of mediation. In the spring of 1951 Morrison proposed a truce whereby all belligerents would respect the thirty-eighth parallel. The Americans were unwilling to commit themselves, and, stung by the warning that MacArthur would be vindicated if the Chinese attacked UN forces and Britain did not sanction immediate retaliation, Attlee and Morrison agreed that air strikes against targets inside China should go ahead in response to such an attack.[56]

Truman still faced domestic disapproval, however, and in the Attlee government there was growing unease about the impact of rearmament. The British had been urged by Washington DC to spend more on defence, but once Britain's rearmament drive took off in 1951 it damaged the economy, affected social programmes and led to a cabinet split. Attlee and Morrison insisted that rearmament had to continue not only for national security reasons but also as a sign of the government's commitment to Anglo-American co-operation. Britain backed sanctions against China and agreed that there could be no question of America abandoning Taiwan while the Korean War was in progress, and although Morrison repeated his wish to be consulted about US plans, he let the matter drop because the British government did not wish to be obliged to consult the Americans before taking action in the disputes with Iran and Egypt. When further quarrels broke out between the British and Americans about the Japanese peace treaty, Morrison again decided to give way. During 1951, therefore, if Britain and America were still standing together in the Far East this was primarily because of British concessions.[57]

In parliament the Attlee government came under more pressure from the Conservatives and from the Labour left. Some MPs wanted to know why more had not been done to control MacArthur. There was a questioning of

American leadership. The possibility that the Americans would employ atomic weapons was also discussed at length. India, Australia and other members of the Commonwealth backed Attlee's efforts to reason with the Americans, as did France and the Netherlands. Whenever Washington DC asked Britain to take on more of the burden in Korea, London maintained that with other overseas responsibilities and a fragile economy, it was impossible for Britain to do more.[58]

Labour was defeated at the general election of October 1951. The Conservatives took office under Churchill. Both of the main parties had declared for peace in Korea during the election campaign. Churchill focused on the need for a summit with the Soviets while most of his cabinet colleagues wanted to prioritize the economy. Cuts in spending were announced and it was hoped that peace in Korea would help by making raw materials cheaper and enabling the United States to spend more on economic aid. The Churchill government also believed that the Korean War had to be ended if the Americans were to be persuaded to extend their commitment to European security.[59]

As arrangements were finally made for peace talks, British and US leaders disagreed on points of detail and procedure. The Americans, suspecting that the communist camp would not stick to a ceasefire, favoured a military response if it was broken. Eden did not want any prior commitment to bombing or a blockade, and, when the Americans insisted on the need for a statement of aims, he argued that any such document would have to be approved by all the countries that had participated in the UN's military effort. The Americans agreed to consult more widely. Negotiations began but Moscow was uncooperative and the Chinese and North Koreans stubborn. In January and May 1952 Truman seriously considered using atomic weapons. When Eisenhower succeeded as president early in 1953, the threat of nuclear war was conveyed to China through the government of India. Previous Anglo-American arguments on these points quickly resurfaced. During 1952, with the peace talks reduced to a stalemate, the Americans provoked protests by enlarging their military effort against Chinese and North Korean forces.[60]

Stalin died in March 1953. His successors wanted to end the war in Korea and consolidate their position at home and in Eastern Europe. The US government also wanted to end the war. It was the Koreans, north and south, who wanted carry on. A ceasefire agreement was finally reached, without much enthusiasm on either side, in July 1953. The partition at the thirty-eighth parallel became permanent.[61]

Ending the Korean War was a long and thankless task. American threats were probably counter-productive, as was the focus on voluntary repatriation of prisoners of war. The Americans insisted that prisoners must be given a choice in the matter of repatriation because, having failed to win a military victory over

China and North Korea, they thought they could win a moral victory. That the peace talks produced an agreement probably had less to do with US pressure than with Stalin's death, which altered Soviet policy and in turn affected the communist camp's willingness to prevaricate.[62]

Eden blamed the Americans for the lack of progress. He considered them too inflexible. He also complained that they were making decisions (about bombing raids in Korea, for instance) without consulting Britain. He had not had an easy working relationship with Acheson and he found Acheson's successor as US secretary of state, John Foster Dulles, to be even more disagreeable.[63]

Eden sought to link the Korean settlement with a broader agreement on the Far East. This proposal was not welcomed in Washington DC. The Americans wanted to keep the UN involved and had no intention of joining in a venture that might be taken to imply US recognition of Mao's regime. When the Americans requested British help to coerce China, Eden refused. There was the safety of Hong Kong to consider, Eden insisted, as well as Britain's other economic and political interests in the region, and to provoke China might also be to provoke the USSR. Churchill looked to Moscow rather than Peking. He began to interfere with Eden's diplomacy because he thought he saw an opportunity to improve relations with Moscow now that Stalin was dead. If the Soviets helped to bring peace to Korea, the prime minister thought, other bargains would become possible and the Cold War might be ended. Eisenhower ruled out an approach to the Soviets and desired above all to damage Chinese prestige, though this was balanced by his wish to co-operate with Britain and avoid a rupture in NATO. There was also some common ground between London and Washington DC with regard to the regime in South Korea. Opinion in the United States turned against Rhee and the Americans tried to keep him in line by offering a mutual security pact and economic aid. Churchill assured Moscow that Britain did not support Rhee.[64]

The armistice in Korea was announced in the Commons on 27 July 1953 by Selwyn Lloyd, minister of state at the foreign office, whose mood, like that of other Conservative spokesmen, was one of celebration. Some Labour MPs took exception to this, and on 30 July they resumed their attack, condemning America for failing to consult its allies and arguing that the time had come to admit China to the UN. Lloyd admitted that there were some points on which the British and US governments disagreed, but maintained that these matters were better discussed in private.[65]

Seeking to influence US policy in the Far East, Britain had mixed results. Co-operation with India proved to be unfruitful. Britain and India shared a desire for diplomatic rather than military containment, but there was a fundamental divergence in that India wanted to reduce the role of the Western powers in Asia, while Britain was determined to shore up its position there.[66] Bevin, Attlee,

Churchill and Eden all thought that the West could learn to live with communist China. To them, a relationship with Peking was needed in order to protect British interests and separate China from the Soviet Union. The Americans were difficult to convince.[67]

The Korean War led to significant changes, especially in political and security matters, in both Europe and Asia. America committed combat-ready forces to NATO, which was converted into an effective military alliance. The US government expanded America's national security establishment, pushed for the FRG's involvement in collective defence, and, domestically, overcame the 'Asia first' lobby that advocated traditional American detachment from Europe. US policy in Asia was also transformed. Guarantees were made to South Korea, Japan and Taiwan, and attention was given to the need for a broadly based regional pact. There would be no thaw between Washington DC and Peking.[68]

Historians disagree about whether the changes wrought by the Korean War in Europe were more important than those in Asia.[69] Some argue that the Korean War was not the main reason for the shift from economic to military commitments on America's part, for the Truman Doctrine, Czech crisis and Berlin blockade had already set this in motion. Yet even after the Korean War there were differing opinions in the West about the Soviet threat. During the war, meanwhile, rearmament brought inflation and hampered the Marshall Plan because the resources invested in economic recovery were eroded by the rising cost of raw materials and their diversion to military purposes. Moves for European unity were also affected as the OEEC was subordinated to NATO. American and British leaders agreed that more substance had to be given to NATO, which meant that the OEEC could not emerge as a vehicle for supranational integration. There were objections across Western Europe, and some doubts about NATO's ability to answer the West's security needs.[70]

The Korean War greatly affected Sino-Soviet relations. Disputes arose during the war and the 1950s saw quarrels between China and the USSR on their economic relationship, on foreign affairs, on domestic measures, and on what constituted 'true' socialism. The Korean War also led Mao to decide that he had to make China stronger militarily, which alarmed Moscow, particularly as the Chinese proceeded to develop an atomic bomb.[71]

The British were also uneasy about this, and there was talk in London of extending the West's nuclear umbrella to protect India and deter China. In fact, the Korean War ensured a permanent arms race. American defence spending increased from $17.7 billion in 1950 to over $50 billion in 1953. Britain and the USA's other allies were also rearming in this period, and West Germany was remilitarized.[72]

Britain's inability to match the Americans and Soviets in developing new weapons often came up in parliamentary debates, and there was a testy exchange between Attlee and Churchill on 15 February 1951. Churchill questioned the Labour government's record on defence, but Attlee insisted that years of effort would soon pay off and that Britain would have the atomic bomb. As Attlee pointed out, Churchill could not produce 'any evidence whatever to show that, given the resources and possibilities over here as compared with the resources they have in the United States of America, we could have done more than we have done'.[73] Britain's atomic bomb was ready in 1952, by which time the two superpowers were developing the hydrogen bomb. Once again it seemed that Britain was being left behind. The commitment to an independent deterrent remained, even though many observers argued that it made little difference to the global strategic balance. Labour and Conservative leaders believed that without nuclear weapons it would be even more difficult to influence the Americans. Neither Attlee nor Churchill secured big concessions from the Americans in this period: not on Asian policy, great power summits, US bases in Britain, British interests in the Middle East, or weapons development.[74]

Britain still had *some* influence, however, and generally used it effectively. Co-operating with the Americans in Korea might not have brought all the benefits Britain had hoped for, but the Korean War did not spread and US troops remained in Europe. Washington DC was also impressed by Britain's weapons programme. For London, the programme necessitated further consideration of the relationship between conventional and nuclear forces and the affordability of both. At the end of 1954 Churchill described NATO as an alarm system, and he and his advisers had no wish to see it denuded of conventional forces. Concepts of deterrence were increasingly important to British strategists, though, and to the government, but pressure mounted to bring defence policy into line with Britain's economic condition. Lack of accurate information about Soviet capabilities was another complicating factor, as was the tendency for British planning to reflect future hopes rather than current strength. Though development of the atomic bomb was a significant achievement, did it greatly improve Britain's position? By the time of the British test in 1952, the Americans were thought to have set off thirty atomic bombs and the Soviets at least three. Britain's atomic breakthrough would certainly assist in NATO's defence of freedom and democracy, commented *The Times*, but if the British could now expect more influence, they would also have to take on more responsibility.[75]

In the aftermath of the Korean War the world was more polarized than ever. In the West, much was made of the contrasts between the communist order and the 'free world', while increasing Soviet chauvinism led Moscow to condemn the West as 'corrupt' and 'bourgeois'.[76] Western security and values were reinforced by changes in NATO, but the Korean War had also globalized the confrontation between the superpowers. The Cold War spread decisively into Asia. The Americans were determined to preserve Chiang Kai-shek's regime on Taiwan, and there was more US aid for the French in Indochina.[77] Another significant development was the revival of Japan. The occupation came to an end and the Americans incorporated Japan into the West's strategic planning and trading networks.[78] Japan was treated generously in order to ensure that it remained a regional bulwark against communism.[79]

In London there was initially much relief that the Americans intended to stay in Japan, for this indicated that the main security burden in East Asia and the Pacific would not fall on Britain and the Commonwealth. On the other hand, there were fears about Japanese economic recovery and its impact on British trade in the region, and doubts about the wisdom of certain American proposals for Japan.[80] Britain had expected to participate more in the occupation and there were quarrels as the Americans took charge and minimized the contribution of others. British leaders did not feel able to resist because they needed American help elsewhere. They became less interested in Japanese affairs once they realized that Washington DC intended to guarantee Japan's security and as other regional problems demanded more attention.[81]

The peace treaty that officially ended the war in the Pacific was signed in September 1951. The Soviets refused to accept it because they had demanded the demilitarization of Japan, the removal of US forces and Japanese acceptance of Soviet sovereignty over the disputed Kuril Islands, and on none of these points were they satisfied. Soviet trade with Japan expanded from the mid-1950s, but the Soviets also increased their naval presence in the Pacific to put pressure on Japan as well as on China. British annoyance grew, meanwhile, because although Washington DC had promised that Japan could choose whether to recognize Mao's regime or the government on Taiwan, Dulles made sure that the new Japan followed the US line.[82] The British continued to warn the Americans that the future of Japan should not be settled without consulting Peking, or resolving the Taiwan issue, or erecting economic safeguards to weaken Japanese competition in Asia. The Americans were largely unmoved.[83]

The Churchill government had other complaints against the Americans at this time. They were not seeking a constructive engagement with the USSR; they wanted the commander of NATO's combined Atlantic fleet to be an American; they were expanding their air force strength in Britain without tidying up the agreements relating to the use of British bases and the need for consultation before the use of atomic weapons; they were not helping Britain to deal with Iran and Egypt; they were pushing the British to join in moves for European integration. All this made Britain even more indignant about American policy in Asia. British leaders continued to object to the USA's relationship with Taiwan, the peace process preferred by Washington DC in Korea, and arrangements that had been made for Japan.

Yet the rise of Japan was not entirely unwelcome to Britain. It was some time before the economic consequences were felt, and Japan promised to be a strong pro-Western ally in a strategically important region, which would facilitate the scaling down of Britain's overseas commitments.[84] Before the Korean War, Washington DC had expected the British to take the lead across much of Asia and in parts of the Pacific. The military effort in Korea, ANZUS Pact and Japanese peace treaty made it clear, however, that Britain's responsibilities relative to those of the USA were in decline. America's advance, Britain's lack of resources and the limitation of Britain's containment role to specific areas were linked together, but London was far from despondent. In 1948, faced with the Malayan insurgency and warning about an Asian Cold War, Britain had not been able to secure much US support, but now the Americans were fully involved, and, despite the quarrels between London and Washington DC, there was scope for future co-operation in the region.[85]

If the Korean War was the key to Japanese recovery, it was also significant in interfering with Britain's recovery. After 1945 the Attlee government had done well to lay the foundations for sustained economic progress. In 1950 there was a budget surplus of £297 million. Adjustments had to be made as a result of the Korean War, and Attlee's government announced a rearmament programme in September 1950. The cost was initially estimated at £3,600 million. Soon this figure was raised to £4,700 million. Taxes had to be increased and the decision to introduce charges for health care caused resignations from the cabinet. In 1951 there was a balance-of-payments crisis. The distorting effect of rearmament, a rapid influx of imports, and rising wages and prices brought chaos. There was no decisive response to the growing pressure on sterling. The rearmament policy was eventually reassessed, but it took too long for this to happen.[86]

Some critics of rearmament claimed that the West had more to fear from America than from the USSR, because the spending demanded by Washington DC would lead to economic collapse and undermine the very foundations of democracy. The rearmament plan was excessive, it was said, and health charges were just the beginning: in time the whole welfare system might be swept away.[87] To opponents of government policy, rapid rearmament was unnecessary because the Soviet threat had been exaggerated, and dangerous because it tied Britain to the USA. Against this it was countered that complacency would encourage Soviet aggression and that any disadvantages of the link with America were far outweighed by the advantages. To Attlee and Bevin, America had to be coaxed into making further commitments to Western Europe. They also thought that the economic effects of rearmament would be less damaging than the political costs of refusing to adopt it. They had to show they were determined to rearm, otherwise the US Congress would not grant the assistance Britain needed.[88]

Britain's economic ills were exacerbated by wider international circumstances, especially the Cold War and the conflict in Korea. Trade controls were unlikely to assist recovery, moreover, but the US government wanted to deny products to the USSR and its satellites, and Western Europe suffered because this embargo increased the dollar deficit. America's allies complained that they were being obliged to rearm even while they had to contend with the loss of foreign markets, inflation and severe balance-of-payments problems.[89]

Strengthening the nation's defences remained a key priority for British leaders in the early 1950s. One of the motives was deterrence, to prevent another major war, and there was also a desire to set an example so that European members of NATO would spend more on defence. Moves towards European integration were much less important for Britain.[90] The Attlee and Churchill governments knew that Washington DC wanted Britain to move closer to Western Europe. They may have thought that giving way to the Americans on other issues would buy time with regard to integration, and rearmament went ahead in part because of the risk that US aid might be lost. The Americans were disappointed by Britain's reluctance to participate in European integration, but they did not press Britain too hard, since Britain's wider role in collective recovery and rearmament was too important to be sacrificed for the sake of integration.[91]

This was an uncomfortable time for the British. A number of difficulties had to be addressed, connected with the ANZUS Pact; the disputes with Iran and Egypt; the German question and the course of European integration; the Chinese revolution and Korean War and their international consequences; the evolution of the 'special relationship'; Britain's economic performance and the burdens imposed by rearmament. Although Britain's ability to influence events was not always great, the British still had a dominant role in areas outside Europe and Britain was the strongest European power. Britain was also America's closest ally, despite disagreements. Increasingly, Britain's influence would depend on the ebb and flow within the 'special relationship'. The British *could* shape US policy, but they also needed American support if Britain was to remain a world power, which meant that they had to accept constraints and obligations that they would have preferred not to have.

4

Defence and Diplomacy

In 1954 a left-wing critic of British diplomacy asserted that the government 'has not been compelled to give up national rights through sheer economic pressure from the United States. Sometimes there has been this pressure. But in other cases the rulers of Britain have displayed an extraordinary, almost masochistic zeal, to bow to the US government.'[1] The 1950s saw an increase in the questioning of relations with the United States, in opposition to British foreign policy generally, and in debate about the gap between resources and responsibilities. Despite security concerns and doubts about the condition of the economy, however, this was a time in which Britain continued successfully to deal with European and extra-European problems. Growing reliance on the United States was a fact of life, but this did not mean that independent action could not be conceived and taken when the national interests required.

Churchill had returned to the premiership in October 1951. Eden served as foreign secretary, and then as prime minister from April 1955 to January 1957. Churchill and Eden did well to maintain British influence, but this task was growing more difficult. Economic problems intensified and the rearmament programme introduced by Labour had to be revised. The Korean War and other commitments represented a continuing financial drain, and there were disagreements within the cabinet, particularly between Eden and the chancellor of the exchequer, R.A. Butler, about how best to modify Britain's role in the world in accordance with economic realities.[2]

London and Washington DC quarrelled about US aid to Britain and burden sharing in NATO. The Americans agreed to provide aid so as to limit Britain's balance-of-payments deficit, but an unseemly wrangle arose during 1951–52 because the Truman administration provided only part of what was needed. The Churchill government pointed out that Britain was at full stretch in meeting its NATO commitments while other members were nowhere near meeting their contribution targets, and that British rearmament had diverted resources from key export industries. When Eisenhower became president he continued the aid because he accepted that the enhancement of British military power was in America's interest, but Congress looked for an opportunity to make cuts, and these came in 1953 when the British economy showed signs of improvement.[3]

As the strongest European member of NATO, Britain was centrally involved in further moves to resolve the German question. When Moscow proposed that an all-German council be set up, on which the FRG and the East German state, not recognized by the Western powers, would have equal representation, the West refused. During 1951 Soviet willingness to negotiate was tested by the West's insistence on free elections. In March 1952 the Soviets called for the reunification of Germany and withdrawal of all foreign troops. Under this plan, Germany could rearm but would not be permitted to join any military alliance. There was no enthusiasm for the plan in the West, and talks were disrupted when the Soviets denied a UN commission access into East Germany and ruthlessly suppressed disorder in East Berlin in July 1953. Another international conference early in 1954 achieved nothing.[4]

At the time of the East Berlin rising, the British government's view was that negotiations would inevitably falter unless the Soviets accepted the need for elections and other goodwill gestures. Still, Churchill wanted a settlement with the USSR and claimed that Stalin's death represented opportunity. Eden was unconvinced and there was also scepticism in Washington DC. The Eisenhower administration, the British foreign office and the Adenauer government in Bonn all opposed the idea of a summit and looked for ways to integrate the FRG more tightly into Western structures.[5]

Moscow's proposals for the future of Germany challenged and puzzled the Western powers. British, American and French leaders took more than two weeks to respond to Stalin's offer of March 1952, and this did not go unnoticed in the British press. *The Times* was right when it stated that the allies' delay 'reflects their uncertainty more clearly than their policy'.[6]

Britain and America did not want to be deprived of the power potential of West Germany, upon which NATO's future partly rested. Nor did they wish to recognize the East German regime. They were also worried by the possibility of a vacuum in central Europe, and more Soviet interference there. After Stalin's death, Churchill spoke of the West's acceptance of the USSR's security needs and realized that a thaw would enable Britain to reallocate resources. The Soviet leadership became more conciliatory, a result of rivalries within the Kremlin, but the suppression of the East Berlin rising, the failed conference on Germany and the negotiations in the West that led to another reorganization of NATO got in the way of a comprehensive bargain.[7]

Plans for a European Defence Community (EDC) took shape in 1951–52. The project was pursued by 'The Six': France, the FRG, Italy, Belgium, the Netherlands and Luxembourg. It involved the formation of a European army and gave a boost to European integrationists, but the US government argued that this army should be part of NATO, while Churchill and Eden, though they had declared themselves friendly to European unity, were unwilling to give up sovereignty on defence matters and considered the EDC unworkable, as had their Labour predecessors. Nevertheless, Eden had to make a show of commitment because Washington DC still wanted America's allies to do more for their own security. Therefore, between 1952 and 1954 Eden tied Britain to the prospective EDC by treaties of association. France, however, decided not to go ahead with the EDC. Disappointed that Britain would not join and afraid that the EDC would come to be dominated by the FRG from within and the USA from without, the French also pointed to their colonial responsibilities, and the scheme collapsed.[8]

The American secretary of state, Dulles, had been urging members of the EDC quickly to finalize their arrangements. The French wanted safeguards, so that the FRG could be controlled within the EDC, while Dulles warned that failure to get the EDC into full operation would encourage the US Congress to block any increase in American commitments. Adenauer also complained about French equivocation. He had come to regard the EDC as an instrument for promoting unity in a Western Europe in which the FRG would be an equal partner.[9]

Although Eden had decided that Britain should not join the EDC, he intended to support it from the outside. If it failed, he thought, Britain would have to propose an alternative plan to facilitate West German rearmament and persuade the Americans to remain in Europe. The Churchill government was itself divided between Europhobes and integrationists, but the main problem was the attitude of France. Eden tried to satisfy Paris on many points, to the extent that colleagues accused him of giving the French too much, and an added complication was Churchill's approach to Moscow after Stalin's death, because this prompted Paris to announce that a relaxation of Cold War tensions would remove the necessity for West German rearmament.[10]

Paris had taken a long time to decide what it wanted. Since the French public objected to German rearmament but liked the idea of European integration, the answer was to marry the two together in the form of a European army. This was the basis of the Pleven Plan (named after the French prime minister, René Pleven). Like the European Coal and Steel Community, the EDC was to be administered by an executive commission with supranational powers.[11]

Bevin had decided the best solution would be the inclusion of a West German national army in a combined NATO force, but he recognized that careful bartering would be needed to reconcile the French to this. The key was to avoid alienating France while blocking proposals that would offend the FRG. During 1951 Britain worked with the Americans to this end, with the usual proviso: Britain was willing to join in common European activities provided there was no supranational control. As talks on the European army proceeded, the French demanded full British participation to counterbalance the West Germans. The British remained reluctant.[12] French leaders then claimed that to go too far with a defence system in Western Europe would be to turn Moscow completely against negotiation, though their main excuse for being so obstructive was Britain's policy. They appealed to the Americans, complaining that Britain was not truly committed to European unity.[13]

Churchill had often spoken favourably about integration, and when he returned to 10 Downing Street in 1951 observers in Britain, the United States and Europe waited to see if he would act upon the principles he had espoused. He did not. As for Eden, he preferred to think in terms of an Atlantic rather than a European community, but he liked the idea of a European army and thought that integration offered the only means by which to lessen Franco-German tension and involve the FRG in the West's defence arrangements. Eden was totally opposed to the establishment of any supranational political authority, however, and he did not wish Britain to engage in discussions about such matters until the relationship between NATO and the EDC had been settled.[14]

Some members of the government – notably Harold Macmillan, minister for housing and local government, and the home secretary, Maxwell Fyfe – wanted Britain to move much closer to Europe, but Churchill backed Eden's line that 'The Six' favoured supranational solutions that would undercut British sovereignty. Pro-European cabinet ministers subsequently blamed the prime minister and foreign secretary for throwing away a chance for Britain to gain the leadership of Europe, yet Macmillan, Fyfe and their associates exaggerated,[15] and the role they had in mind for Britain might not even have been possible, for the Europeans were disinclined to accept British leadership on Britain's terms. Indeed, the history of the EDC demonstrates that Paris wanted Britain to join in European projects on French terms.

Churchill's view was summed up by a remark he made in parliament on 11 May 1953: 'We are with them but not of them.' Britain would associate with Western Europe, but not when this affected Britain's independence. When Eden explained the nature of Britain's dealings with the EDC on 14 April 1954, he declared that however much EDC membership suited France, the FRG, Italy, Belgium, Luxembourg and the Netherlands, it did not suit Britain because 'it is part of the intention of the EDC plan as a whole that it should lead to federation between these six countries'.[16]

Although the French pulled out of the EDC primarily because Britain refused to join it, there were many reasons why the EDC collapsed, and British policy was itself influenced by the policy of others. It must also be remembered that the French had intended from the outset to use the EDC for their own ends: they expected to wring concessions out of Bonn, London and Washington DC. It soon became apparent that the scheme involved a range of military, political and legal difficulties, and as the Americans put pressure on them to ratify the EDC treaty, French leaders looked for more inducements. The Americans were worried about the Soviets; the French about the Germans.[17]

If French leaders regarded supranational bodies as the best means to control a revived Germany, the approach was selective. The ECSC suited France, but in its final version the EDC plan did not. In contemplating a European army, the French eventually opted for an intergovernmental rather than a supranational structure. The FRG was not to be an equal partner. As negotiations proceeded the supranational aspects became stronger and discrimination against the Germans was toned down. Britain's unwillingness to join the EDC made the whole thing even less palatable. Meanwhile, arrangements were made for a European Political Community to combine the ECSC and EDC. In August 1954 the EDC treaty was removed from the agenda of French national assembly, which amounted to its rejection. The European Political Community also broke down.[18]

Taken together, these schemes represented an ambitious attempt to harmonize economic and political integration with a military alliance. The attempt was ahead of its time. Washington DC was frustrated, but if the Americans expected that the tendencies promoted by the ECSC and EDC would enable them to reduce their involvement in Europe, they were mistaken. The coal and steel pool was not an unqualified success and the EDC plan never came to full fruition. American leaders wanted integration and pushed for it, though not purely for the sake of Western Europe. The main point was to serve US interests.[19]

The Americans had expected the EDC to provide a framework for German rearmament, essential if US troop numbers in Europe were to be cut as Eisenhower wanted. While Moscow was still hoping to detach the FRG from the West, Eisenhower and Dulles called for greater European unity. The French were unmoved, and even the American offer of more help to the French in Indochina if they ratified the EDC treaty did not work. In fact, relations deteriorated as France threatened to pull out of South East Asia altogether and warned that the French contribution to NATO might have to be reduced. This alarmed both Dulles, who thought that the struggle against communism should focus on Asia, and Eisenhower, who tended to prioritize Europe. Eden was worried that French recalcitrance and the downfall of the EDC would prompt America to detach itself from international problems.[20]

The *Observer* wanted the British government to 'save' the EDC and argued that only Britain could ensure that Franco-German relations would change forever and that Western Europe could know true safety. The answer, according to *The Times*, was for Britain to make proposals that would meet collective defence needs while satisfying the desire of many in France and the FRG for 'at least the germ of a new Europe'. The liking for integration had to be respected, not least because of its security aspects. Eden understood this and was ready to take the initiative. He had already told colleagues that he favoured West German rearmament through NATO, with the restoration of sovereignty for the FRG alongside some limits on military independence. Eden set about swaying the French. Taking up an idea that had been discussed previously, he suggested that the Brussels Pact should be extended to include the FRG and Italy. Western Europe would be reassured about Britain's reliability, supranational institutions could be avoided, and the move would show the Americans that the British were serious about European co-operation and that the Europeans were willing to do more for themselves.[21]

The French expressed reservations and Dulles made matters worse by stating that he would visit London and Bonn to help the talks along, but not Paris. A furious Eden pointed out that this would increase French fears of isolation, and it implied that Washington DC did not trust British diplomacy. Eden also took exception to Dulles' argument that it would be better to persevere with the EDC, and its supranational elements, rather than reorganize the Brussels Treaty Organization (BTO). Finally the French government agreed to West German rearmament and membership of NATO, with controls to be exercised through the Brussels Pact. Eden arranged a conference in London, to open on 28 September 1954, at which the details would be worked out. He suggested that Britain might be prepared formally to guarantee French security and he persuaded the treasury, the cabinet and the chiefs of staff that the envisaged commitment was necessary. It would be made to the non-supranational BTO, and it could be altered (in the event of an emergency overseas, for instance, or financial problems at home) on a majority vote of the Brussels powers, since the French had no right of veto.[22]

Eden broke through an initial deadlock at the London conference with a pledge on British troop numbers in Europe. Adenauer accepted limits on the FRG's manufacture of armaments, and voluntarily ruled out the production of atomic, biological and chemical weapons, while Dulles confirmed that the expanded BTO, now renamed the Western European Union (WEU), would have the benefit of all the USA's previous undertakings to the EDC. The occupation of West Germany was to be ended, the FRG would join NATO, and American and Canadian troops would remain in Europe. The proposed measures were adopted as the Paris Agreements of November 1954. They came into force in May 1955.[23]

Eden reported on the London conference to the Commons on 19 October 1954. The idea of bringing the FRG into NATO was not new, he admitted, but by itself it was insufficient, for the continentals were seeking some way to express 'the European idea'. The British government had decided that the best method would be to reshape the Brussels Treaty Organization. This offered a simpler structure than the EDC, but Britain's participation would more than compensate for whatever was lost by the abandonment of the EDC plan.[24]

The settlement of 1954–55 was largely Eden's triumph.[25] It rested not on original ideas but on a series of connected bargains to which Eden decided that Britain should be a party. His achievement was to persuade Britain's allies to group together the available options in a package that they could all accept. He managed to prevent the isolation of France, the alienation of West Germany, and the weakening of American involvement in European defence. The prime minister and others, notably Macmillan, asserted that Eden should have tried to replace the EDC with another organization under Britain's leadership, but Eden had not seen how such a design could succeed. It would have been condemned by the Americans and Europeans, he thought. The Korean War had only recently been ended, moreover, and the deployment of substantial forces in Korea had raised fears about gaps in Western Europe. These had to be plugged as soon as possible.[26]

Eden and the foreign office had extra reason to congratulate themselves, because they had solved an urgent problem without making concessions to the integrationists. They had separated the question of German rearmament from the question of European unity. Nevertheless, the FRG and France were eager for integration and it continued without Britain. The British, while preserving their interests in the short term, helped to enhance the security without which supranational integration led by Paris and Bonn would have been more difficult.[27] London and Bonn did not prioritize their relations with each other. Their bilateral dealings were really part of a multilateral set of relationships, shaped by the Cold War, and the British cared more about opinion in Washington DC and Paris, while the Bonn government similarly regarded Britain as less important than the United States and France.[28]

Eden's diplomatic success had resource implications. On top of the commitments outside Europe, those in Europe had to be extended. Ending the post-war occupation of Germany brought no relief. Troops, equipment and supplies had still to be provided because Britain had agreed to contribute more to the defence of Western Europe. Conscription continued (the National Service Act of 1947 had set the duration of compulsory military service at one year; this was extended to two years in 1950). Annual defence spending remained at about 10 per cent of national income, an unsustainable amount. The chiefs of staff could tolerate a more precise obligation to Europe only on the grounds that Britain's activity outside Europe was likely to decrease.[29]

The Eisenhower administration welcomed the new arrangements for the BTO and NATO. The president hoped they would lead to a reduction in US defence spending, though American army chiefs resisted and argued that US troops must remain in Europe. Quarrels continued and it was not until 1955 that Eisenhower abandoned the idea that America's support for European defence was only temporary. The American focus on European integration, meanwhile, had unintended consequences. In the long run, by pushing for integration the Americans increased the influence of French and West German leaders who grew reluctant to accept Washington DC's direction.[30] Paris and Bonn worked together on common objectives. Some mutual suspicion remained, however, and one of the main reasons why the French government decided to begin a nuclear weapons programme at the end of 1954 was to strengthen France vis-à-vis the FRG.[31]

Britain's most important links with the continent continued to be those forged in NATO. The commitment cost money, but in return Britain could influence security arrangements and shape the methods of co-operation that were needed to give them effect. Harmonization in one area soon spread to others. The rearmament effort, for instance, necessitated agreement on a common standard for measuring defence expenditure in relation to national wealth. The NATO conference in Lisbon in March 1952 set targets for troop numbers and other aspects of the alliance's military strength. Although these targets were never met, NATO members substantially increased their contributions.[32]

The rise of NATO was not a smooth process. The French tried and failed to gain a share in the leadership of the alliance, while West German rearmament progressed more slowly than had been expected and was complicated by the 'New Look' strategy, which resulted in a growing reliance on nuclear weapons. Adenauer was uneasy, since German territory was bound to be devastated in the event of a nuclear exchange in Europe. The 'New Look' was to a large extent Washington DC's attempt to guarantee security at a bearable cost. It signified that the targets for conventional forces set at Lisbon were too expensive to reach, though Eisenhower was less concerned to cut costs through nuclearization than he was to formalize a defensive plan premised on 'massive retaliation' against attacking enemy forces.[33]

European members of NATO had only accepted the targets set at Lisbon because they were assured that nuclear weapons would be used to counter a Soviet invasion. Then the shift towards the 'New Look' made conventional forces less important.[34] This was quite a relief to the British, who had never been convinced that the Lisbon goals were affordable. Britain now possessed the atomic bomb. The French, meanwhile, had turned against the EDC and entertained serious reservations about America's willingness to protect Western Europe. In the spring of 1954 they asked Eisenhower if he would threaten to use nuclear weapons to prevent the fall of Dien Bien Phu, France's key defensive complex in Vietnam. Eisenhower ruled this out. London was pleased, having advised against it, but the French were incensed, and this was one reason why they destroyed the EDC and embarked upon their own nuclear weapons programme.[35]

London, Paris and Bonn sometimes disagreed in their assessment of security threats, and for the continentals there was the added concern about the credibility of the USA's strategic guarantee to Western Europe. Britain wanted to co-operate with the United States in an interdependent relationship. The French were preparing for independence, while the FRG wanted a system of consultation. For Britain, commitment to NATO, strengthening the 'special relationship' and maintaining an independent deterrent became the core features of defence planning. Critics complained that this was to place prestige before security, yet the methods employed were not entirely ineffective since Britain was able to exert more influence than its military and economic strength should have allowed. Labour and Conservative governments remained pragmatic. Possession of nuclear weapons was a means to other ends, never an end in itself. Gaining more leverage in Washington DC was a permanent goal since so many British interests around the world seemed to depend on pushing or retraining the Americans.[36]

London and Bonn were both committed to NATO and both desired a closer relationship with the United States. France became a nuclear power later than Britain, which meant that strategic matters became mixed up with French demands for an equal voice in international affairs, not so much with Cold War problems. In Britain and the FRG, however, nuclear weapons were not normally discussed separately from these problems. Before the mid-1950s, NATO was very much an Anglo-American affair. From 1955 there was some co-operation between Britain and the FRG, to keep NATO together when American and European interests collided, for instance, and to argue against US force reductions in Western Europe.[37]

Inevitably, security developments in the West in the mid-1950s affected the course of the Cold War. The USSR responded to the Paris Agreements by forming the Warsaw Pact on 14 May 1955. The other members were Poland, the GDR, Rumania, Bulgaria, Czechoslovakia, Hungary and Albania. The formation of the Warsaw Pact was a definitive acknowledgement of the division of Europe, in line with the thinking of Stalin's successor Nikita Khrushchev, who favoured a 'two state theory' with respect to Germany and 'peaceful co-existence' with regard to the Cold War. In the West it was thought that Moscow, with the added protection of a defensive pact, might be more willing to negotiate. This seemed to bear fruit in May 1955 when the USSR agreed to the Austrian State Treaty, which ended the occupation of Austria and established an independent, neutral state with its 1938 borders. In addition, Adenauer was invited to visit Moscow and the Soviets indicated that they were ready to establish diplomatic relations with the FRG.[38]

In the British press the Austrian State Treaty was greeted as a significant development, and it was suggested that the Warsaw Pact was primarily about internal bloc politics and would not necessarily set limits on 'Moscow's new conciliatory mood'. Eden, now prime minister, told parliament that 'there is a definite improvement in the international climate', and he pointed to the possibility of a four-power summit in Geneva in July 1955. When he was asked to confirm that Britain would adhere fully to UN principles of independence, equal rights and non-intervention in the affairs of other states, and mention was made of America's stated wish to promote change in Eastern Europe, Eden reminded MPs that it was not only Britain and America that had a duty to respect UN principles: it was necessary to hold the USSR to account as well.[39] Eden may have been less optimistic about a thaw with the Soviets than he liked to appear.

For years the USSR had pressed for a united and neutral Germany, and Stalin had tried unsuccessfully to tempt the FRG away from the West. After Stalin's death Churchill had called for top-level talks, but the Americans disliked the idea, as did Adenauer, and there was opposition in the foreign office. Nor did the prospect of German unification go down well in Europe. The Soviets signed the Austrian State Treaty, perhaps in the hope that the FRG would want the same kind of settlement as Austria, based on independence and neutrality. Once the FRG was fully incorporated into NATO, however, the Soviets gave up and Khrushchev's 'two state theory' meant that all future moves would be premised on the division of Germany. The goal now was to get the West to recognize the GDR.[40] These developments in Soviet foreign policy owed something to the struggle for ascendancy in the Kremlin after Stalin's death. Other influences included Soviet–East German relations and the idea that any tension between Bonn and Washington DC should be turned to good use.[41]

Adenauer's visit to Moscow in September 1955 was not approved by Britain or the United States, but the West German chancellor was not about to abandon his strongly anti-Soviet standpoint. Nevertheless, the FRG's establishment of diplomatic relations with a government that recognized the GDR was problematic. The answer was the Hallstein Doctrine (named after Walter Hallstein, a senior figure in the West German foreign ministry). This maintained that the USSR, as one of the occupying powers after the Second World War, was a special case: it was acceptable for the Soviets to recognize the GDR, but nobody else should do so.[42]

London supported non-recognition of the GDR. Though there were times when the British wished to increase their trade with the GDR and the rest of Eastern Europe, friendship with the FRG and the USA, and the cohesion of NATO, mattered more. Yet in Bonn there was a notion that Britain might recognize the GDR unilaterally or as part of a collective bargain, and by the late 1950s the British were losing patience. Non-recognition had not prevented the growth of West Germany's trade with East Germany, and the British thought that they should be able to do business with East Germans too. This attitude reflected concern about Britain's relatively poor economic performance compared with that of the FRG.[43]

The Geneva conference, attended by Soviet, US, British and French leaders, took place in July 1955 and was followed by further meetings of the foreign ministers from 27 October to 16 November 1955. Little progress was made on Germany, the arms race, or indeed anything else. Faint hopes for an easing of tension in Europe lasted into 1956, but in October 1956 Soviet forces invaded Hungary to quell a reform movement. The Cold War would continue for some time to come.[44]

Eden had hoped for a resounding success at Geneva that would enhance his government's popularity. Eisenhower was suspicious of Moscow, however, and was determined not to bargain away America's advantage in nuclear weaponry. In fact, Eisenhower and Dulles did not initially wish to attend the summit in Geneva. They were encouraged to go by a CIA report that stressed the USSR's economic problems, the Soviets' awareness that they were militarily weaker than the West, their wish to avoid a nuclear war, and the likelihood that Moscow was ready to do a deal. Eisenhower was also willing to help Eden, whose foreign secretary, Macmillan, had suggested that the Conservative government might lose the upcoming general election if there was no summit.[45]

Eden subsequently claimed that the Geneva conference had been worthwhile. The future of Germany remained the main preoccupation of all who wished for peace in Europe, and Eden repeated Britain's position: there should be reunification and free elections and the Germans must be left to decide for themselves whether to remain neutral or to join alliances. The likelihood was that Germany would prefer the West, and in order to reassure the Soviets, Britain favoured a pact by which the USSR, America, France, Britain and the united Germany would guarantee one another's borders. Britain also wanted an arms limitation agreement, with a thorough system of inspection, and if necessary a demilitarized area between East and West. Unfortunately, at Geneva the Soviets had asked for a security agreement first, while Germany was still divided. Eden admitted that the lack of progress was disappointing, but the key point was that the Soviets were willing to talk. With regard to disarmament, Eden wanted to begin with a 'small practical experiment', the joint inspection of forces along the East-West frontier, which he thought would increase trust and confidence. The prime minister also hoped for greater contact between East and West, with more trade and access for students, tourists and journalists, and he was pleased to confirm that the Soviet leaders Nikita Khrushchev and Nicholai Bulganin would visit Britain in 1956.[46]

In July 1955 the *Manchester Guardian* described many of the proposals made by both sides at Geneva as unrealistic and complained that it was difficult to tell 'substance' from 'shadow'. *The Times* was sanguine, referring to the 'Geneva spirit' and predicting a thaw, but the prognosis by mid-November was less optimistic, following the break-up of the foreign ministers' meeting. It had become obvious that the West and the Soviets were still too far apart on fundamental issues. Talks on disarmament continued, but in December 1955 Eden informed the Commons that no agreement had been reached.[47]

Eisenhower had to accept that one of the main elements in his more flexible approach to the Cold War, negotiation with the Soviets on selected matters, was probably not going to work out as intended. Nevertheless, his time in the White House did see a change in US strategy. Moving on from the containment policy of the Truman era, efforts were made to integrate security goals in a long-term plan and to frame a policy that accommodated such realities as limited funds and limited allied support. Behind it all was the president's premise that the Cold War was not a temporary phenomenon but would probably last for decades.[48] There was also some continuity in US thinking, for Eisenhower retained the bipolar world perspective and did not fully appreciate the variety within the communist camp, and in responding to the communist challenge outside Europe he relied primarily on military action. The consequences of this, especially in Asia, would soon become unmanageable.

Washington DC's determination to make America the arbiter of Europe, the chief container of the Soviets and the guarantor of the FRG's absorption into Western Europe ensured the division of Germany. Without a German settlement there could be no stability, and Moscow came to fear that West Germany would gain nuclear weapons. One of Eisenhower's ideas, to facilitate a scaling-down of the US presence in Europe, was for the main NATO powers, including the FRG, to have nuclear forces under their own control. This was controversial, and in any case America's allies opposed Eisenhower's plans gradually to withdraw US support. In addition, Britain and France did not want the FRG to have nuclear weapons. The dangers posed by German revival can be seen as an excuse that served both sides in the Cold War. It was used to justify measures in the West that were directed against the Soviet Union; it was used by Moscow to justify bloc consolidation.[49]

If America was going to reduce its responsibilities in Europe, assumed Eisenhower, an agreement on nuclear weapons was needed in NATO. Initially the president envisaged only a loose co-ordination within NATO and expected American control to be nominal. Eisenhower was certain that the only way to win a war against the Soviets was to pre-empt their nuclear strikes, but as the Soviets expanded their arsenal, pre-emption no longer promised to protect the United States from a counter-attack. Meanwhile, as Eisenhower and Dulles both realized, the Europeans doubted that the United States would really come to their aid with nuclear weapons, and the Soviet build-up also meant that the West needed a centralized command structure, not loosely arranged independent forces.[50]

The German question involved much more than nuclear weapons and the Cold War was itself much wider than the German question. For the British, indeed, close attention had to be paid to extra-European as well as to European developments. By the mid-1950s, some of Britain's difficulties outside Europe had apparently receded. The Korean War was ended and Britain's quarrel with Iran was settled by negotiation. This outcome was more favourable than it might have been, for British policy had been constrained by Washington DC, which urged London to compromise; by friendly Arab states, which warned against military action; by the spread of Arab nationalism; by Britain's limited capacity to project its military power; and by the specific difficulties that would have beset an attempt to use force in the Middle East in a dispute over oil. On the other hand, the settlement involved the loss of the British monopoly in Iranian oil and undermined British influence. The main beneficiary was America.

If Britain's concern was to safeguard oil supplies, the Americans were anxious above all to forestall Soviet intervention.[51] British objections were brushed aside. In London the American attitude caused consternation. To make concessions, it was argued, would be to reward Iran for seizing Western property, which would encourage similar moves elsewhere.

Whereas Truman had been unreceptive, Eisenhower was willing to listen. It was agreed that Iranian prime minister Mohammad Mosaddeq should be removed. Iran's finances were in turmoil, social unrest was increasing and Moscow had offered aid. After a CIA-sponsored coup and a change of government in Iran, the oil industry there was reorganized in 1954 and placed under the control of an international consortium. Britain owned 40 per cent of the shares in the new venture and American companies also gained 40 per cent. The rest went to Royal Dutch Shell (14 per cent) and the French Petroleum Company (6 per cent). The loss of Britain's monopoly was regretted, but the Churchill government did not want further trouble with the Americans and knew that they would purchase Iranian oil regardless of the claim that it really belonged to Britain. In October 1954, under mounting pressure from Washington DC, the Anglo-Iranian Oil Company reluctantly accepted £25 million in compensation.[52]

The *Economist* pointed to the tricky political and financial issues that would have to be addressed for the deal to hold, not least the organization of marketing and production and the money to be paid to the British by members of the consortium and by Iran. In a notably balanced commentary, *The Times* suggested that the idea of a consortium was sound because it removed Iran's old objection about the country's main source of wealth being controlled by one company. No Iranian leader could go back on the principle of nationalization and now it was up to the consortium to reconcile the need for efficiency with the need to respect Iranian wishes.[53] In the Commons on 12 April 1954 Eden brushed aside complaints about Britain's handover of the Iranian oil industry to 'international big business'. The other companies in the consortium would pay for the interests they stood to acquire, Eden said, and the British government would not give up its holding in the Anglo-Iranian Oil Company, which could expect to be recompensed for parting with full control. The chancellor of the exchequer, R.A. Butler, subsequently reinforced the idea that Britain was still a part of the Middle East oil business when he gave details of the investments, assets and equipment that remained.[54]

On Iran, the Conservative government could at least take some comfort from the fact that a solution had been found. The affair had serious ramifications, though, and Britain's challengers from among the Arab states were not slow to take advantage. Only days after the British had evacuated the Abadan refinery in October 1951, Cairo unilaterally abrogated the Anglo-Egyptian treaty of 1936 upon which Britain's presence in the Middle East largely depended.[55]

Britain's relations with Egypt deteriorated, primarily because of the difficulties surrounding the military complex in the Suez Canal zone. The British decided to remove their regional headquarters from Suez to Cyprus and an agreement of July 1954 provided for joint Anglo-Egyptian control of the canal zone while British forces were withdrawn. It was acknowledged that any emergency in the region would necessitate the immediate return of British troops, and Egypt promised to abide by the established convention regarding freedom of navigation on the canal. Arab nationalists objected to any hint of deference towards Britain, however, and their leader Gamal Abd al-Nasser seized power in Egypt in November 1954. The Suez base agreement did not have an easy reception in the Commons, where some Conservative MPs accused the government of capitulation.[56]

There was a serious disagreement between Churchill and Eden. Churchill favoured a hard line towards Egypt and Eden wanted to negotiate. The Americans, meanwhile, were not convinced that Britain could continue to police the Middle East on the West's behalf, and wanted to increase US influence in the region independently of Britain. By 1954 Churchill was thinking in terms of a unilateral British response to developments in Egypt, and Eden objected so strongly that there was talk of his resignation. In the event the prime minister acquiesced, so as not to harm the 'special relationship' with America, and he was also impressed by the military argument that the large Suez base had been rendered obsolete by the advent of nuclear weapons. He agreed that the 80,000 British troops in the canal zone would be better employed elsewhere and that a presence in Egypt was no longer required, since Turkey was in NATO and the front line of defence for the Middle East had shifted to the 'northern tier'. The Americans pushed Britain into making the Suez base agreement because they were still suspicious of British imperialism and thought (wrongly) that concessions to Arab nationalism would turn its leaders into allies of the West.[57]

Churchill and Eden did agree on a general point: they wished to slow down the pace of change in Britain's colonies and spheres of influence. They realized that Britain's quarrel with Egypt would have an impact across Africa and the Middle East, and hoped that British influence could be sustained by defence agreements within the Commonwealth. These were hampered, however, by South Africa's reluctance to co-operate, although there was an important agreement in 1955 by which Britain could use the Simonstown naval base after it came under South African control.[58]

Departure from Suez did not signify, as far as British leaders were concerned, willingness to accept for Britain a lesser role in the world. The cabinet had already agreed in principle at the end of 1952 to move the regional headquarters to Cyprus, and the refusal to grant Cyprus independence, which led to an anti-British insurrection there, was another sign of the government's determination to maintain British power. The withdrawal from Suez also happened for other reasons. Comparatively, the British economy was not very strong; defence spending was still high; and worldwide commitments had overstretched British forces. Redeployment made sense.[59]

The Suez base agreement was favourably received by sections of the British press. In the Commons the minister of state for foreign affairs, Anthony Nutting, argued that the agreement would help to stabilize the Middle East, strengthen NATO's right flank in Turkey, and uphold Britain's regional influence. Labour MPs were unimpressed and Morrison, the former foreign secretary, declared that as with the dispute over Iranian oil, so with Anglo-Egyptian relations, Churchill and Eden had been all bluster and threat, while Labour had advocated peaceful methods, and it was the latter that had produced results. Morrison also complained about Egypt's interference with Israeli vessels in the Suez Canal. Had the government not gained Egypt's assurance that the convention of 1888, for free passage through the canal, would be respected? Eden replied that this problem had been raised at the UN and that the government would do all it could to improve Arab–Israeli relations.[60]

Little was said about strategic planning in the parliamentary debates about the Suez base, and although new circumstances did prompt changes, Britain's global system remained incoherent. The essential requirement in the Middle East was air power. Garrisons, infantry and operations on the ground were much more important in the Far East. This difference in practice, though appropriate, hindered joined-up thinking, and the tendency of army, navy and air force to focus on separate goals added to the confusion.[61]

That the Cold War was spreading was obvious from events in Indochina. A former French colony, Indochina had been divided into the autonomous states of Vietnam, Laos and Cambodia in preparation for a French withdrawal, but armed struggle began in Vietnam between French forces and the communist Vietminh, backed by China. Although America helped the French with money and supplies, by 1954 it was clear that the French would be defeated. Eisenhower moved towards a more energetic intervention in order to save Indochina from a communist takeover.[62] Support for the French was not unconditional and quarrels between Washington DC and Paris added to the contradictions in US policy: opposition to French colonialism had to be married with an effort to ensure that Indochina remained non-communist. A choice had to be made, and in the end American leaders saw that they must either abandon the region or spend more money and send troops. There was considerable domestic opposition to US involvement.[63]

The decline of the European colonial empires encouraged the Americans to bring Vietnam into an interpretative framework that pitted Soviet-style socialism against the liberal capitalism embodied in US institutions. Economic motivations reinforced political ones. If South East Asia was to be preserved as part of the 'free world', it had to be given economic help, and aid and investment in turn required political stability.[64]

While claiming to be neutral, Attlee's government had hoped for a restoration of French power in Indochina. Bevin had decided that the French should have British assistance if they asked for it, because there would probably be payoffs for Britain in Europe and the re-establishment of French colonial rule in Indochina would have a useful impact in Britain's own possessions in the Far East.[65] In the early 1950s, as the crisis in Vietnam intensified and American involvement increased, it was left to the Conservative government to decide how best to serve British interests.

Tension rose to a new level in April 1954 because of the impending fall of Dien Bien Phu. The Americans wanted the British and other allies to participate in joint military action. Churchill and Eden were unwilling, but they did promise that Britain would join in a defence pact for the region. Churchill and Eden believed that the French position was still strong enough for a favourable bargain to be made at peace talks in Geneva, whereas military intervention could lead to a war with China. The Americans had to accept that there would be no international coalition. Eden recommended that they should press for the best possible terms at Geneva.[66]

Britain's 'special relationship' with the United States was more important to Churchill than it was to Eden. On Indochina, however, there was a meeting of minds, for the prime minister and foreign secretary agreed that the Americans were wrong and that intervention should be ruled out. They knew that British public opinion would oppose another war in Asia, as would the Commonwealth, and were worried about Hong Kong. China and the USSR would not keep out of a war in Indochina, they assumed, and Britain might be dragged in, which would add greatly to the problem of balancing resources and commitments. An agreement was reached at Geneva in May 1954 for the partition of Vietnam along the seventeenth parallel. Free elections would be held to decide the future relationship between North and South Vietnam, and separate treaties guaranteed the independence and neutrality of Laos and Cambodia. These agreements were finalized in July mainly on the initiative of Eden, who was widely praised, but from the start the Americans raised objections. Dulles complained that the Geneva accords marked a victory for China.[67]

Eden's priorities at this time were connected with the EDC, not Indochina, and his resentment about Britain's junior status in the 'special relationship' made him wary of the Americans, but in the weeks leading up to the Geneva conference he realized that the French position in Indochina had become untenable and that he had to prevent US military intervention there, which he thought would be disastrous. Policy was shaped by the desire to demonstrate that Britain still had influence in Asia.[68]

Eisenhower and Dulles were determined not to allow the communists to take all of Vietnam. Elections and reunification did not appeal to Washington DC, and, rather than risk an electoral victory for the Vietminh, America gave massive aid to the separate state of South Vietnam. The British government was annoyed, having regarded Geneva as an excellent opportunity to ease Cold War divisions and separate the USSR and China.[69] There was also a quarrel about the planned security pact for South East Asia. When Eden received a draft version in July 1954 he objected to the use of language that, he said, would offend the communist camp unnecessarily. He also urged the Americans not to establish a military relationship with Laos and Cambodia in case this further antagonized the Chinese. Eden and Dulles disliked each other, but there was more to it than this. For years the British had considered US policy in the Far East to be irresponsible. A major war in the region was bound to damage British interests and London was constantly telling Washington DC to hold back.[70]

The Times suggested that the main point of disagreement between London and Washington DC had long been clear: they had different opinions of the communist regime in China. Instead of dwelling on this, Britain and America should focus on harmonizing their activities and making sure that the West's interests were protected. *The Times* wanted a security pact, to balance the Sino-Soviet alliance, and economic aid for friendly states in the region. Peacemaking in Indochina, commented the *Manchester Guardian*, was being slowed down by the 'lack of cohesion on the non-communist side . . . the West is not acting together as closely as it might'.[71]

When Eden reported on the Geneva talks to parliament he said that a lasting settlement was within reach and that no military action should be taken while outstanding problems had yet to be resolved. Eden also spoke of the possibility of a permanent regional defence organization, stressing that it was important not to prejudge such issues as its scope and membership, because this might hinder agreement on the future of Indochina. The priority had to be a political settlement backed up by international guarantees.[72]

Some American observers were amazed that the British had not only refused to support US designs for the region, but had also acquiesced in communist gains there. They thought that the Churchill government had paid too much attention to the wishes of India and the Commonwealth, and that British policy still had an underlying imperialistic motivation. London seemed to be placing Commonwealth unity above what the Americans saw as the main goal, containment of communism.[73] French prime minister Pierre Mendès-France spoke of Geneva as the end of a nightmare. Mao was confident that he had excluded the Americans from Indochina. The Soviets were satisfied, though not without reservations. Opinion in Washington DC was divided. The Americans were pleased that a blow had been dealt to French colonialism and relieved that expenditure on aid to the French could be discontinued. With French power in the region weakened, thought Eisenhower and Dulles, the United States should build a viable non-communist order there. Critics of the administration claimed that it had not done enough to prevent the loss of North Vietnam.[74]

In London it was thought that a dangerous situation in Asia had been created largely by the Americans. British leaders were already anxious about the weakening of Britain's position in the Middle East, the failure to take full advantage of the leadership changes in Moscow after Stalin's death, and challenges to sterling as the world's main trading currency alongside the US dollar. In London these developments were deemed to be direct consequences of policies conceived and implemented by the United States.[75]

This period also saw the extension of the Cold War in Latin America, with a US-backed coup in Guatemala in 1954. Washington DC decided that the left-wing president of Guatemala, Jacobo Arbenz Guzmán, was planning to lead his country into the Soviet camp, even though Moscow had never had a close relationship with Arbenz. Once the coup was under way, the USA was widely criticized. Dulles had to dissuade the UN from interfering. He warned Britain and France not to meddle. Britain had suggested that Arbenz was no threat, since his focus was on domestic reform. His dispute with the United States, moreover, had led him to drop Guatemala's longstanding claim to British Honduras. As for the French, events in Indochina put them in no mood to side with Washington DC on Guatemala. In addition, both Britain and France were eager to use the UN to reduce tension between the United States and USSR. Dulles condemned them for refusing to back America in the struggle against communism, for endangering the unity of the West, and for seeking to misapply the authority of the UN. At the end of June 1954 it was agreed that Britain would abstain, and advise the French to do the same, the next time Guatemala came up for consideration in the UN security council.[76]

Pressed in the Commons to explain the government's position, Eden pointed out that the situation was unclear, since it had not been established whether Guatemala had descended into civil war or been attacked by an external aggressor. He called for the fighting to cease and expected that the UN would play some role, but without assuming the chief responsibility. Some MPs wanted a direct UN response. Others linked the issue with Indochina and suggested that a serious breach was opening up between the British and US governments. Eden replied that Anglo-American discord was too often misrepresented.[77]

Even so, previous harassment of the Arbenz regime had not met with Britain's approval, and though Eden was not particularly worried about the fate of Arbenz, he did care about the reputation of the UN. In the event the British relented, not wishing to forfeit American help in the Middle East and elsewhere. The crisis divided opinion in Britain. Eden was hard upon the Americans, Churchill welcomed the 'rebellion' against a 'communist' regime, and on the British left there was sympathy for Arbenz. *The Times* came out strongly in support of Dulles' plan to have the Organization of American States investigate the situation in Guatemala, with the proviso that the UN security council should be kept informed.[78]

As the Cold War spread, its nature changed. The events of the 1950s highlighted differences between Britain and the United States on how to deal with the Soviets, and the British were particularly doubtful about American modes of covert action, propaganda and economic warfare. Traditionally, Britain preferred to conciliate strong enemies and favoured a non-ideological approach. Churchill repeatedly tried to arrange talks with the Soviets and the British also wanted to trade with the eastern bloc and hoped that closer economic links would make communist regimes more reasonable. Churchill was sure that if the West tolerated Soviet control over Eastern Europe, eventually the bloc would break up.[79]

To Churchill, negotiation with the USSR in an effort to end the Cold War ranked far above European co-operation. He was willing to sacrifice integration, indeed, in order to get his summit with the Soviets. The main point was for Britain to remain a great power, and by the end of the 1940s he had decided that this required a settlement with the USSR. A settlement would promote peace, which in turn would give time for the restoration of Britain's economic strength. Without a sound economy, Churchill thought, Britain could not expect to be treated as an equal by America and the Soviet Union. If Churchill was genuinely committed to détente, his wish for a summit also owed something to personal vanity: he regarded himself as the only world statesman who could bargain effectively with the Soviets. But it was not until the question of German rearmament was put to rest (May 1955) that Western leaders felt themselves strong enough to negotiate with Moscow, and this was too late for Churchill. He was no longer in office.[80]

During the 1950s the Cold War increasingly became an ideological and technological contest. The Soviets claimed to have true liberty and equality, and there was some affinity with the USSR on the political left in the West, but Khrushchev's denunciation of Stalin in February 1956, and the suppression of the reform movement in Hungary eight months later, created uncertainty about Soviet values and this was exploited by CIA-sponsored organizations in Britain and Europe. Hollywood produced anti-Soviet films and the CIA continued to fund youth groups and other bodies across the West for many years. The BBC and British film-makers, artists and writers also participated in this war of ideas, identifying the West with human rights and civilization.[81]

Britain was fully engaged in the cultural side of the Cold War. One of the leading participants was Christopher Mayhew, formerly a deputy of Bevin at the foreign office, who chaired the Soviet relations committee of the British Council. This committee was established in 1955 and was designed to break down the isolation of the Soviet people and disrupt Moscow's ties with communists and other sympathizers in the West.[82]

Khrushchev, who headed the central committee of the Communist Party of the Soviet Union, and Bulganin, prime minister of the USSR, arrived in Britain for an official visit in April 1956. They were received by Queen Elizabeth II, met with Churchill, and had discussions with senior British ministers and officials. The resulting agreements were limited, but they did indicate a shared wish for economic and cultural interaction. Mayhew wanted the Soviets to give up their ties with 'friendship' societies in Britain. He told Bulganin that it was inappropriate for Moscow to promote Soviet–British cultural relations through communist-controlled organizations. The Soviet leadership subsequently paid less attention to these societies, though the ties were not cut completely.[83]

As well as generating a cultural contest, the Cold War necessitated investment in research and development and the use of scientific advances, but there were questions about the cost, the economic impact, the pros and cons of government direction of research, and the knock-on effects of concentrating resources in military and military-related sectors. Rivalry between groups and institutions for funding also created difficulty, as did arguments between the armed services and the scientists.[84] A related matter was espionage, a great concern to government and a matter of fascination to the general public. Some British secrets were passed to Moscow, while direct penetration of Soviet research proved to be almost impossible. The British and Americans saw no Soviet equipment that was not shown to them or already in service. Even between the United States and Britain, information did not flow freely, although in some respects the Americans needed the British and co-operation was closer. Secret intelligence gathering was one such area. Since 1947 Britain, America, Australia and New Zealand had been sharing their signals intelligence facilities.[85]

There was more to the Cold War than containment and security. Offensive as well as defensive methods were called for: hence the propaganda, strategic trade controls, covert operations and intelligence gathering. Anti-communist attitudes were well established in MI6, Britain's secret intelligence service, but breaches of security undermined morale and damaged Anglo-American relations. Still, the Soviets did not entirely have the upper hand. From 1950 Britain provided bases for US spy planes that covered the USSR and eastern bloc, and MI6 and the CIA often worked together, particularly in the Middle East. Meanwhile, MI5 was devoted to counter-subversion at home in Britain, and the new Government Communications Headquarters in Cheltenham, operational from 1952, worked on breaking Soviet codes. There were further reverses for British intelligence, however, as in May 1956 when Commander Lionel 'Buster' Crabb disappeared while spying on a Soviet cruiser in Portsmouth harbour. Eden refused to give details when pressed by MPs, and insisted that his government had not authorized the Crabb operation. *The Times* called the matter 'unsavoury' and argued that Crabb must have been acting on orders.[86]

Britain's problems with secrecy were most important with respect to the weapons programme. For strategic, diplomatic and political reasons it was necessary to conceal certain facts, technological advances and relationships. Secrecy might have retarded progress, for it imposed extra costs and administrative burdens, but even so, the British wanted to hide as much as possible from the Soviets and convince the Americans that Britain could be trusted with sensitive information.[87]

Various committees were charged with Cold War planning, and the Information Research Department, set up in 1948, continued to develop propaganda and psychological warfare not just against the Soviets and communists but also in response to subversive elements in the empire. Unfortunately, British intelligence gathering was not very effective in the early stages of the Cold War. The British knew relatively little about Soviet weapons, for example, and were surprised by the speed of the Stalin–Tito split.[88]

That the Cold War was not going to peter out was confirmed by the fruitless Geneva summit of 1955. The Western powers proposed disarmament with a focus on conventional forces because they knew that the USSR had the advantage in this area, while the Soviets pressed for a limitation on nuclear weapons because their nuclear arsenal was smaller than that of the United States. The West also wanted freedom of information, to disrupt the eastern bloc, while the Soviets wanted economic agreements, to end the trade controls imposed by the West.[89]

The lack of an accommodation with the Soviets ensured that Britain gained no relief. High defence expenditure continued and the British could not easily step back from their global commitments. Conscription continued until 1962. Rearmament had a significant impact on the post-1945 economic recovery. The British were left with a heavier defence burden compared to their European competitors, which affected the balance of payments, yet some manufacturing sectors did well and although there was a fall in exports during the early 1950s, they rose again later in the decade and in some cases the fall was related to increased sales at home, not a diversion of capacity to meet defence requirements. Nevertheless, Britain's manufacturing exports were shrinking as a proportion of the world total. Britain's share in 1955 was almost the same as that of the FRG and Japan combined, but they enjoyed a much faster rate of growth.[90]

In a report of July 1952, the chiefs of staff stated that Britain lacked the economic means to prepare for a long war. The focus, they argued, should be on maintaining sufficient forces for an intense conflict of short duration. The government initially accepted this report, but the advent of the hydrogen bomb prompted a reassessment.[91] The two superpowers exploded their first hydrogen bombs in November 1952 (the Americans) and August 1953 (the Soviets). The British government decided to develop a hydrogen bomb in 1952, but this was not made public until early in 1955. The British bomb was tested in May 1957. Successive governments were often harried in parliament, in the press and on the platform, especially by anti-nuclear Labour MPs, for a clear statement of the circumstances in which Britain might use the new weapons.[92]

The assumption of both the Attlee and Churchill governments was that new weaponry would deter the Soviets and increase Britain's influence over the United States. This encouraged them to make commitments that might otherwise have been ruled out as too dangerous or expensive. The existence of the US nuclear arsenal, and confidence in the future development of British armaments, directly shaped policy, and without Britain's willingness to make commitments it is possible that the Americans would not have agreed to involve themselves so deeply in collective defence. For his part, Churchill was surprised when news came through of the first hydrogen bomb test by the Soviet Union, but for the rest of his public life he adhered to the view that the hydrogen bomb made another world war impossible.[93]

British enthusiasm for biological and chemical weapons tended to wax and wane according to the changing level of Anglo-American nuclear co-operation. Biological and chemical weapons were considered necessary, as the alternative agents of mass destruction to the atomic bomb and then the hydrogen bomb. The economic context was always important, though, and concerns were raised about Britain's ability to pay for new weapons.[94]

By 1950, there were more US bombers and air bases in Britain than there were anywhere else in Europe. From 1951 Churchill tried to revive the wartime nuclear co-operation. In 1952 the Americans agreed to consult London about the use of US weapons based on British soil, but confusion continued as to the degree of consent that the Americans would need. Once Britain became an atomic power, American leaders grew more amenable. The Eisenhower administration decided that co-operation would be advantageous, though there was no question of waiting for British approval before using nuclear weapons in an emergency. Eisenhower asked Congress to amend the McMahon Act of 1946 and, despite some quarrels, over the following years nuclear co-operation became a hallmark of the 'special relationship'. On the other hand, it could also be argued that American concessions to Britain did not greatly assist the British programme, and that by focusing too much on wooing America the British closed off other avenues, notably nuclear co-operation with France.[95]

For Britain, nuclear weapons were a sign of world status and a means of promoting joint action with the United States. Although Britain's influence in

Washington DC rested on diplomacy, history and Britain's conventional forces and geographical position, not just nuclear weapons, it is clear that the weapons programme became a useful bargaining lever. Congress removed certain limits on nuclear co-operation with Atomic Energy Acts in 1954 and 1958, and the sharing of information and technology was also increased under bilateral agreements of 1955 and 1959. Nevertheless, the prospect of nuclear subjection to America now loomed much larger for Britain. The thermonuclear test of 1957 demonstrated Britain's competence in weapons development, but by this time the Americans and Soviets were building missiles. The arms race had entered a new phase, one in which Britain could not compete without assistance.[96]

The nuclear relationship involved not only governments but also military establishments. The links between the RAF and the US air force were particularly important and appeared to justify British optimism about co-operation with the United States, yet Washington DC quickly realized that conversations would provide an opportunity to influence British policy, and this is what happened.[97] By the late 1950s the independence of Britain's deterrent was debatable.

British defence policy was somewhat unsettled in the mid-1950s with respect to the balance between conventional and nuclear forces and their relative merits and costs. It was assumed that conventional forces could be cut where the same tasks could be done by nuclear forces. Outside Europe, the chiefs of staff thought that Britain should maintain the minimum level of conventional forces and use nuclear to support them. Europe was a different matter. Here there was a substantial commitment of conventional forces, and the chiefs disagreed with reductions in Europe and moves within NATO for greater reliance on nuclear weapons.[98]

Anti-nuclear campaigners staged many protests and the agitation touched even the most privileged sections of British society. In the spring of 1954, for instance, hundreds of undergraduates at the University of Oxford signed a petition against nuclear weapons. Later in 1954, the secretary of the Oxford University Communist Club, Peter Sedgwick, linked the nuclear issue with US exploitation of Britain and the evils of imperialism.[99]

In the Commons in April 1954, Attlee referred to recent hydrogen bomb tests by the United States and called for a meeting of British, American and Soviet leaders to discuss arms control. He also wanted a renewed effort to strengthen international peace through the UN. The Commons approved of Attlee's proposals, although Churchill suggested that American tests were not as dangerous as many people thought and that the Soviets were not far behind America in their weaponry. The good news, the prime minister went on, was that the Americans were willing to exchange nuclear information with Britain, subject to restrictions, and Churchill repeated a point he had often made before: this was a matter that the Attlee government of 1945–51 should have resolved. The Quebec Agreement of 1943 had provided for Britain to be consulted by America as an equal, Churchill said, but Labour had given this up. Attlee rejected Churchill's assertion before the prime minister went on to attack those Labour MPs who wanted the United States to abandon weapons testing. When Churchill was himself condemned for giving way to the Americans and rendering Britain powerless, Eden replied that if Britain had been rendered powerless, this was the result of Labour policies that had left Britain less able to deal firmly with the United States. As for arms control, Eden said that this had long been a British aim, one repeatedly blocked by the Soviet Union. Eden confirmed that the government would continue to seek a breakthrough, whether at the UN, in bilateral talks, or in other ways. The matter could not be separated from other problems, however, and Eden asserted that what was really needed was a thaw which would create a more favourable climate for negotiations.[100]

A thaw would certainly have helped Britain to deal with pressing issues at home and abroad, and to adapt to changing international circumstances. External commitments had to be reorganized and there was a need to lighten the political, financial and manpower burdens imposed by the world role. In détente there were many false starts during the 1950s, and no lasting progress. Nevertheless, British policy was not unsuccessful. Influence was maintained and interests defended. Out of the messy EDC affair came the strengthening of NATO, which could now make use of the military and economic potential of the FRG. No major compromises had been necessary in terms of London's attitude to European integration. Talks on the German question would continue, and, despite the formation of the Warsaw Pact and the fading of the 'Geneva spirit', it seemed that an improvement in East–West relations was not impossible. More certain was the evidence that the Cold War in Europe was changing. Meanwhile, international relations were also affected by extra-European developments, including those in Iran and Egypt, in Indochina and in Guatemala. Britain remained a world power, was treated as such by other powers, and was determined to uphold this status. To have a say in Europe, the Middle East, the Far East and elsewhere was indispensable, as was the effort to continue playing in the nuclear game.

5

East of Eden

Churchill's notion that Britain could remain on a par with the United States and USSR, because of Britain's unique position as a fixture in, and the only link between, the 'three circles' of world power, was beginning to unravel by the late 1950s. Eden and the foreign office had a more accurate view of Britain's position. According to Evelyn Shuckburgh, who was Eden's principal private secretary from 1951 to 1954, Eden understood that 'we were stretched all over the world in places which we had no possibility of continuing to dominate'. In making this point to parliament and public, Eden 'was not helped and he was really rather frightened by the opposite view in the party under the umbrella of the great war leader'.[1] Altering the Churchillian perception was not the least important of Eden's tasks. Britain was still a global power, despite the compromises that had to be made owing to circumstances at home and abroad, but Britain's status, strength and potential, relative to those of other powers, were changing. Eden tried to limit and guide this process. Influence had to be maximized, aggression deterred, and peace preserved.

One way of pursuing these ends was to make alliances. By the Treaty of Manila, signed on 8 September 1954, the United States, Britain, France, Australia, New Zealand, Pakistan, the Philippines and Thailand formed SEATO, the South East Asia Treaty Organization. SEATO had no standing army or joint command, and was a much looser arrangement than NATO. For the Americans it was worthwhile, however, because it demonstrated their commitment to regional security, and in due course the protection of SEATO was extended to include Laos, Cambodia and Vietnam. SEATO helped to preserve Britain's role in the region, but the circumstances surrounding its formation increased the animosity between Eden and Dulles, who disagreed about how and when to unveil the pact. The Chinese protested that the neutrality of Laos, Cambodia and Vietnam, agreed at Geneva, was being violated.[2]

London had been hoping for a new security system in the Far East on the assumption that it would help to settle the future of Indochina and enable British leaders more easily to monitor US policy. Churchill believed that if Britain backed the Americans on Indochina, they would back Britain on other questions. Eden told the cabinet in April 1954 that the new organization would remove the 'anomaly' of Britain's exclusion from the ANZUS Pact and add to the security of Hong Kong, Singapore and Malaya.[3] Eden's thinking was influenced by evidence that French power in the region was broken, and by the prospect that the partition of Vietnam and formation of a defensive alliance would erect a barrier against communism.[4]

When Eden discussed the formation of SEATO in the Commons on 25 October 1954, he was asked about the views of India, Pakistan, Ceylon, Burma and Indonesia. He told MPs that there had been appropriate consultations with these countries, but there followed a tetchy exchange during which the foreign secretary was required to explain 'how the cause of security is advanced by a treaty to which nearly all the nations of South East Asia refuse to adhere'. Eden did not accept this assessment.[5]

SEATO was not exactly what Eden had wanted, but he was satisfied that he had won a success over US policy. Hoping for a NATO-type alliance, he realized that the Americans wanted a simpler affair, like ANZUS, to be supplemented by bilateral agreements with individual states. Meanwhile, Washington DC had to go along with the partition of Vietnam pending elections and reunification, and the formation of SEATO went ahead because the Americans, though they resented Eden's part in the Geneva accords, wanted to be prepared for any future crisis. Though he had envisaged a tighter alliance, Eden was not disappointed because he decided that excessive US involvement had to be avoided. Britain needed better relations with neutrals in Asia, especially India, and they would have been alienated had London shown any sign of endorsing America's posture towards China.[6]

To Washington DC, SEATO was important not only for containment in Asia, but also because it affected relations with France and the fate of the EDC. As for the situation in Vietnam, Eisenhower and Dulles regretted the partition of that country and wanted to make sure that SEATO preserved the freedom of South Vietnam and the non-communist remainder of South East Asia.[7] Disagreements between London and Washington DC suggested that Anglo-American co-operation in the region was likely to remain patchy. The Americans disliked British imperialism and were not prepared to help Britain maintain its interests except when these were shared by the United States.[8]

The Soviets claimed that SEATO was directed against them, and they made the same point about the Baghdad Pact, which later developed into the Central Treaty Organization, CENTO. This grew out of an agreement for mutual defence and economic co-operation between Turkey and Iraq, signed in February 1955. Britain joined in April 1955 and was followed by Iran and Pakistan before the end of the year. The Baghdad Pact meant that the British would be better able to protect their position in the Middle East, and they hoped that the pact might link together other alliances, because Britain and Turkey were also in NATO and Britain and Pakistan were also in SEATO. Such a plan could only work, however, if America joined the Baghdad Pact. Though they wanted to minimize Soviet influence in the Middle East, the Americans wanted no strengthening of British influence there either. They were also cautious because Egypt and Syria both condemned the Baghdad Pact.[9]

Britain had been obliged to give up schemes for collective defence in the Middle East, and the Suez base, owing to Arab sentiment and the lack of US support. The Baghdad Pact offered some compensation, and the 'northern tier' became the centrepiece of a new British strategy for the region. Since British troops were needed in other trouble spots, it made sense to reduce their number in the Middle East, particularly when it was possible to use nuclear weapons against the Soviets if they moved into the region.[10] Eden told parliament in March 1955 that British membership of the Baghdad Pact reflected a wish for agreements on a free and equal basis. He hoped that other nations would join the pact in due course. Labour MPs asked about the possible effects on Israel. Eden maintained that Britain wanted friendship between the Arabs and Israel, that the pact was not directed against Israel, and that its purpose was to protect the Middle East from external aggressors.[11]

Eden's readiness to join the Baghdad Pact was also a readiness to act more independently of the Americans. The British had previously tried to bring America into the Middle East without greatly limiting their own freedom of manoeuvre. The Americans were not about to be used in this way, and Dulles was also aware that several Arab states disliked Britain's plans. Eden feared that the Americans would act unilaterally in the Middle East, damaging British interests and giving Arabs the impression that Britain was content for the USA to take the lead. In theory, the Baghdad Pact enabled Britain to regain the initiative.[12]

Britain urged the United States to join the pact, but Eisenhower and Dulles saw no need. Aid to its members would be sufficient, they said, whereas membership of the pact would hinder more important regional goals, especially the effort to promote a settlement between Israel and the Arabs. No such settlement would be possible without Egypt, and Egypt opposed the Baghdad Pact. Nasser believed that to enter into a defence relationship with the West would be to divide the Arab world and to accept the primacy of Iraq, Britain's ally. Eden hated the idea that Washington DC might defer to Egypt even at the risk of undermining the Baghdad Pact. He said in cabinet in October 1955 that, when necessary, Britain should act alone in the Middle East. American support would be welcome, but British interests came first.[13]

Britain's relations with Turkey were already good and Britain had a military agreement with Iraq dating from 1930. It was important to both the Turks and to Britain that this Anglo-Iraqi co-operation should continue. The new pact ensured that it would. Eden hoped that as the pact was opened to others, it would guarantee stability.[14] Egyptian animosity could not be overcome, however, and although it was obvious that the Baghdad Pact would be more durable if more Arab states joined in, they could hardly be forced to sign, and the best course seemed to be to dissuade them from joining any alternative defence system. When Pakistan joined there was a new wave of protests, notably from India, which created further difficulty for Britain.[15]

It does not follow that British strategy should have been different. The focus on the 'northern tier' was related to the need to manage decolonization carefully in case former colonies or allies fell under Soviet influence. The Middle East remained pivotal, for reasons that were much the same as they had been in earlier decades: oil supplies; global communications and trade; the competition for control of the eastern Mediterranean; air bases that were within striking distance of the Soviet Union; the need for an ongoing presence in the Middle East as a barrier to Soviet expansion; and Britain's prestige as a great power.

At the time of the Suez base agreement, Eden had still entertained hopes that Egypt would agree to participate in a regional defence system. Nasser had other ideas. He suspected that the British would seek to use the Baghdad Pact as a means of control in the Middle East, and he was determined not to show weakness in his dealings with Britain.[16]

When the British joined the Baghdad Pact they also arranged for talks in Washington DC. Although the US chiefs of staff wanted to work with the British in the Middle East, senior figures in the state department and National Security Council assumed that Britain was up to the usual trick of seeking to appropriate American resources. Concern was expressed about the attitudes of Egypt, Saudi Arabia, France and Israel. It was also suggested that the Baghdad Pact had more to do with Britain's own political and economic goals than with the Soviet threat. Nevertheless, the Americans later participated in planning discussions with members of the Baghdad Pact and supplied equipment to Iraq, Pakistan and Iran.[17]

There was a wider problem for the British. They were losing friends, even in formerly reliable states such as Iraq and Jordan. Popular nationalism and Arab politics were eroding old relationships and power structures. A fatal blow came in July 1958, when a revolution in Iraq removed the pro-British government and Iraq left the Baghdad Pact. Meanwhile, from the spring of 1956 King Hussein of Jordan began to distance himself from Britain in an effort to court Arab national- ists and strengthen his position.[18] Eden became convinced that the security of the West, Britain's interests in the Middle East, the viability of the Baghdad Pact, and the need to resist Nasser and Arab nationalism were all linked together.

The strategic utility of the Baghdad Pact was understood from the outset, but there were also doubts. It was not clear that its members could assemble enough military strength to prevent or repel a Soviet attack, and yet the very existence of the pact probably encouraged Moscow to pay more attention to the region. Only months after Britain joined the pact, Nasser concluded an agreement to purchase arms from the eastern bloc.[19]

In Europe there had been some hope that Stalin's death would raise the possibility of new talks. One of the main reasons why a summit had been so elusive was US opposition. The Americans did not think that the death of Stalin made much difference, and they assumed that they could win the Cold War as it became a broader conflict, economic, psychological and political as well as military and nuclear. In January 1954 Dulles announced the policy of 'massive retaliation', whereby Soviet aggression would be met with nuclear attack. Britain generally shared America's faith in a nuclear-based strategy, but other members of NATO were uneasy, and quarrels arose as Britain tried to cut its conventional contribution to NATO.[20]

Eden had disagreed with Churchill about the propriety of a summit, before changing his mind after he became prime minister. His international standing was reinforced as he signed the Austrian State Treaty in May 1955 and tried to come to an understanding with the Soviets at Geneva in July. This was the summit Churchill had been seeking. Previously, Eden had insisted that the timing must be right and that an agenda must be established beforehand, with specific goals. He had also warned that a summit might interfere with the FRG's integration into the Western alliance. By the time he became prime minister, however, this had been resolved and he decided that talks with the Soviets would be a good idea. In the event nothing concrete was achieved at Geneva, and the dominant figure at the summit was Eisenhower, not Eden. Even so, the prime minister told the Commons that the summit had reduced the danger of war in Europe and would probably have an impact elsewhere too, notably in the Far East, where America and the Soviet Union both wanted to ease tension.[21]

Arguments continued about nuclear weapons. The Soviets wanted to narrow the gap between their nuclear forces and those of the USA, which they knew to be superior, while American experts attempted to clarify the distinction between strategic and tactical (battlefield) use of nuclear weapons. Eden and his foreign secretary, Harold Macmillan, considered this an unwelcome distinction, and early in 1956 the British expressed further reservations about 'graduated deterrence' because there was no indication that the Soviets were thinking along the same lines.[22]

During Eden's premiership his reputation began to fade. He did not prove to be a strong leader. According to Anthony Nutting, Eden did not have the temperament, personal strength or political ability to deal with events once they started to go wrong for him at home and abroad.[23] Yet this was not an unpromising era. Adenauer's visit to Moscow and the Geneva talks helped to relax the atmosphere, and Khrushchev appeared to need détente if he was to implement the reforms he wanted in the USSR. The Soviet invasion of Hungary in November 1956 undermined claims about a new spirit in East–West relations, however, while for Britain the difficulties involved in attempts to wield power abroad were made plain at Suez.

The Suez crisis had many causes, including Britain's wish to maintain a strong presence in the Middle East, the hostility between Britain and Egypt, and the lack of confidence between Britain and the United States and between Britain and France. Nasser's assertive policies began to worry the Americans as well as the British. The basic problem was a disagreement about how to deal with him.[24]

Nasser visited Moscow in August 1955 and concluded an arms deal with Czechoslovakia. While showing himself to be independent of the West, he was also negotiating with the United States and Britain in order to pursue the Aswan Dam project. Anglo-American financing was meant to turn Nasser away from the USSR, but he remained just as refractory as before and the Americans cancelled their funding for the Aswan Dam on 19 July 1956 when Egypt established relations with China. The British also withdrew their money, though they were angry about the tactless manner in which Dulles announced America's decision. The British military withdrawal from Suez had been completed in June 1956. On 26 July Nasser nationalized the Suez Canal Company, which was jointly owned by Britain and France, and declared that its revenues would be applied to the Aswan Dam project.[25]

Eden told Dulles and Eisenhower that the West's security and economic interests were at risk, but the Americans argued that the use of force would alienate the Arabs and provide openings for Moscow. Washington DC could not be seen to support military intervention.[26] The British view was rather different. *The Times* accused Nasser of 'an act of international brigandage' and expected Eden to respond with 'firmness'. There had already been occasions when the British government's apparently lax response to Egyptian provocation had been condemned in the House of Commons. Now ministers went out of their way to impress parliament and public with their resolve. On 2 August Eden said that the whole of the democratic world depended on the Suez Canal, that Nasser had accepted the rights of the Suez Canal Company in previous agreements, and that nationalization was a criminal act that contravened these agreements and the convention of 1888, which provided for free passage for every vessel. Labour leader Hugh Gaitskell maintained that force should not be used and that Britain must abide by the UN Charter.[27]

The British had long been pressing the Americans to give more direct help in the Middle East. The cooling of Anglo-Jordanian relations increased Eden's concern about Britain's prestige, and he redoubled his efforts to persuade the United States to join the Baghdad Pact and support the friendly government in Iraq, but all he had from Dulles was a suggestion that the West should try to reason with Nasser. Eden found this useless. Nasser's efforts to undermine

British influence during 1954 and 1955 had turned Eden's growing annoyance into a deep loathing. Evelyn Shuckburgh, now the under-secretary responsible for Middle East affairs at the foreign office, suggested in January 1956 that a bargain with Nasser might still be concluded. Eden disagreed, and by March 1956 the wish for regime change was well established.[28] Anthony Nutting thought that hasty responses should be avoided and that it would be better to err on the side of caution. The prime minister rejected this advice. 'You love Nasser', he thundered, 'but I say he is our enemy and he shall be treated as such.'[29] Eden and his closest colleagues had decided to find a way of striking at Nasser some time before the nationalization of the Suez Canal Company.

In the spring of 1956 American and British leaders agreed that Nasser should be removed, but Washington DC did not expect this to happen for some time. The Americans also thought that the British were still intent on acting independently in the Middle East and that fear of losing influence was making them irritable and panicky. Eisenhower would later confess that he ought to have followed British advice and built up Iraq as the rival to Egypt, but at the time the Americans considered Saudi Arabia to be the best bet.[30]

Eisenhower approved of covert action to destabilize Nasser's regime, but when Nasser nationalized the Suez Canal Company and Eden spoke of a military response, Eisenhower objected. The president decided that another coup in the Middle East, so soon after the coup in Iran, should be avoided. He warned Eden against moves that might turn international opinion against the West, encourage the Soviets to interfere, or ruin the prospects for better relations between the West and the Arab world. The Americans doubted that Britain would seek a military solution, while the British persuaded themselves that Eisenhower would not try to stop them if they did.[31]

Eden's government was in a difficult position. British interests in the Middle East could not be protected without US assistance, but the Americans reserved the right to choose which of these interests to support and which to oppose, and Britain's problems in the region were multiplying. Libya wanted more money for the use of its bases, for instance, and threatened to accept aid from the USSR and Egypt if the British did not pay up. Britain wanted to cut its costs in the Middle East, not increase them. The impression in London was that the Soviet threat was changing. It was becoming more political and economic than military, which pushed oil more clearly to the top of the agenda when it came to British strategy in the Middle East. Eden had ordered a review of policy and this was still in progress when Egypt nationalized the Suez Canal Company. There was an immediate protest, backed strongly by British public opinion, and many in Britain advocated the use of force against Nasser, though Eden was not about to rush into anything. There was the question of whether or not to apply to the UN, and Eden's instinct was to seek a settlement peacefully, which is what Eisenhower and Dulles recommended. The French wanted military action, however, as did large sections of the British public and press. Outraged by Nasser's conduct, and sensitive about any hint of appeasement, Eden decided that Britain could not make concessions. In the Commons on 12 September 1956 the prime minister was unequivocal in his condemnation of Nasser. The crisis had to be ended, Eden said, and although peaceful methods were being tried, these methods might not work.[32]

The Americans urged restraint. Eden maintained that Britain could not give in to Nasser, and on 17 September he wrote that it was more important to be resolute than to wait on the Americans. Dulles was assuring him 'that the United States is as determined to deal with Nasser as we are', but the US presidential election was due to take place on 6 November, and Eisenhower was standing on a peace platform. Dulles and Eisenhower made it plain that they wanted nothing to happen before the election. Eden could not accept such a restriction. Perhaps his previous achievements as foreign secretary (the Geneva accords, the Suez base, Iranian oil, and the expansion of NATO and rearmament of West Germany) made him overconfident.[33]

Some officials in Washington DC were anti-British. They wanted to prevent Arab leaders from turning to Moscow, argued that a conciliatory approach was best, and dismissed London's claim that the Arabs would be more impressed by firmness. There were divergent views of the 'northern tier'. Dulles considered it a barrier against the USSR. So did the British, but they also saw it in the light of inter-Arab politics. Another issue on which the Americans and British disagreed was oil. Britain depended mainly on Iraq and the Persian Gulf, while American oil interests were focused on Saudi Arabia. There was no context, therefore, for closer Anglo-American co-operation in the Middle East at this juncture.[34]

One of the possible justifications for military action was that Nasser had breached international law, yet Egypt was a sovereign state and had offered to compensate Suez Canal Company shareholders, and it was not clear that nationalization was illegal. Eden stressed that the canal must remain open for international use, but it was not clear that the canal would be closed to such use. A more likely goal, undeclared for obvious reasons, was to overthrow Nasser. There were other considerations. The British government decided that to lose control of the Suez Canal would be to surrender influence throughout Africa and Asia as well. As the crisis developed, Eden made plans with the French for joint military action in case negotiations were unproductive. Dulles wavered, insisting that Britain should talk but accepting that force might become necessary if Nasser refused to come to an agreement.[35]

The Americans presumed that any attempt to seek a vote against Nasser at the UN would be vetoed by the Soviets. Worried that a veto would encourage Britain and France to invade Egypt, Dulles suggested other solutions. Chief

among these was the formation of an association of canal users, but the proposal
was not well thought out and Nasser opposed it. Then a plan was taken up by
the UN that involved unhindered use of the canal along with a recognition of
Egyptian sovereignty and an agreement on tolls and the arbitration of disputes.
The British and French accepted the plan, after amending it, but the Soviets
blocked an effort in the UN to make sure that Egypt abided by its terms.[36] Dulles
was trying to check Britain and France while persuading Nasser to agree to new
arrangements for the Suez Canal, but this was to look for a middle way that
did not exist.[37] Nasser's refusal to negotiate and the abortive attempt to reach a
settlement through the UN led Eden to commit Britain to a military solution. He
felt betrayed by Dulles, who, he complained, had not done enough. The French
were pleased with Eden's decision. Their oil came through the Suez Canal and
they wanted to oust Nasser because of his supposed support for rebels in Algeria,
where French forces were engaged in a civil war, and his designs against Israel,
with which France had close military ties.[38]

It took too long for British forces to be readied, and delay made the operation
more risky. Britain's critics had time to respond and international opinion solidified against the resort to arms. Eden probably hoped that if they were alarmed,
the Americans would step in and ensure that Britain got what it wanted without
the need for an invasion, but Washington DC did not seem willing to put pressure on Nasser. There would be no crushing diplomatic victory for Britain and
military action became more likely as a result.[39]

Using the Soviet threat to explain Britain's refusal to give way was designed to
minimize international disapproval. Eden used Cold War language in his dealings with the Americans because he wanted their backing, but defending British
interests in the Middle East was an independent goal and Eisenhower continued
to counsel restraint. While some of Eden's advisers still wanted to negotiate with
Egypt, the prime minister disregarded opinions with which he disagreed. The
foreign office was sidelined. On 14 October Eden finally decided that military
action against Nasser would be preferable to a settlement with him.[40]

The Anglo-French plot involved an Israeli advance into the Sinai region, which
would result in war between Egypt and Israel. British and French forces would
immediately enter the canal zone to secure it and ensure new arrangements for
international control. The scheme was put into operation at the end of October
1956, but within days the US government had forced Britain and France to
abandon it.

Following Israel's attack on Egypt, Eden addressed the Commons on
30 October and declared that the cardinal requirement was to keep the Suez
Canal open. Britain and France, he said, would work together to bring hostilities
to an end as soon as possible. Gaitskell opposed the government's policy and
urged Eden to have the matter properly considered at the UN.[41]

Britain could not co-operate openly with Israel because of the impact this would have in the Arab world, so the main British fleet did not leave Malta until the commencement of hostilities in Sinai on 29 October. This meant further delay, and the diplomatic effort against Britain and France rapidly intensified. The French urged Britain to quicken the pace. The hesitation of Eden and his colleagues, who changed their minds several times about aspects of the Suez venture, did not make for clarity either on the policy side or the operational side.[42]

The pro-Conservative *Daily Mail* and *Daily Express* approved of military action, while *The Times* noted that the government would get no support from the parliamentary opposition and that this was not the only troubling issue. Fighting between Egyptian and Israeli forces was not close to the Suez Canal, and although plenty of people would agree that something had to be done about the nationalization of the Suez Canal Company and relations between Egypt and Israel, 'doubts remain whether the right course has been taken now'. Had there been collusion with Israel? Had Arab leaders been consulted? Why had American and Commonwealth assistance not been sought more energetically?[43]

The war between Israel and Egypt was virtually over by the time British troops arrived, and political and diplomatic circumstances were now so ominous that Eden had to think about drawing back. Egypt had blocked the Suez Canal, there were strikes and riots across the Middle East, Syria closed its oil pipeline to the Mediterranean, and British representatives were having a painful time at the UN. Above all, the US government wanted Britain to back down.[44]

A ceasefire was agreed on 6 November. Eisenhower had reacted angrily when he heard of the Anglo-French intervention and persuaded the UN general assembly to condemn it. The US government put pressure on sterling, obliging Britain to seek American help in restoring financial stability. To make matters worse, the Soviets were threatening to retaliate against Britain and France. It was agreed that a UN force would enter the canal zone as Britain and France withdrew. The French blamed the British for caving in but could not continue alone.[45]

Suez ruined Eden and damaged Britain's reputation around the world. Clearly there were miscalculations. American responses were never accurately assessed, although the mixed signals from Dulles could be cited in expiation. Then again, Eden might have done more to clarify what Washington DC would tolerate. Equally important is the question of whether Britain really needed to take the canal. The world was not convinced by the stated reasons for military action. The Egyptians were unlikely to stop the supply of oil, and although Britain purported to be in favour of international control, this was hardly promoted by a policy that annoyed so many governments. In addition, Eden had previously negotiated the British evacuation of Suez and it was accepted that the Cyprus base was adequate for protecting Britain's interests in the Middle East. Even if the real purpose was to topple Nasser it could be argued that the methods Britain adopted had little to recommend them. The operation was abandoned at a stage when the Egyptians were beaten and Anglo-French forces could have taken the whole of the canal zone. Once Egypt and Israel agreed to stop fighting, however, the excuse for Anglo-French intervention was removed. The final outcome was determined not by Eden but by the Eisenhower administration. Perhaps the British should have waited until after Eisenhower was re-elected. The affair might also have ended differently had there been immediate and bold retribution from Britain after Nasser's nationalization of the company. Instead, there was the collusion with Israel and the delay in working out a justification for the use of force. The military action itself took too long to prepare, although this does not mean that a swifter operation would have succeeded, and military success might not have delivered permanent gains for Britain in view of the situation in the Middle East and the fact that London had no clear idea about what should replace Nasser's regime.[46]

Khrushchev claimed that the operation failed as a direct consequence of Soviet pressure. Anthony Nutting thought that Eden was worried about being isolated at the UN and about Britain's need for oil. With the Suez Canal blocked and pipelines closed, and a run on the pound, Britain was using up its dollar reserves to purchase oil and the Americans were unwilling to offer financial support. Criticism also came from the Commonwealth. As for Eden himself, Nutting noted 'pangs of conscience' and the strain the crisis placed upon the prime minister, who was already in poor health.[47]

According to Nutting, by the time the ceasefire was agreed, 'British policy had become a tissue of contradictions and Britain's leaders seemed to be torn in all directions'. The Times stressed Eden's prior statement that Britain and France would halt if the UN agreed to take over. The government still had questions to answer, though, and The Times also reported that Britain was bracing itself for a reduction in oil deliveries and a 10 per cent cut in consumption.[48]

Some of the government's advisers had predicted the American and UN reactions to the Suez operation, yet Eden and his closest colleagues had decided that they knew better. They saw a chance to restore Britain's position in the Middle East, to deal with more specific issues relating to the Suez Canal and Britain's oil supply, and to quash the threat posed by Nasser. However, even had a pro-British candidate been available to replace Nasser, politics in Egypt had reached a stage beyond which any such manipulation could succeed even for a short time.[49]

Eden never forgave Dulles, whose equivocation on Nasser and the canal in 1956 probably owed something to Eden's role on Indochina in 1954. The Geneva accords had been a defeat for Dulles. Suez was his chance for revenge, though it could also be argued that it was Eden who misled Dulles and that Eden kept the Americans in the dark about British intentions and subsequently blamed Dulles to excuse himself.[50]

Nevertheless, in 1956 and subsequently there were misgivings about American policy. Washington DC's attitude towards Arab states was shaped by fear of communist expansion, and American leaders tended to view the Middle East in a Cold War context, ignoring the internal dynamics of the region. One cause of the Suez crisis was this focus on the global picture, which meant that Eisenhower and Dulles might not have been fully aware of Nasser's regional goals. Eisenhower later admitted that he had made mistakes. Still, US policy was more nuanced than the British appreciated. There was no indiscriminate aversion to all Arab nationalists, but rather a desire to persuade some of them to help contain the Soviets.[51] In London, however, the Americans were thought to lack expertise in Middle East affairs. The British, with their longer experience in the region, believed they understood it better.

The remnants of empire remained important to Britain, particularly the economic aspects: networks of trade, investment and payments overseas; earnings from the management, financing and insurance of world shipping; oil interests; and banking and other facilities available in the sterling area. Beyond the economic ties there were political and strategic reasons for Britain's wish to maintain a global reach. The Americans viewed all this as old-fashioned imperialism, and in late 1956 Eisenhower chose not to make allowances. Even so, the precise role of US financial coercion is not easy to determine. It was only after the ceasefire was agreed that ministers began to worry about a sterling crisis. By the end of November, when the cabinet agreed to withdraw British troops from Egypt, financial pressure had become a problem, but it is unhelpful to confuse the ceasefire and the withdrawal, for they were separate decisions. In addition, sterling was in trouble not only because of the Americans but also because of inflation and an unfavourable balance of trade.[52]

The breach with the United States was all the more unfortunate because it was not in keeping with the pattern of Anglo-American co-operation on Egypt that had been established during and after the Second World War. Once the Suez crisis had passed there was immediate financial help: the Americans offered credit facilities and arranged a large loan for Britain from the International Monetary Fund (IMF).[53] It cannot be denied, however, that the crisis had many negative consequences. It confirmed that Britain's ability to take independent action was limited. British influence had been declining for some time, but this had previously been easier to disguise because of the empire and Britain's trade, historic strength and victory in 1945. There was also a loss of moral authority, an important blow because, traditionally, Britain's moral standing had often brought more influence than would have been possible had the British had to rely solely on their military and economic strength. Suez was a setback in other ways. It strengthened Nasser and made him and his Arab allies eager for a reckoning with Israel. They also became even more overtly hostile to British interests in the region. Britain's position was undermined while American and Soviet influence in the Middle East grew.[54]

Another problem with the Suez operation was that it jeopardized Western solidarity against the Soviets. Anglo-American relations and Anglo-French relations were damaged, and the Soviets took advantage of the crisis to frustrate Hungary's bid for autonomy. Admittedly, even had the West's attention not been focused on the Middle East, it would probably not have been possible to prevent Soviet repression in Hungary, but American leaders believed that Suez gave the Soviets an occasion to crush opposition in the eastern bloc. Suez annoyed most non-aligned states, offended the developing world, and handed the Soviets a propaganda victory.[55]

The mood in Western Europe cannot have been helped by the fact that Britain and France had not consulted their Western European Union partners about the Suez operation. Eden was unconcerned, since the WEU had only been created in 1955 as the means to other ends, but on the continent it was decided that unless the WEU could be strengthened as a promoter of European integration, other institutions would have to be established.[56]

Suez greatly affected British politics and society. Disillusionment with the global role increased and there was an acceptance of decolonization and the scaling down of Britain's commitments, although opinion on these matters continued to be divided. The Conservative Party remained in government, but a small group of Conservative MPs, dedicated to the preservation of empire, repeatedly embarrassed the party leadership. The left wing of the Labour Party became more assertive. Some on the Labour left were sympathetic towards the USSR. They condemned West German rearmament and the Suez operation, and some even appeared to accept the Soviet invasion of Hungary, raising the possibility of a party split in the process. Soon they were arguing for unilateral nuclear disarmament. The moderate core of the Labour Party respected the United States, was attached to NATO, accepted nuclear weapons while supporting multilateral disarmament, and was determined to combat communism at home and abroad.[57]

Labour did not take full advantage of Suez, and divisions within the Conservative Party did not prevent it from increasing its majority at the general election of October 1959. The main political beneficiary of Suez was Harold Macmillan, who had briefly served as foreign secretary before being appointed chancellor of the exchequer in December 1955. Macmillan backed military intervention in Egypt, but changed his mind during the first week of November 1956 and subsequently manoeuvred to replace Eden as premier.[58]

Eden's denial of collusion with France and Israel bought dishonour upon him and the extent of his personal responsibility for the Suez crisis remains a favourite debating point for historians. Was he let down by those around him? Macmillan was in Washington DC in September 1956 for meetings on the IMF and took the opportunity to discuss the Middle East with American leaders. He gave Eden an optimistic account of the US government's attitude. Rather than deliberately deceiving Eden, however, Macmillan might himself have been misled by Dulles, who continued to be ambivalent on the fate of Nasser.[59]

After Eden's resignation, most Conservatives fell in behind Macmillan's programme: forgive the United States for Suez, discuss decolonization with an open mind, and find alternatives to the use of military force abroad. In the Labour Party the strengthening of anti-imperialism proceeded alongside an alternative form of national assertiveness, one based on socialist values. It could no longer be taken for granted that the British people would unite behind a resort to arms, yet public opinion had not suddenly turned against the empire or against the maintenance of Britain's status in the world. Suez did not, by itself, speed up decolonization, and there is opinion-poll evidence to suggest that although the military intervention in Egypt never had an approval rating above 49 per cent, more people agreed with it than disagreed.[60]

Foreign policy quarrels within the main political parties were often more obvious than those between them. Conservative and Labour leaders agreed on the need to reassert British power after Suez. In the late 1950s the foreign office argued for a continued presence in the Far East. In the Middle East the focus began to shift from the 'northern tier' to the Persian Gulf, but the goals remained unchanged: securing oil supplies, keeping lines of communication open, and containing communism.[61] Nevertheless, Suez did exacerbate divisions, especially between the Conservative right and Labour left, and this was seen not only in parliament but also in extra-parliamentary organizations. It reflected a wider rift in British society: the right stood by the government, the centre and left (the Liberal Party, peace movement, trade unions, churches and the Labour Party) did not.[62]

Among the most important international consequences of Suez were those that involved the UN. Not only was there an unsuccessful Middle East peacekeeping effort after 1956, but Suez also offered further evidence of the self-interested uses to which UN procedure could be put by the great powers, and as such tainted the UN's reputation. Britain and France blocked resolutions in the security council against their intervention in Egypt. The Soviets did the same on 4 November 1956 with respect to their invasion of Hungary.[63]

The use of the veto by Britain and France failed to shield them. Still, the establishment of a UN peacekeeping force at least gave them the opportunity to withdraw from Egypt with some dignity. The ceasefire was agreed on the understanding that the UN Emergency Force would replace British and French troops. Eden told the Commons on 9 November 1956 that this accorded with his previous statement that Britain's intention all along had been to separate Egyptian and Israeli forces. He hoped that a comprehensive regional settlement, involving Israel, would now be possible. There were quarrels about the composition of the UN force, and then, when it arrived in December, instead of spreading out along the Suez Canal, part of it moved east behind the retreating Israelis. London and Paris complained that this was not what had been agreed, and the Israelis claimed that the UN force was pushing them back in order to open a route through Sinai for the Egyptians.[64]

The Soviet action in Hungary added to Britain's discomfiture during the Suez crisis. In the first week of November, Labour MPs were quick to make a connection between Suez and Hungary despite a statement from foreign secretary Selwyn Lloyd, who asserted that 'the action in Hungary is an intervention from without to suppress and prevent the independence of a country. Our intervention is to try to prevent a state of war between two countries.' Labour MPs did not accept this.[65]

Why had Soviet forces invaded Hungary? Stalin's death had been followed by some modest reforms in the USSR and eastern bloc. Khrushchev held out the prospect that satellite governments could pursue 'different paths' to socialism. Disturbances in Poland led to concessions, but Poland remained a one-party state and followed the Soviet lead on foreign policy. Reformers in Hungary tried to go further. There were demands for the removal of Soviet troops, a multi-party system and workers' councils in all industries. Moscow decided that change of this kind could not be permitted.[66]

Khrushchev eschewed 'different paths'. Although he still wanted 'peaceful co-existence' with the West, he now thought that this required greater control over the satellites. He had to demonstrate strength in order to secure his own position in the Soviet hierarchy, preserve Moscow's influence in Eastern Europe, and persuade the Americans that they needed to negotiate with him.[67]

The White House did consider a CIA plan for flying in arms and supplies to help the Hungarians, but in view of the Suez crisis and the possibility of war with the Soviets if he pushed them too far, Eisenhower preferred to hold back. He consulted Britain and France and put the matter before the UN. Though Eisenhower and Dulles had spoken a lot about the 'liberation' of Eastern Europe, they did not want to take military action to promote it and they understood the Soviet fear that if Hungary became independent it might join NATO, which could bring on the collapse of the whole eastern bloc.[68]

The British government's response to the unrest in Hungary was cautious. Having to devote attention and resources to Suez, Eden and his colleagues did not wish to get involved in Eastern Europe. The Soviet invasion of Hungary was launched on 31 October 1956. On 1 November the British government announced that it had no intention of using disorder in the bloc to undermine Soviet security.[69] Ministers were so preoccupied with Suez that Hungary was hardly discussed in these days. Eden was disappointed that the international outcry against Britain was far more intense than that against the Soviets.[70] The world seemed to expect a higher standard of behaviour from Britain, while the Soviets were typecast as aggressors, and it was easier for the international community to do something about Suez than it was to protect Hungary.

In the Commons on 7 November, Lord John Hope, under-secretary of state at the foreign office, reported that 'the fighting in Hungary bears the exclusive character of a Soviet campaign of repression'. MPs expressed concern about the plight of refugees, the safety of British nationals in Budapest, and the threat to Austria and other neighbours of Hungary. Hope said that relief supplies were being arranged and that Britain was willing to accept refugees. He confirmed that Moscow had not responded to the UN general assembly's call for a ceasefire, the withdrawal of Soviet troops and admission of UN observers.[71]

The *Manchester Guardian* praised the Hungarian people but added that all reformers in the eastern bloc had to learn a lesson: they had to 'go on prodding the communists towards freedom without prodding them so far that they fall back on brutal repression'. According to *The Times*, the Soviets would have intervened in Hungary whatever was happening elsewhere, but it was true that Suez offered a 'timely smokescreen'. The Soviets would go on using it because they were determined to gain more influence in the Middle East and at the UN, and it was a pity that the UN had acted quickly on the Suez crisis yet seemed unable to help Hungary.[72]

Suez affected the manner in which the UN dealt with the invasion of Hungary. Britain and France pressed for the UN to consider Suez and Hungary together, so as to minimize the censure they were bound to receive, but the Americans blocked this. Quarrels over Suez meant that the West was divided and that the UN could not act firmly against the Soviet Union. On the other hand, it is unlikely that the USSR would have relented. Moreover, the West's passivity was not really caused by Suez but had more to do with the lack of options, the practical difficulties involved in trying to intervene in Eastern Europe, and the unwritten Cold War bargain that the USA and USSR would not normally interfere in each other's spheres of influence.[73]

If Suez allowed the Soviets more easily to intervene in Hungary, it also opened the door for involvement in the Middle East. The USSR was able to establish closer relations with Nasser and he became dependent on Soviet aid, although the Soviets misunderstood him. He believed in central planning but he was not a communist and he had previously hoped to co-operate with the Americans. Egyptian communists were jailed and Nasser, like many of Moscow's friends in the developing world, did not become an amenable client.[74]

Eden discussed Suez in his memoirs, which, though self-serving, are not without value, for they reveal what he was trying to do, what he hoped to achieve in the longer term, and what he wished to prevent. Eden stressed that Britain's military victory over Nasser's forces had made possible a new agreement on the

Suez Canal and a wider Arab-Israeli settlement. The operation was stopped in order for these to be worked out. Eden expected the UN to make the necessary arrangements. Instead, at the behest of the Americans, the UN gave up the advantages gained by military action before talks could begin. Eden's view, therefore, was that the real mistakes occurred *after* the ceasefire, not before it, and they occurred because other world leaders acted in an unexpected and unreasonable manner.[75]

Eden told parliament on 20 December 1956 that that British government had not known in advance of Israel's intention to attack Egypt. Unsurprisingly, collusion with Israel does not feature in Eden's memoirs, but the memoirs do defend the Suez operation as an effort to promote a lasting Arab–Israeli peace. Unfortunately, the situation in the Middle East continued to deteriorate after 1956. Eden did not accept that this was the result of Suez. He argued, rather, that circumstances would have been even worse had Britain and France not acted. Only six months after Suez the British and Americans were co-operating to deal with crises in Jordan and Lebanon. According to Eden, the US government had realized that it ought not to have opposed the British over Suez, for there were anti-Western forces at work in the region that had to be checked. This was dramatically illustrated by the Iraqi revolution of July 1958.[76]

Eden resigned as prime minister on 9 January 1957. He retired from the Commons two days later. He told reporters on 18 January that it was important to see the Suez operation in its proper context: 'The difference between the West and Egypt has not been colonialism – it is the difference between democracies and dictatorship. The British people, with their intrinsic good sense, have understood that. I am sure they will always understand.' In his memoirs he linked this theme with the lessons of the 1930s. The Suez operation, he wrote, marked an open repudiation of appeasement. Britain had taken up 'the opportunity and the responsibility' to break a 'chain of failure', and this made the action against Nasser all the more salutary and important.[77]

These excuses and explanations are not without logic, and the disrepute into which Eden sank after Suez was not wholly warranted. Plenty of governments in world history have tried to topple dangerous dictators. Some have succeeded, and the British effort of 1956 would have worked if not for US policy, which Eisenhower and others later admitted had been inappropriate. Perhaps it is really the morality of the Suez operation that observers find most objectionable – secretly conspiring with foreign leaders, lying to parliament and the international community, presuming to determine the fate of a weaker nation – but again, plenty of other governments have done all this as well, before and after the Cold War as well as during it. Though Suez has negative connotations, the damage it did to Britain was mostly limited and temporary.

The key point is that Eden *had* to act. Military action might have been a gamble, but the chances of success were not bad and for all its shortcomings the military campaign could have been completed. It was the international reaction that ruined it, and from the outset this reaction proved difficult to predict and control. Suez inevitably affected British prestige and influence, and it was the biggest blow suffered by Britain in a period that saw a number of setbacks. There were worthy efforts to defend British interests in South East Asia, the Middle East and Europe. SEATO and the Baghdad Pact were useful but did not achieve all that was hoped for with respect to the stabilization of strategically vital regions and the preservation of a dominant role in those areas for Britain. The Geneva summit was disappointing, though at least it suggested that a European thaw might happen sooner rather than later. Then the Soviet intervention in Hungary raised Cold War tensions once again. After Eden, the Middle East was still a British sphere but it was impossible to recreate there the conditions that had prevailed in the past.

6

Finding a Role?

Harold Macmillan led the government from January 1957 to October 1963 and focused on restoring relations with the United States. He shared Churchill's 'three circles' perspective and hoped to show the Americans that they still needed Britain. Macmillan believed that he could mediate between East and West and that the British had a prominent role to play in global affairs, even if military and economic resources were not what they had been. The Macmillan government envisaged a reorganization of national defence, to save money, and the prime minister wanted to address a range of issues with the Americans: the future of the UN; disarmament; East–West relations; Britain's role in Europe; China; trade with the communist bloc; the Suez and Palestine questions; and Soviet ambitions in the Middle East and Africa.[1]

London had limited influence in Washington DC, but it was natural for Macmillan to speak up Britain's strength and potential. Anglo-American relations did improve, and now that the US elections were over, Eisenhower announced that the situation in the Middle East necessitated intervention. The Eisenhower Doctrine of January 1957 was meant to facilitate this. In April 1957 King Hussein of Jordan appealed for help as the pro-Nasser faction in his country stepped up its destabilization campaign. The coup in Iraq in July 1958 brought down the pro-British leader Nuri el-Said. American troops were sent to protect the government of Lebanon, and disorder in Jordan prompted British military intervention there, with Washington DC's approval.[2] Eisenhower's intention was that US involvement in the Middle East would be selective. The Americans were sure that the British would try to lock them into a heavier commitment, so as to protect Britain's oil supply and undermine Nasser.[3]

The coup in Iraq reinforced London's fears about Arab nationalism. London was also worried about the spread of Soviet influence, as were those states in the Persian Gulf that still regarded Britain as their guardian. The need for a show of force partly explains the intervention in Jordan. Remaining in the Middle East was a strategic necessity for Britain: the problem, by now chronic, was that responsibilities exceeded means. Britain's commitments in the early 1960s would not be significantly fewer than they had been in earlier years.[4]

Continuing British involvement in the Middle East was controversial and Macmillan did not go unchallenged when he explained government policy to the

Commons in July 1958. He argued that friendly Arab states needed reassurance, but Labour MPs objected to Britain's intervention in Jordan and much was made of the UN Charter and the need to refer questions to the security council *before* taking military action, not afterwards. Several MPs expressed concern about the likely Soviet response to British and US activity in the Middle East.[5] *The Times* insisted that a country had the right to ask for help when it was threatened and that refusal to act in Jordan 'would have been a plain dereliction of duty'. Inaction would have damaged British prestige.[6]

British and US troops were withdrawn from Jordan and Lebanon within four months, and a resolution was passed at the UN to promote stability in both countries. Macmillan was satisfied that Washington DC would pay more attention to London's advice about the Middle East in future, though there remained a suspicion that America wanted to replace Britain as the dominant power there. Privately, the British continued to criticize American policy in the Middle East.[7] Nevertheless, Anglo-American relations had certainly improved. In March 1957, Macmillan and foreign secretary Selwyn Lloyd met Eisenhower and Dulles for talks in Bermuda. Later in 1957 Queen Elizabeth II went on an official visit to the United States, and Macmillan and Eisenhower signed a 'Declaration of Common Purpose'.[8]

Despite the recovery of the 'special relationship', this was not an easy time for the British. The hydrogen bomb was tested in 1957, but the weapons programme was very expensive, as was the system of national service. NATO responsibilities had pushed expenditure up by about £50 million a year. A review of April 1957 resulted in reforms that were named after the defence minister, Duncan Sandys. The idea was to cut costs by relying on an independent nuclear deterrent and smaller, better-equipped conventional forces. Before the Second World War, defence spending had taken only 3 per cent of the national wealth and the armed forces numbered fewer than 300,000. By 1957 defence spending was up to 8 per cent and the armed forces up to 700,000. The French were spending 6 per cent of their gross national product on defence and the FRG only 4 per cent. Savings had to be made. Sandys proposed that conscription would cease by 1960, the armed forces would be cut to 400,000 by 1962, and defence spending would be held at 7 per cent of gross national product.[9]

Some commentators were unhappy. Developing British missiles and warheads appeared to make sense in that America's reliability might decline with the proliferation of intercontinental ballistic missiles (ICBMs), but Sandys had also stressed the need for collective defence, and it was plain that Britain could not protect itself without allies. Money saved in one area, moreover, might simply be spent in another, and Sandys had not found a way to balance the nuclear and conventional sides of defence.[10] Sandys told MPs that his was a five-year plan and should be judged as such, and that 'abroad, after some initial doubts, it has in the main been received with understanding and a good deal of respect', but there were protests about the 'undue dependence' on nuclear weapons and a lack of precision in defence planning.[11]

Restructuring was hindered by quarrels, delays and compromises. Government advisers, defence experts, the chiefs of staff and other interested groups disagreed about many of the changes, and however drastic they seemed when first announced, the Sandys reforms were not radical in practice. Savings on the conventional side were smaller than predicted, the nuclear focus entailed greater dependence on the United States, and the continuation of high defence spending exacerbated domestic economic difficulties.[12]

The Eisenhower administration accepted that Britain wished to develop a new defence policy, and talks in Washington DC in October 1957 led to the establishment of two Anglo-American committees to oversee nuclear co-operation. Britain's plan to cut conventional forces and rely more on the nuclear deterrent was not welcomed in Western Europe or by American army chiefs, and indeed British defence policy became part of the debate in Washington DC surrounding the US military's demand for more resources. In Britain the Sandys reforms increased the armed services' already intense competition for money. Some of the projected cuts had to be abandoned.[13]

Eisenhower was sure that the British should have a credible deterrent. He was willing to help, not only because he wanted to restore Anglo-American relations after Suez, but also because he was worried about the rapid increase in the USSR's military strength. Washington DC was impressed when the British tested their hydrogen bomb in May 1957, and alarmed when the Soviets demonstrated their technological progress by launching the Sputnik satellite in October 1957, and the wish for co-operation with Britain effectively curtailed discussions that had been going on between Britain and France about a common security policy for Western Europe.[14] Macmillan prioritized Britain's defence relationship with the Americans and direct requests from the French for joint projects were turned down. Britain now had the hydrogen bomb; accepted intermediate-range ballistic missiles (IRBMs) from the Americans under a dual key arrangement; benefited from bilateral exchanges with the United States; and went on to purchase new US delivery systems on favourable terms. At the same time, Macmillan was under pressure from parliament and public to promote disarmament and a test ban. He was personally committed to these ends, but did not want them to jeopardize Anglo-American agreements or interfere with Britain's weapons programme.[15]

The Anglo-American nuclear relationship did not always run smoothly. Political, strategic, financial and technological problems arose, and there was a difference in motive, for the British wished to maintain an independent deterrent while the Americans viewed the missiles in Britain as a component of the USA's defence system. On weapons testing, moreover, the Americans were not ready to bargain. In the spring of 1958 they rejected a Soviet proposal for the cessation of tests.[16]

The British did not expect their Blue Streak missiles to be ready until the early 1960s. In the meantime, American Thor IRBMs were deployed, as agreed at Bermuda in March 1957. Targeting co-ordination by the RAF and US air force and closer contact in intelligence and planning also resulted from the Bermuda talks.[17] It was partly the success of Britain's nuclear programme that convinced the Americans to co-operate. The value Eisenhower placed on the 'special relationship' was important too, although, had it not been for Sputnik and the increased awareness of Soviet advances, the arrangements described above would not have been so extensive.[18]

Britain and the United States had to take account of NATO policy, which was often inconvenient. Eisenhower wanted to withdraw US troops from Europe and replace them with tactical nuclear weapons for battlefield use. This was in line with Britain's intention to end conscription and downsize the British contingent in West Germany. A review of NATO strategy did not go as London and Washington DC wanted. It was decided that a major war was less likely than smaller conflicts in which nuclear weapons would not be used. Therefore, as the FRG recommended, conventional forces would have to be augmented. A compromise was worked out in March 1958. This entailed 'differentiated responses', to include – but not be confined to – the use of nuclear weapons.[19]

To London, possession of the hydrogen bomb was necessary to contain the Soviets, to prove that Britain was a great power, and to increase Britain's influence over the Americans. The weapons programme was speeded up in order to progress as far as possible before any test ban was agreed. Meanwhile, the Campaign for Nuclear Disarmament (CND) was inaugurated in 1958. Soon its leaders claimed to have 100,000 active supporters. Weapons research became more expensive, a British missile system was never perfected, and there was still a need to station conventional forces abroad.[20] In addition, the 'special relationship' became so obviously unequal that many British observers considered Macmillan's policies not to be in keeping with the national interests. There was also the old problem that the Americans tended to downplay the 'special relationship' and keep it as informal as possible, while the British wanted to make it more formal. On the other hand, greater collaboration between the American and British armed forces probably made the British government less anxious about the loss of nuclear independence. The cancellation of Blue Streak in 1960 indicated that Britain could not afford its own deterrent.[21]

The Sandys reforms did not enable Britain to carry on as a world power at a lower cost. Peter Thorneycroft, chancellor of the exchequer from 1957 to 1958 and subsequently minister of aviation and minister of defence, maintained that the reforms did not go far enough, while the service chiefs complained that Sandys had not consulted them and threatened to resign. After the general election of October 1959, Sandys was moved from the defence ministry to aviation and thence to Commonwealth relations. The new minister of defence was the less assertive Harold Watkinson. Here was a sign that Macmillan did not want further reforms and that he wished to avoid alienating the service chiefs. Spending on overseas commitments actually increased.[22]

Labour MPs continued to challenge government policy. In June 1960, for instance, Watkinson was asked to provide details about Britain's proposed purchase of Skybolt missiles from America. The cost of missiles that did not yet exist could not possibly be estimated, it was asserted, and there was no guarantee that Skybolt would ever be supplied. Meanwhile *The Times* insisted that Britain should not give up nuclear weapons and rejected the idea that NATO should not threaten to use nuclear weapons first in the event of a war. The *Economist* noted the government's nervousness about 'innocent-looking proposals that might rivet millions of pounds of expenditure for weapon development onto the national budget for years ahead'.[23]

Macmillan had decided that it might be possible to increase Britain's influence in Washington DC in one of two ways: either by moving closer to Western Europe, which would involve cutting down Britain's military presence elsewhere; or by maintaining the world role, which is what Macmillan preferred to do, as did most Conservative MPs. Before long, the government arrived at some related conclusions: that decolonization was necessary, that it was politically important to keep some forces in Europe, and that large military operations outside the American orbit were best avoided.[24]

By the early 1960s, however, it seemed that Britain's defence planning was falling into disarray. Britain still spent a higher proportion of its national wealth on defence than did the other European members of NATO. Although by 1963 the British Army of the Rhine (BAOR) had been reduced to 51,000, from 77,000 in 1957, in 1965 there were still more than 60,000 British servicemen and eighty vessels East of Suez, safeguarding trade, keeping order, improving security and performing tasks that benefited the *whole* of the West, not Britain alone. New quarrels over money broke out among the service chiefs and unease increased about dependence on America. More thought was given to combining with France, the fourth nuclear power from 1960, but no new proposals were made.[25]

For Britain this was a difficult period with regard to decolonization. The government wished to prepare colonial peoples for independence but their nationalist leaders grew impatient. Britain also hoped for a smooth transition, with former colonies joining the Commonwealth, but some chose not to. Violence erupted at times, as in Kenya and Cyprus. Though loss of empire had implications for Britain's global influence, policy makers concluded that Britain would gain more from friendship than from control and that decolonization would mollify anti-colonial opinion (in the United States, for instance) and free up resources for fighting the Cold War, while to retain the colonies would be to take on massive expense and increase the likelihood of wars and possible Soviet intervention.[26] Wary of allowing US power to be used to prop up Britain's imperial position, the Americans were nevertheless willing to work with the British in strategically important places, notably the Far East (Macmillan began to treat Hong Kong as a responsibility that could be shared between Britain and the United States).[27]

During the premierships of Churchill and Eden there had been a determination to uphold the empire, not dismantle it. Macmillan had shared this view, but after succeeding Eden he asked his advisers to weigh up the costs and benefits of empire. It was hoped that circumstances would allow a peaceful process of decolonization. Within a few years, however, the pace quickened.[28]

Macmillan's overseas tour of 1958 was both a goodwill exercise and an opportunity to find out more about what was going on in Britain's spheres of influence. He was struck by how fragile the pro-Western leaders were, mainly because of social and economic problems. He decided that Britain and the West had to help the Commonwealth to become a strong barrier against communism. Between 1957 and 1960 Britain's expenditure on aid doubled.

Trade and finance loomed large in the government's calculations. Britain needed more export earnings in order to support the sterling area and invest overseas, and there was an expectation that foods and minerals from the Commonwealth would be in demand and could command good prices. This optimism proved to be misplaced. Perhaps Britain should have been trying to export more to the United States and Western Europe, not pursuing the Commonwealth option, but at the time it was not clear that this option would be damaging.[29]

Macmillan had decided that Africans and Asians had to be treated in a new way, and this was at the core of his policy by the time of his 'wind of change' speech in Cape Town on 3 February 1960. Nevertheless, transfers of power were not invariably smooth or successful. Not all local nationalist leaders were equipped to take over and some of the new states were far from stable. There was uncertainty about the rights of different racial and tribal groups, voting qualifications and the status of the white settlers who stayed behind. There were difficulties at home, notably within the Conservative Party, many of whose members and supporters disliked decolonization. There was also dissent in the older white dominions, for the idea of a multi-racial Commonwealth did not have universal appeal.[30]

Washington DC welcomed decolonization and co-operated with the European colonial powers in arranging for their withdrawal. Newly independent states were encouraged to look to the West, not to the communist bloc, for protection. Eisenhower praised Macmillan's 'wind of change' speech, but Macmillan was disturbed by the unrest across Africa and the racial policies of the South African government. Nor was it clear that the Commonwealth, changed by the entry of numerous weak states, could support Britain's global position.[31]

Although Soviet involvement in Africa was growing, in most of the new states that embraced socialism the Soviet model was not considered applicable. Much more important in shaping British policy was the strength of nationalism. A more assertive nationalism had to be confronted in the Middle East and in Asia, and increasingly in Africa. The British withdrawal from Africa was speeded up from 1959 not so much because of the international environment or conditions within Britain, but because of pressure from the Africans themselves.[32]

Decolonization did not mean that Britain intended to give up the world role and focus more on Europe. This was a period of adaptation. Some commentators might subsequently have liked to call it a retreat, but this is not how British leaders saw it. To them, it was adjustment in order to *avoid* retreat, a realistic response to the problem of limited resources. It involved giving up some rights and commitments while seeking new ones and exerting influence in new ways.[33]

During the last ten to fifteen years of colonial rule there was increased metropolitan involvement, not less, which confirms that British leaders were worried about the consequences of economic weakness and wished to retain links with the colonies for their raw materials and dollar-earning exports. Labour and Conservative governments were equally determined to maintain sterling as a major currency, and for a long time it was assumed that the empire would help. As the empire came to be seen as a liability, opinion changed. The Macmillan government saw no point in delaying decolonization or trying to keep former colonies in the sterling area. The formation of the European Economic Community (EEC) added another complication, for it discriminated against British colonial commodities.[34]

The Macmillan government's preoccupation with American friendship, nuclear weapons and the Commonwealth meant that less attention was paid to Europe, where the EEC was established without Britain by the Treaty of Rome of March 1957. Its founder members were 'The Six': France, the FRG, Italy, Belgium, the Netherlands and Luxembourg. At first British leaders refused to believe that the EEC could succeed, and they still entertained the old idea that Britain, as a world power, did not need closer ties to Europe. The Americans urged Britain to work with Europe, however, and Macmillan and his colleagues saw potential benefit in economic agreements. Their main goal was to create a free-trade area. In pursuing this aim they were obstructed by Charles de Gaulle, prime minister (1958) and subsequently president (1959–69) of France. De Gaulle disliked US leadership of the West, considered that the British were too close to the

Americans, and wished to limit both British and US influence in Europe. He was bolstered by the developing Paris–Bonn axis. France and the FRG co-operated closely on European integration, and de Gaulle was able to use this relationship against Britain.[35]

De Gaulle was determined to foil the British plan for a free-trade area. Adenauer shared de Gaulle's suspicions about the British and Americans but suggested that Britain ought not to be excluded from economic integration, and the FRG's finance minister Ludwig Erhard was strongly in favour of a free-trade area. De Gaulle therefore had to turn the EEC into a Franco-German alliance. His promises on political and economic co-operation impressed the Adenauer government, and although Paris and Bonn did not view the EEC in exactly the same way, Britain's effort to exploit this did not get very far.[36]

For British leaders, the main problem with 'The Six' was that they had accepted supra-nationalism. A free-trade area, with imperial preference on food, was much more to Britain's taste, and London expected the most industrialized parts of Europe to approve. The British presented their plan as a means to promote collective economic progress and integrate the FRG more deeply into Western Europe. Leaders of 'The Six' were intent on a customs union with supranational institutions, however, and had no intention of abolishing tariffs against Britain and accepting British industrial competition while Britain could buy cheap food from the Commonwealth. They accused Britain of trying to wreck the EEC. Perhaps the British made an error, in that they should have negotiated in a more constructive fashion, joined the EEC, and in due course altered it from within.[37] Yet this assumes that suitable arrangements could have been made with the Commonwealth, which is by no means certain, and that 'The Six' were amenable to Britain's recommendations, which they were not. By the summer of 1958 Macmillan was ready to take a hard line, but de Gaulle and Adenauer stood firm. The British government was misled on certain points. For example, the embassy in Paris informed Macmillan that de Gaulle wanted Britain in the EEC. The government consulted Britain's entrepreneurs and industrialists only to find that they had no clear or united opinion on Europe.[38]

Britain went ahead with the formation of the European Free Trade Association (EFTA), which consisted of 'The Seven': Britain, Switzerland, Austria, Norway, Denmark, Sweden and Portugal. The EFTA treaty came into effect in May 1960 and was based on the principle of free trade in industrial goods. EFTA was a loose association, intergovernmental in nature and dominated by a council of ministers. Euro-sceptics in Britain probably supposed that matters could safely be left where they were.[39]

In the negotiations that had produced the Treaty of Rome, the goal seemed to be a tight customs union that Britain, with its extra-European interests, found unappealing. In practice the EEC stopped short of this, but for political reasons it had not been possible to settle every detail in advance. Had this not been so, British policy might have been different. In the event Macmillan and his colleagues overestimated their bargaining position, which affected not only the early history of the EEC, but also the shape of EFTA and the talks about a possible accommodation between the two bodies. There was no fundamental shift in British thinking on Europe. It was hoped that Britain could move closer to 'The Six' without making compromises.[40]

Speculation mounted that Britain would abandon EFTA in order to join the EEC. In the Commons on 26 May 1960 Macmillan declared that Britain would not seek a separate agreement with the EEC, but the government was unsure about how to proceed. Was EFTA to be defended on its own merits, or treated as the means to obtain a deal with the EEC? Macmillan told cabinet colleagues that whatever they said, they should all say the same thing. He was also conscious that although American leaders supported free trade in principle, there were protectionist impulses in America and an aversion to any European arrangements that discriminated against the United States. American leaders were well disposed towards 'The Six' already, because they saw EEC-style integration as politically and strategically useful.[41]

London and Washington DC had been arguing about Europe for years. In the mid-1950s the Americans had made it clear that they wanted negotiations for an economic community to succeed, and they warned Britain not to stand in the way.[42] Eisenhower and Dulles decided that the EEC should establish itself *before* arrangements were made for Britain to join, in case the British frustrated the enterprise. Henceforth, Washington DC's position was that the British should only be encouraged to join if they accepted the necessary elements of supra-nationalism. It was expected that 'The Six' would continue to respect America's wishes, but once the EEC was formed, de Gaulle openly challenged US leadership. This, together with America's own economic problems, meant that sympathy grew for the British view of European integration, and a related development was Christian Herter's appointment as US secretary of state in April 1959. Herter was more of an Atlanticist than Dulles had been.[43]

The British economy experienced periodic downturns and growth rates that were persistently lower than those of other industrial nations. The idea spread that membership of the EEC might be economically beneficial.[44] This was not unanimous, however, and relative economic decline was not the result of any single factor. Assertions were made about complacency and error on the part of policy makers, but structural shortcomings were also to blame; some problems were not confined to Britain, and policy mistakes only became obvious later on. Western Europe experienced a golden age of prosperity from the early 1950s, and this was probably assisted by integration, but by the 1970s the effects of integration were not so impressive.[45] Britain did benefit from the golden age but, importantly, was not part of the integrated order in the years when membership of that order might have been advantageous.

The idea of an industrial free trade area around 'The Six' was attractive because it offered Britain access to the common market without any obligation to accept its common tariff, the common agricultural policy and the loss of national veto rights. The French made sure that Britain's plan was blocked.[46] In September 1960 *The Times* suggested that if 'The Six' and 'The Seven' were going to come together, the most promising method would be political rather than economic.[47] If this meant making EFTA more like the EEC, however, it would not accord with the British government's view of how European integration should proceed.

Despite the economic segmentation of Europe, Macmillan considered his foreign policy successful, especially in relation to his dealings with the Soviets. In November 1958 Khrushchev declared that US, British and French forces should leave West Berlin and that access to West Berlin must be negotiated with the government of the German Democratic Republic. He warned that the USSR would sign a separate peace treaty with the GDR unless the Berlin question was resolved within six months. Macmillan, with an eye on the Conservative Party's election prospects and wishing to raise his own reputation, visited Moscow in February 1959. He gained the publicity he wanted, and the six-month deadline was abandoned because he promised to press the Americans for a summit, but there was no deal on Berlin and the Geneva conference in the summer of 1959 also failed to reach agreement. Nevertheless, Khrushchev did not revive his ultimatum and Macmillan claimed that the talks in Moscow had helped. Macmillan's conduct annoyed the FRG, France and the United States, however, and they rejected his suggestion that the West ought to recognize the GDR and withdraw troops from West Berlin.[48]

To the *Observer*, Macmillan's trip to Moscow was unimportant because he could not speak for the West as a whole, but important because the time was coming when the West would have to choose either to continue building up its alliance against the USSR or to find ways of co-operating with the USSR: 'on this fundamental decision everything else depends'. *The Times* approved of the 'scouting expedition' in Moscow, and the prime minister was sure that he had been right to make the effort, but Britain's allies did not accept that he had gained much from Khrushchev, which isolated Macmillan and opened up a rift in the West. Macmillan had refused to give way to Khrushchev on the West's responsibilities in Berlin, though, and perhaps this reassured Adenauer, de Gaulle and Eisenhower about British intentions. Macmillan hoped to remove their objections to a summit. Khrushchev needed a thaw if he was going to divert resources and improve living standards in the USSR as he wished. The Americans remained cautious, and France and the FRG even more so.[49]

Macmillan repeatedly defended his détente policy in these months. He told the Commons in December 1958 that rights and obligations in Berlin could not be 'unilaterally renounced or changed', and after his visit to Moscow he claimed to have persuaded the Soviets that international problems should be settled by negotiation. Arguments developed about the extent to which the West should compromise in order to secure agreements with the USSR.[50]

Controversial at home, Macmillan's effort to broker an agreement between the West and the Soviet Union continued to irritate other Western leaders. Adenauer was offended by what he took to be Macmillan's arrogant presumption that the British government was best qualified to deal with the Soviets on the West's behalf, and feared that if Macmillan was not stopped, a bargaining process would begin that ran counter to Bonn's interests. As well as doubting the reliability of Macmillan, Adenauer was worried about the Americans. He suspected that Washington DC might choose to recognize the GDR rather than risk a confrontation with the Soviets. De Gaulle had already challenged the United States on nuclear matters and the future of NATO; now he urged the Americans not to compromise on Berlin. Adenauer was grateful, while Dulles does not appear to have realized that de Gaulle had other goals in mind besides resisting Moscow. De Gaulle wanted Adenauer to be closer to Paris than to Washington DC.[51]

Khrushchev's policy was marked by assertiveness and brinkmanship. A German settlement, he thought, would usher in a long period of stability and make possible the peaceful transformation of the world from capitalism to socialism, yet his Berlin ultimatum of November 1958 alarmed the Western powers, and some of his colleagues thought him rash. He was confident, however, that he could do many things at once: strengthen his position at home, impose his authority over Walter Ulbricht's regime in the GDR, ensure the viability of the East German state, prevent the FRG from obtaining nuclear weapons, restrain China in Asia, hide from the West the fact that Moscow's relations with Peking were at breaking point, and convince the Americans to treat the Soviet Union as an equal.[52] Khrushchev's concept of 'peaceful co-existence' rested on a dynamic global competition between the two superpowers that stopped short of war.[53]

The renewed emphasis on Berlin necessitated negotiations, and on this point Macmillan was correct. Eisenhower, while declaring that the West would not give way, invited Khrushchev for talks once the Soviet leader had removed the six-month deadline.[54] Macmillan genuinely believed that an agreement could be reached that would not undermine Western security. Adenauer and de Gaulle were sceptical. Eisenhower had no wish for a summit, and Macmillan continued to think that he should act for the West because nobody else was willing to step into the breach. It was agreed that there should be a conference of foreign ministers in Geneva. Since the Soviets were intent on a great-power summit, Macmillan reasoned, they would not make concessions at Geneva while the Americans were unlikely agree to a summit *unless* something was achieved at Geneva. Macmillan was relieved, but not happy, when Eisenhower invited Khrushchev for bilateral talks in the United States.[55] The invitation suggested that the USA and USSR could bargain by themselves, without Britain, but then it transpired that the Americans were willing to go ahead with a great-power summit after all.[56]

These developments assisted de Gaulle to convince the FRG to rely more on France. The Americans were no better than the British, he argued, for they were ready to speak to Khrushchev over the heads of their allies. What Eisenhower was really doing was allowing Khrushchev room to manoeuvre, while Khrushchev took the invitation to visit the United States as a sign that Soviet pressure was paying off.[57]

Eisenhower and Khrushchev met at Camp David, Maryland, in September 1959. Though they reached no agreement on Berlin, the prospects for a thaw seemed to be improving. In January 1960, Khrushchev announced that the Soviet army was to be reduced in size. Mao accused Moscow of giving in to the West, which widened the rift between China and the USSR. Then the Paris summit of May 1960 proved to be a fiasco. Just before it opened the Soviets shot down an American U2 spy plane.[58]

After the Sputnik shock of 1957, reports had circulated that the USSR was spending more on arms and had a faster rate of economic growth than the United States. Eisenhower provided for a bigger defence budget but also hoped for a test ban and disarmament. The Paris summit represented a welcome opportunity, therefore, and its collapse was doubly embarrassing for Eisenhower, who was already being criticized at home for allowing the Soviets to take the lead in armaments. In fact, Khrushchev had by now decided that the Berlin problem could not be solved and that a test ban would favour the Americans and reveal the true condition of Soviet defences, so he used the spy plane incident to wreck the Paris talks.[59] Eisenhower was disappointed, as was Macmillan. On the eve of the summit, Khrushchev had assured Macmillan that agreements were still possible.[60] After Camp David, Macmillan had looked forward to a significant change in international relations. The election of October 1959 confirmed the Conservatives in office, which buoyed the prime minister's spirits, and despite grumblings from de Gaulle and Adenauer, Macmillan thought that the Paris summit would at least produce an interim agreement on Berlin, which could be followed by military disengagement in the centre of Europe.[61]

There was amazement in Britain about Khrushchev's behaviour in Paris. The Times admitted that the U2 incident was 'a bad business', but added that it gave Khrushchev no excuse for disappointing 'the millions of people everywhere who had hoped that the heads of four great nations could behave like responsible men when they met with the world's destiny in their hands'. Macmillan hoped that events in Paris would not put off an accommodation between the West and the Soviets for too long. He told the Commons on 30 May 1960 that talks about disarmament and nuclear tests would continue.[62] Although he tried to sound positive, there was now no meaningful role for Macmillan as the honest broker between East and West. Eisenhower resisted calls for a prompt resumption of communication with Khrushchev, and de Gaulle refused to help.[63]

Another summit would not be feasible for at least a year, Macmillan thought, and in the meantime he spoke more about interdependence in the West. Since Eisenhower was not seeking re-election, Macmillan focused on de Gaulle, but the French leader wanted to discuss NATO and nuclear weapons while Macmillan was worried about the British economy and Britain's relationship with the EEC. Macmillan thought it would be possible for Britain to lead Europe. Against foreign office advice he began to foment discord within both NATO and the EEC, because he expected this to provide leverage. By the end of 1960 Macmillan had made up his mind that Britain should apply to join the EEC, not only for the sake of the country's finances and export trade but also because the route to British leadership of Europe lay through the EEC.[64]

John F. Kennedy assumed the US presidency early in 1961. Khrushchev still needed a foreign policy success and sought to manipulate Kennedy, while the latter made plain his assertive disposition and promised that America would support liberty all over the world. Soon he announced large increases in military spending. Khrushchev and Kennedy both wished for a further summit.[65]

This took place in Vienna in June 1961. Khrushchev had repeated his threat to push the Americans out of Berlin. Kennedy wanted the opportunity, in person, to make the Soviet leader reconsider, but the meeting was dominated by Khrushchev.[66] Kennedy and his aides believed that the United States should make no concessions. The US state department was sure of this, as was the experienced Dean Acheson, whom Kennedy drafted in as a special adviser. When Macmillan and his foreign secretary, Lord Home, visited Washington DC in April 1961, they were disappointed by the inflexibility they encountered there.[67]

There were many in Britain who agreed with the Soviets that the Berlin question should be settled and that if Germany was to be reunited, it should not be part of the Western military alliance. In the aftermath of the Vienna summit, the parliamentary opposition insisted that the government should not simply fall in behind American policy. On 19 June 1961 these matters were addressed by the lord privy seal, Edward Heath, who upheld the principle of self-determination and declared it to be the essential condition for a German agreement. No immediate or far-reaching results could be expected from the Vienna summit, commented the Guardian (formerly Manchester Guardian), but at least Kennedy and Khrushchev had established a personal contact that would make future talks go more smoothly. According to The Times, the summit left the world 'neither any worse nor any better'.[68]

By the summer of 1961 Moscow had decided that the communist system was losing prestige because so many East Germans were crossing to the West. The Americans had long accepted the division of Germany and their real goal was stability. Since the exodus from East Germany created instability, US politicians began to make speeches in which they suggested that the Ulbricht regime would be within its rights to close East Germany's borders. This situation led to the erection of the Berlin Wall in August 1961.[69] Khrushchev declared that more was gained from the wall than might have been gained from a treaty, yet he could not hide his failure to make the Western powers deal directly with the government of the GDR. He could hardly admit it, but he also feared that the global balance of power was shifting to the USSR's disadvantage. He still wanted a German agreement, which he thought would signify the West's acknowledgement of Soviet ascendancy in Eastern Europe. He had to keep open the possibility of talks. Some of his enemies in Moscow criticized him for giving way to the Americans, others for risking war.[70]

In Britain the erection of the Berlin Wall was greeted with dismay. Edward Heath said that Britain and its allies would not try to settle the matter by force, no matter how 'unpalatable' recent events were 'to all decent people everywhere'. Labour leader Hugh Gaitskell, while condemning the Berlin Wall, suggested that the crisis was attributable to the West's failure to communicate with the Soviets, but Macmillan insisted that his government wished for negotiations to take place. The Soviets knew that the West would not give way, and Macmillan was sure that they would prefer to talk rather than fight.[71]

It was soon recognized that the Berlin Wall changed the Cold War, for it reduced tension. It eased the pressure on Khrushchev for more assertive action. The Americans realized that they could do little about the Berlin Wall. Hard-liners advocated retaliation but Kennedy and his defence secretary, Robert McNamara, did not want war. Khrushchev declared that the USSR was not planning to blockade Berlin and would not deny the Western powers their rights in the city. The British counselled restraint and Kennedy decided that agreeing to talks on Berlin would not be a sign of weakness. These negotiations went on for years.[72]

Macmillan's government claimed that it did not consent to the division of Germany and of Europe, though in practice division was accepted. The government refused formally to recognize the East German state, but again, in practice there was de facto recognition. This irritated Bonn and Paris. Macmillan believed that obstruction from them could be circumvented if Berlin and Germany were dealt with through bilateral US–Soviet talks. This made Bonn and Paris even angrier.[73]

Still there was no consensus about what a settlement in Europe should include. Britain wanted Bonn to accept the existing frontier between Germany and Poland and unreservedly to give up any claim to nuclear weapons. Not only did Washington DC disagree, but de Gaulle told Macmillan that he could not promise never to give the FRG nuclear weapons. Macmillan thought that these matters should be used as bargaining tools, along with issues like recognition of the GDR and the relationship between West Berlin and the FRG, but Kennedy objected that more must be done to satisfy Adenauer, and Britain's plan to apply for membership of the EEC complicated matters further. At a NATO meeting in December 1961 the French opposed the reopening of negotiations with the USSR. Meanwhile the Americans became more concerned about the possibility that the FRG would seek its own nuclear capability.[74]

Knowing that Kennedy was under pressure from hard-liners in Washington DC, Macmillan sought to help him avoid confrontation with the Soviets. According to a report in the *Daily Mail* of 21 July 1961, 71 per cent of Americans were willing to fight over Berlin. The British figure was 46 per cent and in France only 9 per cent of those polled were prepared to support military action. Khrushchev was aware that the Western powers were not united on Berlin, but by keeping up appearances Macmillan and Kennedy dissuaded him from pushing them harder.[75]

Kennedy was encouraged by Khrushchev's abandonment of threats and deadlines and by the withdrawal of a Soviet demand that the office of secretary-general of the UN should be divided into three and shared between nominees of the West, the communist bloc and neutral states. Less welcome was the resumption of Soviet nuclear weapons tests, but even so, it was expected that the Berlin Wall would bring more predictability into the Cold War. Notwithstanding Kennedy's anti-communist '*Ich bin ein Berliner*' speech of June 1963, he wanted agreements with Moscow. Macmillan sought a test ban and also liked the idea of a non-aggression treaty between NATO and the Warsaw Pact, but this was opposed by the FRG because it would involve accepting the division of Germany. Problems like these made Kennedy and his advisers more eager for bilateral arrangements with the Soviets.[76]

Kennedy arrived in London for talks at the end of June 1963. *The Times* suggested that there were two issues that needed attention: 'how to keep Britain as close as possible to Europe until she can actually join it', and 'how to develop between Britain, the United States and Europe a greater degree of trust and agreement on the broad strategy of the Cold War'. Complaints about US policy had been growing for some time, and there was a danger that division would increase. The troubled history of the NATO plan for a multilateral nuclear force (MLF) illustrated this point. Macmillan and Kennedy issued a joint communiqué on 30 June, and on 2 July Macmillan reported on their talks to parliament. He did not say much about Berlin. Instead, the prime minister emphasized his commitment to a test ban treaty.[77]

Some of Kennedy's advisers feared that the '*Ich bin ein Berliner*' speech would undo the work that was being done to promote détente, but different audiences heard what they wanted to hear in Kennedy's speech. For all his talk of victory, meanwhile, Khrushchev did not emerge from the Berlin crisis of 1958–62 with his position at home or his influence abroad greatly enhanced. In Western Europe, and above all in the FRG, the Americans were accused of selfishness and compromise, yet Bonn initially supported America's MLF proposal, while Britain and France opposed because they had their own nuclear capabilities and did not want to share control.[78] A related dispute arose as a result of the American fear of a missile gap. The Americans proposed that their allies should build up conventional forces while the United States focused on upgrading its nuclear arsenal. The allies refused and this quarrel proved that the 'differentiated responses' compromise worked out by NATO in the spring of 1958 would have to be revisited.[79] The MLF proposal was dropped and taken up again several times. For London it represented a challenge to Britain's independent deterrent. For the Americans the multilateral force offered a way of dealing with NATO difficulties, especially the FRG's nuclear aspirations.[80]

Britain's hopes of retaining nuclear independence and reducing defence expenditure were dashed in the early 1960s. By the Nassau Agreement of December 1962, Macmillan and Kennedy arranged for Britain's purchase of Polaris missiles from the United States. Meanwhile, the emergency in Jordan in 1958 had shown that there was still a need to deploy British troops abroad, and crises of 1961 in Kuwait and Berlin prompted an extension of the period of service for the last intake of conscripted troops and the calling up of reserves. A confrontation between Malaysia and Indonesia in 1963 meant that British troops had to remain in the Far East. Nuclear defence did not mean cheaper defence. Blue Streak was abandoned because of the cost. The government appeared to retrieve the situation by applying for US Skybolt missiles, but in 1962 Kennedy's administration scrapped Skybolt. Worried about Britain's international credibility (and his own reputation) Macmillan was determined to obtain Polaris from the USA.[81] Despite the pressure to save money and the growth of anti-nuclear sentiment among the British people, there seemed no alternative to Polaris. The submarines needed to carry Polaris did not suit the East of Suez responsibilities to which Britain was still wedded, however, and navy chiefs continued to stress the need for surface ships, especially aircraft carriers. The RAF complained that its strategic function was passing to the Royal Navy.[82]

Debates about Skybolt, the Nassau Agreement and Polaris were inseparable from concerns about Britain's economic performance. Relative decline became clearer as some of Britain's competitors moved further ahead (especially the FRG and Japan). The economic policies of the period did not help, for there was little consistency, while the world role probably imposed psychological as well as financial burdens.[83] The resources available for defence were not always used effectively. These years saw delay in moving research closer to industry, a failure to concentrate technological effort in areas that would benefit Britain, and the loss of huge sums on cancelled projects. Macmillan's success in gaining American co-operation contributed to his failures elsewhere. De Gaulle's refusal to allow Britain into the EEC and the evolution of strategic arms limitation into basically a US–Soviet affair did not say much for Britain's influence.[84]

The decision to abandon Blue Streak was made in February 1960. The project was going to be expensive to complete and the chiefs of staff had advised that by the time the missile was ready it would be virtually obsolete, whereas the life of Britain's bomber aircraft could be extended by the purchase of Skybolt. By April 1960 Macmillan had a US assurance that Skybolt would be provided. In return, the Americans would be allowed to use a submarine base on the Clyde, not far from Glasgow. Labour MPs, CND protesters and others pointed out that Glasgow was bound to be targeted by the Soviets. On 1 November 1960 Macmillan assured the Commons that the British and US governments would consult closely about the use of the base. Protests against nuclear weapons continued, as did a wider dissatisfaction with what were regarded as negative aspects of Cold War culture.[85]

Some of Kennedy's advisers thought that the sharing of nuclear technology with Britain should cease, in order to encourage the British to co-operate more fully with Europe. During the Cuban missile crisis of October 1962, Kennedy only told America's allies about his decisions *after* they had been made, which suggests that he did not regard them as nuclear partners. This was probably true of Britain, just like the rest, although Kennedy's regard for Macmillan and belief that the USA's relationship with Britain was worth strengthening opened the way for the Nassau meeting at the end of 1962.[86]

The cancellation of Skybolt caused a crisis in Anglo-American relations that, according to some observers, was comparable to Suez. The main point for the British was not the quality of their deterrent but its *independent* status. The Americans had not appreciated this. For them, the main point was that Skybolt was not cost effective and had been rendered unnecessary by new strategic plans, defence systems and long-range weapons.[87]

In London it had been recognized that reliance on an American missile that was still in its experimental stages was far from ideal, yet no contingency plans were made in case Skybolt was cancelled. Macmillan was losing popularity, his government was beset with difficulty on Europe and other issues, and the newspapers were increasingly drawing attention to Britain's declining influence. The prime minister was emboldened by the knowledge that Kennedy was thinking about offering Polaris.[88] It is possible that the president made up his mind to supply Polaris before going to Nassau.[89] Kennedy did not commit himself to anything in advance, though, and when the offer was made the Americans stipulated that Britain's nuclear forces must be linked with NATO. In response,

Macmillan wanted it understood that Britain would have the right to use these forces independently should the nation's security be threatened.[90]

The Polaris missiles would be fitted with British warheads and carried by British submarines, which would be part of a NATO force (the MLF, never in fact formed). However tenuous, the claim to nuclear independence died hard and by the Nassau arrangement neither America nor Britain would use nuclear weapons without consulting the other, though in practice it was clearly much more important for the British to have US consent rather than vice versa. Macmillan came in for some hostile press coverage and the Labour Party announced that it would renegotiate the deal when it came into office.[91]

Though the United States still needed Britain, reflected the *Observer*, this need was diminishing and Macmillan had rightly accepted that Britain could not have security without American help: 'nothing can alter the facts of power'. As for the Nassau Agreement, 'many of the details have been deliberately blurred' and its full implications would only become clear in the fullness of time. *The Times* argued that the Nassau talks would have been much less important had the Skybolt decision been delayed, had the Conservative Party not been 'in deep water at home', and had such a fuss not been created by the recent remarks of Dean Acheson, who, in a speech of 5 December 1962, declared that Britain 'has lost an empire and has not yet found a role'. *The Times* was relieved that the Skybolt controversy had passed, and, in view of Britain's need for US nuclear technology, commented that recent official statements put 'the best face on the inevitable'.[92]

Particularly remarkable is the extent to which Macmillan and Kennedy had to contend with opposition from their own colleagues. Macmillan was warned against over-reliance on the USA. On the American side, many influential figures argued that it would be a mistake to introduce an element of bilateralism into the Polaris programme. Kennedy did impose conditions: Macmillan had to approve the MLF and increase Britain's conventional contribution to NATO. The Americans thought that they could limit trouble within NATO by offering Polaris to France. It did not matter that the French nuclear programme was not sufficiently advanced to make use of the offer: this was a political move designed to reassure Western Europe. Kennedy might also have hoped that de Gaulle would become less obstinate on NATO matters and Britain's bid to join the EEC.[93]

De Gaulle rejected the Polaris offer, vetoed Britain's EEC application, and made it clear that France would not be a party to America's European intentions. Macmillan moved to limit the political impact of these transactions at home. He had no doubt that the Polaris deal was good for him and for Britain. It meant the preservation of the independent deterrent on favourable financial terms, and in order to get Polaris he misled Kennedy. He warned that Britain might have to opt for nuclear co-operation with France. Macmillan was aware by now that de Gaulle would block Britain's bid to join the EEC, but he could not admit this to the Americans. In addition, though they told the Americans otherwise, he and his colleagues never believed that the government would fall over the Skybolt issue.[94]

Some Labour MPs were incensed by a deal that they said would cost too much money and fail to solve the nation's defence problems. Gaitskell's successor as party leader, Harold Wilson, rejected the idea of a unilateral deterrent, but although Labour would go into the general election of 1964 promising to reconsider Britain's commitments, once in office Wilson decided that nuclear deterrence should continue, not least because voters approved of it.[95]

De Gaulle's opinion was that the Nassau Agreement threatened British and perhaps European sovereignty. Still envisaging an independent Europe led by France, he was bound to take a jaundiced view of Britain's application for EEC membership. Kennedy had been encouraging Macmillan to join the EEC on the basis that integration was both economically important and essential to NATO. Talks on British entry during 1962 did not get far. Macmillan tried to divide the FRG from France while telling de Gaulle that there would be no US domination of Europe and making suggestions about European political co-operation, but de Gaulle was furious about the USA's refusal to permit Britain to pass on nuclear information to France and when he issued his veto on 14 January 1963, he explicitly linked together the Nassau Agreement and Britain's bid to join the EEC. Adenauer did not back the British because he considered them soft on the Soviets and did not want to jeopardize the FRG's understanding with France.[96] The need to offer a nuclear bribe to de Gaulle had been central to Macmillan's thinking since the application to join the EEC had been definitely decided upon, but in the event the Americans would not allow him to provide what de Gaulle was thought to want.[97]

The Commons had endorsed the government's decision to make the EEC application on 3 August 1961, but this only entailed a process that would determine whether or not satisfactory terms could be agreed. Macmillan confirmed that the government had no intention of weakening the Commonwealth and that EFTA's interests and the needs of British agriculture would be respected. When asked if he thought the negotiations would succeed, Macmillan described himself as 'hopeful' but 'not confident'. Although the prime minister stated that the membership application related purely to economic matters and did not directly involve defence and foreign policy, he kept telling the Commons that if the talks failed there would be danger for the 'free world'.[98]

That de Gaulle was not ready to let Britain join the EEC became obvious during 1962. Finally Macmillan met him for crisis talks in December 1962 at Rambouillet. The French leader considered the British inflexible. He said they were incapable of making the adjustments that would be needed for membership of the EEC, yet there had been an earlier, apparently more promising meeting at the Château de Champs in June. Nuclear matters featured prominently at Champs, where de Gaulle indicated that something might be worked out. Thereafter, his confidence was boosted by electoral gains for his party and by the rapidly improving relationship between France and the FRG. At Rambouillet, de Gaulle went back on many of the things he had said at Champs.[99]

In conducting the EEC bid Macmillan and his colleagues made mistakes, though it should be remembered that there were many circumstances over which they had no control. They misjudged the depth of integrationist sentiment in Europe, the readiness of 'The Six' to press ahead without Britain, and the strength of Britain's negotiating position. The economic context did not help, since Britain's economic position was getting weaker relative to that of 'The Six'. Had Macmillan shown more enthusiasm for the EEC, things might have been different, but de Gaulle would probably have blocked Britain's application in any case, and there were reasons for Macmillan's equivocation. The British government, parliament, press and public were not united on Europe.[100]

Matters could not be rushed, because of opposition to EEC membership at home and because it was important to take repeated soundings in Washington DC and throughout the Commonwealth. Delay made the government seem less than committed, but at least de Gaulle's conduct meant that Britain did not have to choose between America and Europe: relations with both could still be cultivated. Moreover, de Gaulle had to accept that Britain's perspective on this was shared by others in Europe, especially in the FRG, where the consolidation of the EEC was not considered to be inconsistent with a close security relationship with the United States. What was really at stake between Britain and France was the question of who should lead Europe. The French, already inside the EEC, had advantages that the British lacked.[101]

American policy also had a bearing on what happened. The Kennedy administration wanted Britain to join the EEC as part of a grand design that would reshape Europe in a way that helped the Americans with their own problems (especially nuclear strategy, slow economic growth and a trade deficit). Kennedy and his advisers knew that this would not appeal to Paris and Bonn. Obstruction would be overcome, it was thought, if the USA's principal ally joined the EEC, and if a stable, prosperous, unified Western Europe took on a greater share of world responsibilities. Kennedy was worried that if he agreed to supply Britain with Polaris, Britain's bid to join the EEC would fail, but Macmillan had assured him that the French were more concerned about agriculture than about nuclear weapons.[102]

Though the case presented to different audiences by Macmillan and by Edward Heath, who managed the EEC bid, was selective, it is also true that everything was conditional upon the terms that could be agreed with 'The Six'. It is likely that Macmillan's stress on the Anglo-American link made it more difficult for

Britain to move closer to Europe, but it does not follow that the EEC would have accepted British leadership, or that the 'special relationship' was not as useful to Britain as Macmillan and others thought.[103] In the end, British mistakes and the nature of Anglo-American relations might have mattered less than the conduct of de Gaulle. Then again, perhaps de Gaulle's veto was not inevitable. The responses of 'The Six' to the British application affected and were affected by their policy towards each other. The conditional nature of Britain's application and the discussions within 'The Six' appear over time to have increased de Gaulle's readiness to use the veto.[104] He wanted not only to block what he took to be a British challenge to French leadership of the EEC, but also to re-assert that leadership and overcome resistance to his plans for the EEC's future.[105]

It dawned on 'The Six' that admitting Britain would bring considerable legal and institutional disruption. Britain had also to consider the Commonwealth. The EEC application failed in part because of Britain's need to safeguard Commonwealth interests, although the problem here might not have been in the details but rather in the delay that was caused by Britain's efforts to persuade the Commonwealth to back the EEC bid.[106]

The FRG's willingness to side with de Gaulle was limited by Bonn's attitude towards nuclear strategy, the perceived need to involve Britain more in continental affairs, and the desire to retain US goodwill. Bonn wished to work closely with Paris, but Bonn also wished to take its own path as appropriate, a tendency that was reinforced at this time by American proposals for the MLF. Washington DC conceived of the MLF project as a means to strengthen the FRG's commitment to NATO and prevent Franco-German nuclear coalition under de Gaulle. Bonn wanted to go ahead with the MLF in order to have more say in nuclear decision making, while the British did not want or need a collective deterrent, and neither did the French. Other European members of NATO also had misgivings. Washington DC continued to think that to supply the FRG with nuclear weapons would be to facilitate US military withdrawal from Europe, while Soviet diplomacy was heavily influenced by the desire to prevent the FRG from acquiring a nuclear capability.[107]

Unable to lead Britain into the EEC, Macmillan came under more pressure at home. In February 1963 he was asked about the alternatives to EEC membership, but on the possibility of boosting trade with the Commonwealth, or perhaps with the Soviet bloc, the prime minister was non-committal. MPs were told that de Gaulle used the veto not because negotiations were floundering but because he was afraid they were going to succeed. Harold Wilson protested that Macmillan had offered not 'a breath of justification for his policies over the past eighteen months'. *The Times* claimed that de Gaulle's action had provoked 'shock and disapproval' across Europe: French intransigence had been condemned, a desire had been expressed for the negotiations to continue, and Britain should not give up.[108]

The failed EEC bid added to the impression that the government had lost its way, and the prime minister's fitness to lead was questioned. For all this, however, the EEC application had some favourable results. Macmillan had decided that the attempt was worth making in order to shore up Britain's influence in Washington DC and in Europe, and it was not thought that the failure of the application would be economically damaging. Tariffs were already coming down, Britain's exports to the EEC were increasing, and it was not possible to tell if membership of the EEC would have done much to solve Britain's long-term economic problems. Politically the damage was containable: the government could shift the blame onto de Gaulle and the EEC application divided the Labour Party. The application does not appear to have greatly harmed the Conservatives' electoral prospects, because Europe was not a major issue at the general election of October 1964, which Labour narrowly won. As for the wider foreign policy purpose behind the application, if the plan was to maintain for Britain a status that was higher than that of France and West Germany, this was substantially achieved.[109] The Polaris deal was useful in making the Soviets think that a second centre of command existed in the West, but its main value was as a symbol of Britain's status. Relative economic decline mattered less while Britain had up-to-date weaponry. Macmillan also used the EEC bid to influence the Americans in another way, deepening their dissatisfaction with de Gaulle. Macmillan argued that economic division hindered political unity, and American leaders hoped that Britain would join the EEC in the future.[110]

De Gaulle's confrontational approach assisted Britain while also, by angering others in the EEC and contributing to their disagreements about institutional reform, slowing down European integration. Another useful result of the EEC application concerned EFTA. As 'The Six' began to argue among themselves, members of EFTA became more enthusiastic about the body to which they belonged and Britain won approval for its proposal that all internal tariffs should be abolished by January 1967.[111]

Nevertheless, the failed application was a blow to British prestige and Macmillan feared that the world would soon be divided into an American sphere, the Soviet bloc, and a united Europe of which Britain was not a part. The Test Ban Treaty of July 1963 offered some compensatory indication that Britain was still a great power. The US, Soviet and British governments agreed to stop nuclear testing under water and in the earth's atmosphere.[112]

This treaty was a long time in the making. Talks collapsed several times, but Macmillan repeatedly brought the Americans and Soviets back into the process with new initiatives.[113] Kennedy referred to Macmillan's role in arranging the treaty as 'indispensable' and congratulated the prime minister for doing so much for world peace. Macmillan also had other reasons for pursuing a test ban. Conservative MPs were overwhelmingly in support of it and opinion polls indicated public approval. In addition, the government had long since linked disarmament with the need to reorganize Britain's defences. Once Kennedy had decided to find out if Khrushchev was really prepared to sign a treaty, Macmillan encouraged him to proceed in spite of opposition within the United States.[114]

If the treaty marked a victory for British persistence, it also showed, once again, that the wish for close relations with the United States limited Britain's ability to act independently in the Cold War. Macmillan was motivated largely by domestic political considerations, international opinion (especially that of the non-aligned states) and a desire to stop the arms race. His arguments had some effect in Washington DC, but Kennedy and his advisers thought that it would be better to continue the arms race than to lose it, and the White House had also to listen to military and industrial leaders who wanted to go on testing and developing weapons. In its final form, indeed, the Test Ban Treaty was a partial measure. Underground tests were not covered and the nuclear arms race did not end. Macmillan had hoped for more, and the final outcome was shaped more by the two superpowers than by Britain.[115]

Macmillan only pursued a treaty vigorously *after* the British had tested their hydrogen bomb and the Cuban missile crisis had demonstrated their limited influence during a superpower confrontation. A test ban was certainly in Britain's interests, for Britain could not possibly keep up in a quickening arms race, and negotiating a test ban went hand in hand with securing Polaris from the Americans. Macmillan thought that he would be better able to justify maintaining the British deterrent if he also made an effort to slow down the arms race. The signing of the Test Ban Treaty was a personal success. Macmillan had overcome the reluctance of some of his colleagues and resistance from Kennedy's advisers, and he had raised his own standing as a world statesman.[116]

Acheson's point about Britain's search for 'a role' in the changing international order displeased London, but it was not an entirely inappropriate observation. Britain had mixed fortunes after Suez. Though the 'special relationship' recovered, problems in the Middle East gave Britain no end of trouble, and decolonization, though it was handled well in most places, carried with it some unwelcome implications respecting Britain's status as a world power. Decolonization might have freed up resources for other things, but it complicated Britain's effort to maintain a global reach. National defence, meanwhile, continued to require adjustment and to provoke controversy, and the Sandys reforms brought few of the financial, strategic and political benefits that had been expected. Little could be done, moreover, to arrive at a mutually advantageous accommodation between Britain and Western Europe. The Cold War context was unhelpful. No lasting thaw could be negotiated. On nuclear matters, Britain's deterrent was hotly debated even while Macmillan was pursuing a significant diplomatic accomplishment in the form of the Test Ban Treaty. In view of all these developments, it is not surprising that Britain's role in the world was not as clear as it once was. Britain would remain a major power, but new methods were needed and new challenges had to be met. How could Britain deal with leaders in Africa, Asia and the Middle East who were determined not to succumb to Western control? As America became more active in the world, how could Britain influence Washington DC and obtain US help? Would Britain's non-membership of the EEC be a long-term problem? How important were nuclear weapons to British security, status and influence, and could Britain really afford them? Britain was trying to be a world power, a nuclear power and a European power. It was trying to enhance its economic and military strength and exercise to the full its political and diplomatic expertise. All this brought up questions of identity and potential in what was a testing time between the later 1950s and the mid-1960s. The British still expected to play a role in Churchill's 'three circles', but the nature of this had yet to be settled and opinions differed about how to overcome the relative decline in Britain's international influence and resource base.

7

Losing a Role?

In the 1960s Britain could not sustain its former level of activity overseas and entered into a time of drawing back from and rearranging its global commitments. Retreats were hidden and minimized. Britain remained a great power, and was treated as such, though a large gap had opened up between Britain's capabilities and those of America and the Soviet Union. The British did well to maintain influence and prolong the perception at home and abroad that Britain was still able to shape events across the world, but it was not easy to keep this up. Problems multiplied in the Commonwealth. Cold War tensions increased in Africa, Latin America and South East Asia as well as in Europe.

In trying to keep the Commonwealth happy Britain ran the risk of annoying the United States and Western Europe: the Americans because of Britain's inability to change the anti-Western stance of such Commonwealth countries as India and Ghana, and the Europeans because of the commercial preferences for Commonwealth products.[1] Ethnic, tribal and religious divisions in the colonies sometimes led to violence as Britain withdrew. There was ongoing controversy over apartheid in South Africa, which left the Commonwealth in May 1961. The Commonwealth conference of March 1961 was a stormy affair, mainly because of South Africa, and the conference of September 1962 was overshadowed by Britain's bid to join the EEC. Britain's immigration policy also caused offence after new limits were imposed in July 1962. The Commonwealth expanded, became truly multi-racial, and Britain had to take more account of its members' sensibilities.[2]

Between January 1957, when Macmillan asked for a profit and loss assessment of each colony, and October 1964, when a Labour government took office in Britain for the first time in thirteen years, about half of Britain's formal dependencies became independent or had dates set for independence. The process was complicated by domestic politics, the Cold War, anti-colonial sentiment in the UN, protests against apartheid, Britain's EEC application, war in the Congo, the confrontation between Malaysia and Indonesia, and disorder in Aden and southern Arabia. To many contemporaries, decolonization was economically necessary. Yet it proved to be very expensive. Former colonies expected and received generous financial settlements. In 1961 the colonial secretary, Iain Macleod, argued that these costs could not be avoided if Britain's influence was to be preserved and communism kept at bay. That decolonization was not simply a matter of saving money is further indicated by the debates about it after 1964. Financial motives mattered less than concern about Britain's reputation and pressure from the UN.[3]

Such was the desire not to damage Commonwealth relations that British leaders repeatedly declared that they would not take the country into the EEC unless suitable arrangements could be made with respect to Commonwealth interests. Britain's relative economic decline and the decreasing importance to Britain of trade with the Commonwealth prompted a change of opinion, but this was balanced by Cold War concerns and the need to shore up influence in Africa and Asia. Local and regional conditions also shaped British policy: the pace of change in East Africa owed a lot to the Congo crisis, and the creation of the Federation of Malaysia was dictated largely by defence considerations.

Concern about immigration made Conservative right-wingers less interested in the colonies and former colonies, which helped Macmillan's government to accelerate decolonization. Some ministers had misgivings about limits on immigration. The Labour Party was committed to a multi-racial Commonwealth, although by 1962 there were murmurings against excessive immigration both in the party and in the trade unions.[4]

The Commonwealth needed structural reform, and after several years of discussion a secretariat was established in 1965. The Commonwealth was growing, its newer members wanted more influence, and London decided that it would be better to guide than to resist. It was hoped that administrative adjustments would not reduce Britain's role as leader of the Commonwealth. The economic importance to Britain of the Commonwealth and sterling area was rapidly declining, which prompted further reassessments of Britain's priorities, and it was decided that disengagement would eliminate Britain's most disadvantageous commitments around the world and improve Britain's position politically and economically within the West.[5]

The anti-Western rhetoric of 'racism' and 'imperialism' was one of the most negative aspects of Cold War ideology and was not without impact on newly independent states. Their ill feeling towards the former colonial powers grew, exacerbating the violence and instability to which many of them succumbed. Wars broke out, notably in Congo in the summer of 1960. Congo shared borders with the British territories of Uganda, Tanganyika and Northern Rhodesia, and the political situation in these territories was delicate. With the French and Belgians quitting Africa, Macmillan was sure that it would be unwise for Britain to remain. Dealing with the Congo crisis was not easy, partly because of the wider context: the U2 incident; the unproductive Paris summit of May 1960; the lack of progress on Berlin and the German question and on disarmament.[6]

Congo had been a Belgian colony. Disturbances prompted Belgium to grant independence, but a civil war began as the Congolese government was challenged by secessionists in the mineral-rich province of Katanga. Khrushchev wanted to open a new front in the Cold War and offered to help the government of Congo, led by Patrice Lumumba. The Belgians intervened to protect their assets in Congo and sided with the Katangan rebels. The UN arranged to send in a peacekeeping force, by which time the Americans had become more involved (the CIA had been planning to assassinate Lumumba). Washington DC wished to prevent Soviet gains in Africa, and intended to block the dismemberment of Congo and install a friendly regime there. The war continued into the early weeks of 1963, when the Katangans accepted that there would be no secession.[7]

President Kennedy had argued that the UN's task was not to defeat secession militarily, but to persuade Katanga's leaders to co-operate with the government of Congo. The United States, Britain and Western Europe hoped for negotiations that would allow Katanga a measure of autonomy and preserve their economic interests, while the Soviets and many of the new nations across Africa and Asia, which cared nothing for the West's interests, argued that the secession should be ended by force. Macmillan was not in favour of Katanga's secession, but nor did he want a united Congo to be a communist Congo, and he was also frustrated as serious rifts opened up at the UN.[8]

Events in Congo affected the plans the government was putting together for Britain's colonies in Africa. Macmillan came under pressure to accept Katanga's declaration of independence. British businessmen, Conservative MPs and colonial administrators in Africa all wanted Katanga to be stable and friendly, and there were protests at the end of 1961 when the government announced that Britain would supply UN forces with arms.[9] There was more behind sympathy for Katanga than economic links and mining concessions. Katanga's leaders were would-be allies of the West. Macmillan was concerned, however, that partiality would push Congo's leaders completely over to Moscow, and he did not want to annoy African and Asian opinion, which was still sensitive about colonialism. Then again, to stand by and see the Katangans defeated could be to facilitate the spread of communist influence across central Africa. The promise of independence to Britain's colonies in the region might stop disorder from spreading, but this hope ran up against the growing opposition to majority rule. White settlers, especially in Northern and Southern Rhodesia, claimed that Congo showed what could happen when black rule was established without white supervision.[10]

The Americans told Macmillan that Britain should support UN action against the Katangans. Macmillan urged restraint, but Washington DC had little sympathy for Britain's colonial troubles and accused London of encouraging Katanga's leader, Moise Tshombe, to obstruct a settlement. Tshombe eventually agreed to accept a federal constitution for Congo, but then he repudiated it and Macmillan could no longer defend him in view of Britain's need for Polaris. Tshombe was removed early in 1963. For many in the West, this was regrettable. They regarded Tshombe as a reliable anti-communist and as someone with whom they could bargain for access to Katanga's minerals. Governments in Western Europe were generally more cautious than the Americans about interfering in Congo. The British repeatedly declared that the UN should not use coercive methods, and Britain's reluctance to support the UN's military operation annoyed the Americans.[11]

Congo was the subject of fiery altercations in the House of Commons, as in March 1961 when Labour MP Denis Healey complained that British policy was frustrating the UN effort in Congo. Healey accused the government of alienating African and Asian states, giving them little cause to trust the West on this or any other matter, and associating Britain too closely with the ill-considered Belgian intervention on Katanga's side. Edward Heath protested that Britain was assisting the UN effort and that Africans could hardly question Britain's motives at a time when colonies were being granted independence and aid was being provided to help the continent advance economically, socially and politically.[12] In February 1963 ministers were pressed by their own backbenchers to request a full investigation into the UN's military action in Congo. Allegations were made about looting and other outrages, and it was said that the conflict would not have escalated had UN forces not entered Katanga. Labour MPs were appalled by these attacks on the UN. *The Times* had sympathy for ministers, but suggested that they could have done more to show people at home and abroad that Britain was doing enough. Though the government had not supported Tshombe unconditionally, and had sought 'a reconciliation that would do justice to Katanga's claim to a fair measure of self-determination', Britain's enemies had misinterpreted this.[13]

The fall of the pro-Western secessionist regime in Katanga prompted black African leaders in the British territories to be more demanding. They refused to discuss new political arrangements. The presence of UN forces boosted anti-colonial opinion, created an expectation of imminent freedom, and undermined the authority of the British government and of local white élites. Fear of African nationalism increased as a result of the atrocities committed in Congo. In Southern Rhodesia white leaders were adamant that they would not share power with blacks. Many whites in British areas decided to leave Africa. Britain's plans for decolonization were partly based on the assumption that people of British and European stock would remain in Africa, but it was too late now greatly to alter schemes that were being implemented.[14]

The Cold War made matters worse, for crises in Africa became a part of the Cold War contest. The contest changed in other respects. A gradual retreat from rigid planning gave more scope for market forces in the Soviet bloc, though this was more obvious in some countries than in others. Most trade remained within the bloc and was guided by Comecon. Even so, during the 1960s trade with the West increased and moves toward a relaxation of economic controls in certain parts of the bloc were matched by greater freedom in social and cultural spheres. The state remained supreme and was ready to use repression and terror as necessary, but reform opinion was never entirely suppressed.[15]

Though the West courted Yugoslavia's leader, Tito, this did not cause the bloc to collapse. Albania left Comecon in 1961 and the Warsaw Pact in 1968, but did not turn to the West. Rumanian leader Nicolae Ceauşescu appeared to take a more independent line in foreign policy, and in the West it was thought that his quarrels with Moscow might lead to Rumania's detachment from the bloc. This did not occur, and in any case Rumania's economic underdevelopment and human rights abuses hardly endeared Ceauşescu to the West. At the same time, however, the large private sector in Polish agriculture and ongoing development of a market economy in Hungary did confirm that the eastern bloc was far from monolithic.[16]

Tito was committed to non-alignment. He wanted the benefits of friendly relations with the West and sought at the same time to avoid conflict with Moscow. Britain joined the Americans in offering aid and in the later 1950s the Yugoslavian economy grew stronger. The American attitude hardened in the early 1960s, but a wave of reforms in Yugoslavia led to further loans and trade deals and in 1970, with détente very much the order of the day, Yugoslavia concluded an agreement with the EEC.[17] Once the Western powers, especially the USA, had given up on an ideological approach, strategic interest (specifically Yugoslavia's potential as a defensive shield for NATO's southern flank) became the primary motivation. It became clear that Yugoslavia would not side with the West in the Cold War, and the Americans accepted this. The British thought that aid should be limited so that Tito received just enough to allow his regime to survive. This would prove that a communist state did not have to rely on Moscow. The Americans were more generous. They wanted Yugoslavia's economic success to be exemplary, to demonstrate the full benefits of co-operation with the West.[18]

Yugoslavia was an exceptional case. Other threats to unity in the bloc, and to its ruling élites, were dealt with more easily, and the danger receded as economic growth improved the standard of living. During the 1960s the more backward areas of Eastern Europe began to industrialize, but the bloc never matched the prosperity of Western Europe.[19]

Nevertheless, economic expansion enabled Moscow better to fight the Cold War and extend it beyond Europe. In the Middle East the Soviets improved their links with Egypt, Syria and Iraq. In Asia they promised to help new nations in the struggle against imperialism, and the Soviet Union's strategic preoccupations in Asia continued, not least because of the long border with China. After a brief war in 1962 between China and India, the Soviets drew closer to India. China then protested about the Test Ban Treaty of 1963, which Mao regarded as an attempt to slow down China's nuclear programme. There were several border clashes involving the USSR and China. By 1969 the Soviets were threatening to use nuclear weapons, and both sides were building up their naval strength. China tried to improve relations with the United States because of Soviet hostility.[20]

There were times during the 1960s when the Americans were made to feel vulnerable, and the Cuban missile crisis of October 1962 momentarily increased the likelihood of a full-scale war. Sputnik had revealed to American leaders that the Soviets had the technology for long-range attacks, and nervousness increased as the Soviets made threats about Berlin and involved themselves militarily in Africa.[21] London constantly urged Washington DC not to overreact. Disagreements in the early 1960s made even more important the mutual respect between Macmillan and Kennedy. Good personal relations helped to smooth over some of the problems that arose. This process was aided by David Ormsby-Gore, who was close to the Kennedy family and served as Britain's ambassador in Washington DC.[22]

Khrushchev had decided that Soviet success would come not through nuclear or conventional forces, but though wars of national liberation in Africa, Asia and Latin America. Kennedy's response was to promise to defend freedom everywhere. If his policy was designed to establish US primacy in international affairs, it also had the effect of disturbing them.[23] The fixation with Cuba is best understood in this context. Fidel Castro had taken power in Cuba in January 1959. He embarked on a series of radical reforms and in Washington DC there was little doubt that he was creating a communist dictatorship and would make Cuba heavily reliant on the USSR. Cuba's proximity to the US mainland made it likely that the Americans would respond. When Kennedy assumed the presidency he found the Bay of Pigs scheme already in place: CIA-backed anti-communist Cuban exiles would invade the island and remove Castro. Eisenhower had approved the plot in principle. It was Kennedy who allowed it to go ahead in the spring of 1961, and it was an embarrassing failure. The CIA subsequently plotted in various ways to get rid of Castro.[24]

British newspapers were less than impressed. If Kennedy was going to contain communism, *The Times* suggested, he would have to rely on negotiation rather than military force and settle for 'a workable form of neutrality' for Cuba (and for Laos, where the Americans were resisting Soviet-backed insurgents). To the *Observer*, Kennedy was guilty of 'a disastrous blunder' and the way to win the Cold War was through 'tolerance': Kennedy had to demonstrate to all people everywhere that 'the United States accepts their wish to conduct their own affairs in their own way more genuinely than does the Soviet Union'. Macmillan considered the Bay of Pigs invasion a bad mistake, but as the American focus on Castro intensified, British leaders could do little. Cuba was too close to the United States for Washington DC to allow London to have a say. In the Commons on 18 April

1961 some speakers condemned the Bay of Pigs operation and the government was urged to denounce it openly, but Heath replied that hasty comment was best avoided. On 20 April Labour MPs argued that the Americans, unless they were stopped, would trigger off a major war. The home secretary, R.A. Butler, did not agree with this interpretation.[25]

The Bay of Pigs affair provided valuable propaganda material for the Soviets, whose prestige was also boosted at this time by the first manned flight in space. Khrushchev tried to take advantage at the Vienna summit in June 1961, but on Berlin, nuclear testing, Congo, Laos and other matters, Kennedy refused to make concessions. Khrushchev decided to put more pressure on Kennedy and show the world that the Soviet Union was America's equal. He may have thought he could use Cuba to gain a bargain on Berlin.[26]

Castro's regime moved quickly to the left after the Bay of Pigs, in terms of both policy and personnel. The bond between Havana and Moscow was strengthened.[27] Khrushchev's need for a success abroad was greater than ever. The Sino-Soviet split was now more visible to the West. There was tension within the USSR after a run of deficient harvests. The Americans had based Jupiter missiles in Italy and Turkey and Soviet intelligence had confirmed that the United States was winning the nuclear arms race. It was estimated that the placing of missiles on Cuba would save the USSR perhaps ten years in its pursuit of parity with the USA.[28]

Khrushchev's idea of a bold move had the same flaw as Kennedy's similarly proactive approach: destabilization was dangerous. Moreover, Khrushchev lied to Kennedy, assuring him that only short-range surface-to-air missiles were being sent to Cuba. In fact, the Soviets provided medium- to long-range nuclear weapons, along with 22,000 troops and technicians and twenty-four anti-aircraft missile groups.[29]

Kennedy's administration was initially split between those who advocated a decisive air strike against Cuba, and in due course an invasion, and those who preferred a blockade in the hope that this would be sufficient to make the Soviets relent. After wavering between the two positions, the president opted for a blockade, which was announced on 22 October 1962.[30]

In Britain, as the foreign office issued anti-Soviet statements and confirmed that British and American leaders were in discussions about Cuba, *The Times* declared that Kennedy was right to declare a blockade. True, past US mistakes, Washington DC's aversion to the Castro regime, the Bay of Pigs and Kennedy's 'sudden display of toughness now during a mid-term election campaign in which he has been accused of softness' might lead one to be sceptical, but the main point was that the Soviets intended to station offensive weapons on Cuba despite their previous assurances to the contrary. Many nations would probably dispute the legality of the US blockade. Nor was it likely that Castro would permit

UN observers to supervise the dismantling of Soviet missile bases. The linkage between Cuba and Berlin added another complication. Nevertheless, a deal could be worked out, especially if both America and the USSR agreed to give up a number of their 'forward bases' situated close to each other's territory.[31]

On 25 October Macmillan told MPs that the discovery of missiles with a range of over a thousand miles contradicted previous Soviet assurances that Castro would be provided only with defensive weapons. Clearly Kennedy had to insist on the removal of these missiles, otherwise doubt would be cast on American pledges and commitments all over the world and even greater dangers would arise. Macmillan said that Britain fully supported the attempts that were under way, primarily at the UN, to have the missiles removed. Labour MPs warned that the US blockade would set a damaging precedent.[32]

Reporting the results of a quick and 'unscientific' survey of popular opinion in Britain, the *Guardian* stressed the absence of unanimity. Some thought US policy to be correct, others did not, and though there was an aversion to 'appeasement' there was also a sense that Kennedy had not yet provided enough evidence about Soviet activities on Cuba: 'most people feel emotionally on the side of the president but are unconvinced by his facts, and the "don't knows" are a large proportion'. *The Times* subsequently reported on progress at the UN and argued that it was not advisable for Britain to try to mediate alone. Some hope was offered by the prospect that US missiles in Turkey could be used to make a bargain on the Soviet missiles in Cuba. In a letter to *The Times* dated 25 October 1962, the historian J.B. Conacher, an associate professor at the University of Toronto, complained about those British commentators who opposed the US blockade of Cuba. Conacher also insisted that the bases in Turkey were not to be viewed in the same way as the bases on Cuba, for 'to govern the Cold War by the "fair play" rules that will serve on the playing fields of Eton is surely unrealistic and will only encourage the Russians to write off those who advance such ideas as of no account'.[33]

Kennedy and his advisers gambled that Khrushchev would not go to war. On 26 October, the Soviet leader agreed to remove the missiles in return for a pledge that the Americans would not invade Cuba. The next day Khrushchev added another condition. He demanded the withdrawal of medium-range US missiles from Turkey. Kennedy ignored the second condition and agreed only that Cuba would not be invaded, and Khrushchev accepted this as the basis of a settlement on 28 October.[34]

Both the Soviet and US leaderships claimed victory, but it is not easy to identify meaningful gains on either side. Khrushchev would be deposed in October 1964. His options had been limited in the missile crisis because Cuba was too far away from the USSR to gain the full benefit of Soviet protection. As for Kennedy, despite his undoubted skill in the public relations aspects of the crisis, he did make concessions: US missiles *were* withdrawn from Turkey, and communist Cuba survived intact as a *military ally* of the USSR. On the other hand, the missiles in Turkey were obsolete and would soon have been withdrawn anyway, and in the long run the alliance between Cuba and the USSR did not prevent the Americans from doing the important things they wanted to do in the world. Although the Turkish missiles featured in the arrangements he made with Khrushchev, Kennedy could not be open about the link between them and the Cuban issue in case NATO disapproved, and he had to prevent the Soviets from interpreting any deal on the Turkish missiles as a sign of American weakness.[35]

How important was Britain's role? The core elements of American policy were settled by the Americans themselves. As Kennedy's advisers stressed, Cuba was not close to Britain or Europe, their perspective was bound to be different, and therefore it would not be wise to involve them in the decision-making process. The views of the European members of NATO had also to be blocked out because of the nuclear context. For years Washington DC had worked to deny them the capacity for an independent use of nuclear weapons. The Americans did not want to be dragged into a nuclear war to defend interests that were not vital to the United States. The Cuban missile crisis turned this situation around: now the European members of NATO were worried that they would be involved in a nuclear war caused by decisions taken by the Americans alone.[36]

Plenty of historians have argued that Britain's influence during the crisis was negligible and that, though Kennedy and Macmillan spoke regularly on the telephone, the British did not shape US policy at all, since Kennedy only used them as a sounding board. Indeed, Macmillan opposed the removal of missiles from Turkey and Kennedy rejected Macmillan's suggestion that the Thor missiles in Britain could be immobilized to get the Soviets to talk. According to this line of argument, during the most serious international emergency since the Second World War Britain played no meaningful role.[37]

Yet no other leader had the relationship that Macmillan enjoyed with Kennedy, or the mutual confidence, or the direct communication with the US president during the crisis. Britain's ambassador in Washington DC, David Ormsby-Gore, was also an important participant. British influence at this juncture might not have been decisive, and should not be exaggerated, but neither can it be discounted. Macmillan saw immediately that Britain could help to end the crisis. In his dealings with Kennedy and with European and Commonwealth leaders, he set an example of firmness and restraint. After the crisis he insisted that the British government had done its part, sharing in US decision making and keeping Western Europe together in such a way that complications from that direction were minimized. Nevertheless, it is true that Kennedy and his closest colleagues made the key decisions. Ormsby-Gore later admitted that British advice reassured

Kennedy, but did not change his policy. Still, Kennedy did listen to Macmillan and was influenced by him. Both the president and his secretary of state, Dean Rusk, knew that the British had done invaluable service in preserving NATO's unanimity and placating the governments of Western Europe.[38]

It was Macmillan, backed by Ormsby-Gore, who had pressed Kennedy to publish photographic evidence of the Soviet missiles on Cuba. When Kennedy confided to Macmillan that pressure was building for air strikes against Cuba, and even invasion, the prime minister pointed to the risks involved. When Kennedy decided to impose a blockade rather than order air strikes, Ormsby-Gore suggested that the 'quarantine' line should be five hundred instead of the proposed eight hundred miles off the Cuban coast, so that Moscow would have more time to reflect and Khrushchev could find a way of saving face. Another important contribution was the intelligence provided by Oleg Penkovsky, a Soviet spy who had been recruited as a double agent by the British. As the tension mounted, and Kennedy asked Macmillan what he thought about a US invasion of Cuba, the prime minister replied (25 October 1962) that the time for an invasion had passed and that other means should be tried. On all of these points, British assistance and advice may not have been the main determinant of US policy, but equally, they were not without impact. In these days, the conversations between Kennedy and Macmillan had more to them than simply the passing on of information.[39]

There was a limit to Britain's helpfulness. The government was not slow to criticize those American decisions with which it disagreed. This robust approach was most evident in the foreign office, where US designs against Cuba had long been a source of annoyance. When the Americans suggested that NATO forces should be placed on alert it was Macmillan himself who took the lead in resisting. British leaders also insisted that the blockade of Cuba should not be extended (to cover items other than weapons), and they were sensitive about Britain's maritime rights and the free movement of British shipping. Some Kennedy aides complained about Britain's attitude. They had expected more support.[40]

Although Britain backed the United States in general terms, ministers tried to avoid making specific statements. There were no pronouncements on whether Cuba was really a threat to the USA, or whether the placing of Soviet missiles on Cuba altered the global balance. On both these matters the foreign office entertained doubts, but for the foreign secretary, Lord Home, the main point was not to take sides publicly against the Americans.[41]

If the British government was worried about the possible consequences of the crisis, there was also an idea that the crisis could be used to promote a deal on Berlin. In London's calculations, European security and the status of Berlin mattered more than Cuba, and there was a wish in some quarters to exploit the Cuban missile crisis in order to achieve political goals elsewhere. The snag was

that little could be done in Europe without American co-operation, and US pressure would also be needed to persuade the Soviets and the Cubans to participate
in the desired arrangements.[42]

After the Cuban missile crisis, Macmillan and his colleagues liked people
to think that they had been more influential than they really were, and this
accorded with the continuing desire to present Britain as a great power. Equally,
for Kennedy's administration it was important not to alienate Britain. The
president and his advisers valued British friendship. Indeed, they needed a
close democratic ally all the more at a time when Washington DC's support for
anti-communist dictators around the world was widely condemned. Britain was
also useful because of its links with Western Europe and the Commonwealth.
Although the British could not greatly influence US policy on Cuba, in truth they
had no need to, except in so far as Britain's wider concerns might be affected (the
EEC application, the need to resolve disputes within NATO, and the problems
associated with decolonization and the Commonwealth).[43]

Macmillan's desire to stay close to the Americans is also illustrated by his reaction
to information he received from the intelligence services. Through intermediaries,
the Soviets suggested that if Britain arranged a summit, Khrushchev would accept
the invitation. Macmillan decided not to respond because he thought that Moscow
was trying to drive a wedge between Britain and the United States.[44]

There has been speculation that Britain became more involved in the crisis
than was realized at the time and afterwards. It appears, for instance, that Britain's
nuclear forces were secretly placed on alert. A related matter is the worldwide
alert upon which US forces were placed, which must have involved the American
bases in Britain. The British government might not have been aware of everything
that was going on. Questions also remain with regard to the bargain Kennedy
made with Khrushchev. According to Macmillan, Kennedy could not have made a
deal involving the Jupiters in Turkey because of the possible effect on the strength
and unity of NATO, but this is what Kennedy did. The Soviet ambassador in
Washington DC said so, and Dean Rusk later confirmed it.[45] If the Americans
disguised their intentions with regard to the missiles in Turkey, there were also
good reasons for them to conceal the true extent of their consultation with
Britain. For example, Washington DC thought it wise to play down its discussions
with London in order to avoid offending Paris: the United States needed friends
in October 1962.[46]

Britain's direct influence on the outcome of the Cuban missile crisis was
limited, but the British government knew much more about what the president
and his advisers were doing than did all other governments. Of course, in asking
for advice, Kennedy was not committing himself to act upon it. Kennedy would
try out ideas, think aloud and seek suggestions. This enabled the British quite
freely to express their views. Indeed, the cumulative effect of Macmillan's written

and verbal communications with Kennedy during the Cuban missile crisis was considerable. The transcripts have been published and they indicate the extent of the interaction between the two leaders. Hugh Gaitskell claimed that the British government had been powerless, and told the Commons on 30 October 1962 that better contact would be needed if another such emergency arose, but Gaitskell did not have the transcripts before him. He cannot have known what Kennedy and Macmillan had or had not discussed.[47]

The Bay of Pigs affair and Cuban missile crisis pushed Kennedy closer to Macmillan. The dangers Kennedy encountered in his dealings with Cuba increased his need for approval.[48] British advice gave him more options. It encouraged him to follow his instincts, which pointed towards caution rather than bellicosity, and it helped him to stand up to the hawks in Washington DC, who were pressing for military action. The Cuban missile crisis was quickly followed by the Nassau Agreement. Close Anglo-American co-operation continued into 1963, and the Test Ban Treaty was one result.

The Cuban missile crisis had lasting consequences. American and Soviet leaders agreed to establish a hotline between Washington DC and Moscow, in the hope that ease of communication might help to resolve disputes in the future. They also saw the need for a deal on missile development and proliferation, and the Test Ban Treaty of 1963 marked a useful beginning. Tension over Berlin receded, and although the USSR concluded a separate treaty with the GDR in June 1964, Moscow stressed that this would not affect the rights of the Western powers.[49]

On the other hand, in some respects superpower rivalry became more intense, notably in the 'space race'. Kennedy was keen to outdo the Soviets in this field, especially after the spring of 1961 when the Soviets put the first man in space and America's reputation was affected by the Bay of Pigs. By 1972 the USA and USSR had launched more than 1,200 satellites and probes. Superpower rivalry was also seen in other areas. Khrushchev's successors increased the number of ICBMs on Soviet territory and expanded the Soviet Union's conventional forces. The removal of missiles from Cuba made US leaders overconfident, meanwhile, and they were eager to oppose communism elsewhere. This had unfortunate consequences, not least in Vietnam.[50]

After the Bay of Pigs, the Kennedy administration decided that America had to regain the initiative. The president was convinced that US power would be more credible if South Vietnam could be saved for democracy. Eisenhower and Dulles had rejected the Geneva accords of 1954 and approved massive aid to South Vietnam. The Vietcong emerged and set out to unite the country by force under the communists. By 1961 Vietnam was one of America's largest overseas commitments. There were demands for Kennedy to go back to the Geneva arrangements, but he and his advisers did not wish to appear weak. Kennedy increased the US military presence in South Vietnam and in October 1963 American strategists were predicting that the war would be won before the end of 1965. Though the president was coming to believe that the military effort could not succeed, he never had the chance to strike out in a new direction because he was assassinated on 22 November 1963.[51]

The situation in Vietnam caused arguments between the United States and Britain, where Labour took office in October 1964. Macmillan had resigned in October 1963 through ill health. His successor was Sir Alec Douglas-Home, formerly (as the Earl of Home) foreign secretary, but the Conservatives narrowly lost the general election of 1964 and Labour leader Harold Wilson took over as premier. The foreign secretaries in the Labour government were Patrick Gordon Walker (1964–65), Michael Stewart (1965–66 and 1968–70) and George Brown (1966–68), but often it was Wilson who shaped policy. Much to the annoyance of Labour left-wingers, in foreign affairs the Wilson government for the most part followed the example of its Conservative predecessors. At the heart of the policy was the wish to work with the United States. Britain's influence across Africa and Asia would be used to benefit the West and contain communism; British power would remain operative in regions where the Americans were relatively weak; substantial forces would be committed as necessary to restore order (as during the confrontation between Malaysia and Indonesia); and in return, it was expected, America would treat Britain as its principal ally, co-operate closely on nuclear matters, and offer financial help. Unfortunately the 'special relationship' was complicated by the war in Vietnam. As communist infiltration of South Vietnam increased, the presidency of Lyndon Johnson (1963–69) saw a rapid extension of US involvement in the region. Australia, New Zealand and South Korea also sent troops.[52]

Once Johnson won the presidential election of November 1964 his advisers recommended air strikes and ground reinforcements. In February 1965 Johnson was told that the war would be lost unless the American effort increased, that there was still time to avoid defeat, and that having taken responsibility for the survival of South Vietnam, the United States had to discharge this responsibility in a manner that left the world in no doubt of American strength and reliability. In order to keep as free a hand as possible, the White House hampered the mediation efforts of others. The UN was marginalized.[53]

Some of the most serious disagreements between Washington DC and London in the past had concerned South East Asia. There was a difference between American and British views of regional security. America's priority was to resist communism. With regard to Vietnam, this meant helping the French and then, when that did not work, propping up the non-communist regime in South Vietnam. Rarely did Washington DC make a distinction between communism and nationalism. The British, meanwhile, saw a need for the West to come to terms with nationalism and provide for stability.[54] One of the goals of British decolonization in Asia was to retain influence after the transfer of power, and the spread of anti-imperialist sentiment had increased the need for caution. To British leaders, economic links mattered more than political control.[55] They wanted collaborative networks in the region, not conflict.

Although Macmillan tried to restrain the Americans in Asia, he did not deny that circumstances might arise in which US military intervention there would be appropriate, in which case Britain could gain more influence by supporting US policy. Macmillan shared the American view that South Vietnam was strategically vital. His government acquiesced in the escalation as part of the effort to restore Anglo-American co-operation after Suez. Another reason was the wish to maintain British influence in South East Asia at a time when London's commitment to regional security was being questioned. This had implications for Commonwealth unity, since Australia and New Zealand suspected that Britain was unwilling to meet its regional responsibilities (an impression that was strengthened by Britain's application for EEC membership). Britain's experience in dealing with the insurgency in Malaya was important as well, for British leaders genuinely believed that guerrilla wars could be won in South East Asia. They also looked at the wider context and decided that US action in Vietnam was a Cold War necessity and that by supporting the Americans, Britain could help to contain China.[56]

The British attitude began to change late in 1963. The foreign office concluded that reliance upon military means in Vietnam would lead to a much bigger war that the United States could not win.[57] British advice had limited effect in Washington DC.[58]

Britain's position in South East Asia was challenged when Indonesia moved against the Federation of Malaysia (established in 1963, consisting of Malaya, Singapore, Sabah and Sarawak). London requested backing for a firm response but Washington DC hesitated, fearing that the Indonesian leader, Ahmed Sukarno, would seek allies in the communist camp. From 1963 to 1967 British forces resisted Indonesia's effort to undermine the Federation of Malaysia. This commitment of manpower and money was difficult to sustain.[59]

Wilson's government decided that there could be no question of sending British forces to Vietnam – not least because many Labour backbenchers opposed the US intervention there – but Wilson and his colleagues had publicly to express support for US policy, anxious as they were to retain American friendship. Wilson hoped for a quick end to the war and tried to arrange peace talks. In June 1965 he proposed a Commonwealth peace mission.[60]

The Labour government's small parliamentary majority made for caution while the worrying balance-of-payments situation suggested that Britain might soon need to ask for American financial help. Ministers were also conscious of

Britain's obligations in Asia. As a member of SEATO, indeed, Britain was partly responsible for the integrity of South Vietnam. Wilson was worried that if he objected too strongly to US policy in Vietnam, the Americans would turn against Britain's campaign in Malaysia.[61]

For the Labour left, criticism of US policy was a habit. Wilson did not wish to alienate left-wingers in his party. Nor was he on good terms personally with Johnson. British and American interests were diverging, the disparity in power between Britain and America was becoming more obvious, and Washington DC was not slow to condemn the scaling down of Britain's activities around the world. That the Americans did not react more strongly on the Vietnam issue suggests that Washington DC still thought that British co-operation was worth having on other matters. Nevertheless, American leaders increasingly viewed Britain as only one of several important allies and dismissed British claims to precedence.[62]

As the Americans poured more resources into Vietnam, Britain decided to leave Aden, suffered a sterling crisis, had further trouble with the Commonwealth, and eventually announced an almost complete withdrawal from East of Suez, all of which revealed both the limits on British power and the differences between British and US views of intervention in the developing world. Although Wilson wanted to act as a peacemaker in Vietnam, moreover, his attempt was doomed. Some of his colleagues, notably defence secretary Denis Healey and Richard Crossman, who held several cabinet posts between 1964 and 1970, insisted that Britain could not mediate, since Britain could not denounce the Americans, but Wilson was sure that Britain could help.[63]

What Johnson wanted was not a peace initiative but a contribution to the military effort. Wilson's excuses infuriated him, and he was particularly offended by Wilson's emphasis on Britain's role as co-convenor of the Geneva conference, which, Wilson said, obliged the British not to send troops but to promote a settlement.[64] Wilson played down the division and insisted that his conduct on Vietnam was appreciated by the US government. In fact, Johnson angrily rejected the suggestion that Wilson should visit the United States for emergency talks in February 1965, and although the two leaders did meet in April 1965, Wilson made too much of Johnson's vague promise to support Britain's policy. The Americans did not want to push the British into co-operation with de Gaulle or with UN secretary-general U Thant. If peace was going to be pursued, they wanted to make sure that the methods employed suited them.[65]

During the summer and autumn of 1965 sterling grew weaker, Wilson was embroiled in a struggle over the future of Rhodesia, and Washington DC feared that Britain would drastically scale down its responsibilities in the Middle East, Asia, the Indian Ocean and the Pacific. A new sterling crisis coincided with the arrival of many more US troops in Vietnam. Wilson's pose as a peacemaker became problematic. The Soviet Union, China and North Vietnam refused to believe that he was acting independently of the Americans. By the time Wilson returned to Washington DC in December 1965 he seemed not to be focusing so much on peace plans.[66]

Wilson's conduct generated many quarrels in the government, the Labour Party and parliament. Crossman thought that the prime minister was neglecting domestic difficulties for the sake of a high-profile 'Vietnam stunt' that was unlikely to achieve anything. When Wilson went before the Commons on 17 June 1965 he admitted that one or more of the interested governments might rebuff the peace mission, but added: 'I believe it better to have tried and failed than at this historic, critical moment for us not to have made the effort.' On 5 July foreign secretary Michael Stewart confirmed that North Vietnam had refused to participate.[67]

The *Guardian* and *The Times* both suggested that the communist regime in Hanoi might receive the mission in return for diplomatic recognition. In fact there was nothing that Wilson could do about North Vietnam's intransigence. The North Vietnamese asserted that Wilson was an agent of Washington DC and that the only way to end the war was for US troops to leave Vietnam. *The Times* was subsequently disappointed to learn that US troop numbers in Vietnam were going to be increased. The *Observer* argued that the 'tragedy' of Vietnam could not be ended only by supporting South Vietnam and putting more pressure on Hanoi. What was needed was a clearer indication from the Americans about what kind of settlement they would accept: a neutral Vietnam, with no foreign troops or bases, reunited after free elections, or a Korea-style partition, with South Vietnam defended by US forces?[68]

London was worried that the Americans would allow themselves to be distracted from Western Europe (a concern that had previously influenced British policy in the early and mid-1950s). This suggests that there was more to Wilson's refusal to send troops to Vietnam than personal authority, party infighting, domestic politics, international criticism and lack of resources. Clearly, if British forces were sent, then the war in Vietnam would be further internationalized, which would endorse the American commitment to the region.

Many Labour MPs wanted Wilson and other ministers to speak out against US policy. Anger grew as members of the government avoided making any such remarks, though the prime minister sometimes made gestures. He dissociated himself from the US bombing of North Vietnam in 1966, and the government also suspended the sale of weapons that might possibly be used in Vietnam. In November 1967 the foreign secretary, George Brown, told the cabinet not to receive US policy uncritically. Washington DC went on complaining, but Johnson had already chosen not to exert full pressure. In 1965 and 1966 his advisers suggested that US loans and support for sterling could be used to bring the British into line, but Johnson decided that this would be too extreme.[69]

The British did not remain uninvolved in the war. They provided a medical team, supplied intelligence, gave advice on counter-insurgency, sent weapons (sometimes disguised) and possibly also an élite special unit, and offered South Vietnam economic aid. British personnel trained US and South Vietnamese troops in jungle warfare. Britain also made available port facilities and airfields in the region. Johnson wanted more, but Wilson went on arguing that Britain would be of most service as a mediator.[70]

Wilson persisted in his search for peace in order to deflect American demands for British troops, to raise his own profile, and to mollify Labour MPs who were hostile to US involvement in Vietnam. Johnson could not openly block the peace efforts, which played into Wilson's hands, and difficulties in the Commonwealth help to explain why Wilson preferred to work through that organization when he was able. Some Commonwealth countries were outspoken in their opposition to US policy, while Australia and New Zealand both had troops in Vietnam. It seemed that the Commonwealth might fall apart. Peace offered a unifying cause. Moreover, Wilson could use Vietnam to divert attention away from another divisive Commonwealth issue, Rhodesia, and to show the Commonwealth that Britain could act independently of the United States. Wilson also thought that peacemaking was a matter on which it was difficult for his opponents, Conservative and Labour, to attack him.[71]

Vietnam brought nothing but trouble for Wilson. He offended the Americans. At home he continued to resist pressure from the Labour left and refused publicly to oppose US policy, even though this did not improve his standing in Washington DC. There were times when the conduct of Labour MPs was acutely embarrassing, and outside parliament the government had to contend with popular protests and the Vietnam Solidarity Campaign. After inconclusive talks with Soviet premier Aleksei Kosygin, who visited London in February 1967, Wilson had to face facts. He stopped pushing for peace plans. In fact he lost confidence across the board at the end of the 1960s, weighed down with political problems at home as well as abroad.[72]

Wilson alienated sections of the Labour Party and the British media and public opinion, and damaged Britain's relations with the Commonwealth and Western Europe. De Gaulle's argument that Britain was still too close to America was reinforced. In view of all these disadvantages, the prime minister might have hoped for more sympathy from the US government. Wilson and his colleagues resented the lack of prior warning whenever America made a new move in Vietnam, for this made it harder for them to deal with the fallout in parliament and the press.[73]

The collapse of the peace effort of late 1966 and early 1967 came as a huge disappointment to Wilson and George Brown. During the talks in London in February 1967 it became clear that Washington DC had already been in touch with the Soviets through other intermediaries. Then Kosygin and Soviet foreign minister Andrei Gromyko were surprised when Brown had to tell them that the Americans had changed their minds. The Soviets concluded that the British government did not have American confidence. Wilson had been too anxious for a deal and had failed to check everything out with Washington DC. The US government was itself divided, with hawks and doves struggling to control policy. There was no consistent line, which meant that the British were constantly picking up mixed signals. The process was also hindered by the Soviets, who had less influence than they claimed over North Vietnam.[74]

Although the Americans were irritated by Wilson's actions on Vietnam, they valued Britain's contribution to security arrangements in those parts of the world where the British had traditionally been strong, especially the Indian Ocean and Persian Gulf, and they were even willing to cover some of the costs of Britain's global role. They reacted badly to indications from London that the East of Suez presence might have to be abandoned and they hoped that Wilson would be able to avert the devaluation of sterling. It is possible that Wilson agreed to support US policy on Vietnam and to postpone devaluation in return for American loans. Indeed, for many people in Britain, and especially the Labour left, the prime minister went too far in doing what the Americans wanted. Some Conservative MPs also began to take up this argument, complaining that the government had made Britain subservient, although the leader of the opposition from August 1965, Edward Heath, claimed that Wilson was not backing the Americans strongly enough. As prime minister from 1970, Heath supported US policy on Vietnam because he thought that if the American withdrawal looked like surrender it would encourage the Soviets to destabilize Europe.[75] The devaluation of sterling in November 1967 and confirmation of the withdrawal from East of Suez in January 1968 left the Johnson administration deeply disappointed, as Wilson found when he arrived for meetings in Washington DC in February 1968.[76]

Wilson always maintained that he was not supporting US policy on Vietnam in return for American financial help, yet he did admit that Britain could not do without American money. This created an unfortunate predicament: the United States was helping Britain to meet its overseas commitments, but the reason that the British needed American assistance was the insupportable burden of the commitments that Washington DC wished Britain to maintain. When the withdrawal from East of Suez was announced, the Americans were indignant because they had assumed that this would not happen while they were involved in Vietnam.[77]

The decision to withdraw from East of Suez was taken by Washington DC as a further sign of British unwillingness to police the Far East. Johnson pressed Wilson to reverse the decision, but he was coming to realize that the USA's own role in the Far East needed to be reassessed, and during 1968 there were clear indications that the Americans wished to leave Vietnam. Johnson did not seek re-election in 1968, largely because of Vietnam. In London there was relief but also fear, because a scaling down of US commitments in Asia might lead to a scaling down in Europe, and because Britain could not easily appeal to the Americans to remain in Europe after having refused to help militarily in Vietnam.[78]

Anglo-American defence talks continued, and there was diplomatic co-operation during the Arab–Israeli War of July 1967 and Czech crisis of August 1968, but the ill feeling prompted by disagreements on Vietnam and East of Suez did not quickly fade away. Nevertheless, cultivating the 'special relationship' remained one of Britain's primary tasks, even if its value to Britain came increasingly to be questioned. Britain still had the capacity to act independently in the world in a small way, but on the most vital issues of the day American policy was a determinant of Britain's policy. The Commonwealth was not proving to be the economic and political asset that had been hoped for. During international crises in Congo, Cuba and Vietnam the British were not without influence, but could not expect to get their own way, and the Cold War in Europe meant that there was danger close to home as well as in far-off places. In each of the 'three circles', Britain had to adapt to a sizeable loss of control, opportunity, prestige and status. The Anglo-American 'circle' operated relatively well, but remained problematic. The importance to Britain of engagement with the empire-Commonwealth 'circle' was decreasing. In the European 'circle' there were difficulties relating to East–West rivalry and Britain's exclusion from the EEC.

8

Asia, the Middle East, Europe: No Respite (II)

The world changed so quickly in the 1960s that Britain did not find it easy to respond in a way that preserved influence. Problems with the Commonwealth, economic concerns at home, and a search for ways to strengthen NATO and enhance the national defences added to the uncertainty about how to handle Britain's commitments in the Middle East and Far East. Britain's relations with Europe were much debated as membership of the EEC, diplomatic initiatives from Paris and Bonn, and a Cold War crisis in Czechoslovakia demanded clarity and decisiveness. Trouble grew outside Europe, especially as Arab–Israeli rivalry became ever more intense.

Britain's influence in Washington DC decreased because of quarrels over Vietnam, the scaling down of Britain's overseas activity, and the continuing weakness of the British economy. Maintaining the global role had less appeal when it seemed that the effort would make little difference in Britain's dealings with the Americans. Britain's focus had been shifting towards NATO and Europe for some time. Indeed, the British had been trying to strengthen NATO when the French decided in 1966 to pull out of its military arrangements. Defence secretary Denis Healey sought to revive NATO in 1967, and helped to persuade the NATO council to adopt the strategy of 'flexible response', which provided for each member of the alliance to decide on the type of forces it would contribute. Healey's wish for a clearer European defence identity was reinforced when the Americans failed to consult NATO about the Strategic Arms Limitation Talks (SALT), which began in Helsinki in November 1969. One consequence was the formation of the 'Eurogroup' within NATO.[1]

The Wilson government's reluctance to send forces to Vietnam was related to divisions in the Commonwealth. Among Commonwealth members only Australia and New Zealand sent troops. Other members condemned US policy. Australia welcomed American involvement in Asia and the Pacific, while Britain, committed to decolonization and turning more towards Europe, gave less attention to issues that Australia considered vital. The confrontation between Indonesia and Malaysia led to disagreements within the Commonwealth about how to handle Indonesian leader Sukarno.[2]

The idea that the Commonwealth could be made into more of an asset proved to be unrealistic. Some former colonies were not economically viable and needed subsidies – notably Gambia from 1965. Controversy developed over Gibraltar, whose inhabitants wished it to remain a British dependency while the UN and Spain pressed for a change. In September 1965 the Kashmir dispute between India and Pakistan led to war. Peace talks were arranged in January 1966 by the Soviets, not by Britain. The unilateral declaration of independence (UDI) by white political leaders in Rhodesia, who intended to deny the black majority equal rights, placed the British government in an awkward position. The Commonwealth demanded military intervention, as did the Labour left, but Wilson opted for economic sanctions in the hope that the illegal Rhodesian regime would agree to a new constitutional settlement. Sanctions were evaded. Negotiations failed in 1966 and again in 1968. Another controversy related to arms sales to South Africa. Apartheid continued to provoke the bitter hostility of Commonwealth members and Wilson's government decided to cancel the relevant contracts, but this decision was attacked by the Conservative leader Edward Heath, who also criticized the policy on Rhodesia. Ministers were also condemned when Britain provided support for the Nigerian government during the Biafran war of 1967 to 1970.[3]

The Americans continued to encourage decolonization, but respected Britain's wish to move slowly and avoid conflict. Unfortunately, British moderation made leaders of the white minority in Rhodesia think that London lacked the resolve to prevent them from setting up the kind of government that they wanted.[4]

The changing nature of the Commonwealth prompted questions about the value of the link with former colonies. There were objections to aid for Gambia. Official British aid rose in the mid-1960s, but Britain's exports to Gambia did not show a marked increase. Some important contracts for British companies were announced in the spring of 1968, but these were financed from the British aid.[5] On Gibraltar the government had to steer a middle course between upholding British rights and making conciliatory gestures, as foreign secretary George Brown indicated in the Commons in October 1966.[6] The war over Kashmir led to complaints that the government had not done more to prevent it. In December 1965 the secretary of state for Commonwealth relations, Arthur Bottomley, told MPs that the government was helping the UN to broker a ceasefire and had decided not to act through the Commonwealth for fear of cutting across the UN's efforts. Bottomley welcomed Soviet mediation, but on 25 January 1966, when he was asked why Britain was not taking the lead, he merely repeated that the government would work with others.[7]

Summing up the Rhodesian situation in May 1969, foreign secretary Michael Stewart insisted that 'if the door is now being slammed it is not by us, but by the regime'. Britain had made fair proposals, Stewart said, involving concessions that many in the Commonwealth disliked, but alongside the flexibility there had been adherence to the fundamental requirement: 'unimpeded progress within a reasonable time towards majority rule'. Opponents of sanctions claimed that government policy was harming Britain, pointed out that other countries were not observing the sanctions, and suggested that coercive means were unlikely to bring about a settlement.[8]

On the arms sales to South Africa, the government was condemned both by those who thought that its policy was not stringent enough, and by those who opposed the embargo and claimed that it was damaging British trade. In some quarters it was argued that Britain should have pressed for a mandatory embargo at the UN, though the foreign office view was that no case existed for so extreme a measure. The notion that Britain's overall trade with South Africa had declined as a result of the refusal to supply weapons was denied in July 1969 by the parliamentary secretary to the board of trade, Gwyneth Dunwoody.[9]

When civil war broke out in Nigeria, the Labour government declared itself for non-intervention, yet supplied weapons to the federal government of Nigeria. A humanitarian crisis in Biafra increased the furore over Britain's position. In October 1968 Wilson rejected the claim that Britain had lost moral authority. He regretted that some countries had recognized Biafra as an independent state and supplied it with arms, and defended Britain's 'traditional role' as a supplier of arms to the federal government of Nigeria. 'I cannot accept the doctrine of neutrality in this matter', he went on, 'because here we have a Commonwealth country facing a secessionist revolt.'[10]

Britain's difficulties in these years were to some extent attributable to errors in policy. Some members of the government thought that the prime minister was chiefly to blame. On Kashmir, Wilson made a personal plea for the avoidance of war but India invaded anyway. Wilson's condemnation of Indian aggression meant that Britain could not broker a peace. On Rhodesia, thought Richard Crossman, Wilson acted as if it was 'his Cuba' – a test of his statesmanship. The prime minister did try to prevent UDI, but failed to put together a plan for dealing with it in case it happened.[11] Wilson ruled out military action in Rhodesia. He was worried about party unity and the government's position in parliament, and impressed by opinion polls that indicated a very low level of approval for the use of force against the white Rhodesian regime. Members of the Commonwealth stepped up their denunciation of British policy and Wilson could do little more than buy time by insisting that sanctions would eventually have an impact.[12] As for arms sales to South Africa, George Brown argued that the contracts were in keeping with the Simonstown agreement of June 1955 (under which Britain transferred control of the Simonstown naval base and the South African navy to the government of South Africa, in return for which the Royal Navy could continue to use the base). Britain had to help South Africa to perform those tasks in the region that had formerly been Britain's, Brown contended, and Britain also needed the export revenue. Wilson accepted these arguments but then succumbed to pressure from the Labour Party and suggested that the arms sales should be stopped. This was one of the reasons that Brown resigned as foreign secretary.[13]

Britain's relations with South Africa had long been complicated by arguments over apartheid, attitudes in the Commonwealth, and British party politics. Labour was solidly against apartheid and when in opposition had committed itself to end the arms sales. When Labour took office, Brown and Healey wanted a rethink. This issue, and the devaluation of sterling in November 1967, brought on a cabinet split. Devaluation damaged Wilson, since he had fought hard against it, and some ministers took advantage by recommending the resumption of arms sales to South Africa. Wilson was wary of antagonizing the Labour left and the Commonwealth, however, and the policy on arms sales remained unchanged.[14]

If a difficult balancing act was required with respect to South Africa, the same was true of Nigeria. Britain was the former colonial power, had set up the federal system, and wanted Nigeria and other former possessions in Africa to be stable. Wilson hoped to increase trade with and investment in the country. The decision to supply weapons to Nigeria prompted popular protests. Newspapers, churches, Labour MPs and some Conservatives joined in. Wilson promised to change government policy if it became clear that by doing so he could bring closer a peace settlement.[15] Crossman wrote in his diary on 5 December 1968 that attacks on the government were unfair, because serious efforts *were* being made to end the war. It was not clear what else Britain could do. The USSR was sending weapons to the Nigerians, the French were arming the Biafrans, and meanwhile the British public was demanding that food and medical aid should be provided for Biafra. Above all, what was needed was a joint Anglo-French-Soviet agreement that no more weapons would be supplied. Crossman thought that Britain should set an example and stop arms sales in the hope that others would follow suit. Wilson, however, would not risk offending Nigeria's leaders.[16]

In later years Wilson asserted that his foreign policy had been consistent and successful, but he was more equivocal than he liked to admit. Though he hated apartheid and opposed arms sales to South Africa, for example, he also needed a solution to the Rhodesian crisis and decided that the best way to pressurize Rhodesia's white leadership was through South Africa. Therefore he wanted to conciliate the regime in Pretoria. A complicating factor with respect to Nigeria was oil. The war in the Middle East in June 1967 created the need for an alternative source. Nigeria had oil, but the civil war disrupted the supply. Wilson also had to contend with quarrels in his party, for many Labour MPs sympathized with the separatists as victims of an oppressive federal government.[17]

In the background, continually, was concern about Britain's loss of influence and status. For those companies that had a stake in both Rhodesia and Britain, UDI was unwelcome and dangerous. For the Conservative right, meanwhile, decolonization was regrettable and white rights in Africa had to be respected. UDI in Rhodesia and the war in Nigeria were especially challenging for Britain because they directly affected what had long been regarded as British spheres of influence.[18] There were frequent reassessments of the value of the Commonwealth to Britain. The approach was a little disjointed. Although the government was disillusioned with it, ministers never thought of breaking up or abandoning the Commonwealth and stood firm against threatened departures from it.[19]

This was a period in which Britain's economic problems made for a more acute awareness that the global role could not be paid for. If the gradual withdrawal from overseas commitments saved money, however, it also weakened Britain's influence, especially over the US government.[20] American leaders tried to argue Wilson's government out of a full withdrawal. They feared that they would be obliged to fill the vacuum, and indeed, it would not be long before the United States was intervening in the India–Pakistan war of 1971 and arming Iran as a regional policeman. Nevertheless, it would be wrong to suggest that Britain had lost all influence in sensitive parts of the world. In the Middle East, for example, relatively good Anglo-Jordanian relations persisted into the 1970s.

As Britain faltered, the FRG took advantage of its growing importance to the Americans. West Germany became the strongest European member of NATO, with larger armed forces than Britain. The FRG also had a leadership role in the EEC. By the end of the 1970s Britain's gross domestic product would be only half that of the FRG.[21] The rise of the FRG would have been less alarming had the British economy been stronger, for economic success was an obvious contributor to political weight, diplomatic influence and military power. The Wilson government inherited a large trade deficit in 1964 and had only a small majority in the Commons, which ruled out drastic measures, including manipulation of the exchange rate. The general election in the spring of 1966 gave the government a bigger majority. Instead of promptly devaluing the pound in order to facilitate economic recovery, however, the government delayed until late 1967.[22]

The overvaluation of sterling had become more perceptible as the balance-of-payments deficit continued to defy remedial efforts, but even when the pound was finally devalued the balance-of-payments situation was not improved for long. The collapse of the Bretton Woods system in 1971 led to freely moving exchange rates (in 1944, Bretton Woods had fixed these to the US dollar). Sterling was floated in June 1972, which effectively put an end to the sterling area. The value of the pound against the dollar continued to fall, and its fall against the Japanese yen and West German Deutschmark was even more pronounced. Britain's trade was affected and government adviser Alec Cairncross noted tensions in policy making and was sceptical about the planning for faster growth.[23]

As the world economy expanded after the Second World War, Britain's share of total trade decreased. The key problem for Britain was the balance of payments, and it proved to be very difficult to make British goods and services more competitive.[24] According to Cairncross, Britain's relatively poor economic performance was largely attributable to the resurgence of West Germany and Japan and to Britain's decision to stay out of European integration. Less important, though some contemporaries did not think so, was the high level of defence spending.[25] To the extent that some problems could be mitigated by state action, the Labour government did have choices. It is widely thought that it made the wrong choices. Even so, the government did not have complete freedom of manoeuvre. Domestic and international conditions saw to that.

The devaluation of 1949 was important because sterling was central to world trade at that time. In 1949 there was no trade deficit and devaluation was designed to remove a wartime control, assist with economic planning, earn more dollars and redirect exports. In 1967 there was a trade deficit and the goal was to restore Britain's competitive position. The exchange rate was intimately bound up with British prestige, but a stringent policy of deflation was not politically advisable or likely to provide much relief, for the basic problem was the lack of competitiveness abroad at the existing exchange rate. Therefore deflationary measures could only have a temporary impact, whereas devaluation was thought to promise more, particularly if accompanied by international financial assistance. Fortunately, foreign governments agreed not to alter their own economic policies in response to devaluation.[26]

Compromises had to be made regarding military strength and the global role. Wilson and his colleagues saw that government spending was too high, especially abroad. Defence took one-third of a total outlay that was still growing. Expenditure overseas had gone up from £50 million in 1952 to £400 million in 1964. To cut this spending was an urgent task. Efforts were made, which angered other NATO members, especially the FRG, whose government complained whenever it seemed likely that troops would be withdrawn from the BAOR. At the end of the 1960s the need to send troops to Northern Ireland added yet another burden. As Macmillan had done, Wilson hoped that by relying on nuclear forces, Britain could be defended in a more cost-effective way. Although the Labour manifesto of 1964 had condemned the Nassau Agreement, Wilson had decided that the purchase of Polaris missiles should go ahead.[27] In October 1964 Wilson met with the new foreign and defence secretaries, Patrick Gordon Walker and Denis Healey, to examine the Polaris question 'in the light of the information now available to us'. The result was that the leaders of the Labour Party not only accepted Polaris but went on to make it the mainstay of Britain's defences. They misled the cabinet when they said that the Polaris programme was past the point of no return.[28]

The government tried to put off retreats for as long as possible. Arguments in favour of devaluation were continually resisted, precisely because Wilson and his closest colleagues believed in the world role and regarded devaluation as a sign of weakness. The prime minister also dismissed claims that he should not have been so attached to the nuclear deterrent, although in order to mollify Labour's left-wingers he openly eschewed the Conservatives' rhetoric about an *independent* deterrent. On the British presence East of Suez, most ministers accepted that Britain had a responsibility to remain, which accorded with the preference for a world role rather than just a European one.[29]

The government's aims and professions were to be sorely tested as the resource gap widened and as trade and consumption turned Britain away from Africa and Asia.[30] Decolonization was part of the retreat from the global role. Means and opportunities that might previously have been available were gone by the 1960s, when Britain ceased to be an imperial state. Outside Europe, Britain was no longer able to use military protection and economic aid to retain influence, even in former colonies.[31]

There was a growing sense that excessive defence spending was harming the British economy, yet the governments of the 1960s did not bring about a real reduction. All they could do was slow down the increase. The British continued to spend more on defence, as a share of the national wealth, than all their main allies and economic competitors except the United States. These other countries did not feel the need to spend so much on defence. They were able to specialize in their military commitments. They did not have to protect widespread global interests. They did not require a capacity for long-range intervention. Britain's retrenchment efforts in the 1950s and 1960s were prompted by the belief that high defence expenditure would hinder economic growth, but there was little specific knowledge about this, and it is not possible to assess the effects of the world role by looking only at the direct economic impact of high military expenditure.[32]

Rather like Sandys had done in the late 1950s, Labour's defence secretary, Healey, tried to find a way in which Britain could remain a great power while bringing down the cost. The government's position was clarified in the Statement on the Defence Estimates of February 1965, which pointed to the problem of overstretch and looked forward to a defence policy that was affordable and in keeping with Britain's political and strategic objectives.[33]

Wilson and other senior Labour figures were still committed to the world role, however, and it was a long time before they reconciled themselves to the abandonment of responsibilities East of Suez. One of the reasons for this was the importance they attached to the 'special relationship' with the United States. Patrick Gordon Walker was particularly insistent on the need to remain useful to the United States. The Americans, meanwhile, though they were aware of Britain's resource problems, objected whenever there was any talk of withdrawal from East of Suez. In 1965 the British secured financial assistance from the United States on the understanding that there would be no devaluation of sterling and no British withdrawal from East of Suez.[34]

The general election of March 1966 returned many new Labour MPs to the Commons, and they demanded savings, while scepticism about British interests East of Suez was also prevalent in the Europhile lobby led by the home secretary, Roy Jenkins. In the summer of 1966 there was a sterling crisis and the government, preferring not to devalue, had to reduce spending, raise taxes and freeze wages. Labour's popularity plummeted. Healey accepted that defence spending was too high, but doubted that commitments could be greatly reduced.[35] He was sure in 1966 that Britain could and should remain East of Suez in some form. The government line was still that Britain would definitely stay.[36]

In February 1967 the chancellor of the exchequer, James Callaghan, took up an American proposal that Britain should apply for a large international loan in order to cover exiting debts and end the 'inhibiting' concerns about sterling. The Johnson administration attached 'political conditions' to the deal, however, insisting that Britain must remain East of Suez. The British government could not accept this. To Callaghan, 'it was not sensible to maintain a worldwide influence on borrowed money'. The question of EEC membership had also to be resolved. Any attempt to carry on a global role would undermine the government's claim to be committed to Europe. Healey was obliged to accept that the withdrawal might be quicker and more substantial than he had envisaged.[37] This led to the supplementary statement on defence policy of July 1967 and Wilson's remark that 'in the last resort, the strength of a nation's resources can never be greater than the strength of its economic base'.[38]

Reports from Washington DC suggested that although American leaders were unhappy about the prospect of a British withdrawal from East of Suez, they thought that this withdrawal need not be complete, that the British base at Singapore might be retained, and that the defence statement of July 1967 'left the door open to persuasion'. Labour left-wingers had other ideas. They pressed Healey to speed up the withdrawal. Conservative defence spokesman Enoch Powell ridiculed the government for offering no intelligible picture of Britain's future defence posture: 'It is to be simply the death by a thousand cuts.' *The Times* distinguished between the Middle East and the Far East. Withdrawal from the former would be inadvisable, in view of the instability there. Withdrawal from the Far East might be easier, but would still need careful consideration.[39]

According to the supplementary statement of July 1967, it was not needful for British forces to remain East of Suez in large numbers. Instead, Britain would help its allies in the Middle East and Far East to do more for their own security and prosperity. The bases in Singapore and Malaysia would be abandoned and the total number of personnel in the armed forces reduced. Decisions about the Persian Gulf were less clear, and the possibility that British forces might have to return to the Far East in an emergency was recognized. The chiefs of staff were comforted by this, and by the realization that a future Conservative government might reverse Labour's decisions. Another financial crisis in November 1967, however, plunged Wilson and his colleagues into even deeper political trouble. Some ministers objected, but Wilson and Jenkins, who was now chancellor of the exchequer, prevailed and early in 1968 the government confirmed that there would be a complete withdrawal from East of Suez by 1971.[40] Jenkins, relatively untainted by devaluation and the confused defence policy, was in a much stronger position than before and took advantage of this to press for an end to the global role and an attempt to join the EEC. With Wilson concerned above all for the survival of his government, Jenkins was able to determine the priorities for further cuts in spending. Brown and Healey tried to resist but it was too late.[41]

January 1968 marks an important turning point. The government was admitting that Britain's status and role in the world had changed. Though savings did result, Britain continued to spend more on defence than did the countries of Western Europe, and in economic performance the British could not match their main competitors. The targets set in 1968 were not met. Some commentators believe that a clear opportunity existed for a radical restructuring of defence and that the government was wrong not to take it. Most of the forces withdrawn from East of Suez were given roles in NATO. Reorganization did not go further, in part because of the influence of military and industrial interests and the entrenched attitude among Britain's political leaders that Britain could remain a great power.[42]

The East of Suez decision was not purely about economics. It was also determined by political and strategic considerations, many of which had not been effectively addressed by the government's Conservative predecessors. External events played their part as well. The end of the confrontation between Indonesia and Malaysia, for instance, affected British thinking about Singapore. The withdrawal policy did not mean that all of Britain's responsibilities were suddenly given up, for Britain still had the ability to act in many parts of the world.[43] Wilson confirmed that British forces would leave the Far East and Persian Gulf by the end of 1971 in his statement to the Commons of 18 January 1968. On 25 January Healey stated that British forces could still operate outside Europe if necessary, but that national defence would now have a European emphasis.[44]

Relative economic decline cannot entirely explain the withdrawal from East of Suez, for British leaders had been aware of the decline for years and it did not stop them from thinking of Britain as a global power. Short-term political and domestic causes were therefore of special importance. The shift in Wilson's cabinet and the influence of the pro-European Jenkins had a direct bearing on what happened, as did the financial crises of the period. Many Labour backbenchers were sceptical about the global role, moreover, and ministers grew worried about revolts on various issues, and for Wilson there was the added desire to remain as premier and nullify rival claimants to this office. In addition, in the Conservative Party, in the press and in the country generally, doubts had arisen about the global presence, in part a legacy of Suez.[45]

The government was never quite in control of the process of withdrawal. Rather, it was at the mercy of events and the merging of economic and strategic problems proved too much for it. In fairness, it should be remembered that these problems were to some extent inherited and that no government could insulate itself against external developments. The British had been adapting their role in the world for decades. Until 1957, the tendency was to treat South East Asia as a discrete unit. The same was true of the Middle East. There was no uniform approach to some larger entity called 'East of Suez'. This changed as a result of the Suez crisis. Different units were brought together, which probably made it easier to justify general withdrawal in the late 1960s, although with regard to the Persian Gulf the opposition to withdrawal was considerable (Gulf states met almost half of Britain's energy needs and had been promised British protection). The Wilson government, however, had financial worries, and Arab animosity towards Britain also influenced its deliberations, as did a ministerial bargain, whereby limits on social spending would be accompanied by cuts in defence.[46]

The East of Suez decision did not go down well abroad. There were complaints from the Commonwealth. Australia was especially angry, and Singapore threatened to withdraw its sterling balances from London. Some of Britain's oil-rich allies in the Persian Gulf offered money to help the British to remain. The Americans told Wilson in January 1968 that if Britain did pull back, the United States would no longer regard the British as reliable allies in any part of the world, including Europe.[47]

Wilson looked to Europe for an opportunity to regroup. He hoped that the retreat from the world role would make it easier for Britain to join the EEC, and wished to appease the pro-Europe members of the cabinet. Since the Americans wanted Britain to join the EEC, moreover, he thought he could find a way of compensating them for the East of Suez decision.[48] Yet Wilson was less enthusiastic about European unity than the Conservative leader, Edward Heath, who saw economic integration as the beginning of a process by which Western Europe could make itself a centre of power linked to America but also more independent of America. Wilson seemed not to care much for this process. Nor was the prime minister completely sure that membership of the EEC would strengthen the British economy and restore Britain's influence, though Labour's Euro-sceptics proposed no alternative method of achieving these ends.[49]

Wilson had previously declared that he would only consider entry if the terms were right. After taking office in 1964, however, he recognized that Britain was growing weaker in relation to other powers. He relaxed his demands in order for the EEC to admit Britain, although, as he stressed in March 1966, there could be no 'unconditional acceptance of whatever terms we are offered'. Despite clear signs that French objections to British membership had not been assuaged since de Gaulle's veto of January 1963, the government's eagerness to make its bid increased, only for de Gaulle to declare on 16 May 1967 that Britain was still not ready to join the EEC.[50]

The *Economist* deplored the French leader's 'threadbare ratiocination' and put his conduct down to 'an old man's conservative objections to any disturbance of things as they are'. *The Times* looked forward to the day when de Gaulle was no longer president of France, and hoped in the meantime that the British government could satisfy the other members of the EEC that Britain's adherence to the common market would be mutually advantageous. As for Wilson, he did not accept de Gaulle's announcement as a final answer. He thought that persistence would pay off. In fact, de Gaulle confirmed the veto of Britain's second EEC application on 27 November 1967.[51]

The Wilson government's EEC bid owed something to Cold War calculations. Washington DC continually pressed for greater European unity, to counter the Soviets, and in London it was agreed that co-operation would bring added strength. Moreover, as the EEC had prospered since the late 1950s, the British were conscious of being left out. Britain lacked the will, allies and ability to break the EEC up, and the only choice seemed to be to influence it from within. This was the view of George Brown, Britain's foreign secretary from August 1966 to March 1968, who, like Wilson, decided that EEC membership could help Britain to remain a great power. That they knew what de Gaulle thought, but went ahead anyway, probably shows how desperate they had become as the Commonwealth waned, as Britain's position East of Suez was effectively given up, as the British economy continued to under-perform, and as Britain's importance to the United States declined.[52]

Wilson's government was similar to Macmillan's in that there was no conversion to the ideals behind the EEC or to some 'European vision' (by which many continental politicians claimed to be guided). Labour's bid was a pragmatic affair, and it was presented as such to the British people. National identity was not to be undermined. Nor were the 'special relationship' with America and the pledges to NATO. Though Wilson realized that French opposition would not be easy to break down, he hoped for help from those in the EEC who wanted Britain to be admitted. In the event these other members were swayed by de Gaulle's opinion that Britain's economic weakness was a barrier to membership.[53]

If Britain's second EEC bid was largely motivated by economic concerns, political goals were important too. Indeed, there was a suspicion that membership of the EEC would have some detrimental economic effects. These economic costs were considered by Wilson to be worth paying in order for Britain to preserve an international role. With the Commonwealth divided and the Americans unwilling to treat Britain as an equal, new ways to exercise influence had to be found. Economic determinants, while not unimportant, might have been less important than political motives, since the economic benefits of membership of the EEC could only be guessed at, while the fact that Britain's position East of Suez was being reassessed probably reinforced the political arguments for the EEC bid.[54]

Despite all this, Wilson's approach was cautious and his commitment to the EEC bid was temporary rather than permanent. Britain's application remained active, which gave Wilson the flexibility he wanted. If circumstances changed and it no longer seemed appropriate for Britain to join the EEC, he could withdraw the application. Wilson was also pleased because the bid had been politically useful. Labour's pro-European section was grateful that the attempt had been made; those in the government and party who had opposed the application were satisfied, since they had been vindicated; and the Conservatives could no longer claim that they alone had the desire and ability to forge a closer relationship with Europe. When de Gaulle resigned in 1969, Wilson remained cautious because opinion within the government, the Labour Party and the trade unions had become less favourable towards the EEC and a general election was approaching.[55]

De Gaulle's ongoing aversion to British membership of the EEC reflected his wider agenda and his taste for active diplomacy, and affected not only Britain's status but also the course of the Cold War. The French president was pursuing a thaw with the Soviets. From 1960 he started to withdraw French units from NATO exercises, and in March 1966 he took France out of the integrated military command. Determined to end what he regarded as Western Europe's dependency on the United States, and convinced that the USSR wanted to bargain, de Gaulle offended London and Washington DC in equal measure.[56] The damage he was doing to NATO was particularly irresponsible, claimed the British, for it jeopardized the safety of all, but de Gaulle was intent on forcing a reorganization of NATO and moving international affairs away from a bipolar basis.[57]

Responding to the French withdrawal from NATO's military command, Britain's foreign secretary Michael Stewart told the Commons that NATO would remain 'an effective and credible military organization' and that its members were determined to resolve matters related to European security, a German settlement and East–West relations. *The Times* suggested that even if de Gaulle had reason to complain about American domination of NATO, his behaviour was intolerable. He was damaging the alliance psychologically, undermining unity and discouraging individual members of NATO. Still, the alliance – unlike the EEC – could survive without France. In the EEC, concessions always had to be made to the French, but de Gaulle would find that he could not bully NATO.[58]

Britain helped to keep NATO together and the bid to join the EEC had an impact, improving Britain's standing in Europe. Wilson's government was keen to act boldly in NATO, in order to prove to the Americans that Britain was still important. One result was an increase in tension between London and Moscow.[59]

Discussion of nuclear issues continued. Wilson's government was no more sympathetic to the MLF than its Conservative predecessors had been, but the Americans persisted because they wanted to lower the status of the British deterrent and merge Britain's nuclear forces with others in a body that would be under US control. The British government sought to wreck the MLF plan by proposing an alternative, the ANF, or Atlantic Nuclear Force, which would consist of Britain's nuclear submarines, an equivalent number of US submarines, and a small mix-manned element, loosely assigned to NATO. The Americans were unenthusiastic and the proposal was not developed.[60]

Nuclear weapons and East–West relations continued to provoke heated debate in Europe, particularly in West Germany. To some extent de Gaulle's independent line and anti-Americanism suited the FRG. West German leaders opposed the Vietnam War and resented the way in which US policy seemed to be based on an acceptance of the division of Germany. They also wanted more say in NATO's nuclear strategy.[61]

During the entire life of the MLF plan, nobody in Britain or Western Europe had anything like the same liking for it as officials in Washington DC. To the latter, multilateralism offered a way forward in US–European relations and in discussions about the future of NATO. The British wished to devote resources to their Polaris fleet, not to the MLF, and could not afford to do both. Meanwhile, discussions about nuclear co-operation between France and the FRG did not get very far either.[62]

If American leaders disapproved of de Gaulle's efforts to deal with the Soviets, they were similarly uncomfortable about West Germany's self-assertion. In May 1967, for instance, the FRG agreed to pay more towards the cost of maintaining US and British troops on NATO's front line, which removed the leverage associated with the threat to withdraw them on financial grounds. The FRG also improved relations with the eastern bloc in May 1969 by abandoning the Hallstein Doctrine. Willy Brandt became chancellor of the FRG in October 1969 and energetically pursued a thaw with his 'Ostpolitik'. White House national security adviser and future US secretary of state, Henry Kissinger, warned that closer ties between the FRG and the eastern bloc would only strengthen the Soviets and their allies.[63]

The situation in Europe continued to be complicated by events in Vietnam. In France and the FRG, opposition to American policy in Vietnam reinforced the desire to act independently of the USA, as Moscow was quick to notice.[64] De Gaulle's goal for Europe was independence from America and leadership from

Paris. British membership of the EEC had no place in this scenario. The FRG chose France over Britain without much hesitation, but could de Gaulle persuade Bonn to choose France over the United States? This proved to be a step too far. De Gaulle tried to control Bonn through his dealings with the USSR and its satellites.[65] The 'Ostpolitik' frustrated him. 'Ostpolitik' developed around the idea that German reunification was not an end in itself, but had to be part of a general thaw that would overcome the Cold War division of Europe. Policy adjustments began before Brandt became chancellor, and he was able in due course to extend them. He favoured British membership of the EEC because he preferred economic union to political integration and feared that the latter would get in the way of 'Ostpolitik'. Bonn's willingness to recognize the GDR and renounce territorial claims in Eastern Europe made the FRG stronger in international affairs, while the Soviet Union co-operated primarily in order to obtain economic benefits.[66]

International circumstances facilitated thaw in Europe. The Soviets were looking to ease tensions in Europe because they were worried about China, and the Americans hoped to gain Soviet help in ending the war in Vietnam. As 'Ostpolitik' evolved, aided by and related to East–West détente in general, the two superpowers sought to influence the actions of their respective allies. The idea that détente ought to be given a try had been gaining ground in the Kremlin: it would better enable the USSR to take advantage of the Vietnam War and exploit quarrels within NATO, and more trade with Western Europe would boost the Soviet economy and provide opportunities to weaken Western Europe's dependence upon the United States. Though the Soviets responded favourably to de Gaulle's overtures, French friendship never mattered more to them than their wish to improve relations with the USA and FRG.[67]

Most Western leaders still wanted a more robust and unified NATO. A review of NATO strategy was completed in January 1967 and brought about the consolidation of 'flexible response', extending the principle of 'differentiated responses' not only between nuclear and conventional but also between different forms of nuclear action. The wish to keep options open, however, made for ambiguity. More specific guidelines were not issued until November 1969. These covered the first and follow-on use of nuclear weapons, but not a full strategic assault (which was no longer seen as occurring at the beginning of a war).[68]

To sections of the British press, NATO strategy was flawed and the balance of conventional and nuclear forces unsatisfactory. The USSR's continuing superiority in conventional forces, and defence secretary Denis Healey's view that NATO should have sufficient conventional forces to guard its frontiers, led *The Times* to argue that the conventional alternative to nuclear weapons had to be properly maintained.[69]

When Richard Nixon succeeded Johnson as president of the United States early in 1969, one of his first steps was to revive NATO. Kissinger had advised him that a constructive relationship with Western Europe would be facilitated if he reaffirmed the USA's commitment to NATO and expressed support for European unity. In the effort to strengthen NATO, Nixon and Kissinger enlisted the backing of Britain and the FRG. The Americans also tried to woo de Gaulle, and not only for NATO purposes: like his predecessors as president, Nixon was keen for Britain to join the EEC, and if de Gaulle became more flexible, it was thought, he might be useful in other ways (in talks with China and North Vietnam, for example).[70] De Gaulle soon gave way to a new French president, Georges Pompidou. By the mid-1970s, de Gaulle's earlier realization that France lacked influence in Moscow was confirmed in French policy making, and Pompidou also tried briefly to befriend Britain as a counterweight to the FRG.[71]

London welcomed the prospect of a thaw in Europe. After talks with Brandt in March 1970, Wilson recorded that these discussions 'showed a total identity of views' on the EEC, European security and 'Ostpolitik'. The prime minister expressed support for Brandt's policy in the Commons and denied that EEC regulations would hinder Britain's trade with Eastern Europe, if and when Britain joined the common market. The *Guardian* praised Brandt for the 'feat of leadership' that was changing the two Germanys and the rest of Europe: he had been 'bold without being reckless or flashy', focusing on a few core goals and pursuing them relentlessly. *The Times* hailed Brandt for 'breaking out of the rigidities of the past twenty years'.[72]

Though Wilson had always spoken in favour of détente, as prime minister he did little to promote it and he had an exaggerated notion of his standing in Moscow. There were trade deals with the Soviets and various conferences, and a hotline between London and Moscow was established in October 1967 (after de Gaulle had one), but the Czech situation in 1968 damaged Anglo-Soviet relations and it was clear that underlying animosities remained. As for countries in the eastern bloc, Britain was slow to establish closer links with them. A beginning was made, though little was achieved before the general election of 1970, which Labour lost.[73]

De Gaulle's diplomacy and Brandt's 'Ostpolitik' added a new twist to international relations. These years also saw a dramatic increase in tension as a result of war in the Middle East and crisis in Czechoslovakia. Israel won the Six Day War of June 1967, defeating Egypt, Jordan and Syria. American and Soviet leaders arranged a ceasefire through the UN. Washington DC refused to provide weapons when these were requested by Israel. The war was so brief that the USSR was not able to re-supply the Arabs until the fighting stopped.[74]

In Britain there was fear about the economic consequences of another Arab–Israeli war, and debate in the cabinet about moving British warships into the region to put pressure on Israel. Before June 1967 London and Washington DC both warned the Israelis not to take unilateral action but to be patient and give diplomacy a chance. Wilson's sympathies were with Israel, as were those of other members of the cabinet and many Labour backbenchers. Brown was more favourable to the Arabs, but, like his colleagues, he did not want a war.[75]

As the crisis intensified in May 1967 intervention had considerable support in the cabinet, though Crossman and Healey pointed out that such action would alienate African and Asian representatives in the UN and might be seen as an attempt to re-establish control over the Middle East. Israel launched its offensive on 5 June and the British government opted for a policy of strict neutrality. Crossman was pleased that the non-interventionists had won: 'if we had not been neutral our oil would have been stopped and a large part of our sterling balances would have been withdrawn'. The chiefs of staff also opposed intervention, while Brown lamented the unfavourable international circumstances that restricted Britain's influence. The Six Day War demonstrated that the British no longer had a significant role in Arab–Israeli relations, despite their need for the region's oil and their dependence on the Suez Canal for trade and communications.[76]

Some Arab states suspended oil shipments and severed relations with Britain, but ministers called for a peace settlement that would not favour one side over the other. The essential requirements were the withdrawal from occupied territory, freedom of passage through international waters, and an agreement on the refugee question. When Conservative MPs condemned the government's policy as weak and apologetic, Brown taunted them with references to the Suez crisis. Outside parliament there were notable outbursts from prominent figures, including the historian Max Beloff, of All Souls' College, Oxford, who insisted that Britain should openly support Israel.[77]

The Arab–Israeli war of 1967 posed problems for the Americans. They had tried to prevent the war but were torn between the established policy of supporting Israel and the need to restrain Israel, and there were concerns about oil supplies, instability in the region, and the USSR's influence there. Israel doubted that the United States could really construct a peace settlement. The Arabs would not recognize Israel, after all, and the Americans could not make them do so. American policy was confused. Johnson was preoccupied with Vietnam, and while many of the president's friends and advisers were pro-Israel in sentiment, US ambassadors in the Middle East were urging the White House not to antagonize Egypt.[78]

Israel was not unwilling to fight in 1967, owing to Arab threats, acts of terrorism, and interference with Israeli shipping. Though the war might not have been intended or planned by any of the participants, none of them wanted to negotiate or compromise. The major powers and the UN were also to blame, perhaps, for they had had spent years trying to stabilize the region and they had signally failed to do so.[79]

Israel's rapid victory in 1967 impressed the *Observer*, which challenged Israel to turn its success into 'a political settlement to end the strife of decades'. In order to assist, the West had to accept that Moscow wanted to play a part in peace talks, that the Arabs would not make a deal while they were so much weaker than Israel militarily, and that Israel could not be expected to exist under a constant state of siege. The Arabs and Israelis both had to feel safe, argued the *Observer*, which made a new 'international peace-keeping system' the only solution. According to *The Times*, the Six Day War proved that Britain's status in the world had fallen. It was not clear how 'past assurances that Britain's presence in the Middle East would safeguard our oil supplies and other interests' could be reconciled with 'the fact that oil supplies are now curtailed, petrol prices threatened, and trade with Arab countries damaged'. Evidently, the future of the region would depend mainly on the Americans and the Soviets.[80]

After the war George Brown was largely responsible for a UN security council resolution of November 1967, which was designed to facilitate Arab recognition of the state of Israel. Brown's idea was that each side would give something up, but that this would be expressed in non-specific terms. According to the resolution, Israel was to withdraw from conquered territories and the Arabs and Israelis were to terminate 'all claims or states of belligerency'. One of the problems was that the word 'all' was not used in connection with the occupied areas from which Israel was going to withdraw, the implication being that the withdrawal would be less than complete.[81]

Defeat in the Six Day War was a blow to Nasser, but he recovered and Soviet president Nikolai Podgorny visited Cairo after the war, demonstrating the USSR's continuing support for Nasser's regime. Arms and equipment followed. The Israelis accepted the UN resolution of November 1967 because they expected to have security guarantees from the West. Nasser wanted to rearm and to unite the Arabs in order to negotiate from a position of strength, so he stalled. Clashes continued. In August 1970 the Nixon administration proposed a ceasefire. Israel agreed, as did Nasser, but still there was no peace settlement. Both sides prepared for another war, and the Americans were drawn further into the region's difficulties in the absence of any breakthrough at the UN.[82]

Britain remained involved in the Middle East, not least as an arms vendor. Wilson's government tried to impose a balance, so that neither the Arabs nor Israel gained special treatment, and to minimize the supply of offensive weaponry. When Israel placed an order for tanks in 1968 the government approved the deal in order to safeguard jobs and businesses, but the tanks were subsequently held back on foreign office advice. British peace efforts also caused trouble. 'Land for peace', upon which Brown's activity in the UN had been based, annoyed Israel and provoked quarrels within Wilson's cabinet. As time passed and a general election approached, the prime minister was reluctant to do anything that might cause a stir.[83]

The Soviets also became cautious. China condemned Moscow for encouraging the Arabs to fight and then abandoning them, but despite this Soviet
leaders decided against commitments that could possibly become expensive
and dangerous. The plan all along had been to restrict US influence in the
Middle East. The Soviets respected Nasser for his leadership of the Arab states,
but were less impressed by Anwar Sadat, who succeeded Nasser as president of
Egypt in 1970.[84]

The situation in the Middle East continued to disturb international affairs.
Instability and tension were also raised by the Czech crisis of 1968. A reform
movement had developed in Prague. Alexander Dubček rose to become leader
of the Czech Communist Party, and his was a more thorough programme than
the one the Hungarians had proposed twelve years earlier, though the Czechs did
not wish to pursue their own foreign policy as the Hungarians had. Believing that
Soviet control over the eastern bloc would be undermined if Dubček gained the
latitude he was seeking, Moscow sent troops into Czechoslovakia on 20 August
1968 and a pro-Soviet regime was restored in Prague.[85]

Western leaders were reluctant to lose the benefits of détente and this affected
their responses to the invasion of Czechoslovakia. In addition, the West was more
impressed by signs of disunity in the Soviet bloc than by prospects of reform:
hence the continuing overtures to Nicolae Ceaușescu of Rumania, who was trying
to pursue his own line within the bloc.[86] The Czech crisis came at a difficult time
for the West, as had the invasion of Hungary in 1956. Then, the Western powers
had been distracted by Suez. Now, in 1968, all the controversy over US involvement in Vietnam made the Soviets think that they could act in Czechoslovakia
without fear of a vigorous Western response. Moscow did not want to damage
East–West relations any more than necessary, and sent conciliatory notes to
the governments of America, Britain and the FRG on the eve of the invasion of
Czechoslovakia.[87]

Soviet leaders had condemned Dubček's reforms in the spring of 1968. In July
the British government decided not to get involved. The invasion in August came
as a surprise. London issued a protest and some links with the eastern bloc were
abandoned. At the same time, there was no wish to destabilize central Europe or
damage British trade with the region. In the West, the main results of the invasion were that NATO unity was enhanced, that de Gaulle's independent contact
with the Soviet Union was shown to be unproductive, and that Washington DC
shelved plans to cut the number of US troops in Europe. British leaders still
thought that a thaw was worth pursuing. This opinion was particularly strong
in the foreign office.[88]

What did the Soviets expect to achieve by invading Czechoslovakia? *The Times*
assumed that Moscow aimed to enforce conformity in the eastern bloc, prevent
reforms there and make an example of the Czechs, but coercion could not

succeed every time: eventually people would resist. *The Times* wanted a forceful British condemnation of the USSR and a strengthening of NATO.[89] George Brown was reminded of what Khrushchev had said in 1956 to the effect that no satellite could be allowed to remove itself from Moscow's influence, while Richard Crossman focused more on the unwillingness of America and France to act and on Wilson's unimpressive performance. The prime minister had parliament recalled for an emergency sitting on 26 August and his remarks, though 'decent', were 'superficial'. For the Conservatives, Edward Heath said that mere protests would not stop the Soviets. What would happen if a similar emergency arose in the Middle East or the Far East, or affecting a member of the Commonwealth: would Britain do nothing except protest? Heath also wondered about détente. The assumption had been made that détente was now a permanent feature of international affairs, but the Czech crisis showed how quickly circumstances could change.[90]

Members of the NATO alliance agreed to expand their armed forces. There was a limit to what some of them could do, however, in a period when domestic political and economic concerns ruled out significant increases in defence spending. The British government set an example. Healey announced an increase in funds for the British contingent in West Germany. The Czech crisis also saw closer diplomatic co-operation between London and Washington DC than had been seen for some time.[91]

The invasion of Czechoslovakia confirmed that Leonid Brezhnev, who had taken over as Soviet leader after the fall of Khrushchev in 1964, was a much more conservative figure than his predecessor had been. He was determined to keep the Warsaw Pact and Eastern Europe's 1945 frontiers intact. The expansion of nuclear arsenals during the 1960s and a new generation of intercontinental ballistic missiles had enabled the USSR to catch up with the United States, and Brezhnev also reversed Khrushchev's plans to reduce the Soviet Union's conventional forces. According to the Brezhnev Doctrine of 1968, governments within the eastern bloc were required to maintain an acceptable socialist outlook internally and externally. This was also called the 'doctrine of limited sovereignty'.[92]

In the international arena the short-term consequences of the invasion of Czechoslovakia were unhelpful to the Soviet Union. NATO was reinvigorated. A European security conference, which Moscow had been hoping would commence early in 1970, was put in jeopardy, as were Soviet thaw policies, especially those involving the FRG. Western Europe again saw its need for the USA. In Japan the opponents of the security pact with America, which was due for renewal in 1970, were weakened. Across the developing world the invasion was condemned. On nuclear questions, ratification of a non-proliferation agreement was delayed as opposition to it increased in the United States, the FRG and Japan, and the opening of the Strategic Arms Limitation Talks was delayed.[93]

Nevertheless, détente did not collapse. East–West trade increased, visits and exchanges resumed, several Western governments followed the example of Brandt's 'Ostpolitik', and Nixon's administration decided to go ahead with SALT. The British were not directly involved in SALT, but they favoured arms limitation because they did not wish to fall further behind the two superpowers in military capability.[94]

Although the Brezhnev Doctrine was condemned in the West, it did not signify a marked change in Moscow's attitude towards the eastern bloc. It did make more difficult the expression of diversity in the communist camp, yet diversity was a fact, even if it could not readily be expressed. Some governments in Eastern Europe could not avoid making compromises, especially in economic and social spheres, in the period that followed the Czech crisis of 1968.[95] Contact between East and West meant that problems in the West began to affect the bloc, and this was seen most clearly in relation to trade and finance. The system (Bretton Woods) that had fixed the value of the US dollar to gold and other currencies to the dollar was dismantled. While the USA had a strong economy there was no reason why its national interest would conflict with its role as currency regulator, but the American economy began to experience difficulties in the 1960s and Washington DC unilaterally suspended gold convertibility in 1971. International trade was flagging. Across Eastern Europe, state socialism was increasingly questioned. National interests were put before bloc harmony owing to pressures created by the links with money, food and energy markets in the West.[96]

Détente also undermined the established order in the bloc. To Moscow, détente was about competing as well as co-operating with the West, and Soviet leaders were loath to prioritize the co-operative aspects. Even so, these aspects gave the West opportunities. In America, Britain and Western Europe, while conservatives often condemned détente, its authors used it to change the enemy.[97]

There can be no denying Britain's loss of influence in each of the 'three circles' of world power. The 'special relationship' remained vital to Britain, but some serious quarrelling between London and Washington DC meant that it was not clear how helpful the Americans would be in return for British loyalty and approval. In the empire-Commonwealth 'circle', British efforts to supervise and strengthen had mixed results. There were reforms, and London devoted a lot of attention and resources to Commonwealth affairs, but none of this prevented disputes, particularly over Rhodesia, South Africa and Britain's policies East of Suez. As for Europe, the British found little about which to comfort themselves. The Czech crisis and the Brezhnev Doctrine appeared to prolong the Cold War. Britain could not gain entry into the EEC, whose members explicitly pointed to British economic weakness. Relations with Europe remained contentious at home, and the situation was not helped by the increased diplomatic weight and activity of France and the FRG. Perhaps British leaders should have done better.

Certainly they opened themselves up to accusations about 'death by a thousand cuts'. On the other hand, they could have done much worse. Though their options were limited and international conditions were not favourable, they persevered. Some specific measures might have been flawed, but the general policy was not, and the endeavour to shore up British influence for as long as possible was not ineffective. In the 1970s Britain clearly ranked below and lacked the sway and independence of the USA and USSR, but it still had the chance and potential to play an important role in the 'three circles'.

9

Years of Frustration

Along with retreats there was also resilience. In dealing with the new contexts of the 1970s, a frustrating time for *all* of the world's major powers, British leaders were as determined as they had ever been to meet commitments and maintain influence. A basic hindrance remained: Britain was losing the ability to carry events in a chosen direction and had instead to respond to crises in the solution of which others had more input. The British did draw closer to Europe, but were continually engaged in disputes over integration, NATO, détente, and US involvement in European affairs. Commonwealth relations troubled London, and although a residual presence in the Persian Gulf and Far East was thought to be sustainable, there was no going back on the general withdrawal from East of Suez. All this was controversial, and the effort to increase Britain's prestige and reshape Asian politics through a thaw with China did not bring all the expected benefits. More turmoil in the Middle East, and the resulting oil shock, added to Britain's problems in this period, and through it all there was constant anxiety about what Washington DC was doing in the Middle East and in Europe, Asia and Latin America.

Edward Heath's Conservative government, in office from 1970 to 1974, finally managed to negotiate Britain's entry into the EEC, which took effect on 1 January 1973, but the issue remained contentious. (The EEC had merged with the European Coal and Steel Community and European Atomic Energy Commission to form the 'European Communities', or EC, in 1967.) On other matters there was failure. The foreign secretary, former prime minister Alec Douglas-Home, did work out a settlement on Rhodesia that would eventually have established wide African voting rights, but an inquiry of 1972 showed that the Africans were not satisfied. Economic sanctions against the white Rhodesian regime remained in place, a policy that divided the Conservative Party.[1]

The Rhodesia question continued to sour Britain's relations with the Commonwealth. Heath lost patience with the latter, in part because he was sure that Britain's future lay in Europe. Matters were not helped by the ease with which sanctions were evaded. The bigger picture for Britain was one of relative economic decline. The use of economic means to support diplomatic pressure had offered viable options in previous times. The Heath government did not have this advantage. The United States shared London's view of the white Rhodesian regime, but was not committed to sanctions and rarely intervened to shield British policy from international disapproval.[2]

In Britain there were popular demonstrations and many public figures involved themselves in the controversy. In the autumn of 1972, eighty-three members of the House of Lords signed a statement to the effect that the Rhodesian people, black and white, had to be allowed to sort out their own problems. Sir Dingle Foot, QC, protested that the blacks were being denied free expression. Writer and journalist Roy Lewis argued that parliament should remove Rhodesia from the queen's dominions and continue sanctions in line with Britain's membership of the UN. This would not make Rhodesia independent or transfer power to the illegal regime led by Ian Smith. The effect, rather, would be to pass authority to the UN.[3]

As tempting as this solution might have seemed, the government considered it too radical. An abdication of responsibility on Britain's part was bound to affect the country's international standing and embroil ministers in even greater trouble at home. In July 1973, Home told the Commons that he was still pushing for talks between the Smith regime and Rhodesia's black leaders. A lot depended on the Rhodesians themselves: they had to want to reach an agreement. Meanwhile, sanctions would continue, in line with UN recommendations. Some MPs objected. Sanctions had been in place for eight years, they complained, and Britain had been a big loser.[4]

Britain's arms sales to South Africa were allowed to go ahead when Heath's government reversed the decision of the previous Labour cabinet. The main reasons were economic (the wish to prevent other countries from gaining contracts that should have been Britain's) and strategic (concern about the growth of the Soviet navy). The loudest protests were from African members of the Commonwealth. Immigration policy was a related problem. Britain was accused of discriminating against non-whites, although the government's hands were tied to some extent because EEC membership meant that more Europeans had to be allowed in.[5]

Heath had dismissed the Labour years of 1964–70 as years of surrender. He had spoken of restoring Britain's world position. It was not long before he accepted that this would not be possible, and limited resources made him even more determined to make Britain truly a part of Europe, where a collective diplomacy could be forged.[6]

In opposition Heath had attacked Labour for weakness, but as prime minister the same charge was to be made against him. Conservative right-wingers disliked the cabinet's decisions on Rhodesia and East of Suez. Under pressure from the right, the prime minister was also criticized by moderate opponents and those on the political left. He refused to condemn French nuclear tests in the Pacific, for example, even though Commonwealth and other nations did, and his wish for Anglo-French nuclear co-operation, which he thought would aid

European integration and reduce British and European reliance on America, ran aground on France's determination to preserve its nuclear independence. Heath also caused offence when he welcomed Portugal's right-wing leader Marcello Caetano to Britain in July 1973 at a time of press reports about 'massacres' in the Portuguese colony of Mozambique. Home explained to MPs that although Portugal had to be respected as an important member of NATO and as an old ally of Britain, the government did not endorse Portuguese actions in Africa.[7]

In opposition the Conservatives pledged themselves to reverse some of Labour's cuts East of Suez. This was partly for electoral purposes. Heath and his colleagues also sought to win over those Conservative MPs and activists who had doubts about the move towards Europe, so they stressed that Britain would continue to live up to its proud history as a global power. It was hoped that a party split on foreign policy could thereby be avoided (Harold Wilson had a similar problem with the Labour Party, which is why he promised to hold a referendum on British membership of the EEC).

In office, Heath and his colleagues accepted that Britain could not afford to remain East of Suez. In order not to leave a vacuum into which the Soviets could move, it was decided that wherever possible a token presence should continue, but most of the cuts announced by the Labour government went ahead. Iran, Iraq, Saudi Arabia and Kuwait all wanted Britain to leave the Persian Gulf, and the small states of the region did not wish to be seen as dependent on Britain. In the Far East it was different, because Singapore and Malaysia, and the Americans, wanted the British to stay.[8] Here, the British arranged for the formation of a joint defence force. This would involve Britain, Australia, New Zealand, Malaysia and Singapore. The agreement was primarily consultative in nature, and the government was embarrassed when revelations were made about haggling over money, particularly between Britain and Australia.[9] Britain would still have troops in Singapore, a small garrison in Hong Kong and five surface ships stationed permanently in the Far East, but the commitment to SEATO was fading. The wish was to pass responsibilities on to others: Australia and New Zealand in South East Asia; America and Iran in the Gulf. In the Indian Ocean the British allowed the Americans to develop a base on the island of Diego Garcia.[10]

At a time when Britain seemed to be losing prestige, the thaw in relations with China was a welcome distraction. Britain and the People's Republic of China agreed to exchange ambassadors in March 1972, and in the following October Home made an official visit to China. The Chinese foreign minister Chi Peng-fei visited Britain in June 1973. The British had not had normal diplomatic relations with China since the communist takeover there in 1949. The Anglo-Chinese thaw was partly a by-product of President Nixon's effort to foster friendship between the United States and China.[11]

London had not been informed by Washington DC about US contact with

China and this annoyed the foreign office, which had been negotiating for the establishment of full relations with Peking. American policy undercut Britain's negotiating position. This explains why Britain finally broke with the United States on Taiwan. Washington DC maintained that Taiwan should continue to sit on the UN security council as 'China', but Britain and most other members of the UN were unwilling any longer to put up with this anomaly.[12]

The government had been thinking about improving Britain's links with China, as a means of safeguarding Hong Kong and of contributing to a global thaw. Heath was impressed by the 'increasing fluidity' in relations between the United States, Western Europe, Japan, the USSR and China, and the view in London was that China needed interaction with the West. For Britain, the prospect of trade was a big incentive. In due course arrangements were made for Heath to visit China.[13]

The normalization of Anglo-Chinese relations had diplomatic, political, commercial and cultural sides to it. The process was made easier by Nixon's policy, but was not dependent upon it. Indeed, some advances had been made before Heath became prime minister and before Nixon made overtures to the Chinese. Still, Nixon's rapprochement with Peking was important, as was China's wish to come out of isolation and Britain's status as co-author of arrangements made in 1943 and 1945 concerning the post-war settlement in the Pacific. The context was also shaped by instability in South East Asia. In January 1973, in Paris, a tentative agreement was reached for peace in Vietnam, but in the following period the Khmer Rouge overthrew a pro-US regime in Cambodia, the Pathet Lao took control of Laos, and North Vietnamese forces overran the whole of Vietnam and reunified the country in June 1975.[14]

Anglo-Chinese relations steadily improved. The issue of China's UN seat was resolved and there were agreements on trade and industry, science and technology, sporting links, and air services. Chinese students were invited to study in Britain. Between 1971 and 1974 the value of Britain's exports to and imports from China more than doubled.[15]

The new understanding with China was shaped by détente and the course of Anglo-European and Anglo-Soviet relations. In 1971 the Heath government demonstrated that it was not unwilling to stand up to Moscow when it expelled Soviet diplomats for spying. This impressed Chinese leaders. It also helped Heath to reassure those in Europe who thought that Britain was too close to the United States, for this was a time when US–Soviet tension was being eased. European détente was relevant too, and London wanted the Europeans to deal with the USSR collectively rather than approach Moscow individually and try to outbid one another with concessions. Heath and Home advocated a common negotiating position, which is why they favoured the process of European Political Co-operation (EPC). They also insisted that a joint policy was needed with respect to the Conference on Security and Co-operation in Europe (CSCE).[16]

Despite Home's claim late in 1972 that contact with China would bring benefits, there was scepticism, especially with regard to trade. *The Times* took a different tack, insisting that Britain's friendship was important to the Chinese because Britain was shortly to join the EEC: 'the image of a politically mature and stable power playing a part in the new Europe engages China's interest'. The *Guardian* echoed this, adding that China respected Britain's refusal to trust the Soviet Union. Meanwhile, Home and Heath had cause to lament the unhelpful nature of US policy. Washington DC often told the British to stand aside at key moments so that US–Chinese negotiations could proceed. The British had little choice because America and China gave precedence to their bilateral relationship.[17]

That Britain was at the mercy of international events, and not controlling them, was made clearer by the Arab–Israeli War of October 1973. Britain's position was further undermined as the war in the Middle East affected oil supplies from a region that met half of all Britain's energy needs. Prices rose and Britain's oil imports were reduced by about 15 per cent.[18]

The outbreak of war in the Middle East alarmed Heath, though he did not think that Moscow would interfere. He was worried more by the Americans, who placed their forces in Europe on alert without consulting their allies. The Americans also wished to use their bases to supply Israel during the war. Britain and its European partners refused to permit this, with the exception of the Netherlands. The Heath government made much of its even-handed approach. Home announced that Britain would not supply any of the combatants with arms. This was not enough for the Arabs, who declared that oil supplies would be cut until Israel withdrew from occupied land and the Palestinians were granted self-government. There was a complete embargo on the sale of oil to the Americans and the Dutch.[19]

A ceasefire was agreed on 24 October, but the end of the fighting did not mean that the problems behind it, or the wider effects, had been properly tackled. On 6 November the EC called upon Israel to leave the occupied territories and respect Palestinian rights. Britain's position was that Europe had to remain neutral, to earn Arab goodwill. The idea was for London and Paris to take the lead in an effort to get oil flowing again, but members of the EC began to quarrel with one another and the British and French were accused of putting their own interests first.[20] Moscow had not encouraged the embargo. Kosygin, the Soviet prime minister, and Gromyko, the foreign minister, feared that it would provoke Western military intervention, but after the war they came to see the oil weapon in a more positive light.[21]

The oil crisis damaged the British economy and impeded Britain in Europe, as when the FRG insisted that, in view of the financial pressures of the time, the planned Regional Development Fund could not be as large as Britain wanted. In addition, a serious dispute arose between the British government and the oil companies, which Heath thought should be doing more to help. The balance-of-payments problem was exacerbated, and the wage demands of the powerful miners' union further inconvenienced the government.[22]

The Europeans continued to bicker as each country tried to safeguard its own oil supplies. Heath was disappointed, though not to the extent that he offered to share North Sea oil. All this made plain some differences of approach with regard to EPC, which had been intended to provide for foreign policy co-ordination. London, and also Paris, saw EPC as a supplement to national foreign policy and as a way of gaining support for a wider, extra-European role, but for Bonn, EPC was a vehicle for national policy and potentially also a substitute for it. The FRG wanted to act primarily as a member of the EC.[23]

Home advocated a peace in the Middle East that would combine security for Israel with the return of occupied Arab land, and he approved of Heath's determination to stand up to Britain's European allies on the oil question. Home differed with the West Germans about the US military alert. Bonn fancied that there had been collusion between London and Washington DC and complained that the alert was inappropriate: it affected US troops in West Germany and might have triggered off a nuclear exchange. Home tried to calm Bonn while telling US secretary of state Henry Kissinger that Britain should be free to object to certain aspects of American policy in order to make British support on other aspects more useful.[24]

The oil crisis raised concerns about Britain's economic security.[25] The British stepped up their efforts to exploit North Sea oil in the 1970s, while France and the FRG rapidly expanded their generation of nuclear power. All were aware of the sensitivity of national economies to events outside the national boundary. The fact that the British economy was vulnerable to external disturbances also contributed to the breaking down of distinctions between domestic and foreign policies.[26] Britain's activity abroad was heavily influenced by successes and failures in economic management at home.

Lack of resources bedevilled Britain's attempts to preserve status. In the 1970s many commentators specifically denied that the nuclear deterrent was worth the money. They did not think that it influenced the Soviets and by 1979, when Britain agreed to buy Trident from the United States, the West seemed to be threatened less by the nuclear capabilities of the USSR than by rogue regimes, like those in Libya and Iraq, which were thought to possess nuclear weapons. The Trident deal was important to Britain, nonetheless, and the Americans offered generous terms that they were unlikely to offer anyone else, which confirmed the survival of a 'special relationship' in defence.[27]

The development of Trident worried Moscow. To some historians, the Soviets were essentially cautious in this period and not as strong militarily as they appeared.[28] If true, however, this can only have become apparent with the passing of time. In the 1970s and 1980s there was an undercurrent of suspicion in all of London's contacts with Moscow.

Britain's global role was diminishing. The British were not involved in the major East–West summits of 1972 to 1974, which were attended by Nixon and Soviet leader Leonid Brezhnev. Britain could do nothing about the loss of control over old imperial lines of communication through the Mediterranean and Red Sea: Somalia became a Soviet ally in 1969; Malta's government requested the departure of British forces in 1971; and the Libyans, led from 1969 by Muammar Gaddafi, ended their defence treaty with Britain in 1972. British forces did not leave Malta completely, but the negotiations were difficult and Britain had to pay more for the use of facilities there.[29]

As Washington DC and Moscow began to deal directly with each other, Britain's opportunities to influence events were fewer. This made it easier for Heath to think about distancing Britain from America and using the superpower thaw further to reduce Britain's commitments around the world. There was a change in these years, in that Britain joined the EEC, yet there was a limit to what could be done in terms of shifting policy onto a new basis. Britain's need for American help remained constant.[30]

Heath was not fond of the Americans. He took a neutral line during the Arab–Israeli War of 1973, but it was difficult, not to say impolitic, to try to exercise independence in other respects, and the importance of US support for British and European security was underlined as pressure grew within America for a scaling down of US military involvement overseas. Washington DC was angered by the efforts of America's allies to take their own path. The Europeans were thinking in terms of greater co-operation among themselves and Washington DC was worried that they would no longer care about reconciling their own interests with those of the United States. The Americans wanted a stronger 'European pillar' and expected the money and manpower to come from the Europeans, but they also feared that if Western Europe did do more to defend itself, American influence would be lost. Under pressure from Washington DC, the Europeans accepted that they would have to do more and the trend was for NATO to become more 'European' while the Warsaw Pact was 'Sovietized'.[31] Heath wanted Britain to go its own way more often, but his attitude towards the Americans was not entirely negative and the tendency to distinguish Britain's interests from those of the United States soon petered out. Heath understood that British policy would always have to take account of US power, and his misgivings about the 'special relationship' were balanced by Home's enthusiasm for it.[32]

Britain's troubles continued. Wilson's Labour government of 1974 to 1976 renegotiated the terms of Britain's membership of the EEC, gaining nothing substantial but adding to the acrimony of the European debate in Britain and offending Britain's European partners. The dire economic situation had also to be dealt with. The rise in oil prices had knock-on effects for several years, and slow economic growth combined with inflation created 'stagflation'. This, and the promise of 'mutually assured destruction' (MAD) held out by the nuclear stand-off between the two superpowers, made for a pessimistic outlook.[33]

The 1970s were difficult for all the advanced economies, but Britain suffered more than most. At the time of the oil shock in 1973 Britain already had a large trade deficit and inflation was out of control. Heath's Labour successors were unable to redress the situation and a sterling crisis in 1976 forced the government to seek assistance. Washington DC offered credit but imposed conditions. The package did not really help and the Labour government then applied to the International Monetary Fund. Again the Americans made demands. They wanted rigorous deflationary measures. Washington DC had less reason to lend a hand now that Bretton Woods had been dismantled and the British military presence East of Suez had virtually ended. Though the Labour government subsequently claimed that it had intended to set deflation targets anyway, the affair damaged Britain's reputation.[34]

The increasing capacity of nuclear weapons suggested that no government could defend its citizens against attack, although in practice, it was hoped, this realization would promote stability. MAD was still shaping military thinking in the mid-1980s. One of the reasons that America's Strategic Defence Initiative (SDI, or 'star wars') would be so controversial was because it was a destabilizing departure that seemed to make nuclear war more likely. The arms race intensified in the late 1970s and early 1980s on the basis that it was unwise to seek bargains with an adversary without first gaining a position of strength.[35]

British sensitivity about the loss of status and power was palpable in the 1970s. Entry into the EEC was taken by some as a sign that Britain counted for less in the world, yet the British still had their 'special relationship' with the United States, still had extra-European interests, and did not wish to be confined to a European role. In Western Europe Britain was blamed for blocking quicker integration for the sake of an unequal relationship with the Americans. Quarrelling on this score continued as the British chose not to join in the projected European Monetary System (EMS) and argued in favour of a broader approach to international monetary problems, that would include the United States, rather than purely a European one. Nevertheless, there were opportunities for British and European governments to work together, especially on security matters, and the 'Eurogroup' sometimes agreed on joint measures before full sessions of the NATO council.[36]

Despite the pessimism of the 1970s, the Helsinki Accords of August 1975 did inspire a belief that détente was working. The West recognized Soviet interests in Eastern Europe and the Soviets agreed to open up the eastern bloc for trade and to respect human rights. There was no end, however, to the disputations over defence in Britain. The Labour left pressed again for nuclear disarmament, convinced that the Soviet threat had been exaggerated. Wilson's government agreed that the British deterrent would not be replaced. Instead, an attempt was made to update Polaris. This was called the Chevaline project, and it began under Heath. The decision to go ahead with it was made by a small committee of ministers, in secret, shortly after Wilson's return as premier in March 1974. The cabinet was informed that the cost would be about £250 million. Within two years the cost had soared to four times this amount. Wilson's successor as prime minister, Callaghan, decided that so much had been spent on Chevaline, and it had progressed so far, that it should not be discontinued. Callaghan established a good rapport with US president Jimmy Carter, who occupied the White House from January 1977, and this affected British nuclear planning. However, economic decline could not be halted, and, as Callaghan himself had said in April 1974 when he was foreign secretary, Britain's role in the world was shrinking because long-term political influence depended on economic strength, and that was running out. In May 1977 the members of NATO agreed to augment their defence spending, which had obvious implications for Britain and proved that détente had not ended military competition with the Soviets after all.[37]

Carter announced a bigger increase in 1979 when the Soviets invaded Afghanistan. For the British, defence spending continued to impose a heavy burden. The Chevaline project made sense, in that Britain could retain the ability to strike targets in the USSR while postponing a decision on the new generation of submarine-launched missiles, but the Labour government appointed in 1974 could not easily balance the need to finance Chevaline with the need to cut public expenditure. This government inherited a huge balance-of-payments deficit from its Conservative predecessor, and predictions about trade, oil prices and economic performance were not very encouraging.[38]

As well as keeping up their nuclear deterrent, the British had also to give attention to conventional strength. Heath's defence secretary, Lord Carrington, had insisted that even in a time of thaw it was necessary for the West to improve its conventional forces, without which 'flexible response' would be unworkable. Eventually NATO reached the decision of May 1977 for a 3 per cent increase in defence spending each year for five years from 1979. This was a tall order for Britain. It is likely that the agreed targets would have been forgotten had it not been for the fall of Nicaragua to the left-wing Sandinistas in June 1979 (which for Washington DC raised the spectre of another Cuba); the Kremlin's threat to retaliate when NATO deployed Cruise and Pershing to counter the USSR's SS20 intermediate-range ballistic missiles, and the Soviet invasion of Afghanistan. Britain worked hard to meet NATO targets. Callaghan thought that the money could be taken from North Sea oil revenues. The soaring cost of Chevaline was worrying, however, and even more money was needed in due course for Trident, which Britain had to have, it was decided, if the deterrent was to remain credible and if Britain was to retain influence in Washington DC.[39]

Officially, Britain remained committed to détente. Wilson and Callaghan had done much to bring about the agreements reached at Helsinki in 1975.[40] The Conference on Security and Co-operation in Europe had been launched with preparatory talks in November 1973. Initially, Britain's view was negative. It was assumed that the Soviets intended to use CSCE to reinforce their position in Eastern Europe, retard economic and political co-operation in Western Europe, and weaken NATO. Nevertheless, in Western Europe there was a desire for conversations with the USSR and eastern bloc on a range of issues, and the Nixon administration, under pressure domestically to withdraw US troops from Europe, was interested in mutual and balanced force reductions (MBFR). Brezhnev agreed that there could be two sets of negotiations, CSCE and MBFR. Though the Soviets wanted to confine CSCE to security matters, the West insisted that humanitarian issues should be included.[41]

The British foreign office saw that 'Ostpolitik', SALT, MBFR and CSCE were all pointing in the same direction. It was not thought that Britain could stem this tide, but there was a determination not to accept a CSCE agenda shaped by Moscow or by wavering allies. At the same time, it was admitted that Britain would have to compromise. Refusal to do so would be to risk isolation and loss of influence, while working with European partners on CSCE would help to promote EPC, in which there might be some benefits for Britain.[42]

Britain's attitude towards European détente was equivocal, for it coincided with adjustments in Britain's international role. There was an acceptance that in world status Britain now ranked far below the two superpowers and an acceptance that Britain's importance related more to transatlantic relations than to internal European questions, on which the FRG was the main player. The FRG had more to offer the USSR and its allies in Eastern Europe, especially economically, while Britain lacked common interests with the USSR and eastern bloc. London's relationship with Moscow normally depended on the general state of East–West relations. In view of all this, Britain had little incentive and few opportunities to try to take a lead in European détente.[43]

In the early 1970s British leaders wanted Nixon to talk to the Soviets, though they were eager to prevent US–Soviet bargains that damaged the interests of America's allies. In London there was support for MBFR, which, it was hoped, would nullify pressure in the US Congress for the American military presence in Europe to be reduced unilaterally. As for CSCE, the Americans were wary while the British pressed for US participation. London did have some of the same reservations as the Americans, for CSCE had long been a staple feature of Soviet propaganda and many British as well as American observers did not see why the USSR should be forgiven for Czechoslovakia in 1968, or why the Soviets should be provided with the means to gain legitimacy for their control over Eastern Europe.[44]

The British argued that close attention should be paid to the details of proposed agreements with the Soviets, and like the Americans thought that CSCE should not be legally binding (so the Helsinki Final Act would not be a formal treaty registered with the United Nations). In London it was assumed that economic and cultural links could be improved quite easily. Security issues and human rights were less straightforward, and the key here was to make sure that concessions to the USSR on the political and military side were made only in response to Soviet concessions on the humanitarian side. Some disputes broke out in NATO on tactics and goals. The Americans were determined that MBFR should not be delayed and that preparatory arrangements for CSCE should only be made after or alongside discussions on MBFR.[45]

An agreement on MBFR was not to be finalized until 1986. All through these years Moscow was determined to preserve the Warsaw Pact's superiority in conventional forces, but was willing to talk about reductions in order to gain leverage on other matters. In NATO the prevailing opinion was that substantial reductions would be dangerous. Western governments had to negotiate, however, in order to maintain domestic support for their defence policies. Divisions within NATO became more obvious. For a time the FRG pushed for radical force reductions across the board. In due course the French also called for a new approach.[46]

With regard to CSCE, the Kremlin wished to bargain only on non-military aspects of security, had little interest in economic and technological co-operation, and was totally opposed to any serious negotiation on humanitarian issues. On human rights London was disposed to be bold, but it was not easy to forge a common position with allies. Addressing the Commons in December 1972, Home had stressed that it would be wrong to expect too much from the different negotiations that were in progress or soon to commence. With the approach of the official opening of the CSCE talks, it was procedural difficulties that most vexed the British government. Committee I was to deal with security, Committee II with economic, scientific, technological and environmental co-operation, and Committee III with humanitarian and other matters. Britain's position, outlined by Home in October 1973, was that the humanitarian and security strands should 'proceed as far as possible in parallel'.[47]

After taking office in 1974 Labour leaders, thinking that CSCE had made insufficient progress, sought to inject new impetus. Wilson and Callaghan had both visited the USSR in the past and Callaghan had a fairly good working relationship with Gromyko. With the Americans Callaghan discussed 'Basket III' (humanitarian issues) and confidence-building measures (such as the idea that NATO should give Moscow prior notification of its military exercises). Callaghan did not want the West to reveal too much in its dealings with the Soviets: a distinction had to be privately maintained between what the West proposed and what the West would be willing to settle for.[48] In February 1975, Wilson and Callaghan arrived in Moscow for talks with Brezhnev and Kosygin. Wilson focused on trade, Callaghan on security and stability in Europe. Human rights, left-wing subversion in Portugal and the need for a CSCE agreement were among the matters discussed. The visit facilitated agreement at the CSCE summit in Helsinki in August 1975.[49]

Wilson liked to present himself as a world statesman who could communicate effectively with both the Americans and the Soviets. He considered his visit to Moscow in February 1975 a great success: among its results were agreements on economic and industrial co-operation, science and technology, health and medicine; a protocol on consultation; and a joint declaration against the proliferation of nuclear weapons. Although Brezhnev dismissed the human rights aspects of CSCE as unimportant, Wilson and Callaghan hoped that these could be pursued in the Helsinki process, and Callaghan was glad that Kissinger seemed willing to give the process a chance. Anglo-Soviet relations improved, with more trade and cultural links, and talks with Gromyko in the spring of 1976 led to the relaxation of restrictions on dissidents. None of this represented an independent course on Britain's part, however, for the government remained committed to NATO and much of what Callaghan did in these years was discussed beforehand with Kissinger.[50]

British ambivalence about détente in Europe did not fade away. Bonn's 'Ostpolitik' was recognized as significant, not least because it removed the assumption that the reunification of Germany had to precede a thaw, but there was concern in London as the FRG pushed ahead to improve its relations with the East German regime, the USSR and the eastern bloc. Washington DC decided to get more involved, for fear of losing control over détente. While British leaders hoped that contact between the superpowers would lessen the risk of nuclear war, they continued to worry, as the Europeans did, that the Americans and Soviets would bargain above their heads. If London wanted the Helsinki process to develop, moreover, there was still a belief that the cohesion of NATO mattered more than the conclusion of a comprehensive settlement with the USSR and its satellites. This reflected a sense of marginalization. The British contribution to CSCE was clearer on human rights and economic co-operation than it was on the serious political issues.[51] Even on human rights, doubts have been raised as to whether British policy makers were genuinely interested in promoting change.[52]

London made good use of the machinery that was put in place to review the implementation of the Helsinki Final Act. One by-product was the growth of

EPC, which gave Britain new ways of exercising influence. Certain goals could be pursued through EPC that could not be achieved by acting as a mediator between America and its allies. By 1977, when the first CSCE follow-up meeting opened in Belgrade, the British were pushing EPC as the way to balance the need to continue European détente with the need to preserve the unity of the West.[53]

Britain's initial caution was vindicated as détente lost its impetus. Little progress was made with MBFR or stage two of SALT, and the Americans and Soviets went on competing with each other in Africa and Asia. After 1975 the Soviets complained about the way the Helsinki Final Act was being used against them. Neither East nor West wanted CSCE to collapse, however, because it provided negotiating tools. In addition, there was still a lot of ambiguity and both sides could claim that they had made gains, whether to do with the recognition of frontiers in Eastern Europe, the role the EC was able to take up in international affairs, the prospect of regular review meetings, or the opportunity the West had to encourage reform in the communist bloc. There were follow-up conferences at Belgrade (1977–78), Madrid (1980–83) and Stockholm (1984), though these were marked by disagreements that reflected the wider course of international events.[54]

Britain's position was clarified by Callaghan in July 1976, when he said that the Helsinki Final Act should not be treated as a static document, and by the British foreign secretary David Owen, who declared in March 1977 that Helsinki had created a long-term framework that was always evolving. To Margaret Thatcher, who at this time was leader of the Conservative Party, the principal requirement was for the West to match the USSR militarily. She thought that the Soviets were using détente to gain strength.[55] Moscow was ready to discuss disarmament, while the Americans prioritized human rights, on which the West had the advantage. The CSCE meeting at Madrid worked out a compromise in September 1983 and disarmament talks were arranged, but NATO missile deployments went ahead and the USSR asserted that it had no choice but to respond.[56]

From the outset the Helsinki process meant different things to different people. What Brezhnev had in mind was a transitional period during which tension could be lowered despite the increase in armaments. The end in view was a shift in the global balance in favour of the USSR. For the Americans the main point of détente and trade was to bring the USSR into interdependence. CSCE was less important to the USA than it was to the Europeans, who were seeking a way to overcome the division of Europe and reduce the importance of the military aspects of East–West relations. NATO's rearmament programme and Soviet objections to it overshadowed the Madrid conference, and although disarmament talks subsequently opened in Stockholm, the Soviets pulled out of meetings on other issues and the West's effort to reinforce the human rights section of Helsinki was met, as before, with Soviet intransigence.[57]

The West's reaction to the Soviet invasion of Afghanistan was robust, and this coincided with a shift to the right in British and American politics. A Conservative government took office in Britain in May 1979 under Thatcher. In November 1980 the Republican candidate, Ronald Reagan, gained a landslide victory over Carter in the US presidential election. Thatcher and Reagan went on to forge the closest working relationship between Britain and America since the days of Macmillan and Kennedy. They were determined to take a tough line against the Soviets, although the situation took a new turn after Mikhail Gorbachev became Soviet leader in 1985. In the meantime, Britain was still struggling to maintain influence. The West German economy had been more successful than Britain's for some time, and by 1979 the FRG was making a larger contribution to Western Europe's defences, and at a relatively lower cost, than were the British, who had to impose further limits on their spending.[58]

When Thatcher became prime minister she and her cabinet inherited a defence budget that was on the increase. The economy was in recession, unemployment rose, the cost of social welfare mushroomed, and through it all the Conservatives preached and practised public retrenchment. It became difficult to sustain the responsibility Britain had to increase defence expenditure, though the attempt was made and by the mid-1980s Britain was one of the few NATO countries to meet the agreed target. Then there were reductions. In absolute terms Britain's expenditure was about the same as that of the FRG and France, but as a proportion of national wealth it was much higher. Britain's smaller economy was subjected to greater pressure. Britain still had a variety of obligations, more like America's than those of NATO's European members. There was the continental commitment, and the need for ships and aircraft in the Atlantic and the waters around the British Isles. There was Britain's own security to attend to, which was based primarily on air defence. There was the nuclear deterrent. There were also forces beyond the NATO area, notably in Hong Kong, Belize, the Persian Gulf and the Falklands.[59]

Quarrels intensified in NATO as some members reached the 3 per cent target and others did not, and there were disagreements about how the money should be spent and about burden sharing. During the 1980s it was recognized that new imbalances had resulted from the USA's relative economic decline, and the Americans were doubly sensitive because they were in economic competition with their military allies. Uneasiness also grew in Western Europe, where governments worried that Washington DC, in projecting American power throughout the world, might act against their wishes.[60]

High defence spending caused divisions in the Thatcher government. The chancellor of the exchequer between 1979 and 1983, Geoffrey Howe, proposed wide-ranging cuts. Thatcher saw defence as a special case, however, and defence secretary Francis Pym insisted that the 3 per cent NATO commitment was one that Britain was bound to honour. At first Thatcher approved the large defence budget, though she backed Howe on the need to limit the Trident programme.[61]

As well as spending more on defence than most other advanced industrial nations, Britain also maintained larger professional military forces. France and the FRG, for example, relied on conscripts, while Britain had no compulsory military service. In the mid-1980s Britain was the world's third-largest spender on defence. In 1984 the Thatcher government announced that it would not be continuing with the 3 per cent annual increase in defence spending from 1986. Significant extra burdens had been taken on, notably the cost of Trident and the cost of maintaining forces in the South Atlantic after the Falklands War of 1982.[62]

The Falklands crisis demonstrated that a military venture outside the NATO area could have a significant long-term impact. The United States had also experienced a distant war that brought with it enormous difficulty. For the Americans, Vietnam cast a long shadow. Edward Heath had come to see their involvement in Vietnam as a source of humiliation which would prompt them to reassess their activities around the world and pull forces out of Europe. He considered it vital that the Americans should not be defeated and insisted that they had to leave Vietnam in such a way as to dispel any idea that US power was waning. If they failed in this the Soviets might grow bolder and Western Europe would come under more pressure as a result. The Americans were pleased that a small British force remained in the Far East as part of the defence agreement between Britain, Australia, New Zealand, Malaysia and Singapore. Nevertheless, there were US troop reductions in Europe.[63]

By the early 1970s the Soviets had more ICBMs than the Americans, while the United States had superiority in other types of nuclear weapon, as well as a strategic bomber force, and Britain and France also had nuclear weapons. Still, Nixon could not ignore the Soviet armaments programme or the spread of Soviet influence. He wanted to remove tension and his approach to China was part of this, as was his wish for a shared US–Soviet understanding that the bipolar Cold War world no longer existed. Nixon was fortunate in that an opening already existed, SALT, which he was sure could be linked with other initiatives. He was hoping in particular to secure Soviet help with the Vietnam peace plan.[64]

Nixon's concept of multi-polarity had a mixed reception in Britain. Would it bring a dramatic alteration in world affairs? Would it restore confidence in the USA's leadership role? British leaders were unused to the language that Nixon was employing. British policy was still shaped by the 'realist world-view', which gained added force when the thaw slowed down, when the disadvantages of multi-polarity became clearer, and when tension rose again. To the 'realist', international relations were determined by power struggles, the world was anarchic, each state had to rely on its own efforts and resources, and conflict was inevitable. These assumptions featured in the debates of the 1970s and 1980s, but so did other ideas and models, and the need for pragmatism meant that no single formula could determine policy. This was also true of Washington DC. Indeed, Nixon's apparently more flexible approach might not have represented much of a shift at all, for multi-polarity came to be seen as a source of instability.[65]

Nixon's thaw with the Soviets divided the West. Kissinger repeatedly told America's allies that they should confine themselves to supporting US efforts, that they should make no unilateral overtures to Moscow, and that if they entered into a competition with the United States for better relations with the USSR they would lose. Western Europe reacted angrily to such pressure. Heath's inclination to co-operate more with Europe than with America, meanwhile, did not go down well in the White House.[66]

Even if there was scepticism in London about Nixon's policy, Heath and Home saw opportunity in the changing relationships of the early 1970s. They agreed that Britain should try to establish better relations with Moscow and Peking. Willing to negotiate, they also demonstrated firmness, as when Home expelled Soviet diplomats in September 1971 and when Heath supported US bombing of North Vietnam at the end of 1972.[67]

The Soviets gave détente a chance in order to see what they could get out of it. To begin with, the focus was on SALT, which officially opened in Vienna in April 1970. The USSR wanted to cover only those weapons that could hit Soviet and American territory, so as to exclude Soviet missiles aimed at Western Europe and expose rifts within NATO. Another dispute arose over whether to discuss offensive weapons or to bargain only on defensive anti-ballistic missiles.[68] America and the Soviet Union had different weaponry and it proved impossible to create conditions in which each side had an equal chance of responding to a first strike. If offensive weapons, ICBMs and multiple independently targeted re-entry vehicles, or MIRVs, raised the tension, so did defence systems, because a stable deterrent relationship required that civilians on both sides were hostages against an attack by the other.[69] One of the Soviets' main concerns, as the SALT sessions progressed, was the damage that could be done if an agreement was not concluded. Any serious blow to US–Soviet détente was bound to help China. The Americans, too, were concerned about China's ambitions, and this gave them a shared interest in a bargain. A related goal for Moscow was thaw in Europe.[70]

British commentators looked forward to an arms limitation treaty, although it was clear that an agreement would not be easy to arrange. The Americans wanted a comprehensive deal; the Soviets wanted to limit anti-ballistic missiles and leave offensive systems for SALT II. As well as this divergence on substantive issues, the two sides differed in general attitude. The Soviets preferred broad restraints that would have maximum political impact. The Americans wanted specific measures that would stabilize the strategic balance. The American tactic of 'linkage', whereby different goals were grouped together, caused problems, as did domestic political pressures, which continually affected US and Soviet negotiating positions.[71]

Eventually it was agreed that there would be a restriction on anti-ballistic missiles and a freeze on the development of offensive nuclear weapons. Nixon announced this outcome in May 1971. In September 1971 the Americans, Soviets, British and French signed a new treaty regulating the status of West Berlin, but during the war between India and Pakistan late in 1971 the Soviets helped one side and the Americans the other. This war underlined the fact that Britain was no longer the West's peacekeeper in the Indian Ocean and Persian Gulf, and indicated that American leaders were still thinking in Cold War terms: to them the war resulted from Indian aggression, backed by the USSR, when in fact the war had more to do with tensions that had mounted since India's partition in 1947 and the impending break-up of Pakistan. Neither the USA nor the USSR wanted the thaw to end, however, and Nixon went ahead with a visit to Moscow in May 1972.[72]

SALT I was signed by Nixon and Brezhnev on 26 May 1972. British and French nuclear weapons were not included. Some of the arrangements were of an 'interim' nature, to last for five years, which ensured that talks would carry on. The Moscow meeting also resulted in a trade agreement. On Vietnam, though, the Americans and Soviets had to agree to disagree, and the Soviets drew up the 'Basic Principles of Mutual Relations', which stated their readiness to defend their interests by all means short of war. Neither side expected SALT I to make a huge difference. The arms race continued. SALT I did oblige the superpowers to limit their armaments to a particular level, but Moscow declared that if the USA's allies increased their nuclear forces, the USSR would match this increase.[73]

If the Americans and Soviets were unwilling to give way on essentials, the same was true of Britain. London was suspicious not only of Moscow but also of Washington DC. The notion that the Americans might enter into agreements that did not suit Britain was ever present. The Heath government had to prevent this from happening while making confident remarks about British influence: hence the official statement that Britain had been properly consulted about SALT. While Heath and Home favoured détente, they wished to guide it in a certain direction. Readiness to work with the United States was combined with the idea that Britain should withstand the Americans when necessary. *The Times* welcomed the SALT treaty on the grounds that it would enhance superpower détente and lead to agreements on Vietnam, the Middle East and other international problems. The *Economist* detected a hint of 'You need this deal just as badly as I do' in the SALT process and Moscow summit.[74]

Heath was concerned when negotiations were interrupted by crises, because he thought that Washington DC had a tendency to overreact. The war between India and Pakistan in December 1971 was one example. Britain had attempted to reduce tension between these two members of the Commonwealth before hostilities commenced. Washington DC saw India as a Soviet-backed aggressor. By helping Pakistan the Americans hoped to prevent the USSR from dominating the region while assisting the thaw between the United States and Pakistan's protector, China. Home had some sympathy for American policy and regretted that Heath did not. When a ceasefire was arranged *The Times* argued for a speedy resolution of outstanding issues, including independence for Bangladesh, formerly East Pakistan. With US and Soviet warships in the Bay of Bengal, it was also incumbent on the UN security council to ensure that the ceasefire would hold. As for the Americans, they 'seem to have misunderstood the political tensions at work in the sub-continent and to have mistimed almost all their interventions'.[75]

For Moscow one of the key aims at this time was to show the world that the Soviet Union could do more for its allies than Peking could do for the friends of China.[76] The Americans, meanwhile, were victims of their own 'linkage' approach, in which Pakistan and India, the desire for a settlement in Vietnam, the opening to China and détente with Moscow were all connected together.[77]

Notwithstanding US involvement in the India–Pakistan war, Nixon could respond to claims that he was not doing enough to promote détente by pointing to SALT (though his personal desire for arms control was weaker than the desire to strengthen his position as president). Moscow remained in SALT as a means of checking US power. In their dealings with America the Soviets were not inflexible. At the same time, they had a fixed idea about Europe: here they wanted protection. One of the main reasons why MBFR did not get far was that Soviet security doctrines entailed a decisive conventional advantage in Europe.[78]

Although the Heath government publicly approved of US–Soviet negotiations, it resented Britain's exclusion and disliked the competition in détente, as when Western governments scrambled for access to markets in the communist bloc. This also annoyed the Wilson government of 1974–76. When an Anglo-Soviet trade agreement was arranged in 1975, British negotiators were frustrated by Moscow's insistence that they should offer more credit. The Soviets made much of the fact that France had been generous in this respect, but they would not reveal the terms the French had offered, and neither would Paris.[79]

The British also had misgivings about SALT. The Americans and Soviets were discussing matters that directly affected Britain, but Britain was not participating in the talks. There were implications, too, for Britain's role in détente. The superpowers had less need to use Britain as an intermediary, and Britain increasingly saw the FRG dealing with Washington DC, whereas Britain had long acted as the bridge between the American and European pillars in NATO. After SALT I British leaders pressed for a comprehensive test ban. The Americans grew angry with

London's wish for strict terms and warned in June 1979 that if the British did not compromise, the USA and USSR would agree a test ban without them. In fact, Carter and Brezhnev had already decided that SALT II should take priority.[80]

Difficulties with SALT led the British to think that they had been right all along to view détente with caution. Still, in general they were satisfied by SALT I. They had to make a decision about the future of their deterrent, and instead of having to replace Polaris completely they were enabled to take a cheaper option, the updating of Polaris. Had the deployment of anti-ballistic missiles not been restrained, the ability of Polaris to penetrate Soviet defences would have been reduced. London continued to monitor SALT, making sure that Britain's nuclear forces were excluded and manoeuvring as necessary to preserve Anglo-American strategic co-operation.[81]

Although there were aspects of Nixon's détente that gratified British leaders, it appeared that any withdrawal of US forces from Europe would mean that Britain would be expected to do more for collective security. The financial contingencies of this complicated Heath's plan to work with the Europeans. Nixon was determined that neither European integration nor European détente should interfere with the superpower thaw, while Kissinger was sceptical about EPC and wanted to bring it into line with NATO policy. To Heath, this was an attempt to control the Europeans and give Washington DC more leverage in its dealings with Moscow.[82]

Nixon's attitude towards SALT was in some ways far from conciliatory: this was the mindset that favoured more bombing of North Vietnam in order to get Hanoi to negotiate. Alongside the equivocal attitude towards Europe and the notion that Pakistan was a barrier against the Soviets, moreover, came similar ideas that were acted upon in other parts of the world. Washington DC remained sensitive about communism in Latin America, and in the early 1970s its main target was Salvador Allende's government in Chile. Allende was overthrown by army officers in 1973. His opponents had US backing, and with Allende gone Chile went on to enjoy substantial American aid. The right-wing dictatorship of Augusto Pinochet was to last for seventeen years. The Nixon approach was briefly reversed by Carter, who withdrew US support for repressive regimes in Latin America. In the 1980s the former pattern was restored.[83]

The British had reservations about the USA's bullying of Allende and the Labour governments of 1974 to 1979 imposed sanctions against Pinochet's regime. Thatcher's government resumed diplomatic relations with Chile, encouraged trade, and lifted Labour's arms embargo. Thatcher justified all this with the claim that the human rights situation in Chile was improving, even though the UN, Amnesty International and other bodies suggested otherwise. Thatcher's policy was in keeping with that of the Heath government shortly after the coup against Allende. Heath recognized the new Chilean leadership and the official British verdict was that recent events represented 'essentially a Chilean dispute settled by Chileans'.[84] In Moscow there was outrage at the coup against Allende. The US government was held responsible, but there was no desire on the Kremlin's part to endanger the gains made through détente, and Chile was too far away for the Soviets to make much difference there.[85]

The furore over Chile was embarrassing for the US government, but greater difficulty was to follow with the Arab–Israeli war of 1973. Nasser's successor in Egypt, Anwar Sadat, had in mind a limited war to regain the territories lost in 1967. The attack came on 6 October 1973, during the Jewish festival of Yom Kippur. The United States assisted Israel and then, when the tide turned against the Arabs, pressed for a ceasefire. The Soviets threatened to help Egypt and Syria, however, and Arab governments used their oil to pressurize the West. Kissinger went to Moscow, then to Israel, and the USA and USSR co-operated to pass a ceasefire resolution at the United Nations, but the Israelis now had the upper hand and refused to stop fighting. Soviet naval and air force activity was stepped up in the Mediterranean and US forces were suddenly placed on alert.[86] Brezhnev's suggestion that a joint US-Soviet force should be sent in to separate the belligerents, and that the Soviets might act alone if the Americans refused to participate, was the main cause of the US alert. It was called off on the understanding that a UN force would be put together, composed of contingents from non-nuclear powers.[87]

Opinion in the UN was against the Americans and their support for Israel. Unmoved, Kissinger was determined to take the lead in arranging peace talks and was irritated by suggestions from Western Europe. As he later recalled, 'unwilling to draw attention to the fact that they still enjoyed preferential status in Washington, British officials did nothing to stem the tide of criticism from the other allies – and fell in with the prevailing brouhaha over inadequate consultation'. The French tried to bolster anti-Americanism and within NATO there arose a greater willingness to object to US initiatives.[88]

Kissinger hardly communicated with America's allies as he worked for peace. His main tasks, he thought, were to persuade Moscow to allow him a free hand, and to persuade Israel to enter into discussions with the Arabs. A settlement was put together in stages during 1973 and 1974. Egypt and Israel came to an agreement, but a deal between Israel and Syria was more difficult to accomplish. President Hafez al-Asad of Syria accused Kissinger of deceit and decided that, despite the promises that had been made, Kissinger never had any intention of persuading Israel to return to its 1967 borders and to respect Palestinian rights. From the US perspective, however, Kissinger had done well, for he had kept the Soviets out of the war and the peace process. This was all the more remarkable in view of the Watergate scandal, which eventually led to Nixon's resignation.[89]

Governments in Western Europe were certain that the USA was wrong to side with Israel, but they could pursue no alternative common policy and rapidly lost Arab respect. They disagreed with one another and with Washington DC. American leaders complained that a fixation with Arab oil had produced a blinkered short-termism in Western Europe.[90] Kissinger's conduct offended Moscow, though the Kremlin did not automatically tar Britain with the same brush. Soviet leaders did not consider British policy to be as dangerous as that of the United States, and Home's visit to the USSR in December 1973 went well.[91]

Nixon toured the Middle East in June 1974. The beleaguered president hoped that an active foreign policy would help him to shore up his reputation at home. This hope was not to be realized. Arab and particularly Israeli intransigence hampered American attempts to promote stability in the region. The SALT II negotiations, meanwhile, had been going on for over a year, and Nixon made another high-profile visit to Moscow in search of a breakthrough. The Soviets expected him to make concessions but the Moscow talks achieved little.[92]

On SALT II the US government was divided. Those who were committed to arms control and saw in SALT a way to relax East–West tension argued against those who rejected the whole principle of SALT, and there were many advisers who insisted that whatever Moscow proposed had by definition to be contrary to US interests. The events of 1973–74 encouraged the revival of containment thinking. Flexibility, détente, SALT, Vietnam policy and other vital activities began to lose support.[93]

Kissinger visited London in July 1974 for discussions with the British foreign secretary, Callaghan. SALT was the main topic of conversation. Callaghan agreed with Kissinger that a way should be found to keep the process going, although the Soviet desire to include British and French nuclear forces presented a problem. When he was challenged in the Commons, Callaghan tried to sound optimistic about SALT and insisted that closer links with Europe would not prevent the British government from working with the Americans 'at any stage' it liked. *The Times* was unimpressed by the latest US–Soviet talks.[94]

Leaders in Western Europe wanted détente to continue, despite continuing tension on human rights and trade. The economic side of détente was not working as expected. Trade did not at first provide much political influence over the eastern bloc. Poland, Rumania and Hungary borrowed large sums from the West and invested in its technology, but were unable to use this technology to best effect, while 'stagflation' hit the West, interest rates rose and increased the size of the bloc's debts, and the West did not buy Eastern Europe's products in large quantities. Nevertheless, the commitment to CSCE was strong because of security and other concerns. The British, as before, went along with their allies while doubting that much would be accomplished.[95] This was also a period in which British defence experts became anxious about the possible impact of SALT on the Anglo-American nuclear relationship. Indeed, the US joint chiefs of staff did not see the need to help Britain on the same scale as before, and Kissinger had doubts about nuclear co-operation with Britain because he thought it might interfere with SALT.[96]

The problems of the 1970s did not go away. Some of them, indeed, grew worse. Despite the European and extra-European challenges of this time, however, British power did not collapse, and though its prestige and influence might have been more limited than before, Britain still had a role in most of the regions, institutions and relationships that determined the course of world affairs. These were years of frustration, and there was some pessimism when thoughts turned to what the future held for Britain. How long could further retreats be avoided? As a military power Britain was not in bad shape. There was continuity in defence policy, with high expenditure and the survival of multiple commitments, and Britain remained militarily strong. In this sphere there was not so much a decline as an adjustment to new conditions. Yet Britain's influence did not depend only on the nature and strength of its armed forces. Influence was lost less because of military weakness than because of an inability to mobilize other sources of power, especially economic and technological.[97] Diplomatic skill and political leadership were important as well. It remained to be seen whether Britain would be able so to organize all of its resources that they could be used to manage the situations that lay ahead.

10

Towards a New Order

The Cold War changed direction several times during the 1970s and 1980s. Negotiation increased, faltered, and then another thaw developed, with more flexibility and bargaining. Britain participated in these developments and in the 1980s there was a more self-confident tone in British diplomacy. Such is the nature of power, however, that it remained relative and contingent, and there was a limit to what Britain could do. On détente the British counselled their allies not to expect too much. They agreed that Western leaders should talk to the Soviets, but added that security had to be enhanced as well, and that Moscow should be subjected both to military pressure and to increased demands with respect to human rights. Through the 1970s and 1980s Britain was concerned to limit the concessions made by the West. The British continued to value the 'special relationship', and their main goals in international organizations – the EC, the UN security council, NATO – were to uphold British interests and to promote agreements in order to make these bodies function more efficiently. There were disputes, which sometimes obstructed British policy, and Britain was partly responsible for the quarrelling on nuclear weapons and arms control, superpower and European détente, the future of NATO, European integration, extra-European problems, and the meaning of reform within the USSR and eastern bloc.

Gerald Ford became US president in August 1974. Kissinger remained as secretary of state. Both men realized that a SALT II agreement was vital if détente was to continue. Ford and Brezhnev met for a summit in November 1974 at Vladivostok and declared a wish for continuity in US–Soviet relations, but tension was building not only over SALT but also over such questions as the Middle East peace process. Domestic politics in the United States also got in the way. Kissinger, who worked hard to keep SALT going, had to contend with pressure from Congress and opposition from other members of the Ford administration.[1] At Vladivostok it was agreed that the Americans and Soviets would each observe a limit of 2400 missiles and bombers, including no more than 1320 MIRVed missiles. This framework was incomplete because it did not cover the Cruise missiles of the USA and the Soviet 'Backfire' bomber. Ford grew worried that his rivals would use détente against him at election time, and this weakened his desire to complete SALT II.[2] Brezhnev's planned visit to the USA in 1975 never took place. The US–Soviet trade agreement of 1972 was cancelled by Moscow in January 1975 and three months later North Vietnamese forces reached Saigon, turning American opinion even more firmly against the idea of bargaining with communist regimes.[3]

British experts had always doubted that détente would achieve all the things expected of it. They assumed that the Kremlin still saw itself in a continuous struggle, with thaw a matter of tactical manoeuvre. *The Times* insisted that SALT I had to be followed up and feared that tension in one aspect of US–Soviet relations would affect all the others. Opinions differed about what had been achieved at Vladivostok, noted the *Guardian*, and even if the 'broad political context' had been improved, there was no sign of an end to the arms race.[4]

Eventually, five years after Vladivostok, a SALT II agreement was signed. Vladivostok proved to be important, therefore, because it laid down the basic principle: an equal overall limit on Soviet and US offensive strategic forces. Nevertheless, Brezhnev's criticism of US policy grew more insistent after Vladivostok; nuclear arsenals continued to expand; American arms sales abroad actually increased during Carter's presidency; and the Kremlin objected whenever Washington DC made trade and credit dependent on Soviet compromises with respect to human rights.[5]

Keen to demonstrate that he could still play a part in world affairs and that his government was committed to arms control, Wilson took some interest in SALT II during his premiership of 1974–76. As US–Soviet relations soured, however, there little that Wilson could do to redeem the situation. By this time, the British had a settled approach to SALT. Their main concerns were to keep Britain's deterrent out of the talks and to prevent restrictions on the exchange of information and technology from cutting across Anglo-American nuclear co-operation. These matters were relatively unimportant to Britain's European allies, and disagreements on SALT made for some awkward NATO meetings. When Thatcher became Britain's prime minister in May 1979 she publicly endorsed SALT, despite private reservations, and sought to take advantage of the Carter administration's wish to show NATO and US domestic opinion that the United States would look after its allies. This suggested that Washington DC would be generous when it came to negotiating the deal to replace Britain's Polaris force with Trident.[6]

British and American leaders were alarmed by Soviet and Cuban involvement in Africa. The rise of the left-wing Sandinistas in Nicaragua was also a worrying development. Soviet assertiveness was underlined by the expansion of the USSR's navy, and the Soviets had also maintained their superiority in conventional forces in the European theatre.[7] Yet the Cold War had reached something like equilibrium, based on the superpowers' respect for each other's spheres of influence. Both sides found it expedient to maintain the established distribution of power. Kissinger's chief adviser on the Soviet Union, Helmut Sonnenfeldt, told

US ambassadors in Europe in December 1975 that the unity of the USSR and eastern bloc suited American interests because it promoted stability. Here was a frank admission that stability mattered more than trying to win the Cold War, or at least, this was how Sonnenfeldt's remarks were reported. Opponents of détente seized on what they saw as weakness. At the same time, however, efforts were made to expose Soviet economic inefficiency through East–West trade, so the model of stability did allow for elements of change.[8]

Change could also be pursued through CSCE. Though Kissinger resented what he took to be the unhelpful attitude of the Europeans, who were more regularly challenging US policy and who acted in CSCE not as a single entity but as individual states, ready to bargain with the USSR and the countries of Eastern Europe,[9] he was satisfied with the Helsinki Final Act. Existing borders had been confirmed, but the Brezhnev Doctrine had been contradicted because the Act obliged all its signatories to respect one another's freedom to develop their own political, cultural, social and economic systems. Moscow went on arguing that human rights were strictly an internal matter for each individual state, but this did not silence the dissidents and reform movements in the communist bloc or the many 'Helsinki Watch' groups in the West. Washington DC did not want MBFR to be complicated by any confidence-building measures that were agreed as part of the Helsinki process, but did come round to the view that CSCE could be used against Moscow. Still, the Americans never attached the same importance as their allies did to the Helsinki process. European détente had deeper roots than superpower détente.[10]

The British could take a consistent line on CSCE because they were more detached than others. CSCE issues were less urgent for Britain than they were for the FRG, for example, and British governments did not have to contend with the ethnic lobbies, partisan rivalries and moralizing over foreign policy that affected the White House. The British saw that CSCE embraced potentially contradictory tendencies. It covered inter-state relations, and here the purpose was to reduce tension, which meant showing respect for the existing order in Europe. It also covered relations between the individual and the state, and here the agenda was for change. In effect, the British sought a middle way between acceptance of a political freeze in Eastern Europe and rejection of the Soviet claim to dominion there. In contrast, the Americans did not pursue a consistent line. Although Sonnenfeldt had suggested in 1975 that the West should accept the existence of the Soviet sphere, for example, at the Stockholm CSCE review meeting of 1984 US secretary of state George Shultz declared that the USSR's position in Eastern Europe had no legitimacy whatsoever.[11] For the British, in the 1980s as in the 1970s, détente could not be the main priority. Though ready to promote it, they continued to insist that the West had to attend to self-defence as well as to thaw.[12]

In June 1979 the SALT II treaty was finally signed. It was to last until the end of 1985 and its primary function was to limit the size of offensive arsenals. Perhaps its main significance was political: US–Soviet relations appeared to have improved again; both sides felt strong enough to strike a bargain; and public opinion across the world had become much more interested in and informed about arms control.[13]

When Callaghan was Britain's foreign secretary and prime minister, he believed that whatever Soviet leaders might say in public, the truth was that they wanted peace. Soviet policy was more pragmatic than ideological, he thought, and increasingly organized around détente, trade and East–West contacts. Outside Europe, however, in parts of Africa, Asia and Latin America, this was a time of war and revolution during which competition between the West and the Soviets continued unabated. The Americans aided their friends and harassed their enemies in Latin America, supported anti-communist factions in Angola, and encouraged South Africa to intervene in Angola and Mozambique. It seemed that the tide was turning against the United States in the developing world, as Vietnam, Laos, Cambodia, Ethiopia, Angola, Mozambique, Nicaragua and Afghanistan either moved into the Soviet sphere or came under the control of left-wing leaders. Although the British were less worried about these regimes, they tended to back US diplomatic and military action.[14]

The Americans were disappointed by the failure of détente as a method of restraining the USSR. The Soviet invasion of Afghanistan late in 1979 led them to shelve the SALT II treaty and begin a rearmament programme. According to the Carter Doctrine, the United States would resist Soviet intervention in the oil states of the Persian Gulf. Carter's successor went further. Convinced that the Soviets could be tamed, Reagan massively increased the US defence budget and pursued an assertive anti-Soviet policy. Tension rose, then fell again as Gorbachev's rise to ascendancy in Moscow opened the door for a new period of negotiation. One result was the Intermediate Nuclear Forces (INF) Treaty of 1987.[15]

These were years in which America's allies complained ever more loudly that they were not being properly consulted. As Carter made human rights central to East–West relations, the British pointed out that this was unlikely to promote harmony. Though Callaghan agreed that the Soviets should be reminded of their obligations under the Helsinki Final Act, he advised that they should not be pushed too hard, but Carter opted for a public policy of rewards and penalties. President Giscard d'Estaing of France became a firm opponent of US policy. There were sharp disagreements over détente, with Paris and Bonn frequently taking a view that was distinct from that of Washington DC.[16]

More questions were raised about America's willingness to look after its allies' interests. These were linked with moves for greater European co-operation, seen in the revival of the WEU and the development of EPC. Britain involved itself mainly to prevent France and the FRG from taking the lead. The British valued the US military presence in Europe and opposed the anti-American line taken by others. Clearly, the American domestic consensus on the importance of NATO could not be allowed to break down, which made it crucial for the Europeans to convince America that burdens were being shared. Europe's double-mindedness with regard to the USA was evidenced on other matters. Reagan's Strategic Defence Initiative was condemned, for instance, and yet there was a scramble for contracts and the allies accepted the American decision to deal with them individually rather than collectively.[17]

For hard-liners in America and Britain, Soviet willingness to compromise from the mid-1980s was a consequence of the courage and firmness of the conservative leaderships in Washington DC and London. This version of events was quite persuasive at the time, but it was coupled with misgivings. British defence planners gave plenty of thought to the question of what might happen if Gorbachev's conciliatory stance was replaced by a hawkish attitude in Moscow, and tensions within NATO continued to grow on INF and the bilateral arrangements being made by the United States and USSR. Despite her respect for Gorbachev, Thatcher insisted that the Soviets were still dangerous. The 'Eurogroup' looked for ways to reinforce NATO and compensate for the loss of US weapons under the INF Treaty.[18]

European leaders were not slow to distance themselves from the United States when they saw advantage in doing so, but Britain's influence held up quite well in these circumstances and the British achieved their main goals: holding NATO together; framing agreements that combined British, European and US preferences; preventing a fatal rupture between America and its allies; and keeping the Americans involved in Western Europe's security system.[19]

From the mid-1980s Moscow paid more attention to Western Europe, not only in an effort to get the INF talks moving but also because the EC was regarded as an important body in international affairs. Gorbachev knew of the possibility of common defence planning and foreign policy in the EC. He thought this might be used as leverage in his negotiations with Reagan. He also wanted to see how friendly Bonn, Paris and London were disposed to be, and to increase the USSR's trade with Western Europe.[20]

The western half of Europe had been transformed over the preceding years. All the talk was of a 'new Europe', typified by the rise of the FRG. The French were worried and it was with much relief that Paris had reconstructed a positive working relationship with Bonn during the 1970s. West German chancellor Helmut Schmidt and French president Giscard d'Estaing both took office in 1974. Their co-operation resulted in such initiatives as EMS, a key element of economic convergence about which Britain remained unenthusiastic.[21] Meanwhile, 'Ostpolitik' had altered Europe's political complexion. The Americans were not particularly pleased about Bonn's independent line, and the French were conscious that it had not been necessary for the FRG to gain their approval.[22]

By the end of the 1970s Britain had a long record of constructive, if limited, engagement with the Soviets, mainly trade agreements and scientific, technical and cultural exchanges. The Heath government had extended these contacts to Poland, Hungary, Czechoslovakia, Rumania and the GDR. In non-military spheres, it was thought, concessions might be appropriate, provided that strong defences were maintained. The FRG proceeded on the same basis. 'Ostpolitik' was praised in the British press and in some ways it increased the pressure on the British government to participate in the wider détente. British leaders could not ignore the domestic popularity of détente. Nor could they remain idle while France, the FRG and the USA were all working to improve their own contacts with the USSR.[23] 'Ostpolitik' made the Heath government more active in seeking better relations with the eastern bloc, and Callaghan consistently supported 'Ostpolitik' as useful in itself and as a means of facilitating more trade and other links between Britain and the bloc.[24] The Soviets were aware of Britain's relative economic and military decline and did not attach the importance to British opinion that they once had, but in London it was assumed that British influence would grow if something could be made of the USSR's economic difficulties, the gradual loss of cohesion in the eastern bloc, the moves for common policies in Western Europe, and the USA's internal problems.[25]

Under Carter, America's relations with other countries increasingly depended on their human rights records. There were complaints from the Soviets, from some of the USA's allies who found the policy unhelpful, and from Carter's opponents at home, while for Britain the human rights aspects of détente were central, as Wilson had made plain at the Helsinki conference in August 1975. There were disagreements about the Helsinki process in Britain. While he was prime minister, Wilson argued that it would bring positive results. *The Times* gave the Helsinki conference a mixed review, and Thatcher argued at the time that much more would be needed to alter the 'underlying position' in Europe. In the long run Helsinki turned out to be more significant than Thatcher predicted. The fact that the humanitarian strand was open-ended proved to be advantageous to the West.[26]

By the end of the 1970s the American government was taking a harder line and argument was increasing between Washington DC on one side and Bonn and Paris on the other, with London frequently stuck in the middle. Thatcher could do little to break the influence in Europe of the Franco-German axis and feared that the Americans might one day elevate their relations with Bonn above those with London.[27] Her wish to show loyalty to the Americans was related to her notion that Britain's usefulness to the United States had been fading. While she was not prepared to support the Americans on every issue, Thatcher did insist that without closer ties between London and Washington DC Britain could not expect to be safe or successful.[28]

Thatcher disliked Helmut Kohl, chancellor of the FRG from 1982, and saw that détente would bring serious problems if it led to the withdrawal of US forces from Europe and the creation of a Europe in which the Germans were supreme. Nicholas Ridley, a member of Thatcher's cabinet from 1983, eventually complained that Kohl wanted to take over everything. In July 1990 Ridley declared that to give sovereignty to European institutions would be like giving it to Hitler. He had to resign, yet his thinking on these matters was close to that of the prime minister.[29]

According to Geoffrey Howe, chancellor of the exchequer from 1979 and foreign secretary between 1983 and 1989, Thatcher *was* anti-German, Bonn knew it, and this was part of a bigger problem: the prime minister's reluctance to work constructively with Britain's European partners. From the beginning of her premiership, indeed, Thatcher had made a point of challenging them. She claimed that Britain was paying too much into the EC budget and managed to get a new financial agreement. Lord Carrington, foreign secretary from 1979 to 1982, thought that although she was right to make an issue of Britain's contribution, her conduct created a negative atmosphere and hindered efforts to achieve other goals. In 1990 the British government was embarrassed not only by the Ridley affair but also by a leaked report about a high-level meeting at which negative remarks were made about the German character. Controversy increased as news came through from Moscow, where Gorbachev and Kohl were discussing German reunification. Labour leader Neil Kinnock described Thatcher as a 'Cold War nostalgist . . . philosophically unwilling to undertake the co-operation necessary in these new times'.[30]

British politics were increasingly dominated by the struggle between Europeanists and Euro-sceptics. According to the *Economist*, this schism could be seen in the government, in the Conservative and Labour parties, and in the nation as a whole. Somehow, argued *The Times*, Britain would have to embrace European integration while remaining on guard against the dangers it posed. In one sense Ridley was right, *The Times* suggested, because the changes that were in prospect would make the Germans even more powerful.[31]

Thatcher warned that German reunification would have negative effects on Gorbachev's position, his negotiations with the West, and the stability of Eastern Europe. The people of East Germany would choose democracy by themselves, she thought, because communism was collapsing, and reunification was a separate issue. She appealed to Reagan's successor in the United States, George Bush, and to French president Francois Mitterrand, pointing out that the question of territorial adjustments had been addressed in the Helsinki Final Act: Europe's borders were to be respected, not subverted. When Kohl came out strongly for reunification, however, Washington DC and Paris gave cautious support, linking the matter with further European integration.[32]

Circumstances had changed remarkably and quickly. In the early 1980s American fears about the loss of influence in Europe had deepened. The US government imposed sanctions on the USSR following the invasion of Afghanistan in 1979, and within a year America's exports to the USSR fell by half. In the same period British, French and West German exports to the Soviet Union increased by 30 per cent. Of special concern was a pipeline that would carry gas from Siberia into Western Europe. At the end of 1981 the Reagan administration tightened the sanctions against the Soviets following the imposition of martial law in Poland. In June 1982 the Americans decided to include pipeline technology in these sanctions. Kohl and Mitterrand, and even Thatcher, insisted that the pipeline contracts should be respected, and Washington DC relented in November 1982.[33]

Thatcher generally supported the Americans in their firm line against the USSR, but she was unsure about the usefulness of sanctions and argued that the Soviets should not be punished only by economic measures. Moreover, Reagan's sanctions ran counter to the sale of massive amounts of US grain to the Soviets.[34]

In the summer of 1982 the Thatcher government insisted that a way would be found to safeguard the pipeline contracts won by British companies. To some observers the dispute presaged a trade war between the EC and the United States, for there was bound to be increased rivalry in a time of global economic difficulty. Although the prime minister was concerned about Afghanistan and Poland, she told the Americans that the pipeline was not relevant and that this was an issue on which NATO might become fatally divided. Bonn and Paris were not going to give way. Thatcher also denied that the pipeline would make the FRG and France dependent on Soviet energy and amenable to Moscow's wishes. Britain's own interests were at stake too. Thatcher was certain that the pipeline would benefit the British economy, and, in view of the loans made by Britain to Poland, she was anxious about America's threat to force the Poles to default on their international debts. She advised Reagan that contention over the pipeline would be more disadvantageous than allowing the pipeline to go ahead.[35]

The Americans were surprised by the strength of this reaction to sanctions. The quarrelling made plain a fundamental difference between the USA and its allies on East–West relations, and tensions remained even after the pipeline crisis had passed. In Western Europe, linkage with the economies of the USSR and eastern bloc was deemed to be appropriate, while the Reagan administration chose to bring its trade policy more into line with US military and geopolitical interests.[36]

This helps to explain why the 1980s were quite unlike the 1970s. The Nixon, Ford and Carter administrations had all favoured a thaw in the Cold War. For this reason, they were willing occasionally to make concessions to America's allies. Willingness to bargain was in large measure a consequence of the USA's economic difficulties. In time, though, Carter's annoyance with the French and West Germans increased, with Callaghan often acting as go-between.[37] The détente of the 1970s lost support. Late in 1979 NATO adopted the 'dual track' policy: the Soviets would be pressed to withdraw their SS20 missiles aimed at Western Europe, and, if there was no deal on this, equivalent US weapons would be deployed, mainly in West Germany. The deployment of Cruise and Pershing missiles proved to be very controversial. Some Europeans accused the Americans of overreacting to events in Europe and to the wars in Angola and Ethiopia and the Soviet invasion of Afghanistan. Even in Britain there was both a strong peace movement and a high level of scepticism about certain US policies.[38]

Thatcher considered the 1970s to be a period of US weakness and was glad when Reagan took over as president. She wanted more toughness from the Americans, but in Western Europe there was little enthusiasm for this. Opposition to the deployment of Cruise and Pershing increased and governments had to try harder to maintain domestic support for their defence programmes.[39] Moscow attempted to forestall the 'dual track' decision. Brezhnev wished to avoid an increase in East–West tension while there was still a chance that the US Senate would ratify SALT II. The Kremlin soon ran out of patience and issued threats. In the West there were calls for the deployment of missiles to be postponed.[40]

The Soviets assumed that NATO would sooner or later fall into line with what Washington DC wanted. Therefore it did not seem worthwhile for Moscow to try to exploit popular opposition to deployment. Instead, the Soviets focused on SALT III and pressed for a speedy resumption of US–Soviet contacts. Lord Carrington later insisted that European leaders never doubted the need to deploy Cruise and Pershing and that the deployment was purely a response to the SS20s. *The Times* backed NATO policy and argued that the alliance could not afford to delay its security measures. Though Brezhnev claimed to want an agreement, he was not offering enough to justify any such postponement.[41]

The 'dual track' entailed a commitment to talks as well as to deployment, and it was natural for governments and peoples to attach great importance to negotiation in the context of 'Ostpolitik', CSCE, SALT and MBFR. Moreover, Washington DC could hardly disappoint the Europeans in their desire for meaningful talks if it wished to restore their confidence in US security guarantees. Chancellor Schmidt was not alone in thinking that arms-control talks would make new Soviet deployments less likely, and all interested parties knew that without progress on this, Cruise and Pershing would not be politically acceptable in Western Europe. At the same time, it was thought that Moscow would have no incentive to make a bargain unless NATO deployed Cruise and Pershing.[42] Thatcher was insisting by 1987 and the signing of the INF Treaty that NATO's fortitude had forced the Soviets to withdraw their SS20s and that the whole exercise had therefore been worthwhile.[43]

Problems outside as well as inside Europe caused continuing disagreements in the West. On Angola there was no common policy with regard to recognition of the left-wing regime established in 1975. Nor was there unity on Afghanistan. The Americans expected support for their policy of suspending East–West dialogue and imposing punitive measures upon the USSR, but leaders in Western Europe were unwilling to oblige, for they would not give up hope for an end to the Cold War. Against American wishes, French president Giscard d'Estaing met with Brezhnev in Warsaw in May 1980 to discuss Afghanistan.[44] This meeting and the divisions within NATO and the EC did not please the British government or the British press. An air of unity was restored, but when Carrington went to Moscow to propose an international conference on Afghanistan, Soviet foreign minister Gromyko refused to entertain the idea.[45]

The Thatcher government did not find it easy to reconcile differing needs in the early 1980s, and the situation in Afghanistan made matters worse. The prime minister was convinced that the Soviets had to be resisted, but she also wanted to cut Britain's defence budget. Carrington had no doubt that détente could be salvaged, and found the Reagan administration too confrontational. On Afghanistan, Carrington thought, it was necessary to offer the Soviets a way out, perhaps through arrangements for the neutralization of Afghanistan. He did not win much support for this among Britain's allies.[46]

Leaders in Western Europe were not going to abandon their pursuit of détente just because Britain or America said they should. They did not regard the invasion of Afghanistan as a final straw and they were not prepared to stop talking to Moscow. For them, détente could not be sacrificed for the sake of problems outside Europe. The Americans had in due course to agree to carry forward the INF talks with the Soviets.[47] Brezhnev claimed that relations were ruptured not because of Afghanistan but because there were powerful groups in the United States and in NATO that opposed détente.[48] His words were not without effect in the West.

In Moscow the idea had developed since the late 1960s that détente would deliver tactical and possibly lasting advantages, but a thaw abroad did not entail reform at home. Inside the Soviet Union the Brezhnev regime was firmly entrenched. Most of the measures that had been introduced by Khrushchev, including the relaxation of censorship and the criminal code, had been reversed. A new constitution adopted in 1977 reinforced the totalitarian system.[49] This made even more important the human rights aspects of CSCE, much to Moscow's dissatisfaction. Internal repression in the USSR and eastern bloc featured ever more prominently in the diplomacy and propaganda of the West.[50] Soviet leaders continued to warn that détente was being jeopardized, while the West maintained that all parts of the Helsinki Final Act were interdependent. There was disagreement about how to promote change in the Soviet Union, and Thatcher decided that the West was becoming complacent. As she saw it, the willingness to make concessions remained strong even though Soviet prisons and labour camps were filling up. When Brezhnev defended the 1977 constitution against its critics in the West, *The Times* pointed out that it prescribed no limits on state power and that 'rights' in the USSR had more to do with obligation than freedom. Similar comments were made in the *Observer*.[51]

The Kremlin was essentially unmoved by all the talk of human rights. Soviet leaders considered that they had no option but to maintain discipline and stability at home, not least as a platform for growing influence abroad, especially in the developing world.[52] Washington DC responded, often clumsily, as was the case with Nicaragua. The USA had been supporting the right-wing dictator Anastasio Somoza, and after he was overthrown a political, economic and military struggle was carried on against the Sandinista government, beginning under Carter and intensified by Reagan. The Conservative government and press in Britain backed US policy, accepting that even if Moscow was reluctant to interfere in Latin America, Washington DC could not be sure that this would remain the Soviet position.[53] American support for the insurgency against Nicaragua's left-wing regime had an impact in Western Europe. Here was a sign of how Washington DC viewed the wider relationship between the West and the USSR. The question of how to handle Nicaragua merged into the question of how to handle Moscow. On the other hand, since Britain and the other European members of NATO had little at stake in Latin America, they saw no point in risking an open breach with the United States.[54]

This is not to suggest that they were oblivious to Soviet designs and communist advances outside Europe. Anxiety did grow about Nicaragua, Africa, Soviet naval strength and a host of related problems, including Soviet success in the international arms trade. By 1980 the USSR was the biggest seller of arms in the world. There were quarrels in NATO, meanwhile, because the Americans tried to push their allies into buying US weapons. Commercial competition in this regard meant that there was little chance of standardizing conventional armaments within the alliance.[55]

The arms trade was a matter of no small concern to the British. In the relationship with South Africa, for instance, the sale of weaponry had come to play a key part. The Labour government appointed in 1974 reintroduced the embargo on sales that Heath had removed, which caused an outcry, since Britain was losing a good customer.[56] Soviet and Cuban involvement in Africa complicated matters. South Africa had long been a reliable anti-communist ally.

The Americans regularly consulted Callaghan about Africa. Soviet involvement there featured in his discussions with Kissinger, and events in Angola and Mozambique affected Britain's effort to find a settlement in Rhodesia.[57] Callaghan expected Soviet activism to recede. He was confident that Helsinki would influence Soviet policy and that the USSR's economic strength would wane. His successor as prime minister was not convinced. Thatcher pointed to 'communist subversion throughout the Third World', yet in one respect Callaghan was right. For all its signs of vigour, the USSR's economic growth slowed down, and by the time the West placed limits on trade in response to the invasion of Afghanistan, the eastern bloc was heavily indebted to the West. Moscow began to see the satellites as a burden. Soviet agricultural policy, meanwhile, had been failing for years.[58] The economic side of détente was important to Callaghan, who had envisaged East–West co-operation on the world's economic problems, direct contact between businessmen, the exchange of useful commercial information, improved services for individual firms, and, in time, the erosion of distinctions between the economic systems of the West and those of the communist bloc.[59]

As leader of the opposition, Thatcher had accused Labour of gullibility and eschewed the optimism that surrounded the Helsinki process. She continued in this vein as prime minister, rejecting the conciliatory attitude of some in Europe and praising the hard-line approach of the Americans (with reservations). She also began to emphasize human rights and the CSCE review conferences. In various ways the Thatcher government sought to re-establish Britain as a world power, and one of the reasons that a task force was sent to the South Atlantic in response to Argentina's invasion of the Falklands was to show that Britain was strong.[60]

In the early 1980s the prime minister saw no need for overtures to Moscow. She did not attend Brezhnev's funeral in 1982, and although she was at the funeral of Brezhnev's successor, Yuri Andropov, in 1984, she did not speak to or even shake hands with the new Soviet leader Konstantin Chernenko. Cultural exchanges between Britain and Eastern Europe at this time were limited, as was trade. In the mid-1980s only about 2 per cent of Britain's total trade was with the USSR and eastern bloc. Attitudes began to soften after the Conservatives were confirmed in office by the general election of 1983. Reappraisal suited Thatcher. She was confident after victory in the Falklands War and her electoral success, and aware that international circumstances were changing. The foreign secretary from 1983, Howe, was strongly in favour of a thaw with Moscow.[61] He visited most of the countries in the eastern bloc. In December 1984 a Soviet delegation arrived in Britain, led by Gorbachev, the coming man in Soviet politics. During 1985 and 1986 several British representatives went to Moscow to discuss trade, energy and other matters.[62] Criticism of the Soviets was now combined with agreements with them. There were arrangements for economic co-operation, an accord on finance and credit, and exploratory talks on the prevention of terrorism. Thatcher and Gorbachev met for a summit in Moscow in March 1987. There were further efforts to expand trade. In December 1987 Gorbachev stopped in England on his way to sign the INF Treaty in Washington DC. Thatcher's claim to be more than merely a European leader irritated Paris and Bonn, but here was Gorbachev, treating her as someone who could influence the Americans and whose views on international affairs really mattered.[63]

British power, measured in economic and military terms, was still limited, but power also depended on perception and presentation. If Britain's importance in East–West relations had diminished since the days of Eden and Macmillan, Thatcher's conduct suggested otherwise. On the other hand, Britain was only the junior partner in the 'special relationship' with America, and London's determination to stay close to Washington DC set limits on the improvement of Anglo-Soviet relations. Neither Britain nor the USSR considered these relations to be of primary importance. Moscow focused more on Bonn and Paris than on London in an effort to facilitate European détente. Although the Soviets occasionally thought of using London to test opinion in Washington DC, Britain's influence in Moscow fell behind that of the FRG and France.[64]

Nevertheless, the emergence of 'new Europe', the vision of a multi-polar world, and related changes in the international situation meant that the two superpowers were not so dominant, and they recognized this. They knew they had to show more respect towards other powers. Nixon's détente had been partly based on the premise that America needed friends. The Americans engaged in talks with Peking and Moscow simultaneously in the early 1970s, and claimed that they wanted 'an open world' in which no state was isolated. The Carter administration established full diplomatic relations with China in 1978 and ended the USA's mutual defence treaty with Taiwan, and during the 1980s there was a large increase in US–Chinese trade. The international order *did* change, but how much? Despite the strength of China, Japan and the FRG, talk of a new configuration was in some ways premature. In the military sphere, indeed, it is difficult to detect a shift away from bipolarity. The USA and USSR still had military supremacy, with their nuclear arsenals and large conventional forces.[65]

Yet the general assumption was that bipolarity was giving way to multi-polarity. What were the implications of this for Britain? The British were aware that they could no longer exert much direct influence in the Middle East and Far East, but they still expected to play a role as opportunities arose. Heath had characterized the early 1970s as a period when circumstances changed more quickly than they had for many years.[66] Thereafter, economic realities necessitated more co-operation and the leading nations of the non-communist world, the G7 (Group of Seven, consisting of the United States, Britain, Canada, Japan, the FRG, France and Italy) held regular summits from the mid-1970s. In time the G7 took up political as well as economic concerns. Reagan used the G7 to put pressure on the Soviets. Economic rivalry had always been part of the Cold War.

Now, in the 1980s, economic help for the USSR from the G7 could be withheld unless the Soviets made concessions (only with the break-up of the USSR and eastern bloc after 1990 did the G7 become the G8, with Russia as a member). The Reagan administration was certain that economic pressure should be employed against Moscow. Some leaders in Western Europe disagreed, while Japan's fear of Soviet assertiveness increased, leading Tokyo to favour a united front.[67]

For the Americans the use of economic pressure became more difficult, and on economic matters Moscow was influenced less by US policy than by the price of oil, the indebtedness of the USSR and its satellites, and the pressure for economic liberalization created by the success of the FRG, Sweden and Japan and by reforms in Eastern Europe. Indeed, the Reagan years saw the USA's relative economic position deteriorate. Never again would the United States dominate the global economy as it once had.[68]

The changing international situation also affected the United Nations. By the mid-1960s the majority of UN members were from Africa and Asia. Although America, Britain and France were permanent members of the security council and could influence its deliberations, the UN seemed increasingly anti-West in attitude. The G7 certainly made this charge. The Americans resorted to undermining the UN, while many observers protested that the G7, UN security council, IMF and World Bank were all being used selfishly by the rich nations of the West. The framing of international economic arrangements became the subject of ongoing disputation between the G7 and UN. Increasingly, G7 countries moved outside formal frameworks for exchange rates, credit flow, tariffs and related matters and set their own rules.[69]

Britain's experiences in the G7 were not particularly happy. A quarrel developed from late 1975 over energy policy, with Britain insisting that as the EC's only oil producer, it had to speak for itself and not as part of the EC. The G7 conference hosted by Britain in May 1977 was marred by tension, especially between America and the FRG. From 1979 Thatcher condemned French and West German ideas on how to promote economic and financial stability. She was unenthusiastic about concerted programmes for growth, all the more so as European integration picked up speed. The weakness of sterling and Britain's economic decline relative to the rest of the G7 meant that there were few opportunities to shape collective policy. Nor is it likely that membership of the G7 increased Britain's importance to the Americans. Still, there were occasions when Britain benefited from G7 decisions, as when an effort was made in the mid-1980s to limit the variability of exchange rates.[70]

The G7's tendency to address important political issues, not only economic ones, was confirmed during the 1980s. The summit of 1983 considered arms control and endorsed NATO's deployment of Cruise and Pershing missiles, though France and Canada had misgivings. The summit of 1986 discussed international terrorism. The summit of 1987 looked again at arms control, and was notable for a quarrel between Britain and the FRG on the question of short-range nuclear weapons.[71]

British dissatisfaction with the UN increased, meanwhile, and there was a link here with Britain's attitude towards developing countries, some of which were members of the Commonwealth. The overseas aid budget was cut under Thatcher. She was attacked for this, for her opposition to sanctions against South Africa, and for Britain's withdrawal from UN initiatives in education, science and culture, but the Commonwealth and the developing world were not important to Britain in the 1980s, and even if the British saw some need to remain involved in parts of Africa and Asia in order to contain communism, the means and the will were decreasing. London had complained in the 1970s that the UN's measures disregarded and disadvantaged the advanced countries. Thatcher used the fortieth anniversary meeting of the UN in 1985 to call for dramatic improvements in the body's policy making and practical action. These years also saw mounting discord over UN peacekeeping efforts.[72]

Criticism of the UN arose in some quarters because it seemed incapable of halting the spread of nuclear weapons. While established powers like Japan and the FRG were happy to remain non-nuclear because they had US security guarantees, an increasing number of states had developed nuclear capability, including China, India, Pakistan, Israel and South Africa. Japan chose not to endanger economic progress by trying to keep up with all the latest weaponry, though there was a snag in that Washington DC became concerned about the trade imbalance between America and Japan.[73] Tokyo was an interested observer of US negotiations with the USSR and China in the 1970s and the subsequent INF negotiations between the Americans and Soviets. China's development of nuclear weapons was a worry, as was the prospect that if Moscow promised to reduce the number of SS20s aimed at Western Europe, these missiles might be transferred to Asia.[74] The Japanese respected Washington DC's desire to stop the spread of nuclear technology, but Japan's energy needs prompted the development of nuclear facilities and although the United States tried to delay this, it was clear that the West had less to fear from Japan than it had from the nuclear aspirations of unstable regimes in the developing world.[75]

While Japan kept out of the arms race Britain had taken a different course, relying on the Americans for up-to-date weaponry and desiring the closest possible military and strategic co-operation with the United States. The Callaghan government of 1976–79 pursued two goals simultaneously: international disarmament and the modernization of the British deterrent. These were not considered to be contradictory, since a viable deterrent would be a useful bargaining tool in disarmament talks with the Soviets. Bonn was not so sure, and as Carter and Schmidt clashed over how to persuade the Soviets to remove their

SS20s,[76] Callaghan convinced Carter that the United States should renew Britain's deterrent. Carter decided that supplying Britain with a successor to Polaris would enhance Western security and assist with SALT. Britain's military experts thought that Trident missiles represented the best option, but discussions were still in progress when Callaghan's government fell in May 1979.[77]

As in previous years, Britain's desire to preserve its deterrent was combined with a desire to check nuclear proliferation. Agreements were in place to halt the spread of nuclear weapons. The Test Ban Treaty of 1963, Outer Space Treaty of 1967 and Non-Proliferation Treaty of 1968 were followed by SALT I and II, but nothing could prevent the development of marginal nuclear capacity by unstable regimes and states that felt insecure or inadequately protected by alliances. The main nuclear powers were pressed to make a commitment that they would not use nuclear weapons against any non-nuclear state. Special meetings took place at the UN on this matter, but no agreements were reached.[78]

For Britain a chief difficulty was that more robust non-proliferation treaties would get in the way of planned defence projects. When he was prime minister, Callaghan was personally in favour of a test ban agreement, but he saw no easy way to resolve such matters as enforcement, coverage and duration. Preventing the transfer of information and technology from civilian to military establishments also seemed impossible. Quarrels continued about the exportation of nuclear plant and technology: the Americans repeatedly urged France and the FRG to discontinue these exports.[79] Britain's purchase of Trident appeared to some commentators to be incompatible with non-proliferation, but British leaders responded by pointing out that Trident represented continuity, in keeping with the established policy of modernization, and insisted that there was no conflict between deterrence and non-proliferation.[80]

Attention was increasingly focused on SALT II. In Western Europe there was some disquiet at the prospect of a US–Soviet deal that would limit the long-range weapons the superpowers could use against each other while hardly affecting weaponry designed for use in Europe. Tension within NATO increased on this and on other matters.[81] Carter implored America's allies to keep their nerve, for he needed their help if he was going to ask the US Senate to ratify SALT II. He then intended to move on quickly with SALT III, which he knew would require an agreed position in NATO. The question arose as to whether NATO's nuclear forces should be modernized before, during or after the talks for SALT III.[82]

When Thatcher went to Washington DC in December 1979, one of the results was a joint statement of support for the British deterrent and Anglo-American strategic co-operation. The British were still concerned about the impact of SALT on the USA's role as protector of Western Europe, however, and this in turn had implications for the upgrading of Britain's deterrent. The British deterrent was excluded from SALT II, but US negotiators assumed that it would feature in SALT III, provided the Soviets made concessions.[83] Former British prime minister Edward Heath complained that not enough was done to revive the negotiating process after SALT II. The American failure to ratify SALT II, and the belief that the USSR had benefited from a shift in the nuclear balance during the 1970s, did not make for a helpful context.[84]

In 1980 the Thatcher government confirmed that Britain would be purchasing Trident at a cost of about £5 billion (on terms that were similar to those in the Nassau Agreement concluded by Macmillan and Kennedy in 1962).[85] Then the Reagan administration announced plans to develop an improved version, Trident II. This introduced new difficulties: it was argued that Britain could not afford Trident II and did not really need it, that it would not be possible to exclude it from future arms-control arrangements, that it would provoke a Soviet reaction, and that British public opinion would not accept it. By January 1982, however, Thatcher had decided that Britain had to have the same system as the Americans, instead of relying (as had happened with Polaris) on weaponry that was no longer used by the USA and for which there was no production and support network. The government admitted that Trident II would exceed the nation's defence requirements, but calculated that, rather than develop independent facilities, it would be cheaper to have the Americans service the weapons. Thatcher therefore concluded a new agreement with Washington DC that was expected to cost £10 billion. Labour MPs condemned the policy, as did peace campaigners and anti-nuclear protesters. Controversy continued as the running costs of Polaris and the expenditure on Trident swallowed up an ever-bigger share of the defence budget.[86]

Trident was one of the key issues in the general election of June 1987, which the Conservative government easily survived. Having frustrated their domestic opponents, however, ministers now had to cope with allies in Europe who claimed that Trident was interfering with arms control and that Thatcher's determination to have Trident was part of a scheme to cut Britain's conventional contribution to NATO.[87]

Developments in British strategy influenced and were influenced by the debate surrounding intermediate-range nuclear forces. NATO's 'dual track' policy involved the strengthening of defences while seeking an arms-reduction deal with the USSR. Despite considerable domestic opposition, the British government agreed that Cruise missiles would be stationed in Britain, but London also pressed Washington DC on the other side of the 'dual track' policy and insisted that greater efforts should be made to negotiate with the USSR. The Americans put forward the 'zero option': if the Soviets abandoned their INF systems there would be no NATO deployments. Matters were complicated by Reagan's 'star wars' programme, announced in the spring of 1983. The Soviets wanted all elements to be brought together in a comprehensive treaty, but the Americans wanted to keep them apart, as did the British.[88]

The INF Treaty was signed by Reagan and Gorbachev late in 1987. As a settlement became likely, Britain's ambivalence had been increasingly exposed. The government wanted a treaty and sought to remove such obstacles as SDI, but at the same time there was a determination to prevent the 'decoupling' of American and European defence, which seemed inevitable if all intermediate-range weapons were withdrawn from Europe. Thatcher sought assurances from Reagan, especially at the time of the Reagan–Gorbachev summit at Reykjavik in October 1986. Reagan alarmed her when he spoke of a deal for the abandonment of all nuclear weapons.[89]

The British government and chiefs of staff did not want all intermediate-range missiles to be removed from Europe, but they knew they would have to accept a treaty of some sort, and they did not wish to annoy Washington DC in case they jeopardized the Trident deal. Thatcher focused on one main priority: in order to preserve a credible British deterrent, she insisted that the idea of eliminating all ballistic missiles should be given up. Luckily for her, the US government was itself divided on the matter. She took advantage and a joint statement was agreed. It advocated an INF treaty, a 50 per cent reduction in strategic forces over five years, a ban on chemical weapons, continuing SDI research, the NATO strategy of mixed arsenals including nuclear, and modernization of Britain's deterrent.[90]

While refusing to abandon SDI, or to admit that his earlier opinions about the Soviets had been mistaken, Reagan admitted that the USSR was changing and that a thaw was possible. His administration was coming under more pressure domestically and needed a foreign policy success to compensate (particular embarrassment was caused by the 'Iran-Contra' affair: weapons had been sold illegally to Iran and the proceeds used to fund anti-communist insurgents in Nicaragua). Another reason for making a bargain, as far as Reagan was concerned, was his belief that America was winning the Cold War.[91]

The INF Treaty and the prospect of a bigger strategic arms agreement fostered doubts about Britain's Trident programme and NATO's strategy of 'flexible response'. Thatcher argued that disarmament had gone far enough. In 1988 NATO confirmed its commitment to 'flexible response', but while the United States and Britain favoured the updating of short-range nuclear weaponry, the FRG did not.[92]

The Thatcher government was coming under increased pressure at home, meanwhile, because of the high cost of defence. Back in 1981 a defence review had arranged for considerable cuts in spending. One of the main reasons for the reallocation of resources, however, was to find enough money for Trident, which was controversial, and the Falklands War of 1982 meant that some of the cuts promised in the defence review had to be cancelled.[93] Manpower and financial burdens caused problems for the government. So did the closeness of Anglo-American defence relations. For example, in retaliation for acts of terrorism that were allegedly sponsored by Colonel Gaddafi, the Americans bombed Libya in April 1986 using aircraft based in Britain. Thatcher was widely criticized for allowing the US bases to be used in this way. Another divisive issue was SDI, which represented a shift from deterrence to defence, in contradiction to British strategic thinking. SDI also threatened to make existing offensive weapons obsolete, which would be disastrous for Britain and its comparatively small nuclear force. Howe condemned SDI in March 1985, but Thatcher was quite willing for British companies and experts to participate in the 'star wars' programme and told Reagan that she had not given her blessing for Howe's speech. Howe was applauded in Europe, however, and persuaded Thatcher that the Americans must revive START, the Strategic Arms Reduction Talks, which had commenced in 1981 (Reagan initially referred to START as SALT III).[94]

Thatcher's unwillingness to quarrel with the Americans on SDI was related to her fear that any large discrepancy between US and European security interests might lead to the effective removal of the deterrence she considered essential for the protection of Britain and Western Europe. She was also aware of the pressure that was building up in the US Congress for the withdrawal of American forces from Europe. She therefore sought to influence US policy by emphasizing her reliability. Sometimes she worked with the Europeans, though the end in view was to gain more influence over Washington DC. When she spoke of common European initiatives, she presented them as a way of strengthening NATO, not as an alternative position.[95]

In the late 1980s Thatcher was forced into some difficult manoeuvring as Britain's bargaining position became weaker. While pleased that NATO's deployment of Cruise and Pershing had been effective, in that the USSR had agreed to withdraw its SS20 missiles, Thatcher repeated her misgivings about the removal of land-based intermediate-range missiles from Western Europe and the possible 'decoupling' of US and European defence planning. She supported 'flexible response' because she wanted NATO to preserve the ability to escalate through each level of conventional and nuclear weaponry. The INF Treaty would leave a hole in NATO's defences, she insisted, and this brought up the question of short-range nuclear forces, or SNF. Bonn wanted early talks on the reduction of SNF. Thatcher wanted to delay, to buy time for the development of new missiles that would strengthen NATO's short-range nuclear forces, and Reagan agreed.[96]

In February 1988 Gorbachev announced that Soviet troops would begin to leave Afghanistan within three months. In March 1988 a NATO meeting in Brussels was overshadowed by talk (encouraged, Thatcher thought, by Soviet propaganda) of the denuclearization of Germany. Kohl agreed with Thatcher on the need to uphold 'flexible response', but opposed Thatcher's view that quick action was needed to modernize NATO's short-range nuclear forces. All through this period Thatcher continued to argue that it was the West's resolve that had prompted the Soviets to negotiate. The French weighed in with objections to denuclearization: French security concepts did not embrace such a goal.[97]

Thatcher maintained that strong defence and thaw with the Soviets should go together. On arms control she advocated a step-by-step process, but direct superpower contact was now well-established, making London's bilateral relationships with Washington DC and Moscow less significant, and Thatcher was quarrelling with her counterparts in Western Europe over the shape of the EC. Thatcher repeatedly discussed SNF with Kohl and with Reagan's successor Bush. When Gorbachev visited London in April 1989 and warned against SNF modernization, Thatcher insisted that it could not be avoided. Relations between London and Bonn deteriorated. Kohl told Thatcher that it was politically impossible for him to accept that there should be no negotiations to control those categories of weapon that most affected the FRG. Thatcher told him that if he persisted, he would pull NATO apart, but in May 1989, without consulting London, Washington DC decided that SNF negotiations with Moscow should go ahead.[98]

Disputes about arms control – and the wider problem of nuclear weapons proliferation – outlasted the Cold War, which finally came to an end with the economic and political collapse of the USSR and eastern bloc. The Gorbachev reforms in the Soviet Union had a swift impact on the bloc, and the most dramatic change was the fall of the communist regime in the GDR, for there were no more potent or emotive symbols of the Cold War than the division of Germany. The GDR's premier, Erich Honecker, disliked Gorbachev's reforms, but his government and others in the eastern bloc could not turn the clock back. They were ultimately dependent on Soviet readiness to intervene if they were challenged by internal opponents, and Gorbachev had announced the phased withdrawal of Soviet troops from the bloc.[99]

Thatcher welcomed change in the communist bloc, but added a note of caution, pointing out that the establishment of economic and political liberty in Eastern Europe would take many years. Instability might increase, she warned, with border disputes and ethnic conflicts. Another problem for Thatcher was the probability that change in Europe would further increase Bonn's influence at London's expense.[100]

The disintegration of the eastern bloc had been coming for some time, and it was largely a matter of economics. Sustained growth between 1950 and 1970 enabled the USSR and bloc to narrow the gap with the West, but along with growth came chronic deficiencies.[101] Economically, communist countries were outperformed by the West. Gradually more flexibility was allowed in the bloc as growth rates began to fall. Elements of a market economy crept in alongside the planning. More consumer goods became available, as did foreign loans and imports. By the 1980s over half of the bloc's trade was realized outside Comecon.[102]

The situation became more difficult because of the USSR's own stagnating economy. Among other things, there had to be cutbacks in arms production at a time when the contest with America was growing more intense, and ten years of war in Afghanistan also represented a serious drain, on top of other commitments. Afghanistan was a defeat, moreover, which affected Soviet prestige. Economic exhaustion, political repression and knowledge of the alternative life available in the West sapped the authority of the conservative Brezhnev regime. Gorbachev became Soviet leader in 1985, arranged the withdrawal from Afghanistan, inaugurated a period of reform, and suspended the Brezhnev Doctrine.[103] In fact the Brezhnev Doctrine was virtually obsolete before Gorbachev took power. The key development here was the crisis in Poland in 1980–81. Civil unrest led to the imposition of martial law, but it was the Polish government that acted, not the Soviets. The Brezhnev Doctrine no longer offered an effective means to influence events in the bloc. Détente had altered the context fundamentally and the bloc's leaders had come to realize that their interests and those of the USSR did not always coincide. It is possible that the eventual ending of the Cold War had more to do with long-term processes inside the USSR, and the Gorbachev reforms, than with pressure from the West. *The Times* commented that under Brezhnev the USSR had been 'frozen'. In contrast, Gorbachev seemed to be a man of energy and ideas. Afghanistan was the big test, and Bush's promise that the United States would stop sending weapons into the country facilitated the Soviet withdrawal, after which there were to be free elections under UN supervision. The details were worked out in June 1990.[104]

Western leaders were willing and able to do business with Gorbachev, and this showed how much the world had changed since the Czech crisis of 1968. In the early 1970s, when Home was Britain's foreign secretary, it was not generally thought that the nature of the Cold War could be dramatically altered, although Callaghan subsequently predicted that the Soviets would have to come to an understanding with the West because their economy could not support the aggressive momentum of Brezhnev's regime. Carrington later wrote that despite the intelligence concerning Soviet military power, the USSR was probably weaker than the West supposed. Even so, there is little indication that the Thatcher government really expected the changes that occurred at the end of the 1980s, although failure to anticipate the end of the Cold War did not mean that there was a lack of awareness of the USSR's problems.[105]

Carrington, both as British foreign secretary between 1979 and 1982 and as secretary-general of NATO from 1984 to 1988, shared Thatcher's view that the Soviets posed a continuing danger. He welcomed the agreements between Reagan and Gorbachev in the mid-1980s.[106] In due course it became clear that the Soviets were indeed suffering the effects of over-extension and economic failure. The states of the eastern bloc began to go their own way. There were more protests about human rights abuses. Some dissidents became famous in the West, and Thatcher insisted on meeting them when she visited the bloc. The Helsinki conference of 1975 may have been a false dawn, but memories of that time and that mood revived in the 1980s.[107]

Britain often used its dealings with eastern bloc countries in the 1970s and 1980s to bring up humanitarian issues, but the impact was limited. The GDR, for instance, remained close to the USSR and its government was one of the most repressive in the bloc. Although London expected trade to provide a way of influencing the GDR's internal policies, the volume of trade between Britain and the GDR remained small. Whenever the British mentioned human rights the Soviets made the same response, invoking the principle of non-intervention in each other's internal affairs. Nevertheless, Callaghan repeatedly brought up the plight of dissidents and minorities and managed to obtain small concessions by avoiding publicity. Howe did the same after his appointment as foreign secretary. Thatcher spoke more about human rights during the later 1980s than she had previously, because she considered it important to challenge as well as to bargain with Gorbachev.[108]

Her government had elucidated its position on these matters back in June 1979, describing the CSCE review conference at Belgrade as 'disappointing' and expressing the hope that the next meeting would be better. Early in 1980 *The Times* suggested that Moscow did not care about international opinion, but soon the Gorbachev period brought a relaxation of internal discipline inside the USSR. Britain's importance also increased in Soviet eyes, owing to the victory in the Falklands War, Thatcher's strong leadership, and the evidence of Britain's economic progress.[109]

After the CSCE meeting in Belgrade, which had been a confrontational affair, the Helsinki process looked to be at a standstill. The West had to rethink its position in advance of the next follow-up conference, which opened in Madrid in November 1980, a time when East–West relations were strained owing to the invasion of Afghanistan, the Polish crisis, crackdowns in the USSR and eastern bloc, the rise of the conservative right in America, NATO's decision on missile deployments, and the suspicion in the West that Moscow intended to pull out of CSCE. At Madrid the West chose not to focus so heavily on humanitarian issues and a concluding statement was agreed, reinforcing the commitments made in the Helsinki Final Act. The change in tactics therefore paid off. Moscow was still to be pressed on human rights, but less stridently than before. Madrid was also significant because it was the place where the Soviets struck back, obliging the West to take more account of different concepts of human rights.[110]

Whatever the consequences of the West's campaigning on humanitarian issues, economic difficulties had more impact on the course of the Cold War. There was a link between human rights and the economic situation, in that increasing East–West contact contributed to the undermining of the communist order. A key problem for those bloc regimes that tried to cast off economic weakness was the tendency to associate prosperity with the capitalism and even the political institutions of Western Europe and America. Another problem was that communist reform failed. [111]

The bloc's indebtedness helps to explain why Britain opposed tougher sanctions against Poland and the USSR in the aftermath of the imposition of martial law in Poland in December 1981. If the Poles defaulted on their debts, Thatcher warned, this would have a domino effect throughout Eastern Europe, with potentially disastrous consequences for the banking system in the West. She saw at first hand the distress in Poland when she visited the country in 1988. She was convinced that people in the bloc would not take up 'economic responsibility' unless they were granted the freedoms enjoyed in the West. Carrington had come to a similar conclusion when he visited Poland in 1980.[112]

The Wilson and Callaghan governments had tried hard to increase Britain's trade with the USSR and Eastern Europe, but questions were frequently raised about this in parliament. Some MPs complained that the Soviets were taking credit in order to produce items that they then sold back to the West at fixed prices. There was also discussion about the extent to which Britain could use economic pressure as a means of influencing Moscow. By the end of the 1970s the trade balance was heavily in the USSR's favour.[113] In the early 1980s trade was affected by Thatcher's economic policies and the stronger pound and higher interest rates. Inflation in the West made its goods more expensive, the Soviet Union and Eastern Europe were finding it hard to sell their products in the West, and the creditworthiness of some of the communist states was in doubt. Nevertheless, France and the FRG were winning major contracts in the Soviet Union, and in them the USSR found eager trading partners. The volume of Britain's trade with the Soviets did rise, but it still accounted for only a tiny share of the USSR's total trade and Britain's total trade.[114] In the mid-1980s British companies were eager to take up opportunities in the USSR and bloc, and the government encouraged this, although – as in the 1970s – there was no wish to make concessions that might damage the British economy, in which certain sectors remained fragile.[115]

Eastern Europe was affected by decisions made by the G7. In some respects the international economic order was shaped so that other nations would have to fit in with what the G7 did, and this was the context within which bloc countries underwent economic transformation. Changing economic relationships within the bloc were also important. Soviet priorities shifted; Eastern Europe wanted things that the USSR could not provide, but the West could; and the gradual relaxation of controls within Comecon reversed the previous trend towards integration. Economic developments alone do not explain the break-up of the bloc, however, because political and military relationships also changed. The longer Gorbachev remained in power, the more the Soviet attitude towards Eastern Europe altered.[116]

If difficulty and divergence within the bloc affected the course of the Cold War, so did economic circumstances in the West. Oil crises in 1973 and 1979 meant that the price of almost everything soared. Output fell and hundreds of thousands of industrial jobs were lost during the 1970s. After the end of the Bretton Woods system in 1971, exchange rates were in disarray and the stability of the major currencies less assured. Greater rivalry in trade, technology and investment developed between Western Europe and the USA. The economic growth rates of the 1950s and 1960s proved impossible to sustain.[117]

The British economy was suffering from structural and long-term flaws that successive governments could not correct, and this situation was exacerbated by the short-term perspective of most ministers and by policy mistakes. There was no consensus on broad questions of economic management. The concept of 'decline' took firm root. In fact, Britain was probably not performing far below other industrial powers, and claims about 'decline' were often politically motivated. They were used as a party weapon, especially by Thatcher.[118] Even so, the fact that Britain sometimes lacked confidence on the international stage was partly due to economic weaknesses. Needing money for other purposes and concerned about the impact of the military burden, Thatcher's government tried to bring down defence spending, but this necessitated adjustments, including government intervention, not least to soften the effect on individual industries and regions. It was also clear that reductions could not be carried too far too quickly, for fear of weakening the national defences. The problem of bringing military commitments into line with the available resources was no less challenging in the 1980s than it had been in the 1970s.[119]

High defence spending was not the only reason for Britain's comparatively poor economic performance between the 1950s and 1980s. It was probably not even the main reason. Indeed, as a share of total public expenditure, defence saw a marked reduction over the long term, while spending on welfare, health and education increased.[120] Substantial sums were still being spent on defence in the 1980s, though, and the general economic situation was less helpful than it had been in earlier decades. Britain was forced to change its conduct. From the late 1960s the tendency was to be more flexible and less ambitious. During the 1970s it proved impossible to restore the economic supports of British power. Thatcher's ideological approach, a departure from the pragmatism of the Heath, Wilson and Callaghan governments, might have made things worse. She believed in market forces, and after the early 1980s Britain's economic position did show signs of recovery, but was this due to Thatcherism? Or were economic growth and a healthy balance of payments the result not of government policy but of North

Sea oil? What is clear is that, as in the 1970s, Britain was affected more and more by external events that were beyond its control.[121]

Thatcher's ambivalent attitude towards international affairs in the late 1980s, and her continued use of Cold War rhetoric, showed that she preferred stability and gradualism. She thought that the world was changing too quickly. She was worried that the new situation would further reduce Britain's influence and did what she could to guide what was happening, especially in the EC, in European détente and in Anglo-American relations.[122] She had a personal stake in this, because her image as the 'Iron Lady', how she defined herself, and what made her appealing to British voters were linked with the Cold War and with a positive view of British power.

Nevertheless, Britain's influence and status were sustained into the 1990s. Britain had problems, but it suffered nothing like the political and economic breakdown experienced by the USSR. British power did not collapse. Britain was able to adapt and to retreat as necessary. The USSR did not demonstrate this capability. Over the years Britain had almost perfected the art of damage limitation so as to manage decline.

In the 1990s the Americans could do things against Britain's wishes. So could Moscow. So could the EC, NATO, the UN, the G7, and the Commonwealth. But no government or organization could ignore Britain's wishes on matters that affected British interests. Britain still had the ability to influence. Douglas Hurd, who was British foreign secretary from 1989 to 1995, used the phrase 'punching above its weight' to describe Britain's performance in international affairs. Though it had long since ceased to be a power of the first rank, Britain was one of the leaders of the chasing pack. It had a role and status beyond its real economic and military strength. Resources and opportunities, limited as they were, were used effectively. Britain did decline relative to other great powers, but the decline was resisted, minimized, controlled, hidden, denied, slowed up and deferred as well as it possibly could have been in the circumstances.

Conclusion

By the 1980s, Britain's activity and influence in the 'three circles' of world power – the Anglo-American relationship, the empire-Commonwealth, and Europe – were possibly more limited and more contingent on circumstance than they had ever been, and yet the essential fact is not Britain's relative decline over the course of the twentieth century, but Britain's success in managing decline so well. For the British, this was a century of ever-decreasing circles: the political, economic and military capacity to control events in each circle shrank; Britain's fields of action became more restricted; status, opportunity and influence in each circle were gradually eroded. There was no headlong retreat, however, and Britain's determination and ability to 'punch above its weight' remained fundamentally intact, even if British power rested increasingly on co-operation with others and not on independent decision making.

Britain's ongoing involvement in extra-European affairs is worthy of note. Although British activity had a European focus in the late twentieth century, there were still political and economic links with Africa, the Middle East and Asia. To a large extent these were shaped by the Cold War. Soviet and Cuban intervention in Africa, for instance, created a need for Britain and its allies to monitor the situation there. Gorbachev's ascendancy in Moscow from the spring of 1985 brought a period of relaxation as the Soviets became less adventurous in Africa. This was a time of transition. Britain finally secured a Rhodesian settlement in December 1979, and this led to the emergence of the independent state of Zimbabwe. British aid for Commonwealth countries in Africa continued. In South Africa apartheid was eventually dismantled. Britain's role in this development was controversial, mainly because Thatcher held that reform was best promoted through trade and contact, not sanctions.

Stability remained a major concern in Asia. Tension between the USSR and China created opportunities but also problems for the West. The safety of Japan was important, and for London a key issue was the future of Hong Kong. This was resolved by the Anglo-Chinese agreement of December 1984: the colony was to come under Chinese sovereignty but with safeguards for its economic and political institutions. An even more significant breakthrough in international affairs was Gorbachev's decision to withdraw Soviet forces from Afghanistan.

Hopes for stability in the Middle East were raised temporarily by US-led peace efforts. Carter sponsored the Camp David agreement of September 1978, which led to a treaty between Israel and Egypt, but other Arab states were not satisfied with this framework and regional discord was not mitigated. Israel refused to relinquish occupied land, while most Arab leaders declared themselves unable to accept Israel's right to exist. The British played a useful supporting role in the diplomatic efforts of the 1970s and 1980s, but the withdrawal from East of Suez meant that Britain was no longer a military power in the Middle East. Even the residual presence in the Persian Gulf had to be reduced for financial and political reasons.

Questions were asked at home and abroad about the international role to which Britain was best suited. This debate was dramatically affected by events in the South Atlantic in 1982. Britain still had distant responsibilities, and the Falklands crisis showed that Britain was able to act militarily outside the NATO area in times of emergency. Nevertheless, some commentators saw the whole affair as an unfortunate mistake, argued that the war could have been prevented and that the Falklands were not worth fighting over, and pointed to the expensive commitment Britain took on thereafter to defend the islands from future aggression. There is a sense in which the war for the Falklands seems incongruous. Perhaps it did not prove that Britain was still a great power, but rather prevented an appreciation of Britain's real place in the world.

Any fair assessment of Britain's role and influence, and the changes that had to be accommodated in the years between the 1890s, when Britain was the strongest power, and the 1990s, by which time Britain had ceased to be dominant anywhere, must balance the failures with the successes. It must explain why some options were taken and others abandoned, and investigate the prevailing international circumstances which at any given time conditioned Britain's conduct.

The two world wars had a lasting impact on Britain. They destroyed systems of trade, finance, imperial authority and international relations that the British had done much to shape and from which Britain benefited. The crisis of summer 1914, and the final breach between Britain and Germany, had been a long time coming. Despite many efforts in the preceding years, an understanding with Germany had not been achievable and from the British perspective the main stumbling block was German intransigence. Wider circumstances were not helpful, because two power blocs had emerged and neither would tolerate gains by the other. Britain entered the war in 1914 for European reasons, and to defend the empire, and because of fear about what might happen if Britain did not fight.

After the First World War, Britain was a maker and keeper of peace. Optimism grew. It seemed that international co-operation would usher in a new age of progress and stability. This mood was lost: as one historian puts it, 'under a veneer of greater civility, relations remained strained'.[1] Appeasement was meant to limit danger; to buy time; to influence foreign leaders; and to impose order on malfunctioning structures and the unpredictable course of international relations. It was affected by error, inefficiency and disunity. It did not prevent another world war, but it was not a policy of weakness and it was not based on a failure to identify and pursue Britain's vital interests in difficult times.

It is often argued that the Second World War bankrupted Britain. Certainly it placed an unprecedented strain on the nation's resources. It did not begin Britain's relative economic decline, but it did accelerate it. Yet it did not relegate Britain to a much lower status in the world. Instead, it gave the British an international standing they might not otherwise have had. As one of the victors, Britain gained prestige and position. Britain was a founder member of the United Nations, for example, with a permanent seat on its security council. Despite the shock of war, moreover, there was no weakening of the British determination to retain a global reach. In the foreign office it was axiomatic that Britain had to have a say in what happened in all regions of the world.[2]

This is why the empire-Commonwealth remained so important. Colonies, dominions, dependencies and the associated spheres of influence were regarded as assets and it was not unrealistic for British leaders to think that the empire-Commonwealth could be used to bolster Britain's position after 1945. The white dominions, in particular, had given considerable support during the Second World War, and despite some quarrels they chose to stay close to Britain because this suited them better than divergence.[3]

Britain's influence in distant regions was not entirely lost to the United States as a result of the Second World War. London was unhappy about American competition in the Far East and Pacific, about Washington DC's anti-colonial rhetoric, and about the USA's success in using the war to gain concessions from Britain.[4] At the same time, London was confident that British power could be preserved. Even if India was granted its independence, it was assumed, a network of relationships could be constructed to compensate. A new treaty system was envisaged, one that would deliver economic and strategic gains for Britain, but local circumstances frustrated this plan, as did the differences between British and US interests.[5] British influence in the Middle East and Far East began noticeably to decrease. The ANZUS Pact, problems with SEATO, an inability to attract wider support for the Baghdad Pact, and the Suez affair and its ramifications were some of the indicators signifying the gap between British goals and British capability.

Correlli Barnett has argued that the period between 1918 and 1940 saw British power 'decay' and that the years 1940–45 saw its 'collapse'.[6] It is important to keep a sense of proportion: taking the long view, from the late nineteenth century to the late twentieth century, British decline was not rapid or massive, but 'relatively gradual and relatively gentle'.[7] The decline and fall of the Soviet

Union and eastern bloc was a much quicker process. If it is logical to suppose that 'decay' leads to 'collapse', in Britain's case the interconnection is hardly neat or straightforward.

Consider this scenario: the First World War exposed Britain's economic and military weaknesses and left the country financially reliant on the United States; loss of confidence and dissatisfaction with the peace settlement made British leaders reluctant to enter into commitments abroad and fashioned a cautious foreign policy in the 1920s and 1930s; in the empire the idea spread that Britain was slipping; the dominions did not wish to be involved in another European war; and across Africa and Asia British rule was challenged. Does all this explain British decline? A different interpretation is possible, one that regards Britain as stronger between the wars than it had been for generations. Indeed, an argument can be made that Britain was still the only world power. Britain alone had a global reach, and Britain dominated the main international organization of the day, the League of Nations. Taking up Barnett's thesis, the Second World War was a long and expensive conflict that Britain could not afford to fight, and after 1945 the British came under pressure from friends as well as enemies and lost influence and empire. There will probably never be a consensus about the nature and timing of these changes in status, though, and the main point is not to pre-date or to exaggerate British decline.[8]

There were British politicians and strategists who imagined that Britain would emerge from the Second World War as powerful as ever. After all, for most of the war Britain carried the biggest share of the fight against Hitler's Germany, and Britain still had the empire and a presence across the globe. Treasury officials did warn that Britain's capacity to remain a great power would depend on resources, and in the foreign office there was a distinction between those who feared the revival of Germany and those who focused on the threat posed by the USSR. The chiefs of staff were worried about the Soviets long before the end of the war. Political leaders were also ranging themselves on different sides of the debate about defence and foreign policy. Bevin was criticized, especially by Labour left-wingers who thought that he should have been more conciliatory towards Moscow, but this did not deflect him from his priority: to obtain American support for Britain and for Western Europe.

There were domestic and international constraints within which Bevin had to operate, and he did so with some dexterity. A sure sign of his effectiveness is the extent to which Stalin and Molotov disliked him.[9] Bevin managed to achieve much of what he wanted after 1945 because of Soviet conduct. This is not to suggest that the Soviets alone were responsible for the Cold War. Some historians think that the Cold War suited the West rather more than it suited the USSR. If it is accepted, for the sake of argument, that the West wanted the Cold War, this provides a framework for understanding the breakdown of diplomacy with the

Soviets in the post-war years. Bevin, it might be added, was a leading mover in this development. America's role in the Second World War had indicated that, in future, the West's struggle for security and stability would have to be US-led. An East–West rupture was the means to get the Americans more involved in world affairs, and, beyond this, to pursue a military-industrial build-up in the West that would lead, over much of the globe, to a new hegemony. This did happen, though opinions differ about how much was a matter of design or otherwise. What is clear is that Bevin secured American assistance, and, by skilful manoeuvring, took advantage of events so that the Soviets could not obstruct it. He accepted that Europe would be divided. In fact, most political leaders in Britain agreed that the Soviet threat must be countered, and there was less criticism of heavy defence spending.[10] It was hoped that US involvement would ensure that British resources were not stretched too far. There was much relief that responsibility for protecting Western Europe would not rest on Britain alone.

The transactions of the early months of 1947 were crucial. The British government's decision respecting assistance to Greece and Turkey, followed by the Truman Doctrine and Marshall Plan, moved international affairs into new territory. Bevin alone was not responsible for this, and British policy was only one factor in Washington DC's calculations. Still, it was an important factor. Attlee encouraged Bevin to be firm with the Americans. The prime minister also sided with Bevin in internal Labour Party disputes: many on the left wanted greater reductions in the armed forces and a quicker retreat from Britain's overseas role.[11] Attlee was no hawk.[12] He and Bevin disagreed about the speed at which Britain should scale down its commitments, though this never caused a breakdown in their relationship.

A former under-secretary of state at the foreign office, Christopher Mayhew, later recalled 'the bitter, unrelenting opposition to Bevin from a sizeable proportion of our own backbenchers'.[13] Bevin was repeatedly a target of the 'Keep Left' group, which was proud of its anti-capitalist credentials and condemned US economic and military ambitions. Its members wanted to continue Britain's wartime alliance with the USSR, but Stalin's policies in Eastern Europe prompted a reassessment, and, as a result, there was more support for Bevin as foreign secretary, outside as well as inside the Labour Party. He basically agreed with Churchill's 'three circles' idea, that Britain was in a unique position as the link between America, Europe and the empire-Commonwealth. He never wavered in his belief that Britain had a pivotal part to play against the Soviets.[14] All the same, Bevin's opinion that Britain should remain a major force in world affairs would have been impossible to sustain had it not been for the change in US attitudes. The Truman administration had made plain its wish to detach the USA from Britain after the Second World War. Bevin helped the Americans to realize that they needed a partner.[15]

The security arrangements that led to the formation of NATO were not meant to deal only with the immediate post-war situation. A long-term alliance with America and Western Europe represented a significant break with the British past and helped to determine the policies of the future. Collective defence was essential for the restoration of confidence and prosperity. By promoting security, Bevin allowed his successors to respond to new circumstances as they arose later. Had he not done so, their options would have been much narrower.[16] Still, Bevin's effectiveness should not be exaggerated. The Americans did not need his encouragement to adopt an anti-Soviet line, and was NATO really his triumph? Bevin was not particularly keen on NATO at first and would have preferred a 'third force' – a Western Europe that was equal to and independent of the USA and part of a wider anti-Soviet coalition combining the British-led Commonwealth and British-led Europeans.[17] In addition, Bevin did not decide the course of European integration.[18] He misjudged opinion in Europe, thinking he could get co-operation on Britain's terms without any pooling of sovereignty. In time, moreover, the British would voice the same complaints about American policies that were heard on the continent. Britain and the nations of Western Europe wanted US help and they knew that they could not defend themselves alone, but they regretted being so reliant upon the Americans.[19]

By the end of the 1940s, the British had decided that the 'third force' was not a viable option. The strength of nationalism in Western Europe, its need for continued US economic and military support, and Britain's reluctance to make commitments, taken together, meant that Western Europe would not become the equal of the USA and the USSR. Nor was it realistic to think in terms of a power bloc that combined Western Europe with the Commonwealth. Instead, Bevin looked to the 'three circles': the Commonwealth, America and Western Europe would grow together naturally, with Britain as the link between them, and the British and Europeans would help each other as necessary to prevent US domination.[20]

In these years the British managed to limit the damage to their interests. The imperial dimension became less important as the Atlanticist orientation of Bevin's policies became more pronounced, but the idea of global influence was still present. Instead of pursuing it independently, Britain entered into a dependent relationship, though a 'special' one, with the United States.[21]

The assumption that Britain's economic problems were only temporary was probably indulged for too long. Attlee decided some time before Bevin did that independent action across the globe would not be possible. Though the British decision on Greece and Turkey prompted the Americans to increase their international responsibilities, Attlee thought that the real turning point was not this decision but rather the Berlin airlift, which brought the United States irreversibly into European affairs. Some historians have pursued this line of reasoning.

John Gaddis argues that the Truman Doctrine did not signify a commitment to contain communism on a global basis and that no such commitment existed until the Korean War. [22]

British politicians (Conservative as well as Labour), military experts, diplomats, strategists and advisers generally thought that Britain would remain a world power. It is true that the convertibility crisis of 1947 and devaluation of the pound in 1949 led a number of observers in Washington DC to conclude that Britain was no longer able to finance a world role, yet Britain's economic recovery after the Second World War was not unimpressive and it was primarily rearmament, for which the Americans had been pushing, that held the recovery back. In addition, British leaders' confidence about the world role was not necessarily misplaced: they knew that Britain could remain a great power even if its activities had to be gradually reduced.[23] The early part of the Cold War was shaped largely by British policy. It was London that was most suspicious about Moscow's intentions. The Americans came to share the British view.[24] If some American leaders were willing to admit that Britain had a unique place among the USA's allies, however, others were not, and there was no possibility that the USA would share primacy within the West. To the Americans, the 'special relationship' was a means to organize international affairs as they wanted. The British defined it more expansively and saw it as their means to maintain status. This difference did not prevent co-operation but did determine its character.[25]

Arguments about the extent to which Britain refused or failed to face up to its weakened position have been rightly dismissed as 'sterile'. John Kent insists that British leaders were aware of Britain's decline. The key point is that they considered it reversible. They expected economic recovery. They expected Britain to regain lost influence. They saw the empire as an essential prop for the economic and military efforts that would be necessary if Britain was to retain a global reach and combine with other states in the type of alliances that would confirm Britain's place in the first rank of world powers. None of this seemed strange or impracticable. Indeed, Anne Deighton has pointed out that British policy after 1945 worked well in most respects. The Attlee government was 'in the vanguard' when it came to bringing the Americans into and keeping the Soviets out of Western Europe.[26]

Britain was still operating a global system. If we acknowledge Kent's point, that there was no 'imperial retreat', and that new relationships were being forged to replace direct rule and formal control, it becomes easier to see why a loss of influence in one area strengthened Britain's determination to maintain it in another. The British responded to new circumstances by trying to rebuild their global system along different lines, and, as such, they were leading players in the Cold War. By pursuing their own interests, the British exacerbated the tensions that developed into the Cold War. Britain was not simply reacting to the Soviet threat, nor focusing only on the need to obtain US protection for Western Europe.

British leaders often based decisions not on concern about Britain's vulnerability, but on concepts of status. Instead of being determined by real security needs, therefore, certain measures had more to do with the desire to act like a great power. Perhaps this diverted attention away from other options, including closer links with Europe. Nevertheless, the decisions were sensible in the circumstances of the time. If there was a serious flaw in the late 1940s, it was the failure more quickly to adapt and to plan for the longer term. When George Kennan attended talks on security and European integration in the spring of 1949, he noted the familiar British approach: 'the usual pragmatic, tentative one, distrustful of logic and of hypothetical considerations, and directed primarily to the short term'.[27]

While contending with economic difficulties, the British continued to spend heavily on defence and to meet multiple commitments overseas. To the obligations imposed by imperial defence and membership of NATO were added extra burdens associated with British involvement in the Korean War, and the economic impact of rearmament was exacerbated by rising prices, particularly of raw materials. A trade deficit made rearmament even more problematic. The British were paying 42 per cent more for their imports in 1951 than had been paid in 1950, and export prices had only risen by 18 per cent. The increased cost of imports was almost the same as the total expenditure on rearmament for 1951. It was proving to be very expensive to pursue Britain's international objectives.[28] *The Times* in February 1947 had pointed out that it would not be easy to preserve the capacity to act as a great power, and that it would be even harder to increase this capacity.[29]

Britain sent troops to Korea in order to promote containment, to demonstrate the type of commitment that was expected from a world power that had important interests in Asia, and to gain more influence over the Americans. The Korean War stimulated international rivalry and changed inter-state relations in both Asia and Europe. It taught Mao that he could not trust Stalin. The US government approved a massive increase in American military might. The presence of US troops in Western Europe was confirmed and extended. West Germany rearmed and was admitted to NATO. Japan experienced an economic boom and became a core part of US strategy in Asia and the Pacific.

Concerns about British power and identity came more prominently to the fore during the mid-1950s. The relationship between Britain and America, and that between Britain and Western Europe, were complicated by an uneasy mix of ideas and methods. William Wallace has highlighted what he takes to be a fundamental dichotomy in British attitudes: the 'Anglo-Saxon' inclination competed with the 'European' option. For many contemporaries the former was preferable, since it accorded with British culture and tradition and pointed towards the 'special relationship' with America. This 'Anglo-Saxon' sentiment brought ideology and symbolism into British foreign policy, whereas Britain's dealings with Europe remained pragmatic. There was no sense of common identity. Wallace considers this regrettable,[30] but it bears repeating that British leaders had good reason for their scepticism about European integration. Even in the early 1960s, by which time it appeared that much could be gained from entry into the EEC, government, parliament, press and public were all divided on Macmillan's membership application and it became clear that 'The Six', especially France, were unwilling to make concessions in order to ease Britain's qualms about joining.

The first EEC bid was part of a post-Suez reassessment process. Though Suez did not turn Britain towards Europe and away from empire or the world role, it did foster a less negative view of European integration, even if there was no ideological conversion to the Europeanist agenda and no decision to prioritize Europe at the expense of the other two 'circles' of power (the Anglo-American and the empire-Commonwealth). Churchill's saying about the Europeans still held true: Britain was with them but not of them. Pursuing the possibility of joining the EEC was really a question of practical advantage: what was in it for Britain?

One historian of British foreign policy, writing only five years after the Suez operation, deemed it 'a serious miscalculation'. Most commentators agree with F.S. Northedge's verdict. None of the after-effects were as serious as was feared, however, for the Commonwealth survived, Anglo-American relations were restored, and NATO was relatively unaffected.[31] The Suez affair has often been regarded as the ultimate marker of British weakness and a confirmation of the end of empire, but as Ritchie Ovendale has pointed out, Britain was already retreating from empire in 1956.[32] The crisis did not force British leaders to think more about Britain's future in Europe, as opposed to thinking about Britain as a global power. Macmillan only committed himself to the turn to Europe in 1961, as he pondered over South Africa's departure from the Commonwealth and as opinion grew in London that the Commonwealth was not the asset that had been expected. Suez did annoy Washington DC, but if this was a nadir it was soon left behind. Eisenhower later admitted that his policy had been inappropriate, and this was also the view of Kissinger, secretary of state in the 1970s under Nixon and Ford. A lot changed for Britain because of Suez, but there was an essential continuity in that British leaders were still confident about the future, still expected recovery, and still believed that Britain would remain influential across the world, including in the Middle East.[33]

Suez did not eradicate British aversion to European integration. Conservative and Labour leaders shared a determination not to be drawn into supranational bodies. Although they were willing to consider a limited involvement if the terms were acceptable, they did not see a closer relationship with Europe as the best vehicle for promoting British interests. For generations Britain had enjoyed the luxury of choice, based on the underlying security of the British Isles and the existence of a large empire.[34] After 1945 these supports were known to be getting weaker. Though the context changed, however, the old reluctance to be closely tied to Europe remained.

The Suez crisis did not mark the end of British involvement in the Middle East and was not the last occasion on which Britain was willing and able to take the initiative in international affairs. For example, efforts to broker a deal between the West and the USSR in the late 1950s and early 1960s, especially on Berlin and the German question, would not have been made had it not been for the perception that Britain was still a great power.

The discrepancy between resources and commitments could not be borne indefinitely, of course, and after the early 1960s the British presence in the Far East, Pacific, Indian Ocean, Middle East and Persian Gulf became increasingly contentious. Malcolm Chalmers has argued that the withdrawal from East of Suez should have come much sooner. He blames poor leadership and thinks that the success in securing US support after 1945 pushed British governments down the wrong path: there should have been 'drastic adjustments', but Britain avoided these by using American money to pay for a global role. Resources were not diverted to domestic economic improvement, and the effort to remain a world power distorted Britain's view of European integration.[35]

Though not unreasonable, this line of argument relies on hindsight. If we remove the premise of poor decision making, and accept that British leaders evaluated the available options, usually based their choices on good advice and information, and kept abreast of the opportunities presented by international circumstances, a less negative interpretation emerges. On the other hand, it is difficult not to accept the point that earlier and bolder adjustments would have mitigated the difficulties of the late 1960s. Even with the cuts that were made in the 1950s and 1960s, Britain was spending a greater proportion of the national wealth on defence than were its European allies. There was an opportunity to reduce spending to European levels, Chalmers claims, but it was not taken.[36]

This is debatable. Britain had to meet its NATO commitments and could not easily abdicate its established role in providing for the defence of Western Europe. In order for Britain to do less in this respect, the Europeans would have had to do more. They were not willing. It can be argued, therefore, that Britain was unable fundamentally to rearrange its defence policy and make the savings that would have helped to ease its economic problems because of the attitude of the Europeans. It might also be argued that no government could have done more in these years. Other policies might have made some difference, but not much, if Britain's relative decline is to be understood primarily in terms of structural economic weaknesses and other long-term problems. In weighing up social, cultural, imperial, political, economic and financial conditions, and the

interpretations that have been offered to explain what happened, Paul Warwick
has suggested that the real answers lie in the late nineteenth century.[37] What
governments did or did not do after the Second World War, and in the 1960s,
assumes less importance in this scenario.

The withdrawal from East of Suez seems inevitable, given the available
resources, but we need not focus only on Britain's relative economic decline.
The decision to withdraw was also a political one. Economic pressures were
constant after the Second World War, while withdrawal was an admission that
a long-existing global military network had to be given up. Jeffrey Pickering
contends that such a shift cannot be explained by referring only to a constant.
Indeed, Britain's role East of Suez might have ended sooner had it not been
for non-economic considerations. Attlee had wanted to scale down Britain's
overseas commitments but was resisted by the foreign office and service chiefs.
The commitments continued because there was a belief that Britain could
remain a world power. Later, at the time of the Suez crisis and despite all the
difficulty that ensued, Britain chose not to withdraw from East of Suez. Although
economic problems mounted during the Macmillan years, Pickering stresses
that 'overstretch' is natural for great powers and that Britain had managed to
cope with it for over a century. The Wilson government came into office in 1964
committed to the preservation of Britain's status and prestige. In 1966–68 it was
the weakness of sterling that created the political context for the East of Suez
decision. Devaluation in November 1967 was a blow and withdrawal from East
of Suez, 'not consciously planned or debated by leading members of the cabinet',
was 'largely an indirect result of the scramble for political survival'.[38]

Pickering's analysis is useful, but attention must also be paid to other influences on British policy, especially Anglo-American relations and the multifarious
arrangements between the two allies on Malaysia, Vietnam, trade, sterling,
nuclear weapons and Europe. Another important consideration is the anti-
imperial tradition of the Labour Party. This shaped the attitude of many Labour
MPs and supporters in the 1960s. Looking back on this period, Denis Healey
and Michael Stewart later described the East of Suez presence as anachronistic.
Wilson also opined that it had been a mistake to cling to the global role.[39]

Healey came to think that it would have been impossible to remain East of
Suez, because of the growth of nationalism there and the economic situation at
home, but he denied that the Labour government had been too slow to withdraw
and that it should have made the necessary arrangements soon after taking office
in 1964. While British troops were fighting in southern Arabia and Borneo,
assisted by forces from the Commonwealth, it would have been irresponsible
abruptly to leave, especially without consulting Britain's partners. The context
was also important, because in the mid-1960s there was still an attachment to
the global role. Healey always maintained that the Labour government was to be

commended for the way it managed the withdrawal from East of Suez. Twenty years earlier, in managing Britain's withdrawal from India, the Attlee government had not been able to prevent catastrophe. Millions of people became refugees and tens of thousands lost their lives. The government of 1964–70 did better than this, Healey thought, and its withdrawal from East of Suez was also more impressive than the American performance in Vietnam.[40]

In some respects this was a government that acted firmly and effectively. It made the tough decisions that were needed to ensure that Britain's role in the world would henceforth be based on a better sense of balance between ends and means. John Young writes that greater reliance on non-military methods to maintain influence in the world as 'a primarily European power' meant that in the 1970s, in contrast to earlier years, Britain had 'international ambitions that did match resources to aims'. It is worth remembering, though, that even after the withdrawal Britain still had nuclear weapons and overseas bases, and Anglo-American co-operation remained close (neither Britain nor the USA had such a relationship with any other power). Britain was far from a nonentity in world affairs, even if, by 1970, the focus was on NATO and Europe.[41]

The financial crises of 1966 and 1967 revealed Britain's weakness both to the government and to everyone else, but Young suggests that even more decisive might have been an earlier event, the decision of November 1964 to hold defence spending at £2 billion. This set a target that could not be met without abandoning external commitments. Wilson and those of his colleagues who cherished the world role did not at first expect that role to end. It was a long time before they accepted the need for a general retreat, and even in 1968 some ministers opposed a rapid withdrawal from East of Suez.[42]

Any hope that Britain's options would increase as a result of economic recovery were dashed as international commercial and financial relationships became more rather than less problematic. No single government could do much about this. The 1970s would see further currency problems, inflation and economic stagnation. In Britain the Wilson government had to contend with the early stages of this global downturn. It is possible that an earlier retreat from East of Suez might have helped. Then again, measures were taken that did shore up key sectors of the British economy, and it was better that withdrawal from the global role was as orderly and careful as circumstances allowed, rather than rushed and chaotic. Despite their objections to Labour's policy in the late 1960s, the Conservatives did not reverse the East of Suez decision when they took office in 1970.[43]

It was natural for Wilson and his colleagues to put a favourable spin on what they were doing, and make a virtue of necessity, because it would have damaged them politically to admit that they had no choice. Still, the stuttering performance of the British economy did not inspire confidence. In the second half of the twentieth century the economy enjoyed unprecedented growth, yet the rate of growth was much slower than that of Britain's competitors. Peter Clarke suggests that the most important British mistake was the failure to join the EEC much sooner. Britain thereby missed out on the benefits of membership.[44] But this assumes that Britain could and should have joined in or shortly after 1957, which is not clear, and when Britain did apply to join the French blocked the way, which was hardly Britain's fault.

Even so, British leaders might have taken more seriously the moves for unity in Western Europe after 1945. At first the main motive behind these moves was related to mutual security and the pressures created by division of Europe and the Cold War.[45] Britain played a leading part in the development of a security system, but was not able to control or agree with the path taken by those who wished for economic and political integration. There was not enough preparation for what might happen in the future. By the early 1960s official attitudes had moved on. Discussion focused more on the terms rather than the principle of entry into the EEC. Nevertheless, Europe remained a divisive issue and British political leaders were concerned to keep their parties united and to link European policy with electoral advantage. A persistent idea was that Europe needed Britain more than Britain needed Europe. The Europeans saw things differently. Indeed, Britain would not have emerged as the leader of Europe even had there been a much earlier British commitment to integration. 'The Six' acted on their own initiative and did not want or expect to have to accept British leadership.[46]

Britain's history had a direct bearing on policy towards Europe. The British view of the continent had long been ambivalent. Knowing that they had to be involved in some way but not always able to decide how best to proceed, the British were 'reluctant Europeans', and after 1945 concerns grew about how to preserve Britain's independence.[47] Did decolonization make Europe the only option? Was it really worth getting closer to Europe, despite the costs? On these questions there was disagreement, and the debate went on long after the withdrawal from East of Suez and Britain's entry into the EEC.

Britain was not the only power to be in difficulty in the late 1960s and early 1970s. The United States also went through a time of crisis, division and policy shifts. American strength affected British strength. The British still had a say in the Middle East and Far East, but were unable to influence the course of events just by themselves. Nor could they use international organizations to change the situation. The United Nations, for example, was often a hindrance rather than a help.

During the 1950s and 1960s, the UN was marginalized as the Americans and Soviets used other means to address problems.[48] The UN's role and authority declined largely because of the attitude of the United States. Decolonization and associated changes in the international order led to arrangements at the UN in the mid-1950s whereby the organization quickly grew in size. New independent states were admitted to the UN almost automatically, which transformed it into a forum for the developing world. These new members used the UN to gain influence. Western dominance of the UN was ended and the Americans became disillusioned. The United States eventually became the most frequent user of the veto in the security council, having not used it at all before 1970.

Though the British disliked American unilateralism they did share Washington DC's disappointment about the way the UN had developed, and whatever transpired at home or abroad, nothing mattered more to the British in terms of status, influence and planning than the 'special relationship' with the United States. Though there were quarrels, Anglo-American co-operation carried on. On Britain's side, giving support to and gaining support from the Americans offered the means to remain a world power. The 'special relationship' tended to slow down and hide Britain's decline, even if the British and Americans saw it differently. London tried to formalize it while Washington DC preferred informality; London wanted it established as a common priority while Washington DC increasingly treated Britain as only one of several important allies. Some observers claimed that the relationship was not 'special' at all. On the other hand, there are those who argue that the bonds were always stronger than the disagreements.

At both an élite and a popular level, the Americans cared less about the 'special relationship' than did the British. Co-operation was, in truth, conditional. It rested on common needs and on separate goals that could be served by the same course of action. When there was no mutual gain, it was only maintained because rivalry, or lack of co-operation, would have been detrimental. For Britain, the weaker of the two partners, attention had always to be paid to the risk that US hostility might damage British interests. Dependence upon the USA did not prevent Britain's relative decline as a world power, though it slowed the process. Paradoxically, dependence also contributed to Britain's decline, since independence is probably the foremost quality of a great power. One does not have to be a pro-European, moreover, to think that by relying on the partnership with America, the British isolated themselves from other necessary partnerships. On the other hand, it cannot be denied that the 'special relationship' brought significant benefits to Britain, especially American political support and loans and investment. The British invested heavily in America (more foreign investment in the USA came from Britain than from anywhere else) and the sharing of nuclear technology and information was absolutely vital to Britain.

The Polaris deal ensured that Britain would have a credible deterrent while also guaranteeing the British considerable influence in their dealings with the Americans and the other members of NATO.[49] Polaris meant that the world role would continue for a while longer. As this role was reduced, however, the Americans came to view the British as less useful, and the East of Suez decision inevitably led Washington DC to downgrade the 'special relationship'. For his part, while he was prime minister Heath became more willing to challenge US policies because he expected Europe to provide a better basis for British influence. Heath was particularly annoyed by America's conduct during the Arab–Israeli war of 1973.[50]

Thatcher was fully committed to the 'special relationship', yet there were times when she criticized the United States. When the Soviets invaded Afghanistan she agreed that the West should make a firm response, but even while lamenting the lack of support from Europe she advised Washington DC against carrying sanctions too far. Although she thought it important for Britain to stand with America, she sometimes found this difficult, as on the question of the Siberian gas pipeline. When US forces invaded Grenada in October 1983 she felt betrayed (there had been a coup in Grenada and Washington DC was concerned both for the safety of American students on the island and about the presence there of advisers from Cuba, the USSR, North Korea and Libya). Britain was not consulted, even though Grenada was a Commonwealth country. A comparison with Afghanistan suggested itself: how could the West condemn the Soviets for aggression when the Americans were guilty of the same crime?[51]

The international scene was greatly altered by European and superpower détente. In the 1970s London was convinced that a thaw was worth pursuing, with the proviso that this had to be done from a position of strength. The British did not want to make substantial concessions and insisted on the need to avoid any weakening of NATO's cohesion and capabilities. In the CSCE process the British focused mainly on human rights, thinking that this was the way to subject the Soviets to maximum pressure. When the West imposed sanctions following the Soviet invasion of Afghanistan, domestic repression in the USSR increased. Soviet leaders did not care about salvaging détente at this juncture, believing that the thaw of the 1970s was already being reversed: Soviet and Cuban involvement in Africa had been resisted, arms-limitation talks had reached an impasse, and the USSR's human rights record had been condemned at the CSCE review meeting in Belgrade in 1977–78.[52]

British governments continued to challenge Moscow on humanitarian and other issues, but now there were fewer opportunities to intercede between the two superpowers, a change that was epitomized by SALT and the growth of direct, bilateral US–Soviet negotiations. In addition, the Americans increasingly looked upon the FRG as the key ally in Europe, owing to the FRG's position in NATO and the EC. American attitudes were also shaped by recent history: British policy on Vietnam (no combat troops; failed peace efforts); Britain's retreat from East of Suez; Britain's economic and financial weakness; Heath's decision to give British policy a more European and less Atlanticist slant.[53]

Despite all this, the British made good use of the influence they still possessed. When Callaghan was prime minister he contributed to détente, often mediated between the Americans and Europeans, and made progress with his main objectives: to keep disarmament talks going, to promote the 'dual track' in connection with this, and to safeguard the future of the British deterrent. Callaghan knew that British preferences carried less weight abroad than they had in former times, but he managed to provide for the nation's defence needs as they were seen in the late 1970s, while keeping the cabinet together and resisting pressure from the Labour left. These were important achievements, even if his conduct was 'reactive and not particularly inspired'.[54]

The early years of the Thatcher government were notable for a more assertive policy and a hard-line approach to East–West relations, but during the mid-1980s Thatcher became more flexible, especially after Gorbachev became the Soviet leader. Britain began to enjoy a more constructive relationship with the USSR, although less was done than might have been possible on Anglo-Soviet trade and on including Britain in a common EC position on East–West relations. One reason for this was the persistent idea of Britain as an independent force in international affairs.[55] Equally relevant was Thatcher's wish to stay close to the Americans and her awareness that they had doubts about détente. When foreign secretary Geoffrey Howe went to Washington DC in July 1983 for talks with Reagan and senior US officials, he noted their lack of enthusiasm for closer East–West links, which disappointed him.[56]

Mark Curtis has contended that Thatcher was too deferential to the Americans and supported them when she should have done otherwise. This links in with the general Curtis theme that British policy departed from the values and goals it purportedly had with respect to promoting democracy, human rights and justice. Curtis points to Britain's backing for American military action and collusion with brutal dictators, and efforts to maintain an international order that suited the West's selfish political and economic interests.[57]

Though it is no doubt the case that Britain's policy was often less enlightened and benevolent than those responsible for it liked to admit, Curtis exaggerates and his view of 'Anglo-American power' and the world it had fashioned by the late 1990s is problematic.[58] Curtis condemns Britain and the United States for increasing poverty across the globe, concentrating power in the hands of unaccountable private organizations, and prospering a minority at the expense of the rest. A few scholars stick to these facts, Curtis argues, whereas 'establishment scholarship' is corrupt. As with his other claims, however, this is simplistic and overstated. There were important differences between Britain and the United States. Sometimes there were conflicts between them. Curtis appears not to appreciate the difficulties that faced policy makers, or to be very interested in the reasons that some options were taken and others rejected. He is too eager to dismiss the work of other scholars. He cannot accept that some of the decisions made by British and US leaders might have been appropriate and justified; nor does he recognize that other regimes might be partly responsible for the world's problems.

Thatcher was not incorrect to attach importance to the relationship between Britain and the United States. In Reagan she found a leader with whom she could readily co-operate. Then the rise of Gorbachev made her think that a thaw was possible, and she was willing to promote it while trusting also in the British deterrent and a strong NATO. By the late 1980s she was growing dissatisfied, however, because in her opinion processes of bargain and change were moving too quickly. She argued with Britain's European partners and with the Bush administration. She called for a reassessment so that the USSR would be challenged more directly on its human rights record, and declared that the Western powers should not be so eager to lavish their economic aid on the Soviets and the eastern bloc. Thatcher's stance on the EC solidified as well. She thought that reforms in the EC and the continuation of détente would reduce British influence. As France and the FRG pushed ahead with détente and developed the EC in ways that Britain opposed, they were encouraged by the realization that the British government could no longer rely on US support. Bush preferred to see Britain as part of the EC and part of NATO, not as a special ally with a unique importance to the United States.[59]

Gorbachev's wish to integrate the Soviet economy into world trade, and his domestic reform and international détente agenda, added to the confusion of the late 1980s. Soon popular revolutions broke out across Eastern Europe. The question of German reunification came to the fore and needed a solution. Security structures and negotiating procedures were changing and the old military balance between East and West had gone, for Soviet troops were leaving the eastern bloc. NATO seemed to be losing its raison d'être. This, along with Eastern Europe's desire to merge economically with Western Europe, rapidly raised the importance of the EC. Previously in the West, Atlantic institutions had covered security and European institutions had covered economics, but this distinction broke down. The British were unsure how to react. They could no longer separate détente and security issues from EC matters and European integration: all became mixed together in a debate about Britain's future.[60]

Thatcher rejected the suggestion that the EC should deal with security problems and maintained that NATO must supervise détente. In a speech of 20 September 1988, delivered at the College of Europe in Bruges, she warned against the creation of 'a European super state' and argued that individual countries could not fit into 'some sort of identikit European personality'. Thatcher wished to preserve the Europe of independent states. She preferred the clarity of NATO's security function to what she saw as vague pan-European concepts. Although British goals and opinions still mattered, however, the ability to determine outcomes was limited.[61]

With some justification, Thatcher and her supporters regarded her premiership as a time of British resurgence. The economic weaknesses, political compromises, loss of prestige and shrinkage of influence that had affected Britain since the early 1960s had apparently been overcome, so that Britain could again act and expect to be treated as a great power. The most telling sign of this, so the argument ran, was victory in the Falklands, but at the time and afterwards questions were raised about British policy and about the circumstances surrounding Argentina's invasion of a small, far-off and relatively unimportant British possession. London and Buenos Aires misinterpreted each other's actions: British leaders assumed that Argentina would not invade the Falklands; the ruling military junta in Argentina could not believe that the British would go to war.[62]

Thatcher always maintained that the Falklands War involved more than just the islands and their inhabitants. It also concerned 'our honour as a nation' and the fundamental principles 'that aggressors should never succeed and that international law should prevail over the use of force'. The war had positive results, not least by enhancing Britain's reputation and boosting British self-confidence. Moreover, 'years later I was told by a Russian general that the Soviets had been firmly convinced that we would not fight for the Falklands, and that if we did fight we would lose. We proved them wrong on both counts, and they did not forget the fact.'[63] It is easy to meet these remarks with a 'well she would say that, wouldn't she?' type of response, but the Falklands victory did have some of the effects Thatcher claimed. It was a sign of boldness and vigour that was at odds with the decline in influence and the resource gap that had restricted British policy for many years. While victory fostered a lot of self-congratulation, though, it did not alter the fact that Britain ranked far below America and the USSR in power. It was a reminder to the world that Britain still mattered. It did not permanently change the international order.

Nor was the Falklands campaign an independent operation, for Britain requested and, after some equivocation in Washington DC, received US assistance (intelligence, diplomacy, refuelling facilities, weaponry). Reagan's secretary of state, Alexander Haig, thought that even without America's help, Britain would have won the Falklands War. But the task would have been much more difficult.[64]

The Falklands crisis erupted in the middle of a long and sometimes painful process of adaptation, from the late 1960s through to the end of the century, during which Britain continually rebalanced commitments and capabilities. Michael Clarke noted in the early 1990s that change was, if anything, gaining more speed.[65] He pointed to the paradox that while there was more interdependence and homogeneity in the world, societies and nations were breaking up and political instability was on the increase. Clarke highlighted the impact of non-institutional influences, particularly public opinion and the media, and of developments associated with legal frameworks, international mobility, multiculturalism, market forces and trans-national economic links. Britain's leaders had to be more flexible in order to manage many complex issues. For good or ill, the European dimension was even more important by the 1990s than it had been in the 1970s. Indeed, membership of the EC had become probably the most important single influence on British foreign policy. This was problematic, not only because of the opposing views on Europe in domestic politics, but also because of its implications for Britain's international role. The rise of 'hybrid sovereignty' meant that foreign policy was becoming less distinct. So was Britain's role. For example, in the 1970s Britain accepted the loss of empire and tried to act as an 'Atlantic manager'. In the 1990s the end of the Cold War deprived Britain of this function.[66]

Clarke did not think that accommodating new pressures and needs would be easy. Indeed, the pessimism of some experts in the 1990s struck a similar chord to that of William Wallace in the 1970s. One of Wallace's main contentions was that policy making was a deliberate mystery, too secretive and conservative and too far removed from outside debate and research. The solution, Wallace thought, was to acknowledge that international affairs no longer represented a separate field of policy. Instead, they should be treated as part of domestic politics.[67] Such shifts in perspective do not happen quickly. One reason for this has been the limited understanding of foreign affairs in parliament. A study carried out in 1988 revealed that more than 80 per cent of MPs could not name the secretary-general of NATO.[68]

By this time Britain, though it could still 'punch above its weight', had accepted many limits on its influence. That Britain was less able to compete in the world politically and economically was clear enough, but nobody knew what the future held and Britain's posture was the subject of enormous speculation in the 1990s.[69] The end of the Cold War, when it came, was quick and unexpected. This was a time of uncertainty. Decisions had to be made about Britain's security and about how to restructure defence forces to suit new circumstances. Attention had to be given to the pros and cons of taking scarce resources from defence and using them for other purposes. Potential threats had to be assessed: would a post-Gorbachev Russia be dangerous, or was the main threat likely to come from somewhere else; and if the most serious trouble was likely to arise outside the NATO area what part should Britain play in collective defence through NATO? There was disagreement about Britain's role in collective defence, especially on the question of whether or not the British should go for greater specialization. Some experts thought that Britain should maintain its military capacity across the board and that the armed forces represented a unique national asset and should not have their scope and capability narrowed. Others wanted a major reorganization in pursuit of adequate forces at an affordable price.

Discussions about the military, economic and political foundations of British power will continue. As for the twentieth century, it was a century of relative decline for Britain, but that decline was in most respects well managed. Of course there is a place in scholarly discourse for criticisms of British policy making and for questions about motives and goals, methods and guiding principles, perception and reality. Overly negative assessments of Britain's international role and activity ought to be eschewed, however, for influence was preserved even in the most difficult circumstances, and although Churchill's 'three circles' of power became ever-decreasing circles – in the sense that British involvement in and manipulation of each of them gradually diminished – in the 1990s Britain was still being consulted and still making its wishes known about issues and events near and far.

Endnotes

Notes to Introduction

1   *The Conservative Party since 1945*, S. Ball (ed.) (Manchester, 1998), pp. 143–4.
2   Correlli Barnett interview, July 1996, in *Rethinking British Decline*, R. English and M. Kenny (eds) (Basingstoke, 2000), p. 45.

Notes to Chapter 1: The Era of the Two World Wars

1   P.W. Schroeder, 'International Politics, Peace and War, 1815–1914', in *The Nineteenth Century: Europe, 1789–1914*, T.C.W. Blanning (ed.) (Oxford, 2000), pp. 158–209; J.A.R. Marriott, *A History of Europe from 1815* (London, 1952), pp. 312–13, 423; M.S. Anderson, *The Ascendancy of Europe, 1815–1914* (Harlow, 2003), Ch. 5; W.R. Keylor, *The Twentieth Century World and Beyond* (New York, 2006), pp. 1–36; F.R. Bridge and R. Bullen, *The Great Powers and the European States System, 1814–1914* (Harlow, 2005), pp. 252–9; R.W. Winks and R.J.Q. Adams, *Europe: Crisis and Conflict, 1890–1945* (New York, 2003), Ch. 2; J.M. Roberts, *Europe, 1880–1945* (Harlow, 2001), Ch. 4; M. Rapport, *Nineteenth-Century Europe* (Basingstoke, 2005), pp. 297–363; J. Joll, *Europe since 1870: An International History* (Harmondsworth, 1983), pp. 84–5, 87, 96, 101; J.W. Young, *Britain and the World in the Twentieth Century* (London, 1997), Ch. 1; D. Reynolds, *Britannia Overruled: British Policy and World Power in the Twentieth Century* (Harlow, 2000), pp. 63–8; J. Davis, *A History of Britain, 1885–1939* (Basingstoke, 1999), pp. 115–16; T.W. Heyck, *A History of the Peoples of the British Isles from 1870 to the Present* (London, 2002), pp. 85–96.
2   A. Booth, *The British Economy in the Twentieth Century* (Basingstoke, 2001), pp. 23–6, 53–9; M. Daunton, *Wealth and Welfare: An Economic and Social History of Britain, 1851–1951* (Oxford, 2007), pp. 168–76; C. More, *The Industrial Age: Economy and Society in Britain, 1750–1995* (Harlow, 1997), Part 2; R. Lloyd-Jones and M.J. Lewis, *British Industrial Capitalism since the Industrial Revolution* (London, 1998), Chs 5 and 6.
3   T.H. Parsons, *The British Imperial Century, 1815–1914* (Lanham MD, 1999); A.G. Hopkins, 'Overseas Expansion, Imperialism and Empire, 1815–1914',

in Blanning, *Nineteenth Century*, pp. 210–40; H.L. Wesseling, *The European Colonial Empires, 1815–1919* (Harlow, 2004), Chs 4–6; A. Porter, 'The Empire and the World', in *The Nineteenth Century*, C. Matthew (ed.) (Oxford, 2000), pp. 135–60.

4   K. Jeffery, 'British Isles/British Empire: Dual Mandate/Dual Identity', in *The British Isles, 1901–51*, K. Robbins (ed.) (Oxford, 2002), pp. 13–19; A. Porter, 'The South African War: Context and Motive Reconsidered', *Journal of African History, 31* (1990), pp. 31–57; I. Smith, *The Origins of the South African War, 1899–1902* (London, 1996); B. Nasson, *The South African War, 1899–1902* (London, 1999); D. Judd and K. Surridge, *The Boer War* (New York, 2003), Part 1.

5   F.R. van Hartesveldt, *The Boer War: Historiography and Annotated Bibliography* (Westport CT, 2000); Judd and Surridge, *Boer War*, Parts 3, 5; P. Brendon, *The Decline and Fall of the British Empire, 1781–1997* (London, 2007), pp. 214–17; P.J. Cain and A.G. Hopkins, *British Imperialism, 1688–2000* (Harlow, 2002), pp. 318–27, 383–6; D.G. Boyce, *Decolonization and the British Empire, 1775–1997* (Basingstoke, 1999), pp. 60–4; E.R. Kantowicz, *The Rage of Nations* (Grand Rapids MI, 1999), pp. 5–8; Heyck, *History of the Peoples*, pp. 96–9; *The South African War Reappraised*, D. Lowry (ed.) (Manchester, 2000); *The Impact of the South African War*, D. Omissi and A. Thompson (eds) (Basingstoke, 2002); *Writing a Wider War*, G. Cuthbertson, A. Grundlingh and M. Suttie (eds) (Athens OH, 2002); *The International Impact of the South African War*, K. Wilson (ed.) (Chesham, 2001).

6   D. Read, *The Age of Urban Democracy: England, 1868–1914* (Harlow, 1994), pp. 354–7, 363–4; Marriott, *History of Europe*, p. 397; K. Robbins, *Britain and Europe, 1789–2005* (London, 2005), pp. 160–1, 172–81; Reynolds, *Britannia Overruled*, Ch. 3; Young, *Britain and the World*, Ch. 1; Heyck, *History of the Peoples*, pp. 99–101; Anderson, *Ascendancy of Europe*, p. 49; Roberts, *Europe, 1880–1945*, pp. 96, 109–10, 203; T.G. Otte, 'Old Diplomacy: Reflections on the Foreign Office before 1914', *Contemporary British History, 18* (2004), pp. 31–52.

7   K. Neilson, '"Greatly Exaggerated": The Myth of the Decline of Great Britain before 1914', *International History Review, 13* (1991), pp. 695–725. For an alternative view – that Britain's relative weakness created a conscious need for allies – see P. Kennedy, *The Rise of the Anglo-German Antagonism, 1860–1914* (London, 1980), and G. Monger, *The End of Isolation: British Foreign Policy, 1900–1907* (London, 1963). Another useful contribution is K. Wilson, *The Policy of the Entente: Essays on the Determinants of British Foreign Policy, 1904–14* (Cambridge, 1985).

8   Z. Steiner, 'British Power and Stability: The Historical Record', *Diplomacy and Statecraft, 14* (2003), pp. 23–44.

9   H. Temperley, *Britain and America since Independence* (Basingstoke, 2002), pp. 68–88; A.P. Dobson, *Anglo-American Relations in the Twentieth Century* (London, 1995), pp. 17–31; K. Hildebrand, 'The Transformation of the International

System: From the Berlin Congress to the Paris Peace Treaty', in *The Quest for Stability: Problems of West European Security, 1918–57*, R. Ahmann, A.M. Birke and M. Howard (eds) (Oxford, 1993), pp. 25–6; S.A. Cordery, *Theodore Roosevelt: In the Vanguard of the Modern* (Belmont CA, 2003), Ch. 4; N. Ferguson, *Colossus: The Rise and Fall of the American Empire* (London, 2005), pp. 41–60.

10 Joll, *Europe since 1870*, p. 97; G.A. Craig, *Germany, 1866–1945* (Oxford, 1991), pp. 311–14.

11 Young, *Britain and the World*, pp. 25–7; Boyce, *Decolonization and the British Empire*, pp. 65–6; Kantowicz, *Rage of Nations*, pp. 64–5; Davis, *Britain, 1885–1939*, pp. 115–16; Reynolds, *Britannia Overruled*, p. 70; Roberts, *Europe, 1880–1945*, pp. 203–4; Read, *Age of Urban Democracy*, pp. 472–3; Marriott, *History of Europe*, pp. 362–4; A. Thompson, *Imperial Britain: The Empire in British Politics, 1880–1932* (Harlow, 2000), p. 115; J.N. Westwood, *Endurance and Endeavour: Russian History, 1812–2001* (Oxford, 1993), Ch. 6; W.G. Beasley, *Japanese Imperialism, 1894–1945* (Oxford, 1987), pp. 77–100.

12 Joll, *Europe since 1870*, pp. 91–2, 176; Reynolds, *Britannia Overruled*, pp. 73–80; Young, *Britain and the World*, Ch. 2; Read, *Age of Urban Democracy*, pp. 363–4, 475; Heyck, *History of the Peoples*, pp. 101–2; Marriott, *History of Europe*, pp. 395–403; Anderson, *Ascendancy of Europe*, pp. 28–48; Bridge and Bullen, *Great Powers*, pp. 266–72; Roberts, *Europe, 1880–1945*, pp. 63–4, 93–4, 96, 175–6, 203, 209–10; Craig, *Germany*, pp. 303–10; J. Steinberg, 'The German Background to Anglo-German Relations, 1905–14', in *British Foreign Policy under Sir Edward Grey*, F.H. Hinsley (ed.) (Cambridge, 1977), pp. 193–215.

13 P. Kennedy, *The Rise and Fall of British Naval Mastery* (London, 2004), Ch. 8; Reynolds, *Britannia Overruled*, pp. 58, 73–80; Read, *Age of Urban Democracy*, pp. 363–5, 474–6; Young, *Britain and the World*, Ch. 2; Craig, *Germany*, pp. 311–14; Joll, *Europe since 1870*, pp. 96–7, 176–7; Thompson, *Imperial Britain*, pp. 112–13; Wilson, *Policy of the Entente*, Ch. 6.

14 Joll, *Europe since 1870*, p. 172; Kantowicz, *Rage of Nations*, pp. 61–9; A.L. Macfie, *The Straits Question, 1908–36* (Thessaloniki, 1993). On the relative positions of the great powers of the late nineteenth and early twentieth centuries – Britain, France, Germany, Austria-Hungary, Italy, Russia, the USA, Japan – see P. Kennedy, *The Rise and Fall of the Great Powers* (New York, 1987), pp. 202–49.

15 Kennedy, *Rise and Fall of the Great Powers*, pp. 195, 250–1; Young, *Britain and the World*, pp. 17–18; Joll, *Europe since 1870*, pp. 86–7, 98.

16 Roberts, *Europe, 1880–1945*, pp. 205, 207; Joll, *Europe since 1870*, pp. 98–100, 178; Davis, *Britain, 1885–1939*, pp. 116–17; Read, *Age of Urban Democracy*, pp. 478–80; Reynolds, *Britannia Overruled*, pp. 70–1; Marriott, *History of Europe*, pp. 404–10; Bridge and Bullen, *Great Powers*, pp. 272–8; Young, *Britain and the World*, pp. 28–9; Kennedy, *Rise and Fall of the Great Powers*, pp. 250–2; Anderson, *Ascendancy of Europe*, pp. 49–51.

17 Roberts, *Europe, 1880–1945*, pp. 207–8; Kennedy, *Rise and Fall of the Great Powers*, p. 252; Young, *Britain and the World*, pp. 31, 36–7; Reynolds, *Britannia Overruled*, p. 75; Davis, *Britain, 1885–1939*, pp. 116–17; Anderson, *Ascendancy of Europe*, p. 51; Cordery, *Theodore Roosevelt*, pp. 127–8; Craig, *Germany*, pp. 318–21; Bridge and Bullen, *Great Powers*, pp. 278–82; Marriott, *History of Europe*, pp. 410–12; Joll, *Europe since 1870*, pp. 99–100, 177–9.

18 Young, *Britain and the World*, pp. 43–4; Read, *Age of Urban Democracy*, pp. 476–8; *The British General Staff: Reform and Innovation, c. 1890–1929*, D. French and B.H. Reid (eds) (London, 2003); Roberts, *Europe, 1880–1945*, p. 110.

19 Z. Steiner and K. Neilson, *Britain and the Origins of the First World War* (Basingstoke, 2003), Ch. 4; A.S. Tuminez, *Russian Nationalism since 1856: Ideology and the Making of Foreign Policy* (Lanham MD, 2000), Ch. 4; Westwood, *Endurance and Endeavour*, pp. 201–2; Marriott, *History of Europe*, pp. 415–17; Roberts, *Europe, 1880–1945*, pp. 208–9; Kennedy, *Rise and Fall of the Great Powers*, pp. 252–3; Young, *Britain and the World*, pp. 40–3; Reynolds, *Britannia Overruled*, pp. 69, 72–6; Read, *Age of Urban Democracy*, p. 480; Joll, *Europe since 1870*, pp. 100–1, 177, 179; Anderson, *Ascendancy of Europe*, pp. 51–2.

20 Reynolds, *Britannia Overruled*, pp. 73–80; Young, *Britain and the World*, pp. 40–51; Joll, *Europe since 1870*, pp. 100–1, 179; Roberts, *Europe, 1880–1945*, p. 209; Marriott, *History of Europe*, pp. 417–18; Bridge and Bullen, *Great Powers*, pp. 282–6; Westwood, *Endurance and Endeavour*, p. 202; Craig, *Germany*, p. 321.

21 K. Wilson, 'British Power in the European Balance, 1906–14', in *Retreat from Power: Studies in Britain's Foreign Policy of the Twentieth Century*, D. Dilks (ed.) (2 vols, London, 1981), Vol. 1, pp. 21–41; J. Charmley, 'Splendid Isolation to Finest Hour: Britain as a Global Power, 1900–50', *Contemporary British History*, 18 (2004), p. 135; J. Joll and G. Martell, *The Origins of the First World War* (Harlow, 2007), Chs 3, 5.

22 Joll, *Europe since 1870*, pp. 98–101, 175–9; Read, *Age of Urban Democracy*, p. 479; Young, *Britain and the World*, pp. 46–51; Reynolds, *Britannia Overruled*, pp. 79–80; D. Stevenson, *1914–18: The History of the First World War* (London, 2004), pp. 9–10.

23 S. Crowe and E. Corp, *Our Ablest Public Servant: Sir Eyre Crowe, 1864–1925* (Braunton, 1993) gives a favourable assessment of Crowe but pays little attention to the wider determinants of British foreign policy.

24 J.W.M. Chapman, 'British Use of "Dirty Tricks" in External Policy Prior to 1914', *War in History*, 9 (2002), pp. 60–81.

25 Joll, *Europe since 1870*, pp. 172–4; Young, *Britain and the World*, p. 42; Bridge and Bullen, *Great Powers*, pp. 286–94; Roberts, *Europe, 1880–1945*, pp. 210–13; Craig, *Germany*, pp. 321–4; Anderson, *Ascendancy of Europe*, p. 52; Marriott, *History of Europe*, pp. 425–34; Westwood, *Endurance and Endeavour*, p. 202.

26 Reynolds, *Britannia Overruled*, pp. 76–7; Young, *Britain and the World*, pp. 47–8;

Anderson, *Ascendancy of Europe*, pp. 52–3; Bridge and Bullen, *Great Powers*, pp. 303–10; Kennedy, *Rise and Fall of the Great Powers*, p. 253; Roberts, *Europe, 1880–1945*, pp. 213–14; Joll, *Europe since 1870*, pp. 171, 177; Marriott, *History of Europe*, pp. 418–21; Craig, *Germany*, pp. 328–9; Wilson, *Policy of the Entente*, Ch. 7; Heyck, *History of the Peoples*, p. 103; Read, *Age of Urban Democracy*, pp. 480–1; Davis, *Britain, 1885–1939*, pp. 117–18.

27 A. Thorpe, *A History of the British Labour Party* (Basingstoke, 1997), pp. 9, 35–6, 42–3; Read, *Age of Urban Democracy*, p. 500; G.R. Wilkinson, *Depictions and Images of War in Edwardian Newspapers, 1899–1914* (New York, 2003).

28 L. Sondhaus, 'Naval Power and Warfare', in *European Warfare, 1815–2000*, J. Black (ed.) (Basingstoke, 2002), pp. 179–83; Thompson, *Imperial Britain*, p. 112; Wilson, 'British Power in the European Balance', p. 39; Read, *Age of Urban Democracy*, pp. 475–6, 481–2; Joll, *Europe since 1870*, pp. 177–9; Roberts, *Europe, 1880–1945*, pp. 209–10, 214; Young, *Britain and the World*, pp. 39–40, 46–51; Reynolds, *Britannia Overruled*, pp. 76–81; Craig, *Germany*, pp. 329–31; K. Larres, *Churchill's Cold War: The Politics of Personal Diplomacy* (New Haven CT, 2002), p. 28.

29 M. Stibbe, *German Anglophobia and the Great War* (Cambridge, 2001).

30 Steiner and Neilson, *Britain and the Origins*, Ch. 3.

31 Joll, *Europe since 1870*, pp. 174–5; E. Ginio, 'Mobilizing the Ottoman Nation during the Balkan Wars (1912–13): Awakening from the Ottoman Dream', *War in History*, 12 (2005), pp. 156–77; Marriott, *History of Europe*, pp. 443–61; Bridge and Bullen, *Great Powers*, pp. 310–24; Young, *Britain and the World*, p. 51; Roberts, *Europe, 1880–1945*, pp. 214–15; Read, *Age of Urban Democracy*, p. 498; Steiner and Neilson, *Britain and the Origins*, Ch. 6.

32 Kantowicz, *Rage of Nations*, Ch. 6; Roberts, *Europe, 1880–1945*, pp. 215–16; Joll, *Europe since 1870*, p. 175; Craig, *Germany*, pp. 331–4; Westwood, *Endurance and Endeavour*, pp. 202–3; P. Hayes, 'Russia and Austria-Hungary: Empires under Pressure', in *Themes in Modern European History, 1890–1945*, P. Hayes (ed.) (London, 2004), pp. 55–82. On Moltke's role in shaping German policy, see A. Mombauer, *Helmuth von Moltke and the Origins of the First World War* (Cambridge, 2001).

33 Joll, *Europe since 1870*, pp. 180–1; Craig, *Germany*, pp. 335–6; H.H. Herwig, *The First World War: Germany and Austria-Hungary, 1914–18* (London, 1997), pp. 8–23; Roberts, *Europe, 1880–1945*, pp. 217–18; Marriott, *History of Europe*, pp. 487–8; S. Marks, *The Ebbing of European Ascendancy* (London, 2002), pp. 27, 34.

34 Stevenson, *1914–18*, pp. 10–43, and idem, 'International Relations', in *Europe, 1900–45*, J. Jackson (ed.) (Oxford, 2002), pp. 16–20; Kennedy, *Rise and Fall of the Great Powers*, pp. 253–6; Roberts, *Europe, 1880–1945*, pp. 218–19; Joll, *Europe since 1870*, pp. 181–5; Marriott, *History of Europe*, pp. 488–92; Read, *Age of Urban Democracy*, pp. 498–9; Westwood, *Endurance and Endeavour*, pp. 203–4;

Craig, *Germany*, pp. 335–7; A.J.P. Taylor, *The First World War* (London, 1966), pp. 13–21; M. Ferro, *The Great War, 1914–18* (London, 2002), Ch. 6; F. Fellner, 'Austria-Hungary', J.C.G. Rohl, 'Germany', K. Neilson, 'Russia', and J.F.V. Keiger, 'France', all in *Decisions for War, 1914*, K. Wilson (ed.) (London, 1995), pp. 9–25, 27–54, 97–120, 121–49.

35 P.G. Lauren, G.A. Craig and A.L. George, *Force and Statecraft* (New York, 2007), pp. 228–32; Hildebrand, 'International System', pp. 29–31.

36 S. van Evera, 'The Cult of the Offensive and the Origins of the First World War', in *Offence, Defence and War*, M. Brown, O. Cote, S. Lynn-Jones and S. Miller (eds) (Cambridge MA, 2004), pp. 69–118.

37 Young, *Britain and the World*, pp. 51–6; Reynolds, *Britannia Overruled*, pp. 84–8; Read, *Age of Urban Democracy*, pp. 498–500; Marriott, *History of Europe*, pp. 493–4; Roberts, *Europe, 1880–1945*, p. 219; Steiner and Neilson, *Britain and the Origins*, Ch. 9; Joll and Martell, *First World War*, Ch. 1.

38 Read, *Age of Urban Democracy*, pp. 498–500; Joll, *Europe since 1870*, pp. 185–6; Heyck, *History of the Peoples*, pp. 104–5; Wilson, *Policy of the Entente*, Ch. 8.

39 P. Hayes, *Modern British Foreign Policy: The Twentieth Century, 1880–1939* (London, 1978), pp. 170–1.

40 Davis, *Britain, 1885–1939*, pp. 117–18.

41 Read, *Age of Urban Democracy*, pp. 499–500; Sir E. Grey, *Speeches on Foreign Affairs, 1904–14* (London, 1931), pp. 297–315.

42 P. Bell, *The Origins of the Second World War in Europe* (Harlow, 1997), p. 21; P.W. Doerr, *British Foreign Policy, 1919–39* (Manchester, 1998), pp. 43–4; C. Barnett, *The Collapse of British Power* (Stroud, 1993), pp. 312–13; Young, *Britain and the World*, p. 76.

43 Marks, *Ebbing of European Ascendancy*, pp. 31–6; Joll, *Europe since 1870*, pp. 169, 171; P. Bell, 'Origins of the War of 1914', in Hayes, *Modern European History*, pp. 114–18. Joll and Martell, in *First World War*, Ch. 5, point out that a government would have been very unwise to start a war in order to divert attention from domestic problems, since there was no way of knowing in advance that war would have the desired consequence. On domestic issues in Europe before 1914, see E.D. Brose, *A History of Europe in the Twentieth Century* (Oxford, 2005), Ch. 2.

44 On domestic politics see M. Bentley, *Politics without Democracy, 1815–1914* (Oxford, 1996), pp. 223–65; D. Powell, *British Politics, 1910–35: The Crisis of the Party System* (London, 2004), Ch. 2; G.R. Searle, *The Liberal Party: Triumph and Disintegration, 1886–1929* (Basingstoke, 1992), Chs 5 and 6; P. Clarke, *Hope and Glory: Britain, 1900–2000* (London, 2004), Chs 1 and 2; D. Dutton, *A History of the Liberal Party* (Basingstoke, 2004), pp. 14–55; Read, *Age of Urban Democracy*, pp. 483–97; T.O. Lloyd, *Empire, Welfare State, Europe: History of the United Kingdom, 1906–2001* (Oxford, 2002), Chs 1 and 2; P. Thompson, *The Edwardians: The Remaking of British Society* (London, 1975), Chs 15 and 16;

E. Hopkins, *Industrialization and Society: A Social History, 1830–1951* (London, 2000), Ch. 6.

45 Boyce, *Decolonization and the British Empire*, Ch. 3; N. Ferguson, *Empire: How Britain Made the Modern World* (London, 2004), pp. 288–93; Thompson, *Imperial Britain*, p. 157.

46 A. Mombauer, *The Origins of the First World War: Controversies and Consensus* (London, 2002), pp. 23–4, 51, 57–69, 92, 138, 212; H. Afflerbach, 'Wilhelm II as Supreme Warlord in the First World War', *War in History*, 5 (1998), pp. 430–3, 448.

47 N. Ferguson, *The Pity of War* (London, 1998); T.G. Otte, 'Neo-Revisionism or the Emperor's New Clothes: Some Reflections on Niall Ferguson on the Origins of the First World War', *Diplomacy and Statecraft*, 11 (2000), pp. 271–90.

48 Charmley, 'Splendid Isolation to Finest Hour', pp. 130–46, and idem, *Splendid Isolation? Britain and the Balance of Power, 1874–1914* (London, 1999).

49 R. Shannon, *The Crisis of Imperialism, 1865–1915* (London, 1974), p. 427; Steinberg, 'German Background', pp. 214–15.

50 Thompson, *Imperial Britain*, p. 157.

51 Heyck, *History of the Peoples*, pp. 99–101.

52 C.J. Bartlett, *British Foreign Policy in the Twentieth Century* (London, 1989), Ch. 2; R.J.Q. Adams, *British Politics and Foreign Policy in the Age of Appeasement, 1935–39* (London, 1993); W. Rock, *British Appeasement in the 1930s* (London, 1977); P. Calvocoressi and G. Wint, *Total War: Causes and Courses of the Second World War* (London, 1972), pp. 71–2; S. Marks, *The Illusion of Peace: International Relations in Europe, 1918–33* (Basingstoke, 2003); Robbins, *Britain and Europe*, Ch. 9; F. McDonough, *Neville Chamberlain, Appeasement and the British Road to War* (Manchester, 1998), Part 2; I. Kershaw, *Making Friends with Hitler: Lord Londonderry and Britain's Road to War* (London, 2005), pp. 340–50; G. Robb, *British Culture and the First World War* (Basingstoke, 2002), Ch. 8; H. James, *Europe Reborn: A History, 1914–2000* (Harlow, 2003), Ch. 5; S.C. Tucker, *The Second World War* (Basingstoke, 2004), pp. 1–29.

53 Barnett, *Collapse of British Power*, pp. 152–60, 193–5, 198–200, 205–8, 224–6, 240, 267–73, 287–90, 298–305, 317–18, 335–40, 373–5, 395, 401–6, 446–8, 452–5, 462–8, 470–4, 512–51, 567–8, 570–2, 589–92.

54 D. Wright, *The Great War: A Useless Slaughter?* (Huddersfield, 1991) summarizes some differing viewpoints. For overwhelmingly negative interpretations of the First World War see T. Travers, *The Killing Ground* (London, 1990); J. Keegan, *The First World War* (London, 1999); R. Graves, *Goodbye To All That* (London, 1929); and James, *Europe Reborn*, in which the First World War shatters the confident, progressive, modernizing Europe of the late nineteenth century and ushers in a period of insecurity and crisis. That the war was not simply tragic and futile is a theme pursued in J.M. Bourne, *Britain and the Great War, 1914–18*

(London, 1989), T. Wilson, *The Myriad Faces of War* (Cambridge, 1986), and *Evidence, History and the Great War: Historians and the Impact of 1914–18*, G. Braybon (ed.) (New York, 2003). There are also useful discussions in S. Hynes, *A War Imagined* (London, 1990); L. Macdonald, *1914–18: Voices and Images of the Great War* (London, 1988); J. Fuller, *Troop Morale and Popular Culture in the British and Dominion Armies, 1914–18* (Oxford, 1991); Robb, *British Culture*, Ch. 8, and B. Bushaway, 'Name upon Name: The Great War and Remembrance', in *Myths of the English*, R. Porter (ed.) (Cambridge, 1994), pp. 136–67.

55   M. Kitchen, *Europe Between the Wars* (Harlow, 2006), Ch. 5; P. Johnson, *A History of the Modern World* (London, 1984), pp. 30–5, 147–8; Calvocoressi and Wint, *Total War*, pp. 29–33, 56–7; Joll, *Europe since 1870*, pp. 289–90; Roberts, *Europe, 1880–1945*, pp. 270, 281–3; Brose, *History of Europe*, Ch. 4; Keylor, *Twentieth Century World*, Ch. 3; Barnett, *Collapse of British Power*, pp. 59–60, 64, 237–8, 241–4, 254, 331–4; Doerr, *British Foreign Policy, 1919–39*, pp. 78–107; R. Graves and A. Hodge, *The Long Weekend: A Social History of Great Britain, 1918–39* (London, 1991), p. 161; Heyck, *History of the Peoples*, pp. 171–88; Kennedy, *Rise and Fall of the Great Powers*, Ch. 6; Stevenson, 'International Relations', pp. 23–9; Marks, *Illusion of Peace*, Chs 3 and 4, and idem, *Ebbing of European Ascendancy*, pp. 291–4; M. Lamb and N. Tarling, *From Versailles to Pearl Harbour: The Origins of the Second World War in Europe and Asia* (Basingstoke, 2001), pp. 56–8; Dobson, *Anglo-American Relations*, pp. 48–50; Hildebrand, 'International System', p. 33; Temperley, *Britain and America*, pp. 106–12; R.H. Zieger, *America's Great War: World War I and the American Experience* (Lanham MD, 2001), pp. 215–19; Young, *Britain and the World*, pp. 75–6, 89–99; Reynolds, *Britannia Overruled*, pp. 109–12; Bell, *Origins of the Second World War*, Ch. 3; D. Richardson, *The Evolution of British Disarmament Policy in the 1920s* (London, 1989); Powell, *British Politics*, pp. 142–78.

56   D. Cannadine, *History in Our Time* (London, 1998), p. 218; A. Sharp, 'Adapting to a New World? British Foreign Policy in the 1920s', *Contemporary British History*, 18 (2004), pp. 74–86; B. Morris, *The Roots of Appeasement: The British Weekly Press and Nazi Germany during the 1930s* (London, 1991).

57   Barnett, *Collapse of British Power*, and idem, *The Audit of War* (London, 1986); P. Kennedy, *The Realities behind Diplomacy: Background Influences on Britain External Policy, 1865–1980* (London, 1981), and idem, *Rise and Fall of the Great Powers*.

58   J. Ferris, '"The Greatest Power on Earth": Great Britain in the 1920s', *International History Review*, 13 (1991), pp. 726–50.

59   The effects of Versailles, especially on Germany, are discussed in P. Bobbitt, *The Shield of Achilles: War, Peace and the Course of History* (London, 2002), pp. 570–608. On Germany in the 1920s see T. Balderston, *Economics and Politics in the Weimar Republic* (Cambridge, 2002). Stresemann was a nationalist, but

according to J. Wright, *Gustav Stresemann: Weimar's Greatest Statesman* (Oxford, 2002) this does not mean that he was insincere about peace and co-operation.

60 Craig, *Germany*, pp. 511–24, 673–8; J. Hiden, *Germany and Europe, 1919–39* (Harlow, 1993), pp. 33–4, 43–6, 70–5, 77–80, 84–90, 119–25, 146–51, 169, 171–3, 176, 194–6; Barnett, *Collapse of British Power*, pp. 276–7, 323, 330, 333; Temperley, *Britain and America*, p. 132; Young, *Britain and the World*, pp. 93, 106–8; Calvocoressi and Wint, *Total War*, pp. 47–9, 57–8; Bell, *Origins of the Second World War*, pp. 41, 82–97, 103; Reynolds, *Britannia Overruled*, pp. 112–13; Stevenson, 'International Relations', pp. 27–37; Roberts, *Europe, 1880–1945*, pp. 281–4, 407–8; Kitchen, *Europe Between the Wars*, Chs 2, 9, 13; Winks and Adams, *Europe: Crisis and Conflict*, pp. 135–50; B. Lightbody, *The Second World War: Ambitions to Nemesis* (London, 2004), pp. 10–17; J. Ploughright, *The Causes, Course and Outcomes of World War II* (Basingstoke, 2007), Chs 1 and 2; A. Bullock, *Hitler: A Study in Tyranny* (London, 1981), Ch. 6.

61 P. Towle, 'British Security and Disarmament Policy in Europe in the 1920s', in Ahmann, Birke and Howard, *Quest for Stability*, pp. 127–53. See also, in the same volume, M. Vaisse, 'Security and Disarmament: Problems in the Development of the Disarmament Debates, 1919–34', pp. 173–200, which usefully points out that disarmament is not the same thing as peace.

62 Mombauer, *Origins of the First World War*, p. 97.

63 R.H. Haigh, D.S. Morris and A.R. Peters, *German-Soviet Relations in the Weimar Era: Friendship from Necessity* (Aldershot, 1985); S.C. Salzman, *Great Britain, Germany and the Soviet Union: Rapallo and After, 1922–34* (Rochester NY, 2003).

64 C. Fischer, *The Ruhr Crisis, 1923–24* (Oxford, 2003).

65 For a vindication of the treaty see M. MacMillan, *Paris 1919: Six Months that Changed the World* (New York, 2002). Versailles is condemned in C.L. Mee, Jr., *The End of Order: Versailles, 1919* (New York, 1980) and R.M. Watt, *The Kings Depart: The Tragedy of Germany, Versailles and the German Revolution* (New York, 1968). A more balanced account is A. Sharp, *The Versailles Settlement* (Basingstoke, 1991).

66 C.J. Kitching, *Britain and the Geneva Disarmament Conference: A Study in International History* (New York, 2003).

67 Beasley, *Japanese Imperialism*, Chs 10–12; Barnett, *Collapse of British Power*, pp. 267–73, 298–305; Doerr, *British Foreign Policy, 1919–39*, pp. 61–5, 109–14, 120–2; Thompson, *Imperial Britain*, pp. 175–6; I. Nish, *Japan's Struggle with Internationalism: Japan, China and the League of Nations, 1931–33* (London, 1993), and idem, *Japanese Foreign Policy in the Interwar Period* (Westport CT, 2002), pp. 58, 76, 108, 127, 132; A. Gordon, *A Modern History of Japan* (Oxford, 2003), Part 3; Marks, *Illusion of Peace*, pp. 131–6; Lamb and Tarling, *Versailles to Pearl Harbour*, pp. 62–70, 81–91; Dobson, *Anglo-American Relations*, pp. 50–2, 57–8; Temperley, *Britain and America*, pp. 115–17; Johnson, *Modern World*,

pp. 310–13; Kantowicz, *Rage of Nations*, pp. 352–8; Bell, *Origins of the Second World War*, p. 228; Reynolds, *Britannia Overruled*, pp. 119–22; Young, *Britain and the World*, pp. 103–6; Lightbody, *Second World War*, pp. 3–7; Calvocoressi and Wint, *Total War*, pp. 591–609, 623–6.

68   C. Ward, *Stalin's Russia* (London, 1999), Ch. 5; J. Jacobson, *When the Soviet Union Entered World Politics* (Berkeley CA, 1994); Kantowicz, *Rage of Nations*, pp. 320–5; A.A. Kokoshin, *Soviet Strategic Thought, 1917–91* (Cambridge MA, 1999), pp. 19–43, 80–98, 147–65; Westwood, *Endurance and Endeavour*, pp. 349–51, 355–6; E.H. Carr, *The Russian Revolution from Lenin to Stalin, 1917–29* (London, 1979), pp. 84–105, 173–84; I. Deutscher, *Stalin: A Political Biography* (Harmondsworth, 1972), pp. 383–414, 417; Bell, *Origins of the Second World War*, pp. 124–38, 220–3; Winks and Adams, *Europe: Crisis and Conflict*, pp. 160–74; Roberts, *Europe, 1880–1945*, pp. 272–4, 284, 347–9, 423–5.

69   Doerr, *British Foreign Policy, 1919–39*, pp. 173–4; Barnett, *Collapse of British Power*, p. 407; Johnson, *Modern World*, p. 351; Young, *Britain and the World*, pp. 106–9; Calvocoressi and Wint, *Total War*, pp. 61, 71–2, 83; Bell, *Origins of the Second World War*, p. 249; Bullock, *Hitler*, pp. 336–8; Craig, *Germany*, pp. 684–8; Hiden, *Germany and Europe*, pp. 90–3; Lamb and Tarling, *Versailles to Pearl Harbour*, pp. 80–1, 92–5; Joll, *Europe since 1870*, pp. 359–60; M. Howard, 'British Military Preparations for the Second World War', in Dilks, *Retreat from Power*, Vol. 1, p. 103.

70   N. Medlicott, 'Britain and Germany: The Search for Agreement, 1930–37', in Dilks, *Retreat from Power*, Vol. 1, pp. 80–1, 85, 91; Young, *Britain and the World*, pp. 91–2, 97, 99, 101, 105, 107–9, 116; Reynolds, *Britannia Overruled*, pp. 45–6, 114–19; Bell, *Origins of the Second World War*, pp. 18, 39, 143–4, 146–9, 162–5, 196–7; Doerr, *British Foreign Policy, 1919–39*, pp. 145–6, 150, 152; Lauren, Craig and George, *Force and Statecraft*, pp. 58–60; McDonough, *Chamberlain, Appeasement and the Road to War*, Ch. 9; Barnett, *Collapse of British Power*, pp. 294–5, 416–17; G. Schmidt, *The Politics and Economics of Appeasement, 1931–37* (Leamington Spa, 1986).

71   S. Pollard, 'Economic Interdependence and Economic Protectionism: From the Conference of Genoa (1922) to the Conference of London (1933)', in Ahmann, Birke and Howard, *Quest for Stability*, pp. 157–71. On the effects of international indebtedness, the disruption of trade and the Great Depression, see also Temperley, *Britain and America*, pp. 117–19, 122–31.

72   G. Peden, *British Rearmament and the Treasury, 1932–39* (Edinburgh, 1979); J.P. Levy, *Appeasement and Rearmament: Britain, 1936–39* (Lanham MD, 2006), Chs 2 and 3; Reynolds, *Britannia Overruled*, pp. 45–6, 114–19; Bell, *Origins of the Second World War*, pp. 18, 39, 143–4, 146–9, 162–5, 196–7; Young, *Britain and the World*, pp. 91–2, 97, 99, 101, 105, 107–9, 116.

73   Doerr, *British Foreign Policy, 1919–39*, pp. 166–7; Barnett, *Collapse of British Power*,

pp. 416–17; Young, *Britain and the World*, pp. 105, 107, 114; Reynolds, *Britannia Overruled*, pp. 114–19. Broader economic contexts are examined in Clarke, *Hope and Glory*, Ch. 5; P.K. O'Brien, 'Britain's Economy Between the Wars: A Survey of a Counter-Revolution in Economic History', *Past and Present, 115* (1987), pp. 107–30; Bell, *Origins of the Second World War*, Chs 9 and 10; Daunton, *Wealth and Welfare*, pp. 176–90; Lloyd-Jones and Lewis, *British Industrial Capitalism*, Ch. 7; More, *Industrial Age*, pp. 215–21, 230–46; Booth, *British Economy*, pp. 59–69; Hopkins, *Industrialization and Society*, Ch. 8. On the Conservative Party in the 1930s see R. Blake, *The Conservative Party from Peel to Churchill* (London, 1970), pp. 235–46.

74   Medlicott, 'Britain and Germany', p. 86; Johnson, *Modern World*, p. 351; Doerr, *British Foreign Policy, 1919–39*, pp. 168–9; Barnett, *Collapse of British Power*, pp. 313, 397–407; Joll, *Europe since 1870*, p. 276; Roberts, *Europe, 1880–1945*, p. 416; Bell, *Origins of the Second World War*, p. 249; Craig, *Germany*, pp. 683–4; Hiden, *Germany and Europe*, p. 94; Bullock, *Hitler*, p. 331. On Vansittart's opinions see Michael L. Roi, *Alternative to Appeasement: Sir Robert Vansittart and Alliance Diplomacy, 1934–37* (Westport CT, 1997).

75   Barnett, *Collapse of British Power*, pp. 327–31; A. Adamthwaite, *France and the Coming of the Second World War* (London, 1977); M. Adam, *The Little Entente and Europe, 1920–29* (Budapest, 1993); Roberts, *Europe, 1880–1945*, pp. 278–9; Joll, *Europe since 1870*, pp. 289–90, 296–7, 363; Calvocoressi and Wint, *Total War*, pp. 50–1, 54.

76   This is illustrated in *Anglo-French Defence Relations between the Wars*, M.S. Alexander and W.J. Philpott (eds) (Basingstoke, 2002). See also R. Davis, *Anglo-French Relations before the Second World War: Appeasement and Crisis* (London, 2001) and M. Dockrill, *British Establishment Perspectives on France, 1936–40* (London, 1999).

77   Medlicott, 'Britain and Germany', pp. 85–8, 95–6; Doerr, *British Foreign Policy, 1919–39*, pp. 158–9, 168–70, 172, 186–7, 205; Johnson, *Modern World*, pp. 319–21; Joll, *Europe since 1870*, p. 353; Young, *Britain and the World*, pp. 109–12; Reynolds, *Britannia Overruled*, pp. 112–13; Bell, *Origins of the Second World War*, pp. 228–32; G. Johnson, 'Sir Eric Phipps, the British Government and the Appeasement of Germany, 1933–37', *Diplomacy and Statecraft, 16* (2005), pp. 651–9; Calvocoressi and Wint, *Total War*, pp. 49, 54–8, 74; Bullock, *Hitler*, pp. 331–5; D. Mack Smith, *Mussolini* (London, 1983), pp. 221–6, 238–9.

78   R. Ahmann, '"Localization of Conflicts" or "Indivisibility of Peace": The German and Soviet Approaches towards Collective Security in East Central Europe, 1925–39', in Ahmann, Birke and Howard, *Quest for Stability*, pp. 201–47; Barnett, *Collapse of British Power*, pp. 331–4.

79   Mack Smith, *Mussolini*, pp. 220–35; Bell, *Origins of the Second World War*, pp. 70–6, 230–8; Medlicott, 'Britain and Germany', pp. 94–5; Bullock, *Hitler*, pp. 341–6;

Hiden, *Germany and Europe*, pp. 93–5; Craig, *Germany*, pp. 687–90; Roberts, *Europe, 1880–1945*, pp. 410–17; Lightbody, *Second World War*, pp. 17–23, 28–9; Calvocoressi and Wint, *Total War*, pp. 60–4; Joll, *Europe since 1870*, pp. 358–61; Lamb and Tarling, *Versailles to Pearl Harbour*, pp. 95–102; Young, *Britain and the World*, pp. 109–12; Reynolds, *Britannia Overruled*, pp. 112–13, 122–3; Doerr, *British Foreign Policy, 1919–39*, pp. 179–87, 189–94; Barnett, *Collapse of British Power*, pp. 350–86, 408–9; D. Dutton, *Anthony Eden: A Life and Reputation* (London, 1997), pp. 63–6; D.R. Thorpe, *Eden* (London, 2003), pp. 175–7; Kitchen, *Europe Between the Wars*, pp. 395–7; Johnson, *Modern World*, pp. 320–1, 349, 351–2; Kantowicz, *Rage of Nations*, pp. 368–9, 371–4.

80 R. Mallett, *Mussolini and the Origins of the Second World War, 1933–40* (Basingstoke, 2003).

81 Medlicott, 'Britain and Germany', pp. 89, 91–3, 97–8; Calvocoressi and Wint, *Total War*, pp. 47–8, 73; Bullock, *Hitler*, pp. 358, 366; A. Crozier, *Appeasement and Germany's Last Bid for Colonies* (London, 1988); Young, *Britain and the World*, p. 111; Hiden, *Germany and Europe*, p. 94; Dutton, *Anthony Eden*, pp. 60–1; Thorpe, *Eden*, pp. 174–5; Barnett, *Collapse of British Power*, p. 453; Roberts, *Europe, 1880–1945*, p. 415 n.14.

82 Howard, 'British Military Preparations', pp. 113–14; Reynolds, *Britannia Overruled*, pp. 114–19; Barnett, *Collapse of British Power*, pp. 402, 412–19, 438–9, 475–504, 551–2, 554, 558; Young, *Britain and the World*, pp. 105, 107–8, 111–12, 114–16, 124; Bell, *Origins of the Second World War*, pp. 193–204. For more detailed discussions of defence policy and rearmament, see R.P. Shay, *British Rearmament in the Thirties* (Princeton NJ, 1977); B. Bond, *British Military Policy between the Two World Wars* (Oxford, 1980); M. Howard, *The Continental Commitment* (London, 1972).

83 G. Post, *Dilemmas of Appeasement: British Deterrence and Defence, 1934–37* (Ithaca NY, 1993).

84 Howard, 'British Military Preparations', pp. 102–4; Doerr, *British Foreign Policy, 1919–39*, pp. 164–7, 173, 204; Barnett, *Collapse of British Power*, pp. 250–3, 257, 273, 299–300, 345–50, 440–2, 445–6; Beasley, *Japanese Imperialism*, Chs 13 and 14; Lamb and Tarling, *Versailles to Pearl Harbour*, pp. 102–11; Calvocoressi and Wint, *Total War*, pp. 66, 626, 634–60; R. Chandavarkar, 'Imperialism and the European Empires', in Jackson, *Europe, 1900–45*, pp. 138–72; L.J. Butler, *Britain and Empire: Adjusting to a Post-Imperial World* (London, 2002), Ch. 1; P. Lowe, *Great Britain and the Origins of the Pacific War, 1937–41* (Oxford, 1977); Cain and Hopkins, *British Imperialism*, pp. 16, 594, 596, 600–12; Brendon, *Decline and Fall of the British Empire*, Chs 13–15; Robb, *British Culture*, Ch. 1; R. Johnson, *British Imperialism* (Basingstoke, 2003), Ch. 11; Young, *Britain and the World*, pp. 102–9, 112, 116–17, 121–3, 125; Reynolds, *Britannia Overruled*, pp. 119–22, 127, 137; Bell, *Origins of the Second World War*, pp. 183, 228, 283; Bullock, *Hitler*, pp. 354–5,

362; Mack Smith, *Mussolini*, pp. 249–52; Jeffery, 'British Isles/British Empire', pp. 18–35; I. Cowman, 'Defence of the Malay Barrier? The Place of the Philippines in Admiralty Naval War Planning, 1925–41', *War in History*, 3 (1996), pp. 398–417; Lightbody, *Second World War*, pp. 3–9; Boyce, *Decolonization and the British Empire*, Ch. 4; T.G. Fraser, *The Arab-Israeli Conflict* (Basingstoke, 1995), pp. 9–14; J.L. Gelvin, *The Modern Middle East: A History* (New York, 2005), pp. 208–12; J. Norris, 'Repression and Rebellion: Britain's Response to the Arab Revolt in Palestine of 1936–39', *Journal of Imperial and Commonwealth History*, 36 (2008), pp. 25–45. On Comintern and its links with Soviet espionage and intervention in Western Europe, Asia, and Britain and its empire, see D. McKnight, *Espionage and the Roots of the Cold War: The Conspiratorial Heritage* (London, 2002).

85 Temperley, *Britain and America*, pp. 132–3; G. Kennedy, *Anglo-American Strategic Relations and the Far East, 1933–39* (London, 2002), Chs 1, 4–6; *Chinese Collaboration with Japan, 1932–45: The Limits of Accommodation*, D.P. Barrett and L.N. Shyu (eds) (Stanford CA, 2001).

86 U. Bialer, *The Shadow of the Bomber: The Fear of Air Attack and British Politics, 1932–39* (London, 1980); Howard, 'British Military Preparations', pp. 104–5, 110; Morris, *Roots of Appeasement*, Ch. 3; Barnett, *Collapse of British Power*, pp. 436–8; Reynolds, *Britannia Overruled*, p. 117; Bell, *Origins of the Second World War*, pp. 198–9; Young, *Britain and the World*, p. 107; J. Buckley, *The RAF and Trade Defence, 1919–45: Constant Endeavour* (Keele, 1995).

87 Howard, 'British Military Preparations', pp. 106–7, 111–12; Reynolds, *Britannia Overruled*, p. 124; Young, *Britain and the World*, pp. 107–8, 116; Barnett, *Collapse of British Power*, pp. 414–16; Doerr, *British Foreign Policy, 1919–39*, p. 209.

88 K. Neilson, 'The Defence Requirements Sub-Committee, British Strategic Foreign Policy, Neville Chamberlain and the Path to Appeasement', *English Historical Review*, 118 (2003), pp. 651–84; Howard, 'British Military Preparations', pp. 108–10; Doerr, *British Foreign Policy, 1919–39*, pp. 164–5, 166–7; Barnett, *Collapse of British Power*, pp. 345–7, 412, 414–16; Young, *Britain and the World*, pp. 107–8. On the situation in the Far East see also P. Bell, *Chamberlain, Germany and Japan, 1933–34* (Basingstoke, 1996); Lowe, *Britain and the Origins of the Pacific War*; W.R. Louis, *British Strategy in the Far East, 1919–39* (Oxford, 1971).

89 D. Dilks, 'Appeasement and Intelligence', in Dilks, *Retreat from Power*, Vol. 1, pp. 139–69; J. Ferris, 'Intelligence', in *The Origins of World War II: The Debate Continues*, R. Boyce and J.A. Maiolo (eds) (Basingstoke, 2003), pp. 308–29; W. Wark, *The Ultimate Enemy: British Intelligence and Nazi Germany* (London, 1985); R. Overy, 'Strategic Intelligence and the Outbreak of the Second World War', *War in History*, 5 (1998), pp. 451–79; Barnett, *Collapse of British Power*, pp. 417–19; Reynolds, *Britannia Overruled*, pp. 115, 127, 129–30, 132, 307; Young, *Britain and the World*, p. 117; J.A. Maiolo, *The Royal Navy and Nazi Germany*,

1933–39: A Study in Appeasement and the Origins of the Second World War (Basingstoke, 1998).

90   A. Best, *British Intelligence and the Japanese Challenge in Asia, 1914–41* (Basingstoke, 2002).

91   The attitudes of dominant groups in British society are explored in Part 2 of Barnett's *Collapse of British Power*, in line with his overarching theme of British decline. See also Calvocoressi and Wint, *Total War*, pp. 49–50, 71–3; Young, *Britain and the World*, pp. 118–19; Bell, *Origins of the Second World War*, pp. 111–22; Reynolds, *Britannia Overruled*, pp. 57–8, 62–3, 108–14; Marks, *Ebbing of European Ascendancy*, Ch. 15; Johnson, *Modern World*, p. 349; Lightbody, *Second World War*, p. 28; *Pacifism is Not Enough: Collected Lectures and Speeches of Lord Lothian*, J. Pinder and A. Bosco (eds) (London, 1990).

92   Kershaw, *Making Friends with Hitler*, pp. 152, 221–3.

93   Medlicott, 'Britain and Germany', pp. 80, 90–1. On opinion in the foreign office in these years, see Doerr, *British Foreign Policy, 1919–39*, Ch. 6. Though Wigram gained a reputation as an opponent of appeasement, his position was not straightforward: P. Neville, 'A Prophet Scorned? Ralph Wigram, the Foreign Office and the German Threat, 1933–36', *Journal of Contemporary History*, 40 (2005), pp. 41–54.

94   B.J.C. McKercher, '"Our Most Dangerous Enemy": Great Britain Pre-eminent in the 1930s', *International History Review*, 13 (1991), pp. 751–83.

95   P. Neville, 'The Foreign Office and Britain's Ambassadors to Berlin, 1933–39', *Contemporary British History*, 18 (2004), pp. 110–29, and idem, *Appeasing Hitler: The Diplomacy of Sir Nevile Henderson, 1937–39* (Basingstoke, 2000); Doerr, *British Foreign Policy, 1919–39*, pp. 158, 217; Reynolds, *Britannia Overruled*, p. 126; Young, *Britain and the World*, pp. 120–1; D.C. Watt, 'Diplomacy and Diplomatists', in Boyce and Maiolo, *Origins of World War II*, pp. 330–41.

96   Reynolds, *Britannia Overruled*, p. 126; Young, *Britain and the World*, pp. 120–1; Doerr, *British Foreign Policy, 1919–39*, pp. 217, 227–8, 230, 242; Barnett, *Collapse of British Power*, pp. 238–9, 460–2, 467, 472, 514, 544; Calvocoressi and Wint, *Total War*, pp. 49–50, 72.

97   A.J.P. Taylor, *Europe: Grandeur and Decline* (Harmondsworth, 1971), p. 259, and for the context see the same author's *English History, 1914–45* (Oxford, 1987), pp. 445–50.

98   Ward, *Stalin's Russia*, Ch. 5; Deutscher, *Stalin*, pp. 408–29; Westwood, *Endurance and Endeavour*, pp. 351–3; Barnett, *Collapse of British Power*, pp. 556–72; Lauren, Craig and George, *Force and Statecraft*, pp. 67, 182–5; Reynolds, *Britannia Overruled*, pp. 55, 104, 128, 131–2, 142; Johnson, *Modern World*, pp. 357–62; Doerr, *British Foreign Policy, 1919–39*, pp. 246–64; Young, *Britain and the World*, pp. 125–7; Bell, *Origins of the Second World War*, pp. 45, 48, 93, 109, 118–19, 124, 130–1, 137–8, 176–7, 223, 265–6, 286–7, 291–4, 294–7, 326–8, 332, 339–40, and

idem, 'Hitler's War? The Origins of the Second World War in Europe', in Hayes, *Modern European History*, pp. 240–2; Roberts, *Europe, 1880–1945*, pp. 435–7; Bullock, *Hitler*, pp. 513–25; Calvocoressi and Wint, *Total War*, pp. 83–9. For a Soviet view of British policy in the 1930s, see I. Maisky, *Who Helped Hitler?* (London, 1964). Lord Strang's 'The Moscow Negotiations, 1939', in Dilks, *Retreat from Power*, Vol. 1, pp. 170–86, is a participant's account.

99   D. Carlton, *Churchill and the Soviet Union* (Manchester, 2000), pp. 46–7, 63–6.

100   Doerr, *British Foreign Policy, 1919–39*, pp. 157–64, 175–8; Lauren, Craig and George, *Force and Statecraft*, pp. 54–7; Barnett, *Collapse of British Power*, pp. 359–60, 420–4; Johnson, *Modern World*, pp. 349–50; Graves and Hodges, *Long Weekend*, pp. 441–6; Bell, *Origins of the Second World War*, pp. 112, 114, 116; Reynolds, *Britannia Overruled*, pp. 116, 122; Young, *Britain and the World*, pp. 105–6; P. Bell, 'Peace Movements', in Boyce and Maiolo, *Origins of World War II*, pp. 273–85; R.B. McCallum, *Public Opinion and the Lost Peace* (Oxford, 1944), pp. 177–80; J. Morris, *The Oxford Book of Oxford* (Oxford 2002), pp. 374–5; Q. Hogg, *The Left was Never Right* (London, 1945), p. 50; M. Ceadel, 'Interpreting East Fulham', in *By-Elections in British Politics*, C. Cook and J. Ramsden (eds) (London, 1997), pp. 94–111, idem, 'The "King and Country" Debate, 1933: Student Politics, Pacifism and the Dictators', *Historical Journal, 22* (1979), pp. 397–422, and idem, *Pacifism in Britain, 1914–45* (Oxford, 1980). Insights into contemporary opinion are also provided by F. Gannon, *The British Press and Nazi Germany, 1936–39* (Oxford, 1971); Morris, *Roots of Appeasement*; D. Birn, *The League of Nations Union, 1918–45* (London, 1981); and P. Kyba, *Covenants Without the Sword: Public Opinion and British Defence Policy, 1931–35* (Waterloo, Ontario, 1983).

101   Lord Cecil, *A Great Experiment: An Autobiography* (London, 1941), pp. 257–60.

102   Doerr, *British Foreign Policy, 1919–39*, p. 209; Barnett, *Collapse of British Power*, pp. 411, 439–40; Young, *Britain and the World*, pp. 91, 110, 116, 122–5; Reynolds, *Britannia Overruled*, pp. 115, 124–7, 131; Lamb and Tarling, *Versailles to Pearl Harbour*, p. 125.

103   Doerr, *British Foreign Policy, 1919–39*, pp. 228–38; Reynolds, *Britannia Overruled*, pp. 126–8; Young, *Britain and the World*, pp. 123–5; Howard, 'British Military Preparations', pp. 113–15; Calvocoressi and Wint, *Total War*, pp. 70–1, 74–9; Bell, *Origins of the Second World War*, pp. 258–75; Lightbody, *Second World War*, pp. 30–2; Barnett, *Collapse of British Power*, pp. 505–17, 546–50, 556; Bullock, *Hitler*, pp. 448–9, 454–71; Johnson, *Modern World*, pp. 353–6; Kitchen, *Europe Between the Wars*, pp. 402–11; Joll, *Europe since 1870*, pp. 368–73; Roberts, *Europe, 1880–1945*, pp. 425–34; Craig, *Germany*, pp. 702–8; Hiden, *Germany and Europe*, pp. 96–104, 162–6; P. Vysny, *The Runciman Mission to Czechoslovakia, 1938: Prelude to Munich* (Basingstoke, 2003), pp. 342–3.

104   Dutton, *Anthony Eden*, Ch. 4; Thorpe, *Eden*, Ch. 7; Medlicott, 'Britain and

Germany', pp. 99, 101; Calvocoressi and Wint, *Total War*, pp. 73–4; Temperley, *Britain and America*, pp. 133–5; Doerr, *British Foreign Policy, 1919–39*, pp. 165–7, 207–10, 213–20; Barnett, *Collapse of British Power*, pp. 444–8, 470–2; Reynolds, *Britannia Overruled*, pp. 121–5; Young, *Britain and the World*, pp. 110–12, 119; Lloyd, *Empire, Welfare State, Europe*, pp. 181–3; Mack Smith, *Mussolini*, Chs 11 and 12; Roberts, *Europe, 1880–1945*, p. 421. On Anglo-American relations and the complications caused by appeasement, see C.A. MacDonald, *The United States, Britain and Appeasement* (London, 1981); W. Rock, *Chamberlain and Roosevelt, 1937–40* (Columbus OH, 1988); D. Reynolds, *The Creation of the Anglo-American Alliance, 1937–41* (London, 1981).

105 Z. Steiner, 'The League of Nations and the Quest for Security', in Ahmann, Birke and Howard, *Quest for Stability*, pp. 35–70; B.J.C. McKercher, 'The Foreign Office, 1930–39: Strategy, Permanent Interests and National Security', *Contemporary British History*, 18 (2004), pp. 87–109.

106 Doerr, *British Foreign Policy, 1919–39*, pp. 207–10; J.D. Doenecke, *Storm on the Horizon: The Challenge to American Intervention, 1939–41* (Lanham MD, 2000), pp. x–xi, 1–8; Dobson, *Anglo-American Relations*, pp. 67–70; Young, *Britain and the World*, pp. 114–27; Bell, *Origins of the Second World War*, pp. 197–204, 264–74; Reynolds, *Britannia Overruled*, pp. 108, 113, 117–34, 138, 141, 147; Heyck, *History of the Peoples*, pp. 188–92; Davis, *Britain, 1885–1939*, pp. 222–35.

107 Calvocoressi and Wint, *Total War*, pp. 74–9; Doerr, *British Foreign Policy, 1919–39*, pp. 223–38; Lauren, Craig and George, *Force and Statecraft*, p. 57; Barnett, *Collapse of British Power*, pp. 505–51; Lloyd, *Empire, Welfare State, Europe*, pp. 183–6; Kantowicz, *Rage of Nations*, pp. 374–7.

108 J. Lawson, *A Man's Life* (London, 1949), pp. 180, 181–2.

109 Doerr, *British Foreign Policy, 1919–39*, Ch. 10; Thorpe, *Labour Party*, pp. 89–91, 96; Barnett, *Collapse of British Power*, p. 556.

110 T.C. Imlay, *Facing the Second World War: Strategy, Politics and Economics in Britain and France, 1938–40* (Oxford, 2003).

111 Calvocoressi and Wint, *Total War*, pp. 92–6.

112 Bell, 'Hitler's War?', pp. 239–40.

113 An early, hostile assessment of Chamberlain's performance is *The Guilty Men* (London, 1940), written by 'Cato' – actually three journalists who opposed appeasement: Michael Foot, the future Labour MP and party leader; Frank Owen, a former Liberal MP; and Conservative supporter Peter Howard. K. Feiling, *The Life of Neville Chamberlain* (London, 1946) views him in a more positive light. M. Gilbert and R. Gott, *The Appeasers* (London, 1963) is negative, but Gilbert's *The Roots of Appeasement* (London, 1966) less so. A.J.P. Taylor's *Origins of the Second World War* (London, 1961), while agreeing that Chamberlain was outfoxed by Hitler, contends that no other British leader could have done better, and draws attention away from personalities to the complexities of policy making and the

difficult problems that the British government had to deal with in this period. On changing interpretative fashions see R.J. Caputi, *Neville Chamberlain and Appeasement* (Selinsgrove PA, 2000).

114 Dilks, 'Introduction', in *Retreat from Power*, Vol. 1, p. 18, and idem, '"We Must Hope for the Best and Prepare for the Worst": The Prime Minister, the Cabinet and Hitler's Germany, 1937–39', *Proceedings of the British Academy*, 73 (1987), pp. 309–52. For a strong defence of Chamberlain, see J. Charmley, *Chamberlain and the Lost Peace* (London, 1989).

115 Levy, *Appeasement and Rearmament*, pp. 157–71.

116 E.g. R. Self, *Neville Chamberlain: A Biography* (Aldershot, 2006).

117 I. Colvin, *The Chamberlain Cabinet* (London, 1971), p. 263. Other negative accounts include K. Middlemass, *The Diplomacy of Illusion* (London, 1972), and L. Fuchser, *Neville Chamberlain and Appeasement* (London, 1982).

118 J. Ruggiero, *Neville Chamberlain and British Rearmament: Pride, Prejudice and Politics* (Westport CT, 1999), pp. 2–3, 8, 154, 181, 183; R. Cockett, *Twilight of Truth: Chamberlain, Appeasement and the Manipulation of the Press* (London, 1989), pp. 186, 188.

119 R.A.C. Parker, *Chamberlain and Appeasement: British Policy and the Coming of the Second World War* (London, 1993), pp. 1–2, 23, 347.

120 D. Dutton, *Neville Chamberlain* (London, 2001), Ch. 7.

121 McDonough, *Chamberlain, Appeasement and the Road to War*, Ch. 10.

122 Gilbert, *Roots of Appeasement*, pp. 187–8.

123 J. Charmley, *Churchill: The End of Glory* (London, 1993); Barnett, *Collapse of British Power*, pp. 587–8.

124 D. Reynolds, *In Command of History: Churchill Fighting and Writing the Second World War* (London, 2005), pp. 172–4. On the possibility of an early peace see also Reynolds, *Britannia Overruled*, pp. 138–9; Young, *Britain and the World*, pp. 127–30; Ploughright, *World War II*, pp. 37–40; Calvocoressi and Wint, *Total War*, p. 50.

125 E.g. J. Lukacs, *Churchill: Visionary, Statesman, Historian* (New Haven, Connecticut, 2002).

126 On Japan's conquests see N. Tarling, *A Sudden Rampage: The Japanese Occupation of South East Asia, 1941–45* (Honolulu, 2001), Chs 1–2.

127 See Correlli Barnett's remarks in English and Kenny, *Rethinking British Decline*, pp. 37–49, and on the imperial aspects R. Ovendale, 'The End of Empire', in the same volume, pp. 257–78.

128 Carlton, *Churchill and the Soviet Union*, Ch. 5; D. Reynolds, 'Great Britain and the Security "Lessons" of the Second World War', in Ahmann, Birke and Howard, *Quest for Stability*, pp. 299–325; J. Kent, 'British Policy and the Origins of the Cold War', in *Origins of the Cold War: An International History*, M.P. Leffler and D.S. Painter (eds) (New York, 2005), pp. 155–66.

Notes to Chapter 2: Post-war Adjustments

1 S. Morewood, 'Divided Europe: The Long Post-War, 1945–89', in *Themes in Modern European History since 1945*, R. Wakeman (ed.) (London, 2003), pp. 15–16; M.P. Leffler, 'Bringing it Together: The Parts and the Whole', in *Reviewing the Cold War: Approaches, Interpretations, Theory*, O.A. Westad (ed.) (London, 2000), pp. 43–63; E.R. Kantowicz, *Coming Apart, Coming Together* (Grand Rapids MI, 2000), p. 284; J.L. Gaddis, *We Now Know: Rethinking Cold War History* (Oxford, 1997), pp. 31, 292; M. Fulbrook, 'Introduction: Europe since 1945', D. Sassoon, 'Politics', H. Kaeble, 'Social History', and K. Larres, 'International and Security Relations within Europe', all in *Europe since 1945*, M. Fulbrook (ed.) (Oxford, 2001), pp. 3, 7, 16, 55, 187.

2 E.g. J. Baylis, *The Diplomacy of Pragmatism: Britain and the Formation of NATO, 1942–49* (Basingstoke, 1993).

3 K. Burk, 'Introduction', in *The British Isles since 1945*, K. Burk (ed.) (Oxford, 2003), p. 1; S. Greenwood, *Britain and the Cold War, 1945–91* (Basingstoke, 2000), pp. 3–4; R. Merrick, 'The Russia Committee of the British Foreign Office and the Cold War, 1946–47', *Journal of Contemporary History*, 20 (1985), pp. 453–68.

4 J. Kent, *British Imperial Strategy and the Origins of the Cold War* (London, 1993), pp. 212–14.

5 D. Reynolds, 'Britain and the World since 1945: Narratives of Decline or Transformation?' in Burk, *British Isles since 1945*, p. 159; C. Coker, 'Foreign and Defence Policy', in *Britain since 1945*, J. Hollowell (ed.) (Oxford, 2003), p. 3; Young, *Britain and the World*, p. 223. The media played its part too: e.g. A. Foster, 'The British Press and the Coming of the Cold War', in *Britain and the First Cold War*, A. Deighton (ed.) (Basingstoke, 1990), pp. 11–31.

6 Winning support abroad was bound to be difficult when there were differing assessments of Soviet intentions. See Greenwood, *Britain and the Cold War*, p. 2.

7 C. Wilson (Lord Moran), *Winston Churchill: The Struggle for Survival, 1940–65. Taken from the Diaries of Lord Moran* (London, 1966), p. 133; T. Morgan, *FDR: A Biography* (New York, 1985), pp. 693–6; *The Roosevelt Letters*, E. Roosevelt (ed.) (3 vols, London, 1953), Vol. 3, pp. 453–4. Despite their disagreements there was great respect between Churchill and Roosevelt. See D. Reynolds, 'Roosevelt, Churchill and the Wartime Anglo-American Alliance, 1939–45: Towards a New Synthesis', in *The 'Special Relationship': Anglo-American Relations since 1945*, W.R. Louis and H. Bull (eds) (Oxford, 1986), pp. 17–41.

8 Johnson, *Modern World*, p. 433; Burk, *British Isles since 1945*, p. 2; T.H. Anderson, *The United States, Great Britain and the Cold War, 1944–47* (Columbia MO, 1981), p. 4; R. Garson, 'The Atlantic Alliance, Eastern Europe and the Origins of the Cold War: From Pearl Harbour to Yalta', in *Contrast and Connection: Bicentennial Essays in Anglo-American History*, H.C. Allen and R. Thompson (eds)

(London, 1976), pp. 298–9; M. Gilbert, *Churchill: A Life* (London, 1991), pp. 826, 828, 832, 835; F.J. Harbutt, *The Iron Curtain: Churchill, America and the Origins of the Cold War* (New York, 1986), Chs 3 and 4; J. Wheeler-Bennett and A. Nicholls, *The Semblance of Peace: The Political Settlement after the Second World War* (London, 1972), p. 290; J. Lewis, *Changing Direction: British Military Planning for Post-War Strategic Defence, 1942–47* (London, 1988), Ch. 4.

9   Reynolds, *Britannia Overruled*, pp. 146–7; W. Churchill, *The Second World War* (6 vols, London, 1948–54), Vol. 6, Ch. 22; Johnson, *Modern World*, pp. 433–5; A. Harriman and E. Abel, *Special Envoy to Churchill and Stalin, 1941–46* (New York, 1975), pp. 390–1; A.B. Ulam, *Stalin: The Man and His Era* (New York, 1973), p. 596.

10 Anderson, *United States, Britain and the Cold War*, pp. 47, 50; Johnson, *Modern World*, p. 435; T.G. Fraser and D. Murray, *America and the World since 1945* (Basingstoke, 2002), p. 2.

11 Johnson, *Modern World*, p. 436; H.S. Truman, *Memoirs* (2 vols, New York, 1965), Vol. 1, pp. 79–80; Anderson, *United States, Britain and the Cold War*, pp. 15–16; Harbutt, *Iron Curtain*, p. 105; D. McCullough, *Truman* (New York, 1992), p. 399; Wilson, *Churchill: Struggle for Survival*, pp. 273, 347; Gilbert, *Churchill*, p. 838.

12 Coker, 'Foreign and Defence Policy', p. 4; J. Hollowell, 'From Commonwealth to European Integration', in Hollowell, *Britain since 1945*, p. 60.

13 J.L. Gaddis, *The United States and the Origins of the Cold War, 1941–47* (New York, 1972), Ch. 6; Fraser and Murray, *America and the World*, pp. 10–11; Truman, *Memoirs*, Vol. 1, pp. 523–5; A.L. Hamby, *Man of the People: A Life of Harry S. Truman* (Oxford, 1995), p. 319.

14 T. Burridge, *British Labour and Hitler's War* (London, 1976), pp. 95–6; A. Sked and C. Cook, *Post-War Britain: A Political History* (London, 1993), pp. 49–51; C. Mayhew, *Time to Explain* (London, 1987), pp. 99, 114; Reynolds, *Britannia Overruled*, p. 148; A. Bullock, *Ernest Bevin: Foreign Secretary, 1945–51* (London, 1983), pp. 839–40.

15 I. Clark and N. Wheeler, *The British Origins of Nuclear Strategy, 1945–55* (Oxford, 1989), p. 120; Reynolds, *Britannia Overruled*, pp. 150–1, 154, 170; Fraser and Murray, *America and the World*, pp. 10–11, 34–5; Young, *Britain and the World*, p. 154; J. Darwin, *Britain and Decolonization: The Retreat from Empire in the Post-War World* (Basingstoke, 1988), p. 43; R. Ovendale, 'Britain and the Cold War in Asia', in *The Foreign Policy of the British Labour Governments, 1945–51*, R. Ovendale (ed.) (Leicester, 1984), pp. 122–3; D. Armstrong and E. Goldstein, 'Interaction with the Non-European World', in Fulbrook, *Europe since 1945*, p. 242.

16 Sked and Cook, *Post-War Britain*, pp. 51–2; Sassoon, 'Politics', p. 23–4; M. Hanagan, 'Changing Margins in Post-War European Politics', in Wakeman, *Modern European History*, p. 125.

17 Anderson, *United States, Britain and the Cold War*, pp. 4, 152; *Roosevelt Letters*, Vol. 3, p. 493; Johnson, *Modern World*, p. 433; Burk, *British Isles since 1945*, p. 2; Fraser and Murray, *America and the World*, p. 2; Sked and Cook, *Post-War Britain*, pp. 52–3.

18 Anderson, *United States, Britain and the Cold War*, pp. 46–7, 50, 80; A. Cairncross, *Years of Recovery: British Economic Policy, 1945–51* (London, 1985), Ch. 5; R. Gardner, *Sterling-Dollar Diplomacy in Current Perspective* (New York, 1980), Chs 9–12; E. Barker, *The British between the Superpowers, 1945–50* (London, 1983), pp. 25–7; A.P. Dobson, *US Wartime Aid to Britain, 1940–46* (London, 1986), p. 226; Fraser and Murray, *America and the World*, pp. 10–12; Reynolds, 'Britain and the World since 1945', p. 159, and idem, *Britannia Overruled*, pp. 144, 151; Young, *Britain and the World*, p. 155; Sked and Cook, *Post-War Britain*, pp. 53–5.

19 W.R. Louis, *The British Empire in the Middle East, 1945–51: Arab Nationalism, the United States and Post-War Imperialism* (Oxford, 1988), pp. 419, 459–60, 467. On British policy see also E. Monroe, *Britain's Moment in the Middle East, 1914–56* (London, 1984), Ch. 7, and R. Ovendale, *The Origins of the Arab-Israeli Wars* (Harlow, 1984), Chs 4–6.

20 Mayhew, *Time to Explain*, pp. 115–20; Young, *Britain and the World*, pp. 163, 230; Coker, 'Foreign and Defence Policy', p. 9; Sked and Cook, *Post-War Britain*, pp. 54–9; Fraser and Murray, *America and the World*, pp. 35–8; Reynolds, *Britannia Overruled*, pp. 156–7, 158–9, and idem, 'Britain and the World since 1945', p. 159; Kantowicz, *Coming Apart, Coming Together*, p. 182. British policy is explored alongside US and Soviet involvement and Zionist and Arab perspectives in *The End of the Palestine Mandate*, W.R. Louis and R.W. Stookey (eds) (London, 1986).

21 Jeffery, 'British Isles/British Empire', p. 40; Bullock, *Bevin*, Ch. 6; T. Kaplan, 'Britain's Asian Cold War: Malaya', in Deighton, *Britain and the First Cold War*, pp. 201–19; Barker, *British between the Superpowers*, pp. 48–52; Sked and Cook, *Post-War Britain*, p. 62; Reynolds, *Britannia Overruled*, pp. 149, 153–4, 157–8; Young, *Britain and the World*, p. 160; C.J. Bartlett, *The Long Retreat: A Short History of British Defence Policy, 1945–70* (London, 1972), pp. 13–21; M. Dockrill, *British Defence since 1945* (Oxford, 1988), pp. 28–32.

22 F.S. Northedge, 'Britain and the Middle East', in Ovendale, *Foreign Policy of the Labour Governments*, pp. 149–80; N. Owen, 'Britain and Decolonization: The Labour Governments and the Middle East, 1945–51', B. Maddy-Weitzman, 'A New Middle East? The Crystallization of the Arab State System after the Second World War', and A. Sela, 'Britain and the Palestine Question, 1945–48: The Dialectic of Regional and International Constraints', all in *Demise of the British Empire in the Middle East: Britain's Responses to Nationalist Movements, 1943–55*, M.J. Cohen and M. Kolinsky (eds) (London, 1998), pp. 3–22, 79–92, 220–46.

23   J. Kent, 'Britain and the Egyptian Problem, 1945–48', and M.J. Cohen, 'The Strategic Role of the Middle East after the War', both in Cohen and Kolinsky, *Demise of the British Empire*, pp. 23–37, 142–61.

24   J. Pickering, *Britain's Withdrawal from East of Suez: The Politics of Retrenchment* (Basingstoke, 1998), pp. 87, 178.

25   D.K. Fieldhouse, 'The Labour Governments and the Empire-Commonwealth', in Ovendale, *Foreign Policy of the Labour Governments*, pp. 83–120; Reynolds, 'Britain and the World since 1945', pp. 160, 168; Sked and Cook, *Post-War Britain*, pp. 59–63; Hollowell, 'Commonwealth to European Integration', pp. 61–2; J. Jordi, 'The Collapse of World Dominion: The Dismantling of the European Colonial Empires and its Impact on Europe', in Wakeman, *Modern European History*, pp. 41–2; Young, *Britain and the World*, pp. 142, 160–2; Kantowicz, *Coming Apart, Coming Together*, p. 104; Burk, *British Isles since 1945*, p. 5; Jeffery, 'British Isles/British Empire', pp. 36–7, 41; N. Owen, 'War and Britain's Political Crisis in India', in *What Difference Did the War Make?* B. Brivati and H. Jones (eds) (London, 1993), pp. 106–29; and idem, '"Responsibility without Power": The Attlee Governments and the End of British Rule in India', in *The Attlee Years*, N. Tiratsoo (ed.) (London, 1991), pp. 167–89; Ovendale, 'Britain and the Cold War in Asia', p. 121.

26   On these and related matters see F. Ansprenger, *The Dissolution of Colonial Empires* (London, 1989), and Darwin, *Britain and Decolonization*, especially Ch. 3.

27   D. Volkogonov, *Stalin: Triumph and Tragedy* (London, 1991), pp. 497–508; Fraser and Murray, *America and the World*, pp. 13–15; Reynolds, *Britannia Overruled*, pp. 146–8; Larres, 'International and Security Relations', pp. 199–200; V. Zubok and C. Pleshakov, *Inside the Kremlin's Cold War: From Stalin to Khrushchev* (Cambridge MA, 1996), p. 22; A.B. Ulam, *Expansion and Coexistence: Soviet Foreign Policy, 1917–73* (New York, 1974), Ch. 8, and idem, *Stalin*, pp. 623–6.

28   Larres, 'International and Security Relations', pp. 194–5, 199; Fraser and Murray, *America and the World*, pp. 10, 16–17; Reynolds, *Britannia Overruled*, pp. 148–9; Bullock, *Bevin*, pp. 19–30, 138, 268–9, 358; K.O. Morgan, *Labour in Power, 1945–51* (Oxford, 1985), p. 235.

29   N.M. Naimark, *The Russians in Germany: A History of the Soviet Zone of Occupation, 1945–49* (Cambridge MA, 1995), pp. 465–6.

30   A. Deighton, *The Impossible Peace: Britain, the Division of Germany and the Origins of the Cold War* (Oxford, 1993), pp. 23–40, 54–7, 88–125; Kantowicz, *Coming Together, Coming Apart*, pp. 13–14; J.H. Backer, *The Decision to Divide Germany: American Foreign Policy in Transition* (Durham NC, 1978), Chs 3–7; H.A. Turner, *Germany from Partition to Reunification* (New Haven CT, 1992), pp. 12–14, 68; Naimark, *Russians in Germany*, Ch. 3; A. Cairncross, *The Price of War: British Policy on German Reparations, 1941–49* (Oxford, 1986), Chs 4 and 5.

31   Cairncross, *Price of War*, p. 146; Reynolds, *Britannia Overruled*, p. 149; Larres,

'International and Security Relations', pp. 194, 199; Kantowicz, *Coming Apart, Coming Together*, pp. 14–15; Turner, *Germany from Partition to Reunification*, pp. 8–16, 55–6; A. Crawley, *The Rise of Western Germany, 1945–72* (London, 1973), Chs 2 and 3; Young, *Britain and the World*, p. 155.

32   Hollowell, 'Commonwealth to European Integration', p. 62; Sked and Cook, *Post-War Britain*, p. 64.

33   *Hansard*, 5th series, 433 (1947), col. 2303; Bullock, *Bevin*, pp. 528–9.

34   Sked and Cook, *Post-War Britain*, p. 65; Larres, 'International and Security Relations', p. 199; Young, *Britain and the World*, p. 155; L. Fawcett, 'Invitations to Cold War: British Policy in Iran, 1941–47', in Deighton, *Britain and the First Cold War*, pp. 184–200; Reynolds, *Britannia Overruled*, p. 148; Coker, 'Foreign and Defence Policy', p. 9.

35   Merrick, 'Russia Committee', pp. 453–68; Greenwood, *Britain and the Cold War*, p. 15; R. Smith, 'Ernest Bevin, British Officials and British Soviet Policy, 1945–47', in Deighton, *Britain and the First Cold War*, pp. 32–52; Lewis, *Changing Direction*, pp. 359–63.

36   *The Speeches of Winston Churchill*, D. Cannadine (ed.) (London, 1990), pp. 296–308; M. McCauley, *The Origins of the Cold War, 1941–49* (Harlow, 2003), pp. 69–82; Young, *Britain and the World*, p. 154; Sked and Cook, *Postwar Britain*, pp. 65–6; Reynolds, 'Britain and the World since 1945', p. 159; Fraser and Murray, *America and the World*, pp. 23–4; Harbutt, *Iron Curtain*, Ch. 7.

37   Kent, *British Imperial Strategy*, pp. 133, 148. On the sterling crisis, see Cairncross, *Years of Recovery*, Ch. 6.

38   R. Smith and J. Zametica, 'The Cold Warrior: Clement Attlee Reconsidered, 1945–47', *International Affairs*, 61 (1985), pp. 237–52; Bullock, *Bevin*, pp. 368–70.

39   Reynolds, *Britannia Overruled*, p. 159; G.M. Alexander, *The Prelude to the Truman Doctrine: British Policy in Greece, 1944–47* (Oxford, 1982), pp. 240–4; McCullough, *Truman*, pp. 539–41; Truman, *Memoirs*, Vol. 2, pp. 122–4.

40   Louis, *British Empire in the Middle East*, pp. 98–100, 102.

41   A. Gorst, 'Facing Facts? The Labour Government and Defence Policy, 1945–50', in Tiratsoo, *Attlee Years*, pp. 190–209; K. Harris, *Attlee* (London, 1982), pp. 303–4, 306–7; *The Times*, 1, 3 March 1947.

42   Young, *Britain and the World*, p. 154; Reynolds, *Britannia Overruled*, pp. 149, 164; Hollowell, 'Commonwealth to European Integration', p. 63; Sassoon, 'Politics', pp. 24–5; Hanagan, 'Changing Margins', p. 125; Johnson, *Modern World*, pp. 437–8; Fraser and Murray, *America and the World*, pp. 19–21; Larres, 'International and Security Relations', pp. 199–200, 203–4; Hamby, *Man of the People*, Chs 20, 22; G.F. Kennan, *Memoirs, 1925–50* (Boston MA, 1967), Ch. 11; Truman, *Memoirs*, Vol. 2, p. 117; Gaddis, *United States and Origins of the Cold War*, Ch. 9; W.D. Miscamble, *George F. Kennan and the Making of American Foreign Policy, 1947–50* (Princeton NJ, 1992), p. 27.

43 Johnson, *Modern World*, p. 438; Gaddis, *United States and Origins of the Cold War*, pp. 338–41; Reynolds, *Britannia Overruled*, pp. 149–50; Fraser and Murray, *America and the World*, pp. 22–3; Truman, *Memoirs*, Vol. 1., pp. 606, 609–16; *The Forrestal Diaries The Inner History of the Cold War*, W. Millis (ed.) (London, 1952), pp. 206–9; D. Acheson, *Present at the Creation: My Years in the State Department* (New York, 1969), pp. 190–2. R.J. Walton, *Henry Wallace, Harry Truman and the Cold War* (New York, 1976), pp. 98–117; A.L. Hamby, 'Henry A. Wallace, the Liberals and Soviet-American Relations', *Review of Politics, 30* (1968), pp. 153–69.

44 M.J. Hogan, *A Cross of Iron: Harry S. Truman and the Origins of the National Security State, 1945–55* (Cambridge, 1998).

45 Johnson, *Modern World*, p. 439; Sked and Cook, *Postwar Britain*, pp. 66–7; Acheson, *Present at the Creation*, Ch. 25; Fraser and Murray, *America and the World*, pp. 27–8; Larres, 'International and Security Relations', pp. 203–4.

46 See J.L. Gaddis, 'Was the Truman Doctrine a Real Turning Point?' *Foreign Affairs, 52* (1973–74), pp. 386–402, and idem, *United States and Origins of the Cold War*, pp. 351–2. In another of his books, *Strategies of Containment* (New York, 1982), Gaddis argues that US policy after 1947 cannot be reduced to a simple anti-Soviet formula.

47 McCullough, *Truman*, pp. 541–9; M.P. Leffler, *A Preponderance of Power: National Security, the Truman Administration and the Cold War* (Stanford CA, 1992), pp. 142–4.

48 *Hansard*, 5th series, 434 (1947), cols 454–6, 1491–95; 435 (1947), cols 15–20.

49 Bullock, *Bevin*, p. 371; R. Frazier, 'Did Britain Start the Cold War? Bevin and the Truman Doctrine', *Historical Journal, 27* (1984), pp. 715–27; Alexander, *Prelude to the Truman Doctrine*, pp. 245, 249–52; *The Times*, 13 March 1947; *Manchester Guardian*, 13 March 1947.

50 Anderson, *United States, Britain and the Cold War*, pp. 144, 171–7, 180–1, 184.

51 Bullock, *Bevin*, Ch. 10; Fraser and Murray, *America and the World*, pp. 22–31; Johnson, *Modern World*, pp. 439–40; Sked and Cook, *Post-War Britain*, p. 67; Hollowell, 'Commonwealth to European Integration', p. 63; Acheson, *Present at the Creation*, Ch. 26; Truman, *Memoirs*, Vol. 2, pp. 136–41; Hamby, *Man of the People*, Ch. 22.

52 Acheson, *Present at the Creation*, pp. 227–30; Kennan, *Memoirs*, p. 325; Mayhew, *Time to Explain*, pp. 100–2.

53 Sked and Cook, *Post-War Britain*, pp. 67–8; Fraser and Murray, *America and the World*, p. 26; Gaddis, *We Now Know*, pp. 41–3; Acheson, *Present at the Creation*, Ch. 26; Zubok and Pleshakov, *Inside the Kremlin's Cold War*, pp. 29–30, 50; Ulam, *Stalin*, pp. 657–1; Volkogonov, *Stalin: Triumph and Tragedy*, pp. 531, 534.

54 Ulam, *Stalin*, pp. 660–1; Volkogonov, *Stalin: Triumph and Tragedy*, pp. 533–4; Zubok and Pleshakov, *Inside the Kremlin's Cold War*, Ch. 4; Gaddis, *We Now*

Know, pp. 41–3, 46–7; Hamby, *Man of the People*, pp. 395–6; Fraser and Murray, *America and the World*, pp. 26, 29; Kantowicz, *Coming Apart, Coming Together*, p. 18; Johnson, *Modern World*, p. 440; Sassoon, 'Politics', pp. 26–7; Morewood, 'Divided Europe', pp. 17–18; Hanagan, 'Changing Margins', pp. 125, 128.

55 D. Reynolds, 'The "Big Three" and the Division of Europe, 1945–48: An Overview', *Diplomacy and Statecraft*, 1 (1990), pp. 111–36; Morewood, 'Divided Europe', p. 18; B. Eichengreen, 'Economy', in Fulbrook, *Europe since 1945*, pp. 105, 117; Larres, 'International and Security Relations', pp. 197–8; Fraser and Murray, *America and the World*, pp. 26–7; Gaddis, *We Now Know*, pp. 48–9; Volkogonov, *Stalin: Triumph and Tragedy*, pp. 535–6; Ulam, *Stalin*, pp. 663–8.

56 Fraser and Murray, *America and the World*, pp. 27, 39; Larres, 'International and Security Relations', pp. 198–200; Morewood, 'Divided Europe', pp. 18–19; Young, *Britain and the World*, p. 155; Reynolds, *Britannia Overruled*, p. 165.

57 Naimark, *Russians in Germany*, pp. 328–9; Fraser and Murray, *America and the World*, pp. 28–9; Hanagan, 'Changing Margins', p. 125.

58 Reynolds, *Britannia Overruled*, pp. 151, 154, and idem, 'Britain and the World since 1945', p. 159; Young, *Britain and the World*, p. 155; Turner, *Germany from Partition to Reunification*, Ch. 1; Fraser and Murray, *America and the World*, pp. 11–12; Deighton, *Impossible Peace*, Ch. 5; Harris, *Attlee*, pp. 270–6; D.C. Watt, 'Britain, the United States and the Opening of the Cold War', in Ovendale, *Foreign Policy of the Labour Governments*, pp. 43–60; Crawley, *Western Germany*, Chs 3 and 4.

59 Larres, 'International and Security Relations', pp. 187, 194–5; Reynolds, *Britannia Overruled*, p. 148.

60 Reynolds, 'The "Big Three" and the Division of Europe', pp. 124–8, and idem, *Britannia Overruled*, pp. 164–5; Fraser and Murray, *America and the World*, p. 26; Sked and Cook, *Postwar Britain*, pp. 67–9; Larres, 'International and Security Relations', p. 195; Morewood, 'Divided Europe', p. 18; Eichengreen, 'Economy', pp. 103–7; Burk, *British Isles since 1945*, p. 9.

61 A.S. Milward, *The Reconstruction of Western Europe, 1945–51* (Berkeley CA, 1984), Chs 2 and 3, and idem, 'Was the Marshall Plan Necessary?' *Diplomatic History*, 13 (1989), pp. 231–53.

62 L. Reichlin, 'The Marshall Plan Reconsidered', and H. Berger and A. Ritschl, 'Germany and the Political Economy of the Marshall Plan, 1947–52: A Re-Revisionist View', both in *Europe's Post-War Recovery*, B. Eichengreen (ed.) (Cambridge, 1995), pp. 39–67, 199–245.

63 M.J. Hogan, *The Marshall Plan: America, Britain and the Reconstruction of Western Europe, 1947–52* (Cambridge, 1987), Chs 4–6.

64 C. Newton, 'The Sterling Crisis of 1947 and the British Response to the Marshall Plan', *Economic History Review*, 37 (1984), pp. 391–408.

65 Milward, 'Was the Marshall Plan Necessary?', pp. 242–3, 250.

66 Leffler, *Preponderance of Power*, pp. 3, 15–16, 19, 135, 364, 443, 446, 498, 500–1, 511, 513, 515–16, 518.

67 Bullock, *Bevin*, pp. 125, 403, 405; D. Healey, *The Time of My Life* (London, 1989), p. 114; Acheson, *Present at the Creation*, p. 234.

68 Mayhew, *Time to Explain*, pp. 106–12.

69 Larres, 'International and Security Relations', p. 203; Reynolds, *Britannia Overruled*, p. 181.

70 M. Charlton, *The Price of Victory* (London, 1983), p. 162; J.W. Young, *Britain, France and the Unity of Europe, 1945–51* (Leicester, 1984), pp. 126–7.

71 Baylis, *Diplomacy of Pragmatism*, Chs 4 and 5, Appendices 1 and 3, and idem, 'Britain, the Brussels Pact and the Continental Commitment', *International Affairs*, 60 (1984), pp. 615–29; G. Warner, 'The Labour Governments and the Unity of Western Europe, 1945–51', in Ovendale, *Foreign Policy of the Labour Governments*, pp. 61–82; Barker, *British between the Superpowers*, pp. 112–27; Young, *Britain, France and the Unity of Europe*, Chs 5–9, and idem, *Britain and the World*, p. 155; Reynolds, 'Britain and the World since 1945', p. 163, and idem, *Britannia Overruled*, pp. 165, 182, 184; Sked and Cook, *Post-War Britain*, pp. 71–2; Hollowell, 'Commonwealth to European Integration', pp. 62–3; Larres, 'International and Security Relations', p. 202; Dockrill, *British Defence*, pp. 32–4; Bartlett, *Long Retreat*, pp. 45–8; Bullock, *Bevin*, pp. 357–9, Ch. 13.

72 *The Times*, 1 March 1947, 30 April 1948; G. Warner, 'The Reconstruction and Defence of Western Europe after 1945', in *Troubled Neighbours: Franco-British Relations in the Twentieth Century*, N. Waites (ed.) (London, 1971), pp. 261–2.

73 Mayhew, *Time to Explain*, pp. 112–13.

74 *Hansard*, 5th series, 450 (1948), cols 1107–12.

75 Sked and Cook, *Post-War Britain*, pp. 73–4; Young, *Britain and the World*, pp. 155–6; Reynolds, *Britannia Overruled*, p. 166; Larres, 'International and Security Relations', p. 202; Kantowicz, *Coming Apart, Coming Together*, p. 19; Turner, *Germany from Partition to Reunification*, pp. 22–4.

76 Bullock, *Bevin*, pp. 571–80, 588–94, 692–8; Kantowicz, *Coming Apart, Coming Together*, pp. 19–20; Sked and Cook, *Postwar Britain*, p. 74; Fraser and Murray, *America and the World*, pp. 39–40; Reynolds, *Britannia Overruled*, p. 166; Larres, 'International and Security Relations', p. 202; Hamby, *Man of the People*, pp. 402, 444–5, 460; Millis, *Forrestal Diaries*, Ch. 12; Zubok and Pleshakov, *Inside the Kremlin's Cold War*, pp. 51–3.

77 *Hansard*, 5th series, 452 (1948), cols 2221–34; Harris, *Attlee*, p. 312; *The Times*, 26 June 1948, 12 May 1949; *Observer*, 15 May 1949.

78 *Hansard*, 5th series, 467 (1949), cols 1571–72, 1595.

79 C.J. Bartlett, *'The Special Relationship': A Political History of Anglo-American Relations since 1945* (London, 1992), p. 36; J. Baylis, *Anglo-American Defence*

Relations, 1939–84 (London, 1984), p. 40; Reynolds, *Britannia Overruled*, pp. 166, 170; Fraser and Murray, *America and the World*, p. 40.

80 Kantowicz, *Coming Apart, Coming Together*, p. 20; Sked and Cook, *Post-War Britain*, p. 74; T. Prittie, *Konrad Adenauer, 1876–1967* (London, 1972), Ch. 7; R.H. Lieshout, 'The Politics of European Unification', in Wakeman, *Modern European History*, p. 214; Turner, *Germany from Partition to Reunification*, pp. 33–46, 104–37; K. Adenauer, *Memoirs, 1945–53* (London, 1966), Chs 11 and 12.

81 Morewood, 'Divided Europe', pp. 16–17; M. McCauley, *The German Democratic Republic since 1945* (London, 1983), Chs 1 and 2; Turner, *Germany from Partition to Reunification*, Chs 2 and 3.

82 W. Loth, *Stalin's Unwanted Child: The Soviet Union, the German Question and the Founding of the GDR* (Basingstoke, 1998); W.R. Smyzer, *From Yalta to Berlin: The Cold War Struggle over Germany* (Basingstoke, 1999).

83 Backer, *Decision to Divide Germany*, pp. 172–3, 176–8; C.W. Eisenberg, *Drawing the Line: The American Decision to Divide Germany, 1944–49* (Cambridge, 1996), Chs 9–11.

84 Deighton, *Impossible Peace*, pp. 6–7, 124, 234–5.

85 Turner, *Germany from Partition to Reunification*, Ch. 4; Sassoon, 'Politics', pp. 28, 31–2, 35; M. Donhoff, *Foe into Friend: The Makers of the New Germany from Konrad Adenauer to Helmut Schmidt* (London, 1982), pp. 26–86; Prittie, *Konrad Adenauer*, Chs 8–10; R. Irving, *Adenauer* (Harlow, 2002), Chs 3 and 4; R.J. Granieri, *The Ambivalent Alliance: Konrad Adenauer, the CDU/CSU and the West, 1949–66* (New York, 2003), Ch. 1; Johnson, *Modern World*, pp. 581–5; Crawley, *Western Germany*, Chs 5–7, 10–12; H.P. Schwarz, *Konrad Adenauer: From the German Empire to the Federal Republic, 1876–1952* (Providence, Rhode Island, 1986), Ch. 5; Adenauer, *Memoirs*, p. 200; R. Wakeman, 'The Golden Age of Prosperity, 1953–73', in Wakeman, *Modern European History*, pp. 67–8; Eichengreen, 'Economy', p. 111.

86 Bullock, *Bevin*, Chs 16–17.

87 L.S. Kaplan, *The United States and NATO: The Formative Years* (Lexington, Kentucky, 1984), Appendix B.

88 Fraser and Murray, *America and the World*, pp. 41–2; Sked and Cook, *Post-War Britain*, pp. 75–6; Bartlett, *Long Retreat*, Ch. 2; Dockrill, *British Defence*, Ch. 3; Kaplan, *United States and NATO*, Chs 4–6 (and Appendices A and C for the texts of the Brussels Pact and the North Atlantic Treaty); T.P. Ireland, *Creating the Entangling Alliance: The Origins of the North Atlantic Treaty Organization* (Westport CY, 1981), Chs 2 and 3; Baylis, *Diplomacy of Pragmatism*, Chs 6–9, Appendix 5. On the perspectives of the North American and European participants in these developments, as well as those of the British, see *The Western Security Community, 1948–50: Common Problems and Conflicting National Interests*

during the Foundation Phase of the North Atlantic Alliance, N. Wiggershaus and R.G. Foerster (eds) (Oxford, 1993).

89   N. Henderson, *The Birth of NATO* (London, 1982), pp. 113–14; Baylis, 'Britain, the Brussels Pact and the Continental Commitment', pp. 627–9.

90   L.S. Kaplan, *The Long Entanglement: NATO's First Fifty Years* (Westport CT, 1999), pp. 1–2; Miscamble, *Kennan and the Making of American Foreign Policy*, p. 134.

91   P. Boyle, 'Britain, America and the Transition from Economic to Military Assistance, 1948–51', *Journal of Contemporary History*, 22 (1987), pp. 521–38.

92   *The Times*, 5 April 1949.

93   Reynolds, *Britannia Overruled*, p. 166; Sked and Cook, *Post-War Britain*, p. 76; Burk, *British Isles since 1945*, p. 2; Larres, 'International and Security Relations', pp. 202–3.

94   Warner, 'Labour Governments and the Unity of Western Europe', pp. 66–7; Baylis, *Diplomacy of Pragmatism*, p. 50.

95   Kennan, *Memoirs*, pp. 456–7.

96   Kaplan, *United States and NATO*, pp. 114–15; Henderson, *Birth of NATO*, pp. 39, 51; Ireland, *Creating the Entangling Alliance*, p. 88; Barker, *British between the Superpowers*, p. 130.

97   Baylis, *Diplomacy of Pragmatism*, pp. 124–6.

98   Burk, *British Isles since 1945*, p. 2. On Ismay's involvement with NATO see R. Wingate, *Lord Ismay: A Biography* (London, 1970), Ch. 9.

99   Morewood, 'Divided Europe', p. 16; Bartlett, *Special Relationship*, pp. 34–6; Leffler, *Preponderance of Power*, pp. 198–218; McCauley, *Origins of the Cold War*, pp. 92–4, 105–6.

100 Baylis, *Anglo-American Defence Relations*, pp. 30–4; Dockrill, *British Defence*, pp. 23–6; Bartlett, *Long Retreat*, pp. 29–32; N. Wheeler, 'The Attlee Government's Nuclear Strategy, 1945–51', in Deighton, *Britain and the First Cold War*, pp. 130–45; Young, *Britain and the World*, pp. 149, 156–7; Burk, *British Isles since 1945*, pp. 2–3; Reynolds, *Britannia Overruled*, pp. 152–3; Coker, 'Foreign and Defence Policy', p. 11.

101 The discordance between personal and formal modes of atomic weapons development is explored in S.H. Paul, *Nuclear Rivals: Anglo-American Atomic Relations, 1941–52* (Columbus, Ohio, 2000).

102 L. Freedman, *Britain and Nuclear Weapons* (London, 1980), p. 1; Bullock, *Bevin*, pp. 188–9, 245–6.

103 J.L. Gormley, 'The Washington Declaration and the "Poor Relation": Anglo-American Atomic Diplomacy, 1945–46', *Diplomatic History*, 8 (1984), pp. 125–43.

104 Lewis, *Changing Direction*, pp. 220–41; Bullock, *Bevin*, p. 352; Harris, *Attlee*, pp. 286–91. The most detailed account of Britain's atomic weapons programme is M. Gowing and L. Arnold, *Independence and Deterrence: Britain and Atomic Energy, 1945–52* (2 vols, London, 1974), but see also Clark and Wheeler, *British Origins of Nuclear Strategy*, Chs 3–5, and A.J.R. Groom, 'The British Deterrent',

in *British Defence Policy in a Changing World*, J. Baylis (ed.) (London, 1977), pp. 120–55.

105 Kennedy, *Realities behind Diplomacy*, p. 334; Clark and Wheeler, *British Origins of Nuclear Strategy*, pp. 39–40, 120–1.

106 See Lewis, *Changing Direction*, especially Ch. 4.

Notes to Chapter 3: Asia, the Middle East, Europe: No Respite (I)

1 Sked and Cook, *Post-War Britain*, p. 88; Young, *Britain and the World*, p. 148; Reynolds, *Britannia Overruled*, p. 167; Jeffery, 'British Isles/British Empire', p. 40; Hamby, *Man of the People*, pp. 534–9.

2 B. Donoughue and G.W. Jones, *Herbert Morrison: Portrait of a Politician* (London, 1973), pp. 478, 496, 514; Morgan, *Labour in Power*, pp. 464–5; Sked and Cook, *Post-War Britain*, pp. 61, 89; Young, *Britain and the World*, p. 142; Bartlett, *Long Retreat*, p. 87; D. Sanders, *Losing an Empire, Finding a Role: British Foreign Policy since 1945* (Basingstoke, 1990), p. 169; J. Frankel, *British Foreign Policy, 1945–73* (London, 1975), p. 128; R. Ovendale, *British Defence Policy since 1945* (Manchester, 1994), pp. 90–4.

3 Morgan, *Labour in Power*, pp. 465–71; Donoughue and Jones, *Herbert Morrison*, pp. 491–2; T. Burridge, *Clement Attlee: A Political Biography* (London, 1985), pp. 301–2; P. Darby, *British Defence Policy East of Suez, 1947–68* (London, 1973), p. 26; Monroe, *Britain's Moment*, p. 172; Ovendale, *British Defence Policy*, p. 13; Louis, *British Empire in the Middle East*, pp. 632–89.

4 M. Curtis, *The Ambiguities of Power: British Foreign Policy since 1945* (London, 1995), pp. 87–91.

5 Sanders, *Losing an Empire*, pp. 89–90; Ovendale, *British Defence Policy*, pp. 83–4, 86–7, 94–6; Frankel, *British Foreign Policy*, pp. 122, 128–9; Bullock, *Bevin*, pp. 831–2; Morgan, *Labour in Power*, pp. 471–4; Louis, *British Empire in the Middle East*, pp. 691–735.

6 See R. Wilson, 'Economic Aspects of Arab Nationalism', and M. Thornhill, 'Britain and the Politics of the Arab League, 1943–50', both in Cohen and Kolinsky, *Demise of the British Empire*, pp. 41, 43, 60, 76; Owen, 'Britain and Decolonization', pp. 3–5, 18–19; Maddy-Weitzman, 'A New Middle East?', pp. 79–92.

7 Ovendale, *British Defence Policy*, pp. 94–6; D.R. Devereaux, 'Britain and the Failure of Collective Defence in the Middle East, 1948–53', in Deighton, *Britain and the First Cold War*, pp. 237–52.

8 Wilson, 'Economic Aspects of Arab Nationalism', pp. 67–8, 76–7; Kent, 'Britain and the Egyptian Problem', pp. 32–5; Cohen, 'Strategic Role of the Middle East', pp. 142, 154; C. Tripp, 'Egypt, 1945–52: The Uses of Disorder', in Cohen and Kolinsky, *Demise of the British Empire*, pp. 112–41.

9   Ovendale, *British Defence Policy*, pp. 98–102.

10 M. de Leonardis, 'Defence or Liberation of Europe: The Strategies of the West against a Soviet Attack, 1947–50', in *The Atlantic Pact Forty Years Later: A Historical Reappraisal*, E. Di Nolfo (ed.) (Berlin, 1991), pp. 176–206; W.F. Hanrieder and G.P. Auton, *The Foreign Policies of West Germany, France and Great Britain* (Eaglewood Cliffs NJ, 1980), pp. 4–5, 97–102, 189–91; Kaplan, *Long Entanglement*, pp. 59–62, and idem, *United States and NATO*, Ch. 8; E. Fursdon, *The European Defence Community: A History* (London, 1980), Ch. 3; Sked and Cook, *Post-War Britain*, pp. 88, 90–1; Reynolds, *Britannia Overruled*, p. 167; Bartlett, *Special Relationship*, pp. 40, 42–3, and idem, *Long Retreat*, pp. 51–2, 59, 92; Young, *Britain and the World*, p. 158; Baylis, *Anglo-American Defence Relations*, pp. 57–60, 63; Ovendale, *British Defence Policy*, pp. 83–4; Truman, *Memoirs*, Vol. 2, pp. 290–8; S.E. Ambrose, *Eisenhower: Soldier and President* (New York, 1990), pp. 249–58; R.H. Ferrell, *Harry S. Truman: A Life* (Columbia MO, 1994), pp. 355–7; Bullock, *Bevin*, pp. 810–12; Barker, *British between the Superpowers*, pp. 225–9, 238.

11 Bullock, *Bevin*, pp. 796–801, 804–11.

12 Larres, *Churchill's Cold War*, pp. 146–9; H. Pelling, *Winston Churchill* (London, 1974), pp. 569–70, 586–7.

13 W. van Eekelen, *Debating European Security, 1948–98* (The Hague, Netherlands, 1998), pp. 5–6; Irving, *Adenauer*, pp. 92–8; Granieri, *Ambivalent Alliance*, pp. 38–42; Prittie, *Konrad Adenauer*, pp. 158–63; Adenauer, *Memoirs, 1945–53*, Chs 15 and 16.

14 M. Peter, 'Britain, the Cold War and the Economics of German Rearmament, 1949–51', in Deighton, *Britain and the First Cold War*, pp. 273–90.

15 J.R. Gillingham, 'Introduction', I.M. Wall, 'France and the North Atlantic Alliance', D. Brinkley, 'Dean Acheson and European Unity', and T.A. Schwartz, 'Dual Containment: John J. McCloy, the American High Commission and the European Integration, 1949–52', all in *NATO: The Founding of the Atlantic Alliance and the Integration of Europe*, F.H. Heller and J.R. Gillingham (eds) (Basingstoke, 1992), pp. 1, 45–56, 129–60, 193–212; A.K. Henriksen, 'The Creation of the North Atlantic Alliance, 1948–52', *US Naval War College Review*, 32 (1980), pp. 27–30.

16 Gillingham, 'Introduction', in Heller and Gillingham, *NATO*, pp. 1, 12–13; K. Schwabe, 'The Origins of the US Engagement in Europe, 1946–52', in Heller and Gillingham, *NATO*, pp. 161–92.

17 Fraser and Murray, *America and the World*, pp. 32–4; Kantowicz, *Coming Apart, Coming Together*, pp. 69, 71; Armstrong and Goldstein, 'Interaction with the Non-European World', pp. 244–5; R. Terrill, *Mao: A Biography* (New York, 1980), Chs 10 and 11; J.K. Fairbank and M. Goldman, *China: A New History* (Cambridge MA, 1998), Chs 16 and 17; O.E. Clubb, *Twentieth Century China* (New York, 1978), pp. 316–25; N. Jun, 'The Origins of the Sino-Soviet Alliance', in *Brothers in Arms: The Rise and Fall of the Sino-Soviet Alliance, 1945–63*, O.A. Westad (ed.)

(Washington DC, 1998), pp. 47–89, and see also Westad's 'Introduction' in the same volume, especially pp. 7–25.

18 Sked and Cook, *Post-War Britain*, pp. 93–4; Reynolds, *Britannia Overruled*, p. 172; Armstrong and Goldstein, 'Interaction with the Non-European World', p. 242; R. Dingman, 'Truman, Attlee and the Korean War Crisis', in *The East Asian Crisis, 1945–51: The Problem of China, Korea and Japan*, I. Nish (ed.) (London, 1982), pp. 5–6; P. Lowe, *The Origins of the Korean War* (London, 1997), pp. 119–30.

19 *Hansard*, 5th series, 469 (1949), cols 2012–14; 470 (1949), cols 1527–28; 476 (1950), col. 1266; *The Times*, 2 January 1950.

20 Ovendale, *British Defence Policy*, pp. 62–3, 65–71; Z.P. Feng, *The British Government's China Policy, 1945–50* (Keele, 1994).

21 R. Ovendale, *The English-Speaking Alliance: Britain, the United States, the Dominions and the Cold War, 1945–51* (London, 1985), Ch. 7; Barker, *British between the Superpowers*, pp. 169–73; Bullock, *Bevin*, pp. 743–4; R. Edmonds, *Setting the Mould: The United States and Britain, 1945–50* (Oxford, 1986), Ch. 11; Gaddis, *We Now Know*, pp. 62–5; Acheson, *Present at the Creation*, pp. 355–8.

22 Barker, *British between the Superpowers*, pp. 198–9.

23 Truman, *Memoirs*, Vol. 2, pp. 457–66; Bartlett, *Special Relationship*, pp. 41, 50; Baylis, *Anglo-American Defence Relations*, p. 61.

24 Reynolds, *Britannia Overruled*, pp. 172–3; Dingman, 'Truman, Attlee and the Korean War Crisis', pp. 6–30; Sked and Cook, *Post-War Britain*, pp. 92–3; Kaplan, 'Britain's Asian Cold War', pp. 201–19.

25 M. Gowing, 'Britain, America and the Bomb', in Dilks, *Retreat from Power*, Vol. 2, pp. 121–37; Bartlett, *Long Retreat*, pp. 29–32, 47, 53, 58–9, and idem, *Special Relationship*, pp. 48, 52–3; Sked and Cook, *Post-War Britain*, pp. 94–5; Reynolds, *Britannia Overruled*, pp. 152–3; Coker, 'Foreign and Defence Policy', p. 11; Baylis, *Anglo-American Defence Relations*, pp. 66–70; M. Gowing, 'Nuclear Weapons and the Special Relationship' and J. Eberle, 'The Military Relationship', both in Louis and Bull, *The 'Special Relationship'*, pp. 122–4, 153–4; Bullock, *Bevin*, pp. 351–3.

26 Lewis, *Changing Direction*, p. 339; R. Aldrich and M. Coleman, 'The Cold War, the Joint Intelligence Committee and British Signals Intelligence', *Intelligence and National Security*, 4 (1989), pp. 540–1; Clark and Wheeler, *British Origins of Nuclear Strategy*, pp. 130–5, 182.

27 Young, *Britain and the World*, pp. 156–7; Reynolds, *Britannia Overruled*, pp. 163, 170; Sked and Cook, *Post-War Britain*, pp. 95–6; Bartlett, *Long Retreat*, pp. 64–5; Baylis, *Anglo-American Defence Relations*, p. 60; P. Boyle, 'The "Special Relationship" with Washington', in *The Foreign Policy of Churchill's Peacetime Administration, 1951–55*, J.W. Young (ed.) (Leicester, 1988), pp. 29–54.

28 *Hansard*, 5th series, 468 (1949), cols 1326–28; *The Times*, 9 February 1950; *Manchester Guardian*, 13 September 1950.

29 E.R. May and G.F. Treverton, 'Defence Relationships: American Perspectives', in

Louis and Bull, *The 'Special Relationship'*, p. 172; Fraser and Murray, *America and the World*, pp. 43–5; Larres, 'International and Security Relations', p. 204; P.H. Nitze, *From Hiroshima to Glasnost: At the Centre of Decision* (New York, 1989), pp. 87, 91–2, 94–8; Acheson, *Present at the Creation*, pp. 344–9, 373–80.

30 See the comments of policy makers and historians in *American Cold War Strategy: Interpreting NSC-68*, E.R. May (ed.) (Boston MA, 1993), pp. 94–6, 99–107, 109–16, 140–6, 156–9, 160–4. See also Gaddis, *Strategies of Containment*, pp. 106, 359; B. Heuser, 'NSC-68 and the Soviet Threat: A New Perspective on Western Threat Perception and Policy Making', *Review of International Studies*, 17 (1991), pp. 17–40; M. Cox, 'Western Intelligence, the Soviet Threat and NSC-68: A Reply to Beatrice Heuser', *Review of International Studies*, 18 (1992), pp. 75–83, and Heuser's response on pp. 85–6.

31 G.D. Kim, *Foreign Intervention in Korea* (Aldershot, 1993), Chs 1–3; Kantowicz, *Coming Apart, Coming Together*, pp. 128–9; W. Stueck, *The Korean War: An International History* (Princeton NJ, 1995), Ch. 1; Lowe, *Origins of the Korean War*, Chs 1 and 2.

32 Stueck, *Korean War: An International History*, pp. 17, 22; Lowe, *Origins of the Korean War*, Ch. 3; Kantowicz, *Coming Apart, Coming Together*, pp. 130–1; Truman, *Memoirs*, Vol. 2, pp. 360–76; Gaddis, *We Now Know*, p. 71; J. Merrill, *Korea: The Peninsular Origins of the War* (Newark NJ, 1989).

33 Zubok and Pleshakov, *Inside the Kremlin's Cold War*, pp. 54–64; Kantowicz, *Coming Apart, Coming Together*, pp. 131–2; Gaddis, *We Now Know*, pp. 70–5; S.N. Goncharov, J.W. Lewis and X. Litai, *Uncertain Partners: Stalin, Mao and the Korean War* (Stanford CA, 1993), Chs 5–7; H.J. Kim, 'China's Non-involvement in the Origins of the Korean War: A Critical Reassessment of the Traditionalist and Revisionist Literature', in *The Korean War in History*, J. Cotton and I. Neary (eds) (Atlantic Highlands NJ, 1989), pp. 11–32; Lowe, *Origins of the Korean War*, p. 182. See also J.L. Gaddis, 'Who Really Started the Korean War?' *Atlantic Monthly*, 8 May 1994, pp. 2–3.

34 Johnson, *Modern World*, pp. 448–50; B. Heuser, *Western 'Containment' Policies in the Cold War: The Yugoslav Case, 1948–53* (New York, 1989), Ch. 1; D. Wilson, *Tito's Yugoslavia* (Cambridge, 1979), Chs 5 and 6; I.T. Berend, 'The Central and Eastern European Revolution', in Wakeman, *Themes in Modern European History*, p. 190; Stueck, *Korean War: An International History*, Chs 2 and 3; Fraser and Murray, *America and the World*, p. 41; Bartlett, *Long Retreat*, p. 52.

35 G.D. Kim, 'Who Initiated the Korean War?' in Cotton and Neary, *Korean War in History*, pp. 33–50; Gaddis, 'Who Really Started the Korean War?', p. 3.

36 M. Schaller, *The American Occupation of Japan: The Origins of the Cold War in Asia* (New York, 1985), pp. 278–80; Truman, *Memoirs*, Vol. 2, p. 381; D. Acheson, *The Korean War* (New York, 1971), p. 3; Johnson, *Modern World*, pp. 450–1; Kennan, *Memoirs*, p. 490.

37   A. Parsons, 'Britain and the Security Council', and C. Tickell, 'Present and Future: A British Perspective', both in *The United Kingdom – The United Nations*, E. Jensen and T. Fisher (eds) (Basingstoke, 1990), pp. 52–3, 277; M.V. Naidu, *Collective Security and the United Nations* (London, 1975), pp. 45, 58–9, 98, 100.

38   Naidu, *Collective Security and the United Nations*, pp. 133–5; Kantowicz, *Coming Apart, Coming Together*, p. 133; Kim, *Foreign Intervention in Korea*, Chs 4 and 5; Stueck, *Korean War: An International History*, pp. 12, 41–4, 54–61; Lowe, *Origins of the Korean War*, Ch. 7; Ferrell, *Harry S. Truman*, pp. 322–5; *The Truman Administration: A Documentary History*, B. Bernstein and A. Matusow (eds) (New York, 1968), pp. 437–9; Hamby, *Man of the People*, pp. 537–9.

39   P.G. Pierpaoli, *Truman and Korea: The Political Culture of the Early Cold War* (Columbia MO, 1999), Ch. 1; Johnson, *Modern World*, p. 451; Fraser and Murray, *America and the World*, pp. 45–9; Kantowicz, *Coming Apart, Coming Together*, pp. 136–7; Young, *Britain and the World*, pp. 147, 158; Reynolds, *Britannia Overruled*, p. 172; Sked and Cook, *Post-War Britain*, p. 93; Bernstein and Matusow, *Truman Administration*, pp. 442–83; Truman, *Memoirs*, Vol. 2, pp. 490–510; Ferrell, *Harry S. Truman*, pp. 328–6; Kim, *Foreign Intervention in Korea*, Chs 7, 9; Gaddis, 'Who Really Started the Korean War?', p. 4, and idem, *We Now Know*, pp. 79–80; Bullock, *Bevin*, pp. 820–4; Burridge, *Attlee*, pp. 244–7; M. Dockrill, 'The Foreign Office, Anglo-American Relations and the Korean War, June 1950 – June 1951', *International Affairs*, 62 (1985–86), pp. 462–6; Lowe, *Origins of the Korean War*, pp. 229–40; Ovendale, 'Britain and the Cold War in Asia', pp. 135–9, and idem, *British Defence Policy*, pp. 84–5; Goncharov, Lewis and Litai, *Uncertain Partners*, pp. 281–2.

40   Hamby, *Man of the People*, pp. 542–6.

41   Ovendale, *British Defence Policy*, pp. 84–6; Bartlett, *Special Relationship*, pp. 48–9; Barker, *British between the Superpowers*, pp. 222–4; Gowing, 'Nuclear Weapons and the Special Relationship', p. 122; Truman, *Memoirs*, Vol. 2, pp. 466–7; C. MacDonald, *Britain and the Korean War* (Oxford, 1990), pp. 43–4; Dockrill, 'The Foreign Office, Anglo-American Relations and the Korean War', p. 465; Kim, *Foreign Intervention in Korea*, Ch. 8; Acheson, *Present at the Creation*, pp. 478–85; Dingman, 'Truman, Attlee and the Korean War Crisis', pp. 19–30, 33–4.

42   Stueck, *Korean War: An International History*, pp. 73–4; S. Greenwood, '"A War We Don't Want": Another Look at the British Labour Government's Commitment in Korea, 1950–51', *Contemporary British History*, 17 (2003), pp. 1–24.

43   Bullock, *Bevin*, p. 791; MacDonald, *Britain and the Korean War*, pp. 13–14, 19–20; Ovendale, 'Britain and the Cold War in Asia', pp. 131–2.

44   Ovendale, *British Defence Policy*, pp. 12, 73–80.

45   *Hansard*, 5th series, 476 (1950), cols 1904–5, 2159–61; MacDonald, *Britain and the Korean War*, p. 20.

46 Bullock, *Bevin*, pp. 793, 795; Stueck, *Korean War: An International History*, pp. 51, 140; Kim, *Foreign Intervention in Korea*, Chs 7 and 8.

47 *Economist*, 8 July 1950; *The Times*, 3, 5 July 1950.

48 Dockrill, 'The Foreign Office, Anglo-American Relations and the Korean War', pp. 459–62; Bullock, *Bevin*, pp. 792–3, 795; MacDonald, *Britain and the Korean War*, pp. 20–1.

49 Stueck, *Korean War: An International History*, pp. 76–8.

50 Bartlett, *Long Retreat*, pp. 55–7.

51 Ovendale, *British Defence Policy*, pp. 82–3; R. Jong-yil, 'Political Settlement in Korea: British Views and Policies, Autumn 1950', and P.N. Farrar, 'A Pause for Peace Negotiations: The British Buffer Zone Plan of November 1950', both in Cotton and Neary, *Korean War in History*, pp. 51–65, 66–79.

52 Baylis, *Anglo-American Defence Relations*, pp. 58–63; B. Perkins, 'Unequal Partners: The Truman Administration and Britain', in Louis and Bull, *The 'Special Relationship'*, pp. 61–3; Bartlett, *Special Relationship*, pp. 43, 48–51; P. Lowe, 'The Frustrations of Alliance: Britain, the United States and the Korean War, 1950–51', in Cotton and Neary, *Korean War in History*, pp. 80–99; *Hansard*, 5th series, 481 (1950), cols 1161–66, 1256, 1258–59.

53 Bartlett, *Special Relationship*, pp. 40–1.

54 Dockrill, 'The Foreign Office, Anglo-American Relations and the Korean War', pp. 464–5; MacDonald, *Britain and the Korean War*, pp. 40–2.

55 Stueck, *Korean War: An International History*, pp. 181–2, 184; Acheson, *Present at the Creation*, pp. 521–8.

56 Dockrill, 'The Foreign Office, Anglo-American Relations and the Korean War', pp. 466–76; MacDonald, *Britain and the Korean War*, pp. 44–8.

57 MacDonald, *Britain and the Korean War*, pp. 48–51.

58 Stueck, *Korean War: An International History*, pp. 131–2, 194–5.

59 Stueck, *Korean War: An International History*, p. 239.

60 Stueck, *Korean War: An International History*, pp. 244, 249, 279; Kantowicz, *Coming Apart, Coming Together*, p. 137.

61 Lowe, *Origins of the Korean War*, pp. 240–6; Stueck, *Korean War: An International History*, Ch. 9; MacDonald, *Britain and the Korean War*, Ch. 8.

62 M. Dockrill, 'The Foreign Office, Anglo-American Relations and the Korean Truce Negotiations', and C. MacDonald, '"Heroes Behind Barbed Wire": The United States, Britain and the POW Issue in the Korean War', both in Cotton and Neary, *Korean War in History*, pp. 100–19, 135–50; M.A. Ryan, *Chinese Attitudes toward Nuclear Weapons: China and the United States during the Korean War* (New York, 1990), p. 164; R. Foot, *A Substitute for Victory: The Politics of Peacemaking at the Korean Armistice Talks* (Ithaca NY, 1990), pp. 177–8, 213–14.

63 Dutton, *Anthony Eden*, p. 332.

64 P. Lowe, 'The Settlement of the Korean War', in Young, *Churchill's Peacetime*

Administration, pp. 207–31; Kim, *Foreign Intervention in Korea,* Chs 9 and 10.

65   *Hansard,* 5th series, 518 (1953), cols 893–8, 1547–1610.

66   A.I. Singh, 'Britain, India and the Asian Cold War, 1949–54', in Deighton, *Britain and the First Cold War,* pp. 220–36.

67   On these points see Q. Zhai, *The Dragon, The Lion and The Eagle: Chinese-British-American Relations, 1949–58* (Kent OH, 1994); M. Schaller, *The United States and China in the Twentieth Century* (New York, 1990); C. Jian, *China's Road to the Korean War* (New York, 1996).

68   R. Accinelli, *Crisis and Commitment: US Policy towards Taiwan, 1950–55* (Chapel Hill NC, 1996).

69   E.g. L.S. Kaplan, 'The Korean War and US Foreign Relations', and the response by R. Dallek, both in *The Korean War: A Twenty-Five Year Perspective,* F.H. Heller (ed.) (Lawrence KS, 1977), pp. 36–75, 76–8.

70   See T.A. Wilson's comments in Heller, *Korean War,* pp. 93–6.

71   See essays in Westad, *Brothers in Arms,* especially K. Weathersby, 'Stalin, Mao and the End of the Korean War', pp. 90–116; S.G. Zhang, 'Sino-Soviet Economic Co-operation', pp. 189–225; C. Jian and Y. Kuisong, 'Chinese Politics and the Collapse of the Sino-Soviet Alliance', pp. 246–94; C. Pleshakov, 'Nikita Khrushchev and Sino-Soviet Relations', pp. 165–88; O.A. Westad, 'The Sino-Soviet Alliance and the United States', pp. 226–45; and S. Goncharenko, 'Sino-Soviet Military Co-operation', pp. 141–64. See also Terrill, *Mao,* p. 210; M. Sheng, *Battling Western Imperialism: Mao, Stalin and the United States* (Princeton NJ, 1997); S.R. Schram, *Mao Tse-Tung: A Preliminary Reassessment* (New York, 1983), pp. 54–5; D. Zagorin, *The Sino-Soviet Conflict, 1956–61* (London, 1964); A. Farrar-Hockley, 'The China Factor in the Korean War', in Cotton and Neary, *Korean War in History,* pp. 4–10; Johnson, *Modern World,* p. 451; Armstrong and Goldstein, 'Interaction with the Non-European World', pp. 244–5.

72   Bartlett, *Long Retreat,* p. 196; Johnson, *Modern World,* p. 452; Larres, 'International and Security Relations', pp. 203–4; S.F. Wells, 'The First Cold War Build-up: Europe in United States Strategy and Policy, 1950–53', and N. Wiggershaus, 'The Decision for a West German Defence Contribution', both in *Western Security: The Formative Years: European and Atlantic Defence, 1947–53,* O. Riste (ed.) (Oslo, 1985), pp. 181–97, 198–214; Kaplan, *United States and NATO,* p. 173.

73   *Hansard,* 5th series, 484 (1951), cols 630–1.

74   Reynolds, *Britannia Overruled,* pp. 170–1; Young, *Britain and the World,* p. 157; Baylis, *Anglo-American Defence Relations,* Ch. 3; D.C. Watt, *Succeeding John Bull: America in Britain's Place, 1900–75* (Cambridge, 1984), pp. 129–30; Bartlett, *Special Relationship,* pp. 48–56; MacDonald, *Britain and the Korean War,* pp. 95–6.

75   Bartlett, *Long Retreat,* p. 104; Clark and Wheeler, *British Origins of Nuclear Strategy,* Ch. 6; Aldrich and Coleman, 'Cold War, JIC and British Signals Intelligence', pp. 538, 541; *The Times,* 4 October 1952.

76 R.C. Tucker, 'Swollen State, Spent Society: Stalin's Legacy to Brezhnev's Russia', *Foreign Affairs*, 60 (1981–82), pp. 414–35; R. Hingley, *Joseph Stalin: Man and Legend* (London, 1974), pp. 379–82, 393–6, 404, 414, 416; L. Kolakowski, *Main Currents of Marxism: Its Origins, Growth and Dissolution* (3 vols, Oxford, 1978), Vol. 3, Ch. 4; R. Conquest, *Power and Policy in the USSR: The Study of Soviet Dynastics* (London, 1962), Chs 5–8.

77 Johnson, *Modern World*, pp. 453–6; Reynolds, *Britannia Overruled*, p. 167; Sked and Cook, *Post-War Britain*, p. 96; R. Jeffreys-Jones, *The CIA and American Democracy* (New Haven CT, 1989), Chs 2–4; Henriksen, 'Creation of the North Atlantic Alliance', p. 38, n. 103; Kantowicz, *Coming Apart, Coming Together*, pp. 141–2; Armstrong and Goldstein, 'Interaction with the Non-European World', pp. 244–5.

78 Lowe, *Origins of the Korean War*, Ch. 4; Kantowicz, *Coming Apart, Coming Together*, pp. 127–8; Fraser and Murray, *America and the World*, pp. 34–5; Johnson, *Modern World*, p. 447; Kennan, *Memoirs*, pp. 375–7; Schaller, *American Occupation*, pp. 58, 61; T. Ito, *The Japanese Economy* (Cambridge MA, 1992), pp. 52–69; Johnson, *Modern World*, pp. 447, 719–20; D.B. Smith, *Japan since 1945: The Rise of an Economic Superpower* (Basingstoke, 1995), Chs 2 and 3; G.D. Allinson, *Japan's Post-War History* (London, 1997), Ch. 2; J.W. Dower, *Empire and Aftermath: Yoshida Shigeru and the Japanese Experience, 1878–1954* (Cambridge MA, 1979), Chs 9 and 10; W.G. Beasley, *The Rise of Modern Japan* (London, 1995), Ch. 13.

79 M. Schaller, *Altered States: The United States and Japan since the Occupation* (New York, 1997); T. Eiji, *Inside GHQ: The Allied Occupation of Japan and its Legacy* (New York, 2002).

80 Ovendale, 'Britain and the Cold War in Asia', pp. 122–3; Schaller, *American Occupation*, p. 51.

81 P. Bates, *Japan and the British Commonwealth Occupation Force, 1946–52* (London, 1993); P. Lowe, *Containing the Cold War in East Asia: British Policies towards Japan, China and Korea, 1948–53* (Manchester, 1997); Bullock, *Bevin*, pp. 150–1, 211–12, 748; Schaller, *American Occupation*, pp. 100–1, 135–6, 169–70, 215–16; Bartlett, *Long Retreat*, p. 14.

82 Smith, *Japan since 1945*, pp. 67–9, 86–90; M. Kajima, *A Brief Diplomatic History of Modern Japan* (Rutland VT, 1965), pp. 83–95; Fraser and Murray, *America and the World*, pp. 49–50; Schaller, *American Occupation*, pp. 288–9; Armstrong and Goldstein, 'Interaction with the Non-European World', pp. 245–6; H.S. Parmet, *Eisenhower and the American Crusades* (New Brunswick NJ, 1999), pp. 271–2; Beasley, *Rise of Modern Japan*, pp. 223–6; D. Rees, 'The Korean War and the Japanese Peace Treaty', in Cotton and Neary, *Korean War in History*, pp. 163–74; D. Mayers, *George Kennan and the Dilemmas of US Foreign Policy* (New York, 1988), p. 187.

83 Stueck, *Korean War: An International History*, pp. 201, 254–5.

84 Bartlett, *Long Retreat*, p. 216.

85 Ovendale, 'Britain and the Cold War in Asia', pp. 139–42.

86 Bartlett, *Long Retreat*, pp. 61–4; Sked and Cook, *Post-War Britain*, pp. 96–8; Ovendale, *British Defence Policy*, pp. 12–13, 89–90; D. Dutton, 'Unity and Disunity: The Price of Victory', in Robbins, *British Isles*, pp. 157–8; Morgan, *Labour in Power*, pp. 433–5, 456–60.

87 M. Foot, *Aneurin Bevan: A Biography* (2 vols, London, 1973), Vol. 2, Ch. 8; P.M. Williams, *Hugh Gaitskell: A Political Biography* (London, 1979), pp. 237, 259, 278.

88 Williams, *Hugh Gaitskell*, pp. 278–80; Cairncross, *Years of Recovery*, pp. 232–3.

89 V. Sorenson, 'Defence without Tears: US Embargo Policy and Economic Security in Western Europe, 1947–51', in Heller and Gillingham, *NATO*, pp. 253–81.

90 Baylis, *Anglo-American Defence Relations*, pp. 58–9; Barker, *British between the Superpowers*, pp. 208–10, 212, 214–16, 219–20, 228–30.

91 H. Leigh-Phippard, *Congress and US Military Aid to Britain: Interdependence and Dependence, 1949–56* (London, 1996), p. 76.

Notes to Chapter 4: Defence and Diplomacy

1 P. Sedgwick, 'America over Britain', *Oxford Left*, Michaelmas 1954, p. 7.

2 Young, *Britain and the World*, pp. 148–9, 153; Reynolds, *Britannia Overruled*, p. 173; Coker, 'Foreign and Defence Policy', p. 15; Pelling, *Churchill*, pp. 596–7; Sked and Cook, *Post-War Britain*, p. 104; D. Carlton, *Anthony Eden: A Biography* (London, 1981), pp. 294, 296–7; Thorpe, *Eden*, p. 363; H. Macmillan, *Tides of Fortune, 1945–55* (London, 1969), pp. 375, 378; Bartlett, *Long Retreat*, pp. 76–81.

3 Boyle, 'Special Relationship with Washington', pp. 39–43.

4 Sked and Cook, *Post-War Britain*, pp. 109–10.

5 *Hansard*, 5th series, 518 (1953), cols 248–9, 513–14; K. Larres, 'Preserving Law and Order: Britain, the United States and the East German Uprising of 1953', *Twentieth Century British History*, 5 (1994), pp. 320–50.

6 Zubok and Pleshakov, *Inside the Kremlin's Cold War*, pp. 159–63; R. Steininger, *The German Question: The Stalin Note of 1952 and the Problem of Reunification* (New York, 1990); G. Wettig, 'Stalin and German Reunification: Archival Evidence on Soviet Foreign Policy in Spring 1952', *Historical Journal*, 37 (1990), pp. 411–19; *The Times*, 26 March 1952.

7 Kaplan, *United States and NATO*, p. 174; Hanrieder and Auton, *Foreign Policies of West Germany, France and Britain*, pp. 52–3, 193–4.

8 Barker, *British between the Superpowers*, pp. 212, 216–17, 221, 225–7; Sked and Cook, *Post-War Britain*, pp. 110–13; Reynolds, *Britannia Overruled*, pp. 183–4; Hollowell, 'Commonwealth to European Integration', pp. 65–6; R.H. Immerman, *John Foster Dulles: Piety, Pragmatism and Power in US Foreign Policy* (Wilmington

DE, 1999), pp. 99–102; F.W. Marks, *Power and Peace: The Diplomacy of John Foster Dulles* (Westport CT, 1995), pp. 54–8; Larres, 'International and Security Relations', p. 206; Bartlett, *Long Retreat*, pp. 91–3.

9   Adenauer, *Memoirs*, pp. 433, 435–7; Prittie, *Konrad Adenauer*, pp. 190–1; Granieri, *Ambivalent Alliance*, pp. 76–80; Irving, *Adenauer*, pp. 98–100, 106–7; F.R. Willis, 'Germany, France and Europe', in *West German Foreign Policy, 1949–79*, W.F. Hanrieder (ed.) (Boulder CO, 1980), pp. 96–9.

10 J.W. Young, 'German Rearmament and the European Defence Community', in Young, *Churchill's Peacetime Administration*, pp. 83–95.

11 Van Eekelen, *Debating European Security*, pp. 6–7.

12 *Britain and European Integration, 1945–98: A Documentary History*, D. Gowland and A. Turner (eds) (London, 2000), pp. 26–7; Warner, 'Labour Governments and the Unity of Western Europe', pp. 74–8; G.H. Soutou, 'France and the German Rearmament Problem, 1945–55', in Ahmann, Birke and Howard, *Quest for Stability*, p. 502; G. Bossuat, 'The French Administrative Elite and the Unification of Western Europe, 1947–58', in *Building Post-War Europe: National Decision-Makers and European Institutions*, A. Deighton (ed.) (Basingstoke, 1995), p. 27.

13 Warner, 'Reconstruction and Defence of Western Europe', p. 276.

14 *Speeches of Churchill*, pp. 309–14; *Documents on British Policy Overseas*, Series II, R. Bullen and M.E. Pelly (eds) (4 vols, London, 1986), Vol. 1, pp. 742–4; Gowland and Turner, *Britain and European Integration*, pp. 28–9.

15 J.W. Young, 'Churchill's "No" to Europe: The "Rejection" of European Union by Churchill's Post-War Government, 1951–52', *Historical Journal*, 28 (1985), pp. 923–37.

16 Warner, 'Reconstruction and Defence of Western Europe', p. 280; Charlton, *Price of Victory*, pp. 137–9; S. Greenwood, *Britain and European Co-operation since 1945* (Oxford, 1992), Ch. 5; J.W. Young, *Britain and European Unity, 1945–99* (Basingstoke, 2000), pp. 32–9; *Hansard*, 5th series, 526 (1954), cols 1141–47.

17 H. Young, *This Blessed Plot: Britain and Europe from Churchill to Blair* (Woodstock NY, 1998), pp. 74–7; Hanrieder and Auton, *Foreign Policies of West Germany, France and Britain*, pp. 5–7, 100–3; Kaplan, *Long Entanglement*, pp. 60–2, and idem, *United States and NATO*, pp. 163, 170; Fursdon, *European Defence Community*, Chs 7 and 8; W.I. Hitchcock, *France Restored: Cold War Diplomacy and the Quest for Leadership in Europe, 1944–54* (Chapel Hill NC, 1998), pp. 100–1, 203.

18 Lieshout, 'Politics of European Unification', pp. 216–17; Larres, 'International and Security Relations', pp. 205–6.

19 E. Fursdon, 'The Role of the European Defence Community in European Integration', in Heller and Gillingham, *NATO*, pp. 213–40; S. Duke, *The Elusive Quest for European Security: From EDC to CFSP* (Basingstoke, 2000), pp. 14–36; Brinkley, 'Acheson and European Unity', pp. 129–60; Schwartz, 'Dual Containment', pp. 193–212; Gaddis, *Strategies of Containment*, pp. 152–3; G. Lundestad, *'Empire'*

by Integration: The United States and European Integration, 1945–97 (Oxford, 1998), pp. 4, 43–9.

20   Bartlett, *Special Relationship*, pp. 43, 55, 66; Baylis, *Anglo-American Defence Relations*, pp. 62–5; Fraser and Murray, *America and the World*, pp. 52–3, 58–60; Reynolds, 'Britain and the World since 1945', p. 163; Thorpe, *Eden*, pp. 313–14; Dutton, *Anthony Eden*, pp. 302–6; Sanders, *Losing an Empire*, pp. 63–4; S.F. Wells, 'The United States, Britain and the Defence of Europe', in Louis and Bull, *The 'Special Relationship'*, pp. 130–2; W. Kaiser, *Using Europe, Abusing the Europeans: Britain and European Integration, 1945–63* (Basingstoke, 1996), pp. 14–17; W. LaFeber, *The American Age: US Foreign Policy at Home and Abroad* (New York, 1994), p. 554; K. Ruane, *The Rise and Fall of the European Defence Community: Anglo-American Relations and the Crisis of European Defence, 1950–55* (London, 2000), Ch. 7.

21   *Observer*, 22 August 1954; *The Times*, 31 August 1954; Young, 'German Rearmament and the European Defence Community', pp. 95–6.

22   A. Eden, *Full Circle* (London, 1960), p. 159; Ovendale, *British Defence Policy*, pp. 106–7; Young, 'German Rearmament and the European Defence Community', pp. 97–8.

23   Young, *Britain and the World*, p. 149, and idem, 'German Rearmament and the European Defence Community', pp. 98–9; Sked and Cook, *Post-War Britain*, pp. 113–14; Van Eekelen, *Debating European Security*, pp. 8–10; Bartlett, *Long Retreat*, pp. 93–5; Reynolds, *Britannia Overruled*, pp. 184–5; Hollowell, 'Commonwealth to European Integration', p. 66; Gowland and Turner, *Britain and European Integration*, pp. 30–2; Larres, 'International and Security Relations', pp. 206–7; Lieshout, 'Politics of European Integration', pp. 217–18; Duke, *Elusive Quest*, pp. 36–41; Eden, *Full Circle*, pp. 146–74; Thorpe, *Eden*, pp. 313–14; Dutton, *Anthony Eden*, pp. 302–6; Fursdon, *European Defence Community*, Ch. 9; Hanrieder and Auton, *Foreign Policies of West Germany, France and Britain*, pp. 7–8, 193; A. Cahen, *The Western European Union and NATO* (London, 1989), pp. 1–4; Kaplan, *United States and NATO*, pp. 163, 168, 170; S. Dockrill, 'Britain and the Settlement of the West German Rearmament Question in 1954', in *British Foreign Policy, 1945–56*, M. Dockrill and J.W. Young (eds) (Basingstoke, 1989), pp. 149–72.

24   *Hansard*, 5th series, 531 (1954), cols 1037–39.

25   It has been suggested that it was Dulles who did most to shape the various arguments about European security in the mid-1950s. An alternative interpretation is that while Dulles' role was important, on crucial points he reluctantly followed Eden's lead. See Immerman, *John Foster Dulles*, pp. 99–105, and Marks, *Power and Peace*, pp. 54–61.

26   Young, 'German Rearmament and the European Defence Community', pp. 100–2; Hollowell, 'Commonwealth to European Integration', p. 67; Reynolds, *Britannia*

Overruled, p. 173; Kaplan, *Long Entanglement*, pp. 59–63; Fursdon, *European Defence Community*, pp. 268–71.

27 A. Deighton, 'British-West German Relations, 1945–72', in *Uneasy Allies: British-German Relations and European Integration since 1945*, K. Larres and E. Meehan (eds) (Oxford, 2000), pp. 36–7; S. George, *An Awkward Partner: Britain in the European Community* (Oxford, 1990), p. 39; J.W. Young, 'Towards a New View of British Policy and European Unity, 1945–57', in Ahmann, Birke and Howard, *Quest for Stability*, pp. 455–7.

28 K. Larres, 'Uneasy Allies or Genuine Partners? Britain, Germany and European Integration', in Larres and Meehan, *Uneasy Allies*, pp. 1–2, 6, 11–12, 15–16; W. Loth, 'The Korean War and the Reorganization of the European Security System, 1948–55', in Ahmann, Birke and Howard, *Quest for Stability*, pp. 465–86.

29 Bartlett, *Long Retreat*, pp. 93–4.

30 May and Treverton, 'Defence Relationships: American Perspectives', p. 168; D.C. Watt, 'Demythologizing the Eisenhower Era', in Louis and Bull, *The 'Special Relationship'*, pp. 76, 78–9, 81.

31 Lieshout, 'Politics of European Integration', p. 218; Soutou, 'France and the German Rearmament Problem', p. 512. See also S.A. Kocs, *Autonomy or Power? The Franco-German Relationship and Europe: Strategic Choices, 1955–95* (Westport CT, 1995).

32 C.S. Maier, 'Finance and Defence: Implications of Military Integration, 1950–52', in Heller and Gillingham, *NATO*, pp. 335–51; Van Eekelen, *Debating European Security*, p. 7.

33 See K.A. Maier, 'The Anglo-Saxon Triangle, the French and Western European Integration', W. Abelshauser, 'The Causes and Consequences of the 1956 West German Rearmament Crisis', P. Fischer, 'West German Rearmament and the Nuclear Challenge', R.A. Wampler, 'Conventional Goals and Nuclear Promises: The Truman Administration and the Roots of the NATO New Look', and M. Trachtenberg, 'The Nuclearization of NATO and US-West European Relations', all in Heller and Gillingham, *NATO*, pp. 311–14, 353–80, 381–401, 403–12, 413–30; Gillingham, 'Introduction', in Heller and Gillingham, *NATO*, p. 13; C.S. Maier, 'The Making of "Pax Americana": Formative Moments of United States Ascendancy', in Ahmann, Birke and Howard, *Quest for Stability*, pp. 421–2, 432, 434.

34 B. Heuser, *NATO, Britain, France and the FRG: Nuclear Strategies and Forces for Europe, 1949–2000* (Basingstoke, 1997), pp. 32–6.

35 Heuser, *NATO, Britain, France and the FRG*, pp. 93–4, 125–6.

36 British, French and West German attitudes are compared in B. Heuser, *Nuclear Mentalities: Strategies and Beliefs in Britain, France and the FRG* (New York, 1998). According to M. Navias, *Nuclear Weapons and British Strategic Planning, 1955–58* (Oxford, 1991), the policy fashioned by Britain at this juncture was one

of 'independence in concert' and it had two main determinants – lack of money and the desire to preserve the 'special relationship' with the USA.

37 Heuser, *Nuclear Mentalities*, pp. 1, 100, 264, 266.

38 Larres, 'International and Security Relations', pp. 207, 210; C. Kennedy-Pipe, *Stalin's Cold War: Soviet Strategies in Europe, 1943–56* (Manchester, 1995), Ch. 6; Morewood, 'Divided Europe', p. 18; Duke, *Elusive Quest*, p. 41; Sked and Cook, *Post-War Britain*, p. 114; Fraser and Murray, *America and the World*, p. 70; Hanrieder and Auton, *Foreign Policies of West Germany, France and Britain*, pp. 50–9; W.F. Hanrieder, *Germany, America, Europe: Forty Years of German Foreign Policy* (London, 1989), Ch. 5.

39 *The Times*, 21 April, 10, 11, 16 May 1955; *Hansard*, 5th series, 542 (1955), cols 76–7, 755–6.

40 Larres, 'International and Security Relations', pp. 207–9; Thorpe, *Eden*, p. 386; Dutton, *Anthony Eden*, pp. 336–42, 348–51; Immerman, *John Foster Dulles*, pp. 132–6, 142–3; Marks, *Power and Peace*, pp. 26, 60, 48–9, 77; Hanrieder, *Germany, America, Europe*, pp. 151–63; Kennedy-Pipe, *Stalin's Cold War*, pp. 184–6; Lundestad, *'Empire' by Integration*, pp. 137–8.

41 Conquest, *Power and Policy in the USSR*, Part 3; M.J. Sodaro, *Moscow, Germany and the West from Khrushchev to Gorbachev* (London, 1991); Zubok and Pleshakov, *Inside the Kremlin's Cold War*, pp. 157–8, 169–71.

42 Larres, 'International and Security Relations', pp. 209–10; H.P. Schwarz, 'Adenauer's Ostpolitik', in Hanrieder, *West German Foreign Policy*, pp. 127–43; W.G. Gray, *Germany's Cold War: The Global Campaign to Isolate East Germany* (Chapel Hill NC, 2003); Hanrieder, *Germany, America, Europe*, Chs 5 and 6.

43 K. Larres, 'Britain and the GDR: Political and Economic Relations, 1949–89', in Larres and Meehan, *Uneasy Allies*, pp. 63–98.

44 Larres, 'International and Security Relations', p. 210; Thorpe, *Eden*, pp. 445–6, 463; Fraser and Murray, *America and the World*, pp. 70–2; Marks, *Power and Peace*, pp. 103, 130; Immerman, *John Foster Dulles*, pp. 135–43.

45 Ambrose, *Eisenhower*, Ch. 16; Parmet, *Eisenhower and the American Crusades*, pp. 401, 403, 405–6; S. Dockrill, *Eisenhower's New Look National Security Policy, 1953–61* (Basingstoke, 1996), Ch. 7; *Cold War Respite: The Geneva Summit of 1955*, G. Bischoff and S. Dockrill (eds) (Baton Rouge LA, 2000); D. Eisenhower, *Mandate for Change, 1953–56* (New York, 1963), pp. 527–30.

46 *Hansard*, 5th series, 544 (1955), cols 1212–21.

47 *Manchester Guardian*, 23 July 1955; *The Times*, 25 July, 17 November 1955; *Hansard*, 5th series, 547 (1956), cols 352–4.

48 R. Bowie and R.H. Immerman, *Waging Peace: How Eisenhower Shaped an Enduring Cold War Strategy* (New York, 1998), pp. 3, 256; M. Bose, *Shaping and Signalling Presidential Policy: The National Security Decision Making of Eisenhower and Kennedy* (College Station TX, 1998), Part 1.

49 On these points see Lundestad, *'Empire' by Integration*, pp. 137–8, and especially M. Trachtenberg, *A Constructed Peace: The Making of the European Settlement, 1945–63* (Princeton NJ, 1999).

50 Trachtenberg, *Constructed Peace*, pp. 179–83, 198–200.

51 J. Darwin, *The End of the British Empire* (Oxford, 1991), pp. 68–9.

52 Bartlett, *Long Retreat*, pp. 82–3; Young, *Britain and the World*, p. 164; Dutton, *Anthony Eden*, p. 359; Immerman, *John Foster Dulles*, pp. 65–8; Marks, *Power and Peace*, pp. 116–18; Sked and Cook, *Post-War Britain*, p. 115; B.H. Reid, 'The "Northern Tier" and the Baghdad Pact', in Young, *Churchill's Peacetime Administration*, pp. 164–70; B. Lapping, *End of Empire* (London, 1985), pp. 204–24; Monroe, *Britain's Moment*, pp. 172, 174; C. Andrew, *For the President's Eyes Only: Secret Intelligence and the American Presidency* (New York, 1995), pp. 202–6; Curtis, *Ambiguities of Power*, pp. 87–96; Jeffreys-Jones, *CIA and American Democracy*, pp. 89–90.

53 *The Times*, 8 April 1954; *Economist*, 17 April 1954.

54 *Hansard*, 5th series, 526 (1954), cols 796–9; 532 (1954), cols 223–6, 333–5, 1037–38.

55 Darwin, *Britain and Decolonization*, pp. 159–63.

56 Young, *Britain and the World*, pp. 164–5; Lapping, *End of Empire*, pp. 244–60; Darwin, *Britain and Decolonization*, pp. 206–9; Sked and Cook, *Post-War Britain*, pp. 115–16; Bartlett, *Long Retreat*, pp. 81–6; Thorpe, *Eden*, pp. 420, 424, 426–7; Dutton, *Anthony Eden*, pp. 354–63; Sanders, *Losing an Empire*, pp. 89–90; Frankel, *British Foreign Policy*, pp. 122, 128–9; Monroe, *Britain's Moment*, pp. 175–7; R. McNamara, *Britain, Nasser and the Balance of Power in the Middle East, 1952–67: From the Egyptian Revolution to the Six Day War* (London, 2003), p. 4.

57 Ovendale, *British Defence Policy*, pp. 105–6, and idem, 'Egypt and the Suez Base Agreement', in Young, *Churchill's Peacetime Administration*, pp. 135–55; Darwin, *End of the British Empire*, p. 69; Lapping, *End of Empire*, p. 308.

58 D. Goldsworthy, 'Keeping Change within Bounds: Aspects of Colonial Policy during the Churchill and Eden Governments, 1951–57', *Journal of Imperial and Commonwealth History*, 18 (1990), pp. 83–5, 88, 91–3, 95–6.

59 Goldsworthy, 'Keeping Change within Bounds', pp. 99–102.

60 *The Times*, 28 July 1954; *Hansard*, 5th series, 532 (1954), cols 221–3, 232–6, 325–3.

61 Darby, *Defence Policy East of Suez*, pp. 57, 89–93.

62 Armstrong and Goldstein, 'Interaction with the Non-European World', pp. 251–2; A. Clayton, *The Wars of French Decolonization* (Harlow, 1994), Ch. 4; M. Kahler, *Decolonization in Britain and France: The Domestic Consequences of International Relations* (Princeton NJ, 1984), pp. 30, 78, 81–3, 85–6, 89–90, 173–6, 200, 274, 300; D. Marr, 'Vietnam: Harnessing the Whirlwind', in *Asia: The Winning of Independence*, R. Jeffrey (ed.) (London, 1981), pp. 163–207; Jordi, 'Collapse of

World Dominion', p. 42; J.L. Gaddis, *The Long Peace: Inquiries into the History of the Cold War* (Oxford, 1987), pp. 129–33; Immerman, *John Foster Dulles*, pp. 87–93; Marks, *Power and Peace*, pp. 33–8, 63–4; E.J. Hammer, *The Struggle for Indochina, 1940–55* (Stanford CA, 1966), Ch. 12.

63 Ambrose, *Eisenhower*, pp. 357–63; Parmet, *Eisenhower and the American Crusades*, pp. 353–63; G.C. Herring, 'Franco-American Conflict in Indochina, 1950–54', in *Dien Bien Phu and the Crisis of Franco-American Relations, 1954–55*, L.S. Kaplan, D. Artaud and M.R. Rubin (eds) (Wilmington DE, 1990), pp. 23–43; Hamby, *Man of the People*, p. 570; Schaller, *American Occupation*, pp. 287–8; A. Stephanson, *Kennan and the Art of Foreign Policy* (Cambridge MA, 1989), p. 166. Growing US involvement in Indochina marked a clear reversal of earlier policy: W. LaFeber, 'Roosevelt, Churchill and Indochina, 1942–45', *American Historical Review*, *80* (1975), pp. 1277–95; G.C. Herring, 'The Truman Administration and the Restoration of French Sovereignty in Indochina', *Diplomatic History*, *1* (1977), pp. 97–117.

64 A.J. Rotter, *The Path to Vietnam: Origins of the American Commitment to South East Asia* (Ithaca NY, 1987); R.B. Smith, *An International History of the Vietnam War* (3 vols, New York, 1985–91), Vol. 2, pp. 142–3. The international context receives less attention in G.M. Kahin's *Intervention: How America Became Involved in Vietnam* (New York, 1987), which stresses the continuity between French and US involvement.

65 J. Springhall, '"Kicking out the Vietminh": How Britain allowed France to Reoccupy South Indochina, 1945–46', *Journal of Contemporary History*, *40* (2005), pp. 115–30.

66 G.C. Herring, *America's Longest War: The United States and Vietnam, 1950–75* (New York, 1986), pp. 35–7.

67 Watt, *Succeeding John Bull*, pp. 127–31; D. Reynolds, 'Eden the Diplomatist, 1931–56: Suezide of a Statesman?' *History*, *74* (1989), p. 71, and idem, *Britannia Overruled*, p. 173; Sked and Cook, *Post-War Britain*, pp. 116–18; Armstrong and Goldstein, 'Interaction with the Non-European World', p. 252; Young, *Britain and the World*, pp. 149, 158; Bartlett, *Long Retreat*, p. 87, and idem, *Special Relationship*, pp. 63–5; Baylis, *Anglo-American Defence Relations*, p. 62; Thorpe, *Eden*, pp. 401–12; Dutton, *Anthony Eden*, pp. 343–54; Marks, *Power and Peace*, pp. 62–7; Immerman, *John Foster Dulles*, pp. 93–6; Gaddis, *We Now Know*, pp. 162–3.

68 K. Ruane, 'Anthony Eden, British Diplomacy and the Origins of the Geneva Conference of 1954', *Historical Journal*, *37* (1994), pp. 153–72, and idem, 'Containing America: Aspects of British Foreign Policy and the Cold War in South East Asia, 1951–54', *Diplomacy and Statecraft*, *7* (1996), pp. 143–62; Singh, 'Britain, India and the Asian Cold War', pp. 220–36.

69 Fraser and Murray, *America and the World*, pp. 61–4; Kantowicz, *Coming Apart, Coming Together*, pp. 305–6; Reynolds, *Britannia Overruled*, p. 173; Armstrong

and Goldstein, 'Interaction with the Non-European World', p. 242; Immerman, *John Foster Dulles*, pp. 97–9; Parmet, *Eisenhower and the American Crusades*, pp. 378, 392–6; Ambrose, *Eisenhower*, pp. 370–1; Herring, *America's Longest War*, Ch. 2; Marks, *Power and Peace*, p. 67.

70 G. Warner, 'The Settlement of the Indochina War', in Young, *Churchill's Peacetime Administration*, pp. 255–7; J. Cable, *The Geneva Conference of 1954 on Indochina* (Basingstoke, 1986), pp. 123–4, 134–5; Hammer, *Struggle for Indochina*, pp. 327–9.

71 *The Times*, 4, 17 May 1954; *Manchester Guardian*, 17 May 1954.

72 *Hansard*, 5th series, 529 (1954), cols 429–1.

73 Darwin, *End of the British Empire*, p. 69.

74 Cable, *Geneva Conference*, pp. 125, 127–8; Herring, *America's Longest War*, pp. 41–2; M.B. Young, *The Vietnam Wars, 1945–90* (New York, 1991), Ch. 3; D.L. Anderson, *Trapped by Success: The Eisenhower Administration and Vietnam, 1953–61* (New York, 1991), p. 44.

75 Watt, 'Demythologizing the Eisenhower Era', p. 74.

76 Fraser and Murray, *America and the World*, pp. 68–70; Ambrose, *Eisenhower*, pp. 377, 474; Parmet, *Eisenhower and the American Crusades*, pp. 379–80; Kantowicz, *Coming Apart, Coming Together*, pp. 327–30; Andrew, *For the President's Eyes Only*, pp. 206–11; Jeffreys-Jones, *CIA and American Democracy*, pp. 90–2; N. Cullather, *Secret History: The CIA's Classified Account of its Operations in Guatemala, 1952–54* (Stanford CA, 1999), pp. 7–8, 21–2, 24–7, 56, 95–6, 107, 111; P. Gleijeses, *Shattered Hope: The Guatemalan Revolution and the United States, 1944–54* (Princeton NJ, 1991), Ch. 7; documents of June 1954 in *Foreign Relations, 1952–54: The American Republics, Guatemala Compilation*, N.S. Kane (ed.) (Washington DC, 1983); Immerman, *John Foster Dulles*, pp. 113–14.

77 *Hansard*, 5th series, 529 (1954), cols 32–4, 546–50.

78 Gleijeses, *Shattered Hope*, pp. 313, 330–1, 340, 371; J. Colville, *The Fringes of Power: Downing Street Diaries, 1939–55* (London, 1985), p. 694; Sedgwick, 'America over Britain', p. 5; *The Times*, 21, 24, 29 June 1954.

79 Young, *Britain and the World*, pp. 158–9; Coker, 'Foreign and Defence Policy', pp. 8–10. Churchill's position is discussed at length in Larres, *Churchill's Cold War*, Chs 8–15. On the wider context for Anglo-American disagreements about how to deal with Moscow, see Bartlett, *Special Relationship*, Ch. 3; Parmet, *Eisenhower and the American Crusades*, Ch. 27; Baylis, *Anglo-American Defence Relations*, Ch. 3; Watt, 'Demythologizing the Eisenhower Era', pp. 65–85; R.H. Ullman, 'America, Britain and the Soviet Threat in Historical and Present Perspective', in Louis and Bull, *The 'Special Relationship'*, pp. 103–14; M.S. Fish, 'After Stalin's Death: The Anglo-American Debate over a New Cold War', *Diplomatic History*, 10 (1986), pp. 333–55.

80 K. Larres, 'Integrating Europe or Ending the Cold War? Churchill's Post-War Foreign Policy', *Journal of European Integration History*, 2 (1996), pp. 15–49; J.W. Young, 'Cold War and Détente with Moscow', in Young, *Churchill's Peacetime Administration*, pp. 55–80.

81 J. Turner, 'Governors, Governance, and Governed: British Politics since 1945', and J. Harris, 'Tradition and Transformation: Society and Civil Society in Britain, 1945–2001', in Burk, *British Isles since 1945*, pp. 27–8, 120–1; Young, *Britain and the World*, p. 223; R. Eatwell, 'The Currents of Political Thought', in Hollowell, *Britain since 1945*, pp. 166, 169; I.B. Neumann, *Russia and the Idea of Europe: Identity and International Relations* (London, 1996); *Cold War Propaganda in the 1950s*, G.D. Rawnsley (ed.) (Basingstoke, 1999).

82 Mayhew, *Time to Explain*, pp. 135–40.

83 Mayhew, *Time to Explain*, pp. 141–3.

84 *Cold War, Hot Science: Applied Research in Britain's Defence Laboratories, 1945–90*, R. Bud and P. Gummett (eds) (London, 2002).

85 J. Agar, 'Science and Information Technology', in Hollowell, *Britain since 1945*, pp. 349–51; J. Agar and B. Balmer, 'British Scientists and the Cold War: The Defence Research Policy Committee and Information Networks, 1947–63', *Historical Studies in the Physical and Biological Sciences*, 28 (1998), p. 248; R. Williams, *The Nuclear Power Decisions: British Policies, 1953–78* (London, 1980), Chs 2–4; D. Vincent, *The Culture of Secrecy: Britain, 1832–1998* (Oxford, 1998), pp. 194–210; R.J. Aldrich, 'Policing the Past: Official History, Secrecy and British Intelligence since 1945', *English Historical Review*, 119 (2004), pp. 922–53; Jeffery, 'British Isles/British Empire', p. 40; Aldrich and Coleman, 'Cold War, JIC and British Signals Intelligence', pp. 540–1.

86 Young, *Britain and the World*, p. 150; R.J. Aldrich, 'Secret Intelligence for a Post-War World: Reshaping the British Intelligence Community, 1944–51', and R.J. Aldrich and J. Zametica, 'The Rise and Decline of a Strategic Concept: The Middle East, 1945–51', both in *British Intelligence, Strategy and the Cold War*, R.J. Aldrich (ed.) (London, 1992), pp. 15–49, 236–74; C. Andrew, *Secret Service* (London, 1985), Chs 1 and 2, pp. 495–6; G. Murray, *Enemies of the State* (London, 1993), p. 118; *Hansard*, 5th series, 552 (1956), cols 1220, 1751–82; *The Times*, 10 May 1956.

87 Gowing and Arnold, *Independence and Deterrence*, Vol. 1, pp. 210–11, 302–3, Vol. 2, pp. 116–17, 134.

88 Merrick, 'Russia Committee', pp. 453–68; Lewis, *Changing Direction*, pp. 262, 338; Reynolds, *Britannia Overruled*, p. 149; Young, *Britain and the World*, pp. 151–2; W.S. Lucas and C.J. Morris, 'A Very British Crusade: The Information Research Department and the Beginning of the Cold War', in Aldrich, *British Intelligence*, pp. 85–110; Aldrich and Coleman, 'Cold War, JIC and British Signals Intelligence', pp. 538, 540–1; Agar and Balmer, 'British Scientists and the Cold War', pp. 209–52.

89 Young, *Britain and the World*, pp. 149, 152.

90 Reynolds, *Britannia Overruled*, p. 173; Young, *Britain and the World*, p. 153; Bartlett, *Long Retreat*, pp. 76–81; Coker, 'Foreign and Defence Policy', p. 15; Dockrill, *British Defence*, pp. 41–7; Ovendale, *British Defence Policy*, pp. 13, 97, 98–102; Cairncross, *Years of Recovery*, pp. 231–2.

91 Ovendale, *British Defence Policy*, pp. 97–102, 104–5.

92 Sked and Cook, *Post-War Britain*, p. 118; Reynolds, *Britannia Overruled*, p. 170; A.J. Pierre, *Nuclear Politics: The British Experience with an Independent Strategic Force, 1939–70* (London, 1972), pp. 86–94; Clark and Wheeler, *British Origins of Nuclear Strategy*, pp. 210–15; Agar, 'Science and Information Technology', pp. 349–50; Bartlett, *Long Retreat*, pp. 99–100, 102–3, 106, 128.

93 E.R. May, 'The Impact of Nuclear Weapons on European Security, 1945–57', in Ahmann, Birke and Howard, *Quest for Stability*, pp. 530, 532; Colville, *Fringes of Power*, pp. 676, 685–6.

94 Agar and Balmer, 'British Scientists and the Cold War', p. 248.

95 Dockrill, *British Defence*, pp. 46–7, 51–2, 56–8, 64, 67–71; Bartlett, *Long Retreat*, p. 99; Reynolds, *Britannia Overruled*, pp. 170–1; Young, *Britain and the World*, p. 157; Boyle, 'Special Relationship with Washington', pp. 44–9; L. Goldman, *Britain and Nuclear Weapons* (London, 1980), Ch. 1; G.M. Dillon, *Dependence and Deterrence: Success and Civility in the Anglo-American Special Nuclear Relationship, 1962–82* (Aldershot, 1983), pp. 13–14; Watt, *Succeeding John Bull*, pp. 129–30.

96 R. Osgood, *NATO: The Entangling Alliance* (Chicago, 1962), p. 267; E. Spiers, 'The British Nuclear Deterrent: Problems and Possibilities', in Dilks, *Retreat from Power*, Vol. 2, pp. 156–7; Gowing, 'Nuclear Weapons and the Special Relationship', p. 126; Eberle, 'Military Relationship', pp. 151–9; Baylis, *Anglo-American Defence Relations*, pp. 66–72, 85–94; Bartlett, *Special Relationship*, pp. 68–71, 92–4; R. Holland, *The Pursuit of Greatness: Britain and the World Role, 1900–70* (London, 1991), pp. 251–3.

97 S. Ball, 'Military Nuclear Relations between the United States and Britain under the Terms of the McMahon Act, 1946–58', *Historical Journal*, 38 (1995), pp. 439–54.

98 M. Navias, 'Nuclear Weapons and British Alliance Commitments, 1955–56', in Deighton, *Britain and the First Cold War*, pp. 146–61.

99 Sedgwick, 'America over Britain', pp. 4–9.

100 *Hansard*, 5th series, 526 (1954), cols 36–153.

Notes to Chapter 5: East of Eden

1 Lapping, *End of Empire*, p. 308.

2 Dutton, *Anthony Eden*, pp. 343–4; Thorpe, *Eden*, pp. 401–2, 424, 427; Young,

Britain and the World, pp. 149, 165; Baylis, *Anglo-American Defence Relations*, p. 62; Fraser and Murray, *America and the World*, pp. 63–4; Sked and Cook, *Post-War Britain*, p. 119; Immerman, *John Foster Dulles*, pp. 96–7, 117; Marks, *Power and Peace*, pp. 33–4, 36, 62–5, 158–60; Warner, 'Settlement of the Indochina War', pp. 257–8.

3   Warner, 'Settlement of the Indochina War', pp. 242–4.

4   Sanders, *Losing an Empire*, pp. 70–1; Watt, *Succeeding John Bull*, p. 130.

5   *Hansard*, 5th series, 531 (1954), cols 1593–94.

6   K. Ruane and J. Ellison, 'Managing the Americans: Anthony Eden, Harold Macmillan and the Pursuit of "Power by Proxy" in the 1950s', *Contemporary British History*, *18* (2004), pp. 149–51.

7   Ambrose *Eisenhower*, pp. 362–3, 368, 370–1; Parmet, *Eisenhower and the American Crusades*, pp. 395–6; Bartlett, *Long Retreat*, pp. 87, 162.

8   J.D.B. Miller, 'The "Special Relationship" in the Pacific', in Louis and Bull, *The 'Special Relationship'*, pp. 383, 385–6.

9   R. Ovendale, *Britain, the United States and the Transfer of Power in the Middle East, 1945–62* (London, 1996), Ch. 5; Sked and Cook, *Post-War Britain*, pp. 119–20; Young, *Britain and the World*, pp. 164–5; Bartlett, *Long Retreat*, pp. 116–19; Baylis, *Anglo-American Defence Relations*, pp. 72–3; Monroe, *Britain's Moment*, pp. 183–91; N. Ashton, 'The Hijacking of a Pact: The Formation of the Baghdad Pact and Anglo-American Tensions in the Middle East, 1955–58', *Review of International Studies*, *19* (1993), pp. 123–37.

10   Ovendale, *British Defence Policy*, pp. 103–4.

11   *Hansard*, 5th series, 539 (1955), cols 379–85.

12   Ruane and Ellison, 'Managing the Americans', pp. 151–2.

13   Ruane and Ellison, 'Managing the Americans', pp. 153–4. American concerns about Arab–Israeli enmity are explored in A. Ben-Zvi, *Decade of Transition: Eisenhower, Kennedy and the Origins of the American-Israeli Alliance* (New York, 1998).

14   Marks, *Power and Peace*, pp. 48, 52, 153; Immerman, *John Foster Dulles*, pp. 147–8; Thorpe, *Eden*, p. 426; Dutton, *Anthony Eden*, pp. 360–1, 365–71.

15   Reid, 'The "Northern Tier" and the Baghdad Pact', pp. 176–8.

16   Lapping, *End of Empire*, pp. 257–60; Darwin, *Britain and Decolonization*, pp. 210–11.

17   Ovendale, *Transfer of Power in the Middle East*, pp. 121–3.

18   M. Eppel, 'The Decline of British Influence and the Ruling Elite in Iraq', and I. Pappe, 'British Rule in Jordan, 1943–55', both in Cohen and Kolinsky, *Demise of the British Empire*, pp. 185–97, 198–219.

19   Bartlett, *Long Retreat*, pp. 117–19.

20   Pelling, *Churchill*, pp. 601–2, 607–8, 610–11; F.I. Greenstein, *The Hidden-Hand Presidency: Eisenhower as Leader* (New York, 1982), pp. 89–90; Gaddis, *Strategies of Containment*, pp. 189–90; Reynolds, *Britannia Overruled*, p. 174; Sked and Cook,

Post-War Britain, pp. 120–1; Fraser and Murray, *America and the World*, pp. 52–8; Bartlett, *Long Retreat*, pp. 101–2.

21 Carlton, *Anthony Eden*, pp. 372, 376–82; Macmillan, *Tides of Fortune*, pp. 586–7, 611–25; Eden, *Full Circle*, pp. 289, 295–311; Thorpe, *Eden*, pp. 445–6; Dutton, *Anthony Eden*, pp. 351, 411, 462; Sked and Cook, *Post-War Britain*, p. 125; Young, *Britain and the World*, p. 149; Reynolds, *Britannia Overruled*, p. 174.

22 Bartlett, *Long Retreat*, pp. 103–4.

23 Sked and Cook, *Post-War Britain*, pp. 126–8; A. Nutting, *No End of a Lesson: The Story of Suez* (London, 1967), Ch. 1.

24 Ovendale, *Transfer of Power in the Middle East*, Ch. 6; Monroe, *Britain's Moment*, Chs 7 and 8; M. Thornhill, 'Britain, the United States and the Rise of an Egyptian Leader: The Politics and Diplomacy of Nasser's Consolidation of Power', *English Historical Review*, 119 (2004), pp. 892–921; P. Woodward, *Nasser* (London, 1992), pp. 28–44; Kantowicz, *Coming Apart, Coming Together*, pp. 194–5; Fraser and Murray, *America and the World*, p. 73; Sked and Cook, *Post-War Britain*, pp. 128–9; Darwin, *Britain and Decolonization*, pp. 210–11; H.S. Wilson, *African Decolonization* (London, 1994), pp. 154–60; Young, *Britain and the World*, p. 165; Armstrong and Goldstein, 'Interaction with the Non-European World', pp. 256–7; Sanders, *Losing an Empire*, pp. 89–90; A. Roussillon, 'Republican Egypt Interpreted: Revolution and Beyond', in *Cambridge History of Egypt*, C.F. Petry and M.W. Daly (eds) (2 vols, Cambridge, 1998), Vol. 2, pp. 334–93.

25 Reynolds, *Britannia Overruled*, p. 191; Kantowicz, *Coming Apart, Coming Together*, pp. 195–6; Sked and Cook, *Post-War Britain*, p. 129; Fraser and Murray, *America and the World*, p. 73; Armstrong and Goldstein, 'Interaction with the Non-European World', p. 257; D. Carlton, *Britain and the Suez Crisis* (Oxford, 1988), pp. 27–8, 31–3; K. Kyle, *Suez* (London, 1991), pp. 132–4, and idem, 'Britain and the Crisis, 1955–56', in *Suez 1956: The Crisis and its Consequences*, W.R. Louis and R. Owen (eds) (Oxford, 1989), pp. 105–13; R. Lamb, *The Failure of the Eden Government* (London, 1987), Ch. 8; H. Beeley, 'The Middle East', in Louis and Bull, *The 'Special Relationship'*, p. 288; Woodward, *Nasser*, pp. 45–9.

26 Immerman, *John Foster Dulles*, pp. 149–50.

27 *The Times*, 28 July 1956; *Hansard*, 5th series, 544 (1955), cols 353–5, 821–3; 545 (1955), cols 64–5; 557 (1956), cols 411, 918–21, 1602–1721.

28 Ovendale, *Transfer of Power in the Middle East*, pp. 147–8; Carlton, *Britain and the Suez Crisis*, pp. 23–5; Nutting, *No End of a Lesson*, pp. 21–2; E. Shuckburgh, *Descent to Suez: Diaries, 1951–56* (London, 1986), pp. 155, 327, 346; A. Adamthwaite, 'Suez Revisited', *International Affairs*, 64 (1988), pp. 451–2, 463.

29 Nutting, *No End of a Lesson*, pp. 27, 29; Lapping, *End of Empire*, p. 316; Carlton, *Britain and the Suez Crisis*, pp. 28–30.

30 Ovendale, *Transfer of Power in the Middle East*, pp. 148–51, 154.

31 Andrew, *For the President's Eyes Only*, pp. 224–7.

32 Shuckburgh, *Descent to Suez*, p. 336; Ovendale, *Transfer of Power in the Middle East*, pp. 152–5, and idem, *British Defence Policy*, pp. 97, 110–11; Kantowicz, *Coming Apart, Coming Together*, pp. 196, 199; Reynolds, *Britannia Overruled*, pp. 191–2; Kyle, *Suez*, Ch. 7, and idem, 'Britain and the Crisis', pp. 113–23; M. Vaisse, 'France and the Suez Crisis', in Louis and Owen, *Suez 1956*, pp. 131–43; Carlton, *Britain and the Suez Crisis*, Ch. 3; Lamb, *Failure of the Eden Government*, Chs 9 and 10; Thorpe, *Eden*, pp. 463–4, 465–6, 473–87; Dutton, *Anthony Eden*, pp. 372–89; *Hansard*, 5th series, 558 (1956), cols 5–6, 15.

33 Thorpe, *Eden*, p. 508; Reynolds, 'Eden the Diplomatist', p. 73.

34 Ovendale, *Transfer of Power in the Middle East*, pp. 171–2.

35 Kyle, 'Britain and the Crisis', pp. 113–15, and idem, *Suez*, p. 199; Kantowicz, *Coming Apart, Coming Together*, pp. 196, 200–1; Sked and Cook, *Post-War Britain*, p. 130; Reynolds, *Britannia Overruled*, p. 192; Dutton, *Anthony Eden*, pp. 389–415; Fraser and Murray, *America and the World*, p. 74; Immerman, *John Foster Dulles*, pp. 149–51; R. Bowie, 'Eisenhower, Dulles and the Suez Crisis', in Louis and Owen, *Suez 1956*, pp. 189–214; Marks, *Power and Peace*, pp. 29–30, 125–7.

36 Immerman, *John Foster Dulles*, pp. 149–51; Marks, *Power and Peace*, pp. 30–2; Sked and Cook, *Post-War Britain*, pp. 130–1; D.B. Kunz, 'The Importance of Having Money: The Economic Diplomacy of the Suez Crisis', in Louis and Owen, *Suez 1956*, pp. 215–32.

37 Bowie, 'Eisenhower, Dulles and the Suez Crisis', pp. 202–7; Kyle, *Suez*, pp. 212–13; L.D. Epstein, *British Politics in the Suez Crisis* (London, 1964), pp. 32–5.

38 A. Gorst and L. Johnman, *The Suez Crisis* (London, 1997), pp. 90–103; Carlton, *Britain and the Suez Crisis*, pp. 42–4, 47, 49, 52–3, 56–7, 58–68; Reynolds, *Britannia Overruled*, p. 192; Kantowicz, *Coming Apart, Coming Together*, p. 200; Sked and Cook, *Post-War Britain*, p. 131; Vaisse, 'France and the Suez Crisis', pp. 131–43; Kyle, *Suez*, Ch. 17; M. Larkin, *France since the Popular Front: Government and People, 1936–96* (Oxford, 1997), Ch. 13; R.F. Betts, *France and Decolonization, 1900–60* (Basingstoke, 1991), p. 96.

39 Bartlett, *Long Retreat*, pp. 120–2; Beeley, 'Middle East', p. 289.

40 W.S. Lucas, 'The Path to Suez: Britain and the Struggle for the Middle East, 1953–56', in Deighton, *Britain and the First Cold War*, pp. 253–72. There are detailed accounts of the deliberations of Eden and his colleagues in Dutton, *Anthony Eden*, Chs 12 and 13, and Thorpe, *Eden*, Chs 17–19.

41 *Hansard*, 5th series, 558 (1956), cols 1274–76.

42 Bartlett, *Long Retreat*, pp. 122–4.

43 *Daily Mail*, 1, 2 November 1956; *Daily Express*, 31 October, 7 November 1956; *The Times*, 1 November 1956.

44 Bartlett, *Long Retreat*, pp. 123–4.

45 Kyle, *Suez*, Chs 24–5, 27; Bartlett, *Special Relationship*, pp. 77–87; Baylis, *Anglo-*

American Defence Relations, pp. 72–3; Armstrong and Goldstein, 'Interaction with the Non-European World', pp. 242, 257; Fraser and Murray, *America and the World*, p. 74; Kantowicz, *Coming Apart, Coming Together*, pp. 197–8; Naidu, *Collective Security and the United Nations*, pp. 139–42; W.R. Louis, 'American Anti-Colonialism and the Dissolution of the British Empire', in Louis and Bull, *The 'Special Relationship'*, pp. 273–9; Parmet, *Eisenhower and the American Crusades*, pp. 470–87; Ambrose, *Eisenhower*, pp. 415–16, 420–34; Sked and Cook, *Post-War Britain*, p. 132; Beeley, 'Middle East', pp. 289–90; D. Goldsworthy, *Colonial Issues in British Politics, 1945–61* (Oxford, 1971), pp. 295–300; Gorst and Johnman, *Suez Crisis*, pp. 122–3, 126–33, 137–45; Carlton, *Britain and the Suez Crisis*, pp. 69–92.

46 Coker, 'Foreign and Defence Policy', pp. 6–7; Young, *Britain and the World*, pp. 165–7; Armstrong and Goldstein, 'Interaction with the Non-European World', p. 257; Bartlett, *Long Retreat*, pp. 122–3; Darwin, *Britain and Decolonization*, pp. 228–9; Sked and Cook, *Post-War Britain*, pp. 132–3; Immerman, *John Foster Dulles*, p. 151; R.R. James, *Anthony Eden* (London, 1986), p. 373; Reynolds, *Britannia Overruled*, pp. 191–4, and idem, 'Eden the Diplomatist', p. 72.

47 *Khrushchev Remembers*, S. Talbott (ed.) (Boston MA, 1970), pp. 435–56; Nutting, *No End of a Lesson*, pp. 133–4.

48 Nutting, *No End of a Lesson*, pp. 141, 145; *The Times*, 7, 8 November 1956.

49 Bartlett, *Long Retreat*, pp. 125–7, 161–2.

50 Watt, 'Demythologizing the Eisenhower Era', pp. 77–8; Cable, *Geneva Conference*, p. 135; Immerman, *John Foster Dulles*, pp. 151–2; Dutton, *Anthony Eden*, pp. 390–1, 412, 444, 481; Thorpe, *Eden*, p. 500.

51 B.I. Kaufman, *The Arab Middle East and the United States: Inter-Arab Rivalry and Superpower Diplomacy* (New York, 1996); W.S. Lucas and R. Takeyh, '"Alliance" and Balance: The Anglo-American Relationship and Egyptian Nationalism, 1950–57', *Diplomacy and Statecraft*, 8 (1997), pp. 631–51; R. Takeyh, *The Origins of the Eisenhower Doctrine* (Basingstoke, 2000).

52 Watt, 'Demythologizing the Eisenhower Era', p. 83, and idem, *Succeeding John Bull*, pp. 131–3; Dutton, *Anthony Eden*, p. 390; Bowie, 'Eisenhower, Dulles and the Suez Crisis', pp. 213–14; Reynolds, 'Eden the Diplomatist', pp. 79–83.

53 P.L. Hahn, 'Discord or Partnership? British and American Policy toward Egypt, 1942–56', in Cohen and Kolinsky, *Demise of the British Empire*, pp. 162–82; Kunz, 'Importance of Having Money', p. 231.

54 Reynolds, *Britannia Overruled*, p. 193; Sked and Cook, *Post-War Britain*, pp. 135–6; Adamthwaite, 'Suez Revisited', p. 448; Darwin, *Britain and Decolonization*, pp. 228–32; Coker, 'Foreign and Defence Policy', p. 6; Bartlett, *Long Retreat*, p. 121; Fraser and Murray, *America and the World*, pp. 74–5; Marks, *Power and Peace*, p. 153; W.P. Kirkman, *Unscrambling an Empire: A Critique of British Colonial Policy, 1956–66* (London, 1966), p. 152.

55   Larres, 'International and Security Relations', p. 212; Sked and Cook, *Post-War Britain*, pp. 135–6; Coker, 'Foreign and Defence Policy', p. 7; Reynolds, *Britannia Overruled*, p. 193; Dockrill, *Eisenhower's New Look*, p. 163; Clayton, *Wars of French Decolonization*, pp. 124–5; Kantowicz, *Coming Apart, Coming Together*, p. 203; Immerman, *John Foster Dulles*, p. 152; Armstrong and Goldstein, 'Interaction with the Non-European World', pp. 257–8; S. Gopal, 'Nehru and the Commonwealth', in Dilks, *Retreat from Power*, Vol. 2, pp. 142–7.

56   Van Eekelen, *Debating European Security*, p. 10; M. Vaisse, 'Post-Suez France', in Louis and Owen *Suez 1956*, pp. 335–40; Betts, *France and Decolonization*, Ch. 7.

57   Adamthwaite, 'Suez Revisited', pp. 455–63; Kirkman, *Unscrambling an Empire*, pp. 202–3; Goldsworthy, *Colonial Issues in British Politics*, p. 300; Kennedy, *Realities behind Diplomacy*, pp. 332–7; Sked and Cook, *Post-War Britain*, p. 136; Turner, 'Governors, Governance, and Governed', pp. 27–8; Harris, 'Tradition and Transformation', p. 121; Epstein, *British Politics in the Suez Crisis*, p. 140; L. Black, '"The Bitterest Enemies of Communism": Labour Revisionists, Atlanticism and the Cold War', *Contemporary British History*, 15 (2001), pp. 26–62.

58   Lord Beloff, 'The Crisis and its Consequences for the British Conservative Party', in Louis and Owen, *Suez 1956*, pp. 319–34; Gorst and Johnman, *Suez Crisis*, pp. 147–9.

59   Lamb, *Failure of the Eden Government*, p. 243; Carlton, *Britain and the Suez Crisis*, pp. 67–8, 93; Dutton, *Anthony Eden*, pp. 456–8; Thorpe, *Eden*, p. 542; A. Horne, *Macmillan* (2 vols, London, 1988–89), Vol. 1, pp. 418–25; McNamara, *Britain, Nasser and the Balance of Power*, p. 283; Ruane and Ellison, 'Managing the Americans', pp. 147–67.

60   Carlton, *Britain and the Suez Crisis*, pp. 106–8; Epstein, *British Politics in the Suez Crisis*, pp. 28–9, 142; R. Skidelsky, 'Lessons of Suez', in *The Age of Affluence, 1951–64*, V. Bogdanor and R. Skidelsky (eds) (London, 1970), pp. 188–9; Darwin, *Britain and Decolonization*, pp. 166, 228–32; A. Low and B. Lapping, 'Did Suez Hasten the End of Empire?' *Contemporary Record*, 1 (1987), pp. 31–3; Goldsworthy, 'Keeping Change within Bounds', pp. 81–108; Darby, *Defence Policy East of Suez*, pp. 56–68.

61   Pickering, *Britain's Withdrawal from East of Suez*, pp. 88–9, 100, 102, 115–17.

62   Lord Ennals, 'The United Nations Association: The People's Voice', in Jensen and Fisher, *United Kingdom – United Nations*, pp. 261–3.

63   Naidu, *Collective Security and the United Nations*, pp. 47–8, 58, 67, 72–3, 81, 103–4.

64   Parsons, 'Britain and the Security Council', pp. 52–3; B. Urquhart, 'UN Peacekeeping: From Observers to the Peace Prize', in Jensen and Fisher, *United Kingdom – United Nations*, pp. 71–3; M.G. Fry, 'Canada, the North Atlantic and the UN', in Louis and Owen, *Suez 1956*, pp. 285–316; *Hansard*, 5th series, 560 (1956), cols 421–7; Kyle, *Suez*, p. 512.

65 *Hansard*, 5th series, 558 (1956), cols 1882–86, 1946–55; 560 (1956), cols 48–9.

66 G. Schopflin, *Politics in Eastern Europe, 1945–92* (Oxford, 1993), Ch. 5; Sassoon, 'Politics', pp. 30–1; Larres, 'International and Security Relations', pp. 210–11; Kantowicz, *Coming Apart, Coming Together*, p. 345; G. Swain and N. Swain, *Eastern Europe since 1945* (Basingstoke, 1998), pp. 79–89; I.T. Berend, *Central and Eastern Europe, 1944–93* (Cambridge, 1996), pp. 99–126, and idem, 'Central and Eastern European Revolution', pp. 190–1; Fraser and Murray, *America and the World*, pp. 71–2; Gaddis, *We Now Know*, pp. 208–11.

67 Zubok and Pleshakov, *Inside the Kremlin's Cold War*, pp. 183, 186–7; Kantowicz, *Coming Apart, Coming Together*, p. 348; Larres, 'International and Security Relations', pp. 210–11; Sassoon, 'Politics', p. 31; Fraser and Murray, *America and the World*, p. 72; Marks, *Power and Peace*, p. 89; Parmet, *Eisenhower and the American Crusades*, p. 486; C. Gati, *Hungary and the Soviet Bloc* (Durham NC, 1986), pp. 219–21; T. Hoopes, *The Devil and John Foster Dulles* (Boston MA, 1973), p. 131.

68 Ambrose, *Eisenhower*, pp. 422–3; Dockrill, *Eisenhower's New Look*, pp. 154, 158–67; Immerman, *John Foster Dulles*, pp. 152–4; G. Litvan, J.M. Bak and L.H. Legters, *The Hungarian Revolution of 1956* (London, 1996), pp. 91–4.

69 Litvan, Bak and Legters, *Hungarian Revolution*, pp. 94–5.

70 Thorpe, *Eden*, pp. 520, 524; Dutton, *Anthony Eden*, p. 434.

71 *Hansard*, 5th series, 560 (1956), cols 113–17.

72 *Manchester Guardian*, 5 November 1956; *The Times*, 8 November 1956.

73 Litvan, Bak and Legters, *Hungarian Revolution*, pp. 96–99.

74 Kantowicz, *Coming Apart, Coming Together*, pp. 201–2; Woodward, *Nasser*, Chs 4 and 5; H.F. Eilts, 'Reflections on the Suez Crisis: Security in the Middle East', R. Owen, 'The Economic Consequences of the Suez Crisis for Egypt', and R. Khalidi, 'Consequences of the Suez Crisis in the Arab World', all in Louis and Owen, *Suez 1956*, pp. 347–61, 363–75, 377–92; S. Bialer, *Stalin's Successors: Leadership, Stability and Change in the Soviet Union* (Cambridge, 1980), p. 271.

75 Eden, *Full Circle*, p. 558.

76 Eden, *Full Circle*, pp. 558–9, 577.

77 Eden, *Full Circle*, pp. 558–9, 584.

Notes to Chapter 6: Finding a Role?

1 Sked and Cook, *Post-War Britain*, pp. 138–9; Fraser and Murray, *America and the World*, p. 74; Dobson, *Anglo-American Relations*, pp. 117–20; Bartlett, *Special Relationship*, pp. 88–90; Sanders, *Losing an Empire*, pp. 171–3; H. Macmillan, *Riding the Storm, 1956–59* (London, 1971), pp. 240, 242; Horne, *Macmillan*, Vol. 2, pp. 45–51.

2   Reynolds, *Britannia Overruled*, pp. 199–200; Sked and Cook, *Post-War Britain*, p. 140; Young, *Britain and the World*, p. 181; F.S. Northedge, *Descent from Power: British Foreign Policy, 1945–73* (London, 1974), p. 290; Dobson, *Anglo-American Relations*, p. 119; Bartlett, *Special Relationship*, pp. 89–91; Fraser and Murray, *America and the World*, pp. 75, 79–81; Dockrill, *British Defence*, pp. 78–9.

3   D. Eisenhower, *Waging Peace, 1956–61* (New York, 1965), pp. 178–83; S.E. Ambrose, *Eisenhower The President* (London, 1984), pp. 381–8; T.G. Fraser, *The USA and the Middle East since World War Two* (Basingstoke, 1989), pp. 73–6; N. Ashton, 'Macmillan and the Middle East', in *Harold Macmillan and Britain's World Role*, R. Aldous and S. Lee (eds) (Basingstoke, 1996), pp. 51–3.

4   G. Balfour-Paul, *The End of Empire in the Middle East* (Cambridge, 1991), pp. 118, 144–5; Ashton, 'Macmillan and the Middle East', p. 61; Darby, *Defence Policy East of Suez*, pp. 145–56.

5   *Hansard*, 5th series, 591 (1958), cols 1438–39, 1506–60. Britain's relationship with Jordan remained close in subsequent years, but it was no mere throwback to the imperial past, for the initiative often came from the Jordanian side. N. Ashton, '"A *'Special Relationship'* Sometimes in Spite of Ourselves": Britain and Jordan, 1957–73', *Journal of Imperial and Commonwealth History*, 33 (2005), pp. 221–44.

6   *The Times*, 17, 18 July 1958.

7   Horne, *Macmillan*, Vol. 2, pp. 94–8; Macmillan, *Riding the Storm*, pp. 243, 516–26; J. Turner, *Macmillan* (London, 1994), pp. 205–7; Baylis, *Anglo-American Defence Relations*, pp. 63–4; Ovendale, *British Defence Policy*, pp. 119–21; Watt, *Succeeding John Bull*, pp. 134–5; Ambrose, *Eisenhower The President*, pp. 462–7, 469–75.

8   Sked and Cook, *Post-War Britain*, pp. 137, 139–40; Baylis, *Anglo-American Defence Relations*, pp. 57–63; Dobson, *Anglo-American Relations*, pp. 118–19; Bartlett, *Special Relationship*, pp. 88–90; Ovendale, *British Defence Policy*, pp. 10–11, 113–16; Eisenhower, *Waging Peace*, pp. 121–5.

9   Coker, 'Foreign and Defence Policy', p. 13; C. Gordon, 'Duncan Sandys and the Independent Nuclear Deterrent', in *Politicians and Defence: Studies in the Formulation of British Defence Policy, 1845–1970*, I. Beckett and J. Gooch (eds) (Manchester, 1981), pp. 132–53; Dockrill, *British Defence since 1945*, pp. 51, 65–71; Young, *Britain and the World*, p. 171; Reynolds, *Britannia Overruled*, pp. 198–9, and idem, 'Britain and the World since 1945', p. 168; Northedge, *Descent from Power*, pp. 289–91; Ovendale, *British Defence Policy*, pp. 8, 10, 13, 16, 113–15; Sked and Cook, *Post-War Britain*, pp. 141–2; Bartlett, *Long Retreat*, pp. 132–44; Turner, *Macmillan*, pp. 128–9, 133, 137–9, 154; Horne, *Macmillan*, Vol. 2, pp. 45–51; Pierre, *Nuclear Politics*, pp. 161–2, 194–5.

10   *The Times*, 17 April 1957.

11   *Hansard*, 5th series, 568 (1957), cols 1758–1878, 1929–2059.

12   M. Navias, 'Terminating Conscription? The British National Service Controversy, 1955–56', *Journal of Contemporary History*, 24 (1989), pp. 195–208; W. Rees, 'The 1957 Sandys White Paper: New Priorities in British Defence Policy?' *Journal of Strategic Studies*, 12 (1989), pp. 215–19; Pickering, *Britain's Withdrawal from East of Suez*, p. 103; M. Chalmers, *Paying for Defence: Military Spending and British Decline* (London, 1985), pp. 66–72.

13   Dobson, *Anglo-American Relations*, pp. 119–20; Bartlett, *Special Relationship*, pp. 92–4, and idem, *Long Retreat*, p. 137; Sked and Cook, *Post-War Britain*, p. 142; Reynolds, *Britannia Overruled*, p. 198; Navias, 'Terminating Conscription?' pp. 202–5; Northedge, *Descent from Power*, p. 291; Dockrill, *British Defence since 1945*, pp. 68, 71–2; May and Treverton, 'Defence Relationships: American Perspectives', p. 168; E.J. Grove, *Vanguard to Trident: British Naval Policy since World War Two* (Annapolis MD, 1987), pp. 200, 203, 213–15.

14   Baylis, *Anglo-American Defence Relations*, pp. 60–1; A.L. Friedberg, 'The United States and the Cold War Arms Race', in Westad, *Reviewing the Cold War*, pp. 209–10; R. Dietl, 'Une déception amoureuse? Great Britain, the Continent and European Nuclear Co-operation, 1953–57', *Cold War History*, 3 (2002), pp. 29–66.

15   D. Murray, *Kennedy, Macmillan and Nuclear Weapons* (Basingstoke, 2000) pp. 18–19; T.J. Botti, *The Long Wait: The Forging of the Anglo-American Nuclear Alliance, 1945–58* (Westport CT, 1987), pp. 175, 182–3, 187, 199–200, 210.

16   Botti, *Long Wait*, pp. 185–6, 196, 226–7, 229, 234, 238–9.

17   J. Simpson, *The Independent Nuclear State: The United States, Britain and the Military Atom* (London, 1983), pp. 124–5.

18   Bartlett, *Long Retreat*, pp. 147–8; Pierre, *Nuclear Politics*, pp. 142–4; Simpson, *Independent Nuclear State*, pp. 226–7, 238–9; Botti, *Long Wait*, pp. 240–1; Ovendale, *British Defence Policy*, pp. 117–19.

19   B. Heuser, 'The Development of NATO's Nuclear Strategy', *Contemporary European History*, 4 (1994), pp. 44–5.

20   K. Pyne, 'Art or Article? The Need for and Nature of the British Hydrogen Bomb, 1954–58', *Contemporary Record*, 9 (1995), pp. 562–85; Sked and Cook, *Post-War Britain*, p. 143; Ovendale, *British Defence Policy*, pp. 113–16; Young, *Britain and the World*, p. 171; Reynolds, *Britannia Overruled*, p. 200; Horne, *Macmillan*, Vol. 2, pp. 275–7, 428–3; H. Macmillan, *Pointing the Way, 1959–61* (London, 1972), pp. 249–56; Kennedy, *Realities behind Diplomacy*, pp. 374–5; J. Dumbrell, *A Special Relationship: Anglo-American Relations in the Cold War and After* (Basingstoke, 2001), p. 48; Dobson, *Anglo-American Relations*, p. 120; Bartlett, *Special Relationship*, pp. 93, 98, and idem, *Long Retreat*, pp. 154–6; Murray, *Kennedy, Macmillan and Nuclear Weapons*, Ch. 2.

21   Watt, *Succeeding John Bull*, pp. 135–6; A.P. Dobson, 'Informally Special? The Churchill-Truman Talks of January 1952 and the State of Anglo-American

Relations', *Review of International Studies, 23* (1997), pp. 27–47, and idem, *Anglo-American Relations*; Ball, 'Military Nuclear Relations', pp. 439–54; Pierre, *Nuclear Politics*, pp. 196–9, 321.

22   Navias, 'Terminating Conscription?' pp. 195–208; Rees, 'Sandys White Paper', pp. 225–6; Pickering, *Britain's Withdrawal from East of Suez*, pp. 103–7.

23   *Hansard*, 5th series, 625 (1960), cols 394–406; *The Times*, 26 September 1960; *Economist*, 22 October 1960.

24   S. Ball, 'Macmillan and British Defence Policy', in Aldous and Lee, *Macmillan and Britain's World Role*, pp. 74–5, 91–2.

25   Pierre, *Nuclear Politics*, p. 320; Coker, 'Foreign and Defence Policy', p. 6; Dockrill, *British Defence since 1945*, pp. 71–7; Young, *Britain and the World*, p. 171; Reynolds, *Britannia Overruled*, pp. 198–9, 202–3; Gowing, 'Nuclear Weapons and the Special Relationship', pp. 123–4; Pierre, *Nuclear Politics*, pp. 217–43; Baylis, *Anglo-American Defence Relations*, p. 77; Simpson, *Independent Nuclear State*, pp. 137–8; M.M. Harrison, *The Reluctant Ally: France and Atlantic Security* (London, 1981), pp. 96–7.

26   Darwin, *End of the British Empire*, pp. 7, 114–22; Lapping, *End of Empire*, pp. 317–49, 405–44; Kahler, *Decolonization in Britain and France*, pp. 142–60; Holland, *Pursuit of Greatness*, pp. 295–302; M. Kitchen, *The British Empire and Commonwealth* (Basingstoke, 1996), pp. 103–4, 111, 123–4, 128, 147; Young, *Britain and the World*, pp. 180–3; Kantowicz, *Coming Apart, Coming Together*, pp. 255–7; Sked and Cook, *Post-War Britain*, pp. 143–7; Reynolds, *Britannia Overruled*, pp. 209–10; Hollowell, 'Commonwealth to European Integration', pp. 68–9; J.D. Hargreaves, *Decolonization in Africa* (London, 1996), pp. 170–81, 200–7; P.E. Hemming, 'Macmillan and the End of the British Empire in Africa', in Aldous and Lee, *Macmillan and Britain's World Role*, p. 118.

27   C.K. Mark, 'Defence or Decolonization? Britain, the United States and the Hong Kong Question in 1957', *Journal of Imperial and Commonwealth History, 33* (2005), pp. 51–72.

28   Goldsworthy, 'Keeping Change within Bounds', pp. 81–108; D.J. Morgan, *The Official History of Colonial Development* (5 vols, London, 1980), Vol. 5, pp. 100–2, and Ch. 5 for the period from 1957 to 1961 as a whole.

29   Wilson, *African Decolonization*, pp. 171–2; D.K. Fieldhouse, *Black Africa, 1945–80: Economic Decolonization and Arrested Development* (London, 1986), pp. 7–9; R. Holland, *European Decolonization, 1918–81* (Basingstoke, 1985), Chs 7–9; P. Kennedy, *Strategy and Diplomacy: Eight Studies* (London, 1989), pp. 217–18.

30   W.D. McIntyre, *The Commonwealth of Nations: Origins and Impact, 1869–1971* (Minneapolis MN, 1977), pp. 389, 450; R. Ovendale, 'Macmillan and the Wind of Change in Africa, 1957–60', *Historical Journal, 38* (1995), pp. 455–77; Holland, *Pursuit of Greatness*, p. 301.

31   J. Kent, 'United States Reactions to Empire, Colonialism and Cold War in Black

Africa, 1949–57', *Journal of Imperial and Commonwealth Affairs, 33* (2005), pp. 195–220; Macmillan, *Pointing the Way*, pp. 155–60, 163–4; Hargreaves, *Decolonization in Africa*, p. 204.

32 A. Mohiddin, *African Socialism in Two Countries* (London, 1981), pp. 54, 56, 73, 83; A. Low, 'The End of the British Empire in Africa', in *Decolonization and African Independence: The Transfers of Power, 1960–80*, P. Gifford and W.R. Louis (eds) (London, 1988), pp. 70–2; D. Austin, 'The British Point of No Return?' in *The Transfer of Power in Africa: Decolonization, 1940–60*, P. Gifford and W.R. Louis (eds) (London, 1982), pp. 231, 238, 246–7.

33 Darwin, *Britain and Decolonization*, Ch. 6.

34 S. Strange, *Sterling and British Policy: A Political Study of an International Currency in Decline* (London, 1971); A. Hinds, *Britain's Sterling Colonial Policy and Decolonization, 1939–58* (Westport CT, 2001); G. Krozewski, *Money and the End of Empire: British International Economic Policy and the Colonies, 1947–58* (Basingstoke, 2001).

35 Hollowell, 'Commonwealth to European Integration', pp. 59–60; Sked and Cook, *Post-War Britain*, pp. 147–50; G. de Carmoy, 'Defence and Unity of Western Europe since 1958', in Waites, *Troubled Neighbours*, pp. 346–8; Greenwood, *Britain and European Co-operation*, pp. 62–78; Gowland and Turner, *Britain and European Integration*, pp. 49, 51–60, 88–90; P. Messmer, 'De Gaulle's Defence Policy and the United States', in *De Gaulle and the United States: A Centennial Reappraisal*, R.O. Paxton and N. Wahl (eds) (Oxford, 1994), pp. 351–7; W.C. Cromwell, *The United States and the European Pillar: The Strained Alliance* (Basingstoke, 1992), pp. 26–37; M. Camps, *Britain and the European Community, 1955–63* (London, 1965), Chs 4 and 5; H. Simonian, *The Privileged Partnership: Franco-German Relations in the European Community, 1969–84* (Oxford, 1985), p. 34; J. Lacouture, *De Gaulle: The Ruler, 1945–70*, translated by A. Sheridan (London, 1991), pp. 333–4.

36 F. Lynch, 'De Gaulle's First Veto: France, the Rueff Plan and the Free Trade Area', *Contemporary European History, 9* (2000), pp. 111–35; Simonian, *Privileged Partnership*, pp. 24, 33–4; M.P.C. Schaad, *Bullying Bonn: Anglo-German Diplomacy on European Integration, 1955–61* (New York, 2000).

37 Young, *Britain and European Unity*, pp. 44–56, and idem, 'The Parting of the Ways? Britain, the Messina Conference and the Spaak Committee, June-December 1955', in Dockrill and Young, *British Foreign Policy, 1945–56*, pp. 197–224; Kaiser, *Using Europe*, Ch. 3; Lamb, *Failure of the Eden Government*, pp. 96–8, 101.

38 Lamb, *Failure of the Eden Government*, pp. 99–101; Gowland and Turner, *Britain and European Integration*, pp. 88–9; S. Greenwood, 'Not the "General Will" but the "Will of the General": The Input of the Paris Embassy to the British "Great Debate" on Europe, Summer 1960', *Contemporary British History, 18* (2004), pp. 177–88; A. McKinlay, H. Mercer and N. Rollings, 'Reluctant Europeans? The

Federation of British Industries and European Integration, 1945–63', *Business History, 42* (2000), pp. 91–116.

39   Young, *Britain and European Unity*, pp. 57–71, and idem, *Britain and the World*, p. 188; Eichengreen, 'Economy', pp. 119, 121; Sked and Cook, *Post-War Britain*, pp. 150–1; P.M.R. Stirk, *A History of European Integration since 1914* (London, 1996), pp. 146–9; Camps, *Britain and the European Community*, Chs 6 and 7; Kaiser, *Using Europe*, Ch. 4; Greenwood, *Britain and European Co-operation*, pp. 71–3; Gowland and Turner, *Britain and European Integration*, pp. 51–3, 89–90; D.W. Urwin, *A Political History of Western Europe since 1945* (London, 1998), Ch. 9.

40   Charlton, *Price of Victory*, pp. 215–17; Camps, *Britain and the European Community*, pp. 506, 510–12.

41   *Hansard*, 5th series, 624 (1960), cols 677–9; Macmillan, *Pointing the Way*, pp. 57–9.

42   S. George, *Britain and European Integration since 1945* (Oxford, 1991), pp. 42–3; Kaiser, *Using Europe*, pp. 105–6; Gowland and Turner, *Britain and European Integration*, pp. 49, 51–3.

43   J.G. Giauque, 'The United States and the Political Union of Western Europe, 1958–63', *Contemporary European History, 9* (2000), pp. 93–110; Lundestad, 'Empire' by Integration, pp. 51–2; Gowland and Turner, *Britain and European Integration*, pp. 49, 51–60, 88–90.

44   N. Crafts, 'Forging Ahead and Falling Behind: The Rise and Relative Decline of the First Industrial Nation', *Journal of Economic Perspectives, 12* (1998), pp. 193–210; C. Bean and N. Crafts, 'British Economic Growth since 1945: Relative Economic Decline . . . and Renaissance?' in *Economic Growth in Europe since 1945*, N. Crafts and G. Toniolo (eds) (Cambridge, 1996), pp. 142–3.

45   See the essays in Crafts and Toniolo, *Economic Growth in Europe*, and also G. Toniolo, 'Europe's Golden Age, 1950–73: Speculations from a Long-Run Perspective', *Economic History Review, 51* (1998), pp. 252–67.

46   U. Kitzinger, *The European Common Market and Community* (London, 1967), pp. 24–5.

47   *The Times*, 27 September 1960.

48   Larres, 'International and Security Relations', pp. 211–12; Sked and Cook, *Post-War Britain*, p. 151; Young, *Britain and the World*, p. 175; J.G. Richter, *Khrushchev's Double Bind: International Pressures and Domestic Coalition Politics* (Baltimore, MD, 1994), p. 118.

49   *Observer*, 22 February 1959; *The Times*, 6, 20, 27 February 1959; J.M. Schick, *The Berlin Crisis, 1958–62* (Philadelphia PA, 1971), p. 60; J.P.S. Gearson, *Harold Macmillan and the Berlin Wall Crisis, 1958–62: The Limits of Interest and Force* (Basingstoke, 1998), pp. 75–8; R.W. Stevenson, *The Rise and Fall of Détente: Relaxations of Tension in US-Soviet Relations, 1953–84* (Basingstoke, 1985), pp. 81–2.

50   *Hansard*, 5th series, 596 (1958), cols 1022–23; 601 (1959), cols 448–53; 610 (1959), cols 11–12.

51   Johnson, *Modern World*, pp. 586–87, 599; Prittie, *Konrad Adenauer*, pp. 173, 236, 262–70; Granieri, *Ambivalent Alliance*, pp. 111–27; P. Alter, *The German Question and Europe: A History* (London, 2000), pp. 121–3, 127–8; Irving, *Adenauer*, pp. 130–9; M. Roseman, 'Division and Stability: The FRG, 1949–89', in *German History since 1800*, M. Fulbrook (ed.) (London, 1997), pp. 371–6; Lacouture, *De Gaulle*, pp. 333–9; E.A. Kolodziej, *French International Policy under De Gaulle and Pompidou: The Politics of Grandeur* (Ithaca NY, 1974), pp. 264–8; Simonian, *Privileged Partnership*, Ch. 2; Harrison, *Reluctant Ally*, pp. 105–6; G. Ambrosius and W.H. Hubbard, *A Social and Economic History of Twentieth-Century Europe* (Cambridge MA, 1989), pp. 298–301; Hanrieder, *Germany, America, Europe*, pp. 13–14, 163–9; A. Sampson, *Macmillan: A Study in Ambiguity* (London, 1967), p. 146; R. Challener, 'Dulles and De Gaulle', in Paxton and Wahl, *De Gaulle and the United States*, pp. 161–5.

52   H. Adomeit, *Imperial Overstretch: Germany in Soviet Policy from Stalin to Gorbachev* (Baden-Baden, 1998), pp. 51–7, 100–3, 159; J. van Oudenaren, *Détente in Europe: The Soviet Union and the West since 1953* (London, 1991); Zubok and Pleshakov, *Inside the Kremlin's Cold War*, pp. 194–200; Richter, *Khrushchev's Double Bind*, pp. 101–3, 106–18; Talbott, *Khrushchev Remembers*, pp. 452–4; J.G. Hershberg, 'The Crisis Years, 1958–63', in Westad, *Reviewing the Cold War*, pp. 305–7; Ulam, *Expansion and Coexistence*, pp. 618–22; Gaddis, *Long Peace*, pp. 230–1, W. Taubman, *Khrushchev: The Man and his Era* (New York, 2003), pp. 396–419.

53   Richter, *Khrushchev's Double Bind*, Ch. 5; Kantowicz, *Coming Apart, Coming Together*, pp. 285–9; Larres, 'International and Security Relations', p. 211; W. LaFeber, *America, Russia and the Cold War, 1945–2002* (Boston MA, 2002), pp. 212–14; Urwin, *Western Europe since 1945*, pp. 96–8; Hershberg, 'The Crisis Years' pp. 308–11.

54   Kantowicz, *Coming Apart, Coming Together*, p. 289; Larres, 'International and Security Relations', p. 212.

55   Turner, *Macmillan*, pp. 142–6; Horne, *Macmillan*, Vol. 2, p. 128; Macmillan, *Riding the Storm*, p. 656; W.J. Tompson, *Khrushchev: A Political Life* (Basingstoke, 1995), pp. 195–6, 203–4.

56   Gearson, *Macmillan and the Berlin Wall Crisis*, pp. 79–87; Turner, *Macmillan*, pp. 146–7.

57   Kolodziej, *French International Policy*, pp. 267–8; Ambrose, *Eisenhower*, pp. 482–3; O. Troyanovsky, 'The Making of Soviet Foreign Policy', in *Nikita Khrushchev*, W. Taubman, S. Khrushchev and A. Gleason (eds) (London, 2000), pp. 217–18, 220–1; Tompson, *Khrushchev*, pp. 195–6, 203–4.

58   Kantowicz, *Coming Apart, Coming Together*, pp. 289–90; Young, *Britain and*

the World, p. 175; Fraser and Murray, *America and the World*, pp. 84–6; Richter, *Khrushchev's Double Bind*, pp. 119–22; Taubman, *Khrushchev: The Man and His Era*, pp. 435–9, 443–9, 456–64; Tompson, *Khrushchev*, pp. 210–12, 219–29.

59   Fraser and Murray, *America and the World*, pp. 77–80, 84–6; Bartlett, *Special Relationship*, p. 94; Burk, *The British Isles since 1945*, pp. 2–3.

60   Stevenson, *Rise and Fall of Détente*, pp. 84–94; Ambrose, *Eisenhower*, pp. 492–4, 507–15; Eisenhower, *Waging Peace*, pp. 558–9.

61   Gearson, *Macmillan and the Berlin Wall Crisis*, pp. 118–27, 131–7, 142–56.

62   *The Times*, 18 May 1960; *Hansard*, 5th series, 624 (1960), cols 999–1010.

63   Gearson, *Macmillan and the Berlin Wall Crisis*, pp. 156–7.

64   Gearson, *Macmillan and the Berlin Wall Crisis*, pp. 157–9.

65   Fraser and Murray, *America and the World*, pp. 94–5; Johnson, *Modern World*, pp. 614–15; Kantowicz, *Coming Apart, Coming Together*, pp. 290–1; R. Reeves, *President Kennedy: Profile of Power* (London, 1993), pp. 36–42; Talbott, *Khrushchev Remembers*, pp. 458–9; Troyanovsky, 'Soviet Foreign Policy', pp. 229–31.

66   Fraser and Murray, *America and the World*, pp. 94–6; Bartlett, *Special Relationship*, pp. 95–6; L. Freedman, *Kennedy's Wars: Berlin, Cuba, Laos and Vietnam* (Oxford, 2000), pp. 51–65; Reeves, *President Kennedy*, Chs 13 and 14; J.C. Ausland, *Kennedy, Khrushchev and the Berlin-Cuba Crisis, 1961–64* (Oslo, 1996), pp. 1–12; Troyanovsky, 'Soviet Foreign Policy', pp. 230–1; Tompson, *Khrushchev*, pp. 232–5; F. Costigliola, 'The Pursuit of Atlantic Community: Nuclear Arms, Dollars and Berlin', in *Kennedy's Quest for Victory: American Foreign Policy, 1961–63*, T.G. Paterson (ed.) (New York, 1989), p. 38; Talbott, *Khrushchev Remembers*, p. 458.

67   R.J. Walton, *Cold War and Counterrevolution: The Foreign Policy of John F. Kennedy* (Baltimore MD, 1972), pp. 77–80; J.N. Giglio, *The Presidency of John F. Kennedy* (Lawrence KS, 1991), pp. 45, 72–9; T.G. Paterson, 'John F. Kennedy's Quest for Victory and Global Crisis', in Paterson, *Kennedy's Quest for Victory*, pp. 15–16, 22–3; Freedman, *Kennedy's Wars*, pp. 9, 417.

68   *Hansard*, 5th series, 642 (1961), cols 928–31; *Guardian*, 5 June 1961; *The Times*, 5 June 1961.

69   Fraser and Murray, *America and the World*, pp. 98–9; Ausland, *Kennedy, Khrushchev and the Berlin-Cuba Crisis*, pp. 13–21; Reeves, *President Kennedy*, Chs 17 and 18; Kantowicz, *Coming Apart, Coming Together*, pp. 291–2; H. Harrison, 'The GDR, the Soviet Union and the Berlin Wall Crisis', in *The Berlin Wall Crisis: Perspectives on Cold War Alliances*, J.P.S. Gearson and K. Schake (eds) (Basingstoke, 2002), p. 116.

70   Troyanovsky, 'Soviet Foreign Policy', pp. 232–3; Tompson, *Khrushchev*, pp. 236–7; Taubman, *Khrushchev: The Man and his Era*, p. 506; Talbott, *Khrushchev Remembers*, pp. 455–8, 460; Adomeit, *Imperial Overstretch*, pp. 103–9; Richter, *Khrushchev's Double Bind*, pp. 140–4.

71   *The Times*, 19 August 1961; *Hansard*, 5th series, 464 (1961), cols 26–30, 36, 314–18.

72   R.M. Slusser, *The Berlin Crisis of 1961* (London, 1973), pp. 129–32; Walton, *Cold War and Counterrevolution*, pp. 90–2; Freedman, *Kennedy's Wars*, p. 75.

73   Gearson, *Macmillan and the Berlin Wall Crisis*, pp. 191–4.

74   Gearson, *Macmillan and the Berlin Wall Crisis*, pp. 194–8.

75   D. Nunnerley, *President Kennedy and Britain* (London, 1972), pp. 68–9.

76   K.P. O'Donnell and D.F. Powers, *Johnny We Hardly Knew Ye: Memories of John Fitzgerald Kennedy* (Boston MA, 1972), pp. 304–6; Fraser and Murray, *America and the World*, pp. 99–101; Kantowicz, *Coming Apart, Coming Together*, p. 292; Reeves, *President Kennedy*, pp. 533–7; Ausland, *Kennedy, Khrushchev and the Berlin-Cuba Crisis*, pp. 73–6, 89; Walton, *Cold War and Counterrevolution*, pp. 149–53; Giglio, *Presidency of Kennedy*, pp. 80–8, 216–19.

77   *The Times*, 28 June 1963; *Hansard*, 5th series, 680 (1963), cols 198–200.

78   Freedman, *Kennedy's Wars*, pp. 72–91, 268–9; Troyanovsky, 'Soviet Foreign Policy', pp. 233–4; Tompson, *Khrushchev*, pp. 236–7; Slusser, *Berlin Crisis*, Ch. 9; G. Schild, 'The Berlin Crisis', in *Kennedy: The New Frontier Revisited*, M.J. White (ed.) (Basingstoke, 1998), pp. 91–123; L.F. Kaplan, 'The MLF Debate', in *John F. Kennedy and Europe*, D. Brinkley and R.T. Griffiths (eds) (Baton Rouge LA, 1999), pp. 51–65; Pierre, *Nuclear Politics*, pp. 243–51; Ovendale, *British Defence Policy*, p. 127; Dumbrell, *A Special Relationship*, pp. 125, 137–41; Harrison, *Reluctant Ally*, pp. 83–5.

79   Bartlett, *Special Relationship*, pp. 93, 95, 98–9; D. Brinkley, 'Dean Acheson and John Kennedy: Combating Strains in the Atlantic Alliance, 1962–63', in Brinkley and Griffiths, *Kennedy and Europe*, pp. 288–316; Heuser, 'NATO's Nuclear Strategy', pp. 45–6.

80   Ovendale, *British Defence Policy*, p. 127.

81   Eichengreen, 'Economy', p. 122; Sked and Cook, *Post-War Britain*, pp. 164–5; Coker, 'Foreign and Defence Policy', p. 7; Reynolds, *Britannia Overruled*, p. 200; Young, *Britain and the World*, p. 171; Baylis, *Anglo-American Defence Relations*, pp. 66–75; Dobson, *Anglo-American Relations*, pp. 120, 127–31; Bartlett, *Special Relationship*, pp. 98–100, and idem, *Long Retreat*, pp. 154–6, 175–9; Pierre, *Nuclear Politics*, pp. 217–43; Dockrill, *British Defence*, pp. 71–6.

82   Grove, *Vanguard to Trident*, pp. 242–4, 270, 273; Heuser, *NATO, Britain, France and the FRG*, pp. 70–1.

83   P. Oppenheimer, 'Muddling Through: The Economy, 1951–64', in Bogdanor and Skidelsky, *Age of Affluence*, pp. 117–67; Bean and Crafts, 'British Economic Growth', pp. 142–7; P. Howlett, 'The "Golden Age", 1955–73', in *Twentieth Century Britain: Economic, Social and Cultural Change*, P. Johnson (ed.) (London, 1996), pp. 320–4; J.C.R. Dow, *The Management of the British Economy, 1945–60* (Cambridge, 1970), p. 111. Dow is sceptical about the Conservative measures of

the 1950s, and according to some of the contributors to *The Labour Government's Economic Record, 1964–70*, W. Beckerman (ed.) (London, 1972), the more interventionist Labour approach was better.

84   V. Keegan, 'Industry and Technology', and L. Stone, 'Britain and the World', both in *The Decade of Disillusion: British Politics in the Sixties*, D. McKie and C. Cook (eds) (London, 1972), pp. 125–6, 140.

85   Macmillan, *Pointing the Way*, pp. 251–3; Ovendale, *British Defence Policy*, pp. 121–3; H. Nehring, 'The British and West German Protests against Nuclear Weapons and the Cultures of the Cold War, 1957–64', *Contemporary British History*, *19* (2005), pp. 223–41.

86   B.J. Firestone, 'Defence Policy as a Form of Arms Control: Nuclear Force Posture and Strategy under John F. Kennedy', in *John F. Kennedy: The Promise Revisited*, P. Harper and J.P. Krieg (eds) (Westport CT, 1988), pp. 57–69; Reynolds, *Britannia Overruled*, pp. 202–3; Coker, 'Foreign and Defence Policy', pp. 11–12; Sked and Cook, *Post-War Britain*, pp. 165–6; Baylis, *Anglo-American Defence Relations*, pp. 75–6; Bartlett, *Long Retreat*, pp. 158–60, 176–9; Pierre, *Nuclear Politics*, pp. 224–5; Dumbrell, *A Special Relationship*, p. 58.

87   R.E. Neustadt, *Report to JFK: The Skybolt Crisis in Perspective* (Ithaca NY, 1999); Murray, *Kennedy, Macmillan and Nuclear Weapons*, pp. 66–71.

88   Murray, *Kennedy, Macmillan and Nuclear Weapons*, pp. 74–80.

89   This is the line taken in I. Clark, *Nuclear Diplomacy and the Special Relationship: Britain's Deterrent and America, 1957–62* (London, 1994).

90   Neustadt, *Report to JFK*, p. 88.

91   Pierre, *Nuclear Politics*, pp. 231–72; Simpson, *Independent Nuclear State*, pp. 162–4, 167; Dobson, *Anglo-American Relations*, pp. 128–31; Baylis, *Anglo-American Defence Relations*, pp. 72–85; Dockrill, *British Defence*, pp. 74–88; Bartlett, *Long Retreat*, pp. 179–80; Reynolds, *Britannia Overruled*, p. 202; Sked and Cook, *Post-War Britain*, pp. 166–7; Horne, *Macmillan*, Vol. 2, pp. 437–43; Ovendale, *British Defence Policy*, pp. 125–7.

92   *The Times*, 22 December 1962; *Observer*, 23 December 1962.

93   Murray, *Kennedy, Macmillan and Nuclear Weapons*, pp. 93–8.

94   Nunnerley, *Kennedy and Britain*, pp. 144–5, 149, 160–1; Murray, *Kennedy, Macmillan and Nuclear Weapons*, pp. 98–103.

95   *Hansard*, 5th series, 670 (1963), cols 955–1074, 1139–1270; Thorpe, *Labour Party*, p. 155; P. Ziegler, *Wilson: The Authorized Life of Lord Wilson of Rievaulx* (London, 1993), pp. 148–9, 208.

96   Greenwood, *Britain and European Co-operation*, pp. 79–90; Sked and Cook, *Post-War Britain*, pp. 167–8, 173; Reynolds, *Britannia Overruled*, p. 203; Young, *Britain and the World*, p. 175; Bartlett, *Special Relationship*, pp. 99–101; Gowland and Turner, *Britain and European Integration*, pp. 54–60, 88; Harrison, *Reluctant Ally*, pp. 69, 79–80, 102.

97 Kaiser, *Using Europe*, p. 173; Baylis, *Anglo-American Defence Relations*, p. 73; Pierre, *Nuclear Politics*, pp. 161, 208, 214–15, 222–4, 234–5, 239–40, 245.

98 *Hansard*, 5th series, 646 (1961), cols 928–39, 1493–94, 1785–86.

99 Charlton, *Price of Victory*, pp. 293, 307; C.A. Pagedas, 'Harold Macmillan and the 1962 Champs Meeting', *Diplomacy and Statecraft*, 9 (1998), pp. 224–42.

100 S. Lee, 'Staying in the Game? Coming into the Game? Macmillan and European Integration', in Aldous and Lee, *Macmillan and Britain's World Role*, pp. 140–5.

101 Horne, *Macmillan*, Vol. 2, pp. 444–51; Macmillan, *Riding the Storm*, p. 435; Kaiser, *Using Europe*, pp. 197–9.

102 F. Costigliola, 'The Failed Design: Kennedy, De Gaulle and the Struggle for Europe', *Diplomatic History*, 8 (1984), pp. 227–51; Cromwell, *The United States and the European Pillar*, pp. 16–26.

103 L. Bell, *The Throw that Failed: Britain's 1961 Application to Join the Common Market* (London, 1995), p. 25; W.S. Lucas, 'The Cost of Myth: Macmillan and the Illusion of the "Special Relationship"', and N. Ashton, 'Managing Transition: Macmillan and the Utility of Anglo-American Relations', both in *Harold Macmillan: Aspects of a Political Life*, R. Aldous and S. Lee (eds) (London, 1999), pp. 16–31, 242–54.

104 N.P. Ludlow, *Dealing with Britain: The Six and the First UK Application to the EEC* (Cambridge, 1997), pp. 242, 244, and idem, '"Ne pleurez pas, Milord": Macmillan and France from Algiers to Rambouillet', in Aldous and Lee, *Macmillan: Aspects of a Political Life*, pp. 108–9.

105 On these points see *Britain's Failure to Enter the European Community, 1961–63: The Enlargement Negotiations and Crisis in European, Atlantic and Commonwealth Relations*, G. Wilkes (ed.) (London, 1987), especially M. Vaisse, 'De Gaulle and the British "Application" to join the Common Market', pp. 51–69; G. Schmidt, '"Master-minding" a New Western Europe: The Key Actors at Brussels in the Superpower Conflict', pp. 70–90; P. Gerbet, 'The Fouchet Negotiations for Political Union and the British Application', pp. 135–43; O. Bange, 'Grand Designs and the Diplomatic Breakdown', pp. 191–212.

106 K. Newman, 'Legal problems for British Accession', and S. Ward, 'Anglo-Commonwealth Relations and EEC Membership: The Problem of the Old Dominions', both in Wilkes, *Britain's Failure*, pp. 93–107, 120–32.

107 Cromwell, *The United States and the European Pillar*, pp. 37–41; Trachtenberg, *Constructed Peace*, pp. ix, 281.

108 *Hansard*, 5th series, 671 (1963), cols 239–40, 954–5, 962; *The Times*, 16 January 1963.

109 Kaiser, *Using Europe*, pp. 199–201.

110 Kaiser, *Using Europe*, p. 201; S. Ward, 'Kennedy, Britain and the European Community', in Brinkley and Griffiths, *Kennedy and Europe*, pp. 317–32.

111 Kaiser, *Using Europe*, pp. 201–2.

112 Young, *Britain and the World*, p. 175; Ovendale, *British Defence Policy*, pp. 129–30;

C. Leyzer, 'The Limited Test Ban Treaty of 1963', in Brinkley and Griffiths, *Kennedy and Europe*, pp. 95–115.

113   K. Oliver, *Kennedy, Macmillan and the Nuclear Test Ban Debate, 1961–63* (Basingstoke, 1998), pp. 14–18, 21, 134–7, 157–61, 163–83.

114   P.J. Briggs, 'Kennedy and Congress: The Nuclear Test Ban Treaty, 1963', in Harper and Krieg, *Kennedy: The Promise Revisited*, pp. 35–55; Horne, *Macmillan*, Vol. 2, pp. 503–11, 518, 522, 524–6, 528, 549.

115   Bartlett, *Special Relationship*, pp. 97–8; Oliver, *Kennedy, Macmillan and the Nuclear Test Ban Debate*, pp. 3, 42, 87, 94, 103, 117, 130, 180, 206; Dobson, *Anglo-American Relations*, p. 130; Nunnerley, *Kennedy and Britain*, p. 110.

116   Johnson, *Modern World*, p. 599; Turner, *Macmillan*, pp. 166–73; Sampson, *Macmillan: A Study in Ambiguity*, Ch. 15.

Notes to Chapter 7: Losing a Role?

1   Hemming, 'Macmillan and the End of the British Empire', p. 118.

2   Sked and Cook, *Post-War Britain*, pp. 175–9; Hanagan, 'Changing Margins', p. 129; Young, *Britain and the World*, p. 182; Hollowell, 'Commonwealth to European Integration', pp. 68–9; I.R.G. Spencer, *British Immigration Policy since 1939: The Making of Multiracial Britain* (London, 1997), pp. 129–34; R. Hattersley, 'Immigration', in McKie and Cook, *Decade of Disillusion*, pp. 184–6; Z. Layton-Henry, *The Politics of Immigration* (Oxford, 1992), pp. 75–7; Sampson, *Macmillan: A Study in Ambiguity*, pp. 191–2, 216–17; Dockrill, *British Defence*, p. 87; Kitchen, *British Empire and Commonwealth*, pp. 143–7.

3   These themes, and those in the next paragraph, are discussed in Gifford and Louis, *Decolonization and African Independence*.

4   D. Welsh, 'The Principle of the Thing: The Conservative Government and the Control of Commonwealth Immigration, 1957–59', *Contemporary British History*, 12 (1998), pp. 51–79; Kahler, *Decolonization in Britain and France*, pp. 156–7, 252, 255.

5   W.D. McIntyre, 'Britain and the Creation of the Commonwealth Secretariat', *Journal of Imperial and Commonwealth History*, 28 (2000), pp. 135–58; Darwin, *Britain and Decolonization*, pp. 304–5; R. Holland, 'The Imperial Factor in British Strategies from Attlee to Macmillan, 1945–63', *Journal of Imperial and Commonwealth History*, 12 (1984), pp. 183–4.

6   Reynolds, *Britannia Overruled*, pp. 209–10; Young, *Britain and the World*, pp. 146, 181–2; Hemming, 'Macmillan and the End of the British Empire', pp. 111–12; Macmillan, *Pointing the Way*, pp. 264–6; Darwin, *Britain and Decolonization*, p. 253; Baylis, *Anglo-American Defence Relations*, p. 66.

7   C. Young, *Politics in the Congo: Decolonization and Independence* (Princeton NJ,

1965), Chs 3, 12–13; I. Kabongo, 'The Catastrophe of Belgian Decolonization', in Gifford and Louis, *Decolonization and African Independence*, pp. 381–400; Kantowicz, *Coming Apart, Coming Together*, pp. 276–7, 279–80; Armstrong and Goldstein, 'Interaction with the Non-European World', p. 254; S. Meisler, *United Nations: The First Fifty Years* (New York, 1995), pp. 116–18, Ch. 7; Hargreaves, *Decolonization in Africa*, pp. 190–7; Darwin, *Britain and Decolonization*, p. 252; L.K. Johnson, *America's Secret Power* (New York, 1989), pp. 27–8; V. Marchetti and J.D. Marks, *The CIA and the Cult of Intelligence* (London, 1974), pp. 31, 117–18, 125–6; Jeffreys-Jones, *CIA and American Democracy*, pp. 97, 126–7, 138.

8 M.G. Kalb, *The Congo Cables: The Cold War in Africa from Eisenhower to Kennedy* (New York, 1982), pp. 289–90.

9 Kahler, *Decolonization in Britain and France*, pp. 145–8, 156, 281, 305.

10 Darwin, *Britain and Decolonization*, pp. 253–4.

11 Dumbrell, *A Special Relationship*, p. 51; Baylis, *Anglo-American Defence Relations*, p. 72; Turner, *Macmillan*, pp. 197–8; Nunnerley, *Kennedy and Britain*, pp. 201–4.

12 *Hansard*, 5th series, 636 (1961), cols 1486, 1517–19, 1523, 1525.

13 *Hansard*, 5th series, 671 (1963), cols 677–746; *The Times*, 17 January 1963.

14 Darwin, *Britain and Decolonization*, p. 255; Low 'End of the British Empire in Africa', pp. 42–3, 50, 56–7; Lapping, *End of Empire*, pp. 392, 437–8.

15 Eichengreen 'Economy', pp. 117–18; Berend, *Central and Eastern Europe*, Ch. 5; D.H. Aldcroft, *The European Economy, 1914–90* (London, 1993), Ch. 6; A. Nove, *An Economic History of the USSR, 1917–91* (London, 1992), Ch. 12; R.J. Crampton, *Eastern Europe in the Twentieth Century and After* (London, 2003), Ch. 17; R.L. Tokes, *Hungary's Negotiated Revolution: Economic Reform, Social Change and Political Succession, 1957–90* (Cambridge, 1996), pp. 91–2; Sassoon, 'Politics', pp. 15, 29; A. Korner, 'Culture', in Fulbrook, *Europe since 1945*, pp. 158–9; Larres, 'International and Security Relations', pp. 196, 210; Morewood, 'Divided Europe', p. 17; Z.A.B. Zeman, *The Making and Breaking of Communist Europe* (Oxford, 1991), Ch. 21; D. Bathrick, *The Powers of Speech: The Politics of Culture in the GDR* (Lincoln NE, 1995), pp. 1–10.

16 Sassoon, 'Politics', p. 17; Berend, *Central and Eastern Europe*, Ch. 5, and idem, 'Central and Eastern European Revolution', pp. 190–2; Fraser and Murray, *America and the World*, p. 41; Aldcroft, *European Economy*, Chs 6, 9; Swain and Swain, *Eastern Europe since 1945*, pp. 121–30; J. Adam, *Economic Reforms in the Soviet Union and Eastern Europe since the 1960s* (Basingstoke, 1989), Part 2; Schopflin, *Politics in Eastern Europe*, Ch. 6; M. Tepavac, 'Tito: 1945–80', in *Burn this House: The Making and Unmaking of Yugoslavia*, J. Udovicki and J. Ridgeway (eds) (London, 1997), pp. 66–72; M. Vickers, *The Albanians: A Modern History* (London, 1997), Ch. 9; T. Gilberg, *Nationalism and Communism in Romania: The Rise and Fall of Ceauşescu's Personal Dictatorship* (Oxford, 1990), Ch. 10;

S. Fischer-Galati, *Twentieth Century Rumania* (New York, 1970), pp. 185–200; R. Shen, *Economic Reform in Poland and Czechoslovakia* (Westport CT, 1993), Chs 3 and 4; N. Davies, *Heart of Europe: A Short History of Poland* (Oxford, 1991), pp. 12–13; Tokes, *Hungary's Negotiated Revolution*, Ch. 2; Gati, *Hungary and the Soviet Bloc*, Ch. 7; I.T. Berend and G. Ranki, *Hungary: A Century of Economic Development* (Newton Abbot, 1974), pp. 210–46.

17 Kantowicz, *Coming Apart, Coming Together*, pp. 33–5; Crampton, *Eastern Europe*, pp. 255–60; Swain and Swain, *Eastern Europe since 1945*, pp. 56–60; Tepavac, 'Tito', pp. 66–72; Gaddis, *Long Peace*, pp. 152–64, 187–91; R.L. Russell, *George F. Kennan's Strategic Thought* (Westport CT, 1999), p. 56; R. West, *Tito and the Rise and Fall of Yugoslavia* (London, 1994), p. 271; Wilson, *Tito's Yugoslavia*, pp. 68, 74, 98, 114–15, 123, 134–5, 156, 194–5, 213; J. Ridley, *Tito* (London, 1994), pp. 362–3; W. Zimmerman, 'Yugoslav Strategies for Survival, 1948–80', in *At the Brink of War and Peace: The Tito-Stalin Split in a Historic Perspective*, W.S. Vucinich (ed.) (New York, 1982), pp. 11–28.

18 Heuser, *Western 'Containment' Policies*, pp. 39–42, 47–9, 66–7, 81–2, 88, 149, 154–5, 161–2, 171–2, 204–7.

19 Sassoon, 'Politics', p. 29; Larres, 'International and Security Relations', p. 188; D. Good and T. Ma, 'The Economic Growth of Central and Eastern Europe in Comparative Perspective, 1870–1989', *European Review of Economic History*, 2 (1999), pp. 103–37; Eichengreen, 'Economy', pp. 99–100, 120; Crampton, *Eastern Europe*, Ch. 19; Nove, *Economic History of the USSR*, Ch. 13; Aldcroft, *European Economy*, Ch. 9; Adam, *Economic Reforms*, Chs 6–9; Berend, *Central and Eastern Europe*, Ch. 6.

20 Johnson, *Modern World*, pp. 549–50; Armstrong and Goldstein, 'Interaction with the Non-European World', pp. 244–6; Terrill, *Mao*, pp. 278–88, 337–41; Talbott, *Khrushchev Remembers*, Ch. 18; S.G. Zhang, 'China's Strategic Culture and the Cold War Confrontations', in Westad, *Reviewing the Cold War*, pp. 258–77; Pleshakov, 'Nikita Khrushchev and Sino-Soviet Relations', pp. 165–88; Jian and Kuisong, 'Chinese Politics and the Collapse of the Sino-Soviet Alliance', pp. 246–94; J. Keep, *The Last of the Empires: A History of the Soviet Union, 1945–91* (Oxford, 1996), pp. 147, 227, 415.

21 K.W. Thompson, 'Kennedy's Foreign Policy: Activism versus Pragmatism', in Harper and Krieg, *Kennedy: The Promise Revisited*, pp. 25–34; Johnson, *Modern World*, pp. 614–15; Burk, *The British Isles since 1945*, pp. 2–3; Walton, *Cold War and Counterrevolution*, Ch. 1.

22 Dobson, *Anglo-American Relations*, p. 124–5.

23 Giglio, *Presidency of Kennedy*, pp. 44–7; Johnson, *Modern World*, p. 615; Fraser and Murray, *America and the World*, Ch. 4.

24 H. Thomas, *Cuba or The Pursuit of Freedom* (London, 1971), pp. 1226, 1231–33; T.G. Paterson, *Contesting Castro: The United States and the Triumph of the Cuban*

Revolution (New York, 1994), pp. 10, 12, 241–54, and idem, 'Fixation with Cuba: The Bay of Pigs, Missile Crisis and Covert War against Castro', in Paterson, *Kennedy's Quest for Victory*, pp. 135–6; S.E. Eckstein, *Back from the Future: Cuba under Castro* (Princeton NJ, 1994); Johnson, *Modern World*, pp. 622–5; Fraser and Murray, *America and the World*, pp. 82–3, 91–4; Kantowicz, *Coming Apart, Coming Together*, pp. 298–9; LaFeber, *America, Russia and the Cold War*, pp. 223–4; Gaddis, *Long Peace*, p. 191; S.G. Rabe, *The Most Dangerous Area in the World: John F. Kennedy Confronts Communist Revolution in Latin America* (Chapel Hill NC, 1999), pp. 71–3; R.M. Bissell, *Reflections of a Cold Warrior: From Yalta to the Bay of Pigs* (New Haven CT, 1996), pp. 201, 203; Walton, *Cold War and Counterrevolution*, pp. 58–9; P. Wyden, *Bay of Pigs* (London, 1979), pp. 324–5; T. Higgins, *The Perfect Failure: Kennedy, Eisenhower and the CIA at the Bay of Pigs* (New York, 1987), pp. 172–3; H.S. Dinerstein, *The Making of a Missile Crisis: October 1962* (Baltimore MD, 1976), p. 131; Andrew, *For the President's Eyes Only*, pp. 253–5.

25   *The Times*, 17, 18, 21 April 1961; *Observer*, 23 April 1961; Higgins, *Perfect Failure*, p. 99; *Hansard*, 5th series, 638 (1961), cols 971–4, 1384–87.

26   J.W. Hilty, *Robert Kennedy: Brother Protector* (Philadelphia PA, 1997), pp. 412–31; Giglio, *Presidency of Kennedy*, pp. 48–63; A.M. Schlesinger, *A Thousand Days: John F. Kennedy in the White House* (London, 1965), pp. 211–70; Talbott, *Khrushchev Remembers*, pp. 491–3; Tompson, *Khrushchev*, pp. 232–5, 247–8.

27   Rabe, *The Most Dangerous Area in the World*, pp. 196, 199; R.E. Quirk, *Fidel Castro* (New York, 1993), pp. 385–7; Kantowicz, *Coming Apart, Coming Together*, pp. 297–300; Zubok and Pleshakov, *Inside the Kremlin's Cold War*, pp. 206–7, 245; Dinerstein, *Making of a Missile Crisis*, Ch. 4; Paterson, 'Fixation with Cuba', pp. 136–42; M.J. White, *The Cuban Missile Crisis* (Basingstoke, 1996), pp. 47–59; LaFeber, *America, Russia and the Cold War*, pp. 214–16; Richter, *Khrushchev's Double Bind*, pp. 151–2.

28   Johnson, *Modern World*, p. 625; Kantowicz, *Coming Apart, Coming Together*, p. 300; Dinerstein, *Making of a Missile Crisis*, p. 153–8; White, *Cuban Missile Crisis*, p. 82; Talbott, *Khrushchev Remembers*, pp. 492–9; Quirk, *Fidel Castro*, pp. 414–15; Zubok and Pleshakov, *Inside the Kremlin's Cold War*, pp. 259–61; Ausland, *Kennedy, Khrushchev and the Berlin-Cuba Crisis*, pp. 66–73, 76, 99, 102; Hershberg, 'The Crisis Years' p. 315; M.P. Riccards, 'The Dangerous Legacy: John F. Kennedy and the Cuban Missile Crisis', in Harper and Krieg, *Kennedy: The Promise Revisited*, pp. 83–5; Tompson, *Khrushchev*, pp. 248–9; Thomas, *Cuba*, p. 1393. R.L. Garthoff, *Reflections on the Cuban Missile Crisis* (Washington DC, 1989) contends that Castro's role in the whole affair was essentially passive. On the development of Cuban-Soviet relations in general, see also A. Fursenko and T. Naftali, *'One Hell of a Gamble': Khrushchev, Castro, Kennedy and the Cuban Missile Crisis, 1958–64* (London, 1997).

29   Johnson, *Modern World*, pp. 625–6.

30   Johnson, *Modern World*, p. 626; Kantowicz, *Coming Apart, Coming Together*, pp. 300–1; Hilty, *Robert Kennedy*, Ch. 15; White, *Cuban Missile Crisis*, Ch. 6; Giglio, *Presidency of Kennedy*, p. 194; Paterson, 'Fixation with Cuba', pp. 142–5; Dinerstein, *Making of a Missile Crisis*, pp. 223–5.

31   *The Times*, 23, 24 October 1962.

32   *Hansard*, 5th series, 664 (1962), cols 1053–64.

33   *Guardian*, 24 October 1962; *The Times*, 26, 27 October 1962.

34   Fraser and Murray, *America and the World*, pp. 107–12; Giglio, *Presidency of Kennedy*, pp. 209–14; Johnson, *Modern World*, p. 626; Kantowicz, *Coming Apart, Coming Together*, p. 301; Talbott, *Khrushchev Remembers*, p. 504; A.M. Schlesinger, *Robert Kennedy and His Times* (Boston MA, 1978), p. 531; Paterson, 'Fixation with Cuba', pp. 145–8; White, *Cuban Missile Crisis*, pp. 218–31; Thomas, *Cuba*, p. 1414.

35   For further discussion of the personal, ideological and strategic aspects of the Cuban missile crisis, the role of American and Soviet domestic politics, policy-making methods, the impact on US–Soviet relations and the future of the Cold War, the use of intelligence, and the extent to which actual hostilities were really likely, see Johnson, *Modern World*, p. 627–8; Giglio, *Presidency of Kennedy*, pp. 213–16; Thomas, *Cuba*, pp. 1418–19; P. Nash, *The Other Missiles of October: Eisenhower, Kennedy and the 'Jupiters', 1957–63* (Chapel Hill NC, 1997), pp. 34, 170; G.T. Allison, *Essence of a Decision: Explaining the Cuban Missile Crisis* (New York, 1971), p. 226, and the revised edition of this book (New York, 1999), by G.T. Allison and P.D. Zelikow, pp. 159–60; Schlesinger, *Robert Kennedy*, p. 523; Talbott, *Khrushchev Remembers*, pp. 500, 504; Zubok and Pleshakov, *Inside the Kremlin's Cold War*, pp. 267–70; M. Tatu, *Power in the Kremlin* (London, 1969), pp. 260–73, and Parts 3 and 4 generally; Gaddis, *We Now Know*, pp. 278–9, and idem, *Long Peace*, p. 225; Richter, *Khrushchev's Double Bind*, pp. 153–6; Fursenko and Naftali, 'One Hell of a Gamble'; Garthoff, *Reflections on the Cuban Missile Crisis*, pp. 134, 145, 182–3, 191, and idem, 'US Intelligence and the Cuban Missile Crisis', *Intelligence and National Security*, 13 (1998), pp. 18–63; Dinerstein, *Making of a Missile Crisis*, pp. 230–8; Hershberg, 'The Crisis Years', pp. 311–14, 316–17; Paterson, 'Fixation with Cuba', pp. 148–9, 151–2; Riccards, 'Dangerous Legacy', p. 100; White, *Cuban Missile Crisis*, pp. 238–9; Walton, *Cold War and Counterrevolution*, pp. 141–2; Andrew, *For the President's Eyes Only*, pp. 302–5; Tompson, *Khrushchev*, p. 253.

36   Dobson, *Anglo-American Relations*, pp. 127–8.

37   Reynolds, *Britannia Overruled*, p. 201; Bartlett, *Special Relationship*, p. 97; Dumbrell, *A Special Relationship*, pp. 54–8; Baylis, *Anglo-American Defence Relationship*, pp. 75–6; Pierre, *Nuclear Politics*, pp. 224–5; Nunnerley, *Kennedy and Britain*, pp. 75–7, 83–4, 87.

38　R. Aldous, 'A Family Affair: Macmillan and the Art of Personal Diplomacy', in Aldous and Lee, *Macmillan and Britain's World Role*, pp. 28–9; Horne, *Macmillan*, Vol. 2, pp. 380–4.

39　Andrew, *For the President's Eyes Only*, pp. 292, 296; A. Horne, 'Kennedy and Macmillan', in Brinkley and Griffiths, *Kennedy and Europe*, pp. 8–12; L. Scott, 'Close to the Brink? Britain and the Cuban Missile Crisis', *Contemporary Record*, 5 (1991), p. 511, and idem, *Macmillan, Kennedy and the Cuban Missile Crisis: Political, Military and Intelligence Aspects* (London, 1999), pp. 9, 98.

40　G.D. Rawnsley, 'How Special is Special? The Anglo-American Alliance during the Cuban Missile Crisis', *Contemporary Record*, 9 (1995), pp. 592–5. On the UN's involvement in the Cuban missile crisis, see Meisler, *United Nations*, Ch. 8.

41　Rawnsley, 'How Special is Special?' pp. 595–7.

42　Rawnsley, 'How Special is Special?' pp. 597–8; Horne, 'Kennedy and Macmillan', pp. 4, 8–9.

43　Rawnsley, 'How Special is Special?' pp. 597–9.

44　Scott, 'Close to the Brink?' p. 515; Garthoff, *Reflections on the Cuban Missile Crisis*, p. 79.

45　Horne, 'Kennedy and Macmillan', pp. 11–12; Scott, 'Close to the Brink?' pp. 509–10, 512–14; Garthoff, *Reflections on the Cuban Missile Crisis*, p. 61, n. 99; Talbott, *Khrushchev Remembers*, pp. 493–4; Schlesinger, *Robert Kennedy*, p. 519.

46　Horne, 'Kennedy and Macmillan', pp. 13–14.

47　Fursenko and Naftali, 'One Hell of a Gamble', p. 236; Garthoff, *Reflections on the Cuban Missile Crisis*, p. 73; *The Kennedy Tapes: Inside the White House during the Cuban Missile Crisis*, E.R. May and P.D. Zelikow (eds) (Cambridge MA, 1997), pp. 268–9, 283–7, 384–9, 393–4, 427–30, 480–5; *Hansard*, 5th series, 666 (1962), cols 18–19.

48　Holland, *Pursuit of Greatness*, p. 309.

49　Larres, 'International and Security Relations', p. 211; Kantowicz, *Coming Apart, Coming Together*, p. 303; Horne, 'Kennedy and Macmillan', pp. 13–14; Zubok and Pleshakov, *Inside the Kremlin's Cold War*, pp. 270–1; Gaddis, *Long Peace*, pp. 204–5; Stevenson, *Rise and Fall of Détente*, pp. 118–19; K. Dyson, 'European Détente in Historical Perspective: Ambiguities and Paradoxes', and A. Carter, 'Détente and East-West Relations: American, Soviet and European Perspectives', both in *European Détente: Case Studies of the Politics of East-West Relations*, K. Dyson (ed.) (London, 1986), pp. 38, 57. In his *Détente in Europe*, John van Oudenaren claims that the USSR was constantly seeking a thaw in these years – which, if true, means that Soviet intentions were repeatedly misunderstood in the West.

50　H. Sidey, *John F. Kennedy: Portrait of a President* (London, 1964), Ch. 8; Johnson, *Modern World*, pp. 629–30; Kantowicz, *Coming Apart, Coming Together*, p. 303; Riccards, 'Dangerous Legacy', p. 100.

51　Johnson, *Modern World*, pp. 630–4; Kantowicz, *Coming Apart, Coming Together*,

p. 307; Fraser and Murray, *America and the World*, pp. 114–17; Sidey, *John F. Kennedy*, pp. 57, 286, 386, 411–13; Reeves, *President Kennedy*, pp. 236–7, 255–7, 259–61, 311, 442–50, 519, 528–9, 541–2, 556–77, 586–601, 610, 617–18, 635–52; Young, *Vietnam Wars*, pp. ix, 60–106; Acheson, *Present at the Creation*, pp. 863–4; Kahin, *Intervention*, p. ix; D. Halberstam, *The Best and the Brightest* (New York, 1972), pp. 135, 225–6; Giglio, *Presidency of Kennedy*, pp. 239–54; Freedman, *Kennedy's Wars*, pp. 299–300, 347, 363, 397, 419; L.H. Gelb and R.K. Betts, *The Irony of Vietnam: The System Worked* (Washington DC, 1979), pp. 70–1; R. McNamara, *In Retrospect: The Tragedy and Lessons of Vietnam* (New York, 1995), Chs 2 and 3; R.E. Neustadt, 'Had Kennedy Lived', *Survival*, 43 (2001), pp. 177–8, 181–3; Schlesinger, *A Thousand Days*, p. 848; L.J. Bassett and E.E. Pelz, 'The Failed Search for Victory: Vietnam and the Politics of War', in Paterson, *Kennedy's Quest for Victory*, pp. 223–52.

52 Sked and Cook, *Post-War Britain*, pp. 194, 210–11; R. Taylor, 'The Campaign for Nuclear Disarmament', in Bogdanor and Skidelsky, *Age of Affluence*, p. 248; J.W. Young, *The Labour Governments, 1964–70: International Policy* (Manchester, 2003), p. 3; B. Lapping, *The Labour Government, 1964–70* (London, 1970), p. 86; Young, *Vietnam Wars*, pp. 117–71.

53 Gelb and Betts, *Irony of Vietnam*, pp. 100–12, 116–18; K. Bird, *The Colour of Truth: McGeorge Bundy and William Bundy, Brothers in Arms* (New York, 1998), Chs 11–14; R. Mann, *A Grand Delusion: America's Descent into Vietnam* (New York, 2001); Neustadt, 'Had Kennedy Lived', pp. 178–81; Meisler, *United Nations*, Ch. 9.

54 Dumbrell, *A Special Relationship*, pp. 148–9; N. Tarling, *The Fall of Imperial Britain in South East Asia* (Kuala Lumpur, 1993), p. 195.

55 Tarling, *Fall of Imperial Britain*, p. 187.

56 P. Busch, *All the Way with JFK? Britain, the United States and the Vietnam War* (Oxford, 2003), Chs 3–5.

57 S. Ellis, *Britain, America and the Vietnam War* (Westport CT, 2004), pp. 267–8.

58 See, for example, D.L. DiLeo, *George Ball, Vietnam and the Rethinking of Containment* (Chapel Hill NC, 1991); P.L. Hatcher, *The Suicide of an Elite: American Internationalists and Vietnam* (Stanford CA, 1990); and F. Logevall, *Choosing War: The Last Chance for Peace and the Escalation of War in Vietnam* (Berkeley CA, 1999).

59 Dockrill, *British Defence*, p. 79.

60 Young, *Britain and the World*, p. 178; Sked and Cook, *Post-War Britain*, p. 211; Armstrong and Goldstein, 'Interaction with the Non-European World', p. 242.

61 Ellis, *Britain, America and the Vietnam War*, pp. 268–9.

62 D.C. Watt, 'Introduction: The Anglo-American Relationship', and A. Horne, 'The Macmillan Years and Afterwards', both in Louis and Bull, *The 'Special Relationship'*, pp. 6, 9, 101; Young, *Labour Governments*, pp. 20–2; Dobson,

Anglo-American Relations, pp. 133–5, 138; Bartlett, *Special Relationship*, pp. 112–15.

63   Ullman, 'America, Britain and the Soviet Threat', pp. 105–6.

64   Baylis, *Anglo-American Defence Relations*, pp. 93–5; Young, *Labour Governments*, p. 69.

65   H. Wilson, *The Labour Government, 1964–70: A Personal Record* (London, 1971), pp. 79–80, 95–6; Young, *Labour Governments*, p. 69; Ellis, *Britain, America and the Vietnam War*, pp. 80–2.

66   Ellis, *Britain, America and the Vietnam War*, pp. 91, 101, 103, 109, 133–4.

67   *The Crossman Diaries: Selections from the Diary of a Cabinet Minister, 1964–70*, A. Howard (ed.) (London, 1979), pp. 104–6; *Hansard*, 5th series, 714 (1965), cols 1046–58; 715 (1965), col. 167.

68   *The Times*, 2, 3, 29 July 1965; *Guardian*, 1 July 1965; *Observer*, 1 August 1965.

69   Dumbrell, *A Special Relationship*, pp. 150–1.

70   Young, *Labour Governments*, p. 78; Dumbrell, *A Special Relationship*, pp. 150–3.

71   Young, *Labour Governments*, pp. 70–1; C. Wrigley, 'Now You See It, Now You Don't: Harold Wilson and Labour's Foreign Policy', in *The Wilson Governments, 1964–70*, R. Coopey, S. Fielding and N. Tiratsoo (eds) (London, 1993), pp. 125–6.

72   J. Barnes, 'The Record', and H. Young, 'Politics outside the System', both in McKie and Cook, *Decade of Disillusion*, pp. 38, 40, 45, 48, 64, 218–19, 221–2, 226; Stone, 'Britain and the World', pp. 127–8, 132; Young, *Labour Governments*, p. 79.

73   Ellis, *Britain, America and the Vietnam War*, pp. 270–1, 273.

74   G. Brown, *In My Way: The Political Memoirs of Lord George-Brown* (London, 1971), pp. 141–7; Young, *Labour Governments*, pp. 75–6; Ellis, *Britain, America and the Vietnam War*, pp. 217, 228–9; J. Dumbrell and S. Ellis, 'British Involvement in Vietnam Peace Initiatives, 1966–67: Marigolds, Sunflowers and Kosygin Week', *Diplomatic History*, 27 (2003), pp. 113–49; Young, *Vietnam Wars*, pp. 181–3.

75   Dumbrell, *A Special Relationship*, pp. 154–5.

76   Ellis, *Britain, America and the Vietnam War*, pp. 248–51.

77   B. Pimlott, *Harold Wilson* (London, 1992), pp. 387–8; Ziegler, *Wilson*, pp. 228–9; Young, *Labour Governments*, pp. 55–6, 77; J. Fielding, 'Coping with Decline: US Policy towards the British Defence Reviews of 1966', *Diplomatic History*, 23 (1999), pp. 633–56; Ellis, *Britain, America and the Vietnam War*, p. 274.

78   Baylis, *Anglo-American Defence Relations*, pp. 95–6.

Notes to Chapter 8: Asia, the Middle East, Europe: No Respite (II)

1   Dockrill, *British Defence*, pp. 88, 96–7, 102; Baylis, *Anglo-American Defence Relations*, p. 97.

2   A.P. Thornton, 'The Transformation of the Commonwealth and the Special Relationship', in Louis and Bull, *The 'Special Relationship'*, p. 368; Miller, 'The "Special Relationship" in the Pacific', pp. 383–4; J. Subritzky, *Confronting Sukarno: British, American, Australian and New Zealand Diplomacy in the Malaysian-Indonesian Confrontation, 1961–65* (New York, 2000).

3   Lapping, *End of Empire*, pp. 100–1, 488–505; Young, *Labour Governments*, pp. 101–2; Reynolds, *Britannia Overruled*, pp. 208–12; Sked and Cook, *Post-War Britain*, pp. 211–13, 237–8; Darwin, *Britain and Decolonization*, pp. 303, 308–10, 314–18; Hargreaves, *Decolonization in Africa*, pp. 110, 140, 220, 222, 235–9; Stone, 'Britain and the World', pp. 129–33; Kitchen, *British Empire and Commonwealth*, Chs 7 and 8; McIntyre, *Commonwealth of Nations*, pp. 427–30; B. Porter, *The Lion's Share: A Short History of British Imperialism, 1850–1995* (Harlow, 1996), pp. 341, 349; Holland, *European Decolonization*, pp. 233–5, 249, 279–83; D. Judd and P. Slinn, *The Evolution of the Modern Commonwealth, 1902–80* (London, 1982), pp. 109–10, 113–15; E. Heath, *The Course of My Life* (London, 1998), pp. 276–8, 476–9.

4   Nunnerley, *Kennedy and Britain*, pp. 204, 207.

5   *Hansard*, 5th series, 744 (1967), cols 237–8; 756 (1968), cols 467–8; 760 (1968), col. 133.

6   *Hansard*, 5th series, 735 (1966), cols 34–41.

7   *Hansard*, 5th series, 722 (1965), cols 2140–43; 723 (1966), col. 15.

8   *Hansard*, 5th series, 784 (1969), cols 443–9.

9   *Hansard*, 5th series, 783 (1969), col. 3; 787 (1969), cols 1446–58.

10   *Hansard*, 5th series, 770 (1968), cols 576–8, 1587–89.

11   *Crossman Diaries*, p. 128 n.1, p. 141; Young, *Labour Governments*, pp. 65–6; Pimlott, *Harold Wilson*, pp. 366–81, 450–8; Ziegler, *Wilson*, pp. 229–40.

12   Low, 'End of the British Empire', pp. 62–5; Young, *Labour Governments*, pp. 186–7.

13   Brown, *In My Way*, pp. 170–4.

14   Young, *Labour Governments*, pp. 166–8, 186–7.

15   Young, *Labour Governments*, pp. 196–211.

16   *Crossman Diaries*, pp. 487–8, 622; McIntyre, *Commonwealth of Nations*, p. 403.

17   Wilson, *The Labour Government*, pp. 133–4, 138, 169–71, 179–80, 195, 198, 279, 282, 285, 301–21, 317, 391–2, 424, 470–6, 480, 517, 554–61, 564–70, 575–7, 589–90, 592, 597, 600–2, 623–40, 681–2, 690, 729–32, 744–51; Ziegler, *Wilson*, pp. 280, 287–90, 318, 338–40, 361.

18   Kahler, *Decolonization in Britain and France*, pp. 148, 313–14; Lapping, *Labour Government*, pp. 60–8.

19   S.R. Ashton, 'British Government Perspectives on the Commonwealth, 1964–71: An Asset or a Liability?' *Journal of Imperial and Commonwealth History*, 35 (2007), pp. 73–94.

20   Bartlett, *Special Relationship*, Ch. 5.

21   D. Reynolds, 'A "Special Relationship"? America, Britain and the International Order since the Second World War', *International Affairs*, *62* (1985), p. 13, and idem, *Britannia Overruled*, p. 225; Burk, *The British Isles since 1945*, pp. 9–10; A. Cairncross, *The British Economy since 1945* (Oxford, 1992), pp. 174–7; Kennedy, *Realities behind Diplomacy*, pp. 341–2; W.M. Scammell, *The International Economy since 1945* (Basingstoke, 1983), pp. 105–6, 110–11; Bean and Crafts, 'British Economic Growth', pp. 142–7; Eatwell, 'Currents of Political Thought', p. 173; and on the economic situation more generally see Part 3 of Hollowell, *Britain since 1945*, and the statistical tables in Eichengreen, 'Economy'. On the respective economic performances of Britain and the FRG during the 1960s, see M. Surrey, 'United Kingdom' and K.H. Hennings, 'West Germany', in *The European Economy: Growth and Crisis*, A. Boltho (ed.) (Oxford, 1982), pp. 485–92, 539–47.

22   W. Beckerman, 'Objectives and Performance: An Overall View', in Beckerman, *The Labour Government's Economic Record*, pp. 67–8.

23   Howlett, 'The "Golden Age", 1955–73', pp. 334–5; A. Cairncross, *The Wilson Years: A Treasury Diary, 1964–69* (London, 1997).

24   J. Foreman-Peck, *The British Economy since 1945* (Oxford, 1991), pp. 177–8. For useful summaries of British economic performance in this period, see F.T. Blackaby, 'General Appraisal', in *British Economic Policy, 1960–74*, F.T. Blackaby (ed.) (Cambridge, 1978), pp. 619–55; L.J. Williams, *Britain and the World Economy, 1919–70* (London, 1974), pp. 139–54; B. Supple, 'British Economic Decline since 1945', in *The Economic History of Britain since 1700*, R. Floud and D. McCloskey (eds) (3 vols, Cambridge, 1995), Vol. 3, pp. 318–46. See also the essays in *The British Economy since 1945*, N. Crafts and N. Woodward (eds) (Oxford, 1991). On the importance of investment, see S. Pollard, *The Development of the British Economy, 1914–90* (London, 1992) and idem, *The Wasting of the British Economy: British Economic Policy 1945 to the Present* (New York, 1984).

25   Cairncross, *British Economy since 1945*, Ch. 3 on the 1950s, Ch. 4 on the 1960s, and pp. 302–7 specifically on external factors.

26   Cairncross, *Years of Recovery*, p. 503; Scammell, *International Economy since 1945*, p. 120; Williams, *Britain and the World Economy*, pp. 147–8, 177–80.

27   Reynolds, 'Britain and the World since 1945', p. 168, and idem, *Britannia Overruled*, pp. 197, 211–12, 305; Sked and Cook, *Post-War Britain*, pp. 233–4; Coker, 'Foreign and Defence Policy', p. 7; Young, *Britain and the World*, p. 72; Dockrill, *British Defence*, pp. 91–6; Dobson, *Anglo-American Relations*, pp. 129–39; Baylis, *Anglo-American Defence Relations*, pp. 91–8; Bartlett, *Special Relationship*, pp. 118–19; Kennedy, *Realities behind Diplomacy*, pp. 327–8, 375–6.

28   Wilson, *The Labour Government*, p. 40; Young, 'Politics outside the System', pp. 217–18; Healey, *Time of My Life*, pp. 302–4.

29   Stone, 'Britain and the World', pp. 126–7; Holland, *Pursuit of Greatness*, pp. 318–21.

30   Sanders, *Losing an Empire*, pp. 112–20.

31 Darwin, *Britain and Decolonization*, pp. 329, 333; Holland, *European Decolonization*, pp. 269–70, 271–2; A. Clayton, 'Deceptive Might: Imperial Defence and Security, 1900–68', in *The Oxford History of the British Empire*, J.M. Brown and W.R. Louis (eds) (5 vols, Oxford, 1999), Vol. 4, pp. 293, 304.

32 M. Chalmers, 'British Economic Decline: The Contribution of Military Spending', *Royal Bank of Scotland Review*, 173 (1992), pp. 35–6, 38–43, and idem, *Paying for Defence*, pp. 112–13.

33 P. Nailor, 'Denis Healey and Rational Decision-Making in Defence', in Beckett and Gooch, *Politicians and Defence*, pp. 161–3.

34 Pimlott, *Harold Wilson*, pp. 382, 385–6, 388; Mayhew, *Time to Explain*, pp. 170–2.

35 Chalmers, *Paying for Defence*, pp. 84–6; Healey, *Time of My Life*, pp. 270–1, 277, 280.

36 Healey, *Time of My Life*, pp. 278–80; Darby, *Defence Policy East of Suez*, pp. 290–8, 304; Pickering, *Britain's Withdrawal from East of Suez*, pp. 162–3.

37 J. Callaghan, *Time and Chance* (London, 1987), pp. 211–12; E. Pearce, *Denis Healey: A Life in Our Times* (London, 2002), pp. 324, 341.

38 *Hansard*, 5th series, 751 (1967), cols 985, 1108, 1110–11.

39 *The Times*, 19 July 1967.

40 Ovendale, *British Defence Policy*, pp. 142–4; Chalmers, *Paying for Defence*, pp. 86–8.

41 Pickering, *Britain's Withdrawal from East of Suez*, pp. 163–72, and idem, 'Politics and "Black Tuesday": Shifting Power in the Cabinet and the Decision to Withdraw from East of Suez, November 1967 – January 1968', *Twentieth Century British History*, 13 (2002), pp. 144–70; Brown, *In My Way*, p. 141; Pearce, *Denis Healey*, pp. 353–6; Grove, *Vanguard to Trident*, pp. 304–5; Darby, *Defence Policy East of Suez*, pp. 316–26.

42 Chalmers, *Paying for Defence*, pp. 88–91.

43 Young, *Labour Governments*, p. 56.

44 Ovendale, *British Defence Policy*, pp. 144–6; Bartlett, *Long Retreat*, pp. 260–1, 263; Lapping, *Labour Government*, pp. 89–90.

45 Pickering, *Britain's Withdrawal from East of Suez*, pp. 177–84.

46 C. Ponting, *Breach of Promise: Labour in Power, 1964–70* (London, 1989), pp. 105–6, 397–8; Darby, *Defence Policy East of Suez*; K. Hack, *Defence and Decolonization in South East Asia: Britain, Malaya and Singapore, 1941–68* (Richmond, 2000), Chs 1, 8; W.R. Louis, 'The British Withdrawal from the Gulf, 1967–71', *Journal of Imperial and Commonwealth History*, 31 (2003), pp. 83–108; J.B. Kelly, *Arabia, the Gulf and the West* (London, 1980), pp. 31–2, 101.

47 Pickering, *Britain's Withdrawal from East of Suez*, pp. 172–3; Ziegler, *Wilson*, pp. 331–2.

48 Ziegler, *Wilson*, pp. 329–32.

49   M. Camps, *European Unification in the Sixties* (London, 1967), pp. 191–5.

50   U. Kitzinger, *The Second Try: Labour and the EEC* (Oxford, 1968), pp. 108–12, 179–88; Sked and Cook, *Post-War Britain*, p. 235; Urwin, *Western Europe since 1945*, Ch. 14; Carmoy, 'Defence and Unity of Western Europe', pp. 363–8; Gowland and Turner, *Britain and European Integration*, pp. 112–13, 117–25.

51   *The Times*, 17 May 1967; *Economist*, 20 May 1967; Gowland and Turner, *Britain and European Integration*, pp. 123–5.

52   Young, *Britain and the World*, p. 191; Brown, *In My Way*, pp. 141, 207. Fear of federalism appears to have been rather overblown. In his *History of European Integration*, Peter Stirk points out that the federalists were never able to set the agenda or impose their political vision. The survival into the 1960s of the 'third force' idea is discussed in G. Aybet, *The Dynamics of European Security Co-operation, 1945–91* (London, 1998).

53   Greenwood, *Britain and European Co-operation*, pp. 91–2.

54   A. Daltrop, *Politics and the European Community* (London, 1986), pp. 32–3; Lapping, *Labour Government*, Ch. 6; Young, *Labour Governments*, p. 159; A.D. Morgan, 'Commercial Policy', in Blackaby, *British Economic Policy*, pp. 538–44.

55   Wilson, *The Labour Government*, pp. 327–44, 386–91; Ziegler, *Wilson*, pp. 331–8; Pimlott, *Harold Wilson*, pp. 432–42; Young, *Britain and European Unity*, pp. 100–1, and idem, *Labour Governments*, p. 160.

56   Morewood, 'Divided Europe', pp. 19–20; Wakeman, 'Introduction', p. 4; Larres, 'International and Security Relations', pp. 214–16; Young, *Britain and the World*, p. 178; Heuser, 'NATO's Nuclear Strategy', p. 46; D. Johnson, 'De Gaulle and France's Role in the World', in *De Gaulle and Twentieth-Century France*, H. Gough and J. Horne (eds) (London, 1994), pp. 83–94; Carmoy, 'Defence and Unity of Western Europe', pp. 352–4; Kolodziej, *French International Policy*, pp. 345–75; Lacouture, *De Gaulle*, pp. 363–98; Ulam, *Expansion and Coexistence*, pp. 723–4; W. Laqueur, *Europe in Our Time: A History, 1945–92* (New York, 1992), pp. 323–7; Urwin, *Western Europe since 1945*, pp. 150, 156, 160–3; F. Costigliola, 'Kennedy, De Gaulle and the Challenge of Consultation', and L. Gardner, 'Lyndon Johnson and De Gaulle', in Paxton and Wahl, *De Gaulle and the United States*, pp. 169–94, 257–78; P. Bell, *France and Britain, 1940–94: The Long Separation* (London, 1997), pp. 164–6, 205–6.

57   Harrison, *Reluctant Ally*, pp. 62–71, 129–31; Heuser, *NATO, Britain, France and the FRG*, pp. 120–3.

58   *Hansard*, 5th series, 729 (1966), cols 1248–49; *The Times*, 9, 14 March 1966.

59   Young, *Labour Governments*, pp. 135–6.

60   Ziegler, *Wilson*, pp. 209–10; Young, *Labour Governments*, pp. 116–20, 134–5; Pearce, *Denis Healey*, pp. 232, 264–6; Lapping, *Labour Government*, pp. 92–3; Healey, *Time of My Life*, pp. 304–5; Heuser, *NATO, Britain, France and the FRG*, pp. 84–5, 157–8.

61 Larres, 'International and Security Relations', p. 214; Baylis, *Anglo-American Defence Relations*, pp. 72–4, 77–91; Dumbrell, *A Special Relationship*, pp. 125, 137–41, 223; Dobson, *Anglo-American Relations*, pp. 127–30; Bartlett, *Special Relationship*, pp. 99, 119; Ovendale, *British Defence Policy*, p. 127; Urwin, *Western Europe since 1945*, pp. 163–4, 169; Hanrieder, *Germany, America, Europe*, pp. 45–50; Costigliola, 'Kennedy, De Gaulle and the Challenge of Consultation', pp. 176, 185–6, 190–2; Gardner, 'Lyndon Johnson and De Gaulle', pp. 259–65; Lacouture, *De Gaulle*, pp. 341–4, 354, 359, 374, 376, 413–33; Harrison, *Reluctant Ally*, pp. 83–5.

62 Murray, *Kennedy, Macmillan and Nuclear Weapons*, pp. 151, 155–8; Heuser, *NATO, Britain, France and the FRG*, pp. 151–7.

63 Morewood, 'Divided Europe', pp. 20–1; A. Stent, *From Embargo to Ostpolitik: The Political Economy of West German-Soviet Relations, 1955–80* (Cambridge, 1981), pp. 154–63; T.G. Ash, *In Europe's Name: Germany and the Divided Continent* (London, 1993), pp. 53–67; Swain and Swain, *Eastern Europe since 1945*, pp. 159–61; W.E. Griffith, *The Ostpolitik of the Federal Republic of Germany* (Cambridge MA, 1978), p. 181; Stevenson, *Rise and Fall of Détente*, pp. 148–50; Bartlett, *Special Relationship*, p. 128; H. Kissinger, *The White House Years* (London, 1979), pp. 408–12.

64 A.B. Ulam, *Dangerous Relations: The Soviet Union in World Politics, 1970–82* (New York, 1984), p. 35.

65 Kolodziej, *French International Policy*, Ch. 7; Larres, 'International and Security Relations', pp. 215–18; Simonian, *Privileged Partnership*, pp. 13, 34–5; Morewood, 'Divided Europe', p. 20; L.P. de Menil, *Who Speaks for Europe? The Vision of Charles de Gaulle* (London, 1977), Chs 7–9; Harrison, *Reluctant Ally*, pp. 112–14.

66 M. Kreile, 'Ostpolitik Reconsidered', in *The Foreign Policy of West Germany: Formation and Contents*, E. Krippendorf and V. Rittberger (eds) (London, 1980), pp. 123–46; G.A. Craig, 'Did Ostpolitik Work?' *Foreign Affairs*, 73 (1994), pp. 162–5, 167; M. Sturmer, 'Deutschlandpolitik, Ostpolitik and the Western Alliance: German Perspectives on Détente', in Dyson, *European Détente*, pp. 134–54; Griffith, *Ostpolitik*, Chs 4 and 5; R. Morgan, 'The Ostpolitik and West Germany's External Relations', in *The Ostpolitik and Political Change in Germany*, R. Tilford (ed.) (Farnborough, 1975), pp. 95–108.

67 M.E. Sarotte, *Dealing with the Devil: East Germany, Détente and Ostpolitik, 1969–73* (Chapel Hill NC, 2001); W. Loth, 'Germany in the Cold War: Strategies and Decisions', and J.M. Hanhimaki, 'Ironies and Turning Points: Détente in Perspective', both in Westad, *Reviewing the Cold War*, pp. 254–5, 333; Hanrieder, *Germany, America, Europe*, pp. 186–202, 262–8; Ulam, *Expansion and Coexistence*, pp. 749–55; Sassoon, 'Politics', p. 37; Larres, 'International and Security Relations', p. 217; Lapping, *Labour Government*, p. 94; Simonian, *Privileged Partnership*, pp. 181–2; Lacouture, *De Gaulle*, pp. 467–82; Johnson, 'De Gaulle and France's

Role in the World', p. 94; Carmoy, 'Defence and Unity of Western Europe', pp. 368–70; Kolodziej, *French International Policy*, pp. 375–90; Swain and Swain, *Eastern Europe since 1945*, pp. 144–5; Schopflin, *Politics in Eastern Europe*, pp. 156–8; Adomeit, *Imperial Overstretch*, pp. 112–15.

68 Heuser, 'NATO's Nuclear Strategy', pp. 46–7.

69 *The Times*, 3 February 1969.

70 Kissinger, *White House Years*, pp. 88–91; *The Times*, 3 February 1969.

71 Fraser and Murray, *America and the World*, pp. 148–51; Larres, 'International and Security Relations', p. 217; R. Nixon, *RN: The Memoirs of Richard Nixon* (London, 1978), pp. 370–5; Kissinger, *White House Years*, pp. 80–111; Greenwood, *Britain and European Co-operation*, p. 95; A. Gromyko, *Memories* (London, 1989), pp. 191–3; Stevenson, *Rise and Fall of Détente*, p. 149; Bell, *France and Britain*, pp. 222, 243; Kolodziej, *French International Policy*, pp. 391–425; S. Berstein and J.P. Rioux, *The Pompidou Years, 1969–74* (Cambridge, 2000), pp. 25–6; Young, *This Blessed Plot*, pp. 234–8; J. Campbell, *Edward Heath: A Biography* (London, 1993), pp. 352–60; George, *Awkward Partner*, pp. 55, 74.

72 Wilson, *The Labour Government*, p. 765; *Hansard*, 5th series, 797 (1970), cols 159, 613, 614; *Guardian*, 3 March 1970; *The Times*, 20 March 1970.

73 Young, *Labour Governments*, pp. 129–30, 134; Griffith, *Ostpolitik*, p. 180.

74 Fraser, *Arab-Israeli Conflict*, pp. 81–5; Johnson, *Modern World*, p. 666; Kantowicz, *Coming Apart, Coming Together*, pp. 361, 363, 367; M. Brecher, *Decisions in Israel's Foreign Policy* (London, 1974), Ch. 7; Fraser and Murray, *America and the World*, p. 137; Ulam, *Expansion and Coexistence*, pp. 731–7; F.J. Khouri, 'United Nations Peace Efforts', in *The Elusive Peace in the Middle East*, M.H. Kerr (ed.) (Albany, New York, 1975), pp. 58–63.

75 *Crossman Diaries*, pp. 314–15; Young, *Labour Governments*, pp. 103–4.

76 *Crossman Diaries*, pp. 314–16; Young, *Labour Governments*, pp. 104–5.

77 *Hansard*, 5th series, 749 (1967), cols 2010–20, 2115–18, 2121–23; *The Times*, 6 June 1967.

78 W.B. Quandt, *Decade of Decisions: American Policy toward the Arab–Israeli Conflict, 1967–76* (Berkeley CA, 1977), pp. 39–40, and idem, *Peace Process: American Diplomacy and the Arab-Israeli Conflict since 1967* (Washington DC, 1993), pp. 23–6, 29, 33–5, 37, 40–1, 43–8, 60; N. Aruri, 'US Policy toward the Arab-Israeli Conflict', in *The United States and the Middle East: A Search for New Perspectives*, H. Amirahmadi (ed.) (Albany NY, 1993), pp. 98–9; Fraser, *The USA and the Middle East*, pp. 78–83.

79 E. Hammel, *Six Days in June: How Israel won the 1967 Arab-Israeli War* (New York, 1992), pp. 92, 139, 397; C.W. Yost, 'The Arab-Israeli War: How it Began', *Foreign Affairs*, 46 (1967–68), pp. 304–20; M. Brecher and B. Geist, *Decisions in Crisis: Israel, 1967 and 1973* (Berkeley CA, 1980), pp. 104, 117, 151.

80 *Observer*, 11 June 1967; *The Times*, 27 June 1967.

81 Brown, *In My Way*, pp. 233–4, 279–80.

82 P.J. Vatikiotis, *Nasser and His Generation* (London, 1978), pp. 253–60; Woodward, *Nasser*, pp. 103–27; Kantowicz, *Coming Apart, Coming Together*, pp. 368–9; Aruri, 'US Policy', pp. 99–101; Quandt, *Decade of Decisions*, Chs 2–5, and idem, *Peace Process*, Ch. 3; Nixon, *Memoirs*, pp. 477–83; Fraser and Murray, *America and the World*, pp. 137–9; Ulam, *Dangerous Relations*, p. 40; Brecher, *Israel's Foreign Policy*, Ch. 8; Khouri, 'United Nations Peace Efforts', pp. 63–82, 87–9; J.C. Campbell, 'American Efforts for Peace', in Kerr, *Elusive Peace*, pp. 283–305; Fraser, *Arab-Israeli Conflict*, pp. 85–99, and idem, *The USA and the Middle East*, pp. 83–97; Meisler, *United Nations*, Ch. 10.

83 Young, *Labour Governments*, pp. 106–8.

84 Ulam, *Expansion and Coexistence*, pp. 728, 737; Gromyko, *Memories*, pp. 267–72.

85 Sassoon, 'Politics', p. 38; Kantowicz, *Coming Apart, Coming Together*, pp. 349–51; Schopflin, *Politics in Eastern Europe*, pp. 152–6; Zeman, *Making and Breaking of Communist Europe*, pp. 278–81; L.R. Johnson, *Central Europe: Enemies, Neighbours, Friends* (New York, 1996), pp. 252–4, 257–8; Ulam, *Expansion and Coexistence*, pp. 738–46; Swain and Swain, *Eastern Europe since 1945*, pp. 140–5; G. Stokes, *The Walls Came Tumbling Down: The Collapse of Communism in Eastern Europe* (New York, 1993), pp. 13–14, 65–7; Berend, *Central and Eastern Europe*, pp. 136–46.

86 Zeman, *Making and Breaking of Communist Europe*, pp. 280, 282; K. Williams, *The Prague Spring and its Aftermath: Czechoslovak Politics, 1968–70* (Cambridge, 1997), pp. 5, 110–11.

87 J. Valenta, *Soviet Invasion of Czechoslovakia, 1968: Anatomy of a Decision* (London, 1979), pp. 130, 147.

88 Young, *Labour Governments*, pp. 132–3.

89 *The Times*, 24 August 1968.

90 Brown, *In My Way*, p. 75; *Crossman Diaries*, pp. 467–8; *Hansard*, 5th series, 769 (1968), cols 1274–75, 1277–78, 1281–82; 1284–92.

91 Dockrill, *British Defence*, p. 97; Baylis, *Anglo-American Defence Relations*, p. 96.

92 Morewood, 'Divided Europe', p. 19; Ulam, *Expansion and Coexistence*, pp. 745–6; Larres, 'International and Security Relations', p. 196; J. Dornberg, *Brezhnev: The Masks of Power* (London, 1974), pp. 219–29; Kantowicz, *Coming Apart, Coming Together*, p. 353, 355; Berend, 'Central and Eastern European Revolution', pp. 190–3; Johnson, *Central Europe*, p. 258; Laqueur, *Europe in Our Time*, pp. 354–61; Schopflin, *Politics in Eastern Europe*, p. 157; B. Fowkes, *The Rise and Fall of Communism in Eastern Europe* (Basingstoke, 1995), pp. 132–44; A. Hyde-Price, *The International Politics of East Central Europe* (Manchester, 1996), pp. 16, 23, 27, 31, 34–5.

93   K. Dawisha, *The Kremlin and the Prague Spring* (London, 1984), pp. 315–16;
     P. Windsor and A. Roberts, *Czechoslovakia 1968: Reform, Repression and Resistance*
     (London, 1969), pp. 105, 114, 118–27, 132–6; A. Dubček, *Hope Dies Last: The
     Autobiography of Alexander Dubček* (London, 1993), pp. 203, 205, 213, 219;
     Williams, *Prague Spring*, pp. 132, 251; Valenta, *Soviet Invasion of Czechoslovakia*,
     pp. 160–1.
94   Stevenson, *Rise and Fall of Détente*, pp. 135–6; Young, *Labour Governments*,
     pp. 133–4.
95   R.A. Jones, *The Soviet Concept of 'Limited Sovereignty' from Lenin to Gorbachev:
     The Brezhnev Doctrine* (New York, 1990), pp. 17, 27, 237, 257; M.J. Ouimet, *The
     Rise and Fall of the Brezhnev Doctrine in Soviet Foreign Policy* (Chapel Hill NC,
     2003), pp. 3, 26–7, 36–7; Stokes, *Walls Came Tumbling Down*, pp. 67–8; C. Gati,
     The Bloc that Failed: Soviet-East European Relations in Transition (Bloomington
     IN, 1990), pp. 43–8, 57; H. Friedmann, 'Warsaw Pact Socialism: Détente and the
     Disintegration of the Soviet Bloc', in *Rethinking the Cold War*, A. Hunter (ed.)
     (Philadelphia PA, 1998), pp. 218–19.
96   Friedmann, 'Warsaw Pact Socialism', pp. 226–8; Berend, *Central and Eastern
     Europe*, pp. 153, 222–32.
97   *Dismantling Communism: Common Causes and Regional Variations*, G. Rozman,
     S. Sato and G. Segal (eds) (Baltimore MD, 1993); Fowkes, *Rise and Fall of
     Communism*, p. 194; Friedberg, 'The United States and the Cold War Arms Race',
     pp. 207, 220–2; Hanhimaki, 'Ironies and Turning Points', pp. 333, 337–8; W. Loth,
     'Moscow, Prague and Warsaw: Overcoming the Brezhnev Doctrine', *Cold War
     History*, 1 (2001), pp. 103–18.

Notes to Chapter 9: Years of Frustration

1   Young, *Britain and the World*, p. 224; Sked and Cook, *Post-War Britain*, pp. 265–6;
    C. Hill and C. Lord, 'The Foreign Policy of the Heath Government', in *The Heath
    Government, 1970–74: A Reappraisal*, S. Ball and A. Seldon (eds) (London, 1996),
    pp. 294–7; Judd and Slinn, *Evolution of the Modern Commonwealth*, pp. 112–13,
    118–19, 131–3; D.R. Thorpe, *Alec Douglas-Home* (London, 1996), pp. 420–9; Lord
    Home, *The Way the Wind Blows: An Autobiography* (London, 1976), pp. 251–7,
    302–12; Lord Carrington, *Reflect on Things Past* (London, 1988), pp. 268–73;
    M. Meredith, *The Past is Another Country: Rhodesia, 1890–1979* (London, 1979),
    pp. 75–103; D. Judd, *Empire: The British Imperial Experience from 1765 to the
    Present* (London, 1997), pp. 375, 381–2, 388.
2   Campbell, *Heath*, pp. 337, 339; Heath, *Course of My Life*, pp. 478–80; C. Hill,
    'The Historical Background: Past and Present in British Foreign Policy', in
    British Foreign Policy: Tradition, Change and Transformation, M. Smith, S. Smith

and B. White (eds) (London, 1988), p. 41; J. Mayall, 'Africa in Anglo-American Relations', in Louis and Bull, *The 'Special Relationship'*, p. 324.

3   *The Times*, 31 October 1972.

4   *Hansard*, 5th series, 860 (1973), cols 713–15.

5   Judd, *Empire*, p. 382; W.D. McIntyre, *The Significance of the Commonwealth, 1965–90* (Basingstoke, 1991), pp. 30–2; Judd and Slinn, *Evolution of the Modern Commonwealth*, pp. 112–13, 119; Sked and Cook, *Post-War Britain*, pp. 266, 268–9; Curtis, *Ambiguities of Power*, p. 125; Hill and Lord, 'Foreign Policy of the Heath Government', pp. 292–4; Carrington, *Reflect on Things Past*, pp. 253–4; Layton-Henry, *Politics of Immigration*, pp. 79–89, 91, and idem, 'Immigration and the Heath Government', in Ball and Seldon, *The Heath Government*, pp. 215–34; P.B. Rich, *Race and Empire in British Politics* (Cambridge, 1986), pp. 207–8; Spencer, *British Immigration Policy*, pp. 142–6; Campbell, *Heath*, pp. 299, 337–8, 340, 392–4, 481; Heath, *Course of My Life*, pp. 399, 455–9, 477–8, 481.

6   Hill and Lord, 'Foreign Policy of the Heath Government', p. 286.

7   K. Theakston, 'The Heath Government, Whitehall and the Civil Service', and J.W. Young, 'The Heath Government and British Entry into the European Community', both in Ball and Seldon, *The Heath Government*, pp. 82–3, 272–3; McIntyre, *Significance of the Commonwealth*, p. 33; Sked and Cook, *Post-War Britain*, pp. 267–8; Campbell, *Heath*, p. 341; *The Times*, 11, 26 July 1973; *Hansard*, 5th series, 858 (1973), cols 91, 329, 400, 1168, 1606; 860 (1973), cols 265, 277–8, 280, 284; Hill and Lord, 'Foreign Policy of the Heath Government', pp. 306–7.

8   Hill and Lord, 'Foreign Policy of the Heath Government', pp. 289–92.

9   Sked and Cook, *Post-War Britain*, p. 267; Heath, *Course of My Life*, p. 481; Hill and Lord, 'Foreign Policy of the Heath Government', pp. 290–1; Campbell, *Heath*, pp. 340–1; Carrington, *Reflect on Things Past*, pp. 219–20; Ovendale, *British Defence Policy*, pp. 147–8; *Hansard*, 5th series 815 (1971), cols 347–9; *The Times*, 15 May 1971.

10 Sanders, *Losing an Empire*, pp. 122–3, 229–30.

11 Young, *Britain and the World*, p. 179; Sked and Cook, *Post-War Britain*, p. 267; Thorpe, *Douglas-Home*, pp. 431–2; Home, *Way the Wind Blows*, pp. 263–5, 269–71; S.E. Ambrose and D. Brinkley, *Rise to Globalism: American Foreign Policy since 1938* (New York, 1997), pp. 232–4.

12 R. MacFarquhar, 'The China Problem in Anglo-American Relations', in Louis and Bull, *The 'Special Relationship'*, p. 318; V.S. Kaufman, '"Chirep": The Anglo-American Dispute over Chinese Representation in the United Nations, 1950–71', *English Historical Review*, 115 (2000), pp. 354–77.

13 Campbell, *Heath*, pp. 347, 634–5; Heath, *Course of My Life*, pp. 468, 485, 494–5; P. Cradock, *Experiences of China* (London, 1994), pp. 149–50.

14 R. Boardman, *Britain and the People's Republic of China, 1949–74* (London, 1976), pp. 143–62; J.P. Jain, *China in World Politics: A Study of Sino-British Relations,*

1949–75 (London, 1977), pp. 109–11, 154–7.

15 Jain, *China in World Politics*, pp. 211–14, 245–8, 340.

16 Hill and Lord, 'Foreign Policy of the Heath Government', p. 309.

17 *Hansard*, 5th series, 848 (1972), cols 649–50; *The Times*, 3 November 1972; *Guardian*, 3 November 1972; Boardman, *Britain and the People's Republic of China*, p. 146.

18 Sked and Cook, *Post-War Britain*, p. 280; Thorpe, *Douglas-Home*, pp. 433–4; Fraser, *Arab-Israeli Conflict*, p. 102.

19 Heath, *Course of My Life*, pp. 500–1; Ambrose and Brinkley, *Rise to Globalism*, p. 262; W. Laqueur, *Confrontation: The Middle East War and World Politics* (London, 1974), pp. 207, 209–12.

20 Heath, *Course of My Life*, pp. 501–2; *A Survey of Arab-Israeli Relations, 1947–2001*, D. Lea and A. Rowe (eds) (London, 2002), pp. 9, 47, 282–3; T.G. Fraser, *The Middle East, 1914–79* (London, 1980), pp. 9, 193–4; Harrison, *Reluctant Ally*, pp. 174–77.

21 V. Israelyan, *Inside the Kremlin during the Yom Kippur War* (University Park PA, 1995), pp. 97–8.

22 Campbell, *Heath*, pp. 571–3; Heath, *Course of My Life*, pp. 502–7.

23 Campbell, *Heath*, pp. 557–9, 563; C. Farrands, 'State, Society, Culture and British Foreign Policy', in Smith, Smith and White, *British Foreign Policy*, pp. 62–3; Hill and Lord, 'Foreign Policy of the Heath Government', pp. 301–2, 311; J. Smith and G. Edwards, 'British-West German Relations, 1973–89', in Larres and Meehan, *Uneasy Allies*, pp. 57–60.

24 Thorpe, *Douglas-Home*, pp. 433–4.

25 *The Times*, 20 October 1973.

26 R. Tooze, 'Security and Order: The Economic Dimension', in Smith, Smith and White, *British Foreign Policy*, pp. 131–2.

27 Coker, 'Foreign and Defence Policy', pp. 12–13; Sanders, *Losing an Empire*, pp. 178–9; Bartlett, *Special Relationship*, pp. 142–3; R. Renwick, *Fighting with Allies: America and Britain in Peace and War* (Basingstoke, 1996), pp. 218–19, 221–4; Dobson, *Anglo-American Relations*, p. 146; Ovendale, *British Defence Policy*, pp. 11–12, 158–61; G. Richey, *Britain's Strategic Role in NATO* (Basingstoke, 1986), pp. 118–20; Simpson, *Independent Nuclear State*, p. 198; May and Treverton, 'Defence Relationships: American Perspectives', pp. 174–5; Heuser, *NATO, Britain, France and the FRG*, p. 76; Callaghan, *Time and Chance*, pp. 553–7; N. Bowles, 'The Defence Policy of the Conservative Government', in *The Conservative Government, 1979–84: An Interim Report*, D.S. Bell (ed.) (London, 1985), pp. 189–93; J. Haslam, *The Soviet Union and the Politics of Nuclear Weapons in Europe, 1969–87: The Problem of the SS20* (Basingstoke, 1989), pp. 91, 135.

28 J. Steele, *World Power: Soviet Foreign Policy under Brezhnev and Andropov* (London, 1983), p. 206.

29 Young, *Britain and the World*, p. 180; Sanders, *Losing an Empire*, pp. 121, 123, 229, 242; Carrington, *Reflect on Things Past*, pp. 241–6.

30 R.S. Litwak, *Détente and the Nixon Doctrine: American Foreign Policy and the Pursuit of Stability, 1969–76* (Cambridge, 1984), pp. 191–3; Hill and Lord, 'Foreign Policy of the Heath Government', pp. 313–14.

31 Campbell, *Heath*, pp. 349–50; Heath, *Course of My Life*, pp. 500–1; Sanders, *Losing an Empire*, p. 177; Renwick, *Fighting with Allies*, p. 212; Watt, *Succeeding John Bull*, pp. 152–3, 156; Dobson, *Anglo-American Relations*, pp. 142, 159; H. Kissinger, *Years of Upheaval* (London, 1982), pp. 1000, 1005; Laqueur, *Confrontation*, pp. 185–6, 215; Coker, 'Foreign and Defence Policy', p. 9; Hill and Lord, 'Foreign Policy of the Heath Government', p. 303; Young, *Britain and the World*, pp. 179, 208; P. Cornish, *Partnership in Crisis: The United States, Europe and the Fall and Rise of NATO* (London, 1997), pp. 4, 34; Wells, 'The United States, Britain and the Defence of Europe', pp. 133–4; Bartlett, *Special Relationship*, pp. 130–1; Cromwell, *The United States and the European Pillar*, pp. 101–3; Harrison, *Reluctant Ally*, p. 171; A. Grosser, *The Western Alliance: European-American Relations since 1945* (London, 1980), p. 329; W. Park, *Defending the West: A History of NATO* (Brighton, 1986), pp. 172, 174, 176.

32 Hill and Lord, 'Foreign Policy of the Heath Government', pp. 307, 313; Thorpe, *Douglas-Home*, p. 431.

33 Young, *Britain and the World*, p. 208; W. Wallace, 'The Management of Foreign Economic Policy in Britain', *International Affairs*, 50 (1974), p. 253.

34 A. Cairncross, 'The Heath Government and the British Economy', in Ball and Seldon, *The Heath Government*, pp. 107–38; Dobson, *Anglo-American Relations*, pp. 144–5.

35 T. McGrew, 'Security and Order: The Military Dimension', in Smith, Smith and White, *British Foreign Policy*, p. 101; Ambrose and Brinkley, *Rise to Globalism*, pp. 321–2.

36 D. Allen, 'Britain and Western Europe', in Smith, Smith and White, *British Foreign Policy*, pp. 170–1; Sanders, *Losing an Empire*, p. 237.

37 Larres, 'International and Security Relations', p. 220; Young, *Britain and the World*, pp. 208–9; Carrington, *Reflect on Things Past*, pp. 222–3; Pimlott, *Harold Wilson*, p. 383; Callaghan, *Time and Chance*, p. 326; K.O. Morgan, *Callaghan: A Life* (Oxford, 1997), p. 605; Ovendale, *British Defence Policy*, pp. 11, 151, 159–60; Chalmers, *Paying for Defence*, pp. 103–5; P. Nailor, *The Nassau Connection: The Organization and Management of the British Polaris Project* (London, 1988), p. 68; Dobson, *Anglo-American Relations*, p. 146; Simpson, *Independent Nuclear State*, pp. 171–8; Richey, *Britain's Strategic Role in NATO*, Ch. 5; Heuser, *NATO, Britain, France and the FRG*, p. 76; Haslam, *Soviet Union and the Politics of Nuclear Weapons*, p. 135; McGrew, 'Security and Order: The Military Dimension', p. 117; Ambrose and Brinkley, *Rise to Globalism*, pp. 235, 282–3, 286–7, 321; J. Dumbrell,

American Foreign Policy: Carter to Clinton (Basingstoke, 1997), pp. 3–4, 25; Sanders, *Losing an Empire*, pp. 237–8.

38 W. Stueck, 'Placing Jimmy Carter's Foreign Policy', in *The Carter Presidency*, G.M. Fink and H.D. Graham (eds) (Lawrence KS, 1998), pp. 251–2; C. Coker, *The Future of the Atlantic Alliance* (London, 1984), pp. 7–24, 27; Baylis, *Anglo-American Defence Relations*, pp. 108–9; Freedman, *Britain and Nuclear Weapons*, pp. 43–58; Dockrill, *British Defence*, p. 107; H. Wilson, *Final Term: The Labour Government, 1974–76* (London, 1979), p. 26; Pearce, *Denis Healey*, pp. 408–27; Ziegler, *Wilson*, pp. 460–1.

39 Carrington, *Reflect on Things Past*, pp. 231–2; Morgan, *Callaghan*, p. 618; Sanders, *Losing an Empire*, pp. 238, 244–5, 249; Dockrill, *British Defence*, pp. 107–9.

40 Morgan, *Callaghan*, pp. 450–1.

41 *Documents on British Policy Overseas*, Series III, G. Bennett and K.A. Hamilton (eds) (London, 1997), Vol. 2, pp. vi–vii; Stevenson, *Rise and Fall of Détente*, pp. 150–1, 167–8.

42 Bennett and Hamilton, *Documents on British Policy Overseas*, Vol. 2, p. vii; M. Clarke, 'Britain and European Political Co-operation in the CSCE', in Dyson, *European Détente*, pp. 237–53.

43 M. Clarke, 'A British View', in *European Détente: A Reappraisal*, R. Davy (ed.) (London, 1992), pp. 90–3.

44 Clarke, 'A British View', pp. 93–4.

45 Clarke, 'A British View', pp. 94–5; Bennett and Hamilton, *Documents on British Policy Overseas*, Vol. 2, pp. vii–ix.

46 C. Bluth, 'Détente and Conventional Arms Control: West German Policy Priorities and the Origins of MBFR', *German Politics*, 8 (1999), pp. 181–206; Harrison, *Reluctant Ally*, p. 187.

47 Bennett and Hamilton, *Documents on British Policy Overseas*, Vol. 2, pp. x–xi, 1–15, 191–2; *Hansard*, 5th series, 848 (1972), cols 645–6, 650, 651–2.

48 Bennett and Hamilton, *Documents on British Policy Overseas*, Vol. 2, pp. 330–2.

49 Morgan, *Callaghan*, pp. 452–3; Callaghan, *Time and Chance*, pp. 365–6; Pimlott, *Harold Wilson*, pp. 669–70.

50 Ziegler, *Wilson*, pp. 461–2; Wilson, *Final Term*, pp. 154–60; Bennett and Hamilton, *Documents on British Policy Overseas*, Vol. 2, pp. 419–22, 447–54; Callaghan, *Time and Chance*, pp. 364–6, 368–70; Morgan, *Callaghan*, pp. 453–4.

51 B. White, 'Britain and East-West Relations', in Smith, Smith and White, *British Foreign Policy*, pp. 163–4; Kissinger, *White House Years*, p. 94.

52 See, for example, the (far from unbiased) comments in Curtis, *Ambiguities of Power*, pp. 116, 140–1.

53 Clarke, 'A British View', pp. 95–6.

54 Clarke, 'A British View', pp. 96–7; Ovendale, *British Defence Policy*, pp. 154–6; K. Dyson, 'The Conference on Security and Co-operation in Europe: Europe

Before and After the Helsinki Final Act', in Dyson, *European Détente*, pp. 104–6.

55 B. White, *Britain, Détente and Changing East-West Relations* (London, 1992), pp. 21–2, 137–40.

56 V. Mastny, *The Helsinki Process and the Reintegration of Europe, 1986–91: Analysis and Documentation* (London, 1982), pp. 1–5.

57 Mastny, *The Helsinki Process*, pp. 3–5; Stevenson, *Rise and Fall of Détente*, pp. 172–3, 184; D.M. Kendall, 'US-Soviet Trade, Peace and Prosperity', D. Reisman, 'The Danger of the Human Rights Campaign', and S. Pisar, 'Let's Put Détente Back on the Rails', all in *Détente or Debacle: Common Sense in US-Soviet Relations*, F.W. Neal (ed.) (New York, 1979), pp. 10, 39–44, 56; R. Legvold, 'The Nature of Soviet Power', *Foreign Affairs*, 56 (1977–78), pp. 49–71.

58 Young, *Britain and the World*, pp. 201, 209–10; Hollowell, 'Commonwealth to European Integration', p. 92; Morewood, 'Divided Europe', p. 28; M. Thatcher, *The Downing Street Years* (London, 1993), pp. 65, 68–9, 87–8, 125, 156–8, 160, 452–3, 469–70, 475; G. Howe, *Conflict of Loyalty* (London, 1994), pp. 358–60; D.N. Schwartz, *NATO's Nuclear Dilemmas* (Washington DC, 1983), pp. 197–200; Nailor, *Nassau Connection*, p. 68; Chalmers, *Paying for Defence*, pp. 134–5; Bowles, 'Defence Policy of the Conservative Government', pp. 184–9, 191–6, 198–9.

59 L. Richardson, 'British State Strategies after the Cold War', in *After the Cold War*, R.O. Keohane, J.S. Nye and S. Hoffman (eds) (Cambridge MA, 1993), pp. 158–64; P. Byrd, 'Defence Policy', in *British Foreign Policy under Thatcher*, P. Byrd (ed.) (Oxford, 1988), pp. 171–2.

60 Park, *Defending the West*, pp. 189–91; B.S. Klein, 'Hegemony and Strategic Culture: American Power Projection and Alliance Defence Politics', *Review of International Studies*, 14 (1988), pp. 142–3.

61 Howe, *Conflict of Loyalty*, pp. 144–5, 189.

62 McGrew, 'Security and Order: The Military Dimension', pp. 102–7; Bowles, 'Defence Policy of the Conservative Government', pp. 198–9.

63 Fraser and Murray, *America and the World*, p. 145; W. Bundy, *A Tangled Web: The Making of Foreign Policy in the Nixon Presidency* (London, 1998), pp. 359, 361–2, 364, 371; Nixon, *Memoirs*, pp. 748–51, 753–4, 757; S.E. Ambrose, *Nixon* (3 vols, New York, 1987–91), Vol. 2, pp. 533–5; W. Isaacson, *Kissinger* (London, 1993), Chs 9, 12–13, 20–1; Kissinger, *White House Years*, Chs 31–4; Ambrose and Brinkley, *Rise to Globalism*, pp. 233–4, 236, 270; Heath, *Course of My Life*, pp. 279, 487, 598; Campbell, *Heath*, pp. 228, 335, 343, 346; Curtis, *Ambiguities of Power*, pp. 147–52; Hill and Lord, 'Foreign Policy of the Heath Government', pp. 292, 303, 307, 312; Thorpe, *Douglas-Home*, p. 431; Sanders, *Losing an Empire*, pp. 147, 149.

64 Fraser and Murray, *America and the World*, pp. 146–7, 160–3; Reynolds, *Britannia Overruled*, p. 225; Young, *Britain and the World*, p. 228; Ambrose and Brinkley, *Rise to Globalism*, pp. 228–36, 269; Ambrose, *Nixon*, Vol. 2, pp. 440–1; C. Fisher,

'A Requiem for the Cold War: Reviewing the History of International Relations since 1945', in Hunter, *Rethinking the Cold War*, pp. 94, 108–12.

65   *Hansard*, 5th series, 790 (1969), cols 359, 371–2; *The Times*, 2, 7, 9 November 1972; Home, *Way the Wind Blows*, pp. 246–7, 264; Young, *Britain and the World*, p. 228; Sanders, *Losing an Empire*, pp. 258, 264–8, 270–2; Curtis, *Ambiguities of Power*, p. 185.

66   Bartlett, *Special Relationship*, p. 131.

67   Heath, *Course of My Life*, pp. 468, 486–7; Campbell, *Heath*, pp. 346–7.

68   Fraser and Murray, *America and the World*, pp. 163–4; Ambrose and Brinkley, *Rise to Globalism*, pp. 229–32; Ulam, *Dangerous Relations*, pp. 46–7, 50–2, 65–6, 68–9.

69   R. Edmonds, *Soviet Foreign Policy, 1962–73: The Paradox of Super Power* (London, 1975), pp. 79–80; Steele, *World Power*, pp. 39–40; J.L. Nogee and R.H. Donaldson, *Soviet Foreign Policy since World War Two* (New York, 1988), pp. 279–80.

70   Ulam, *Expansion and Coexistence*, pp. 768, 773; Edmonds, *Soviet Foreign Policy*, pp. 80, 109.

71   *The Times*, 17, 21 April 1970; T.W. Wolfe, *The SALT Experience* (Cambridge MA, 1979), pp. 8–13; Schwartz, *NATO's Nuclear Dilemmas*, pp. 201–4; Litwak, *Détente and the Nixon Doctrine*, pp. 93–5, 110, 112; M. Sheehan, *The Arms Race* (Oxford, 1983), pp. 54–5; Nitze, *From Hiroshima to Glasnost*, pp. 293–5, 303–5; P.J. Murphy, *Brezhnev: Soviet Politician* (Jefferson NC, 1981), pp. 272–3, 275–6.

72   Nixon, *Memoirs*, pp. 524–31, 609–21; Kissinger, *White House Years*, pp. 819–21, 823–918, 1202–57; Bundy, *Tangled Web*, pp. 248–50, 309–12, 322–7, 344–7; Fraser and Murray, *America and the World*, pp. 163–7; Young, *Britain and the World*, p. 178.

73   Fraser and Murray, *America and the World*, pp. 166–7; Sheehan, *Arms Race*, pp. 55–7; Schwartz, *NATO's Nuclear Dilemmas*, pp. 201–3; Litwak, *Détente and the Nixon Doctrine*, pp. 108–16; Nixon, *Memoirs*, pp. 609–21; Kissinger, *White House Years*, pp. 833–41, 1202–57; Wolfe, *SALT Experience*, pp. 12–22; N.K. Calvo-Goller and M.A. Calvo, *The SALT Agreements: Content, Application, Verification* (Dordrecht, Netherlands, 1987), pp. 11–39, 343–61; Nogee and Donaldson, *Soviet Foreign Policy since World War Two*, pp. 280–1; Edmonds, *Soviet Foreign Policy*, pp. 114–16; Steele, *World Power*, pp. 39–40; Ulam, *Expansion and Coexistence*, pp. 768–70, 772–4; Murphy, *Brezhnev*, p. 275; Haslam, *Soviet Union and the Politics of Nuclear Weapons*, pp. 33–4; R.L. Garthoff, *Détente and Confrontation: American-Soviet Relations from Nixon to Reagan* (Washington DC, 1994), pp. 335–7.

74   *Hansard*, 5th series, 838 (1972), cols 135, 191; 839 (1972), col. 158; Heath, *Course of My Life*, p. 617; *The Times*, 27 May 1972; *Economist*, 27 May 1972.

75   Campbell, *Heath*, p. 344; Heath, *Course of My Life*, pp. 485–6; Kissinger, *White House Years*, pp. 852–3, 856, 891, 899; Thorpe, *Douglas-Home*, pp. 430–1; *The Times*, 17, 20 December 1971; *Hansard*, 5th series, 828 (1971), col. 1302;

829 (1972), cols 215–11; P. Spear, *The Oxford History of India* (Delhi, 1994), pp. 875–6; S. Wolpert, *A New History of India* (New York, 1997), pp. 386–90; G.W. Choudhury, *The Last Days of United Pakistan* (London, 1974), pp. 195, 198; D.K. Palit, *The Lightning Campaign: The Indo-Pakistan War of 1971* (Salisbury, 1972), pp. 117–19.

76 Ulam, *Expansion and Coexistence*, pp. 764–6; Nogee and Donaldson, *Soviet Foreign Policy since World War Two*, pp. 184–7; Steele, *World Power*, pp. 157–8; Edmonds, *Soviet Foreign Policy*, pp. 110–11.

77 Litwak, *Détente and the Nixon Doctrine*, pp. 102–5. There are negative comments on US policy in Bundy, *Tangled Web*, pp. 269–92, and Garthoff, *Détente and Confrontation*, pp. 318–22.

78 Kissinger, *White House Years*, pp. 526–7; Isaacson, *Kissinger*, Ch. 15; Ambrose, *Nixon*, Vol. 2, pp. 441–3, 524, 612; Dyson, 'European Détente in Historical Perspective', pp. 43–4; Carter, 'Détente and East-West Relations', p. 63; P. Malone, *The British Nuclear Deterrent* (London, 1984), p. 183.

79 White, *Britain, Détente and East-West Relations*, pp. 126–7; Wilson, *Final Term*, pp. 186–7.

80 White, *Britain, Détente and East-West Relations*, pp. 131, 137; Reynolds, 'A "Special Relationship"?' pp. 14–15.

81 Baylis, *Anglo-American Defence Relations*, p. 109; Thorpe, *Douglas-Home*, p. 431; Dockrill, *British Defence*, p. 97; Freedman, *Britain and Nuclear Weapons*, pp. 96–7; Clarke, 'A British View', pp. 96–8.

82 Hill and Lord, 'Foreign Policy of the Heath Government', pp. 303–8.

83 Kantowicz, *Coming Apart, Coming Together*, pp. 337–40; Bundy, *Tangled Web*, pp. 198–203, 421–3; Litwak, *Détente and the Nixon Doctrine*, pp. 101–2; Kissinger, *Years of Upheaval*, p. 374; *Chile and Allende*, L.A. Sobel (ed.) (New York, 1974), pp. 174–6; P.E. Sigmund, *The Overthrow of Allende and the Politics of Chile, 1964–76* (Pittsburgh, Pennsylvania, 1977), Chs 6–11; A. Valenzuela, 'Party Politics and the Crisis of Presidentialism in Chile', in *The Failure of Presidential Democracy*, J. Linz and A. Valenzuela (eds) (2 vols, Baltimore MD, 1994), Vol. 2, pp. 91–150; Ambrose and Brinkley, *Rise to Globalism*, pp. 230–2, 290; C. Blasier, *The Giant's Rival: The USSR and Latin America* (Pittsburgh PA, 1987), p. 181, and idem, *The Hovering Giant: US Responses to Revolutionary Change in Latin America, 1910–85* (Pittsburgh PA, 1985), pp. 259–60.

84 Sanders, *Losing an Empire*, p. 177; Curtis, *Ambiguities of Power*, pp. 129–36; *Hansard*, 5th series, 865 (1973), cols 462–538; *The Times*, 28 September 1973.

85 Gromyko, *Memories*, pp. 229–30, 282; Steele, *World Power*, pp. 169, 217–19; Blasier, *The Giant's Rival*, pp. 5, 8, 38, 99–100, 159.

86 Litwak, *Détente and the Nixon Doctrine*, pp. 156–67; Fraser and Murray, *America and the World*, pp. 174–7; Bundy, *Tangled Web*, pp. 434–44; Fraser, *Arab-Israeli Conflict*, pp. 98–103; T.G. Paterson and J.G. Clifford, *America Ascendant: US*

Foreign Policy since 1939 (Lexington MA, 1995), pp. 197–9; C. Smith, 'The Arab-Israeli Conflict', in *International Relations of the Middle East*, L. Fawcett (ed.) (Oxford, 2005), pp. 226–8; Israelyan, *Inside the Kremlin*, pp. 115–75.

87 Ambrose, *Nixon*, Vol. 3, pp. 255–6; Ambrose and Brinkley, *Rise to Globalism*, pp. 259–65; A. Bregman, *Israel's Wars: A History since 1947* (London, 2002), pp. 102–41; P. Mansfield, *A History of the Middle East* (London, 1991), pp. 292–6; Fraser, *Middle East*, pp. 126–34; Laqueur, *Confrontation*, pp. 38–75, 129–58.

88 Lea and Rowe, *Arab-Israeli Relations*, pp. 9, 43–7; Kissinger, *Years of Upheaval*, pp. 712–13; Harrison, *Reluctant Ally*, pp. 178–80.

89 Fraser and Murray, *America and the World*, pp. 178–9; Bundy, *Tangled Web*, pp. 444–52; Ambrose and Brinkley, *Rise to Globalism*, pp. 265–7; Paterson and Clifford, *America Ascendant*, pp. 199–200; Lea and Rowe, *Arab-Israeli Relations*, pp. 9–10, 47–52; Fraser, *Middle East*, pp. 131–47, and idem, *Arab-Israeli Conflict*, pp. 105–8; Smith, 'Arab-Israeli Conflict', pp. 228–9; Mansfield, *History of the Middle East*, pp. 295–8; Kissinger, *Years of Upheaval*, Chs 17–18, 21, 23; Isaacson, *Kissinger*, Chs 23 and 24.

90 Laqueur, *Confrontation*, pp. 187–95, 222–31.

91 Israelyan, *Inside the Kremlin*, pp. 216–18; Thorpe, *Douglas-Home*, p. 434.

92 Ambrose, *Nixon*, Vol. 3, pp. 293–4, 347–8, 354–61; Fraser and Murray, *America and the World*, pp. 179–80; Bundy, *Tangled Web*, pp. 462–9; R. Crockatt, *The Fifty Years War: The United States and Soviet Union in World Politics, 1941–91* (London, 1995), pp. 229–30, 260–1; R.A. Melanson, *Reconstructing Consensus: American Foreign Policy since the Second World War* (New York, 1991), pp. 70–1; Schwartz, *NATO's Nuclear Dilemmas*, pp. 202–7; Sheehan, *Arms Race*, pp. 57–8; Kissinger, *Years of Upheaval*, pp. 1123–43.

93 Kissinger, *Years of Upheaval*, pp. 1010, 1144–50, 1153, 1160–76; Ambrose, *Nixon*, Vol. 3, pp. 369–74; Nixon, *Memoirs*, pp. 1023–4; Wolfe, *SALT Experience*, pp. 85–6, 94–5; Litwak, *Détente and the Nixon Doctrine*, pp. 164, 166–7; Carter, 'Détente and East-West Relations', pp. 64–5; Garthoff, *Détente and Confrontation*, pp. 460, 469–79; Nitze, *From Hiroshima to Glasnost*, pp. 340–1.

94 Callaghan, *Time and Chance*, p. 335; *Hansard*, 5th series, 872 (1974), col. 1132; 877 (1974), cols 419, 421–3; *The Times*, 4 July 1974.

95 Carter, 'Détente and East-West Relations', p. 65; Dyson, 'The Conference on Security and Co-operation in Europe', pp. 105–6; P. Williams, 'Britain, Détente and the Conference on Security and Co-operation in Europe', in Dyson, *European Détente*, p. 228; Clarke, 'A British View', p. 96.

96 Malone, *British Nuclear Deterrent*, pp. 68, 78; A.J.R. Groom, *British Thinking about Nuclear Weapons* (London, 1974), pp. 593–5, 598–9.

97 McGrew, 'Security and Order: The Military Dimension', p. 113.

Notes to Chapter 10: Towards a New Order

1 Heath, *Course of My Life*, p. 493; Campbell, *Heath*, pp. 342–3, 346; Fraser and Murray, *America and the World*, pp. 180–2; Paterson and Clifford, *America Ascendant*, p. 193; Sheehan, *Arms Race*, pp. 57–8; Litwak, *Détente and the Nixon Doctrine*, pp. 167–72; Schwartz, *NATO's Nuclear Dilemmas*, pp. 203–4, 210; Crockatt, *Fifty Years War*, pp. 261–4; Haslam, *Soviet Union and the Politics of Nuclear Weapons*, pp. 56–7, 65–6; Ulam, *Dangerous Relations*, pp. 124–5; Kissinger, *Years of Upheaval*, pp. 272–3; Edmonds, *Soviet Foreign Policy*, p. 175; Nogee and Donaldson, *Soviet Foreign Policy since World War Two*, p. 275; Steele, *World Power*, p. 40; Isaacson, *Kissinger*, pp. 621–6.

2 Isaacson, *Kissinger*, pp. 626–9; Garthoff, *Détente and Confrontation*, pp. 494–505; Melanson, *Reconstructing Consensus*, p. 71; A.J. Reichley, *Conservatives in an Age of Change: The Nixon and Ford Administrations* (Washington DC, 1981), pp. 353–4; S. Talbott, *Endgame: The Inside Story of SALT II* (New York, 1979), pp. 31–7.

3 Nogee and Donaldson, *Soviet Foreign Policy since World War Two*, p. 275.

4 White, *Britain, Détente and East-West Relations*, p. 18; Clarke, 'A British View', pp. 98–9; *The Times*, 25 November 1974; *Guardian*, 26 November 1974.

5 Calvo-Goller and Calvo, *The SALT Agreements*, pp. 43–6, 370; Wolfe, *SALT Experience*, pp. 173–97; W.K.H. Panofsky, *Arms Control and SALT II* (Seattle WA, 1979), p. 66; Murphy, *Brezhnev*, pp. 280, 282; Ambrose and Brinkley, *Rise to Globalism*, pp. 231, 282; Gromyko, *Memories*, p. 284.

6 Pimlott, *Harold Wilson*, p. 669; Freedman, *Britain and Nuclear Weapons*, pp. 97–100.

7 Sanders, *Losing an Empire*, pp. 238, 241–2.

8 Kantowicz, *Coming Apart, Coming Together*, pp. 353, 355; Morewood, 'Divided Europe', p. 27; Curtis, *Ambiguities of Power*, p. 47; Stevenson, *Rise and Fall of Détente*, p. 173; Bundy, *Tangled Web*, p. 483; Litwak, *Détente and the Nixon Doctrine*, pp. 89–90; D.H. Allin, *Cold War Illusions: America, Europe and Soviet Power, 1969–89* (New York, 1994), pp. 55–6.

9 Kissinger, *Years of Upheaval*, pp. 702, 710.

10 Isaacson, *Kissinger*, pp. 663–5; Garthoff, *Détente and Confrontation*, pp. 529–33, 549–50, 554; R. Pearson, *The Rise and Fall of the Soviet Empire* (Basingstoke, 2002), p. 95; R. Davy, 'Perceptions and Performance: An Evaluation', in Davy, *European Détente: A Reappraisal*, p. 245.

11 Williams, 'Britain, Détente and the Conference on Security and Co-operation in Europe', pp. 234–6.

12 White, *Britain, Détente and East-West Relations*, pp. 130–3.

13 Wolfe, *SALT Experience*, Ch. 10; Calvo-Goller and Calvo, *The SALT Agreements*, pp. 46–83, 374–413; Panofsky, *Arms Control and SALT II*, pp. 49–53, 67–75.

14 Morgan, *Callaghan*, p. 451; Sanders, *Losing an Empire*, pp. 177, 193; Curtis, *Ambiguities of Power*, pp. 120, 180–1.

15 Morewood, 'Divided Europe', pp. 21–3; Larres, 'International and Security Relations', p. 225; Stevenson, *Rise and Fall of Détente*, pp. 204–5; Allin, *Cold War Illusions*, pp. xii, xiv, 37–41, 59–77, 90–101, 197; Dobson, *Anglo-American Relations*, pp. 147, 150–1, 158; Hanrieder, *Germany, America, Europe*, pp. 363–7; L.T. Caldwell and A. Dallin, 'US Policy toward the Soviet Union', in *Eagle Entangled: US Foreign Policy in a Complex World*, K.A. Oye, D. Rothchild and R.J. Lieber (eds) (New York, 1979), pp. 199–227; Ambrose and Brinkley, *Rise to Globalism*, pp. 272–3, 276–7, 286–9, 320–1, 344–6; Dumbrell, *American Foreign Policy*, pp. 24, 40–5, 48–9, 56–8, 77, 112–13; Melanson, *Reconstructing Consensus*, pp. 105, 109, 118, 123, 142–3, 189, 227–8; Crockatt, *Fifty Years War*, pp. 257, 259, 261, 267, 288, 290, 307–8, 356–62; Garthoff, *Détente and Confrontation*, pp. 1076–86; Paterson and Clifford, *America Ascendant*, pp. 237, 252–3, 261–6; K.E. Morris, *Jimmy Carter: American Moralist* (Athens GA, 1996), pp. 273–4; Stueck, 'Carter's Foreign Policy', pp. 257–8; C. Bell, *The Reagan Paradox: US Foreign Policy in the 1980s* (New Brunswick NJ, 1989), pp. 74–7; S.K. Smith and D.A. Wertman, *US-West European Relations during the Reagan Years* (Basingstoke, 1992), Ch. 3; Haslam, *Soviet Union and the Politics of Nuclear Weapons*, Ch. 7.

16 White, *Britain, Détente and East-West Relations*, pp. 27, 136–7; Carter, 'Détente and East-West Relations', pp. 64–5; R. Davy, 'Up the Learning Curve: An Overview', and F. Bozo, 'A French View', both in Davy, *European Détente: A Reappraisal*, pp. 19–20, 71.

17 Allen, 'Britain and Western Europe', pp. 179–80.

18 Sanders, *Losing an Empire*, pp. 238–9, 248; G. Smith, *Reagan and Thatcher* (London, 1990), p. 121.

19 J. Sperling and E. Kirchner, *Recasting the European Order* (Manchester, 1997), pp. 64–5; Heuser, *NATO, Britain, France and the FRG*, pp. 90–1.

20 Haslam, *Soviet Union and the Politics of Nuclear Weapons*, pp. 153–64.

21 Donhoff, *Foe into Friend*, pp. 131–44; Simonian, *Privileged Partnership*, pp. 85–6, 96, 115–16, 181–4, 186–8, 277–86, 367–70; Daltrop, *Politics and the European Community*, pp. 168–9; Smith and Edwards, 'British-West German Relations', pp. 51–2, 56–7; Larres, 'Uneasy Allies or Genuine Partners?' pp. 1–24; Reynolds, *Britannia Overruled*, pp. 225–6; Wilson, *Final Term*, pp. 94–5, 203; Morgan, *Callaghan*, pp. 614–15, 617, 622; J. Carr, *Helmut Schmidt: Helmsman of Germany* (London, 1985), pp. 90–2, 140–6; D. Hanley, A. Kerr and N. Waites, *Contemporary France: Politics and Society since 1945* (London, 1991), p. 52.

22 Larres, 'International and Security Relations', pp. 209–10, 217–19, 232–3; Ash, *In Europe's Name*, pp. 53–8; W. Brandt, *My Life in Politics* (London, 1992), pp. 170–218; Stent, *From Embargo to Ostpolitik*, pp. 127–8, 180–95; Griffith, *Ostpolitik*, pp. 135, 137, 177–223; Morewood, 'Divided Europe', pp. 20–1; Donhoff, *Foe into Friend*, pp. 131–44; Simonian, *Privileged Partnership*, pp. 180–4; Hanrieder,

Germany, America, Europe, pp. 196–209. For early assessments of 'Ostpolitik' see Morgan, 'Ostpolitik and West Germany's External Relations', pp. 95–108; G. Roberts, 'The Ostpolitik and Relations between the Two Germanies', in Tilford, *Ostpolitik and Political Change*, pp. 77–93. On the long-term impact of the thaw in central Europe see Hyde-Price, *International Politics of East Central Europe*, pp. 142–6.

23   Sanders, *Losing an Empire*, p. 142; *The Times*, 20 October 1973; Bennett and Hamilton, *Documents on British Policy Overseas*, Vol. 2, pp. v–vi; Deighton, 'British-West German Relations', pp. 41–3; Larres, 'Britain and the GDR' pp. 64–5, 88–9.

24   Heath, *Course of My Life*, pp. 361, 486–7; Campbell, *Heath*, p. 346; Home, *Way the Wind Blows*, pp. 249–50; Morgan, *Callaghan*, pp. 399, 403; Callaghan, *Time and Chance*, pp. 295–6.

25   White, 'Britain and East-West Relations', pp. 163–4; Kennedy, *Realities behind Diplomacy*, pp. 382–3.

26   Ambrose and Brinkley, *Rise to Globalism*, pp. 235, 282–4; Dumbrell, *American Foreign Policy*, pp. 17–21; Reisman, 'The Danger of the Human Rights Campaign', pp. 51–7; Callaghan, *Time and Chance*, pp. 363–4, 366, 369–70; Wilson, *Final Term*, pp. 174–5; Bennett and Hamilton, *Documents on British Policy Overseas*, Vol. 2, pp. xxxiv–xxxv; *The Times*, 2 August 1975; A. Heraclides, *Security and Co-operation in Europe: The Human Dimension, 1972–92* (London, 1993), pp. 32–40; *Hansard*, 5th series, 897 (1975), cols 230–42; Hanhimaki, 'Ironies and Turning Points', pp. 326–7, 334–6.

27   Morgan, *Callaghan*, pp. 452–4, 602–3; Larres, 'International and Security Relations', pp. 222, 232–4; Morewood, 'Divided Europe', p. 23; Armstrong and Goldstein, 'Interaction with the Non-European World', p. 242; Young, *Britain and the World*, p. 178; Grosser, *Western Alliance*, pp. 295–321; Hanrieder, *Germany, America, Europe*, pp. 310–16; Thatcher, *Downing Street Years*, pp. 768, 783–4, 789, 794–6; Simonian, *Privileged Partnership*, pp. 292, 333–4, 359–60; D.W. Urwin, *The Community of Europe: A History of European Integration since 1945* (London, 1991), pp. 221, 225, 227–8, 237–41, 245; D. Dinan, *Ever Closer Union: An Introduction to European Integration* (Basingstoke, 1994), pp. 81, 88–93, 95, 105, 108, 110, 114–15, 120, 122, 129–39; K. Dyson, 'Chancellor Kohl as Strategic Leader: The Case of Economic and Monetary Union', and A. Cole, 'Political Leadership in Western Europe: Helmut Kohl in Comparative Perspective', both in *The Kohl Chancellorship*, C. Clemens and W.E. Paterson (eds) (London, 1998), pp. 38, 59–60, 134–5; T. Cutler, C. Haslam, J. Williams and K. Williams, *1992: The Struggle for Europe* (New York, 1989), pp. 7, 141–6, 149, 163; A. Gamble, 'The European Issue in British Politics', in *Britain For and Against Europe*, D. Baker and D. Seawright (eds) (Oxford, 1998), pp. 20–3; Smith and Edwards, 'British-West German Relations', pp. 48, 51–2, 54–61; Richardson, 'British State Strategies',

pp. 150–1; P. Sharp, *Thatcher's Diplomacy: The Revival of British Foreign Policy* (Basingstoke, 1997), pp. 160–2, 168–70, 209–10.

28 Curtis, *Ambiguities of Power*, pp. 156, 162, 180; Sanders, *Losing an Empire*, pp. 177, 192.

29 Reynolds, *Britannia Overruled*, p. 22, and idem, 'Britain and the World since 1945', pp. 174–5; Dinan, *Ever Closer Union*, p. 132; Young, *Britain and the World*, p. 211; L. Kettenacker, 'Britain and German Reunification, 1989–90', in Larres and Meehan, *Uneasy Allies*, pp. 119–22.

30 Howe, *Conflict of Loyalty*, pp. 583, 632–3; Carrington, *Reflect on Things Past*, pp. 319, 323–5; N. Ridley, 'My Style of Government': *The Thatcher Years* (London, 1991), pp. 136–7, 140, 155–6; *The Times*, 16 July 1990.

31 *Economist*, 14 July 1990; *The Times*, 16 July 1990.

32 A. El-Agraa, 'Mrs Thatcher's European Community Policy', in Bell, *The Conservative Government*, pp. 180–2; Thatcher, *Downing Street Years*, pp. 789–96; Simonian, *Privileged Partnership*, pp. 2–6, 32–45; Allin, *Cold War Illusions*, p. 183.

33 Morewood, 'Divided Europe', pp. 23–5; Bartlett, *Special Relationship*, p. 153; Cromwell, *The United States and the European Pillar*, pp. 118–22; Allin, *Cold War Illusions*, pp. 144–54.

34 M. Smith, 'Britain and the United States: Beyond the Special Relationship?' in Byrd, *British Foreign Policy under Thatcher*, pp. 15–16; Smith and Edwards, 'British-West German Relations', p. 58; Ambrose and Brinkley, *Rise to Globalism*, pp. 324–5; Dumbrell, *American Foreign Policy*, pp. 75–6.

35 *Hansard*, 6th series, 26 (1982), col. 1041; 28 (1982), cols 7–9, 240; *The Times*, 30 June 1982; Thatcher, *Downing Street Years*, pp. 253–6; Smith, *Reagan and Thatcher*, pp. 53, 72–5, 96, 99–102; Sharp, *Thatcher's Diplomacy*, pp. 112–16.

36 A.J. Blinken, *Ally versus Ally: America, Europe and the Siberian Pipeline Crisis* (New York, 1987), pp. 104–6, 151–3; Steele, *World Power*, pp. 66–8; P. Savigear, *Cold War or Détente in the 1980s: The International Politics of American-Soviet Relations* (Brighton, 1987), pp. 125–6.

37 T.L. Ilgen, *Autonomy and Independence: US-Western European Monetary and Trade Relations, 1958–84* (Totowa NJ, 1985), pp. 105–36; Morgan, *Callaghan*, pp. 602–6, 617–21; Bartlett, *Special Relationship*, pp. 140–1.

38 Larres, 'International and Security Relations', pp. 222–3; Farrands, 'State, Society, Culture and British Foreign Policy', pp. 155, 165; J.B. Poole, *Independence and Interdependence: A Reader on British Nuclear Weapons Policy* (London, 1990), pp. 112–13, 118–20; Allen, 'Britain and Western Europe', p. 189; Ambrose and Brinkley, *Rise to Globalism*, pp. 282–7, 321–2; Dumbrell, *American Foreign Policy*, pp. 25–7, 44–5, 47–50, 54–9; Paterson and Clifford, *America Ascendant*, pp. 252–3, 262–3; Richey, *Britain's Strategic Role in NATO*, pp. 55–6; Freedman, *Britain and Nuclear Weapons*, pp. 117–26; Heuser, *NATO, Britain, France and the FRG*, p. 82; Ovendale, *British Defence Policy*, pp. 131, 165–6; Baylis, *Anglo-*

American Defence Relations, pp. 113, 127; Dockrill, *British Defence*, pp. 112–13; Sanders, *Losing an Empire*, pp. 177–8, 238; Callaghan, *Time and Chance*, pp. 542–4; Duke, *Elusive Quest*, p. 66; Allin, *Cold War Illusions*, pp. 85–98, 117–34; Grosser, *Western Alliance*, pp. 315–17; Park, *Defending the West*, pp. 109–17; Renwick, *Fighting with Allies*, pp. 240–2. On peace movements and anti-nuclear protests in Britain and Europe see P. Byrne, *The Campaign for Nuclear Disarmament* (London, 1988), pp. 32–4, 37–9, 118–22, 137, 146–55, 161–2, 228–9; J. Mattausch, *A Commitment to Campaign* (Manchester, 1989), pp. 139–48; P. Calvocoressi, *A Time for Peace: Pacifism, Internationalism and Protest Forces in the Reduction of War* (London, 1987), pp. 105–8, 164–5; T.R. Rochon, *Mobilizing for Peace: The Anti-Nuclear Movements in Western Europe* (Princeton NJ, 1988), Chs 1, 4.

39   M. Thatcher, *The Path to Power* (London, 1995), pp. 360–2, 364–6; Cornish, *Partnership in Crisis*, p. 12; Cromwell, *The United States and the European Pillar*, pp. 110, 115; A. White, *Symbols of War: Pershing II and Cruise Missiles in Europe* (London, 1983), pp. 28–30.

40   Schwartz, *NATO's Nuclear Dilemmas*, pp. 237–8; Smith and Edwards, 'British-West-German Relations', p. 58.

41   Haslam, *Soviet Union and the Politics of Nuclear Weapons*, pp. 101–5; Carrington, *Reflect on Things Past*, pp. 385–6; *The Times*, 26 November 1979.

42   Schwartz, *NATO's Nuclear Dilemmas*, p. 246; Sheehan, *Arms Race*, pp. 199–201.

43   Thatcher, *Downing Street Years*, pp. 240–4, 771.

44   E. Regelsberger, 'EPC in the 1980s: Reaching another Plateau?' in *European Political Co-operation in the 1980s: A Common Foreign Policy for Western Europe?* A. Pijpers, E. Regelsberger and W. Wessels (eds) (Dordrecht, Netherlands, 1988), pp. 3, 7–8, 18–19, 22, 27; Ambrose and Brinkley, *Rise to Globalism*, pp. 284, 321, 323; Paterson and Clifford, *America Ascendant*, pp. 252–3; Dumbrell, *American Foreign Policy*, pp. 25–7, 75; Sanders, *Losing an Empire*, pp. 248, 254, 284; Morewood, 'Divided Europe', p. 21; Larres, 'International and Security Relations', pp. 223–4; Crockatt, *Fifty Years War*, pp. 324–30; Bell, *The Reagan Paradox*, pp. 121–30; Smith and Wertman, *US-West European Relations*, pp. 10–11, 93–103; Allin, *Cold War Illusions*, pp. 132–9, 146, 154–9; J. Spanier, *American Foreign Policy since World War Two* (New York, 1983), pp. 209–13.

45   *The Times*, 7, 9 February, 19, 20, 21 May 1980; Hanley, Kerr and Waites, *Contemporary France*, p. 52; Carrington, *Reflect on Things Past*, pp. 318, 325–6; Smith and Edwards, 'British-West German Relations', p. 58.

46   Sharp, *Thatcher's Diplomacy*, pp. 43, 185; A. Hyman, *Afghanistan under Soviet Domination, 1964–91* (Basingstoke, 1992), pp. 161–2; Thatcher, *Downing Street Years*, pp. 87–8, 91; Smith, *Reagan and Thatcher*, pp. 72, 130.

47   Davy, 'Up the Learning Curve', pp. 23–4; Clarke, 'A British View', p. 104; Garthoff, *Détente and Confrontation*, pp. 812–13, 1081–3, 1087–9; Dyson, 'European

Détente in Historical Perspective', pp. 46–7, 51; T.T. Hammond, *Red Flag over Afghanistan* (Boulder CO, 1984), pp. 105–24; H. Jordan, *Crisis: The Last Year of the Carter Presidency* (New York, 1982), pp. 99–101.

48   Garthoff, *Détente and Confrontation*, p. 1103.

49   Johnson, *Modern World*, pp. 677, 680, 682–3; Sassoon, 'Politics', p. 38; Ambrose and Brinkley, *Rise to Globalism*, pp. 282–4; Dumbrell, *American Foreign Policy*, pp. 17–21; Murphy, *Brezhnev*, pp. 260–2, 273.

50   Bennett and Hamilton, *Documents on British Policy Overseas*, Vol. 2, pp. 476, 486–8.

51   T. Beamish and G. Hadley, *The Kremlin's Dilemma: The Struggle for Human Rights in Eastern Europe* (London, 1979), pp. 34–41; Nogee and Donaldson, *Soviet Foreign Policy since World War Two*, pp. 300–2; Steele, *World Power*, pp. 63–4, 74; Tucker, 'Swollen State, Spent Society', pp. 430–5; A. Solzhenitsyn, 'Misconceptions about Russia are a Threat to America', *Foreign Affairs*, 58 (1979–80), pp. 797–834; Keep, *Last of the Empires*, pp. 200–2, 281–3; M.S. Shatz, *Soviet Dissent in Historical Perspective* (Cambridge, 1980), p. 134; Zeman, *Making and Breaking of Communist Europe*, pp. 288–9; R. Medvedev, *On Soviet Dissent* (London, 1980), p. 113; Thatcher, *Path to Power*, pp. 363–4, 371, 388; *The Times*, 4 June, 5 October 1977; *Observer*, 5 June 1977.

52   Johnson, *Modern World*, pp. 539, 684–5; Armstrong and Goldstein, 'Interaction with the Non-European World', p. 246; Ambrose and Brinkley, *Rise to Globalism*, pp. 276–7, 290, 316–17; Dumbrell, *American Foreign Policy*, pp. 23–5, 37–40; Sanders, *Losing an Empire*, pp. 177, 193, 241–2; C. Legum, 'Communal Conflict and International Intervention in Africa', in C. Legum, I.W. Zartman, S. Langdon and L.K. Mytelka, *Africa in the 1980s: A Continent in Crisis* (New York, 1979), pp. 40, 46, 49–51, 53–7, 60–4; W. Freund, *The Making of Contemporary Africa* (Basingstoke, 1998), pp. 237–9; Steele, *World Power*, pp. 32–6, 159–60, 201–2, 219–20, 222–3, 226–44; P. Shearman, *The Soviet Union and Cuba* (London, 1987), pp. 67–75; Ulam, *Dangerous Relations*, pp. 175–6; S.G. Gorshkov, *The Sea Power of the State* (Oxford, 1979), pp. 178–89; Nogee and Donaldson, *Soviet Foreign Policy since World War Two*, pp. 166–8, 199–200, 202–4, 288–91; M. Perez-Stable, *The Cuban Revolution* (New York, 1993), pp. 148–9; Quirk, *Fidel Castro*, Ch. 28.

53   Curtis, *Ambiguities of Power*, pp. 157–65; *Daily Telegraph*, 18 July, 4, 9 August 1979; Blasier, *The Giant's Rival*, pp. 4–6, 144–51, and idem, *Hovering Giant*, pp. 288–9, 291–2.

54   W.D. Rogers, 'The "Unspecial Relationship" in Latin America', in Louis and Bull, *The 'Special Relationship'*, pp. 345–9.

55   Thatcher, *Path to Power*, p. 371; Johnson, *Modern World*, p. 685; T. Taylor, 'Conventional Arms: The Drives to Export', and T. Ito, 'The Control of Conventional Arms Proliferation', both in *The Defence Trade: Demand, Supply*

and Control, T. Taylor and R. Imai (eds) (London, 1994), pp. 117, 124; H. Tuomi and R. Vayrynen, *Trans-National Corporations, Armaments and Development* (Aldershot, 1982), p. 122; D.C. Gompert and A.R. Vershbow, 'Controlling Arms Trade', in *Controlling Future Arms Trade*, A.R. Vershbow (ed.) (New York, 1977), pp. 1–4, 7–8; R.E. Harkavy, *The Arms Trade and International Systems* (Cambridge MA, 1975), pp. 101–3; Grosser, *Western Alliance*, p. 292.

56 Morgan, *Callaghan*, p. 456.

57 Morgan, *Callaghan*, pp. 441, 595–6.

58 Morgan, *Callaghan*, pp. 451–2, 619; Thatcher, *Downing Street Years*, pp. 87, 158, 329; Johnson, *Modern World*, pp. 713–16; A. Sampson, *The Money Lenders* (London, 1981), pp. 262–7; D. Morgan, *Merchants of Grain* (New York, 1979), pp. 242, 255–7, 259–61, 263, 268–71, 273, 275–9; *The Times*, 22 October 1975; E. Rothschild, 'Food Politics', *Foreign Affairs*, 54 (1975–76), pp. 285–307; R.F. Hopkins, 'How to Make Food Work', *Foreign Policy*, 27 (1977), pp. 89–107; Ambrose and Brinkley, *Rise to Globalism*, pp. 236, 245, 268, 284–5, 288–9, 324–5; Dumbrell, *American Foreign Policy*, pp. 48, 73–4.

59 Bennett and Hamilton, *Documents on British Policy Overseas*, Vol. 2, pp. 457, 461–4.

60 M. Clarke, 'The Soviet Union and Eastern Europe', in Byrd, *British Foreign Policy under Thatcher*, pp. 59–64.

61 Clarke, 'Soviet Union and Eastern Europe', pp. 64–5, 67; Howe, *Conflict of Loyalty*, pp. 309–12.

62 Clarke, 'Soviet Union and Eastern Europe', pp. 68–9.

63 M. Gorbachev, *Memoirs* (London, 1996), pp. 160–1; A. Brown, *The Gorbachev Factor* (Oxford, 1996), pp. 75–8; Gromyko, *Memories*, p. 163; Clarke, 'Soviet Union and Eastern Europe', pp. 69–74; *The Times*, 7 December 1987.

64 White, 'Britain and East-West Relations', pp. 164–7.

65 Fraser and Murray, *America and the World*, p. 162; Reynolds, *Britannia Overruled*, p. 225; Young, *Britain and the World*, p. 207; Nixon, *Memoirs*, pp. 522–3, 525, 545; Ambrose, *Nixon*, Vol. 2, pp. 451–3; J.K. Fairbank, *The United States and China* (Cambridge MA, 1979), pp. 457–62; R. Medvedev, *China and the Superpowers* (Oxford, 1986), pp. 98–105; R.S. Ross, 'US Policy toward China: The Strategic Context and the Policy-Making Process', in *China, the United States and the Soviet Union: Tri-polarity and Policy Making in the Cold War*, R.S. Ross (ed.) (New York, 1993), pp. 149–77; M. Schaller, *The United States and China: Into the Twenty-First Century* (New York, 2002), Ch. 9; *The Times*, 21 August 1972; Kissinger, *White House Years*, p. 1049; H.R. Haldeman, *The Haldeman Diaries: Inside the Nixon White House* (New York, 1994), pp. 315, 319, 421–4; Bundy, *Tangled Web*, pp. 304–5; Ambrose and Brinkley, *Rise to Globalism*, pp. 230, 232, 234, 270; Dumbrell, *American Foreign Policy*, pp. 45–6; McGrew, 'Security and Order: The Military Dimension', p. 103.

66 McGrew, 'Security and Order: The Military Dimension', p. 103; White, 'Britain and East-West Relations', pp. 163–4; Heath, *Course of My Life*, p. 468; Hill and Lord, 'Foreign Policy of the Heath Government', pp. 313–14; Campbell, *Heath*, pp. 350–1.

67 Callaghan, *Time and Chance*, pp. 478–81, 483–6, 488–90, 495–7; Armstrong and Goldstein, 'Interaction with the Non-European World', p. 265; W.H. Lash, 'The International Trade Policies of President Reagan', in *President Reagan and the World*, E.J. Schmertz, N. Datlof and A. Ugrinsky (eds) (Westport CT, 1997), pp. 353–64; R.D. Puttnam and N. Bayne, *Hanging Together: The Seven-Power Summits* (London, 1984), pp. 113–14, 153, 190–1.

68 Dumbrell, *American Foreign Policy*, pp. 115–20.

69 Armstrong and Goldstein, 'Interaction with the Non-European World', pp. 265–6; Ambrose and Brinkley, *Rise to Globalism*, pp. 425–6; Dumbrell, *American Foreign Policy*, p. 58; J.W. Holmes, *The Changing United Nations: Options for the United States* (New York, 1977), p. 35; Curtis, *Ambiguities of Power*, p. 183; Sperling and Kirchner, *Recasting the European Order*, pp. 88–92; S. Zamora, 'Economic Relations and Development', in *United Nations Legal Order*, O. Schachter and C. Joyner (eds) (2 vols, Cambridge, 1995), Vol. 1, pp. 537, 573.

70 Morgan, *Callaghan*, pp. 430, 572–3, 600–1; C.F. Bergsten and C.R. Henning, *Global Economic Leadership and the Group of Seven* (Washington DC, 1996), pp. 58, 76; Sanders, *Losing an Empire*, pp. 188, 214–15, 294.

71 Thatcher, *Downing Street Years*, pp. 299–300, 498, 587.

72 J. Vogler, 'Britain and North-South Relations', in Smith, Smith and White, *British Foreign Policy*, pp. 196–9, 208; *The United Nations in 1985: A Report on the Proceedings* (London, 1986), pp. 21–5; J. Chopra, 'United Nations Peace-Maintenance', in *The United Nations at Work*, M.I. Glassner (ed.) (Westport CT, 1998), p. 312.

73 Johnson, *Modern World*, p. 686; Dockrill, *British Defence*, p. 128; D. Fischer, *Stopping the Spread of Nuclear Weapons* (London, 1992), pp. 232–5; *Western Europe and the Future of the Nuclear Non-Proliferation Treaty*, P. Lomas and H. Muller (eds) (Brussels, 1989), Part 3; Ambrose and Brinkley, *Rise to Globalism*, p. 323; Dumbrell, *American Foreign Policy*, pp. 27–8, 78.

74 G. Kemp, *Nuclear Forces for Medium Powers: Strategic Requirements and Options* (London, 1974), pp. 20–1; Haslam, *Soviet Union and the Politics of Nuclear Weapons*, pp. 32, 40, 135–6.

75 M.J. Wilmshurst, 'The Development of Current Non-Proliferation Policies', in *The International Nuclear Non-Proliferation System: Challenges and Choices*, J. Simpson and A.G. McGrew (eds) (London, 1984), pp. 35–7.

76 Ovendale, *British Defence Policy*, pp. 11–12, 131, 151, 158–61, 165–6, 169–79, 180–3; Morgan, *Callaghan*, pp. 616–19.

77 Morgan, *Callaghan*, pp. 619–20; Callaghan, *Time and Chance*, pp. 553–7.

78   Armstrong and Goldstein, 'Interaction with the Non-European World', p. 247;
     Johnson, *Modern World*, pp. 686–7; Crockatt, *Fifty Years War*, p. 363; Ambrose and
     Brinkley, *Rise to Globalism*, pp. 229–32, 269, 284, 286–8, 303, 322, 334–5, 345–7,
     400–2, 418–19; Dumbrell, *American Foreign Policy*, pp. 101, 148, 171, 184, 188;
     Fischer, *Stopping the Spread of Nuclear Weapons*, Ch. 10; R.K. Betts, 'Paranoids,
     Pygmies, Pariahs and Non-Proliferation Revisited', in *The Proliferation Puzzle:
     Why Nuclear Weapons Spread and What Results*, Z.S. Davis and B. Frankel (eds)
     (London, 1993), pp. 100–24; W.C. Potter, *Nuclear Power and Non-Proliferation*
     (Cambridge MA, 1982), Ch. 5; Stockholm International Peace Research Institute,
     Arms Control: A Survey and Appraisal of Multilateral Agreements (London, 1978),
     pp. 7–35, and idem, *Postures for Non-Proliferation* (London, 1979), Ch. 4; Nogee
     and Donaldson, *Soviet Foreign Policy since World War Two*, p. 279; A. Kelle and
     H. Muller, 'Western Europe and the Geopolitics of Nuclear Proliferation', in
     Lomas and Muller, *Western Europe and the Future of the Non-Proliferation Treaty*,
     pp. 93–101.
79   Freedman, *Britain and Nuclear Weapons*, pp. 88–96; Grosser, *Western Alliance*,
     p. 294; Harrison, *Reluctant Ally*, p. 186; A.G. McGrew, 'Nuclear Non-Proliferation
     at the Crossroads', in Simpson and McGrew, *International Nuclear Non-
     Proliferation System*, pp. 9–10.
80   D. Keohane, 'British Nuclear Non-Proliferation Policy and the Trident Purchase',
     in Simpson and McGrew, *International Nuclear Non-Proliferation System*,
     pp. 120–2.
81   Talbott, *Endgame*, pp. 141–2 (and 279–310 for a copy of the SALT II treaty);
     Callaghan, *Time and Chance*, pp. 483–4, 529–30.
82   Callaghan, *Time and Chance*, pp. 542–4, 546–52; Carrington, *Reflect on Things
     Past*, p. 278.
83   Malone, *British Nuclear Deterrent*, pp. 78, 96, 183–4.
84   Heath, *Course of My Life*, pp. 616–17; Smith, 'Britain and the United States',
     p. 16.
85   Dobson, *Anglo-American Relations*, p. 146; Callaghan, *Time and Chance*, pp. 553–7;
     Byrd, 'Defence Policy', p. 159; Baylis, *Anglo-American Defence Relations*, pp. 126–9;
     Freedman, *Britain and Nuclear Weapons*, pp. 66–8; Thatcher, *Downing Street Years*,
     pp. 244–6.
86   Renwick, *Fighting with Allies*, pp. 218–19, 221–4; Dockrill, *British Defence*,
     pp. 113–14; Dobson, *Anglo-American Relations*, p. 152; Thatcher, *Downing Street
     Years*, pp. 246–8; Byrd, 'Defence Policy', pp. 159–63. On the arguments of the 1980s
     about defence, and especially for and against nuclear weapons, see the debate
     between Ken Booth and John Baylis in their *Britain, NATO and Nuclear Weapons:
     Alternative Defence versus Alliance Reform* (Basingstoke, 1989).
87   Byrd, 'Defence Policy', pp. 163–4.
88   Smith, 'Britain and the United States', pp. 16–17; Byrd, 'Defence Policy', pp. 165–7.

89　Byrd, 'Defence Policy', p. 167; Smith, 'Britain and the United States', p. 17; Smith, *Reagan and Thatcher*, pp. 214–20.

90　Smith, *Reagan and Thatcher*, pp. 220–6.

91　B. Glad and J.A. Garrison, 'Ronald Reagan and the Intermediate Nuclear Forces Treaty: Whatever Happened to the "Evil Empire"?' in Schmertz, Datlof and Ugrinsky, *Reagan and the World*, pp. 91–107. For a denial of the pro-Reagan understanding of the Cold War, see in the same volume, J.E. Ullmann, 'Ronald Reagan and the Illusion of Victory in the Cold War', pp. 109–21.

92　Byrd, 'Defence Policy', p. 168; Duke, *Elusive Quest*, pp. 65–6.

93　Chalmers, *Paying for Defence*, pp. 146, 148, 152–3; Sheehan, *Arms Race*, pp. 42–4.

94　Byrd, 'Defence Policy', pp. 168–9; Smith, 'Britain and the United States', p. 18; Byrd, 'Defence Policy', pp. 169–70; Howe, *Conflict of Loyalty*, pp. 316–18, 321–2, 356–7, 388–93, 542–3; Schmertz, Datlof and Ugrinsky, *Reagan and the World*, pp. 125–7, 138.

95　Dobson, *Anglo-American Relations*, pp. 158–9; Byrd, 'Defence Policy', p. 170; White, 'Britain and East-West Relations', p. 166; Allen, 'Britain and Western Europe', pp. 176, 188; Farrands, 'State, Society, Culture and British Foreign Policy', p. 63; Smith, 'Britain and the United States', pp. 15, 19, 32; Thatcher, *Downing Street Years*, p. 60; D. Allen, 'British Foreign Policy and West European Co-operation', in Byrd, *British Foreign Policy under Thatcher*, pp. 35–6, 49, 52; Van Eekelen, *Debating European Security*, pp. 10–11, 14–19.

96　Thatcher, *Downing Street Years*, pp. 771–3.

97　Thatcher, *Downing Street Years*, pp. 774–6; *Hansard*, 6th series, 111 (1987), cols 723–6; 135 (1988), col. 166; Allin, *Cold War Illusions*, pp. 104, 138–9; C. Bluth, 'A West German View', in Davy, *European Détente: A Reappraisal*, pp. 47–8; Bozo, 'A French View', pp. 77–8; Sturmer, 'Deutschlandpolitik, Ostpolitik and the Western Alliance'; P. Cerny and J. Howorth, 'National Independence and Atlanticism: The Dialectic of French Politics', in Dyson, *European Détente*, pp. 198–220.

98　White, *Britain, Détente and East-West Relations*, pp. 142–3, 147–9, 153; Smith, *Reagan and Thatcher*, pp. 56–8, 182, 244, 254, 267–8; Thatcher, *Downing Street Years*, pp. 784–9.

99　Brown, *Gorbachev Factor*, pp. 247–51; Gorbachev, *Memoirs*, pp. 522–7; M. Galeotti, *Gorbachev and His Revolution* (Basingstoke, 1997), pp. 100–1; Larres, 'International and Security Relations', pp. 225–6; Sassoon, 'Politics', p. 47; Kantowicz, *Coming Apart, Coming Together*, pp. 392–3; Swain and Swain, *Eastern Europe since 1945*, pp. 173–4, 183–5; Berend, *Central and Eastern Europe*, pp. 281–3, 287–8, and idem, 'Central and Eastern European Revolution', p. 198; Adomeit, *Imperial Overstretch*, pp. 215–41; Morewood, 'Divided Europe', pp. 29–30; Pearson, *Rise and Fall of the Soviet Empire*, pp. 131–9; Schopflin, *Politics in Eastern Europe*, pp. 220–2, 235, 239–40; Fowkes, *Rise and Fall of Communism*, pp. 184–6; Zeman, *Making and Breaking of Communist Europe*, pp. 312, 324–6; Allin, *Cold War Illusions*, Ch. 7;

Keep, *Last of the Empires*, Ch. 17; D.S. Mason, *Revolution in East-Central Europe: The Rise and Fall of Communism and the Cold War* (Boulder CO, 1992), pp. 49–52, 58–60; M. Fulbrook, *Interpretations of the Two Germanies, 1945–90* (Basingstoke, 2000), pp. 80–1. See also Fulbrook's *Germany, 1918–90: The Divided Nation* (London, 1991), pp. 321–2, and idem, *Anatomy of a Dictatorship: Inside the GDR, 1949–89* (Oxford, 1995), pp. 236–46.

100 *Hansard*, 6th series, 158 (1989), col. 663; 160 (1989), col. 381; *The Times*, 19 October 1989; Clarke, 'Soviet Union and Eastern Europe', pp. 74–5; White, 'Britain and East-West Relations', pp. 150–2; Thatcher, *Downing Street Years*, pp. 789–90; Bartlett, *Special Relationship*, p. 171; Larres, 'Britain and the GDR', pp. 96–7; Kettenacker, 'Britain and German Reunification', pp. 106–22.

101 Wakeman, 'Golden Age of Prosperity', and D. Kalb, 'Social Class and Social Change in Post-War Europe', both in Wakeman, *Modern European History*, pp. 63, 68–9, 96; Hanagan, 'Changing Margins', 124–6; Sassoon, 'Politics', p. 45; Larres, 'International and Security Relations', p. 188; Schopflin, *Politics in Eastern Europe*, Ch. 6; Eichengreen, 'Economy', pp. 117–18, 139.

102 Thatcher, *Path to Power*, pp. 155–6, 355, 600; A. Kahan, 'Some Problems of the Soviet Industrial Worker', and A. Pravda, 'Spontaneous Workers' Activities in the Soviet Union', both in *Industrial Labour in the USSR*, A. Kahan and B.A. Ruble (eds) (Elmsford NY, 1979), pp. 302–3, 333–66; Good and Ma, 'Economic Growth of Central and Eastern Europe', pp. 122, 124–5, 127; Eichengreen, 'Economy', pp. 117, 139; Berend, 'Central and Eastern European Revolution', p. 192; Wakeman, 'Golden Age of Prosperity', p. 69; Sassoon, 'Politics', p. 15; Kalb, 'Social Class and Social Change', p. 93; Hanagan, 'Changing Margins', p. 129; Fowkes, *Rise and Fall of Communism*, pp. 142–4; A. Koves, *Central and East European Economies in Transition* (Boulder CO, 1992), pp. 2–5; D. Lane, *The Rise and Fall of State Socialism: Industrial Society and the Socialist State* (Cambridge, 1996), pp. 98–9, 152–5; D.H. Aldcroft and S. Morewood, *Economic Change in Eastern Europe since 1918* (Aldershot, 1995), Chs 6–8; Schopflin, *Politics in Eastern Europe*, Ch. 7.

103 Swain and Swain, *Eastern Europe since 1945*, pp. 146–74; Berend, *Central and Eastern Europe*, Ch. 6, and idem, 'Central and Eastern European Revolution', p. 195; Armstrong and Goldstein, 'Interaction with the Non-European World', p. 269; Kantowicz, *Coming Apart, Coming Together*, pp. 382–4; Morewood, 'Divided Europe', pp. 25–7; Korner, 'Culture', p. 158; Larres, 'International and Security Relations', p. 226; Ambrose and Brinkley, *Rise to Globalism*, pp. 190, 321, 333, 340, 346, 348–9, 362–4, 370–4; Dumbrell, *American Foreign Policy*, pp. 108–20; Keep, *Last of the Empires*, Chs 11–13 and pp. 335–62; Zeman, *Making and Breaking of Communist Europe*, pp. 312–32; C. Keble, *Britain and the Soviet Union, 1917–89* (Basingstoke, 1990), p. 283 and Ch. 11; Nogee and Donaldson, *Soviet Foreign Policy since World War Two*, p. 352; Steele, *World Power*, pp. 105, 250–1; Koves, *Central and East European Economies*, pp. 6–9; Aldcroft and

Morewood, *Economic Change*, pp. 134–7, 175, 177–8, 183–5; Lane, *Rise and Fall of State Socialism*, pp. 99–103, 106–9, 152–5; R.V. Daniels, *The End of the Communist Revolution* (London, 1993), pp. 124–31, 136–40; M. Mazower, *Dark Continent: Europe's Twentieth Century* (London, 1999), pp. 384–6; Galeotti, *Gorbachev and His Revolution*, pp. 65–6, 77–8; Thatcher, *Downing Street Years*, p. 774.

104 Loth, 'Moscow, Prague and Warsaw', pp. 103–18; Friedberg, 'The United States and the Cold War Arms Race', pp. 221–2; V. Zubok, 'Why Did the Cold War End in 1989? Explanations of "The Turn"', in Westad, *Reviewing the Cold War*, pp. 360–1; *The Times*, 12 November 1982, 12 March 1985; Brown, *Gorbachev Factor*, pp. 233–5, 239–40, 250; Gorbachev, *Memoirs*, pp. 406, 450–2, 458, 541–2.

105 Home, *Way the Wind Blows*, pp. 245, 250–1; Morgan, *Callaghan*, pp. 451, 617–18, 621; Carrington, *Reflect on Things Past*, p. 278; Sanders, *Losing an Empire*, pp. 186, 239, 242; Thatcher, *Downing Street Years*, pp. 87, 158, 329, 801; Steele, *World Power*, p. 105; M. Cox, 'The End of the Cold War and Why We Failed to Predict It', in Hunter, *Rethinking the Cold War*, pp. 157–74.

106 Carrington, *Reflect on Things Past*, pp. 387–9.

107 Wakeman, 'Golden Age of Prosperity', pp. 77–8; Sassoon, 'Politics', pp. 45–6; Eichengreen, 'Economy', p. 139; Armstrong and Goldstein, 'Interaction with the Non-European World', p. 244; Morewood, 'Divided Europe', pp. 26–8; Berend, *Central and Eastern Europe*, pp. 238–60, and idem, 'Central and Eastern European Revolution', p. 198; Swain and Swain, *Eastern Europe since 1945*, pp. 157–8, 167–70; Korner, 'Culture', p. 158; Larres, 'International and Security Relations', p. 220; Kantowicz, *Coming Apart, Coming Together*, p. 384; Zeman, *Making and Breaking of Communist Europe*, pp. 283–8; Beamish and Hadley, *Kremlin's Dilemma*, pp. 73, 84–93; Daniels, *End of the Communist Revolution*, pp. 69–74, 128–9; A. Judt, 'The Dilemmas of Dissidence: The Politics of Opposition in East-Central Europe', in *Crisis and Reform in Eastern Europe*, F. Feher and A. Arato (eds) (New Brunswick NJ, 1991), pp. 253–301; Lane, *Rise and Fall of State Socialism*, pp. 65–8, 120–1; Aldcroft and Morewood, *Economic Change*, pp. 152–3, 189–90; Fowkes, *Rise and Fall of Communism*, pp. 157–66, 175–80, 186; Ambrose and Brinkley, *Rise to Globalism*, pp. 283–4, 304, 363–4; Dumbrell, *American Foreign Policy*, pp. 17–21, 57, 74, 81, 85; Thatcher, *Path to Power*, pp. 351–5, 364–5, 371–2, 508–9, 591; E. Hobsbawm, *The Age of Extremes* (London, 1995), pp. 398–400; J. Krejci and P. Machonin, *Czechoslovakia, 1918–92: A Laboratory for Social Change* (Basingstoke, 1996), Ch. 16; *Czechoslovakia, 1918–88: Seventy Years from Independence*, H.G. Skilling (ed.) (Basingstoke, 1991), pp. 217–22; J. Staniszkis, *Poland's Self-Limiting Revolution* (Princeton NJ, 1984), Chs 2 and 3; T.G. Ash, *The Polish Revolution: Solidarity* (London, 1991), pp. 21–37.

108 Larres, 'Britain and the GDR', pp. 93–7; Bathrick, *Powers of Speech*, pp. 82–3; A.J. McAdams, *East Germany and Détente* (Cambridge, 1985), p. 182; Keble, *Britain and the Soviet Union*, pp. 282–3; Callaghan, *Time and Chance*, pp. 366,

369–70; Morgan, *Callaghan*, pp. 452–3; Howe, *Conflict of Loyalty*, pp. 314–15, 351–2, 433–5; Thatcher, *Downing Street Years*, pp. 452, 460, 477–8; 773–4.

109 *Hansard*, 5th series, 969 (1979), cols 75–83; *The Times*, 24 January 1980; A. Pravda and P. Duncan, 'Soviet-British Relations under Perestroika', in *Soviet-British Relations since the 1970s*, A. Pravda and P. Duncan (eds) (Cambridge, 1990), pp. 232–55.

110 Heraclides, *Security and Co-operation in Europe*, pp. 51–9, 61, 67; A. Bloed and P. van Dijk, 'Human Rights and Non-intervention', A. Bloed and F. van Hoof, 'Some Aspects of the Socialist View of Human Rights', and A. Bloed, 'Détente and the Concluding Document of Madrid', all in *Essays on Human Rights in the Helsinki Process*, A. Bloed and P. van Dijk (eds) (Dordrecht, Netherlands, 1985), pp. 1–3, 31, 34, 61–6, 77.

111 Morewood, 'Divided Europe', pp. 27–8, 32; Sassoon, 'Politics', p. 17; Larres, 'International and Security Relations', p. 200; Berend, *Central and Eastern Europe*, pp. 222–38, and idem, 'Central and Eastern European Revolution', pp. 191–2, 195; Wakeman, 'Golden Age of Prosperity', pp. 77–8; Swain and Swain, *Eastern Europe since 1945*, pp. 162–8, 175, 179; Schopflin, *Politics in Eastern Europe*, Ch. 7; T. Bauer, 'Reforming or Perfecting the Economic Mechanism', in Feher and Arato, *Crisis and Reform*, pp. 99–120; Hobsbawm, *Age of Extremes*, pp. 399–400; Lane, *Rise and Fall of State Socialism*, pp. 65–9, 152–5; Koves, *Central and East European Economies*, pp. 3–6; Aldcroft and Morewood, *Economic Change*, pp. 156–76; Fowkes, *Rise and Fall of Communism*, pp. 142–56; Steele, *World Power*, pp. 5, 20–1, 250–1; Savigear, *Cold War or Détente*, pp. 63, 121; Nogee and Donaldson, *Soviet Foreign Policy since World War Two*, pp. 323, 335–6; Zeman, *Making and Breaking of Communist Europe*, pp. 289–91; S. Haggard and A. Moravcsik, 'The Political Economy of Financial Assistance to Eastern Europe, 1989–91', in Keohane, Nye and Hoffman, *After the Cold War*, pp. 246–85; R. Vinen, *A History in Fragments: Europe in the Twentieth Century* (London, 2002), p. 516.

112 Bartlett, *Special Relationship*, p. 153; Thatcher, *Downing Street Years*, pp. 777–8; Carrington, *Reflect on Things Past*, p. 330.

113 Morgan, *Callaghan*, pp. 451–3; Callaghan, *Time and Chance*, pp. 295–6, 365–7, 369; *Hansard*, 5th series, 941 (1978), cols 8–9; 943 (1978), col. 994; 954 (1978), cols 1135–36; *The Times*, 18, 24 January, 18 March 1980; M.R. Hill, *East-West Trade, Industrial Co-operation and Technology Transfer: The British Experience* (Aldershot, 1983), Ch. 3, pp. 4–5.

114 Hill, *East-West Trade*, pp. 190–1; Keble, *Britain and the Soviet Union*, pp. 281, 290; M. Kaser, 'Trade Relations: Patterns and Prospects', and A. Pravda, 'Pre-Perestroika Patterns', both in Pravda and Duncan, *Soviet-British Relations*, pp. 7–8, 193, 204.

115 Clarke, 'Soviet Union and Eastern Europe', pp. 68, 72, 74; Howe, *Conflict of Loyalty*, pp. 429, 433.

116 Sperling and Kirchner, *Recasting the European Order*, pp. 88–90; Friedmann,

'Warsaw Pact Socialism', pp. 213–31; Gati, *The Bloc that Failed*, pp. 99–103, 132–5, 155–7.

117   Wakeman, 'Golden Age of Prosperity', p. 78; Eichengreen, 'Economy', p. 121; Kalb, 'Social Class and Social Change', p. 91; Armstrong and Goldstein, 'Interaction with the Non-European World', pp. 264–5; L. Neal, 'Impact of Europe', in *The Cambridge Economic History of Modern Britain*, R. Floud and P. Johnson (eds) (3 vols, Cambridge, 2004), Vol. 3, p. 278; A. Boltho, 'Growth', in Boltho, *The European Economy*, pp. 9–37; Hennings, 'West Germany', pp. 492–8; Surrey, 'United Kingdom', pp. 547–52. On the wider context see H. James, *International Monetary Co-operation since Bretton Woods* (New York, 1996), Chs 11 and 12, and Ilgen, *Autonomy and Independence*, Ch. 5.

118   Ovendale, *British Defence Policy*, pp. 144–5; R. Coopey and N. Woodward, 'The British Economy in the 1970s: An Overview', and K. Hartley, 'The Defence Economy', both in *Britain in the 1970s: The Troubled Economy*, R. Coopey and N. Woodward (eds) (London, 1996), pp. 1–33, 212–35; J. Tomlinson, *The Politics of Decline: Understanding Post-War Britain* (Harlow, 2001), pp. 84–94, 96.

119   N. Crafts, 'Economic Growth', in Crafts and Woodward, *British Economy since 1945*, pp. 261–90; R. Middleton, *The British Economy since 1945: Engaging with the Debate* (Basingstoke, 2000), pp. 57–66, 132–5; P. Dunne and R. Smith, 'Thatcherism and the UK Defence Industry', in *The Economic Legacy, 1979–92*, J. Michie (ed.) (London, 1992), pp. 91–111.

120   T. Clark and A. Dilnot, 'British Fiscal Policy since 1939', in Floud and Johnson, *Cambridge Economic History*, Vol. 3, pp. 377–8.

121   Sanders, *Losing an Empire*, pp. 210–14.

122   White, *Britain, Détente and East-West Relations*, pp. 149–54.

Notes to Conclusion

1   Marks, *Ebbing of European Ascendancy*, p. 292.

2   C. Baxter, 'The Foreign Office and Post-War Planning for East Asia, 1944–45', *Contemporary British History*, 21 (2007), pp. 149–72.

3   F. McKenzie, 'In the National Interest: Dominions' Support for Britain and the Commonwealth after the Second World War', *Journal of Imperial and Commonwealth History*, 34 (2006), pp. 553–76.

4   P. Orders, *Britain, Australia, New Zealand and the Challenge of the United States, 1939–46: A Study in International History* (New York, 2003).

5   A.I. Singh, *The Limits of British Influence: South Asia and the Anglo-American Relationship, 1947–56* (London, 1993).

6   Barnett, *Collapse of British Power*, preface.

7   D. Cannadine, *In Churchill's Shadow: Confronting the Past in Modern Britain*

(London, 2003), pp. 26–44. See also the different perspectives in English and Kenny, *Rethinking British Decline*.

8 G. Martell, 'The Meaning of Power: Rethinking the Decline and Fall of Great Britain', *International History Review*, 13 (1991), pp. 662–94. Martell's discussion includes an extended critique of Kennedy's *Rise and Fall of the Great Powers*.

9 Dilks, 'Introduction', in *Retreat from Power*, p. 23.

10 Reynolds, *Britannia Overruled*, p. 167.

11 Harris, *Attlee*, pp. 304–5, 308.

12 Smith and Zametica, 'Cold Warrior: Clement Attlee Reconsidered'.

13 Mayhew, *Time to Explain*, p. 98.

14 Sked and Cook, *Post-War Britain*, pp. 50, 84; Young, *Britain and the World*, pp. 147–8.

15 Bullock, *Bevin*, pp. 839–40. For a similarly positive assessment, see F.K. Roberts, 'Ernest Bevin as Foreign Secretary', in Ovendale, *Foreign Policy of the Labour Governments*, pp. 21–42. Frank Roberts had served in the Moscow embassy before becoming Bevin's principal private secretary, 1947–49. He subsequently held a succession of senior diplomatic posts.

16 Bullock, *Bevin*, pp. 846–7.

17 Young, *Britain and European Unity*, p. 15, and idem, *Britain and the World*, p. 148.

18 Warner, 'Labour Governments and the Unity of Western Europe', pp. 66–7.

19 The same difficulty would frequently lead to disagreements within NATO: the Europeans were 'torn between gratitude for the shelter of American power and resentment over their dependence on that power' (Kaplan, *Long Entanglement*, p. 62).

20 Young, *Britain, France and the Unity of Europe*, pp. 126–7.

21 Kent, *British Imperial Strategy*, p. 216.

22 Kent, *British Imperial Strategy*, pp. 194, 197, 202; Greenwood, *Britain and the Cold War*, p. 67; Gaddis, 'Was the Truman Doctrine a Real Turning Point?'.

23 Cairncross, *Years of Recovery*, p. 277.

24 Watt, 'Britain, the United States and the Opening of the Cold War', p. 59.

25 Perkins, 'Unequal Partners', pp. 43–64.

26 Kent, *British Imperial Strategy*, p. ix; Deighton, *Impossible Peace*, p. 229.

27 Kennan, *Memoirs*, pp. 456–7.

28 G. Warner, 'The British Labour Government and the Atlantic Alliance, 1949–51', in Wiggershaus and Foerster, *Western Security Community*, pp. 166, 168.

29 *The Times*, 15 February 1947.

30 W. Wallace, 'Foreign Policy and National Identity in the United Kingdom', *International Affairs*, 67 (1991), pp. 65–80.

31 F.S. Northedge, *British Foreign Policy: The Process of Readjustment, 1945–61* (London, 1962), pp. 240–1.

32 Ovendale, *Transfer of Power in the Middle East*, p. 140.

33 Pickering, *Britain's Withdrawal from East of Suez*, pp. 88–9, 100, 102, 115–17.

34 Steiner, 'British Power and Stability', pp. 23–44.

35 Chalmers, *Paying for Defence*, p. 40.

36 Chalmers, *Paying for Defence*, pp. 89–90.

37 P. Warwick, 'Did Britain Change? An Inquiry into the Causes of National Decline', *Journal of Contemporary History*, 20 (1985), pp. 99–133.

38 Pickering, *Britain's Withdrawal from East of Suez*, pp. 87, 107, 123, 166.

39 Healey, *Time of My Life*, p. 277; M. Stewart, *Life and Labour* (London, 1980), p. 233; Ziegler, *Wilson*, p. 211.

40 Healey, *Time of My Life*, pp. 299–300.

41 Young, *Labour Governments*, pp. 54–5, 225.

42 Young, *Labour Governments*, p. 55.

43 Young, *Labour Governments*, p. 56; Lapping, *Labour Government*, pp. 91–2.

44 Clarke, *Hope and Glory*, pp. 441–3.

45 This is the line taken in S. Henig, *The Uniting of Europe: From Discord to Concord* (London, 1998) and Aybet, *Dynamics of European Security Co-operation*.

46 See the discussion in Young, *Britain and European Unity*.

47 Steiner, 'British Power and Stability', and for another long-term perspective on Europe see G.H. Soutou, 'Was there a European Order in the Twentieth Century? From the Concert of Europe to the End of the Cold War', *Contemporary European History*, 9 (2000), pp. 329–53.

48 The UN security council met only five times in 1959, compared with its 132 meetings per year, on average, between 1946 and 1948. S. Ryan, *The United Nations and International Politics* (London, 2000), p. 49.

49 A. Priest, 'In American Hands: Britain, the United States and the Polaris Nuclear Project, 1962–68', *Contemporary British History*, 19 (2005), pp. 353–76.

50 Heath, *Course of My Life*, p. 492.

51 Smith, *Reagan and Thatcher*, pp. 72, 130.

52 I. Elliot, 'The Helsinki Process and Human Rights in the Soviet Union', in *Human Rights and Foreign Policy*, D.M. Hill (ed.) (Basingstoke, 1989), pp. 91–114.

53 Reynolds, 'A "Special Relationship"?' pp. 14–15.

54 Morgan, *Callaghan*, pp. 622–3.

55 White, 'Britain and East-West Relations', pp. 150–3, 165–7.

56 Howe, *Conflict of Loyalty*, p. 312.

57 Curtis, *Ambiguities of Power*, pp. 147, 180–1.

58 See M. Curtis, *The Great Deception: Anglo-American Power and World Order* (London, 1998).

59 Garthoff, *Détente and Confrontation*, pp. 1087–9; White, *Britain, Détente and East-West Relations*, Ch. 7; Clarke, 'A British View', p. 107.

60 Clarke, 'A British View', pp. 107–8.

61 Thatcher, *Path to Power*, pp. 508–9.

62 L. Freedman and V. Gamba-Stonehouse, *Signals of War: The Falklands Conflict of 1982* (London, 1991), p. 417.

63 Thatcher, *Downing Street Years*, pp. 173–4.

64 Smith, *Reagan and Thatcher*, p. 92.

65 For what follows see M. Clarke, *British External Policy Making in the 1990s* (London, 1992).

66 Clarke, *British External Policy*, p. 252.

67 W. Wallace, *The Foreign Policy Process in Britain* (London, 1977).

68 For the record, former West German defence minister Manfred Worner succeeded Lord Carrington as secretary-general of NATO on 1 July 1988.

69 E.g. *British Defence Choices for the Twenty-First Century*, M. Clarke and P. Sabin (eds) (London, 1993).

Index